PENGUIN BOOKS

THE TIME OF MY LIFE

'In a class of its own; robust and intellectual, personal and historic, it rings absolutely true ... The best history is good biography, and we get here a view of government, politics, literature and life as Healey traces the motivations, impulses and actions of many players involved in the mosaic of events in Britain and the world during the second half of the 20th century' – Brian Lenihan in the *Irish Times*

'It is a big book by a big man, vigorously written, forthright but generous in its judgments, as concerned with the substance of policy as with personal reminiscences ... Certainly no finer autobiography has been written by a British politician in this century' – *Economist*

'He is candid and self-revealing in a manner free from rancour and petty self-exoneration ... there is a robust integrity to his account which makes it simultaneously worth learning from and worth arguing with' – Peter Clarke in the *London Review of Books*

'Irreverence ... and the sense of a life which goes well beyond politics, are constantly breaking through' – David McKie in the *Guardian*

'An exceptionally serious, thoughtful and well-written reflection on a life lived at a high level of engagement with great affairs ... his knowledge of music, painting, and literature is deployed on every page to illuminate the foreground subjects of international politics and finance ... No reader ... will fail to learn an immense amount from Healey's shrewd, lucid, robust – and often very funny – survey' – John Campbell in *The Times*

Denis Healey was born in 1917 and brought up in Yorkshire. After gaining a double first at Balliol College, Oxford, for six years he was a soldier learning about real life. Another six years as International Secretary of the Labour Party taught him much about politics, both at home and abroad. Since 1952 he has been a Labour Member of Parliament for Leeds, serving thirty-three years on Labour's Front Bench in Government and in Opposition, including long periods as Defence Secretary, Chancellor of the Exchequer and Shadow Foreign Secretary.

He is a prolific journalist and broadcaster. He has published *Healey's Eye*, a book on his life as a photographer, and has contributed essays to many publications for the Fabian Society, including New Fabian essays and Fabian International essays.

His latest book, *When Shrimps Learn to Whistle – Signposts for the Nineties* includes a selection of his earlier writings which are relevant to the world after the Cold War.

The Time of
My Life

DENIS HEALEY

PENGUIN BOOKS

For Edna, of course

PENGUIN BOOKS

Published by the Penguin Group
Penguin Books Ltd, 27 Wrights Lane, London w8 5TZ, England
Viking Penguin, a division of Penguin Books USA Inc.
375 Hudson Street, New York, New York 10014 USA.
Penguin Books Australia Ltd, Ringwood, Victoria, Australia
Penguin Books Canada Ltd, 2801 John Street, Markham, Ontario, Canada L3R 1B4
Penguin Books (NZ) Ltd, 182–190 Wairau Road, Auckland 10, New Zealand

Penguin Books Ltd, Registered Offices: Harmondsworth, Middlesex, England

First published by Michael Joseph 1989
Published in Penguin Books 1990
7 9 10 8 6

Copyright © Denis Healey, 1989
All rights reserved

The moral right of the author has been asserted

Printed in England by Clays Ltd, St Ives plc

The author and publishers wish to thank the following for permission to reproduce
extracts from copyright material:

David Higham Associates Ltd on behalf of J. M. Dent for 'Fern Hill' from *The
Poems* by Dylan Thomas; Faber & Faber Ltd for 'There Will Be No Peace' and 'The
Managers' by W. H. Auden, 'Thalassa' by Louis MacNeice and 'Homage to a
Government' by Philip Larkin reprinted by permission of Faber & Faber Ltd from
Collected Poems by W. H. Auden, *The Collected Poems of Louis MacNeice* and the
High Windows by Philip Larkin; John Murray Ltd for *Summoned by Bells* by John
Betjeman; Jonathan Cape Ltd for 'To Margot Heinemann' by John Cornford from
John Cornford: A Memoir edited by Pat Sloan reprinted by permission of the estate
of Pat Sloan and Jonathan Cape, John Tydeman for 'Lessons of the War' by Henry
Reed; Jonathan Cape Ltd, The Hogarth Press (publishers) and the Executors of the
Estate of C. Day Lewis for 'The Magnetic Mountain' from *Collected Poems* 1954 by
C. Day Lewis; A. P. Watt Ltd, on behalf of Michael B. Yeats and Macmillan
London Ltd for 'Nineteen Hundred and Nineteen', 'Long-legged Fly' and 'Meru'
from *The Collected Poems of W. B. Yeats* and two lines from the *Variorum Edition*;
Laurence Pollinger Ltd and the Estate of Mrs Frieda Lawrence Ravagli for 'The
Mosquito Knows' from *Pansies* by D. H. Lawrence; Penguin Books Ltd for 9 lines
from 'The Awakening' by Zbigniew Herbert, from *Selected Poems* by Zbigniew
Herbert, translated by Czeslaw Milosz and Peter Dale Scott (Penguin Books, 1968)
copyright © Czeslaw Milosz and Peter Dale Scott, 1968, p. 132; and 6 lines from
Selected Poems by Tony Harrison (Penguin Books, 1984), copyright © Tony
Harrison, 1984, reproduced by permission of Penguin Books Ltd.

Every effort has been made to trace copyright material and the publishers wish to
apologize for any omissions to the above list.

Contents

PART FOUR: *New Challenges*

Illustrations

Copyright owners are indicated in italics.

Preface to the Penguin Edition

All changed, changed utterly:
A terrible beauty is born.

– 'Easter 1916'
W. B. Yeats

THE TWELVE MONTHS since I finished *The Time of My Life* have made an *annus mirabilis*. Eastern Europe has been swept by popular revolutions. German unification has begun. The Soviet Union is moving towards political pluralism, and its peripheral republics are demanding independence. To cap it all, Nelson Mandela has been released and is negotiating with the South African Government to end apartheid.

All these stupendous changes were on the way a year ago; indeed I predicted most of them in my final chapter. But no one could have imagined they would happen so fast. After a hundred and fifty years, the spectre of Communism is no longer haunting Europe. It is still stalking the Far East; the massacre in Tiananmen Square has for the time being destroyed my hope that the Hong Kong settlement might provide a precedent, by combining two systems in a single state.

The age of ideology is over in the Soviet Empire, and in South Africa as well. However, the ideology of the Cold War still survives on both sides of the Atlantic. NATO is finding it difficult to admit that its enemy has disappeared. The European Community seems to regard the triumph of democracy in Eastern Europe as a dangerous distraction rather than a welcome challenge. There is still a tendency to indulge in a shallow triumphalism, to say that we are now witnessing 'the end of history' because 'capitalism has won the Cold War'.

Yet in Britain the last year has also seen the myth of Thatcherism exploded, and in Europe it would be more true to say that history is now beginning again. As I point out in my new book *When Shrimps Learn to Whistle*, which may serve as a companion to *The Time of My Life*, many of the problems we now face confronted us during the first twenty years after the defeat of Hitler; the times today are far more propitious for their solution. However, other problems have emerged which go back to the Austro-Hungarian Empire and beyond, to the days when Sweden, Poland and Lithuania were knocking at the gates of Moscow; these may prove more formidable.

History can stimulate the imagination and offer unfamiliar insights into the modern world. It is easy to see Gorbachev as a modern Peter the Great, turning Russia towards a common European home. It is also tempting to recall that Catherine the Great was the daughter of a Prussian officer and that Germany thereafter provided Russia with tsarinas, ministers and generals right up to the Bolshevik Revolution.

The end of the Cold War has reminded us that nationalism remains the most powerful single force in democratic politics; the Balkanisation of Eastern Europe and the revolt of the Russian colonies could lead again to fighting between states, as they did in the past. But the world at the end of the twentieth century is a much smaller place than it was in 1914. Finance and economics have created global networks which transcend national frontiers. Together with nuclear weapons and the manifold threats to the world environment, they make it essential to find new structures on which to build a world society. It is difficult to envisage any long-term solutions except through a revitalised United Nations.

I believe the main threats to the stability of our new world lie in the economic field. The imminent disappearance of the German and Japanese surpluses will compel the United States and Britain to finance their own trade deficits; if mishandled, this could lead to a world recession. Economic failure could turn the democratic revolutions in Eastern Europe and the Soviet Union, like many in the past, to seek salvation in militarist dictatorships. It seems unlikely that the local wars which might then follow would threaten the survival of mankind directly; the many wars which have erupted in the Third World since 1945 did not do so. But they would bring appalling and unnecessary human suffering. They would also rob humanity of its second chance since the defeat of Hitler to create a world society. If the developed countries cannot now start the process by creating the necessary unity among themselves, there may be no third chance. The spread of missiles armed with nuclear and chemical warheads in the developing countries could rule it out.

That is one of many reasons why I believe that the West must take advantage of the end of the Cold War to make massive cuts in its defence spending. Without help from the resources thus released it will be impossible for Eastern Europe and the Soviet Union to overcome their economic problems; moreover, defence cuts will be needed to provide aid for the Third World and to restore social and economic infrastructures which have become painfully inadequate in parts of the West itself.

Even if the daunting economic problems facing the new democracies can be overcome, nationalism will remain a dangerous and destructive force unless it can be directed into channels which transcend the geographical boundaries by which nations have been defined in the past. There is no way of drawing any frontiers for all the existing states, or even for new states which may achieve independence from the Soviet Union, without including irreconcilable national minorities within them. This fact has already brought bloodshed from Kosovo to Baku. That is why it is so important to create wider international structures for security and prosperity in Europe to replace NATO and the Common Market in their present form.

The writer Vaclav Havel has used his new role as President of Czechoslovakia to identify the central problem now facing not only the new democracies but the whole world; it is essentially to restore the sense of responsibility which all human beings owe to one another. 'The human spirit is not a matter of the human intellect alone,' he told a rally in Prague on the forty-second anniversary of the Communist takeover. 'It is also deliberation and forethought as well as conscience and decency, taste and love for one's neighbour, courage and detachment from oneself, as well as doubt and even humour.' He won applause from the Congress of the United States by saying that the new Europe he envisaged 'will enable us to escape from the rather antiquated straitjacket of a bipolar view of the world and to enter into a period of multipolarity, into an era in which all of us – large and small, former slaves and former masters – will be able to create what Abraham Lincoln called the family of man'. And he warned the Czech people in his New Year's address that, having got the single-party state off their backs, they were now face to face with their real enemy: their 'indifference to public affairs, conceit, ambition, selfishness, the pursuit of personal advancement and rivalry'.

Havel is that rare thing in politics, a philosopher-king. His vision is not unique. It also inspired many of the young men and women who led other popular revolutions in Eastern Europe. Fifty years ago it prompted thousands of ordinary citizens to join the resistance movements against Nazi and Fascist occupation. It has been at the root of democratic socialism for well over a century. It is needed more than ever in the Western democracies today.

The problem is to maintain the purity of such insight when dealing with what Traherne called 'the Dirty Devices of this World'. Already in Eastern Germany the idealism of the Civic Forum has been swept aside by the mass hunger for the material benefits which rapid absorption into the Federal Republic was expected to bring. More than ever, political leaders in both East and West need to combine a cold eye with a warm heart. If this account of my own political experience can help others at least to understand the problem, I shall be content.

March 1990

Acknowledgements

As I hope this book makes clear, I owe whatever I have learned since the war to my family, and to those who have worked with me – in Leeds, in Westminster, in Whitehall, and in many other parts of the world.

A few of my anecdotes are drawn from my photographic memoir, *Healey's Eye* (Jonathan Cape, 1980). My account of the landing at Porto di S. Venere first appeared in the *Sunday Express* on February 28th 1984. Documents recently released from the official archives have added a good deal to my personal knowledge of the fifties, in the main confirming views I had already formed. I have been able to compare my own recollections with those of my colleagues, many of whom, from Hugh Dalton to Roy Jenkins, have published prolific diaries.

The research services of the House of Commons Library have answered my questions with unfailing efficiency. As editor for Michael Joseph, Susan Watt has helped me to improve the structure and clarity of my story. I owe a special debt to the Rockefeller Foundation, which has twice allowed me and Edna to spend a month working at its study centre in the Villa Serbelloni at Bellagio above Lake Como. Apart from the physical delights of that earthly paradise, I was immensely stimulated by my fellow scholars there, who included historians, scientists, poets, playwrights, painters and philosophers from many continents.

Finally, I would have been unable to write this book without the help and protection of my secretary, Harriet Shackman, who has tolerated my eccentricities for more than a decade.

I must express my gratitude to the many correspondents who have drawn my attention to errors in the first edition, which I have now corrected.

Introduction

AT ONE TIME I wanted to call this memoir 'A Hitch-hiker's Guide to the Modern World'. My generation has seen it all. I was born at the end of what we used to call the Great War. My childhood and youth were spent during that uneasy peace which saw the rise of Fascism in Europe and the Great Slump. My student years at Oxford were dominated by the imminence of the Second World War. When it finally came, I spent six years in the army, fighting in North Africa and Italy. Since then I have seen Britain move from Churchill and Clement Attlee to Margaret Thatcher, the United States from Roosevelt and Truman to Reagan and Bush, and the Soviet Union from Stalin to Gorbachev.

This is not, however, a history book; it is the story of how one man lived through those turbulent years. As Emerson said: 'There is properly no history – only biography.' Historians, like economists, try to find a consistent pattern in the infinite variety of shifting circumstances which millions of people, alive and dead, have helped to shape. It is often an unrewarding task, for the reader as well as the writer. 'When one has read no history for a time, the sad-coloured volumes are really surprising. That so much energy should have been wasted to believe in something spectral fills one with pity ... The machine they describe; they succeed to some extent in making us believe in it; but the heart of it they leave untouched – is it because they cannot understand it? At any rate, we are left out, and history, in our opinion, lacks an eye.'

Those are the words of Virginia Woolf, a writer who never fails to refresh me. So my memoir is as much about people as about events. Even in political life I have found that the personalities are as important as the programmes. I have tried to describe the men and women with whom I have lived and worked – not just my fellow politicians, but the civil servants, soldiers, trade unionists, businessmen and bankers. They too are human beings; their distinctive personalities matter as much as their professions in deciding what they say and do.

The nicest people are not always the most effective politicians, and the greatest men are never great in everything. Even the strongest character is moulded by his background, and by the history and geography which helped to make that background what it is. It is difficult to understand anyone without knowing something about the furniture of his mind, the experiences which have shaped him, and the issues which have brought you together. Richard Neustadt has written an excellent manual for decision makers which is based on this point; he calls it 'Thinking in Time'. Rather like Monsieur Jourdain, who discovered he had been speaking prose without knowing it all his life, I have been thinking in time without knowing it, ever since I left school.

On the other hand I have not been able to avoid the 'spectral' abstractions altogether in this memoir. I have spent much of my life trying to get to grips with the appalling problems which the world now faces in its search for lasting peace and prosperity. Through hard work in Opposition and through practical responsibility in Government, I think I have learned something about these problems. So I have tried here to explore the lessons of my experience, even though it means dragging the reader through the treacherous swamps of strategy and the tangled jungles of economics. Otherwise I could not explain the nature of my political work as an MP and a minister.

I am a socialist who believes that the Labour Party offers the best hope for Britain's future. More than thirty-seven years in Parliament, and thirty on Labour's front bench, have left me with few illusions. I do not believe that I or my colleagues are perfect; nor have I ever believed in the perfectibility of man. But my faith in the moral values which socialism represents, and in those who try to put them into practice, however imperfectly, remains undiminished. Despite all its frustrations and disappointments, I know that political action is both necessary and worthwhile.

However, politics as I have lived it would have been intolerable without the love of my wife and children. My family has always meant more to me than my profession. And I have always been as interested in music, painting, and poetry as in politics. A surprising number of the politicians I have known share these passions. Winston Churchill and Peter Thorney-croft were painters. Ted Heath and Helmut Schmidt both play the organ. Enoch Powell, like Karl Marx, wrote romantic poetry before he entered politics. In earlier centuries politics and poetry were very much closer; Dante, Marvell, and Heine were active politicians for most of their lives.

I have quoted poetry a good deal in this memoir, because I find that poets often understand the forces which shape politics better than the politicians themselves. Usually I have chosen the poems which head each chapter to reflect my own feelings at the time; sometimes, however, I have picked them to throw a different light on what I have to say myself.

Until I became an MP in 1952, I often kept quite detailed diaries; so I have used extracts from them in my earlier chapters. Thereafter I was too busy to do much more than write a list of my engagements. I would also have been uneasy about writing up my activities in detail every day. Others may be different; I do not believe I myself could act honestly as an MP or minister if I was wondering all the time how I would describe what I was doing day by day for the benefit of future generations. On the other hand, I have written innumerable articles about the issues which concern me; so I have sometimes quoted from them, because they are documentary evidence of what I thought when the events were taking place.

My life seems to have fallen naturally into sections of four to six years each, as I moved from one job to another. This memoir describes each of these sections in order. On the other hand, since all my jobs involved me in a great variety of issues, I have tried here to deal with each major issue separately, although in fact I was usually dealing with them all at the same time. That should make my story easier to follow, though it means making my life appear much more orderly than it really was. One virtue of a political diary is that it can convey far better than a memoir the frantic confusion in which a minister has to take great decisions.

That mighty prophet, William Blake, once wrote of someone:

> His whole life is an epigram smart, smooth and neatly penn'd,
> Plaited quite neat to catch applause, with a hang-noose at the end

Perhaps there is a hang-noose waiting somewhere for me too; but I have not tried in this memoir to give my life an artificial symmetry, still less to suggest that it is now complete. For one thing my life is by no means over yet. I am still learning every day, and my ideas are changing all the time; they must change if they are to reflect a world which itself is changing faster than ever before in history.

When he reached the age of seventy, Benjamin Franklin said that henceforward he planned to get a little younger every day. I regard that as an honourable ambition. I am determined to pursue it during the second half of my life.

PART ONE: Apprenticeship

CHAPTER ONE

The Schoolboy

Now as I was young and easy under the apple boughs
About the lilting house and happy as the grass was green,
    The night above the dingle starry,
      Time let me hail and climb
      Golden in the heydays of his eyes,
And honoured among wagons I was prince of the apple towns
And once below a time I lordly had the trees and leaves
    Trail with daisies and barley
    Down the rivers of the windfall light.

            – 'Fern Hill' Dylan Thomas

NO COMET BLAZED when I was born. But there was a storm all over England. Virginia Woolf records in her diary that it was 'not actually raining, though dark. Trees turned brown, shrivelled on their exposed sides, as if dried up by a hot sun. No autumn tints.'

The comet arrived later, when a German zeppelin was brought down over Blackheath, a few miles from where we lived. It flamed like a meteor in its descent. My father has described it to me so often that it seems as if I saw it myself; but I was a baby only seven months old when it happened. Nor did I realise, on August 30th, 1917, the day of my birth at a nursing home in Kent, that a new world was also struggling to be born.

The first American troops had landed in France a few weeks earlier, to seal the doom of the Kaiser's Germany; their arrival also signalled the beginning of the end of Europe as the centre of international affairs. A few weeks later the Bolsheviks stormed the Winter Palace; before long, communism covered a sixth of the world. Gandhi had just returned to India from South Africa to plan his campaign of non-violence against British rule. In China Sun Yat-sen had become Commander in Chief of the new Republic. My later life was to be dominated by the consequences of these events. I lived in blissful ignorance of them as a child.

In my earliest years we lived on an estate of wooden huts which had been put up as temporary housing for some of the eighty thousand workers needed at Woolwich Arsenal during the Great War. They were still there twenty years later. Ours was not a luxury dwelling – creosoted weatherboards outside and distempered asbestos inside, a gas mantle in the living room and candles to bed. The roads on the estate were unmade and sprinkled with cinders; years later I saw much the same thing in the South African township of Soweto. But inside the chestnut palings which separated our hut from its neighbours there was a little garden which was paradise enough for me – hollyhocks by the fence, a tiny square of lawn where I could sit at a wooden table and draw with coloured chalks, and a forest of artichokes where I hunted tigers with my friend Robin. His father, Arthur Fulton, had been a sniper in Flanders. Later, for three years in succession, he won the King's Prize for shooting; Robin also won it once.

I look back on those days with immense pleasure, though they have left me with only a handful of images. My father used to take me through the hop-fields sitting in a little wicker basket which was strapped to the handlebars of his bicycle. One day we went to Chislehurst caves, which had been used to store ammunition during the war. I was at once frightened and embarrassed when he leaned over a well and shouted: 'Are there any Germans down there?'

One night I awoke to find my father alone in the room, opening a tin of sardines. No sign of my mother. She had gone to a hospital, he told me, to get me a little sister called Pamela. It turned out to be a little brother called Terry.

In fact my mother had hoped that I too should be a little girl called Pamela. I turned out otherwise, so she left my father to choose a name for me. Like many fathers at that time, he picked Denis for my first name. He wanted something more substantial to follow it. Winston Churchill had been his idol for many years. In 1917 Churchill was in disgrace for his part in the Dardanelles disaster. Like many Irishmen, my father was a lover of lost causes. So my middle name is Winston – a source of much ribald comment when I entered politics.

Children can rarely see their parents as others see them. It was not until quite late in life that I began to understand my father and mother as human beings, and to realise how their personalities and mine had been shaped by their circumstances.

My grandfather, John William Healey, was a tailor. He emigrated to England from a village near Enniskillen when my father was a baby. The family settled in Todmorden, a smoky industrial town sunk in a narrow valley on the border between Yorkshire and Lancashire. They lived in a typical two-room back-to-back terraced house in the shadow of the railway viaduct, with the water closet at the bottom of the street.

The boys were all clever. Frank, the eldest, died soon after the Great War. John, the second, became the Labour Mayor of Todmorden in the twenties, but had a row with the local Party and turned Conservative. Russell, the fourth, caught chronic malaria at Salonica; after the war he became head of the textile department at Bradford Technical College. His daughter Joan went to Nairobi after the Second World War. I met her there in the sixties when she was working as a secretary to Daniel Arap Moi, who later became President of an independent Kenya.

Maggie, the only girl in the family, was a cotton operative the whole of her life. We sometimes visited the mill where she worked with hundreds of other women. The clatter of the machines was deafening and the air was full of cotton dust. Nothing much had changed since the early days of the Industrial Revolution. When she died in the back-to-back house she had lived in for eighty years, Maggie had saved a few thousand pounds. But she always set aside enough gold sovereigns to give one to each of her nephews and nieces on their birth and their marriage.

My father, Will, was the third boy. After eight years at the local council school he took evening classes for five years and won an engineering scholarship to Leeds University – quite an achievement in those days. Another five years' apprenticeship as a fitter and turner qualified him to teach engineering. His first job was in Gloucester, where he met my mother, Winnie, at the local tennis club.

Though circumstances led my father into engineering, his temperament was literary. For many years after going to Leeds he kept a commonplace book into which he copied anything which excited him, and wrote his own thoughts about life. Ruskin and Mark Twain were his favourites and he loved the romantic rhetoric of W. E. Henley and Rudyard Kipling. During his years at Woolwich he wrote short stories and poems for the local paper. The stories usually concerned episodes in the war, owing much to the Kipling of *Soldiers Three*. I presented one, an imaginary incident in Churchill's life, to Mary Soames, Winston's youngest daughter, half a century later.

Will's interest in politics was confined to a romantic Irish nationalism. His father had been a Fenian as a young man, and was deeply ashamed that Tim Healy, the persecutor of Parnell, bore the same name, although they were in no way related. So my head was filled with stories of Napper Tandy, Wolfe Tone, and the Sean van Vocht; my father made me rage at the iniquities of the Black and Tans. The legend of Cuchulain, the Hound of Ulster, was my favourite reading as a little boy, long before Yeats gave it a terrible beauty for me as a student.

I did not take my father's Irish nationalism seriously until the general election of 1945. I was supporting the Labour candidate for Keighley in the local school at Riddlesden. When it was time for questions my father suddenly got up and asked me what was the Labour Party's policy on Irish unity. I was flabbergasted. It had never struck me that Irish unity could be a matter for political debate in Britain. Twenty years later I discovered I was wrong.

My father's poetry was suffused with a wistful melancholy which recalled A. E. Housman. This side of his personality is well illustrated in:

'To a Dead Todmordian'

. . . in a tawdry French cottage, full of gimcrack furniture and pictures, three forgotten men stayed and died as if they were defending the Holy Sepulchre, Because Mr – had told them not to leave until he told them to.

– Official account

The wind that blows in Calder Vale
    Will fret his soul no more;
Nor rolling mists on Blackstone Edge
    Nor rainstorms on Whirlaw.

The smell of snow on Gaddens Moor
    Would come to him in dreams;
The ring of clogs in Rochdale Road
    That 'other life' redeems.

The idle boast and bitter jest
    That was his other life
Is ransomed on an alien soil
    Beneath the scourging knife.

The Schoolboy

Nor more to treat the lamplit streets
  Or pace the Burnley Road,
Which summer days made Arcady,
  A promise and a goad.

How then distilled the awful draught,
  When life and hope are naught:
That little gleam of ecstasy,
  The knife-edge thrust of thought.

To die for some forgotten code,
  Returning blow for blow,
And thin-lipped face the acid truth
  That we would never know.

The Dunkirk beach is silent now,
  The seething ranks are gone.
But still across the broken chairs
  He smiles as if he'd won.

It was a long time before I came to understand this element in my
father's nature. A child's vision of his parents does not extend beyond
their special relationship with him. My father's literary romanticism made
it difficult for him to communicate directly with his children. He found it
easier to express his real warmth and humanity to his students than to
Terry and me. I still get letters from them describing his kindnesses. He
could write a long letter to someone he scarcely knew expressing a loving
sympathy at the death of a wife or husband. But the first time I felt I
really made contact with the man underneath my child's image of my
father was on the morning of my wedding. To my amazement he chose
that moment to tell me that he was in a state of terror the day he married
Winnie Powell.

  She was a very different character – intellectual rather than emotional,
with a will of iron which enabled her to survive four strokes at the age of
ninety-seven. She reminded one journalist who interviewed her of Rose
Kennedy, the mother of the President. The only time I ever saw her
weep was the day my father died. I myself weep as easily as Churchill
did.

  Winnie's father, William Powell, was a signalman, and stationmaster at a small village halt, long since closed, at Newnham on Severn in Gloucestershire. The local MP, Sir Charles Dilke, used to give him a brace of pheasants at Christmas. Once a year Sir Charles invited his tenants to a dance in his Hall. Mother once danced with him as a girl – a memory she recalled with mixed feelings in view of the scandal which cost Dilke his promising career.

She loved reading; on visits to her aunt's farm in Herefordshire she would escape from the other children up an apple-tree with her favourite book. After her course at the teachers' training college in Cheltenham, she began to teach at Gloucester, where she met and married my father at the outbreak of the Great War.

Winnie was then a beautiful young woman with lustrous black hair and strong handsome features – the Edwardian ideal. These looks stayed with her till the end of her life; the Royal Academician, Syd Harpley, insisted on making a model of her head when she was ninety-seven. My father was very jealous of any attention paid to her by his friends. But she was never interested in other men.

She had many women friends, some of whom were suffragettes in her youth. After she had accepted Willie's proposal she insisted they went away to Fleshwick Bay in the Isle of Man for a trial marriage. It was months before her mother would speak to her again. Both my parents could have come from an early novel by H. G. Wells – mother from *Ann Veronica* and father, perhaps, from *Kipps* or *The History of Mr Polly*.

Throughout her life mother wanted to learn more – particularly about literature, music, painting and politics. A series of wireless talks by Harold Nicolson in the early thirties fired her with enthusiasm for the Bloomsbury set, D. H. Lawrence and Aldous Huxley. She was immensely excited when I took her to Sissinghurst after the war and she met Harold Nicolson's son, Nigel, who had been a friend of mine at Balliol. Before the war she took WEA classes in literature and current affairs every year. All these enthusiasms, of course, she passed on to me. It was thanks above all to her that I had such a rich and happy childhood.

In 1922, when I was five years old, we moved to the West Riding of Yorkshire; my father had been appointed Principal of Keighley Technical School, at a salary of £600 a year. It was like emigrating to another country, to leave a gimcrack suburb in outer London for the grimy millstone grit of the industrial North. Even the language was different – 'lake' for play, 'spice' for sweets, 'tart' for girl, and so on. The middle of Keighley, where we lived at first, had changed little since Mrs Gaskell had described it sixty-five years earlier:

Grey stone abounds; and the rows of houses built of it have a kind of solid grandeur connected with their uniform and enduring lines. The framework of the doors, and the lintels of the windows, even in the smallest dwellings, are made of blocks of stone; . . . and the stone is kept scrupulously clean by the notable Yorkshire housewives.

However, Mrs Gaskell already noticed a transformation taking place. As a 'populous and flourishing town' Keighley was acquiring 'dwellings for the professional middle class'. We lived in one of them – a nineteenth-century terraced house in Holker Street. It had a few feet of gritty garden by the front door, where I could hear my pet hedgehog crunching worms, and a walled yard at the back, where I could build Fort Winston with my Meccano set.

I used to run along the top of the walls at the back, jumping over the intervening gates, as the old women shouted: 'Ye'll lame yerself!' The bars of the lampposts provided me with swings. On Sundays we dressed up and walked the mile to Utley Congregational Church. My father felt this ritual would commend him to Mrs Craven Laycock, the grand old lady Congregationalist who was Chairman of his Education Committee.

My schooling started at Drake and Tonsons' Kindergarten in Keighley, which the actress Mollie Sugden also attended. It was there that I endured the greatest humiliation of my childhood. One afternoon I returned to school from dinner at home still wearing a pinafore; I had to hide weeping in the cloakroom, until the teacher found me and took it off.

My life-long fascination with films started at this time. I used to sit in the penny seats on the front row of the Cosy Corner picture house; giant images of Tom Mix and Buck Jones reared above me in distorted perspective with the piano thundering away until, as hero and villain rolled together over the cliff-top, there appeared the legend: 'To be continued next week'. Even at the age of seven or eight what made the biggest impact on me were the great German silent films of Fritz Lang – *Siegfried* and *Metropolis*. I can still see in my mind's eye Siegfried dying in a grove of silver birch on a bank studded with daisies.

Sometimes the films left less agreeable memories. My little brother, Terry, and I once saw a film in which there appeared a villainous character in a pith helmet who carried a stock-whip, called Dr Kief. For years afterwards a mention of Dr Kief was enough to send us under the bedclothes.

Both of us were frightened of the dark. In the days before electric light there were always dark passages to be raced through between kitchen and dining room, where nameless horrors lurked in the shadows. For years I used to sleep with the sheet over my head, breathing through a tiny opening over my nose and mouth. We hated being left alone in the house while our parents were out at golf or bridge. On one occasion we had to be rescued by one of my father's teachers with a ladder from the bathroom where we had locked ourselves in. On another I awoke in the dark to find my parents missing. So I dressed my little brother and dragged him next door to tell the old ladies living there that our mother and father had been killed by a golf ball.

When I was eight years old my world changed again. I won a scholarship to Bradford Grammar School, ten miles away, and we moved from the centre of Keighley to the village of Riddlesden just outside, on the edge of Ilkley Moor. For the next ten years Bradford shaped my intellectual development while my personal life centred on Riddlesden.

They were two different universes. Riddlesden was a village with a long history – it had two Elizabethan manor houses; but new building was fast turning it into a suburb of Keighley. We lived in a semi-detached house on the steep hill looking over Keighley towards Haworth and the moors which inspired *Wuthering Heights*. Emily Brontë's poems have a unique resonance for me. A row of sycamores stood between our front garden and the cobbled snicket which led up to farmland and Rivock Edge, on the southern flank of Ilkley Moor.

On Saturday afternoons and Sundays we explored every beck and crag on the moors above us; we built dams with stones and tussocks of grass, and forced our bodies into every rocky cave in the hope of finding hidden treasure. Our favourite walk took us along the escarpment overlooking Ilkley and the Wharfe valley, past the prehistoric Swastika Stone and Windgate Nick, to tea at a farmhouse on paper-thin bread and butter with strawberry jam before the last lap back to Riddlesden.

When I was given a bicycle I was able to ride further afield – for example to Cottingley Glen, which Conan Doyle celebrated in his book on the Cottingley fairies. I could not understand how the creator of Sherlock Holmes should have allowed himself to be deceived by two schoolgirls, who had taken obvious studio photographs of young ladies in Grecian tunics with gauze wings. Years later I discovered one explanation; besides being a spiritualist, Conan Doyle was a descendant of the great Dicky Doyle, whose illustrations make *In Fairyland* one of the greatest of all Victorian picture books.

The Druid's Altar above Bingley, boating on the River Aire, and the swings and slides of Goit Stock were other delights. But my favourite pleasure ground was in the dales – Wharfedale from Bolton Abbey to Grassington and Linton, and Airedale from Skipton to Malham Tarn and Gordale Scar – an area loved by Wordsworth and painted by Turner, Girtin, and Ward.

At all seasons the dales keep their special beauty – summer when the bracken is green and sweet to smell, autumn when it is golden brown and the moors are flooded with purple heather, winter when all is white with snow and an icy wind makes your eyes water. But loveliest of all is spring, when primroses stud the grey stone walls, the lush meadows are sprinkled with cowslips, and pools of bluebells glow luminous in the woods. And above all this the larks rising and falling in the pure sky: 'It was all Adam and maiden, and fire, green as grass' – Dylan Thomas' 'Fern Hill' captures exactly this part of my own childhood.

Every Whitsun we had our school camp in a field by the Wharfe near Appletreewick where, as we walked to church at Burnsall, 'the Sabbath rang slowly in the pebbles of the holy streams'. One day was always set aside for a walk down the river through Bolton woods to the ruined Abbey, then up the Valley of Desolation and over the moors to Simon's Seat, before dropping back into the valley to camp. This part of Wharfedale is for me what Shropshire was for Housman: 'the land of lost content'. I return when I can, though it is sad nowadays to find those quiet roads choked every weekend by cars from Leeds and Bradford crawling bumper to bumper.

The environmental movement claimed me when I was only eleven years old. Over the hill from Riddlesden, outside the village of Morton, there was a lake called Sunnydale surrounded by larch and pine, which had been created to serve a long disused paper mill. It was a favourite haunt for me and my brother. To my horror I discovered it was scheduled to become a reservoir. I wrote a passionate article in my holiday journal for 1929 warning that 'the ogre of industrialisation stretches out his grimy hand towards it'. The threat was withdrawn, to return nearly sixty years later. In 1987 I sent the protesters a copy of that holiday journal to help their case.

Until I had my bike, however, visits to my mother's family in Newnham provided my country heaven. We used to go there once a year while her parents were alive. My grandfather was a tall, gaunt man with a thick beard and deep-set eyes. He could lift me to the ceiling with the palm of one hand. My grandmother had had a stroke and lived in a darkened room downstairs, from which I could sometimes hear an insane cackling.

Years later I discovered she was an alcoholic. My Auntie Dolly was ten years younger than my mother, and deeply devoted to her – she used to shock me by crying when we left.

They had a typical village house with a vegetable garden, a few apple trees and raspberry bushes, and a shed where Dolly hung a piece of seaweed to forecast the weather. I loved the fresh salty air of the Severn Estuary, and played with my brother on the tiny beach below, which was more mud than sand. My grandfather would take us through the orchards to his little station and let us into the signal box when the trains were passing. Once when we were left for a week alone with Auntie Dolly, she came back from shopping to see me and Terry urinating from the window on the landing towards the house next door. She was not amused.

Mother's brother Bert also worked on the railway. He lived in what then seemed to us rather a grand house at Grange Court nearby; it had previously belonged to Dr Saklatvala, Britain's first Communist MP. What I liked most of all was to walk up the hills behind Newnham to Pleasant Stile, which has one of the loveliest views in England. The great silver bend of the Severn lies below, with the Cotswolds blue on the horizon, Gloucester Cathedral just visible on the left, and the little church of Newnham standing out against the river.

A few miles away, at Coleford in the Forest of Dean, there was a little girl called Edna Edmunds who loved the view as much as I. Twenty years later she became my wife.

Because my grammar school was ten miles away in Bradford, and many of my school friends lived a further ten miles on the other side of the city, my life in Riddlesden centred on my family and my friends in Keighley. Since the technical school held its classes mainly at night, my father went down to Keighley an hour after I got home from Bradford, and that hour was spent having tea and listening to Jack Payne or Henry Hall conducting their dance band on the wireless. So I saw much less of my father than most children would.

My memories of him at that time often have a comic flavour. Being passionately fond of birds, he built a miniature aviary for his canaries and linnets at one end of the garden shed, which projected into the open air through the window. Unfortunately he used chicken wire for the cage, and on more than one occasion a hapless bird pushed its head through the wire netting and could not get it back before the neighbour's cat had bitten it off. When the canaries had an attack of red mites, my father bought a bottle of paraffin and painstakingly brushed the fluid all over their unprotesting bodies, in the hope of disinfesting them. Next morning they were all lying on their backs at the bottom of the cage, stone-dead, with their claws in the air.

During the summer, Terry and I often slept in a tent in the garden; my father decided to make it waterproof by drenching it with paraffin wax. The wax melted in the sun, hanging in long stalactites from the eaves; when autumn came and we took the tent down, it cracked open wherever we tried to fold it.

My father loved experimenting. Our first wireless was a crystal set with a free standing curved horn as a speaker; he would spend hours trying to get the right station with his cat's whisker. Feeling that we needed more comfort in the garden he bought the back seat of an old car, complete with folding canopy, and installed it with great effort under the dining room window, christening it Glugs. It was far too uncomfortable for normal use, but my brother and I found Glugs invaluable for our early amatory adventures.

Photography was another of my father's hobbies. He had an ancient folding camera which used glass plates instead of celluloid negatives; but the bellows was full of pinholes, so his pictures were full of flares. When I was eight he bought me my first camera, a Box Brownie 2A, and helped me to develop the film by seesawing it through a bath of chemicals under the stairs, thus laying the foundation for the passion of a lifetime.

Though a trained engineer by profession, in everyday life my father was, I fear, a bodger – a characteristic he passed on to me. But then I sometimes think that God himself is the Great Bodger in the Sky.

Unlike my father, mother was always there to help and advise. She joined us for walks, encouraged our interests, and above all made sure we did our homework. When I developed my enthusiasm for painting and music she kept pace with me, although she had hitherto had no interest in the visual arts, and little in classical music.

As Terry was three years younger, he sometimes found it difficult to keep up with the rest of our gang – until girls entered the scene, when he showed a precocious aptitude. I fear I took pleasure in frightening him occasionally. He has never quite forgiven me for hiding in the wardrobe of his bedroom one evening when our parents were out. Then, just as he had got into bed, I gave a low moan. He saw a ghastly face, green behind the stained glass of the wardrobe door. Then I emerged, my features daubed with flour and soot, and my arms stretched out towards him.

I loved dressing up. Once, when my parents were next door playing bridge, I went round in my father's coat and trilby, a pipe in my mouth, forced my way into their drawing room and pretended to be a drunken stranger for several minutes until I was found out. Our neighbour, a portly and somewhat pompous bank manager, was deeply offended.

My best friend in Keighley was Peter Walker, the son of a local doctor. My first two girl-friends were his sisters, Mary and Pat – in succession! I was badly shaken when Peter died after an accident at football at the age of eighteen. It was our common delight to cheek his elder brother, Jack, particularly when he first wore long trousers; after a gap of forty years I met Jack again in Singapore. I was Defence Secretary; Jack was Chief Surgeon of our Far East Fleet.

Like most small boys, we formed a gang, riding up and down the hills of small coal by the canal, building dens by the road from which to harass the passers-by. One day we made ourselves bows and arrows and went hunting the chickens on a piece of waste ground. That evening there was a ring at our front door. A man was standing there, with a dead hen dangling from one hand. My father paid him the shilling he demanded to avoid a summons, and as the man turned to go addressed him: 'Eh, wait a minute. I'll have the chicken now I've paid for it.'

My proudest possession was an air rifle, which I could use to ping the church bell a hundred yards away. I also used it to knock starlings down the chimneys of the house next door, until I found a bird I had wounded palpitating on the ground. From that moment I have never killed a living thing for sport – not even a fish.

Riddlesden meant freedom and the country. Bradford Grammar School meant hard work and the city. It was another world altogether – a collection of large stone buildings in the middle of the city, smelling of sweat and oil, and surrounded by concrete playgrounds. I used to travel there with some of my friends from Keighley – at first by train, where the big boys used to beat the smaller boys with the window straps. I still have a scar on one knuckle where my fist went through the glass in a vain attempt to punish my tormentor. Later we went by double decker bus; the game then was to throw the other boys' school caps out of the window.

The school was proud of its reputation as one of the best grammar schools in the country, second only to Manchester Grammar. The great majority of the boys had scholarships, and were drawn from a catchment area more than ten miles round Bradford; so the competition was intense. In order to boost its academic record it made the sixth form boys take Higher Certificate in the same subjects three years running. I greatly resented this waste of time, particularly at an age when I was hungry for knowledge. So I spent much of my last two years ignoring the lessons and reading books of my own choice behind my desk.

In those days the cleverest boys had to learn Latin and Greek so as to sit for scholarships at Oxford or Cambridge; after getting their degrees they were expected to join the Home Civil Service, with the Indian Civil Service as second choice. So I met some of my school friends again when I became a government minister.

Of all my contemporaries at Bradford, I most admired Alan Bullock, who later wrote the biography of Ernest Bevin, became the Vice-Chancellor of Oxford University, and produced the Bullock Report on industrial democracy. He was two years older than I, and won the Senior Essay Prize of the National Book Council in 1930, the same year as I won the Junior Essay Prize. His father was a Unitarian minister and leader of the city's Literary Society. Alan had a range of knowledge and interests unique in our school; he seemed equally familiar with Wagner's letters and Joyce's *Ulysses*. So there was more than an element of *Schadenfreude* in my pleasure when our Latin master wrote at the bottom of one of his proses '*Omasum*' – a Gallic word which means bullock's tripe! He has remained a friend throughout the years, the breadth of his wisdom and humanity steadily growing with time.

Another contemporary was Maurice Hodgson, who became Chairman of ICI. He told me how one winter he cycled to Keighley to skate on the frozen Tarn up in the hills above. When he stopped in the middle of the town to ask the way to the Tarn he was told: 'Tha's in it, lad'.

I am often asked whether I would have not done better to learn something other than Latin and Greek. At least for the work I have done since, there is no better training. Everyone can gain from learning Latin. It teaches you to think clearly and express yourself precisely; it also helps you to learn a number of other languages.

The practical utility of Greek is less obvious. In Victorian days Thomas Gaisford pronounced the revolting encomium: 'Greek not only elevates above the vulgar herd, but leads often to positions of considerable emolument'. That is no longer true. However, Greek poetry, drama, and philosophy have no superior in any language. This is the best reason for learning Greek. Politicians have another. The city states of ancient Greece provided the world with models of every political predicament faced by later Western societies; their historians described these predicaments with unrivalled accuracy and understanding. In his *Peloponnesian War*, Thucydides illustrates most of the dilemmas of modern democracies both at home and abroad.

Apart from its lyric poets, particularly Catullus and Horace, I found Latin literature less exciting. But the fall of the Roman Republic and the story of the Caesars had all too many lessons for modern times. Tacitus analysed the social and political background of those days with a penetration only Marx has equalled, and with a stylish concision which has been the envy of all his successors.

The man who first gave me my love for the classics was 'Tock' Lewis, who taught me at Bradford when I was twelve years old. Bald and white bearded, he had been a friend since youth of Gilbert Murray, then Regius Professor of Greek at Oxford, and had written the standard Greek textbook. He retired to live in Cornwall with his sister, a Cambridge don, after my first year of Greek, and I spent a week or two every summer with him there. Besides learning to read Aeschylus' *Agamemnon*, I was introduced to Beethoven and the Elizabethan dramatists in his library.

After a day on the beach or walking the cliff-tops above Bedruthan Steps I would return to his house at Treyarnon Bay, my knees burning from the windy sun, and listen to Schnabel playing the Emperor Concerto on the gramophone, while on the horizon the conical hills of china clay at St Austell glowed white like the mountains of the moon. In the end I realised that his interest in me was not purely intellectual, so I ceased these visits. But those weeks at Treyarnon Bay laid a solid foundation for my love of music and the classics; they also gave me an abiding love for the north coast of Cornwall, where I later took my own family camping for many years.

I read voraciously throughout my schooldays. Indeed when I look back on the list of twenty-four books I read in a single term when I was fourteen, I feel ashamed I give myself so little time to read for pleasure nowadays, and that I allow television to preempt so much of my leisure.

At first I was devoted to G. K. Chesterton, a writer of exceptional style and imagination, though I now find the acuteness of his vision too often obscured by the flamboyance of his paradoxes. He had first met Father O'Connor, the model for his detective Father Brown, when lecturing at Keighley; they became life-long friends while taking my favourite walk over the moors to Ilkley. In his autobiography, Chesterton talks of us having 'at the back of our minds . . . a forgotten blaze or burst of astonishment at our own existence. The object of the artistic and spiritual life is to dig for this submerged sunrise of wonder.' That has always been my object too.

Later my favourite became Virginia Woolf; I devoured her novels with growing excitement as *Jacob's Room* was followed by *To the Lighthouse* and *The Waves*. I was not to discover the unique joys of her essays until later; they led me to all sorts of authors whom otherwise I would never have thought of reading, from Ellen Terry to Marie, Queen of Rumania. Then, when I was sixteen, the great Russian novelists bowled me over like a tidal wave.

I had already been deeply impressed by Merejkowski's historical novels, particularly the trilogy which takes Akhnaton, Julian the Apostate, and Leonardo da Vinci as types of the Antichrist, whom he admired reluctantly rather as Milton admired Satan. He opened my eyes to unfamiliar cultures and civilisations. But the real revelation came with Dostoevsky, Tolstoy and Turgenev, an inexhaustible store of insights into every aspect of life – including politics. The fable of the Grand Inquisitor in *The Brothers Karamazov* provided me with the best key to understanding the authoritarian state. Piotr Verhovensky in *The Possessed* told me all I needed to know about the terrorist tradition in Leninism; that is not surprising, since he is modelled on Nechaev, the ringleader of the revolutionary group to which Lenin's brother belonged when he was executed. Similarly, modern Russians must be impressed by the way in which their campaign in Afghanistan echoed the imperialist wars in the Caucasus described by Tolstoy and Lermontov.

In the sixth form we were taught English and current affairs by a young man just down from Cambridge, where he had studied under Frank and Queenie Leavis. So their magazine *Scrutiny* became my bible. I read T. S. Eliot, D. H. Lawrence and Wyndham Lewis with new respect and explored the Seven Types of Ambiguity with William Empson. I. A. Richards was of course beyond criticism. Modern fashion has been unkind to the Leavisites; they did invaluable service by giving literature a moral dimension. To me their greatest value was in cutting away the undergrowth of the Georgian poets, and revealing that the true greatness of Yeats lies in his later poems.

Just before I left Bradford I found Samuel Beckett's *Murphy* in the local library and began a lifetime's devotion to that 'seedy Irish solipsist'. Indeed by introducing *Murphy* to Iris Murdoch at Oxford I may have dislodged the pebble which started her avalanche. At this time I also discovered Montherlant's tetralogy, *Pity for Women*, which in my ignorance I imagined was the last word in understanding of the other sex, proving the superiority of the French in these matters.

However, my reading was not confined to such improving works. When I first went to Bradford I used to devour the exploits of the detective Falcon Swift and his assistant Chick Conway in *The Boy's*

Magazine. It cost twopence every Friday. I shared the cost with Arthur Spencer, my best friend at school. Arthur was a clean-cut, good looking boy with fair hair and blue eyes, a natural Head of School, and the very model of the naval officer he became during the war. We were at Oxford together, though he was at a different college and never shared my left-wing political views. After the war he joined the secret service. Peter Wright in *Spycatcher* describes how Arthur secretly monitored the telephone conversations of the Soviet spy, Gordon Lonsdale, though as usual Wright gets all the facts slightly wrong.

The Boy's Magazine was followed by *The Wizard*, *The Rover* and *Modern Boy*, with its tin cutouts of racing cars and aeroplanes. Then I turned to the twopenny library for Bulldog Drummond and the Saint, and became hooked for life on thrillers. When I was a young man, Dashiell Hammett and Raymond Chandler replaced John Buchan and Leslie Charteris; today my favourites are Elmore Leonard and George V. Higgins. The peak of my youthful criminal ambition was achieved when my enthusiasm for the forgotten writer John Franklin Bardin led Julian Symons to invite me to present the Golden Dagger award to the Crime Writer of the Year in 1976.

Bradford did not produce only civil servants and business men. The German Jews who came to Bradford in the nineteenth century to set up textile mills were men of culture too. In my time the three most distinguished old boys of the school were the composer Frederick Delius, the painter William Rothenstein, and the poet Humbert Wolfe, now best remembered for his immortal epigram:

> You cannot bribe or twist
> Thank God, the British journalist.
> But, seeing what the man will do
> Unbribed, there's no occasion to.

In recent times David Hockney has been the school's best known painter, but he came after the war. I myself have always enjoyed drawing; I doodle compulsively, always faces or landscapes rather than abstract patterns. At Bradford I took lessons in watercolour painting from the art master after school, and was much influenced by De Wint, Paul Nash, and Ethelbert White. Later I learned more from Ernest Sichel, a friend of Rothenstein, and practised pastels with Alex Keighley, who was still famous for the landscape photographs he had taken in the nineteenth century; they were printed in fuzzy sepia to look as much as possible like oil paintings.

My own watercolour paintings in those days were quite good; but as I grew older I found it more and more difficult to avoid niggling detail. Nowadays I rarely paint more than one picture a year, on my summer holiday, and it looks like the product of a vicarage spinster. Watercolour is the most difficult of mediums, since you have to get it right first time – it is almost impossible to correct. The greatest watercolourists, like Cotman, are able to transform the most complicated subject into a few broad washes of colour. They have an intellectual capacity to organise their insight which soldiers and administrators might envy; Churchill, himself a painter, saw the justice of this analogy.

I loved the Impressionists particularly, and spent my pocket money on postcards of Monet and van Gogh from the church bookshop. Since there were few great paintings nearby, I had to feed my visual taste from books and reproductions. However, in 1932 my parents took me to the great exhibition of French Art at the Royal Academy in London, where for the first time I saw the originals of some of my favourites, including the magical paintings done by Gauguin in the South Seas. Reading my holiday journals of those years, I find I had become exceptionally sensitive to colour in landscape.

By now an incorrigible bookworm, I began to read books on painting – Clive Bell, Roger Fry, and that exotic flower, George Duthuit. This led me to a book which had as much influence on my thinking as any I have read in any field, Woelfflin's *Principles of Art History*. I found that his separation of art into Romantic and Classical through contrasting dichotomies of style had a universal application; I found it a more useful tool for understanding the different types of people than the categories of Freud or Marx. For example, I noticed that a blues chord tended to be a normal chord with one note flattened; this was a typical Romantic device. Aneurin Bevan, the supreme Romantic politician, often adopted it in his rhetoric, by using a word in a slightly inappropriate sense. He would say 'spatchcock', for example, to mean 'add'; by the time you had begun to ask yourself what was the barrel into which this bung was hammered, he had passed on. His oratory kept you so excited by this sort of provocation that its practical meaning, if any, did not matter so much.

Parallel with this explosion of my interest in painting came a new passion for music. I had taken piano lessons for a few years with a teacher in Keighley who felt that Beethoven and Chopin often got it wrong, and made me play his improvements instead. This was somewhat disheartening, and I did not take up the piano again until some years later. Now I find it my most rewarding hobby. Long intervals without playing do not reduce my ability to read music – the problem is in my fingers, which obstinately refuse to obey my mind. I am too often reminded of Donne's words:

> And like a bunch of ragged carrots stand
> The short swoll'n fingers of thy gouty hand.

During my last years at school I went to every performance of the Hallé Orchestra's subscription concerts in Bradford's echoing St George's Hall. They were conducted by Hamilton Harty or John Barbirolli and had the pick of the world's greatest instrumentalists – Szigeti and Huberman on the violin, Cortot, Fischer and Schnabel on the piano. Schnabel was in a class of his own, particularly in the Beethoven sonatas. From the first to last note he had the architecture of the whole piece clearly in his mind.

As soon as I could afford the money, I began collecting records. A symphony would take up four twelve-inch shellac heavyweights, and was far more expensive in real terms than a compact disc today. Moreover, the steel needles wore the records out, so I experimented with fibre or thorn needles which sometimes would not last out a single side. Even worse, my mechanical gramophone would not play a twelve-inch side without rewinding. So at the most critical moment the music would begin to slow down, and I would have to leap out of bed and crank the machine up again. Nevertheless, my gramophone opened a new world to me.

Today, when almost every piece ever composed is available at the touch of a button in near-perfect sound from a choice of several superb performances, it is easy to forget that eighty years ago no one outside the bigger cities knew any orchestral music unless they could read a score, and most music was not even available on printed scores. Similarly, until photographic colour reproductions began to be available at the end of the nineteenth century, most of the world's great paintings were unknown to anyone who could not afford the time or money to visit them on the spot; the only alternative was black and white engravings, often of appalling quality.

The third field in which my interest exploded in those last years at school was film and theatre. Even in Keighley, the local Hippodrome had annual visits from the D'Oyly Carte Opera playing Gilbert and Sullivan, and from some dramatic companies. I remember Sir Frank Benson hamming Shakespeare with his skinny shanks, the melodramatic declamations of Donald Wolfit and the poetic baritone of Ion Swinley. My real favourite, however, was Tod Slaughter as Sweeney Todd, the Demon Barber of Fleet Street: 'I wish the whole world had just one throat, so that I could have the pleasure of slitting it.' At Bradford the choice was far wider. The Carl Rosa performed grand opera at the Alhambra theatre. It was there that I heard Eva Turner sing Turandot, Beecham conduct *Faust* and Carl Brisson perform *The Merry Widow*.

The Bradford Civic Theatre had an amateur repertory company of exceptional quality, performing modern plays like Capek's *R.U.R.* which never appeared in the commercial theatre in the provinces. It had the astonishing good fortune to persuade Komisarjevsky, a refugee from the Moscow Arts Theatre, to produce Chekhov's *Cherry Orchard*. One unforgettable evening, its Film Club, which specialised in foreign films, showed Eisenstein's *The General Line*. I was so excited that, as soon as I got home, I wrote out the whole of the scenario, almost shot by shot. That was when I decided I wanted to be a film director; it is an ambition I have still not finally renounced.

The climax of my theatrical year would come during our annual visit to London, when my father took us all to join him for a few days during his annual Principals' Conference. We had only one seaside holiday during the whole of my childhood; the visit to London more than made up for this. It was quite an expedition in those days – six hours in the train each way, bed and breakfast for five shillings a night at a hotel in Bloomsbury, and a four course dinner with the unfamiliar luxury of hors d'oeuvres, for four and sixpence at a restaurant in Soho.

We would spend the mornings in museums and galleries, and go every afternoon and evening to the theatre, where I saw all the leading actors of the thirties; some, like Gielgud and Emlyn Williams, are still with us. The most enjoyable single evening of my boyhood was at *Helen*, A. P. Herbert's version of Offenbach's *La Belle Helene* with George Robey as Menelaus, another great comic George Graves as Calchas, and Evelyn Laye as Helen, with decor by Messel and choreography by Massine – a meringue glacé with kirsch! One incomparable weekend when I was sixteen we saw the enchanting American husband and wife team of Lunt and Fontanne in *Reunion in Vienna*, Coward and Yvonne Printemps flirting in *Conversation Piece*, Edmund Gwenn in *Laburnum Grove*, Elizabeth Bergner in *Escape Me Never*, Charles Laughton and Flora Robson in *Macbeth*, and Angela Baddeley in *Richard of Bordeaux*.

My own acting ability was limited – I started at school as Polly Perkins in *The Grand Cham's Diamond* and graduated to Sganarelle in *Le Médécin*

Malgré Lui. My talent has always run to comic turns rather than straight drama.

The arts so dominated my life at school that I had little interest in politics. I remember having to cycle to school from Riddlesden during the General Strike in 1926, and hearing our most popular master, who had been an officer in the war, defend the strikers. I made a speech against Nazism in the Debating Society. My one act of political witness was to brave the wrath of all my teachers by resigning from the Officer's Training Corps in 1935. This was mainly because the poets of the Great War, such as Wilfred Owen and Siegfried Sassoon, had converted me to pacifism; but I confess I also found it senseless to train on wooden Lewis guns in an uncomfortable uniform with puttees which always came unwound.

I was always top in English, but rarely came first in my main subjects, Greek and Latin. My energy went more into the school literary and debating societies than into my classes. So I was lucky to get an exhibition to Balliol College at Oxford in my final year, particularly since very few Bradfordians ever won scholarships to Balliol.

It was in 1936, during my summer holiday between school and Oxford that politics first presented me with the challenge which has shaped my life. I spent five weeks cycling through Europe to see Reinhardt's production of Goethe's *Faust* at the Salzburg Festival. Hitler had not been long in power, and since the Olympic Games were being held in Germany, the people were told to be nice to foreigners. So I was able to talk politics even in the youth hostels, which were then full of Hitler Jugend.

Just to be abroad was an excitement beyond belief. Everything was subtly different from what I had known till then – the clothes, the houses, the countryside, and above all the people. I had learned enough French at school to manage quite well in Belgium, and a year's German in the sixth form taught me at least to read the old script which was still used for newspapers and notices in Germany. My German vocabulary increased steadily day by day, and I have the parrot's facility for pronunciation. German grammar, however, defeated me, and I still fight a losing battle with it.

It was the best holiday of my life – and the cheapest. I slept in barns or the local youth hostels, which in Germany then cost a penny a night and a penny for breakfast. Black bread and strawberry jam, without butter, were my staple fare; I usually managed green salad and potatoes once a day, and meat every two days. So the whole five weeks cost me only five pounds, including the cost of my passport, the fare from Harwich to Antwerp, my ticket to *Faust* and presents to take home.

For that meagre sum I had my first visit abroad, saw some of the best art galleries in the world, enjoyed magnificent scenery, and met a cross-section of Europe's youth in the last years before the Holocaust. Ted Heath was also profoundly affected by his own visit to Germany at that time, and Patrick Leigh-Fermor, who had travelled right to the Black Sea a few years earlier, wrote a diary of his journey which produced two exceptional books half a century later.

I too kept a diary of my journey. It devotes more pages to the art galleries in Munich, Frankfurt, Brussels and Antwerp, than to politics. However, I spent every evening arguing in the youth hostels, talked to everyone I met on the road, and often spent a day or two riding with German companions; so the freemasonry of the young gave me an invaluable insight into European society on the eve of war.

Scarcely eighteen years had passed since the Armistice which ended what was still seen as Armageddon. Some of the Germans I met had fought in Belgium against France. One bitter Alsatian cried a plague on both your houses. The young Austrians were Nazi to a man. The Czechs were Socialist or Communist. Most of the Germans idolised Hitler, despised the French and Italians, and claimed to admire the British. One newspaper had a picture of Etonians in their Officers' Training Corps entitled 'The British Youth Movement'.

Yet I also met many young Germans who were staunchly anti-Nazi; they were mainly working men, who assured me that many of their friends simply wore brown shirts over their red shirts; they were called 'beefsteaks' – outside brown and inside red. I had one long talk by the dark green Königsee just outside Berchtesgaden with a Catholic student who was certain the German people would rise against Hitler.

In Munich I stayed in one of the four magnificent youth hostels built by the Nazis for the Hitler Jugend. Discipline was strict and the children were drilled in the yard before breakfast every morning. Years later, during a talk with Franz-Josef Strauss, we discovered that he must have been staying there at the same time, when he was a young butcher's boy from a village outside Munich. He had never been a Nazi, but he told me that only people who like himself had lived under a dictatorship could understand the coded language used nowadays by East Europeans to express their real feelings.

I had fierce arguments with many of the Germans I met, speaking as a democrat, a socialist, and sometimes as a communist – I did not distinguish much between the three at that time. But these arguments never led to personal hostility. Indeed the only unpleasant reaction I had in five weeks was from the owner of an art shop in Munich, when I asked if he had any reproductions of Matisse or Picasso; he regarded them as decadent pornographers.

On the other hand, I found the ordinary Germans I met exceptionally kind; they would help me to mend my bicycle, give me fruit or milk, and guide me to my youth hostel at night. Yet it was impossible to miss the sense of impending war. Wooden models of air bombs stood in every village square, inscribed with the words *'Denke daran'* or *'Luftschutz tut Not'*; they acted as collection boxes for the air force. The Spanish Civil War broke out during my journey, and the newspapers were full of atrocity stories and anti-Soviet propaganda. None of my friends could explain why they were simultaneously demanding a higher birth rate and more living space, while asserting 'Hitler will kein Krieg'.

Even so, the main impression left by those five weeks was of the beauty of the landscape and the friendliness of the people. I cycled through the rolling pastoral countryside of north-west Germany and the enchanted woods and valleys of the Black Forest, then by the silver expanses of the Bodensee to Bavaria. This was my first experience of the Alps. I climbed up the Madelegabel in the Allgäu to a youth hostel on the snow-line, where I met a noisy and drunken Bavarian who tried to sell me kisses from his girl-friend. Surprisingly, I found less support for Hitler in Bavaria than elsewhere. People much preferred the greeting 'Grüss Gott' to 'Heil Hitler'; there was a famous alley near the railway station in Munich which was used by people who did not want to walk past the memorial to the 'martyrs' of the Bierkeller putsch, where they would have to give the Nazi salute. My only disappointment was the river Rhine, which I found, and still find, a dull industrial ditch. That is not the only thing on which I disagree with Bernard Levin.

The climax of my holiday was a few days in Salzburg. I failed, after four hours' queuing, to get a seat for Toscanini conducting the *Deutsches Requiem*. By paying someone to queue six hours for me, I managed to get a standing place at the back of the gallery for Max Reinhardt's production of Goethe's *Faust* in the Fauststadt, a mediaeval village built into the cliff especially for the play. It is still used for opera at the Salzburg Festival. In those days it was open to the sky. So I spent five hours standing there in drizzling rain, trying to follow every word in my imperfect German. It was well worth it. Paula Wessely made a perfect Margarethe, and the production was incomparable. The scenes in the Charnel House and the

Witches' Sabbath provided a suitable prologue for the approaching war.

As a result of that holiday in 1936, for the first time I began to take a continuing personal interest in politics. However, my passion for the arts remained predominant. During my years at Oxford my loves for both the arts and politics ran parallel, and, contrary to Marvell, though infinite, they did often meet.

CHAPTER TWO

The Student

> *Falstaff* We have heard the chimes at midnight, Master
> Shallow . . .
> Blessed are they that have been my friends . . .
>
> *Pistol* 'Where is the life that late I led?' say they:
> Why here it is; welcome these pleasant days!
>
>   – *Henry IV Part Two* William Shakespeare

EXCITEMENT MINGLED WITH apprehension as I took the train to Oxford that morning in October 1936. Oxford had been the goal of all my ambitions at Bradford. I knew it was, in Hopkins' words, a 'towery city and branchy between towers; cuckoo-echoing, bell-swarmed, lark-charmed, rook-racked, river-rounded'. But I also imagined that life there was still as painted by the postwar novelists like Aldous Huxley and Evelyn Waugh – a succession of parties where gilded young men exchanged epigrams with fashionable young women, interrupted only by drunken revellers from the Bullingdon Club. I had never been away from home before, except in the summer holidays. I did not know a single person at my own college, Balliol; most of my school friends were going to Queens.

My first impressions were confusing. Balliol had no dreaming spires. Its nineteenth-century buildings had given their name to an architectural style known as 'Bloody Balliol'. There was none of the luxury I had expected. I had a tiny living room and tinier bedroom with an iron bedstead. The lavatories were in a modern edifice called 'Lady Perriam' in the next quadrangle, and if I wanted a bath I had to shuffle in my dressing gown and slippers more than two hundred yards, where a queue of other shivering undergraduates would be already waiting.

On the other hand, I had a manservant to make my bed and bring me anchovy toast if I had someone to tea – the 'scout' who looked after all the men on my staircase. And there was a superb college library, where I managed to read through practically all the English poets of the sixteenth and seventeenth centuries in my first year or two.

At first I was nervous, as a grammar-school boy from the North of England, about contact with the public-school boys who still predominated. I remember being overawed by Hugh Fraser during the Convocation in the Radcliffe Camera where we were introduced into the University. He was a tall, handsome young man with an aristocratic profile; when he referred in a lordly drawl to one of the officials as the 'chief eunuch' I was dazzled by his sophistication.

So I sought my first friends among the many American, Commonwealth or Scottish undergraduates at Balliol, to whom social class was irrelevant. It was the first time I had met Americans. Most of them were Rhodes Scholars who had already taken degrees in the United States; they were more mature in every way than the rest of us. My closest friend, Gordon Griffiths, was from California. His grandfather had crossed the Rockies on horseback as a preacher, with a bible in one saddlebag and a rifle in the other. I was often asked to rumple Gordon's bedclothes so that our scout would not know he had spent the night outside the college with his girl-friend.

Before long, however, my interests in the arts and politics bridged all barriers. Balliol was above all a meritocracy; its snobbery was intellectual rather than social. For this reason it tended to attract clever young men from every part of the world.

Though it was founded in 1292, and one of its earliest members was John Wyclif, who first translated the Bible into English, its academic reputation was fairly recent – created by Benjamin Jowett, who was elected Master in 1870 after more than thirty controversial years as a fellow. His religious independence led him to' be accused of heresy before the vice-chancellor's court. When a colleague insisted that you either have compulsory religion or no religion at all, Jowett replied: 'I have never been able to see the difference between the two.' He told Margot Asquith as a little girl: 'My dear child, you must believe in God in spite of what the clergy tell you.'

When I went up to Balliol, Jowett had been dead for forty-three years; but his memory still dominated the college, and many of the older fellows had known him. His robust radicalism had made Balliol the first Oxford college to admit coloured students. After a particularly good

dinner the hearties from Trinity, next door, would assemble in front of
Balliol chanting 'Bring out your white man'. There was a riot in a local
cinema when someone shouted, as a boat of Africans appeared on the
screen: 'Well rowed, Balliol!'

At one time Balliol sought revenge for such aspersions by defining the
Balliol manner as 'the conscious tranquillity of effortless superiority' or
'something which only exists in the inadequate imitations of it at New
College'. The late thirties were too serious for such *jeux d'esprit*. Nevertheless, we were all immensely proud of the Balliol tradition.

Balliol was one of the largest colleges at Oxford; while I was there it
had about three hundred undergraduates. They included an astonishing
number and variety of young men who were to reach the top of their
profession. A dozen of us met again as MPs after the war – including
Ted Heath, Julian Amery, Hugh Fraser, Maurice Macmillan and Tony
Kershaw, who became ministers in Conservative governments, and Roy
Jenkins, Niall MacDermott and David Ginsburg who, like me, became
Labour ministers. All of us had been active in student politics. Despite
wide differences on other issues, all of us had fought against Chamberlain's policy of appeasing Hitler. All of us also fought Hitler directly when
appeasement failed.

The American Rhodes scholars at Balliol were also caught up in the
struggle against appeasement and in the war which followed. I found
myself working closely with many of them in later life. Phil Kaiser was
Chairman of the college's Junior Common Room in the year between
Heath and me. He was a good-looking and immensely gregarious young
man. Since he had given us a talk at Balliol on the American labour
unions, I was not surprised to find him Under Secretary for Labour in
the Truman Administration. Later, as second in command of the United
States Embassy in London, he was immensely helpful to me when I was
a Cabinet minister.

Walt Rostow was one of the few American students I met who had the
courage to develop systematic theories about world affairs. He talked to
the Leonardo Society at Balliol on the American Socialist Party, of which
his father had been a founder member; he was called Walt after Walt
Whitman, while his brother was called Eugene after Eugene Debs – an
association which Gene did not advertise during his career in Washington.
Walt later served several United States presidents as an adviser on
security and economic affairs, so I met him again both as Defence
Secretary and Chancellor.

Canada, Australia, New Zealand, South Africa and India also sent men to Balliol who became my close friends through life; many of them went into politics or government when they returned home. There was also a handful of refugees from Central Europe, some of whom had to change their names. One kept his name but changed his nationality. When I was Chancellor of the Exchequer I was astonished to meet my Czech friend, Alex Kafka, as the Brazilian Director of the IMF.

Though the tradition established by Jowett tended to lead Balliol men into public life, the college was also notable for its music. The Balliol Concerts on Sunday evenings were always crowded. George Malcolm used to play the piano there; at that time he was a pale youth covered with puppy fat. I found it difficult later to recognise him in the gaunt dark man who had become Britain's leading harpsichordist. Teddy Heath was the organ scholar; I can still sometimes see him, in John Mair's words, as 'the demented musician playing astonishing voluntaries on his ruined organ.'

My friends and I used to play Duke Ellington records in our rooms. There was no Balliol jazz band. Other colleges made good this deficiency. There was a lively Dixieland group called 'The Bandits', led by Denis Rattle; his son Simon is now Britain's best young conductor. We had one poet, in John Heath-Stubbs, and at least one novelist, in the Canadian, Robertson Davies. Years later, when my wife Edna was on the jury for the Booker Prize, she just failed to get it awarded to Davies for *What's Bred in the Bone*.

The main function of Balliol at that time was to enable us undergraduates to educate one another. Purely academic work took second place to our other interests. There were three terms each year, each of only eight weeks. I used to spend the mornings going to lectures, until I found that I could learn much faster and better by reading than by listening. Afternoons and evenings were free, apart from tutorials two or three times a week after tea.

I read Honour Moderations and Litterae Humaniores – Mods and Greats – which took four years rather than the normal three, but allowed you to claim a Double First if you did well in both parts. Mods required me to read the whole of classical Greek and Latin literature, and to write prose and verse in both languages. Greats was divided into ancient history and ancient philosophy, with a smattering of later philosophers up to Kant.

Though I got my First in Mods, I did not greatly enjoy it, except for a course in translating Greek poetry given by Professor E. R. Dodds, who brought Louis MacNeice to talk to us; he later edited his poems. I scamped my ancient history, relying on philosophy for my First in Greats. We had lectures on moral philosophy from Professor Ross, author of *The Right and the Good*. He had two daughters whom we called 'The Fast and the Loose'; the relationship of moral philosophy with good conduct is no more direct than that of law with justice. Reproached with his sexual misbehaviour, one German professor of morals replied: 'Have you ever heard of a signpost walking the way that it's pointing?'

In my opinion you should study philosophy not to learn rules of good behaviour but in order to understand a little about how the human mind and the nature of language influence your understanding of reality. In that sense it is useful to everyone, and especially to politicians. Unfortunately, the fashion at Oxford in my time was for logical positivism and linguistic philosophy, which I regarded as intellectual nosepicking. My own tastes led me to the forbidden underworld of metaphysics. I was encouraged in this by my tutor, Sandy Lindsay, the Master of Balliol; it was he who got me to read writers like Kierkegaard and Shestov – and even Ouspensky. Their religious mysticism had nothing in common with Lindsay's own writings; it was the extreme of heresy for the young men who then dominated Oxford philosophy, so it was no help at all to me in Greats. But it appealed to something fundamental in my nature. The intellectual foundation of my socialism was laid by Christian thinkers like Berdyaev and Niebuhr rather than by Marx; even as a member of the Communist Party, I found dialectical materialism a superficial triviality, quite unworthy of Hume and Hegel, from whom it was confected. Moreover, both Marx and Lenin argued their philosophy with an aggressive dogmatism totally at odds with the pragmatic principles they claimed to support.

I was more impressed by philosophers like Kant, who, while analysing the nature of pure reason, were prepared to emphasise its limitations – and thus to open the way to deeper forms of understanding. Politicians can learn from Heraclitus: 'Everything is in flux – you can not step into the same river twice.' Both Marx and Mill must sometimes yield to the wisdom of Tertullian: 'I believe it because it is incredible. It is certain because it is impossible.' Hegel tried to overcome the difficulties faced by reason in dealing with a shifting and unknowable reality by inventing his dialectic: he argued that thesis and antithesis produce a synthesis which is different from both. Marx allied the Hegelian dialectic with the pragmatism of Hume to create dialectical materialism. In pre-war days this appealed mightily to the biochemists who were studying the frontiers between organic and inorganic matter: I have always felt that this explains why so many biochemists at that time, like Joseph Needham and 'Sage' Bernal, became Communists. Personally, I prefer the wisdom which admits: 'We cannot see clearly across the river to the other shore. But the darkness does not destroy what it conceals.' What you do not know is sometimes more important than what you do.

The most important mysteries do not yield to science or even to philosophy. Symbol, myth and metaphor can help. That is why poetry sounds depths which academic study cannot reach. It is no accident that Bradley, one of the greatest Oxford philosophers, finally abandoned philosophy for Shakespeare, and that poets like Heine and D. H. Lawrence could recognise the underlying currents in the political life of their times better than the politicians themselves.

In my first year at Balliol I wrote essays on *Murder in the Cathedral* and *Burnt Norton*. This was my first introduction to T. S. Eliot as an Anglo-Catholic; though I could not accept his political conservatism, I then found his religious treatment of the human condition worthy even of the Greek dramatists. I no longer put Eliot alongside Aeschylus or Sophocles; but I am permanently in his debt for articulating many of my own spiritual feelings, and for expressing insights of universal application. No one can believe that politics or economics is a science if he accepts that:

> For every life and every act
> Consequence of good and evil can be shown
> And as in time results of many deeds are blended
> So good and evil in the end become confounded.

Apart from Russell Meiggs, who taught me Roman history in my last year, and Charles Morris, my first guide to philosophy, few of my tutors left a deep impression. The great exception was the Master of Balliol himself. Lindsay was not an outstanding thinker. His books display a decent Christian socialism but generate no excitement. But, besides running Balliol well, he had a genius for understanding the intellectual needs of his students. In that sense he was a worthy successor to Jowett.

He was a tall, shambling, bear of a man. Wisps of white hair floated round a large innocent pink head. He lectured in a light, sing-song voice, twisting the ends of his gown in front of him. As the first confessed socialist to head a college in Oxford, he was regarded as a dangerous revolutionary by many of his colleagues, particularly when he stood as the Popular Front candidate in the 1938 by-election. Nowadays he would be regarded as a left-wing liberal. Many years working for the WEA had given him a devotion to the working class. John Betjeman puts it well:

> While Sandy Lindsay from his lodge looks down
> Dreaming of Adult Education where
> The pottery chimneys flare
> On lost potential firsts in some less favoured town.

It was this desire to help the under-privileged which determined his socialism. He did not want the proletariat to win the class war – on the contrary, as he told us at his farewell dinner after the war, he wanted to spread aristocratic values through the whole of the British people. Exceptionally kind to anyone in need, he managed to find a place in the Senior Common Room for several refugees, including the great Central European sociologist, Karl Mannheim, the Russian psychologist of adolescence, Iovetz-Tereschenko, and the Hungarian economist, Tommy Balogh, who had been working under Schacht in the Reichsbank and warned us not to imagine that the Nazis' economic policies would fail in their objectives.

By introducing me to the Christian mystics, and through his own social commitment, Lindsay had an influence on me more profound and lasting than I imagined at the time. However, the main imprint left on me by Oxford came from other undergraduates, and from older men I met in pursuit of my innumerable interests outside my academic studies. For example, in a single week in the winter of 1938, besides hearing Phil Kaiser on the American labour unions, I goggled at a debate on Ireland between Arthur Pyper, a pale faced Ulster Protestant and Dan Davin, a shaggy Irish New Zealander; it taught me all I have ever needed to know about the insolubility of Ulster's problems. Next day I listened to Solly Zuckerman on the social applications of hormone research. I had heard a lot about Solly's brilliance from Gordon's girl-friend, who was working with him on the techniques of contraception. Solly had already made his name with his book on the social life of monkeys. He preferred to say it dealt with the sexual life of the primates, believing no doubt that its circulation would be increased if people thought it dealt with scandals at Canterbury. As always, he was spellbinding that evening. After a long account of his talk, I noted in my diary: 'Zuckerman is a young good-looking South African Jew with an international reputation in his subject. He is said to have slept with Elissa Landi.' She was a beautiful film star of the day. Solly would never confirm or deny the truth of the rumour.

The one field for which Oxford did not cater when I arrived was that which interested me most – painting. So with some other enthusiasts I set up the New Oxford Art Society. We held an exhibition of the work Picasso was doing at the time he painted his great mural *Guernica*, which was too big to bring over from Paris. I have always regretted not buying one of his best etchings in the Minotaur series. It cost only five pounds in our exhibition. But who had five pounds to spare in those days?

With help from Roland Penrose and Eduard Mesens we showed a good selection of Surrealist paintings and drawings, including Magritte's *Le Viol*; this represented the torso of a woman in a state of extreme sexual excitement, made to resemble a human face. Not surprisingly, we had to cover it with a velvet curtain for fear of shocking the ladies of North Oxford; it was later bought by the journalist and jazz musician George Melly, who worked for some time at Mesens' gallery.

It is surprising how many leading artists made the tiring journey to Oxford, simply to address a handful of us students. Paul Nash, Gilbert Spencer, and John Skeaping were among those who talked about their own work. John Betjeman took us on a guided tour of his beloved Keble. Moholy-Nagy explained the function of the Bauhaus. And Russell Ferguson spent a riotous evening with us discussing the work of the GPO Film Unit. I had failed to get Wystan Auden, who had written the script for Grierson's GPO film *Night Mail*; he was just leaving for sanctuary in the United States. Len Lye, whose brilliant abstract colour films for the GPO we did show, was too shy to talk about them. One unusual visitor was Anthony Blunt, whose political views were then unknown to us. He gave us a lecture on Poussin, his specialism; the nearest he came to hinting at his secret life was a sentence in his letter to me: 'I can at any rate say that I shall certainly need a lantern.'

Coming from the bleaker moorlands of Yorkshire, where spring arrived a month later and autumn a month earlier, I was entranced by the countryside round Oxford. I spent many afternoons cycling to the villages nearby with my watercolours. I was not looking for the elegiac melancholy of Arnold's *Scholar Gypsy*; it was the Impressionist brilliance of Hopkins' Binsey poplars I was after.

I cycled alone, since my girl-friend, Pat, was in Yorkshire. I knew many girls in the Labour Club, and was attracted by a red-cheeked girl called Edna Edmunds; but she had other boy-friends then – indeed she was described as the Zuleika Dobson of St Hugh's. The University did everything possible to discourage sexual activity. Women were not allowed in the men's colleges after tea, and in some of the women's colleges men were not allowed without a chaperone. In one, the bed was physically

removed before a young man came to tea. Tom Harrison, the founder of
Mass Observation and then at Cambridge, infuriated us with his savage
essay on what he called 'Oxsex'. His strictures were not unfair. For
example, one hot summer afternoon in 1938 I was walking in Balliol
Quad with Teddy Heath; I happened to mention that a mutual friend
was going to Bibury with his girl for the weekend. Teddy looked at me in
horror. 'You don't mean to say they are sleeping together?' he whispered.
'I don't know. I suppose so,' I replied. 'Good heavens,' said Teddy, 'I
can't imagine anyone in the Conservative Association doing that.' Heath's
lack of imagination in this field was to have consequences for some of his
Cabinet ministers later.

Separation every term from my girl-friend at home led me for the first
time in my life to write poetry. Devoted as I was to Donne, Shakespeare
and Hopkins, inevitably I chose the discipline of the sonnet form to
express an emotion which would otherwise have overflowed. For
example:

February 10th, 1938

> The old stone slowly glows in the sun
> Or coldly cuts the gusty winter sky;
> Inside I watch the tattered heavens run
> Over the towers, streaming endlessly.
> Dim slid the Wharfe at Christmas, as we walked
> Swimming through green soft grains of misted night,
> Under an arched immobile wave of darkness talked
> About our love, and sipped the old delight.
>   Space, time, and matter crumble in a slow
> Disintegration, have no permanence,
> But in subsiding leave the constant flow,
> Perpetual presence, of experience.
>   Oxford or Burnsall, day or night, the same:
>   The fuel varies, single is the flame.

February 14th, 1938

> Yesterday my cramped soul strained in the mesh
> Of blind uncertainty's constricting death:
> Slow questions plucked and pulled the tortured flesh;
> Strangling anxieties stuffed up my breath

With gasping suffocation; sightless doubt
Squeezed, cracked my chest, and choked my sobbing lungs.
Today your letter came; hope turned about,
Saw me lie heaving, with a thousand tongues
Sang love and freedom, snapped the circling bars,
Bounded exultant in a dazzling dance,
Covered the sky, and made the whistling stars
Shiver with joy at its new brilliance.
      'Cold self-possession'? – Neither am I cold,
      Nor self-possessed if you such power hold.

One of the few times Pat and I managed to meet surreptitiously during term we were badly caught out. We had each gone separately to London – she from Leeds, I from Oxford – for the weekend of the Youth Peace Congress and were photographed together at the rally in Trafalgar Square because, I suppose, we conformed to the newspaper image of a typical student couple. The *Daily Mirror* gave us a half-page spread and the *Daily Mail* did a feature the next day on 'The girl you noticed in your paper yesterday'. Since we had each told our tutors quite different stories about our absence our credibility suffered as much as our reputations.

Though politics inevitably claimed more and more of my attention during those years, they never dominated my life at Oxford as they have later. Young men have so much else to do, and to learn. Both my appetite and opportunity for new experiences were at their peak. The drumbeat of the approaching war was growing more insistent with every week, yet my generation did not feel doomed. Indeed when Arnold Toynbee told us at Balliol's annual dinner on St Catherine's night in 1939 that it was our fate to be broken on the wheel like her, we were irritated rather than alarmed. Auden gave some flavour of our feelings in his poem 'A Summer Night':

      Soon, through dykes of our content
      The crumpling flood will force a rent
         And taller than a tree
      Hold sudden death before our eyes
      Whose river dreams long hid the size
         And vigour of the sea.

Our reaction to the deepening tragedy of the Spanish Civil War and the betrayal of Czechoslovakia was not despair. We simply worked even harder to prevent the ultimate catastrophe. So we were perhaps the most political generation in Oxford's history; and our politics was overwhelmingly of the Left. In the summer term of 1939, out of an undergraduate population of under four and a half thousand, a third were members of the Labour Club; of those, about two hundred were members of the Communist Party.

For the young in those days, politics was a world of simple choices. The enemy was Hitler with his concentration camps. The objective was to prevent a war by standing up to Hitler. Only the Communist Party seemed unambiguously against Hitler. The Chamberlain Government was for appeasement, Labour seemed torn between pacifism and a half-hearted support for collective security, and the Liberals did not count. Everything began to change, of course, with the Stalin-Hitler Pact and the Soviet attack on Finland; but it was at first too easy to rationalise these reversals of Russian policy simply as a reaction to the failure of Britain and France to build a common front against Hitler.

For my first three years, at least, the challenge and response were self-evident. No later generation has enjoyed the same political certainty. Today the atom bomb offers a similar challenge; but the response is far from clear. The modern world cannot be drawn in black and white. It is not surprising that confidence in political solutions is so low, even in the universities. Such political interest as does exist, now tends to focus on single issues. It seems easier to save the whale than save the world.

When I arrived at Oxford in October 1936 my major interest was still in the arts, and I was secretly disappointed to find that politics was so dominant. But art was turning political as well. The most influential poets were Auden, Spender, Day Lewis and MacNeice, with Betjeman a somewhat marginal outsider. The Spanish Civil War had begun to move Picasso in the same direction, and the bombing of Guernica set him firmly in the communist mould. Across the Atlantic, Dave Dubinsky got the Garment Workers' Union to finance the first political musical, 'Pins and Needles', with hits like 'Sing me a song with a social significance'.

It was the poet, Peter Hewitt, who persuaded me to join the Communist Party in the summer of 1937. He was a close friend of another Christ Church man, Philip Toynbee. Philip had just written a novel, *The Savage Days*; it had a hero whose proud boast was actually to have read *The Daily Worker* from cover to cover in the train between Oxford and Paddington.

Peter and Philip, however, belonged to a different generation of communists from me. They had joined the 'October Club' a year or two earlier, when communists were very sectarian, got drunk, wore beards, and did not worry about their examinations. In 1935 the Seventh World Congress of the Communist International switched the line to the Popular Front. From that moment communists started shaving, tried to avoid being drunk in public, worked for first class degrees, and played down their Marxism–Leninism. As a result, membership of the Communist Party increased rapidly on both sides of the Atlantic; but the new type of communist rarely stayed in the Party for more than two or three years. It became a bed-and-breakfast organisation. It was from the earlier generation, particularly at Cambridge, that the Soviet Union recruited its spies.

The hero of that Cambridge generation was John Cornford. His father was a distinguished Professor of Greek, his mother the poetess Frances Cornford. He himself reacted fiercely against the whole culture which his family represented, expressing his views in a poem which stands for many of the public-school communist intellectuals of his time:

> Wind from the dead land, hollow men,
> Webster's skull and Eliot's pen,
> The important words that come between
> The unhappy eye and the difficult scene,
> All the obscene important names
> For silly griefs and silly shames,
> All the tricks we once thought smart,
> The kestrel joy and the change of heart,
> The dark mysterious urge of the blood,
> The donkeys shitting on Dali's food –
> There's none of these fashions have come to stay,
> And there's nobody here got time to play.
> All we've brought are our Party cards,
> Which are no bloody good for your bloody charades.

Cornford was killed in Spain just before I went to Balliol; he had become a martyr of mythic power. Coming from a grammar school in Yorkshire, I found the element of romantic savagery in such middle-class young communists somewhat distasteful. Their Byronic posturing seemed to spring more from the need to sublimate some purely personal or class neurosis, than from the harsh realities which confronted the rest of us. I particularly resented their affectation of the glottal stop, which they regarded as essential to the proletarian image. 'Ours is a Par'y of a new type', they would say.

In my time at Oxford, however, Cornford's sectarianism was discouraged in favour of the broader simplicities of the Popular Front. Almost any undergraduate who wanted to stop Hitler was then easy game for the Communists. However, I know only one who has remained in the Communist Party throughout the past half century. The great majority left in the first months of the war because of the Stalin–Hitler Pact, and most of the remainder during the post-war tragedies in Eastern Europe, which culminated in the Hungarian rising of 1956. A large number of them abandoned politics altogether; some became active supporters of the Labour Party, and a handful joined me in Parliament later – as Conservative as well as Labour MPs.

There were not many outstanding undergraduates on the Left who did not join the Communist Party in those days. Chris Mayhew fought a fairly lonely battle for democratic socialism until he was joined by Roy Jenkins, whose father was Attlee's Parliamentary Private Secretary. Tony Crosland then considered himself a Marxist, but could not nerve himself to join the Communist Party outright. I knew him less well than I knew Roy, because he was at Trinity, though I found his offhand brilliance most engaging.

My parents took my announcement that I had joined the Communist Party without alarm. Mother was already a socialist, and my father, though I suppose he would have accepted the description of Asquithian liberal, took the familiar line that if I was not a Communist at twenty, there was something wrong with my heart; if I was still a Communist at thirty, there was something wrong with my head.

I myself was inevitably cast as the 'culture boss' of the Party, and wrote the art criticism for *Oxford Forward*. In the number for January 21st, 1939 I reviewed an exhibition of Canadian painting, while Iris Murdoch dealt with a performance of Eugene O'Neill's *Anna Christie* and John Biggs-Davison described a Union debate in which Hugh Fraser 'castigated the National Farmers' Union for being an organisation of rich farmers' and 'Mr Jenkins (Balliol) made a promising maiden speech'.

Gilbert Murray, just retired at Boar's Hill as Regius Professor of Greek, became a friend. As a young man, Bernard Shaw had taken him as the model for Adolphus Cusins, the hero of *Major Barbara*. A tall courtly Edwardian, with the exquisite diction of his period, he was an active Liberal, and a supporter of the League of Nations. His daughter married Arnold Toynbee; Philip Toynbee was his grandson. Along with E. R. Dodds, his successor, George Thomson, the Marxist Professor of Greek at Birmingham, and my own tutor Russell Meiggs, he took part in a series of lectures I organised for the Labour Club on 'Greek Drama and Society'.

I was somewhat surprised to be elected Chairman of the Labour Club in the summer of 1939; later I discovered that the apparatchiks decided I was the best man to beat Tom McWhinnie, a working-class Scot at Ruskin, whom they regarded as politically unreliable. In fact Tom remained a Communist through all the crises of the next forty years, and became an official of the World Federation of Trade Unions.

Some of my American friends at Oxford were to suffer totally unjustified victimisation during the McCarthy Red scares. The worst case of such persecution was Penn Kimball, a Balliol colleague who was not interested in politics, but got on to the wrong computer file and had to fight for over thirty years to clear his name.

The climax of our political activities at Oxford was our campaign against the Munich Agreement, which was the main issue at the by-election in September 1938 after the death of the sitting Conservative MP Quintin Hogg was chosen as the Conservative candidate, and Patrick Gordon Walker, a young don, had been nominated earlier by the Labour Party. The Tory majority was far too high for Labour to overturn, so Sandy Lindsay was asked by a number of Labour dons if he would stand instead as a Popular Front candidate, with support stretching from the Communists through the Labour and Liberal parties to dissident Conservatives. When he agreed, undergraduate Communists flooded the meeting of the Oxford City Labour Party and helped to produce the majority which compelled Gordon Walker to stand down so that Lindsay could fight without a rival from the Left, much against his own will and that of the Labour Party's National Agent.

We fought the campaign with enormous enthusiasm. Almost all the undergraduates who took part supported Lindsay; but since they nearly all came from other parts of Britain, and indeed the world, few of them had votes. Lindsay lost, though he greatly reduced the Conservative majority. When Edna gave the news to a tutor at St Hugh's, the lady told her: 'Oh, I am so sorry. I had so wanted Dr Lindsay to win. Of course I voted for Mr Hogg. But Dr Lindsay would have made such a good MP.'

Controversy continues about the Munich Agreement. I am still convinced that Chamberlain's policy was politically and strategically disastrous, as well as morally contemptible. He really believed that he had brought us 'Peace in our time', and continued to trust Hitler until the occupation of the rest of Czechoslovakia the following Easter. As a result of this the Allies lost thirty Czech divisions, as well as fortifications which the German generals admitted at Nuremburg they would have found it very difficult to overcome. Above all, Hitler made far better use of the time he gained to build up his military power than did Chamberlain and Daladier. On the other hand, it is incontestable that the British Parliament and people were not psychologically ready for war in 1938. The most difficult question is whether Hitler would have backed down if Chamberlain had stood firm. No one will ever know the answer. The judgment of historians is no more reliable than that of politicians on such matters.

I cannot say that I am proud of all my political activities at Oxford. When Chamberlain finally announced he would introduce conscription, I organised a mass meeting against it. We held it in the Coop Hall. The caretaker was knocked down by a car while he was cycling to open it, so we had to force the doors. Then we could not find the master-switch so as to turn on the electricity. So we held the meeting by the light of guttering candles, while members of the animal kingdom from Christ Church tried to break it up. The atmosphere was like the early days of the French Revolution. Besides my own, there were speeches from the local Communist leader, Abe Lazarus, and Frank Pakenham, a young don who had just joined the Territorial Army as a lance-corporal. As we left the hall, glowing with pride at the blow we had just struck for freedom, I was button-holed by an older man who said: 'You remember how Hitler exploited the Oxford Union's vote against fighting for King and Country. How do you think he will react to this meeting?' I realised immediately that I had made a bad mistake.

I learned as much about life and politics from my summer holidays in those years as I did at the University itself. In June 1937 I set off for France with a friend in a car he had bought for ten pounds. It worked pretty well, though the water got into the oil from time to time. So I strapped my trusty Rudge Whitworth bike to the side as a lifeboat; it also gave me independence whenever I wanted to travel some of the way on my own.

We drove through the heart of rural France to the Pyrenees, with a short stop in Paris to leave a message for a certain James Klugman, who was organising aid for Spain. He later became famous as an agent of SOE in Cairo and Yugoslavia. He was simultaneously an agent of the Comintern, for which he had started recruiting spies at Cambridge in 1934.

It was my first visit to France. I loved everything about it – the people, the extraordinary variety of the landscape, the food and the drink.

You could then buy a litre of country wine for about a penny. On my way back I paid the first of many visits to the Louvre, the Orangerie, the Petit Palais, and saw the overwhelming exhibition of French art at the Paris Exhibition. During a special journey to Giverny, I climbed over the wall of Monet's garden to see the lily ponds which he painted so often in his final years.

The deepest impression left on me that summer was by two German refugees, Pitt and Yves Kruger, who had been settled by the English Quakers on a derelict farm in the Pyrenees above Mosset, near Prades. They represented all that was best in the Germany of the Weimar Republic, whose image today has been somewhat distorted by artists like Brecht, Grosz, and Dix – not to speak of films like *Cabaret*. Pitt had been a teacher in Potsdam, where he developed his own theories of education after working with mental defectives. He was the first teacher to be dismissed in East Prussia when Hitler came to power, and left Germany with little but the clothes he stood in, three days after the burning of the Reichstag. Yet he was not greatly involved in politics, loathing the Communists and finding the Social Democrats at once too bureaucratic and too theoretical. He had worked with Lotte Reiniger on the silhouette film, *Prince Achmed* and thus came to know Fritz Lang whom I had admired since childhood.

Pitt was small, slight and wiry, with a thin brown head, spectacles, and hair *en brosse*. His wife, Yves, was a Swiss–French gamine who reminded me of the actress, Luise Rainer, but had far more vitality; she was an excellent cook. At first I saw them simply as intelligent country folk living very full lives. But long conversations far into the night soon revealed their real quality. In Germany Pitt had possessed a music room with a piano, violin, cello, and wind instruments; he was able to bring only two flutes with him to France. Before their marriage Yves had been secretary to a wealthy American woman who married a Bavarian prince. They used to commute between Munich and Florence, where she came to know Toscanini. She knew most of Schubert's songs, and used to sing Bach's 'My heart ever faithful' as she did the farmyard chores. In Potsdam they went to musical evenings held by Wilhelm Kempf. They had a little daughter, Jamine, and a naked baby called Kiki.

My days at their farm, 'La Coume', were unforgettable. I spent the mornings and afternoons gathering in the lucerne, tiling the roof, improving the dangerous track up from the road, and picking the enormous yellow cherries – 'bottled sunshine', Pitt called them. At night we would have a simple but perfect meal, with good local wine, finishing with cherries and sweet muscat from Banyuls. Then we would talk, for hours, on everything from Bach to psychoanalysis. Finally my friend and I would walk back to our hut as a brilliant incandescent moon lit the valley, its contours broken by the black trees which rose above it as we advanced, while the snow-capped peaks of the Canigou glistened on the horizon, emerging above a wreath of cloud.

I spent two wonderful, exhausting days climbing the Canigou alone, sleeping in the open in a mossy forest just below the summit. We went several times to the fishing port of Collioure, celebrated by a generation of painters, and drank little cups of strong black coffee with a small tumbler of cognac in the village square, talking to the peasants who spoke a mixture of Catalan and French. It was a wonderful experience.

The next summer holiday I spent hitch-hiking with Pat round France, and sampling the extraordinary variety of French youth hostels. One of them in the Alps above La Grave, appropriately run by Les Amis de la Nature, had only one bed, thirty feet broad, on which everyone piled in together. Another, on the Cote d'Azur at St Raphael, was an old Roman theatre. We all slept on the floor of the stage under the stars.

Inevitably I took Pat to 'La Coume' so that I could have another week with Pitt and Yves. The Krugers and I corresponded regularly until the war broke out. Then we lost touch for a third of a century. In 1970 Edna and I were touring the Pyrenees and decided to see if the Krugers were still at their farm. This time a well-made concrete drive led from the road where in 1937 our car had slipped off a track of crumbling clay. There was a swimming pool set into the hillside and the farm was spick and span. Pitt and Yves were now running a small private school, mainly for the children of well-known musicians such as the guitarist Yepes and the conductor Markevitch. They had looked after the family of the Dalai Lama after his flight from Tibet; he thought they were Bolsheviks when they made his children work with their hands for the first time in their lives. In the summer holidays they ran seminars for mathematicians and astronomers. Jamine was now a woman of thirty-five – a good violinist married to a cellist in Germany.

But the intervening years had been very different. The village priest had denounced Pitt to the Pétain regime as a Communist and he was sent to a concentration camp in Germany. As the war was ending they took him from the concentration camp and put him into a punishment battalion to fight the Russians. The Russians captured him and put him in a prisoner of war camp near Leningrad. He remained there for three years, finally returning home after Yves had given him up for dead. As his gentle voice described the story I was moved to uncontrollable tears.

My last holiday from Oxford was in the summer of 1939. Balliol had given me a travelling scholarship to visit Greece. This time the drumbeat of approaching war was deafening. As I passed through Switzerland on the way to Venice the train was full of conscripts in civilian clothes, carrying the rifles which they kept at home – clean intelligent individuals, proud to belong to a country which, though small, intended to defend its neutrality. Venice was full of Germans; the shops had advertisements in German and a third of the films were German. I did not enjoy that first visit to the Pearl of the Adriatic. On the long tiring journey south to Brindisi the train was crowded with Italian conscripts, lumpen-proletariat, with poor teeth sloping inwards when they smiled, showing their upper gums.

I went from Brindisi to the Piraeus in the hold of a small steamer. The only other passengers were travelling first class – a Greek coming home from the States, and a rich sleek Rumanian with his two sisters. The Corinthian Canal had conveniently fallen in when Italy invaded Albania a few months earlier, so we had to sail round the Peloponnese. By day I chatted to the Rumanians or lay drowsily in the sun; at night the sailors sat with their guitars in the prow and sang beneath a brilliant moon.

Greece itself was an inexhaustible revelation – the people, landscape, and art were all infinitely more exciting than I had expected. There was a striking difference between the city bourgeoisie and the other Greeks. The middle-class Athenians I met appeared corrupt, self-seeking and shallow. My guide was the son of a wealthy mill-owner who had studied textiles under my father in Keighley. Basil was a flashy young man with co-respondent shoes and a rakish green hat, glittering eyes and moist bright teeth, a sort of down-market Omar Sharif. He moved in a circle of wilting, unhealthy, rich men's sons and forceful youths on the make, with a sprinkling of pretty predatory girls, who rarely dined before ten o'clock and went to bed at four in the morning.

Corruption was universal. Basil and many of his friends had paid the standard bribe of twenty pounds to avoid conscription, but the government decided to call them up after all, without refunding their money. He was angling for a £200,000 contract for supplying uniforms to the government. He knew an admiral who was sailing on official business to Egypt the following weekend. As the government was giving the admiral only two pounds to spend, I was asked to do Basil a good turn by changing ten pounds illegally with the admiral, since his gratitude would probably secure the contract. My reward would be an introduction to professors of philosophy whom the admiral knew.

A little dazed by this rigmarole, I followed Basil to the Ministry and the illicit deal was done. But the professors they had promised to deliver were not in Greece, the drachmae the admiral gave me were four hundred and sixty short, and in return for a cup of coffee I had to invite the admiral to dinner. This experience inoculated me for all my dealings with the Levant ever since.

On the other hand I found the Greeks elsewhere admirably straightforward. I met peasants in the countryside, bus-drivers and their families, and ordinary working people on an outing to Sounion, where they danced to the bouzouki under an awning of rushes while the others clapped them on. I was fascinated by the large number of men I met who had returned to Greece after years in the United States and were prevented by new immigration laws from getting back.

One had been a boxing promoter for twenty-five years on the East Side. Tilting back his chair and leaning a handsome stubbled face on his stick, a crape-banded straw hat on his head, he told me a story which might have come from Damon Runyon. Another had joined the American Army at the end of the First World War. Having fought in the Balkans in 1912 when each side had only one aeroplane and fighting was with rifles and small field guns, he abhorred the thought of a modern war with tanks, poison gas, and air-raids. Such conversations added spice to my journey.

In Athens I stayed at the British School of Archaeology, where I found the company a trifle too spicy. The inhabitants were in the main epicene young exquisites with names like Cosmo, Sergei, Lesbia and Camilla, who would have fitted nicely into a corner of Olivia Manning's Balkan trilogy; but there were exceptions. For example, an earnest New Zealander was still reeling at the thought he had stood on the exact spot where Clytemnestra stood when she axed Agamemnon as he stepped out of the bath. I particularly admired Tom Dunbabin, another New Zealander who was the Deputy Director of the School. He later fought heroically with the Resistance in Crete and died in Oxford, tragically young, just after the war.

The landscape was everywhere magnificent. Even Athens, so often ruined nowadays by petrol fumes, shone golden white in the crystalline air. The roads were fewer then, and much worse. I had to walk over the mountains from Sparta to Kalamata, and my Pyreneean espadrilles finally disintegrated on the stony track from the Byzantine monastery of Osios Loukas.

I travelled to the islands mainly by cargo boat, on a deck covered by noisy Greek families, bundles of carpets, folded camp-beds, tethered hens, baskets of live rabbits and a variety of students from France, Britain and Germany. Mykonos was my favourite. At every step I found a new collection of forms in startling white and transparent shadow, given coherence by a girl in red, a spray of leaves, or a painted door, while the solid blue of the sky carved a valance over the buildings. In those days the windmills actually worked, each turned by an enormous wheel with sails flapping from the spokes, the axles creaking and the pulleys rattling.

In Mykonos I met a German painter called Conrad Westpfahrt who was living precariously in Greece as an undeclared refugee from Nazism – a status which gave him the worst of both worlds, since the British would not exhibit his paintings and they were too 'decadent' to show in Germany. Like Pitt Kruger he represented all that was best in the Weimar Republic. My good fortune in meeting such men protected me from any risk of believing that all Germans were Nazis, either during the war or afterwards.

In fact I was myself arrested as a Nazi spy while I was taking photographs at Eleusis, opposite the Greek naval base at Salamis. The little boys who denounced me thought my shorts were conclusive proof that I was German. Fortunately it did not take me long to convince the police of my innocence.

I finally left the Piraeus on July 28th, 1939 and spent what I then described as the most memorable four days of my life travelling fourth class on the *Cairo City*, which shuttled regularly between Alexandria and Marseilles. The fourth class was an inferior dosshouse in the prow of the boat, where men and women slept without distinction on a double layer of steel-frame bunks. We were fed on the leavings from the higher classes, eaten off a rough board table with wooden boxes to sit on. The thin greasy steward sweated profusely, dripping beads of perspiration from his nose and chin on to my plate. The Arab women did not like the food. After a few movements of the jaw, they would remove the offending victuals between finger and thumb and with queenly arrogance drop the half-masticated mess on the floor.

I had two friends from Oxford on the boat, who had travelled out to Greece with Professor Collingwood on the *Fleur de Lys*, a yacht which I had intended to join; unfortunately it arrived at the Piraeus after I had left for the islands. They were in the second class, so I saw less of them than I wished, since class segregation was rigidly enforced; a fourth-class passenger was not allowed to buy even a box of matches in the third-class

store. My friends in the fourth class were good substitutes. There was a
rosy little German Jew from Palestine who made life on a kibbutz
sound like the nineteenth-century Wild West, a Rumanian Jew with a
tiny black yarmulka no larger than an orange skin whom the other
passengers teased and considered mad, a Somali with a delicate womanish
black face who knew no European language, a fourteen-year-old Greek
boy who spoke Cockney. There were Egyptian men who spent day and
night in long nightshirts and berets, Egyptian women who sat permanently still in silent disdain, and a mysterious young Turkish artillery
officer who pretended to be a Soviet citizen from Odessa. I last saw him
pretending to a group of admiring Palestinians that he was an Annamite.

The first day at sea the ship bucked badly in a heavy swell. All over
the dormitory men and women were retching in agony on the dirty floor.
I lay on my bed watching a rat walk timidly out on to the pipes over the
door, then scurry back again as the ship shuddered down again; I listened
to the groans of the men and the wails of the women, all commending
their souls to a different god. There could have been no better preparation
for what was to come.

A month after I got home to Keighley I was working in my bedroom,
racking my brains over Kant's views about the transcendental synthetic
unity of apperception – surely the most difficult page of prose ever
written. Suddenly I heard my mother running up the stairs. She burst
into the room crying: 'Put away your books! War has been declared!' I
found the first sentence far more startling then the second.

I got in touch with Balliol immediately to volunteer for the army. *The
Daily Worker* told me it had turned from an anti-fascist war into an
imperialist war overnight. Neither I nor any of my comrades took any
notice. I was accepted for the artillery. Then came the anti-climax. Day
after day, week after week I waited for them to call me up. Finally, at the
end of November, I, and all who had volunteered with me three months
earlier, were told that we should go back to Oxford and finish our
degrees. So I took the train to Balliol and tried to revive my moribund
interest in Greats.

That fourth year at Oxford was a bizarre experience. I had missed almost
the whole of the first term. My position as Chairman of the Junior Common
Room at Balliol had been filled by someone else. Many of the dons had left
to work in various government departments. All my contemporaries, like
me, were waiting to join the services, with little confidence we would
survive the war; so we were not very concerned with our examinations.
The year of phony war was accompanied by a year of phony academia.

I was greatly irritated by the spectacle of lecturers who had played no part in the struggle to prevent the war, and were on their way to comfortable berths in the civil service, urging their students, most of whom had already volunteered, to fight and die for Britain. It inspired me to satirical verse:

The Patriotic Don

Time was, the Don was satisfied
Constructing cages for the breeze.
    Nor did he care
    How foul the air;
He still got his tuition fees.

But obstinate senility,
The subtle lie, the pious fraud,
    Have put us all
    Against the wall,
And so the Don's become a bawd.

In every Hall his wrath is turned
On pacifist apostasy:
    'Our cause is just.
    Berlin or bust.
Go out and save democracy.

'You've heard about those camps. That's why
We're fighting. – Why not so before? –
    We tried to be
    Their friends, you see;
It was not us began the war.'

He marches on the Siegfried Line
With fifty thousand abstract nouns,
    Armed to kill
    With a goose quill,
And swathed in tattered MA gowns.

Sometimes the light does reach his eyes,
But he's determined not to see:

'I can't be right
To turn and bite
The healing hand that gelded me.'

Oxford politics was now in turmoil. The Stalin–Hitler Pact, the Soviet
attack on Finland, and the volte-face by the Communist Party produced
a split in the Labour Club. Roy Jenkins, Tony Crosland, and Philip
Williams – later Gaitskell's biographer – set up a rival Democratic
Socialist Party. I am sorry to say I opposed them, more from inertia and
indifference than from conviction. I was too busy making up for my lost
term to take much notice of University politics that last year. So I did
not finally break with the Communist Party until the fall of France.

Oxford was now being invaded by civil servants. I had to change my
digs twice during the two terms left me to prepare for Greats. My love
life was also going through a crisis. My affair with Pat was coming to an
end. I sat down in June for the first of twenty-four gruelling papers in
the examination for Greats on that hot summer day when the German
motor cyclists roared into Abbeville, just across the Channel. Louis
Aragon described it perfectly:

> *O mois des floraisons, mois des metamorphoses,*
> *Mai qui fut sans nuage et juin poignarde,*
> *Je n'oublierai jamais les lilas ni les roses.*

It was difficult to concentrate on the papers in front of us. I was one of
many who walked out without finishing the final Greek verse paper.
Fortunately the examiners made allowances and I got my First.

Then came yet another period of waiting to be called up. So I joined
the Home Guard in Keighley, and spent nights on the moors, watching
one of the few air raids on Bradford. A friend from the Oxford Labour
Club, Edna Edmunds, stayed with us in Riddlesden during her interview
for a teaching post at Keighley Girls' Grammar School. She got the job,
and we started our love affair. Then at last, just after my twenty-third
birthday, I received an official command to report at the Royal Artillery
Field Training Unit in Uniacke Barracks outside Harrogate. Another
phase of my life had begun.

CHAPTER THREE

The Soldier

Today we have naming of parts. Yesterday,
We had daily cleaning. And tomorrow morning,
We shall have what to do after firing. But today,
Today we have naming of parts. Japonica
Glistens like coral in all of the neighbouring gardens
　　　And today we have naming of parts.

And this you can see is the bolt. The purpose of this
Is to open the breech as you see. We can slide it
Rapidly backwards and forwards; we call this
Easing the spring. And rapidly backwards and forwards
The early bees are assaulting and fumbling the flowers:
　　　They call it easing the Spring.

　　　　　　　　– 'Lessons of the War' Henry Reed

Flesh falls within sight of us; we, though our flower the same
Wave with the meadow, forget that there must
The sour scythe cringe, and the blear share come

　　　– 'The Wreck of the *Deutschland*' Gerard Manley Hopkins

UNFASHIONABLE THOUGH IT IS to admit it, I enjoyed my five years in the wartime army. It was a life very different from anything I had known, or expected. Long periods of boredom were broken by short bursts of excitement. For the first time I had to learn to do nothing but wait – for me the most difficult lesson of all. To my great relief, I found

I did not get frightened in action – not that I enjoyed being shelled or dive-bombed any more than the next man; but fear never paralysed me or even pushed me off my stroke. On the other hand I was never called on to show the sort of active courage which wins men the VC. A dumb, animal endurance is the sort of courage most men need in war. I was constantly amazed by the ability of the average soldier, and civilian, to exhibit this under stress.

I even enjoyed my first days of training. Uniacke barracks provided a paradoxical escape from the demoralising consciousness of war and the constant peering into an obscure and dangerous future, which had often clouded my years at Oxford. No one talked politics. The war was rarely even mentioned. I had no responsibilities except to myself, and I positively welcomed the regimentation. The only thing which gave me real discomfort was my army boots. One of my favourite stories concerned the recruit with a pair of ill-fitting boots who refused to ask for another pair, explaining:

'You know Uniacke barracks. There isn't a girl within five miles. There isn't a pub within ten. So taking these bloody boots off is the only pleasure I get in life!'

Most of my fellow recruits had been conscripted from industrial towns in Yorkshire and Tyneside. They were older than I, with a slow but salty wit. A hilarious intelligence test ended when three minutes for reading the questions stretched out to quarter of an hour before two sluggards confessed they could not read at all. There were a number of other volunteers like myself, mainly from universities, including a tall, well-made, glistening young man from Rugby of whom Dr Arnold would have been proud. He was called Hugh Sebag-Montefiore, and later became Anglican Bishop of Birmingham.

Military rank was of course all-important. I felt humble even before an acting unpaid lance-corporal. There was none of the brutality or bullying I had been led to expect by novels about the First World War. But there were some familiar caricatures – a padre who described himself as 'a bloke with the collar the wrong way round' and exhorted us: 'For God's sake, don't do anything unworthy of your manhood.' There was also a beastly captain who told us: 'If you meet a German parachutist, don't offer him a cigarette. Kick him in the balls. Treat him as dirty as you know. Never forget, he's a Hun. The Hun knows no law. Shoot as many as you can; but remember to leave a few for our intelligence boys.'

Sufficient to the day was the evil thereof. When they asked me to lead the physical training class I was as proud as of my Double First. Then the blow fell. At the end of the first week we were marched down to the MO for medical regrading. I was told I had a rupture which would grade me B.1, so I must go into hospital immediately for an operation, followed by sick leave. I felt like Lucifer expelled from Paradise. After vainly trying to get the operation postponed until I had finished my basic training, I accepted the inevitable.

At least I had time in hospital to read Malraux' *La Condition Humaine*, one of the great books of the century. After sick leave I was sent to the Artillery Depot at Woolwich, near my birthplace, to await a posting.

When I arrived at King's Cross the underground was filling up with women in slacks and pinafores with their children, seeking protection against the nightly air raids. Woolwich in the last weeks of 1940 was like Dante's Purgatory, with more than a smattering of the Inferno. Damage littered the streets. The barracks of the Artillery Depot were dirty and squalid, the beds made of iron strips with greasy 'biscuits' for mattresses – no sheets of course. There was little to do by day, and we were allowed out for only an hour or so before the blackout. Nevertheless, some of the men managed quite well. One night a stick of bombs fell in the barracks and there was an early parade to discover the casualties. Several hundred were missing; they regularly spent the night out with their girl-friends, returning only for the normal parade in the morning.

At dawn the barrage balloons looked like a swarm of silver bees, fiery with light. After sunset the air raids began with warnings from the sirens like a chorus of sea beasts moaning in the fog. Then a battery of very heavy guns behind the barracks would make the walls tremble with their WHAM, WHAM, WHAM; the more distant guns sounded like slamming doors. Meanwhile the searchlights swept and intersected in the night sky.

One evening about forty of us were sitting in the canteen, when suddenly, as if at a signal, everyone flopped to the floor. The noise of falling chairs and breaking cups made me think a bomb had fallen just outside. The room looked like a Muslim prayer meeting – a mass of khaki backsides raised to heaven and heads hidden under the marble tables. Then suddenly everyone rose again to continue talking and drinking as if nothing had happened. In fact nothing had happened; it was a good example of the psychology of crowds.

There was no talk of politics, but more of war than at my training camp, since many of the men had fought at Dunkirk. The warm-hearted comradeship was impressive. For example, I saw a Bombardier, who was escorting a deserter from the guard room, give him three Woodbines and four rock-cakes he had bought specially for the purpose. I made some new friends and met one old one – a merry-faced, brown-eyed, black-haired ruffian called Lance-Bombardier Cahal who had been at school with me in Bradford.

He found it impossible to keep any promotion he was given. Even during our days together in Woolwich it happened again. He was in a class playing with the heavy medicine balls in the gym.

'Balls to the outer ring,' shouted the Sergeant.

'And arseholes to you,' replied Cahal.

So down he went to the ranks again. I heard that later he distinguished himself behind the enemy lines in the desert, in Burma and in Northern Europe. He was one of nature's irregulars.

The confusion and dislocation of those first months in the army taught me something of lasting value – the ability to drop from one life into another without regret, so that the previous lives have no more reality than a dream. In the army this is even more useful than in civilian life. No one ever tells you in advance what will happen to you – partly because they do not know. In the end, however, after innumerable morning parades in which others were detailed off to the Middle East, India, or West Africa, I got my posting too. I was to replace a drunken Bombardier on Swindon station as a railway checker.

I served at the Railway Traffic Office on Swindon station for the first months of 1941, charged with a heavy responsibility for keeping the war going. I was supposed to count all the service men and women getting on every train, getting off every train, and getting off and on again. That was not easy on six platforms in the blackout before the scar of my operation had fully healed.

So I made up the number getting off and on again, made an informed guess of the number getting on, and asked the ticket collector for the number getting off. After a few weeks I discovered he was making up his figures as well. This gave me a life-long scepticism about the reliability of statistics, which served me well when I became Chancellor of the Exchequer. It also taught me never to take for granted any information I was given unless I was able to check it from another source at least once.

I was billetted with a lady who kept a vegetable stall at Swindon market, so food was plentiful, though I had to use the public baths. From time to time friends from Oxford, such as Roy Jenkins, passed through the station on their way to the officers' training unit at Shrivenham; and I had one glorious evening at a Leonardo Society dinner in Balliol, when the main guest, Professor Denis Brogan, then Britain's leading expert on French and American politics, got hopelessly drunk; his son was being born that night.

Edna and I took every opportunity of being together. Swindon allowed me to spend occasional weekends in the Cotswolds with her on her way from Keighley to her home in Coleford. A secondary benefit was that I learned to read a railway timetable, something which has baffled finer brains than mine.

After a few months I was sent to an officers' selection centre in Scarborough, where many of the others were actors hoping to join the Artists Rifles; one of them was Nigel Patrick who was as debonair in real life as on stage and film. Once commissioned, as a Second Lieutenant in the General List – or Crosse and Blackwell's Hussars, as we called it – I was sent to Derby to be initiated into the mysteries of Movement Control. This was nothing to do with the Kamasutra, but a branch of staff work concerned with planning and organising the movement of armed forces by land, sea or air. We were an odd bunch. A large number were men who had worked on the railways or at ports in civilian life. Some, like myself, had been posted there by accident. There was an opera singer who never got the hang of the army – he even sloped arms on the wrong shoulder on his passing-out parade.

Two young Frenchmen who had escaped to England after the fall of France were there because they had nowhere else to go, since De Gaulle had not yet set up the Free French Forces. They had been obliged to change their names in case their relatives in France were victimised. One of them, who had chosen to call himself George Farnell-Bourne, as the nearest approximation to his real name Farinelli-Boracci, a family of the papal aristocracy, became a close friend. Tall, dark, handsome, and very lively, he had been one of the chauvinist Camelots du Roi who had torn down the Union Jack from the roof of the British Embassy just before the war. He and I, with Charlie Birkin, an Etonian just married to a young actress, used to scour the surrounding towns in search of plays. We saw *Blithe Spirit* in Leeds with two incomparable performances, by Kay Hammond as the ghost of Elvira and Margaret Rutherford as Madame Arcati.

When my course at Derby was over I spent some months as Rail Traffic Officer in Hull, Halifax, York, Leeds and Sheffield, learning more about railways than I knew there was to learn. I still cherish a letter I picked up from a train guard about a passenger who coughed so hard while he was in the lavatory that his false teeth fell on the track below.

In Sheffield I was able to pursue what has since become a consuming interest. An old lady called Mrs Challenger had inherited a second-hand bookshop on the Glossop Road after her husband's death. She regularly put a load of the older books in the dustbin for scrap; but she allowed me to rummage through the piles and buy any I wanted at the price marked;

she gave me a bowl of water and a towel to wash my hands afterwards. So, among scores of other books of immense interest, I got a first edition of Quarles' *Emblems* for one shilling and a first edition of Hume's *Philosophical Essays* for two shillings. When I met Harold Laski at a meeting in Keighley I told him about it. He made a special visit to Sheffield and bought a dozen rare civil war pamphlets for less money than he later received for writing an article in the *New Statesman* about his visit.

Nevertheless, it was boring work, during which only occasional weekends with Edna gave me something to look forward to. In the wastelands of Hull during the air raids I tried to teach myself elementary Russian, until I found that for all my efforts I could scarcely understand a single word in Soviet films. Finally, in the summer of 1942, I was given the chance to volunteer for something more exciting. So I went to Scotland for training in combined operations so that I could become an Assistant Military Landing Officer in a Beach Group.

The training was exiguous in the extreme, since at that time the British Army had little experience of assault landings on a larger scale than a commando raid. The one big landing, at Dieppe, had been a disaster; the planners had not even bothered to discover that Churchill tanks would not be able unaided to cross the shingle beach, still less to climb the walls of the promenade. I enjoyed the physical exertion of exercises on the hills behind Wemyss Bay. My mother thought that the street fighting course at Greenock had made me more mature! One afternoon, while walking on the golf course at Troon, I saw an aircraft carrier across the Firth sink with all hands in a few minutes; it had hit a mine which had been dropped the night before.

I was allowed one piece of practical experience, when I was sent to join an American cargo boat for the landing at Arzeu in Algeria; it was part of the operation which captured Oran from Pétain's forces. Neither I nor the American officers I accompanied had the slightest idea what my function was. So they got on with the job and I watched them. Our boat had been very badly stowed; throughout the journey it was lurching about thirty degrees from one side to the other. I was never seasick. On the contrary, I loved climbing the mast and sitting in the crow's-nest; it was even more fun than the Big Dipper at Blackpool. Apart from desultory bombing from a couple of aircraft, the landing itself was practically uncontested. But on the way home – to take part in a landing in Spanish Morocco if Franco came into the war – I developed a bronchitis so bad that when we reached Britain I could not walk two steps without gasping my heart out. After a spell in hospital I went back to my Beach Group to finish my training.

Boring, mechanical, and irrelevant as a lot of my army training was, I learned much of permanent value. The basic drill, which seemed so senseless at the time, enabled me to carry out standard movements without thinking, thus freeing my mind for more important tasks in a crisis. Army staff training helped me to analyse problems systematically and to prescribe the necessary action clearly. Business schools are supposed to perform a similar role for industry. For someone like me, who had spent his previous life at school and university, the army was a school in practical reality. After loading tanks on to railway flats during the blackout in a blizzard on the moors above Penistone, I will never again go to a job without a pencil and a piece of paper.

For me, as an individualist intellectual, however, the most valuable legacy of war service was the knowledge that I depended on other people and that other people depended on me. It was this knowledge which created the sense of comradeship so characteristic of wartime and so lacking in peace. Combined operations taught me another lesson – that every group in society has its own special contribution to make through its own special knowledge and experience. The average soldier took the navy and air force for granted; they provided him with protection at sea and in the sky, but he did not realise that their job was as complicated and as dangerous as his own. It came at first as a surprise to me to realise that the navy's job in getting the troops on to a beach was quite as complicated as mine in getting them across and off it.

Finally, no one can go through a war without accepting the importance of planning. Individual initiative and personal bravery have of course a vital role. But without the most careful planning, involving consultation with all the interests concerned, no operation has a chance of success. Needless to say, planning can often go badly wrong, as I was to discover in some of the operations I helped to organise. In war, even more than in peace, it is impossible to know all the relevant facts when you make the plan – and you are working against an enemy whose own plans are designed to frustrate yours. But to rule out the desirability or even possibility of planning in principle, as some politicians do, is to accept an intolerable handicap and to betray those for whom you are responsible. No industrial manager would accept such a handicap; yet many governments do. Oddly enough, the magic of the market place on which they prefer to rely, usually depends on the uncoordinated plans of innumerable private groups.

All these lessons were brought home to me when our Beach Group finally embarked in Glasgow to take part in the real war. We left the quayside on the evening of April 13th, 1943 and began a slow drift through the shipyards of the Clyde, the air noisy with the sounds of seagulls and riveting. People on the banks stopped to wave at us. Then some wit shouted 'Hi di Hi!' The whole ship replied with a thunderous 'Ho di Ho!' and the rest of the way the river resounded with prayer and response like a jovial cathedral.

There was little to do on the ship except read and sleep. I raced through novels by Evelyn Waugh, Graham Greene and C. S. Forester and any autobiographies and poetry I could lay my hands on. I filled my diary with jejune philosophising. We did not know for certain where we were going until we passed the rock of Gibraltar. Ten days after leaving Glasgow we disembarked at Algiers, and began slowly moving up the coast from Bouzarea to the Gulf of Tunis as part of 78 Division for the invasion of Sicily.

Those weeks in North Africa were an odd interlude. The war was always ahead of us, but never present. We saw little of the French and not much more of the Arabs. During our days at divisional headquarters in Guelma we were visited by King George VI and the Secretary for War. Dennis Bloodworth, our security officer took bets all round the mess that the King was not coming; then he refused to pay out on the reasonable grounds that he had only been doing his duty in deceiving us. I did not believe him either when he claimed to speak Chinese. There I was wrong; he married a Chinese girl and served with distinction for many years after the war as the *Observer* correspondent in Singapore.

One of my colleagues in the Beach Group was Lord John Hope, of the Scots Guards. Son of Lord Linlithgow, the Viceroy of India, he missed succeeding to the title by a few seconds, since his twin brother was born just before him. When his father thought it was time he learned the facts of life, he gave him a lecture on 'The Life and History of the Trouser Worm'. He was a pale, friendly man, married to the daughter of Somerset Maugham, and was shocked by my political radicalism. I met him later as a junior minister in the Macmillan Government.

I did some painting and a good deal of writing during the weeks of waiting for action. The landscape of Guelma reminded me surprisingly of upper Wharfedale. When a black Berber drove a donkey along the path in front of me, loaded with carrots and cucumbers, he seemed like an intrusion from a dream.

Our camp at Bougie, on the coast, had a truer feel of North Africa. I described the scene in my diary. 'Grasshoppers whirred away like cotton looms. Nearer, a big cicada was tirelessly creaking. Down in the valley a donkey brayed his eternal protest, Punchinello on all fours. The sea was emerald, stained with violet and ochre. Two slender masts projected from its surface beyond the harbour. By a berth a couple of ships lay on their sides embracing one another. High over the port the silver bees were poised, forever motionless on their invisible wires. Behind, a hedge of cactus hid an Arab farm, enclosing a tiny patio where naked babies crawled among the flies and dirt. Pink, saffron, black and scarlet flared in the stony fields below a pool of yellow flowers – it was a woman doubled under a load of hay.'

Our Mediterranean idyll came to an end on the scorching beach at Hammamet, where we were drawn up in a square to hear an inspirational address from General Montgomery. He did not impress us with his sharp, ferret-like face and pale grey-green eyes, wearing his vanity like a foulard. When he told the veterans of 78 Division, who had almost taken Tunis within three days of landing at Algiers, that they should feel proud to be joining the Eighth Army, the temperature dropped below freezing in a second.

We landed in Sicily at Avola three days after the main landing, so did not see action there. After the arid wastes of North Africa, where you could smell the villages miles away, I felt this was Europe again at last. We occupied a farmhouse in extensive lemon groves on the fertile coastal plain. Three times in the next fortnight I was ordered to Tripoli, where they were planning the landing at Salerno in conditions of almost total publicity. Three times the order was cancelled. Finally I was posted to 231 Independent Brigade as Military Landing Officer – or beachmaster – for an assault on the Italian coast north of Reggio: we were intended to cut off the German forces retreating from Sicily, so that they could not reinforce those drawn up against our landing at Salerno.

I was fortunate in that posting. The officer who took my place in Tripoli was killed within hours of reaching Salerno's beach. Exceptionally experienced, 231 Brigade was composed of three battalions from the regular army, with a first-rate commander in General Urquhart, who later commanded the airborne division at Arnhem. I could not have hoped for better company in my first serious operation.

As always, Murphy ruled, and Sod's Law was continually in force. A violent storm compelled our flotilla of landing craft to put in for the night on a beach near Messina, where I had to reload the whole brigade in darkness – a task which Colonel Marcus Sieff, the port commandant was glad to leave to me. I managed to get our whole force into several fewer craft – we had lost some in the storm – including the ambulances, which the Brigadier had been prepared to leave behind. As it turned out, we needed them badly. The day's delay meant changing our objective from Pizzo, to a little town called Porto di Santa Venere, much further up the coast.

Finally we set sail on the evening of September 7th. Within hours we heard on the radio that Italy had surrendered. We did not know whether to believe it or not; in any case it hardly mattered, since we would be fighting Germans, not Italians.

The darkness was complete when I came on deck at half past two. Our landing craft was frozen in its relation to the dim shapes of other craft, so that it seemed we were stationary and the sea was flowing past us. Flashes of green phosphorescence winked out of the receding foam. With difficulty I could construct a black range of mountains ahead. The Commandos should that moment be landing to test the German defences and to secure the beaches for our assault battalion, due to follow an hour later.

I watched for gun-flashes, strained for the sound of firing. But nothing. Only the hiss of the cleft sea and the whirring hum of the engines.

Boots sounded, shuffling on the bridge. I watched and waited. Half past four – still no sign of fighting. The darkness was almost imperceptibly reduced, the mountains larger, with a faint white glow at their foot. On the bridge the Brigadier was trying to contact his leading battalions.

'Hello Drake, hello Drake – are you dry yet, are you dry yet – over to you, over.'

'The Devons are ashore, sir.'

The quiet repetitions continued. Then, like the cast of a fishing line, a soundless red arc of tracer, and another. Everyone watched intently, trying to interpret. Slowly it became clear that nothing was going according to plan. None of the units ashore had yet found a recognisable objective. But opposition seemed slight.

I went down into the operations room and put on my equipment. I felt sober, suppressing my excitement. With my dispatch cases, mapboards, haversack swinging around me I felt absurdly overdressed.

When I came on deck again it was half light. A grey coast of steep high hills on my left, and a long low jetty running out ahead to meet us on our right. We all crowded up against the ramps. There was a small town ahead of us, the beach enclosed between the hills and the jetty, a few craft already discharging and troops running into the streets behind.

BANG! A loud explosion somewhere. I saw spray settling back into the sea astern. BANG! Another explosion this time sent spray like drizzle over us. We crouched down and adjusted our helmets. It was mortar fire from some concealed position in the hills. Everyone looked serious and a little tense.

At last the craft swished into the shingle, down rattled the ramps, and we ran ashore.

It was still about half an hour before dawn. I could see a number of landing craft beached down by the water's edge, their ramps lowering, waiting for track to pour their vehicles over. Something was seriously wrong. Two craft should have beached half an hour before, carrying howitzers and bulldozers, towing sledges loaded with hundreds of yards of wire track.

All the timing had gone to hell. The Commandos had landed nearly two hours late three miles from the correct place, and no one had yet seen or heard them. The assaulting battalion with the Assistant Military Landing Officers and the naval beachmaster, who should have made a reconnaissance for beach exits, had landed on the wrong beach, an hour and a half late; they had been misled by a smouldering heap of sawdust which they thought was a beach limit sign, and by faulty intelligence descriptions of the jetty.

In fact everyone, assault battalion, AMLOs, beachmaster, reserve battalions, vehicles, and brigade headquarters reached the main beach at the same time. And the Germans had simultaneously occupied the hills above us, where they had perfect positions for their 88mm mortars.

As a result we had an extremely unpleasant time on the beach, with many casualties. The naval commander, Admiral McGrigor, had his launch sunk under him, General Urquhart collected shell splinters in his backside, and I myself had my first experience of being dive bombed.

The enemy mortars were still lobbing bombs at us when everyone dropped flat. Dive bombers were falling on us out of the sun. My head was on gritty concrete. Everything was still. I heard two, three descending drones and the grass suddenly blew in my face, the bushes swayed towards me.

I felt myself lifted off the ground, there was a tinkling followed by thuds as debris hit the earth again. I had not heard the explosion.

Then WHOOM, WHOOM, WHOOM, WHOOM, WHOOM. I counted the bursts, my muscles taut, found a helmet lying on the ground an inch or two in front and jammed it on my head.

Stones and earth showered around and I felt a heavy blow on my right ankle. Then the drone faded. I got up and brushed off the dirt. My ankle was numb and not very painful. That was the only injury I suffered.

The mortar bombing continued all day and night. We were sitting targets for the enemy on the hills above, who could see our every move, while we could never see them. I snatched a few hours sleep wedged between concrete blocks on the beach.

Then the Germans moved on. We shipped our two hundred casualties back to base in Sicily. Suddenly the fields outside the town were swarming with Italian peasants. They had descended from the hills to loot a timber yard full of doors and window frames. Staggering under the weight, they looked like a plague of giant ants as they carried them back to their homes.

The Brigade was snatched away immediately for the landing in Normandy, while I returned to my normal work. They left all their vehicles and equipment behind and invited me to take my pick. I chose an amphibious jeep, like a huge bathtub on wheels, which I managed to keep through most of the campaign in Italy.

My next job was on the staff in Bari. I made up for the routine nature of my military duties by buying almost everything published by the local publishing house, Laterza e Figli. They were specialists in philosophy, particularly the works of the anti-fascist Benedetto Croce. Besides getting everything he had written, I bought Italian translations of Nietzsche and Unamuno, who were more to my taste. My opinion of Croce rose substantially, however, when I discovered an excellent essay of his on Gerard Manley Hopkins, complete with good translations of his poems.

Then I was posted to Naples, where I made many life-long friends. My colonel, Jack Donaldson, was as keen on music as I was. So we sought out the decrepit conductor of the San Carlo Opera orchestra, Signor Baroni, and persuaded him to form a string quartet to give concerts for the forces. Jack was an exceptional individual. He had been instrumental in setting up the Peckham Health Centre in the thirties, a pioneer in its field, and had his house designed by the great German architect Gropius. While he was in Persia his wife, Frankie, had drawn out all his money to buy a farm. She then started a brilliant career by writing books on farming, but found her true bent with a biography of her father, Freddie Lonsdale, the playwright; it is unique for its combination of cold objectivity and filial tenderness. Later she was to work with the grandson of one of her father's mistresses, Edward Fox, in the television film of her book on Edward the Eighth. Jack became Minister of the Arts in the Callaghan Government, but was later seduced into the SDP.

Other Colonels in Movement Control with me at that time were Denis Greenhill, who became head of the Foreign Office, Val Duncan, later an outstanding head of Rio Tinto Zinc, and Marcus Sieff, who succeeded his father Israel as head of Marks and Spencers. I was not surprised thirty years later when Greenhill chose Duncan to write a report on the Foreign Office, with Sieff at his side. One of my colleagues had an Italian girl-friend who had known Gorky in Capri fifteen years earlier. I too had a 'dizionario a lunghi capelli'; so my Italian improved by leaps and bounds.

My immediate superior was a Lieutenant-Colonel known by the men as 'Basil the Bastard'. He had been an amateur racing driver before the war and was a compulsive womaniser. He was also an offensive bully, who took pleasure in humiliating anyone of lower rank; it did not work with me, however. Basil did me one lasting service. After working for him I never had trouble with a superior in later life. After the war, Basil found a kindred spirit in Evelyn Waugh, whom he squired round East Africa.

My love for opera took off in Naples. Before the San Carlo Theatre was reopened I heard Ebe Stignani in *Norma* in the tiny Teatro delle Palme, hardly big enough to contain her glorious voice. But for me the revelation was Puccini, whose music-dramas had a special resonance in wartime Italy. *Butterfly* was the story of so many Italian girls under the allied occupation. The tragedy of *Tosca* must have been repeated many times in the Resistance.

It was in Naples, too, that I began to notice the gulf between the middle class in the cities, who had mainly collaborated with fascism, and the peasants and working people among whom the socialist tradition was still powerful – a contrast which had impressed me so much in Greece at the outbreak of war. 'La Dolce Vita' was a reality among the upper class; their decadence was well chronicled by Malaparte. I even met a young woman who injected her baby with cocaine.

In January 1944 I was appointed Military Landing Officer to the British assault brigade for Anzio. We did the planning in the great baroque palace at Caserta; I remember Humphrey Bogart poking his head round a door during a visit to entertain the American forces – a tiny little man, who conveyed none of the power of his film personality. I preferred him as Philip Marlowe.

In planning the landing, we had a long discussion of how to make sure that the tragedy of Sicily was not repeated; many of the American parachutists there had been shot by their own ground troops, who thought they were German. The American commander suggested that the recognition signal should be a Bronx cheer. The British General had no idea what a Bronx cheer was. So we settled for the metal clickers found in children's Christmas crackers.

Wynford Vaughan Thomas was among the press men who joined us for a final party before the landing; his commentary for the BBC was a classic. Next day, on the way to load up at Castellamare, the lorry I was travelling in ran into a concrete post at sixty miles an hour. I was thrown through the windscreen, cut my throat and broke a front tooth, which produced a gigantic gumboil while I was in Anzio. When I returned to Naples I looked like a chimpanzee, the army dentist could not use an anaesthetic, and broke the drill in my tooth. That was the worst pain I suffered in the war.

Unlike my operation in Calabria, the landing at Anzio went exactly according to plan. We lost fewer men than the Americans had lost on the exercise at Salerno the previous week. The surprise we achieved was so complete that we even captured some German officers in their pyjamas. The real trouble came later, in the months when the beach-head was under siege, so brilliantly described by Raleigh Trevelyan in *Rome 1944*.

Though the landing itself went well, Anzio was a tactical failure. Some of the forces which should have taken part were withdrawn for the landing in France, so we never had enough troops to hold both the beachhead and the Colle Laziale, which dominated the beachhead from a few miles inland. Even if, as armchair critics have claimed, a bolder commander could have entered Rome in those first few days, his troops would have been cut off and wiped out at leisure. But the Germans made greater strategic mistakes. They gravely weakened their forces on more important fronts in the vain hope of wiping out the beachhead. So Anzio on balance turned out to be a success. Victory in war, as in politics, often goes to the side which makes fewer or less serious mistakes, not to the side with the greatest positive virtues.

After Anzio I went back to our mess in Naples, where we were joined by Bill de l'Isle, who was recovering from wounds he had received at Anzio, in an action for which he received the Victoria Cross. He had been a friend of Jack Donaldson's at Eton, but regarded him as well as me as a dangerous Bolshevik. His father-in-law, Lord Gort, had won the VC in the First World War; the men who served under him were always a little nervous in case he were aiming at the same distinction.

I next moved over the icy mountains of central Italy to the east coast where I served with the Polish Corps for the capture of Ancona – a victory particularly welcome to them, since the nearby shrine of Loreto had for centuries been a place of pilgrimage for Polish Catholics. The Polish Corps was drawn from the remnants of the Polish Army which had been transported by the Russians into central Asia after the tragedy of 1939 – the so-called Anders Army.

I developed a lasting affection for that oppressed nation, which had so much in common with my Irish ancestors. Even in those days they could be divided into two groups – those from eastern Poland who hated the Russians more than the Germans, and those from western Poland who hated the Germans more than the Russians. The Poles told me, however, that they killed the Russians for business; they killed the Germans for pleasure.

Once Ancona was captured I rejoined our own Eighth Army at Siena, one of the loveliest towns in the world. I had more spare time here, and used it to read and explore the beauties of Tuscany. On one expedition – or 'swan', as we called it – I went to Montegufoni, of which I had read as the Italian home of the Sitwells. When I persuaded the caretaker that my visit arose from simple curiosity, I was let into the drawing room. A shaft of sunlight illuminated Botticelli's *Primavera*. It was the most exciting moment of my life. Montegufoni was used to store the best paintings from the Uffizi Gallery in Florence for the duration of the war. Though at one time the building was used as a German officers' mess, all the paintings survived undamaged.

In Siena itself a young American officer was collecting and restoring the great Sienese paintings. It was the first time I had seen the pink and emerald delicacy of this gentle school. On many of these explorations I was accompanied by a young captain in the First Aid Nursing Yeomanry, called Lavinia.

The FANY were the aristocracy of the women's services, and tended to provide personal assistants for the generals in Italy. They were an exceptional lot, with much broader views and wider interests than I would then have expected. Mary Benson, for example, was the personal assistant to General Brian Robertson, who was in charge of all administration for the British Army. She was a South African. After the war she was profoundly impressed by Alan Paton's novel *Cry the Beloved Country*, and dedicated her life to the struggle for African freedom.

My friend, Lavinia, loved modern poetry. I introduced her to *Leda and the Swan*, since Yeats had already become my favourite. We spent weekends at the mediaeval town of San Gimignano, and later at the enchanting fishing village of Positano south of Naples. It was the combination of Yeats with Lavinia which finally convinced me that

Lindsay's support for aristocratic values was acceptable. But like Yeats himself, I think there is also a place for 'porter drinkers' randy laughter'.

In November I was sent to Pesaro, south of Rimini, to plan a major landing in northern Yugoslavia, which was intended to prevent Tito's partisans from capturing Fiume. It would have been a difficult and complicated operation for the British Army, which could travel nowhere without masses of equipment on heavy lorries. The small number of roads in Yugoslavia were bad, with few places to park great convoys at night. In the end the operation was cancelled, since Tito's partisans, guessing Churchill's intention, captured Fiume before our main forces were due to start landing at Sibenik, miles to the south. I confess I was relieved; I would have been the MLO for an assault landing on the island of Krk, which blocked the way to Fiume. Since it was strongly garrisoned by German troops on steep mountains which dominated all the beaches, I foresaw a repeat of the landing at Porto di S. Venere in even less favourable conditions.

One of my colleagues on the planning group was an architect who had won the Prix de Rome. Another was Nigel Birch, whose savage tongue made him an opponent to be feared when he joined the Tory benches after the war. He resigned from his job at the Treasury with Thorneycroft and Enoch Powell, thus creating the famous 'little local difficulty' for Macmillan, and ended as a sad figure, almost blind, feeling his way along the corridors of the House of Commons, mumbling and alone.

The last months of the war I spent in Florence. For the infantry, they were the worst of the whole Italian campaign. The Appenines were bitter cold, and the Germans fought hard every inch of the way. Men who had come through the desert and Cassino without breaking, collapsed with the strain of the Gothic Line. There was bitter resentment when Lady Astor described them as 'D-Day Dodgers'. They replied with a song to the tune of Lily Marlene:

> We hope the boys in France will soon be getting leave
> After six months service it's a shame they're not relieved;
> But we can still carry on out here
> For another two or three more years,
> For we're the D-Day Dodgers – out in Italy.
>
> Old Lady Astor please listen, dear, to this.
> Don't stand upon the platform and talk a lot of piss;
> You're the nation's sweetheart, the nation's pride,

But your bloody big mouth is far too wide;
That's from the D–Day Dodgers – out in Italy.

If you look around the mountains, in the mud and rain
You'll find the scattered crosses, some which bear no name.
Heartbreak and toil and suffering gone,
The lads beneath them slumber on,
For they were the D–Day Dodgers – who'll stay in Italy.

Meanwhile at the headquarters of 15 Army Group in Florence things went on as usual. William Chappell, the ballet dancer and stage-designer, was an improbable member of our mess. I went to daily intelligence briefings given by Colonel David Hunt, who had been a don at Oxford, and after the war had a distinguished career in the diplomatic service. Jack Profumo was the Air Liaison Officer; he was an intelligent man of exceptional charm, immensely attractive to ladies of the Italian aristocracy wherever we went. However, our morale was declining, as one general after another left for other theatres. We had our own headquarters song, to the tune of 'Onward Christian Soldiers':

We who crossed the ocean
With this mighty host,
Know that quick promotion
Is what matters most.
Don't take hasty action
On letters you receive,
If things get too awkward
You can take some leave.

Onward 15 Army Group
Marching as to war,
With the AMGOT spearhead
Going on before.

Ike and Monty left us,
Jumbo's gone away,
Gone to reign in glory
In the USA.
Even Alexander's
Left the sinking barque.

AAI is left with
General Fucking Clark.

Get into the landing craft.
Get the oars and row.
Row like hell for – anywhere!
If there's anywhere left to row.

Finally Jack Profumo flew our commander to Switzerland to negotiate the surrender of all German forces in Italy. The armistice was signed on May 1st, 1945. Our part of the war was over.

This phase of my life, too, ended with a memorable journey. I decided to make a final 'swan' and to get if possible into Austria and Yugoslavia. So my driver and I left Florence in our jeep on the evening of May 6th to cross the Appenines over the Futa Pass. It was bleak and bare – everywhere foxholes, gunpits, piles of shell-cases and tangles of signal wire. Towards Bologna every village was a shapeless heap of rubble with the strong sweet stench of death heavy in the air.

Italian partisans controlled the whole area of the Po valley. Suddenly we noticed that people were running out to clap and cheer us. Bells were ringing in the villages, and we heard someone shout: 'La guerra e finita!' We were not sure whether to believe it, since two German parachute divisions held out in Italy after the general surrender. We drove through Sirmione to Verona, past Italians waving torches and lighting bonfires, with Verey lights shooting up green and red in the darkness.

Next day we drove through Udine up the Tagliamento valley into Austria. It was another world – great grey precipices, silky waterfalls, turf green and soft, enamelled with cowslips and mountain flowers, peaks glistening with snow. There was no other traffic, but coming down the pass towards us were hundreds, thousands of refugees of every nationality – Russians, Serbs, Poles, Italians, dressed in every possible way, doggedly tramping into Italy.

At the frontier the mailed fist, badge of our Sixth Armoured Division, was planted above a cluster of German soldiers, all armed. We sped through into an incredible dream. Hundreds of German soldiers were marching up the road. There were German officers in staff cars, all armed, yet no attempt was made to molest us. Beyond Villach we called at the Divisional HQ and I found Tony Crosland, slim and handsome in his parachutist's beret. We had been close friends in the Oxford Labour Club; he was now divisional intelligence officer. He told us our forward troops were in Klagenfurt.

So on we went. In every village banners and flags of Free Austria were hanging out. Hordes of refugees were walking down all the roads; among them were individual German soldiers who had simply decided to walk home. The ditches were full of helmets, webbing, and weapons, abandoned as they tried to lighten their load.

In Klagenfurt we stayed with a platoon of the Rifle Brigade doing guard and garrison in one of the offices of the new local government. The Austrian officials were still terrified of reprisals by the SS. The young lieutenant spoke no German and had little idea what he was supposed to do; so I acted as his guide and interpreter. Going over in the dark to the local Gasthaus to brew some tea I was met by a worried Special Forces officer in a jeep; he said that there were two thousand armed Croat Ustachis milling around in the Adolf Hitler Platz, that Tito's troops were infiltrating into the south of the town, and that there might be a major battle during the night unless the Croats were disarmed – fortunately there was not. An Austrian of the *Landesregierung* said he would be murdered on his way home by the SS unless I gave him an escort.

The following morning there were streams of questioners. Two Slovenes afraid of Tito wanted to know if the road to Villach was free from partisans. A young Albanian asked if he could join the British Army so as to avoid partisan vengeance; he burst into tears when I told him the war was over. A German Colonel demanded to know how to evacuate his wounded. Meanwhile the town was filling up with Hungarian troops in retreat from the Russians.

That afternoon I went over a high pass into Gorizia and territory controlled by the partisans. Yugoslav forces were now in every village; there were notices and slogans in Serbian, posters of Tito, flags and triumphal arches of pine branches and flags over the entrance to every hamlet. The situation in Trieste was extremely tense, since the political future of the area had not yet been decided. West of Trieste we passed through one of Tito's divisions on the march – a band of tough, ragged men, women, and boys, all armed with captured weapons or British Sten guns, a few officers on horses and senior officers in German cars, in every type of clothing – peasant rags, or uniforms from the German, Hungarian, or Italian armies, but all wearing the partisan's grey forage cap with the red star.

I spent the next night in Venice, which was already full of troops on day leave, but otherwise little altered since my peacetime visit six years earlier. Then I drove back to my headquarters in crippling heat through Ferrara and Bologna. The shops were shut and there were religious processions everywhere. It was the Feast of the Annunciation. Nine days later I was on the plane to Britain.

The previous year I had received a letter from Ivor Thomas, the right-wing Labour MP for Keighley, who later joined the Tories: 'From conversation with your parents, and knowing your views,' he wrote, 'I wondered if you would be interested in being put on the list of potential Labour candidates.' I agreed, without great excitement. It seemed a very academic prospect at the time. Later I was offered a choice between two safe Conservative seats to fight. I picked Pudsey and Otley, because it was nearer my home.

The selection conference was held in February, while I was planning the abortive landing in Yugoslavia. So I wrote them a letter from Italy:

> A man pushed blindfold into a courtroom with cotton wool in his ears,
> obliged to plead for his life without knowing where the jury was sitting
> or even whether it was in the room at all, would nicely represent my
> position at this moment . . . I am only one of the hundreds of young
> men, now in the forces, who long for the opportunity to realise their
> political ideals by actively fighting an election for the Labour Party.
> These men in their turn represent millions of soldiers, sailors and airmen
> who want socialism and who have been fighting magnificently to save a
> world in which socialism is possible. Many of them have come to
> realise that socialism is a matter of life and death for them. But too
> many others feel that politics is just another civilian racket in which they
> are always the suckers . . . We have now almost won the war, at the
> highest price ever paid for victory. If you could see the shattered misery
> that once was Italy, the bleeding countryside and the wrecked villages, if
> you could see Cassino, with a bomb-created river washing green slime
> through a shapeless rubble that a year ago was homes, you would realise
> more than ever that the defeat of Hitler and Mussolini is not enough by
> itself to justify the destruction, not just of twenty years of fascism, but
> too often of twenty centuries of Europe. Only a more glorious future can
> make up for this annihilation of the past.

Those were indeed my views, and when a friend of my father put them to the selection conference, I was adopted as prospective Labour candidate for Pudsey and Otley. So once the war in Europe was over I was given three months leave to return to England for the election; I arrived just in time for the Labour Party Conference on May 21st.

The Blackpool Conference was remarkable for the number of young candidates in uniform. Few of us had much knowledge or experience of party politics; but we were all determined to make a better Britain and a better world than we had known before the war. John Freeman had been a Brigade Major in Germany. Roy Jenkins, like myself, had served in Italy. My own speech, so often resurrected since by my critics on Right and Left, was typical of many:

'The upper classes in every country are selfish, depraved, dissolute and decadent,' I cried. 'The struggle for socialism in Europe . . . has been hard, cruel, merciless and bloody. The penalty for participation in the liberation movement has been death for oneself, if caught, and, if not caught oneself, the burning of one's home and the death by torture of one's family . . . Remember that one of the prices paid for our survival during the last five years has been the death by bombardment of countless thousands of innocent European men and women.'

When I returned to my seat, my neighbour, George Thomas, later Speaker of the House of Commons and Lord Tonypandy, congratulated me with the words: 'Denis, you have the most wonderful gift of vituperation!' It was that speech which led Hugh Dalton, Philip Noel Baker and Harold Laski, representing Right, Centre, and Left of the Party, to ask me if I would apply for the job of International Secretary of the Labour Party after my defeat in the general election, which they took for granted.

To everyone's surprise, I came close to victory, cutting the Conservative majority by ten thousand, to 1,651. It was a wonderful campaign, fought largely in small towns and villages of the Yorkshire countryside, during the loveliest June since I took Greats in 1940. I spoke with total confidence, based largely on total ignorance. When I was asked a question about Britain's exports I replied that it was disgraceful to send shoes abroad when there were still children in Britain without shoes. Economics had not yet come to dominate British politics as it has ever since that campaign.

However, my central theme was sound enough: we must solve the problems of the peace by applying the same planning techniques as we had used to win the war. The Conservatives were discredited by memories of the Great Slump and of appeasement. Their main asset, Winston Churchill, threw away his potential advantages by accusing Labour of wanting to introduce a Gestapo into Britain; he was handicapped by his obvious inability to understand the men and women he had led in war. For example, in one broadcast he addressed the British people as, 'you, who are listening to me in your cottages.'

In fact, I would probably have won my own seat if my Liberal opponent had taken nearly as many votes as his predecessor in 1935. But Brigadier Terence Clark did not impress. He had been army heavyweight boxing champion, and it showed. Soon afterwards he became Conservative MP for Portsmouth, and was the nearest thing to neanderthal man on the Tory benches.

Labour's landslide victory in the country as a whole was ample compensation for my personal defeat. As, in the last few minutes of our count, the Conservative edged ahead, news came in of one Tory titan toppling after another. The servicemen's vote was overwhelmingly for Labour. War had given us all a new self-confidence and self-reliance. John Freeman spoke for a whole generation when he told the new House of Commons: 'On every side is a spirit of high adventure, of gay determination, a readiness to experiment, to take reasonable risks, to stake high in this magnificent venture of rebuilding our civilisation, as we have staked high in winning the war.'

A few weeks later the first atom bomb was dropped on Hiroshima and Japan surrendered. I was in Bradford with Edna and my parents when the news was announced. On the way back to Riddlesden the bus stopped at every pub it passed. Hours later we were just able to crawl up the hill to home. The war was over at last.

Like everyone else in the services I felt only an enormous relief at the explosion of the first atom bombs. It meant that I would not have to spend the next few years island hopping in the Pacific. But nevertheless once my leave was over I had to return to the army in Italy, where the only thought in anyone's mind was 'When do I go home'. By then it was all too true that:

> Soldiers who want to be a hero
> Are practically zero.
> But those who want to be civilians,
> Jesus, they run into the millions.

For a soldier, the worst feature of a war is separation from family and friends. Most normal people quite enjoy the travel, excitement, and comradeship. When the war is over there is no compensation for the separation. Yet in 1945 getting everyone home and demobilised was a massive task of organisation; it was bound to take not months, but years.

I tried to keep myself occupied at Allied headquarters in Caserta by reading, walking, going to the opera, and talking – mainly to friends like

Tony Crosland and Andrew Shonfield, who were as anxious to get home as I. I had three possible escape routes. The military wanted me to join a team writing the official history of the Italian campaign under David Hunt. That would have meant being promoted to Lieutenant-Colonel, living in an Austrian castle and shooting chamois in my spare time; it was ruled out by the separation required. I had been awarded a senior scholarship at Merton College, just before I went into the army; so I could have gone back to Oxford and written the world's greatest masterpiece on the philosophy of art. But by now I had learned that I could think well only under stress. I would have gone to seed in academia. So I decided to take up the suggestion that I should apply for the job of International Secretary at the Labour Party headquarters in Transport House.

My Brigadier invented an excuse for me to return to London so that I could appear for the interview. I was to take back to the War Office my history of Movement Control's part in the Italian campaign. On November 20th, 1945 I got the job, with strong support from Dalton, Laski, and Aneurin Bevan. There followed a confusing month in which, though still in the army, I was sought out by Left and Right of the Party, by foreign journalists and diplomatists – in fact by anyone with an axe to grind.

Nevertheless, Edna and I had time to arrange our marriage. We had both had affairs during our years of separation, but our love had only grown stronger as a result. We celebrated my last weeks on a Major's pay by going to the theatre almost every night, and saw the stupendous double bill at the Old Vic in which Laurence Olivier played both Oedipus and Mr Puff in Sheridan's *The Critic*. He finished by swinging on the curtain from a box on to mid-stage; I felt he was a man after my own heart. We listened to Myra Hess playing Beethoven in the National Gallery. Finally, in the week before Christmas, I left the army, married Edna, and started work at Transport House.

As I collected my civilian clothes at the demobilisation depot in Reading – a stiff, ungainly three-piece suit and a hard green porkpie hat, which I decided immediately should never touch my brow – I said to myself: 'Now I can forget for ever all that I have learned in the last five years as a soldier.'

I was wrong. Nineteen years later I was Secretary of State for Defence.

CHAPTER FOUR

International Secretary

You that love England, who have an ear for her music,
The slow movement of clouds in benediction,
Clear arias of light thrilling over her uplands,
Over the chords of summer sustained peacefully;
Ceaseless the leaves' counterpoint in a west wind lively,
Blossom and river rippling loveliest allegro,
And the storms of wood strings brass at year's finale:
Listen. Can you not hear the entrance of a new theme?

You above all who have come to the far end, victims
Of a run-down machine, who can bear it no longer;
Whether in easy chairs chafing at impotence
Or against hunger, bullies and spies preserving
The nerve for action, the spark of indignation –
Need fight in the dark no more, you know your enemies.
You shall be leaders when zero hour is signalled,
Wielders of power and welders of a new world.

– 'The Magnetic Mountain' Cecil Day Lewis

CHRISTMAS 1945 was a difficult time to start our married life. The
only place we could find for our honeymoon was the Buck Inn at
Buckden in upper Wharfedale. It was still crowded with middle-aged
ladies from the nearby industrial towns seeking refuge from the war, so
we had to sleep in the loft of the barn next door. As soon as we had got
into bed a trapdoor in the floor would open, and a head would appear,
followed by a body holding a candle. It was the owner of the barn, a little
old lady who wrote poetry and wanted us to hear her works.

If she expected to interrupt us in amorous exercises she must have been disappointed. I had developed a painful boil at the base of my spine, and Edna spent most of our honeymoon bathing it. I did, however, involuntarily give the other guests a certain thrill when I walked into breakfast one morning with the words: 'Christ, my coccyx is painful today!' I suspect their knowledge of anatomy was no match for their imagination.

We were back in London for the New Year and managed to find a bedsitter in an attic off Manchester Square. So I started work at Transport House, and Edna went back to teaching at Bromley Girls' High School.

London was pullulating at that time with change and excitement. Since Britain was the only belligerent to survive the war without suffering enemy occupation, London served as the political and cultural centre for the whole of Europe. Those intellectuals and politicians who had escaped the concentration camps were still working in London, often as journalists and broadcasters. The European service of the BBC at Bush House was full of them. The York Minster in Soho and Berlemont's restaurant above it had been the favourite haunt of the French Resistance, who still dropped in to meet old friends. The Ivy restaurant nearby was preferred by the Italians, since its owner was a life-long anti-fascist. The Poles had bases further west, notably their Club in Green Street; for years afterwards officials of the Warsaw regime who had served in the British forces used to come there to meet old comrades who preferred exile to Soviet domination.

I spent many happy hours with my European friends in such places, eating and drinking better than I had ever expected, or could have afforded myself. My initial salary as International Secretary of the Labour Party, with a Double First and Major's rank behind me, was seven pounds a week with no expenses. As a teacher, Edna earned eleven. But until we started a family we managed well enough. The Old Vic was then at its peak, with Laurence Olivier, Alec Guinness, and Ralph Richardson appearing together almost every night. I do not think we missed a single play. Outside the West End, the Ballet Rambert danced at Notting Hill Gate, and Sonya Dresdel acted in *Hedda Gabler* and *Rosmersholm* at the tiny New Lindsay Theatre. In our attic off Manchester Square we had frugal suppers with army friends like Billy Chappell and Basil Burton, who owned the Academy Cinema, and with writers like Angus Wilson, who was beginning to cast his cold eye on the world outside the British Museum.

Some of my Oxford friends lost their lives in the war; but there was nothing like the holocaust which had wiped out a whole generation in Flanders. However, we survivors had all been changed in some way by our life in the forces. Bob Conquest, who had been a Communist at Oxford, returned from the Balkans with a Bulgarian wife and a burning hatred of the Soviet Union. Robert Browning, a brilliant Greek scholar who had shown no interest at Balliol in politics, returned from a similar wartime role as a committed Marxist. Teddy Heath returned from the war as Ted, with a new toughness which was to take him to the Chief Whip's office and No. 10.

The organisational side of the Labour Party was run by people who had worked there during the war. Morgan Phillips, the General Secretary, was a brisk, efficient bureaucrat who gave a fairly free hand to the young men who had just joined him to work in the policy departments. They were an exceptional lot. Michael Young, the Research Secretary, was a sallow intellectual with lank hair and horn-rimmed spectacles, a product of the experimental school at Dartington Hall. An economist by training, he had an enquiring mind and a roaming imagination. He was later to make his name as a sociologist and the founder of the consumer magazine *Which*. He became a Social Democratic Party peer.

After a few years he was succeeded by Wilfred Fienburgh, who had been badly wounded in Normandy. Wilfred's good looks and big brown eyes often led him astray. After entering Parliament in 1951 he recorded his adventures in a novel, *No Love for Johnnie*. It gives a good picture of the postwar Labour Party and was made into a powerful film. The political character of the hero was based, he told me, in equal parts on himself, Desmond Donnelly, and Jim Callaghan. Wilfred had a pretty wit. When the Spiritualist Association asked what Keir Hardie would have thought if he had known that the Witchcraft Act, which controlled their activities, was still in force, Wilfred replied: 'Why don't you ask him?' In my opinion Fienburgh might have been a candidate for the Labour leadership if he had lived. But some demon made him accident-prone: in 1958 he was killed in a car crash when only thirty-seven years old. When he became an MP in 1951 he was succeeded as head of the Research Department by Peter Shore, later my colleague in the Wilson and Callaghan Cabinets.

One of my ablest and most attractive colleagues was Michael Middleton, who designed the layout of our publications and produced an excellent short guide to typesetting, 'Soldiers of Lead'. Fleet Street pursued him incessantly, offering him several times what he earned at

Transport House. He finally succumbed, to become editor of *Lilliput* and later head of the Civic Trust.

The Labour Party shared Transport House, a modern office block off Smith Square in Westminster, remarkable only for the unreliability of its lifts, with the Trades Union Congress and the Transport and General Workers Union. Two of my Oxford friends had just become heads of the TUC's International and Organisation Departments; Len Murray was Deputy to George Woodcock, then head of its Research Department. I used to play ping-pong with Len and Frank Cousins, then at the TGWU. So my period at Transport House brought me friends in the trade union movement who were to prove invaluable in later life.

Working in an office as part of a large headquarters was something for which my wartime experience had prepared me well. I found my army staff training invaluable – as did other ex-officers at the Conservative Party headquarters, such as Enoch Powell and Reggie Maudling. Indeed postwar politics in both parties was largely shaped by men who had learned a new way of looking at problems as the result of their practical experience in the services during the war. That is why 'Rab' Butler was able to convert the Conservative Party to economic planning and the welfare state. Thatcherism became possible only when the wartime generation was passing from the stage.

The Attlee Government took office with a mandate for fundamental social and economic change. It fulfilled its mandate more successfully than any Labour government before or since. Moreover it managed the difficult transition from war to peace with exceptional skill. I was little involved in these areas of its work, since my international responsibilities took all my time – and more.

For some time I was both head and tail of the International Department of the Labour Party. I had no help except from a charming and intelligent elderly lady, Christine Howie, who had worked there since the end of the Great War. She had been an early Fabian, and always regretted that when George Bernard Shaw addressed her during a ramble in the country, she had a large sweet in her mouth and was unable to reply. She had found the answer to a problem which always tormented me: how to survive two hours in an art gallery without physical collapse. She would limp up the entrance stairs with a heavy stick and demand an invalid chair, thereby ensuring not only comfort, but also a place directly in front of any painting she admired. I later acquired two more secretaries and two assistants. One of the assistants might have been Geoffrey Johnson Smith, who applied from San Francisco but was unable to attend the selection meeting. He assuaged his grief by becoming a leading television star and Tory MP.

My predecessor at Transport House had been Willie Gillies, a cantankerous Scot who distrusted foreigners and hated all Germans. He was compelled to retire a year before I took over; so I had not only a clean slate to work on, but also the inestimable advantage of an incompetent and unpopular predecessor. I needed every advantage I could get, because my responsibilities were daunting in the extreme.

On the one hand I had to rebuild relationships between the Labour Party and socialist parties all over the world, and to help in re-establishing some sort of Socialist International. On the other hand I had to provide a bridge between the Labour Government and the Labour Party outside Whitehall on foreign, commonwealth, and colonial policy.

These two responsibilities were closely related. My relations with socialist parties abroad plunged me into the centre of British foreign policy, since in Europe almost all the new postwar governments contained socialists. In Western Europe the socialists were mainly in coalition with demochristian parties; in Eastern Europe they were compelled to form an alliance with the communist parties.

Even before the fighting was over, Moscow had made the European labour movement a central battleground of its Cold War. Stalin never had the slightest intention of honouring his undertakings at Yalta and Potsdam to allow free elections in Eastern Europe. When Byrnes, the American Secretary of State, warned him that the elections must be like Caesar's wife, above suspicion, he replied with a wolfish grin: 'But we both know, don't we, Mr Byrnes, that Caesar's wife was not above suspicion.' His plan was first to eliminate the bourgeois and peasant parties, then to compel the socialist parties to fuse with the communists in a single party.

In Western Europe Stalin aimed to encourage popular front governments in which the socialists would form a United Front with the communists. He treated any socialists who opposed this objective as his most deadly enemies, since without socialist support his whole plan was bound to collapse.

Britain was as much a target for this strategy as any other European country. The British Communist Party iself was a negligible factor in Parliament, with only two avowed MPs, though a handful of Labour MPs were thought to be secret communists, and there were a larger number of fellow-travellers, such as Konni Zilliacus, who always took the communist line on foreign policy.

In the trade unions, however, the Communist Party had power out of all proportion to its membership. It had total control of a few unions which had vastly expanded their size during the war, like the Fire Brigades Union. In many others its members got into key positions either through their personal ability, like Arthur Horner, the General Secretary of the miners' union, or by exploiting the pitifully low proportion of trade unionists who bothered to vote in union elections. Wal Hannington, for example, was elected National Organiser of the Amalgamated Engineering Union in 1942, only a few months after joining it. He got under 32,000 votes out of a total membership of over 600,000. He was still National Organiser the following year, when the union had over 900,000 members.

When I arrived at Transport House, I found that the prime aim of the Communists was to secure affiliation to the Labour Party, by exploiting the block vote of the unions and the pro-Soviet feeling still strong in the constituency parties. I suggested to Morgan Phillips that we should end the possibility of communist affiliation once and for all, by amending the Labour Party constitution so as to rule out the affiliation of organisations which put up separate candidates at local or national elections. This was done at the 1946 Conference, though it meant also excluding the tiny Independent Labour Party. But communist influence in the Labour Party and the unions remained a major obstacle in my task of winning support for the Government's foreign policy.

Except in Italy, where Togliatti continued the more humane tradition established by Gramsci, and the communists had fought shoulder to shoulder with the socialists in the Resistance, there was little support for the United Front in Western Europe. On the contrary. Many of the socialist leaders had been inoculated, like me, by having once been members of the Communist Party themselves. In Norway the Labour Party as a whole had actually joined the Comintern in the twenties, only to leave during the thirties in disgust at Stalin's purges; it was particularly shocked by the judicial murder of Bukharin, with whom it had exceptionally close ties. Many of the most outstanding postwar leaders of the German Social Democrats, such as Ernst Reuter in Berlin, Fritz Erler and Herbert Wehner in Bonn, had been prominent communists before the war.

Even in Switzerland the Secretary of the Socialist Party, Humbert-Droz, had been an active member of the Comintern. Such men knew at first hand many of the communist leaders in the Soviet Union as well as in Western Europe; they were well prepared for every twist and turn of communist tactics. Yet none of them suffered from the knee-jerk anti-communism so common at that time among Western intellectuals who saw communism simply as the god that failed.

Among socialists on the Continent, the British Labour Party then had a prestige and influence it never enjoyed before or since. Britain was the only big country in Europe where a socialist party had won power on its own, without depending on any coalition partners. Britain had stood out alone against Hitler after the rest of Europe crumbled. And Britain had won.

At that time Britain was also one of the great world powers, with direct responsibilities in Europe which were sustained by British troops. In Germany, Austria, Italy and Palestine we had occupying forces and civilian as well as military administrators. In Greece we were involved willy-nilly in the civil war which followed the defeat of Hitler. As the most important of the European allies, we had to play a leading role both in ensuring that the Yalta and Potsdam agreements were observed, and in solving the many territorial disputes still awaiting settlement – over the Saar, Schleswig–Holstein, Venezia Giulia, Trieste, and the South Tyrol, for example. Finally we were expected by our socialist comrades to help in liquidating the one Fascist regime which had survived the war, in Franco Spain; this was a hopeless task so long as the Spanish socialists themselves were deeply divided by personal feuds as well as by Basque and Catalan nationalism.

For all these reasons, as International Secretary of the Labour Party I appeared to socialists abroad, both in government and opposition, as an obvious channel for influencing the Labour Government in Britain. The Italian and Austrian governments appointed socialists to their embassies in London, who used me as a vehicle for conducting their relations with the British Government as well as with the Labour Party.

Walter Wodak, who had been a refugee in Britain during the war, put the Austrian case over the Tyrol to me as well as to the Foreign Office; he kept me closely in touch with any problems which arose between his government and the occupying powers. Franco Malfatti and his successor Raimondo Manzini, represented in London the Italian socialists as well as the Italian government: they put their case for the return of Libya to me, as well as their Party's problems. They were soon to form the core of Foreign Minister Fanfani's diplomatic young Turks – called the Mau Mau, after their initials. Malfatti later ran the private office of President Saragat, and Manzini became Ambassador in London and head of the Italian Foreign Office. I developed close friendships with all these men, which have lasted all my life.

One special friend was the Finnish Ambassador, Eero Wuori. A large, shambling man with a white face, horn-rimmed spectacles, and a projecting lower jaw which carried a palisade of crooked teeth, he had been a General in the Finnish Red Army at the age of seventeen. He showed great skill later, both as Ambassador in Moscow and as head of the Finnish Foreign Office, in helping to persuade the Kremlin to let Finland remain a democracy, despite its wartime alliance with Germany and its proximity to the Soviet Union. That was not an easy task, especially for a Social Democrat, since most of his Party's leaders had fought bravely against Russia in more than one war. When I asked Unto Varjonen, the Secretary of the Social Democratic Party, if he knew any Russian, he replied: 'Only two words – hands up!'

Special geopolitical factors help to explain Finland's success in maintaining its internal freedom since the war. But no one who has watched the Finnish people over the last forty years can use the word 'Finlandisation' as a term of abuse, to imply a semi-colonial relationship with the Soviet Union.

I was responsible in my work to the International Subcommittee of the Labour Party's National Executive, which met for an hour or two once a month, and between its meetings to the Subcommittee's Chairman, Hugh Dalton, and later Harold Laski. The Subcommittee was not a very effective body. Its political members were nearly all Cabinet ministers, who had little time or inclination to read the papers I submitted, while, with one exception, the trade union members were not of the first rank. The exception was Sam Watson, a Durham miner of unusual intelligence and total integrity; like many prominent trade unionists he had moved from the extreme Left of the party to the hard Centre-Right. A small sturdy figure with balding head and twinkling eyes, he was typical of the working-class intellectuals whom society had denied a university education; but unlike Ernest Bevin, with whom he had much in common, he was a great reader, and for years taught his fellow miners in the Socialist Sunday School. It was he who persuaded Nye Bevan in 1957, after hours of exhausting argument at their hotel in Brighton, to ask the Labour Party not to send him 'naked into the conference chamber' by endorsing a policy of unilateral nuclear disarmament for NATO.

Dalton and Laski took a close interest in my work. Hugh Dalton was a tall man with an egg-shaped head and eyes once described as 'green pools of insincerity' – a most impressive personality, yet fatally flawed. His powerful intellect shines through his memoirs, which are among the best four or five political autobiographies published in Britain since the war.

His pettiness and occasional meanness of spirit are no less evident in his diaries, which were not intended for publication. He was extraordinarily generous to younger men of promise; half the Wilson Cabinet, including me, had at one time or another been under his wing. But he could be brutally cruel to men of his own age, especially if he saw them as potential rivals.

Bombastic and flamboyant when confident, he was also capable of surprising cowardice, as I myself had cause to discover. There was a deep insecurity and sadness at the root of his being, which he sometimes sought to disguise with rough words. He was capable almost at the same moment of displaying a deep and genuine moral commitment and a hair-raising cynicism. He told me how Attlee had offered him the Colonial Office after he had resigned from the Treasury following a budget leak: 'No bloody fear, I told him. A lot of syphilitic niggers. All kicks and no ha'pence. Not me!' He once described the other Labour Party intellectuals of his time as 'Semi-crocks, diabetics, and under-sized semites.' Yet he could heap sincere and unstinted praise on people he admired, like Churchill and Bevin, even though he might know his admiration was not reciprocated.

There was a tragic hollowness in his life. His best friends were killed in the First World War. His marriage collapsed with the death of his little daughter Helen, in 1922, when she was only five years old and he was thirty-five. From that moment an essential part of his personality ceased to develop. Peter Pan was never far away. His capacity for human feeling withered, though he tried to revive it by a series of sentimental attachments to younger men. Many politicians attempt to develop a persona for public show. With Hugh Dalton the persona came to replace the personality. Yet despite his gargantuan weaknesses, Dalton was a seminal force for good in the Labour movement for over forty years. He brought a rational objectivity to its discussions both on economic and foreign policy. He was the most important intellectual influence in guiding the pre-war Party towards a meaningful resistance to fascism – though Ernest Bevin was a much more powerful political influence in the Labour movement as a whole.

Although his opportunism and disloyalty often made Dalton exasperating to work with, I derived much of lasting value from him. His frequent attempts to bully me were water off a duck's back. I had learned how to deal with bullies from my wartime Colonel, Basil the Bastard.

Harold Laski was the only member of the National Executive to represent the constituency parties who was not in the Government; it was not until 1952, after Bevan's resignation and the defeat of the Attlee Government, that the constituency parties turned decisively to the Left, where they have remained for a quarter of a century. Between 1952 and 1987 the constituencies elected only three members who were not from the Left – Jim Callaghan, Jack Ashley and me. None of us survived for more than a few years as constituency representatives. However, the importance of the National Executive can be exaggerated. Bevin and Cripps, arguably the most powerful members of the Attlee Government, never stood for the Party Executive at all in those years.

Laski, like Dalton, taught at the London School of Economics and was a committed Zionist. Otherwise they had nothing in common. A mousy little man with a small moustache and big sorrowful brown eyes, Laski had more than a touch of Charlie Chaplin. He was a brilliant teacher. His lectures and books influenced generations of students all over the world. But he lacked political judgment. When I first met him he was still smarting at Attlee's rebuff for his interventions during the 1945 election campaign: 'A period of silence from you would be welcome.' A very sensitive man, he felt the political humiliation even more keenly than the financial cost when he lost a libel action against a journalist who accused him of preaching revolution.

His most alarming characteristic when I knew him was a tendency to fantasise, which ultimately went beyond neurosis. It is said that when he paid a return visit to Harvard after the war one of the professors asked another if he had noticed any change in Laski. 'Oh yes,' was the reply. 'He has now actually met some of the people he said he had met last time.' I was once acutely embarrassed when I sat on the platform at a mass meeting in Brussels and heard him say, quite seriously, that he had travelled there in a Spitfire crouching against the knees of the pilot.

He was immensely generous and warm hearted. For example, he heard of a clever Jewish boy from Manchester who was working for 17/6d a week in a warehouse, because his parents could not afford to keep him at school. So he arranged the money needed to complete the boy's education, and kept a close interest in him for the rest of his life. The boy concerned, Leo Pliatzky, became a close friend of mine and Edna's at Oxford, and later Secretary of the Fabian Society; as a civil servant he later worked closely with me at the Treasury.

Dalton treated Laski with brutal contempt. Yet, when Dalton was having a difficult time as Chancellor, Laski sent him a note which gives the flavour of the man:

This is merely a word to bid you be of good heart. The dogs bark but the caravan passes on. I know, I suppose as well as most people, the infamy of political rancour. It does hurt. But it does not matter as long as you retain the confidence of those whom you respect. Be quite sure you have that. And be quite sure that those who, like me, have faith in you, will, in their small way, fight your battle. Courage, camarade, le diable va mourir.

That type of magnanimity is not common in political life. To me it does much to make up for Laski's obvious weaknesses.

I found the International Bureau of the Fabian Society a useful source of guidance. My literary idol, Virginia Woolf, had described the Fabians in 1915 as 'earnest drab women, who are thought "queer" at home and rejoice in it, and broad nosed, sallow, shock-headed young men in brown tweed suits . . . the idea that these frail webspinners can affect the destiny of nations seems to me fantastic'. They were much the same thirty years later. But the great benefit of joining the Bureau for me was to meet and know its chairman, Leonard Woolf, Virginia's widower. Then sixty-five, he looked older than his years, a frail, trembling figure with a long brown face wrinkled like a tortoise, the inevitable brown tweed suit and knitted tie, his shock of hair still profuse, but grey.

At the end of his five-volume autobiography, which will live as long as his wife's novels, he summed up his contribution to politics as follows:

> Looking back at the age of eighty-eight over the fifty-seven years of my political work in England, knowing what I aimed at and the results, meditating on the history of Britain and the world since 1914, I see clearly that I achieved practically nothing. The world today and the history of the human anthill would be exactly the same as it is, if I had played ping-pong instead of sitting on committees and writing books and memoranda.

That may be true. But Leonard Woolf made a contribution to history which few successful politicians can match. Besides writing a classic account of his own life, which covered much of what was most valuable in British politics and culture over three generations, he sacrificed his career by dedicating himself to the nurture and protection of his wife's tragic genius. He shares in her lustre.

Another invaluable source of help, particularly in my work with the European socialists, was a group of émigré journalists then working in

London. The *Observer* newspaper harboured some of them. The best was Rix Loewenthal, who covered European politics in general. Eyes bulging in the head of a foetus, he had a way of chewing his words till they became almost incomprehensible. But he was exceptionally intelligent and well-informed, particularly about Germany; before the war he had been a member of the dissident communist sect called Neu Beginnen along with some of the Social Democrat leaders.

Walter Kolarz, a Czech, was the London correspondent of the Associated Press, a typical Central European with a large head, swarthy complexion, and hair en brosse – his wife Shura was Russian and had worked at the Soviet Trade Union headquarters in Moscow. Wolf Schuetz was a German Social Democrat but represented the *Neue Züricher Zeitung*, which was uniquely well-placed to follow politics in Eastern as well as Western Europe. Ruggero Orlando was the correspondent of the Italian *Avanti*, though he was paid rarely, and always late. I liked him particularly because he shared my love of literature and had translated the early poetry of Dylan Thomas into Italian. He had a fruity voice, a somewhat scabrous turn of phrase, short legs and a large head like Buster Keaton's. Later he became famous as a TV correspondent in Washington before dwindling into a senator. My French informants were successive correspondents of the socialist *Le Populaire*, until the glamorous Jean Jacques Servan-Schreiber arrived to represent *L'Express*.

With this wealth of expertise at my service, and my contacts in the Foreign Office, I was well-placed to perform my role in restoring relations with the European Socialists.

My first journey abroad was to Amsterdam, by train and boat, where the Dutch Social Democratic Labour Party was holding a conference, whose main purpose was to eliminate the phrase 'Social Democratic' from its title. By thus signalling a break with its Marxist past it hoped to attract Catholic voters. In the short run it gained nothing by the change, since the Catholic hierarchy threatened to excommunicate any of its flock who voted for the new Labour Party. This was my introduction to the extraordinary sectarianism of Dutch politics; there were then still important groups with names like the Christian Historical Party and the Anti-Revolutionary Party, which commemorated obscure struggles in the distant past. The new leaders of the Labour Party were fine men, such as Koos Vorrink, who had worked in the Resistance until they were caught and put in concentration camps. Five of the ministers in the Government had been in Buchenwald together. Holland had suffered badly under the German occupation; in the last winter before liberation the population kept itself alive on a nauseous diet of tulip bulbs. Anti-German feeling was very strong. Yet it was already obvious that, since Holland's prosperity depended on traffic to and from Germany, Dutch living standards would fall if Germany's industrial capacity was heavily cut, as the allies had prescribed at Potsdam.

Two months later I went back to my wartime haunts in Italy in a Labour Party delegation with Harold Laski. Edna, and Laski's wife, Frida, were with us. It was an extraordinary experience to be back there as a civilian, while most of my friends there were still in the army. Once we had crossed the frontier from Switzerland, our train was met at every station by cheering crowds of working people carrying bouquets of roses. It was an intoxicating experience. We were wonderfully received wherever we went.

When we reached Spezia, however, our driver refused to continue, since the Passo di Bracco was still infested with bandits. At the hotel that evening Harold heard that there was a ship in the harbour carrying Jewish refugees to Palestine, which the British Navy was preventing from sailing. We immediately went aboard; Harold, greatly moved, undertook to get the British Government to let them proceed. He succeeded. I believe it was the only case in which he ever got Bevin to change his mind.

The main feature of the Socialist Party Congress in Florence was its rejection of fusion with the Communists. But the struggle for power between the older leader, Pietro Nenni, and his wartime comrade, Giuseppe Saragat, had already begun. We spent much time with Sandro Pertini, a heroic Resistance leader who became an excellent President of Italy in his eighties, and with the novelist, Ignazio Silone, and his handsome blonde Irish wife, Darina. As a student I had greatly admired Silone's story of fascism in the Abruzzi, *Fontamara*. I was fascinated to meet him as an active member of the Socialist Party after his exile in Switzerland. He was a sleek, morose man who spoke slowly with flashes of humour. After leaving the Communist Party before the war, when he had worked with most of the present communist leaders, he became obsessed by the relationship between morality and politics, moving steadily towards the Christianity which pervades his later novels. Surprisingly, his writing was much less popular in Italy than outside; the Italians found his style rough and clumsy. He was fascinated by football as a team game which symbolised his political ideal; none of his visits to England was complete without a journey to the Fulham ground.

This was the first of many visits to Italy, in which I was trying in vain to keep the Italian socialists united. Just after our visit the socialists fought the municipal elections mainly on joint lists with the communists. They won slightly more seats than their allies; the communists suffered because Stalin supported Yugoslavia against Italy over Venezia Giulia. However, their United Front came ahead of the Christian Democrats, above all in the towns and cities. But the alliance with the communists was already creating strains; they led to the Socialist Party splitting after coming second to the Christian Democrats in the July election that year. The breakaway party went into office with the Christian Democrats, and split again on that issue. So the Socialist Party, which had a real chance of forming a government when the war ended, and to wait nearly forty years before again playing an important role on the national stage; this was a lesson which was to be taught again in France. It was the main reason why I did my best to prevent the Gang of Four from splitting the Labour Party in 1981. I was not surprised by the consequences of that unhappy experiment; right-wing breakaways from left-wing parties have never come to anything. Their only important effect is to weaken the influence of common sense in the party they have deserted, and to keep Conservative governments in power.

Once the Congress was over Edna and I left for a delayed honeymoon in Capri; we had decided that our weekend at Buckden did not count. On the way I showed Edna my old stamping grounds in Siena, Rome and Naples. In Rome we met most of the Italian political leaders of all parties, and dined with Prime Minister De Gasperi, his Communist opponent Togliatti, and the Socialist Romita. It was a wonderful experience for a young man of twenty-eight, and since I spoke Italian I was able to take full advantage of it. Our Ambassador, Sir Noel Charles, was drunk most of the time, but his smoothly efficient labour attaché, Bill Braine, made up for him. On later visits I met the writer Moravia, whose novels give a coldly clinical picture of post-war Italy; he had a pale, pockmarked fox-like face and his conversation was as witty and pointed as his books. I also met the communist painter, Renato Guttuso, whose funeral in 1987 was an occasion for national mourning.

Finally, after looking in at Caserta, where many of my army friends were still impatiently waiting to be demobilised, we began our honeymoon at Sorrento. The army had lent me a jeep, so we were able to tour the mountainous peninsula; we visited my old haunts at Positano, and dined on a terrace facing Capri with oranges hanging over our heads like lamps. It was a honeymoon well worth waiting for. Capri itself was full of families from Naples celebrating the Easter holiday by singing to guitars and accordions. We followed the traditional tourist pattern – a pony-cart to Anacapri, a boat to the Blue Grotto, and walks on the Via Tragara. A visit to Pompeii ended this excursion to paradise.

Few of my political missions were quite so enjoyable, but I usually managed to mix some pleasure with my business. Nor was the business itself all politics in the narrow sense. On one later visit to Italy I went to see the Pope, with Bob Openshaw, the trade unionist on our delegation. His Holiness Pius XII opened the conversation:

'As a leading member of the Labour Party, Mr Openshaw, you have a heavy responsibility.'

'Aye, Pope, and so have you,' was the reply.

Our talk continued for half an hour. Then the Pope opened a drawer in his desk, saying:

'I know you are not a Catholic yourself, Mr Openshaw, but perhaps you would like to take home a rosary for a friend. Would you prefer black or white?'

'Oh, I reckon I'll have one of each,' said Bob.

And so he did, and so did I.

Even my visits to Eastern Europe offered some ancillary delights. In Budapest I was able to visit the art galleries, and see excellent paintings by men then unknown in the West, such as Rippl Ronai, Csontvary, and Derkovits; when I mentioned them to my friends, they thought I had made the names up. I never missed the chance of an opera, especially an unfamiliar one. So I saw Moniuszko's *Halka* in Warsaw, Dvorak's *Rusalka* in Brno, and Moussorgsky's *Khovantschina* in Budapest, where I also saw *Fidelio* played in Hungarian costume, with a Pizarro from the puszta, who seemed to have strayed in from *Zigeunerbaron*.

The atmosphere in Eastern Europe after the war, however, was the opposite of that in the West. It is well illustrated by the poem, *The Awakening*, by the Polish poet, Zbigniew Herbert:

> When the horror subsided the floodlights went out
> we discovered that we were on a rubbish heap in very strange poses
>   some with outstretched necks
> others with open mouths from which still trickled my native land
>   still others with fists pressed to eyes
> cramped emphatically pathetically taut . . .
> We listened to the chirping of streetcars to a swallow-like voice of
>   factories
> and a new life was unrolling at our feet.

My task in these countries was to help the socialist parties to stay alive. It was tragically frustrating. The socialists were clinging on to their separate identities by the tips of their fingers. They knew they were doomed to destruction. I first went to Hungary, in January 1947, and found that the icy winter which gripped the country symbolised its politics. Young soldiers from the Red Army in pointed fur caps stood guard on the snowy runway when I landed from Vienna. Little had yet been done to repair the destruction caused by war.

One night when we were returning in a blizzard through the ruined streets to the clinic where the foreign delegates were staying, our car broke down. After waiting some minutes alone in the darkness we saw a taxi unsteadily weaving its way towards us through the snowy night. Our guide, the Socialist Baroness Hatvany from London, stopped it:

'Comrade,' she said, 'can you take us to the clinic?'

'I am no comrade,' he replied.

'But we are from the Social Democratic Party Congress,' said the Baroness, 'and this is the delegate from the British Labour Party.'

'Oh, are the Social Democrats comrades too?' asked the taxi driver. 'I am a Social Democrat. Get in.'

He then told us his story. He had come into Budapest from a nearby town, and was told he could not have a licence to drive a taxi unless he joined either the Communist Party or the Social Democratic Party:

'Well, no power on earth could make me join the Communists, so I joined the Social Democrats.'

For twenty-five years until the end of the war, Hungary had been a dictatorship under Admiral Horthy. All the pre-war democratic parties had a tiny membership, since they had to work largely underground. The first general election in 1945 was fairly free, and the Smallholders' Party, largely representing the countryside, won fifty-seven per cent of the votes. A United Front of Social Democrats and Communists came next, polling just over thirty-four per cent; the Social Democrats were just ahead of the Communists because they had overwhelming support in the trade unions. But the Soviet occupation authorities made sure that the Communists got the key positions in the government, under a Smallholder Prime Minister. Rakosi, the Communist leader, had been in prison for fifteen years before the war, and was an important member of the Comintern. A small, fat, bald man with the face of a Mongolian torturer, he told me jovially that he had joined the Fabian Society as an émigré in London before the Great War. Supported by the equally sinister Geroe and Revai, he was effectively the Soviet Gauleiter; his job was to eliminate the Smallholders and swallow the Social Democrats, so that Hungary could be a Communist dictatorship when the Red Army went home in 1948. He succeeded by what he called 'salami tactics', dividing the Left from the other parties, then the hard Left of the Social Democrats from the soft Left, forcing the latter into exile and putting hundreds of trade union leaders into jail, and finally organising a fusion of the Social Democratic rump with the Communists.

The political tissue of postwar Hungary was not robust. When I made my first visit in January 1947, the Social Democratic Party had half a million new members to absorb, many of whom had joined for opportunist reasons, like my taxi driver. Living standards were only half as high as in 1939, since in addition to the destruction caused by war, Hungary had to spend forty per cent of its budget on maintaining the Red Army's occupation forces and on reparations to the Soviet Union. Since the Communists controlled all the privileges conferred by the state, they could bribe as well as bully.

As the Labour Party representative, there was little I could do except listen sympathetically to my fellow Socialists and help them personally when they were finally forced into exile. During my visit there was a typical incident. One of the few Social Democrats in the political police was shot twice, in the back and neck, from a passing limousine which proved to belong to the Russians. He then simply disappeared. Budapest was buzzing with rumours about it the whole week I was there. I heard later that he had shot back, killing a Soviet agent, and been spirited across the frontier into Austria.

On the way back to London I met an acquaintance from Oxford who was shortly to become Assistant Military Attaché in Hungary – a Major Michael Hanley. When we next met, some thirty years later, I was Chancellor of the Exchequer and he was head of MI5.

Hungary had spent most of the war in alliance with Nazi Germany, so its fate was not unexpected; yet its people, under the leadership of Rakosi's Communist successors, were to show nobility and courage in fighting Soviet power only nine years later.

There could be no conceivable excuse for Stalin's treatment of the next East European country I visited. Czechoslovakia had been Hitler's first victim, and had done its best before the war to persuade Britain and France to join Russia in resisting him. It had made a military alliance with the Soviet Union when the war ended.

In November 1947 I went to a decisive congress of the Czech Social Democratic Party in Brno. It was winter again. The whole country was gripped by snow and ice. When I landed at the airport in Prague I was told that the Government had called a strike to protest against the conduct of the non-Communists – a typical example of the role of trade unions under Communism. The Social Democrats were under heavy pressure to accept fusion with the Communists, whose leader, Gottwald, was Prime Minister; the Communists had been a powerful party even before the war, and Russia's popularity as the liberator of Prague (thanks to an agreement by the Allies), had made them by far the largest party in the 1946 elections. The Social Democratic leader, Fierlinger, had been Ambassador in Moscow and was universally regarded as a Soviet stooge.

To the amazement of all outside observers, the Social Democratic Party Congress rejected Fierlinger in favour of the centrist, Lausmann, and went on to defeat the motion for fusion by an overwhelming majority. I shall never forget the wolfish snarl with which Fierlinger, white as a sheet, received the announcement of the votes.

It was a Pyrrhic victory for the Social Democrats. Within three months the Prague putsch installed a Communist dictatorship. A week later, the Czech Foreign Minister, Jan Masaryk, fell to his death from a window. No one has ever fully established the cause. He was a charming man, with all the cynicism of his nation's hero, the Good Soldier Schweik, and a lot more urbanity. When someone asked him why, as a good democrat, he had made an alliance with the Soviet Union rather than the United States, he replied: 'Because when the next war comes I would much rather be taken prisoner by the Americans than by the Russians.'

It was twenty years before spring returned again to Prague, and then only for a few weeks.

A month after leaving Brno I found myself in East Europe again. This time I was attending the congress of the Polish Socialist Party in the ruined city of Wroclaw, previously Breslau; it had been transferred with the rest of East Prussia to Poland in compensation for the loss of eastern Poland to the Soviet Union. Again, freezing winter. Again, fusion was the main issue. But the political situation was very different in Poland. In 1939 the Red Army invaded Poland in collusion with Hitler. In 1940 Stalin murdered most of the Polish officer corps at Katyn. In 1944, during the siege of Warsaw, the Red Army sat with its arms folded on the other side of the river, so that the Germans could massacre the men and women who had spent the war fighting Hitler in the underground.

It was not surprising that there were practically no communists in Poland when the war ended, except those brought in from the Soviet Union in the Red Army's baggage train. The congress at Wroclaw was overwhelmingly against fusion with the Communists. There was a great roar of approval when the Socialist leader, Cyrankiewicz, said: 'The Socialist Party is, and will be, essential for the Polish nation.' The Communist leader, Gomulka, listened in silence. People noticed that Cyrankiewicz had brought Gomulka, while his new wife, a well-known actress, had brought her director. 'Chacun son regisseur,' said the cynics.

In fact Gomulka himself was purged by the Russians later that year, in case he made common cause with the Socialists against them. After a show trial of Socialists who had fought in the Resistance, Cyrankiewicz surrendered, and fused his party with the Communists in a new Workers' Party; some believe that he had secretly joined the Communist Party during the war while in a concentration camp. In any case the post-war Socialist Party in Poland represented only those who had worked in the war with the communists, rather than with the government in exile, which organised the Polish underground army from London.

In Western Europe, apart from my fruitless attempt to keep the Italian socialists united, my most important task was to help the German Social Democrats to reestablish themselves both inside Germany and in the European socialist community. Ernest Bevin as Foreign Secretary was anxious to strengthen the German labour movement. He appointed an able young trade unionist, Allan Flanders, to supervise the reorganisation of the German trade unions. Well aware of the weaknesses of the TUC in Britain, Allan produced a centralised structure of industrial unions for the German trade union movement which was one of the keys to Germany's post-war economic miracle. So there were no inter-union disputes; the employers' organisations under successive German governments were able to negotiate constructive agreements with the DGB both on wages and on other industrial problems, and the agreements were kept. This has rarely been achieved in Britain, and never for long. Austen Albu, later a Labour MP, was appointed to help the political and industrial wings of the movement in West Berlin; without his help it is doubtful whether the SPD there could have resisted Communist pressure for fusion. John Hynd, Willie Henderson and Frank Pakenham (soon to become Lord Longford) gave steady support to these efforts as the Ministers responsible for Western Germany in the British Government.

Rebuilding the SPD on the ground was of course the responsibility of its own leaders in Germany. Kurt Schumacher, its first post-war chairman, performed a critically important function in standing up for the Party against all comers, including the occupation powers when necessary. He had lost an arm in Hitler's concentration camps, and in 1948 had to have a leg amputated in London. To many Germans, his thin body, bullet head, bloodshot eye and ravaged face made him appear as a latter-day Frederick the Great; but his nationalistic rhetoric, delivered in a rasping voice, too often reminded the allies of Hitler. While he was leader, only the British Labour Party tried seriously to establish fraternal relations with the SPD.

This was mainly due to my efforts. Dalton had been deeply prejudiced against all Germans since fighting in the Great War. Laski was, of course, a committed Zionist, and could not forget the Holocaust. I had great difficulty in persuading the National Executive to invite Schumacher to London in November 1946. When he arrived I found him much more human and likeable than I had expected, and so did the National Executive. The continental socialists were not so easily reconciled – particularly the French and of course the East Europeans. The SPD was finally admitted to our community in June 1947, at the Zurich Congress of the International Socialist Conference. The vote was nine in favour, five against, with five abstentions – scarcely a declaration of confidence. Disagreements over the SPD continued to trouble our meetings. In 1950 I had to assemble a *cour d'honneur* at the Council of Europe in Strasbourg to dispose of a claim by Guy Mollet, the leader of the French Socialists, that an SPD delegate, Carlo Schmidt, had been responsible for war crimes in Lille.

The Zürich Congress was particularly memorable for me, since it was my first encounter with Golda Meir, later Prime Minister of Israel. She was a powerful, handsome woman who had only recently left New York. She still called herself Goldie Myerson, and represented Mapai, the Labour Party in Palestine. The unpopularity of Britain's Palestine policy with the other socialists had been greatly increased by the *Exodus* incident – the Royal Navy had recently prevented the *Exodus* from discharging its cargo of Jewish refugees in Palestine. All the National Executive members found it convenient to stay away from the Congress debate on Palestine, leaving me alone to answer a devastating onslaught from Golda. I did my best with a bad brief, but she never held it against me afterwards.

The Palestine problem dogged my early years as International Secretary. Bevin believed that a Jewish state would ruin Britain's relations with the Arab world, and deeply resented pressure from Washington to change his policy. The Foreign Office was convinced that a Jewish state would be a Communist state – a ridiculous illusion, then shared by the

Russians themselves. However, the Labour movement was overwhelmingly pro-Zionist; Dalton had a life-long devotion to the Zionist cause. Neither the Labour Party nor the trade unions knew anything about the Arab world, and there were then no socialist movements in the Middle East to put the Arab case. However, the Jewish socialists in Palestine itself were far more sensitive than their supporters in Britain. My best friend at the time among them was Teddy Kollek, who spent some years in London just after the war as unofficial ambassador of Mapai. He had left Vienna for Palestine in the mid-thirties and was a good-looking young man with reddish fair hair and Austrian charm – a typical Yekki. He was far more willing to concede some justice in the Arab case than the average British Zionist. After independence he served for a time as Ben Gurion's private secretary before becoming Mayor of Jerusalem.

The only effective opponents of Zionism in the International were a small socialist party representing Polish Jews – the Bund; it regarded Zionism as a mixture of nationalism and imperialism with which true socialists had nothing in common. After the war it existed only in exile, and soon dwindled away under the impact of the Holocaust and the creation of Israel. Its representative in London was a little man called Lucjan Blit, not unlike Laski in appearance, but with far greater political understanding. He had spent some years after the fall of Poland in a Soviet concentration camp in the Arctic Circle, before being sent to Kuybishev to join the Anders Army. I learned from him about the Gulag long before Solzhenitsyn wrote his book; his calm judicious mind made him an invaluable source of information on Eastern Europe and the Soviet Union.

I enjoyed one unique privilege during those years at Transport House – the opportunity to meet some of those socialist leaders who had started their political careers before the Great War, in a world not yet dominated by statistics, when it was possible to be a politician without abandoning one's other interests. Louis de Brouckère, for example, who had helped to found the Second International, was a mathematician of world standing; he was tall and erect at eighty, with a long white beard, twinkling eyes and a penetrating intellect. His fellow Belgian, Camille Huysmans, was a figure from *La Boheme*, with a black cloak, black beret, and a sallow, cunning face. Martin Tranmael, then editor of the Norwegian newspaper, *Arbeiderbladet*, for which I was later to work myself, was a little man of demonic energy straight out of Ibsen, who had been a close friend of Bukharin. In Austria the President, Otto Renner, and the Mayor of Vienna, General Koerner, had both been important figures in the Austro-Hungarian Empire. Leon Blum in France was a tall, elegant lawyer who had written a witty treatise on marriage before becoming Prime Minister of the Front Populaire Government before the war. All these men had a serene humanity and a broad culture which is all too rare in modern politics. They were also gentlemen in the truest sense of the word. The only man I knew in Britain with a similar quality was Gilbert Murray.

Another exceptional figure from that vanished world was the Russian revolutionary socialist, Angelica Balabanoff, who had been forced into exile in Italy before the Great War, and had been Mussolini's mistress while he was still a socialist. I would meet her at every socialist congress I attended in Italy, withered and white-haired, but as energetic and committed as ever, a character from Turgenev's *On the Eve*. My Italian duties also allowed me to meet Bernard Berenson in his lovely villa, *I Tatti*, on the hills above Florence, a frail old man with a little beard. He was very much under the thumb of his secretary, whom he married just before he died. Much has since been written of his alleged readiness to take money for offering a false attribution to a painting. He was, nevertheless, a great connoisseur and art historian, who communicated his enthusiasm for the Renaissance to millions of young men and women who would have been poorer without it.

As human beings, the postwar generation of socialist leaders rarely had the distinction of the pioneers. We had to comfort ourselves by saying with Yeats:

> Though the great song return no more,
> There's keen delight in what we have:
> The rattle of pebbles on the shore
> Under the receding wave.

The change was not surprising. Many potential leaders had been killed in battle or died in concentration camps. New technology was already creating the need for more and faster decisions, and electorates were demanding more and more of their representatives. Few politicians now had the leisure needed for a rounded personality. And it must be admitted that in some countries, particularly Italy, the Resistance movements had attracted many of the best and brightest on the Left into the Communist Party.

Leon Blum was soon replaced as leader of the French Socialists by the bureaucratic Guy Mollet, under whom the party's support was restricted mainly to teachers and minor civil servants; so it could offer no effective challenge either to the Communists or to the Gaullists. It had to wait thirty years for Mitterrand to recover a wider appeal; the Italian Socialists had to wait even longer for Craxi. After Schumacher's death, the SPD was led mainly by decent but unexciting individuals who had spent the war in England, like Erich Ollenhauer, Fritz Heine, and Herta Gotthelf. Men of superior quality who might have led it, like Reuter and Erler, died tragically young. It was twenty years before Willy Brandt was able to rekindle the flame, and Helmut Schmidt to keep it glowing.

Some of the smaller countries had outstanding socialist leaders, such as Spaak in Belgium and Lange in Norway, but their stage was too small for them to have a major impact, though some of them were able to exercise an important influence through international institutions. In Greece the civil war inflicted heavy damage on the labour movement, which remained deeply divided until in 1963 Andreas Papandreou returned from academic exile in California, to take up the torch left barely flickering by his father, George.

I went to Greece myself in January 1949 with a Belgian colleague, Victor Larock, to try to identify the most effective socialist leader. We agreed on Professor Svolos, a mild and decent man; when I described him in my report as an outstanding intellectual, Victor asked me to strike out the phrase, on the grounds that it would prejudice the Labour Party against him. As editor of *Le Peuple* Larock had acute observation and a mordant wit. When I was walking with him in the streets of Brussels during the first Berlin crisis, he asked me if I had noticed the difference between the cars in Brussels and those in Paris, which we had just visited together. In Paris the cars had been fitted with roof racks for a quick getaway to the South when the war started. In Brussels everyone had simply bought another car.

My contacts with the socialist parties outside Europe were much less frequent. There were occasional visitors from Japan who carried little conviction. I developed a close friendship with some of the Burmese socialists, and with the outstanding Indian, Jayaprakash Narayan, who at one time seemed capable of assuming the mantle of Mahatma Gandhi; he had much of Gandhi's spiritual and intellectual force, but little of his political skill. Roy Welensky called on me as leader of the Rhodesian Labour Party. We accepted the Cooperative Commonwealth Federation of Canada, forerunner of the present New Democratic Party, into the socialist community. It was well led by David Lewis and had a permanent representative in London, Graham Spry, who was the Agent General for

Saskatchewan, where the CCF held power – at that time it had little following in the rest of the country. Before long it sent other delegates to the international socialist meetings in Europe. The first was a voluble, bespectacled, roly-poly intellectual, Captain Bob Mackenzie, later known to millions as a TV commentator on British elections and author of a seminal work on the British party system. The second was a dark, saturnine young journalist, Major Milton Shulman, still a leading dramatic critic in London.

For some time we had no contact with China. But one day I was visited by a young Englishman with a Chinese wife who said I knew his father. It was Michael Lindsay, son of the Master of Balliol, who had spent the war with the Eighth Route Army in Yenan and knew Mao Tse-tung well. He established a link between the Labour Party and the Chinese Communists; it was not very fruitful, since at that time they were strict followers of the Cominform.

One of my jobs was to organise the meetings which finally led to the establishment of the Socialist International at Frankfurt in 1951. It was a thankless task. The meetings were too often ruined by interminable wrangles on procedural questions, and the job of drafting the necessary compromise usually fell to me. I wrote the first draft of the Declaration of Socialist Principles for the International in one night, over two bottles of Dutch gin; it has survived for over thirty years.

It was still possible in those days for me to write a speech for Morgan Phillips which proclaimed that the Labour Party owed more to Methodism than to Marxism. In the intervening period the continental parties have adjusted much better to social and political change than the Labour Party. Because it is still the most conservative party in the world, much of the Labour Party now appears more wedded to a primitive sort of Marxism than any of the others. The pre-war Left Book Club has a lot to answer for. Young men and women hungry for political guidance fell on its pink or orange volumes as revealed truth. It was essentially inspired by the Popular Front Communism of the later thirties; but it had a lasting influence on a whole generation of the Left in Britain.

I learned much about European politics in those years, which it would have been difficult to learn in any other way. Many of the difficulties which troubled our relations with the continental socialists arose from differences in mental and linguistic patterns which were not central to the real issues at stake. We British still tended to regard a juridical commitment as defining the minimum you guarantee to fulfil. The continentals tended to see it as setting an objective at which you aim, although you may well fail to achieve it. Much of the tedious argument about federalism which divided us when we discussed the path to European unity was unnecessary once this was understood.

This was brought home to me at a meeting in Copenhagen when we had to decide whether to accept two of the Italian socialist parties into the International; both were undeniably democratic, and both had split from Nenni's party over relations with the Communists. The constitution of the International insisted that there should never be more than one party represented from each country. On this occasion the British argued pragmatically that we should admit both, while insisting that this should not create a precedent. The French argued furiously against such a constitutional breach, and finally gave in – strictly on the condition that the meeting simultaneously passed a *motion prealable* stating that under no circumstances should there be more than one party from a single country. We were both saying exactly the same in practice, but different legal traditions made each seem a hypocrite to the other.

I owe one unique experience to my work for the International. A delegation of Swiss socialists had visited Marx's tomb in Highgate cemetery and was shocked to find it in poor repair. They collected some money to restore it, and asked me to make the necessary arrangements. Since Highgate was a private cemetery, I had to get the consent of Marx's nearest surviving relative. This proved to be a Dr Edgar Longuet, his grandson.

The next time I was in Paris I went with the Chairman of the Swiss party to the suburb where Longuet lived. We found a tiny nineteenth-century house in a quiet street, rang the bell, and were let in by an aged maidservant. She gave us sweet sherry as we waited in a small parlour stuffed with plush furniture and dripping with aspidistras. At last Dr Longuet entered, a little old man with a white military moustache. After a courtly greeting he asked us the purpose of our mission. We explained that we were from the Socialist International and wanted permission to restore his grandfather's grave. He exploded with fury:

'It would be an insult to Karl Marx's memory to let a modern socialist party look after his grave.'

So we were frustrated. Some time later the Soviet Communist Party succeeded where we failed; they planted a monstrous headstone over the grave; a massive bust of the great man now looks down on pilgrims from all over the world. I later took Roy Jenkins and Tony Benn to see it with Walter Lippman; Tony has never recovered from the experience.

Ruggero Orlando once told me another story. Signore Leone, the owner of the Quo Vadis restaurant in Soho, decided during the war that he needed another small dining room in the building. He told a waiter to clear out the attic, which had been unoccupied for many years, to take the furniture to a junk shop and to sell the old books in nearby Charing Cross Road. The waiter sold the furniture, but brought the books back again. No one would buy them because they were hopelessly outdated works on economics and sociology, badly defaced by scribbled notes in the margins. So they were burnt. A few weeks later Leone was approached by two men in long black overcoats. They were from the Marx-Engels Institute in Moscow and had reason to believe that Karl Marx had lived for some time at that address; he had probably left a large part of his library in the attic!

Looking back on my work with the European socialists, I can feel some satisfaction. The Labour Party made good use of the exceptional influence it enjoyed after the war as the only socialist party to hold power on its own in a major country. The period of the Attlee Government marked the high point of the Labour Party's role in Europe; our lowest point came in the eighties. However, I was prevented from making full use of the Attlee Government's unique standing by Britain's post-war economic weakness. Even in the European labour movement, the American trade unions, strongly supported with money and diplomatic assistance by the Truman administration, were often able to exert more influence than the British Labour Party or TUC. Their efforts were directed by the fanatically sectarian Jay Lovestone, who had been expelled for heresy by the American Communist Party, and his able representative Irving Brown; they had a single objective – to mobilise the European Left against the local Communist Parties and against the Soviet Union, often with little regard to the facts of the local situation.

Moreover, in the more important continental countries the socialists were either in opposition or in coalition governments with other parties, mainly the Catholic Christian Democrats. Apart from Britain, Scandinavia was the only part of Europe with majority socialist governments. These governments worked closely with Attlee and Bevin, but, like the Labour Party in those days, were pragmatic rather than ideological in their attitudes. They rejected the federal approach to European unity which was endorsed by most of the continental parties and their Christian Democratic partners, and strongly promoted by the Americans.

Working with the European socialists inevitably had an immense impact on my views about the foreign policy which post-war Britain should pursue, and powerfully influenced me in my other role, as a bridge between Ernest Bevin and the British labour movement.

My years at Transport House saw the outbreak of the Cold War, with the Communist putsch in Prague, the Soviet blockade of Berlin, and the war in Korea. They saw the United States commit itself to help Europe's economic recovery through the Marshall Plan and to defend Western Europe through NATO. They saw the European empires crumbling overseas, and the first steps towards what was planned as a European federal union in the Schuman Plan for coal and steel. In all these revolutionary developments the Attlee Government played a central role, and I had to act as its interpreter.

CHAPTER FIVE

Cold Warrior

> What have you done to them?
> Nothing? Nothing is not an answer:
> You will come to believe – how can you help it? –
>   That you did, you did do something;
> You will find yourself wishing you could make them laugh,
>   You will long for their friendship.
>
> There will be no peace.
> Fight back, then, with such courage as you have
> And every unchivalrous dodge you know of,
>   Clear in your conscience on this:
> Their cause, if they had one, is nothing to them now;
>   They hate for hate's sake.
>
> – 'There will be no peace' W. H. Auden

As INTERNATIONAL SECRETARY it was my job to explain the Government's foreign policy to the Party and the world. To fulfil this task I had first to understand the policy myself. No one in the Government would talk much in public, or even to me in private, about the underlying principles and objectives of their policy, as distinct from justifying their position on particular issues. So I had to learn for myself, from observation, both about the nature of foreign policy as such, and about Britain's specific problems in the postwar world and how the Government planned to deal with them.

I was only dimly conscious of the massive problems facing the Attlee Government when I first went to Transport House as a young man of twenty-eight. Like most of my generation, I was fired with the determina-

· tion to play my part in building a new Britain based on social justice. After five years in the army, it was enough to be back in England and free to live my own life again. Edna and I were used to food rationing; the gimcrack 'utility' chairs and tables, with which we furnished our flat, fully met our modest needs. What our children would see as our economic privations were more than made up for by the excitement of living for the first time in London, surrounded by the theatres and galleries which offered inexhaustible delights.

It took me only a few months in my new job to discover that the Second World War had changed Britain and the world for ever. A century earlier Karl Marx had forecast that, if there was no power in Central Europe to resist her, the western frontier of Russia would run from Stettin to Trieste. Earlier still de Tocqueville had said that the Russians and Americans seemed 'marked out by the will of Heaven to sway the destinies of half the globe'. It was Adolf Hitler who made these prophecies come true – helped by the failure of the other European powers to stop him in time. In 1945 the Russian and American armies stood face to face across the middle of a divided Europe; its ruins were still smoking.

Since Britain was the only big European power to survive the war comparatively undamaged, the responsibility for coming to terms with the Soviet presence in Central Europe lay inevitably with Britain in the first place. Yet everyone responsible for Britain's postwar foreign policy knew that Britain was no longer in a position to perform her traditional role as arbiter of the European balance of power.

We had exhausted ourselves economically to win the war. Having spent most of our sterling balances to finance the war effort, we faced appalling difficulties simply in paying for the imports we needed for our postwar reconstruction. Meanwhile the British Empire was seething with revolt, encouraged by our wartime ally, the United States. And the moment the war ended, Washington broke its wartime agreement to continue nuclear cooperation with London.

I remained a firm believer in collective security. But looking back on the appalling history of attempts to create collective security in the interwar years, which Ernest Bevin once described to me as a period when British diplomacy reached rock-bottom, I soon came to some basic conclusions.

First, whether I liked it or not, the basic unit in world affairs was the nation state. Attempts to base policy on the international solidarity of social classes had broken down in two world wars. A common ideology was no more likely than class solidarity to override the realities of national feeling. I learned that quickly from my contacts with the postwar socialists in Europe. It soon became clear that communists were no more immune to nationalism than democratic Socialists. Starting with Tito in 1948, no Communist Party which won power by its own efforts has accepted Soviet leadership for long; even those installed by Soviet power would achieve independence if the Red Army allowed it. When Khrushchev made his ex cathedra denunciation of the infallibility of the Red Pope, he dissolved the ideological cement of international communism. From that moment, even communist parties out of power began to renounce their subservience to Moscow.

My second conclusion was that in a world of nation states, order could not be maintained by law alone; nor could treaty obligations by themselves guarantee how governments would behave in a crisis. The League of Nations had failed to prevent nations from breaking its Charter by resorting to war; and the alliances which followed its failure had been ignored by their members when their obligations fell due. On the one hand, Britain and France simply ignored their treaty commitments to keep Germany out of the Rhineland and Czechoslovakia. On the other, the anti-Comintern Pact did not prevent Hitler from making a treaty with Stalin, and did not bring Mussolini into the war when fighting started between Germany and the allies. When Japan finally entered the war it was to fight the United States, not the Soviet Union – and Russia did not join the war against Japan until it was practically over. Fascism was no more reliable a bond than communism; Franco remained stubbornly neutral throughout the war.

The insanity of the pre-war international anarchy reached its peak in 1939, when Chamberlain, having already declared war on Germany, decided to fight Russia as well; his plan to send troops to Finland failed only because Sweden refused to allow them passage. No one who lived through this period, like me, could imagine that the traditional type of alliance was any basis for collective security.

In my thinking about power politics I was much influenced by American realists like Hans Morgenthau and William Fox, and by Christian pessimists like Reinhold Niebuhr and Herbert Butterfield. I expressed my general views as they developed in pamphlets for the Labour Party, such as *Approach to Foreign Policy* in January 1947, and in my chapter on 'The Labour Party and Power Politics' in *New Fabian Essays* in 1951. In a later Fabian essay, 'Beyond Power Politics', I suggested that the way to overcome the weaknesses of the pre-war alliances was to develop a form of functional cooperation between allies, through which a network of interdependence would grow, in economic as well as military matters, so as to make the vested interest in cooperation proof against crisis.

As I saw it, both the Marshall Plan, with the European Recovery Programme through which it operated, and the Atlantic Alliance, with the integrated military structure imposed by the North Atlantic Treaty Organisation, were prototypes for a new type of international cooperation which would meet this need. I hoped that the functional organisations of the United Nations would perform a similar role. But the Soviet Union and its client states refused to join any of them; so once the Cold War was under way the West preferred to work through its own institutions instead.

To me, as to millions of others, Soviet behaviour after the war came as a bitter disappointment. We had thought, as Bevin told the Labour Party Conference in 1945, that 'Left could speak to Left'. What I saw for myself in Eastern Europe was typical of Stalin's approach to all who did not accept his dictates.

Revisionist historians have argued that the West was primarily responsible for the Cold War, and that the Attlee Government betrayed the peace by meekly falling in behind American anti-communism. They are wrong on both counts. Soviet policy after the war was based on the Leninist doctrine of the Two Camps, formulated even more strongly by Zhdanov. This held that the communist and capitalist worlds were condemned to a struggle which must end in the victory of one side or the other, perhaps after a war to which the capitalists might resort as the only way of avoiding defeat in peaceful competition. It rejected in principle the concept of a single world society, on which the United Nations was based.

Moreover, Britain, not America, was the first target of Soviet hostility, because it was British troops which stood on the frontiers of Soviet power in Greece, Trieste and Persia, while the United States was trying to disengage from its wartime positions all over the world as fast as possible. In those days Russia concentrated its propaganda overwhelmingly against Britain. For example, on June 8th, 1946, Moscow radio told its listeners in Norway:

'This little country (Britain) went to war because it and its fascist reactionary leaders love war and thrive on war. The attack on Hitlerite Germany was purely incidental.'

The United States remained undecided about its policy towards the

Soviet Union until late in the day. At first it often took the Russian side against Britain in Germany, hoping that Stalin would join in a common recovery programme for both halves of Europe. This illusion survived right up to Marshall's fruitless visit to Moscow on the eve of announcing his Plan in June 1947, when Stalin vetoed the Czechoslovak government's decision to join the European Recovery Programme.

Like most Western observers at this time, I believed that Stalin's behaviour showed he was bent on the military conquest of Western Europe. I now think we were all mistaken. We took too seriously some of the Leninist rhetoric pouring out from Moscow, as the Russians took too seriously some of the anti-Communist rhetoric favoured by American politicians.

Moreover, Stalin concealed the full extent of Russia's wartime losses. We now believe that twenty million Soviet people died and another twenty-eight million were made homeless in the Second World War. In some parts of western Russia the death-roll was one in three, and two thirds of the wealth was destroyed. This makes it most unlikely that Stalin could have contemplated another war against the West. But it does much to explain his determination to create a buffer zone in Eastern Europe extending his direct control to the line which Marx had described as the boundary of 'the Slavonic Empire which certain fanatical Pan-Slavistic philosophers have dreamed of'. It also accounts for his merciless extraction of reparations from Germany, Austria, and Hungary. Above all, it explains the universal hatred of war among the Russian people.

However, German reparations and the dismantling of German industry imposed an economic burden on Britain which we had no means of sustaining. The bulk of West Germany's industry and population was in the British zone. Refugees from East Germany were soon to total twelve million. To allow starvation and mass unemployment in the British zone would be to court a social breakdown and political disaster in which Germany's behaviour would be unpredictable; the memory of cooperation between Germany and the Soviet Union against the Versailles Treaty under the Rapallo Pact was still alive in Whitehall. On the other hand, to pour British economic aid into Germany only to see it drained off into the Soviet Union was equally unacceptable – like feeding the cow in the West and having it milked in the East, as we used to say.

It was this above all else which compelled the Labour Government to opt for separating the Western zones from the Soviet zone, so confirming the division of Europe. Though that division was really implied by Yalta and Potsdam, in the early postwar years the Government still hoped to avoid the division of Europe from crystallising into something permanent, as I argued in my pamphlet *Cards on the Table* in 1947. But the logic of events was inexorable.

Britain was desperately over-extended. In the Middle East, India, and South East Asia we faced nationalist movements already in arms against us. Our domestic economy was badly overstrained, our foreign assets liquidated. We had to reduce our commitments as fast as possible. With Russia hostile and our European neighbours even weaker than ourselves, there was only one possible answer: we had to find some way of engaging the United States in helping to fill the vacuum which the retreat of British power must leave, at least in Western Europe.

Washington, however, was deeply divided on its postwar role. Among both conservatives and liberals, there were forces highly suspicious of the British as imperialists who wanted America to pull their chestnuts out of the fire. Many Republicans and Democrats longed to return to the isolationism of the thirties; it was, after all, only nine years since the United States had committed itself to permanent neutrality by Act of Congress.

Even among the experts in the State Department, who recognised that America could not avoid playing a major role in the years immediately ahead, there were some, like Ben Moore, who saw this as a temporary responsibility, to be off-loaded within ten years or so – once Western Europe had restored its economic strength and achieved political unity, hopefully under British leadership. Others, like Secretary Byrnes, believed that America's monopoly of nuclear weapons would enable her to dictate the peace on her own. Henry Stimson, however, the Secretary for War, with strong support from the elder statesman, Bernard Baruch, believed no less fervently that it was essential for the United States to share the control of nuclear technology with the Soviet Union.

It was Soviet intransigence which finally determined the direction of American policy in the postwar world. That policy was shaped, however, by the diplomatic skill and foresight of a small group of men, both in Washington and London. These men had learned to trust one another during the war; they were now determined to work together so as to secure the peace, by avoiding the mistakes which had helped to make that war inevitable. I was lucky, in Dean Acheson's words, to have been 'present at the creation' as their efforts bore fruit. In Britain, however, the key figure was Ernest Bevin, whose personal experience of world affairs was limited, and who had hoped and expected to be Chancellor of the Exchequer instead of Foreign Secretary. Bevin was the illegitimate son of a Somersetshire girl who earned her living as a domestic servant and village midwife. She died when he was only seven years old. He left school at eleven and after some years as a farm boy went to Bristol, where he worked as a drayman until he was twenty-nine, when he joined the Docker's Union as an organiser. I was twenty-nine when we first met. The fact that I had started my marriage and career at about the same age as he, gave our relationship a flying start.

Though short in stature, he was built like a battle tank, with the rolling gait and thick stumpy fingers typical of a stevedore. Slow and soft of speech in private, he could roar like any sucking-dove at a public meeting. He had shown a ruthless ambition in getting to the top of his union and could be brutally arrogant in debate, as in 1935, when he told the revered pacifist, George Lansbury, to stop hawking his conscience around from conference to conference. When he became Foreign Secretary after the 1945 election, he was sixty-four. Except for the last five years as Minister of Labour in the coalition government under Churchill, he had spent his whole life as a trade unionist.

Nevertheless, his experience as a trade unionist was a far better training for his postwar role than that of many other foreign ministers. He had acquired a deep understanding of human beings through an unparalleled experience in negotiation and organisation. A constructive imagination and the ability to think long-term had enabled him to build the Transport and General Workers' Union into the largest and most powerful labour organisation in the world. The same qualities led him to reorganise Western Europe and North America into an Atlantic community, in which economic and political cooperation were no less important than the military alliance.

I heard his great speech at the Blackpool Conference of the Labour Party without fully appreciating its meaning; as a soldier just back from Italy I was bursting to express my own feelings. He insisted again and again that nations could not work together successfully for peace unless they also worked together for prosperity. He had already worked with foreigners in the trade union movement and the International Labour Organisation, and his restless, enquiring mind would analyse and file away every chance contact or experience for future reference.

Sometimes his trade union experience could lead him astray. He was confident at first that he could solve the Palestine problem by negotiation – an illusion in which he was not alone: Senator Warren Austin at the United Nations was appealing to the Jews and Arabs to behave like

Christians. There was also some insight in the jibe that Bevin thought the Soviet Union was a breakaway from the Transport and General Workers' Union. But even on such issues he showed more insight than most of his contemporaries; he feared that if Palestine became a Jewish state it would become a ghetto in a hostile Arab world, and his familiarity with communist tactics in his own union prepared him well for dealing with Molotov and Stalin.

It was not anti-communism which made him oppose Soviet policy. Indeed, as a young man he led a dockers' strike against loading supplies for the Western forces which were trying to suppress the infant Russian revolution. He was determined to judge people on their behaviour, not by the labels applied to them by others. So he told the Labour Party at Blackpool that General Sikorski was not a Fascist, and rejected complaints the following year that there were too many public-school men in the Foreign Office, saying: 'I am not one of those who decry Eton and Harrow. I was very glad of them in the Battle of Britain.'

Those conference speeches were a nightmare for his civil servants. He would arrive at his hotel the night before he was due to speak, and ask me what had been happening and how he should respond. Then he would make a few notes, sometimes with the help of his private secretary, sometimes not. When he got to his feet next day, and found himself once again facing the sort of audience he had known for forty years, he would surrender to his stream of consciousness. For example, he told the Bournemouth Conference in 1946:

'There has been agitation in the United States, and particularly in New York, for a hundred thousand Jews to be put into Palestine. I hope I will not be misunderstood in America if I say that this was proposed with the purest of motives. They did not want too many Jews in New York.'

Rambling and ill-constructed though they were, such conference speeches invariably won overwhelming support from his audience, whatever the price paid by his diplomatic advisers in nervous breakdowns. He was less successful in the House of Commons, where his speeches often collapsed into tedious obscurity, though he was never guilty of 'clitch after clitch after clitch' – to quote his description of Eden's speeches.

Though he read little except his red boxes of government documents, he listened to his academic adviser, Sir Charles Webster, and ploughed through Webster's great study of the foreign policy of Castlereagh, for he had a great interest in how his predecessors had dealt with the sort of problems which he now faced himself.

Merciless to those he saw as disloyal to him, he was exceptionally loyal to his staff and friends; for example, he brutally rebuffed a conspiracy to get him to step into Attlee's shoes after the dock strike. I had a personal reason to be grateful for this loyalty. On a visit to the Italian Socialist Congress in 1949 I had criticised the breakaway socialist leader, Saragat, for attacking Bevin's policy on the Italian colonies. The Prime Minister, de Gasperi, complained to the British Ambassador, Sir Victor Mallet, who complained to Bevin. I sent Bevin a copy of my speech and awaited his summons. He received me alone in his great room overlooking St James's Park, dismissing his foreign office advisers, who had looked forward to witnessing my come-uppance. I tried to appear calm, and prepared to argue my case, though I did not relish the thought of an argument with the great man.

'Well, Denis,' he said, in his soft Somersetshire accent, 'have you anything to say about this speech you sent me?'

'I don't think so,' I replied. 'It's all there.'

'All right then, I'll tell Mallet to stop whining.'

That was all he had to say about Italy, and we passed to other matters.

The smooth sophisticates of the Foreign Office still describe Bevin as the most loved and respected of all Britain's foreign ministers this century. He formed a close personal friendship with his American partner, Dean Acheson, who in social and intellectual background might have appeared his antithesis. Jim Baker, who became America's Secretary of State forty years later, wrote his dissertation at Princeton in praise of Ernest Bevin, though by focussing on his pragmatism he gave too little importance to his long-term vision.

However, Bevin had enormous difficulty in winning the approval of the Labour Party itself while he was still alive, and had to contend with at best grudging acquiescence from many of his Cabinet colleagues. Much of the Party still took a Utopian view of world politics. Many at every level of the movement still had their pre-war illusions about Stalin's Russia as the workers' paradise. An even larger number distrusted the United States. Above all, there was a general reluctance to accept that the defeat of Hitler and Mussolini had not in itself created the conditions for a lasting peace. With so much to do at home, the idea of continuing to divert resources to defence was universally unwelcome.

When I published my pamphlet, *Cards on the Table*, in 1947 to explain what I thought lay behind his policies, it was fiercely attacked at the Labour Party Conference and received little support in the National Executive; Dalton had in fact approved it, but refused to admit this until the very end of a stormy meeting. Oddly enough, I do not think Bevin himself had seen it until he arrived at the conference, but he took care to give it a word of endorsement in his speech.

However, I had taken care to make sure it was approved by Hector McNeil and Chris Mayhew, Bevin's junior ministers, who were my main channel of communication with him. They were both exceptionally able men, little older than I. Hector's ability was rewarded by promotion to the Cabinet as Secretary for Scotland. He found the job unexciting after the Foreign Office, lost interest in national politics, and died a few years later, without realising his early promise.

Chris Mayhew was one of the few socialists at Oxford in my time who never joined the Communist Party. He had been in the intelligence unit, Phantom, during the war, with Norman Reddaway, who became his private secretary and later worked in Singapore for the so-called Information Research Department; this was set up to organise propaganda for Britain abroad, but in the end destroyed its usefulness by spreading disinformation. Chris himself was something of a boy-scout, seeing issues always in black and white; this made him one of the best early television presenters. Two decades later he was my Navy Minister, and resigned over my decision to phase out the aircraft carriers, afterwards leaving the Labour Party and becoming a Liberal peer.

McNeil and Mayhew were immensely helpful to me at Transport House. I was less impressed by Philip Noel-Baker, who preceded McNeil as Bevin's Minister of State. Of Quaker background, he started his career as a pacifist and was decorated for bravery while serving in Italy with the Friends Ambulance Unit in the Great War. In the interwar years he worked for a time in the League of Nations before becoming a Labour MP and devoting himself to the cause of disarmament and collective security. He had been a champion runner as a youth, and was passionately keen on dancing, never missing a chance of whirling Edna round a ballroom. Yet, though he was given the Nobel Peace Prize in 1959, he was an ineffective politician. When his utopianism was confronted with the world of power politics, he tried to ride both horses at the same time. Thus the former pacifist found himself as Secretary for Air in 1946-7, presiding over the first moves towards producing Britain's atom bomb. When, as Philip Baker, he married Irene Noel, the daughter of a great landowner in Greece, he added her family name to his own; so the passionate socialist inherited most of the island of Euboea as his personal estate. I found it distasteful when at the end of his life he asked me to intercede with Prime Minister Papandreou to spare his estate from a long-overdue land reform.

While Noel-Baker was Bevin's Minister of State, he appointed to his private office a number of brilliant and attractive intellectuals who had been in Victor Rothschild's circle before and during the war. They included Stuart Hampshire, the code-breaker and philosopher, Tessa Mayor, who later married Rothschild, and Pat Llewelyn-Davies, who became Labour Party Whip in the House of Lords. They were to be greatly discomfited when Guy Burgess and Anthony Blunt were discovered to be Soviet spies, since that couple had also been members of the Rothschild circle, and Guy Burgess was one of Hector McNeil's private secretaries while they were with Noel-Baker. I saw a good deal of Burgess in those days, finding him louche and slovenly, with none of the charm others saw in him. It was he who actually wrote the chapter attributed to Hector McNeil in Herbert Tracey's mammoth *Book of the Labour Party*. If his despatches to the NKVD were equally boring, he may have done the West less harm than he is given discredit for.

Bevin gave me a pretty free run of the Foreign Office, and I made many friends among its officials – notably Gladwyn Jebb, a lordly radical who had been Dalton's diplomatic adviser at the Special Operations Executive, which organised sabotage and resistance in occupied Europe, and the intellectual Evelyn Shuckburgh; he once startled me, in a discussion of Tito's break with Stalin, by suggesting that it might have been a trick to deceive the West. No one with any political understanding could believe that governments, even when led by Communists, can conduct their affairs as if they are secret agents. Yet the illusion persists; there was a group of experts in Washington who believed for years that China's break with Moscow was such a trick. Though I found, as in any organisation, cases of bad judgment, in my experience political party bias rarely played a role in the Foreign Office. Throughout my career in politics I have found civil servants, if anything, overscrupulous to avoid party prejudice.

As one of Bevin's links with the Labour Party I saw a lot of the backbench Labour MPs in the External Affairs Group; most of them were hostile to his policy, particularly on Palestine and Germany. Not surprisingly, their quality was mixed since the Government itself had scooped the cream of the 1945 intake, and few of the survivors from the thirties had taken much interest in foreign policy.

This was the beginning of a long relationship with Dick Crossman – a large man with spectacles, mousy hair falling lank on each side of his forehead, and a mouth which turned down at the corners with the expression of Burglar Bill in the dock. I was impressed by his brilliance, until Hector McNeil reminded me: 'It's easy to be brilliant if you are not bothered about being right.' Crossman had a heavyweight intellect with a lightweight judgment. He was an exciting teacher, and would have made a magnificent successor to Laski at the London School of Economics. As a politician, and even more as a minister, he left much to be desired.

Herbert Hart, who was at Bradford Grammar School just before me, and was at New College with Crossman, told me years later, when he was Professor of Jurisprudence at Oxford, that he once went to a football match between Winchester College and the Old Wykehamists. He swore that he heard a little boy say to his friend on the touch-line: 'You see that big chap over there? That's Dick Crossman. Before long I bet he'll score a goal; and it'll be against his own side.'

Crossman found it difficult to listen to others. He and I once visited General von Bonin on the hills outside Bonn after disagreements on strategy had caused his dismissal from the job of setting up the postwar German army. Von Bonin favoured defence in depth supported by mobile tank forces as *Sperrverbände* or blocking groups. I described his theory in my report to the National Executive. Dick wrote an article the same week for the *New Statesman*, in which he put all his own arguments into the mouth of von Bonin.

Like a Greek sophist, Dick was always more interested in the process of argument than in its conclusion. He and I once ruined dinner with a friend by a fierce four-hour wrangle about what Dick considered to be a socialist's duty, automatically to oppose anything which was being proposed. The next night my friend heard Dick lecturing a Fabian meeting with equal ferocity that whether or not a socialist should oppose a proposal depended on whether or not the proposal made sense – the obvious point I had been making the night before.

At the height of the crisis over Palestine Dick suddenly shocked his Zionist friends by insisting that Britain should get out of the Middle East altogether, and concentrate on exploiting the economic and political opportunities in Africa. He once appalled an audience in Germany by proposing that the West should abandon Berlin for the sake of a peace treaty on Austria; a week later Russia finally agreed the Austrian Peace Treaty without any conditions on Berlin.

An uncovenanted luxury, which Edna shared with me, was our occasional weekend at Buscot Park, a beautiful country house near Swindon. It was the home of Gavin Faringdon, an active Fabian and Labour peer. He was a slim and epicene young man who was dedicated to reform, especially in the colonies. His eighteenth-century house stood in large grounds on a hill which overlooked the Cotswolds in one direction and a lovely lake with a heronry in the other. There was no trace anywhere of dirt or dilapidation; every detail was perfect in beauty and comfort. It was an unearthly paradise in postwar Britain. The paintings were mainly Victorian, some already familiar to me from my mother's book *Classic Myth and Legend*. One weekend we slept with Lord Leighton's *Daedalus and Icarus* on the wall, on another we were surrounded by Burne-Jones' lovely frieze of *The Sleeping Beauty*.

The other guests were never exclusively political. Benn Levy, an ex-naval officer with a black spade beard and a soft friendly voice, was a playwright as well as a Labour MP; he brought his beautiful wife, the actress Constance Cummings. Peter Rodd arrived fresh from Italy without his wife Nancy Mitford, but with all the sardonic, raffish charm which was said to have made him one of the models for Evelyn Waugh's hero, Basil Seal. The bizarre balletomane, Lord Berners, was another visitor from that vanished world.

Moving in these exalted circles, and regularly attending functions in foreign embassies, I decided, or Edna decided for me, that I needed a decent suit. Since I had not the slightest idea how to get one, I consulted my old friend Ted Heath. After a short spell in the civil service following demobilisation, he was working as news editor of the *Church Times*. He had also become a Conservative candidate, so I assumed he knew the ways of the ruling classes. He gave me the name of his tailor, Watson Fagerstrom and Hughes in Hanover Street. I bought an expensive suit from them about once or twice every ten years, until I was prominent enough not to care what people thought of my clothes.

Such extravagances were more than I could afford on my Transport House salary, particularly when we started our family with Jenny in 1948, so I had to begin a parallel career as a journalist and broadcaster. Bush House, the headquarters of British broadcasting overseas, became my second home. I did a weekly commentary in French on whatever caught my fancy in the news; I broadcast occasionally in German and Italian, and before long I was doing a great deal in English, for audiences abroad. Believing that no one I knew would ever hear me, I spoke my mind without respect for the Labour Party line. This nonchalance came to an end, however, when the Chinese invaded Tibet. The Dalai Lama sent an emissary from the Himalaya to plead his cause in London. Mr Sen entered my office with open arms and embraced me, exclaiming: 'Ah, Mr Healey, at last. I have been listening to you in Lhasa every week on London Forum.'

Since then I have had many similar experiences of the influence and reputation of the BBC abroad. It baffles me why so many British governments have wanted to cut the foreign services of the BBC. Their value is even greater when Britain's economic and military influence is in decline.

The producer of my French broadcasts was a sallow, twitching young man with a drooping moustache, called Edward Ashcroft. After working with me for a year or two he said that his sister would like to have lunch with me. I agreed without enthusiasm, wondering what his sister was like and what on earth had brought her to this pass. We climbed the stairs from the York Minster pub and entered Berlemont's restaurant to find his sister already there. It was Peggy Ashcroft, who was and remains my theatrical idol – the greatest British actress of her generation. At that time she was married to Jeremy Hutchinson, a brilliant young lawyer who had stood for Labour in 1945.

Since I was already writing regularly for Labour Party publications, the switch to commercial journalism was easy enough. I wrote at first mainly for foreign papers. The Labour daily in Norway, *Arbeiderbladet*, could not afford to keep its own correspondents abroad, so I did a weekly report for them from London for over fifteen years, until I became Defence Secretary. Willy Brandt did the same from Berlin, until he became Lord Mayor; he had spent the war in Norway and Sweden, and had a Norwegian wife. *Arbeiderbladet* paid me three pounds a week for my service, which was little even in those days, but before long I was sending my piece also to *Le Peuple* in Belgium, *Arbeiterzeitung* in Vienna, *Il Punto* in Rome and *To Vima* in Athens. Since Athens got the fifth carbon copy, typed on flimsy paper by a Hermes portable, I suspect the editor of *To Vima* had to exercise a good deal of imagination in deciphering it.

In England I wrote frequently for *Tribune*, then a mainstream socialist paper edited by an able German refugee, Evelyn Anderson. I also wrote occasionally for *The Economist*, though since they demanded high quality articles, paid little, and did not publish their writers' names, I found it unrewarding both financially and politically.

I have written a great deal for newspapers ever since, almost always about the problems I am facing as a politician, so my journalism has helped me politically as well as financially; it compels me to think my problems through more carefully than if they had to wait for the occasional speech. There are some dangers for a politician in confining his journalism to belles-lettres; it may lead people to take his views on political matters less seriously than they deserve. However, since I have enjoyed making a fool of myself on television with comedians such as Dame Edna Everage, and my *Doppelgänger* Mike Yarwood, perhaps that observation is a trifle pompous.

My closest friends throughout my years at Transport House were not in the Labour Party, nor even British. They were American. Howard K. Smith, who had preceded me as Chairman of the Oxford Labour Club in 1939, had settled in London as the CBS correspondent, following Ed Murrow. He had spent the previous five years as a war correspondent in Europe, when he became a close friend of the Silones, and brought with him an exceptionally beautiful Danish wife, Benny, with long legs, silky auburn hair, and a milky complexion – the soldier's dream of a Petty Girl from *Esquire* magazine. She was also deadly serious, had no eyes for anyone but Howard, and had the capacity to do anything she chose after reading the relevant book. During treatment for tuberculosis in Switzerland she taught herself to paint with academic efficiency. Back in Washington many years later, when Howard was under a cloud for having invited Alger Hiss on to one of his programmes, she decided to earn money herself. So she bought a book on growth stocks and before long was making more than her stockbroker. They had a house overlooking Regent's Park which Benny's perfectionism turned into an eighteenth-century jewel. Later she did the same with their home by Chain Bridge in Washington.

Howard kept me in touch with events in America and Europe; but he and Benny were above all close personal friends. I was delighted years later to be able to help their son Jackie, who is now himself a leading TV correspondent, to get a place at Merton after he had been badly wounded in Vietnam.

Our closest friends were Dave and Anne Linebaugh, at the United States Embassy; indeed Dave was probably my closest personal friend till the end of his life. A slow-speaking country boy from Oklahoma, with a handsome brown face and impish brown eyes, he had immense human warmth and total intellectual integrity. He was also a fine athlete, who had played tennis with Arthur Ashe. His wife, Anne, had the fair hair and fine bones of the actress Miriam Hopkins, allied with a feisty radicalism and a fierce wit. Their children grew up with ours, and when Edna had our second baby, Tim, while I was away at the Party Conference, it was Dave who raced her to the hospital. In later life, whenever I was in Washington I made a point, however busy my ministerial schedule, of having at least a breakfast with Dave and Anne.

Dave was marked out for the top rank of the State Department when he was struck down by tragedy. His spine was snapped in a car accident and for nearly a year he was totally incapable of any movement. Adequate treatment by private medicine in the United States was impossibly expensive. I was preparing to draw out my own meagre savings to help him when Anne phoned with good news. The President's wife, Jackie Kennedy, had been greatly impressed by Dave in Pakistan a few years earlier. Hearing by chance that he was paralysed, she had him moved at her own expense into Johns Hopkins hospital where he got the best treatment America could offer. Before long some of the nerves in his spine knitted together again.

He remained badly paralysed for the rest of his life, however, with no feeling whatever in the lower half of his body. But once strapped up in his steel frame – a painful and exhausting process which Anne had to start at five o'clock every morning – he was actually able to go back to work full-time in the official Arms Control and Disarmament Agency, even making one visit to Moscow. Later he worked with Paul Warnke's private disarmament organisation, until a series of physical malfunctions forced him on to a life support machine in Georgetown hospital. I saw him there for the last time just before he died in 1987. His son, Peter, a student radical in the sixties, gave a moving address over his grave:

> In 1965, when I was doing everything, by hook or by crook, to avoid getting drafted and sent to the Vietnam jungles, I asked him what he thought. Instead of telling me, he put another thought into my head by asking a question again: Do you want to be a part of the major experience of your generation?
>
> Dad did not himself have answers to these questions. He wanted me to think for myself. He had confidence that I would. He also knew about life and death struggle. From such like questions I make some inferences about him in order to determine his legacy to me. He was not afraid of questions he could not answer. That is one. He had faith in other people. That is the other. To me they both form part of his legacy and I shall draw courage from his life by honouring them.

There was a luminous goodness about David Linebaugh which radiated far beyond his own family circle. He was immensely helpful to me in those early postwar years when we were both trying to understand the new world. For example, early in 1948 he heard that the Secretary of the Czech Social Democratic Party, Blasej Vilim, had escaped into West

Germany and was being held in a CIA intelligence centre in Frankfurt. Since we were holding a meeting with the Polish Socialists in London the next day, I asked Dave if he could conceivably arrange for Vilim to come to London to confront his former colleagues. Dave rang Bob Murphy, the American political adviser in Berlin, who arranged for him to be flown that afternoon to London, where his story made a real impact on our meeting.

About six weeks later another of my Czech friends arrived in London from Frankfurt. He had escaped from Prague with Vilim, so I asked why it had taken him so long to reach us. He answered that he had been interrogated for over a month by the CIA to discover how Vilim had managed to get out of their hands. I wonder if cooperation between the different arms of the American Government is any better today.

Other close friends in the US Embassy were the Labour Attaché, Sam Berger, and his wife Margie. Sam was a small man with a large, V-shaped head, pointed ears and a pockmarked face which usually wore an expression of irony or sarcasm. In fact he had a warm heart and was deeply committed to working people. He had studied labour history with the redoubtable Selig Perlman in Wisconsin, the seedbed of many level-headed liberals in modern America. By developing good personal relations with many key figures in the British Labour movement at the end of the war, including Sam Watson and Hugh Gaitskell, he exerted an enduring influence on British foreign policy. Later he fell foul of Richard Nixon while serving in Tokyo and was banished to New Zealand; he was never again able to exercise his full potential.

People like Sam Berger and Dave Linebaugh show that there is still an important role for the diplomatist serving abroad, even in the age of information technology and Concorde, when ministers try to conduct so much diplomacy themselves. Good British diplomatists are particularly valuable in Washington, where it is often impossible for a visiting minister to meet the men who actually decide policy, and is sometimes difficult for our embassy to identify them. The American system is exceptionally open to outside advice from individuals whose integrity is trusted and whose knowledge and intelligence are respected. Lord Harlech, as British Ambassador, was practically a member of Kennedy's cabinet during the Cuba crisis; I have known quite junior members of the embassy staff who made an important input to American strategic thinking – such as John Thompson, who served later as our Ambassador to the United Nations. For this reason, both as Defence Secretary and as Chancellor of the Exchequer, I made a point of seeing as much as possible of the officials who advised my foreign colleagues, whether chiefs of staff or central bankers or civil servants.

In those Transport House years, without my wide range of contacts, both in London and on the Continent, I would have found it much more difficult to understand the development of Bevin's foreign policy and to interpret it to the Labour movement.

Essentially, Bevin was trying to involve the United States long-term in the recovery and security of Western Europe. He accepted new British commitments on the continent only when he was satisfied that America would share them, or as a means of securing an American commitment. By withdrawing British troops from Greece he stimulated the first major American commitment after the war, in the Truman Doctrine. When Truman refused to support his policy in Palestine he handed the Mandate back to the United Nations. He saw the Brussels Treaty in 1948, which committed Britain to keep a large number of troops in Germany for fifty years, as the sprat necessary to catch the whale of NATO in 1949.

Perhaps his most important achievement in this field was his part in the Marshall Plan. When Marshall made his Harvard speech on June 5th, 1947, offering to provide American support if the Europeans themselves would take the initiative in devising a recovery programme, it is doubtful if he personally realised how fast events would move. Dean Acheson, then his deputy, who played a key role in drafting the speech, briefed a few selected British correspondents on its potential importance, and asked them to make sure Bevin was aware of his views. In fact Bevin was ahead of him. The moment he heard a report of the speech on his bedside radio, Bevin decided to act, without even, as his officials suggested, trying to find out what Marshall meant.

He first consulted his French colleague, George Bidault, then approached the Russians. On June 27th he met Bidault and Molotov in Paris to discuss the preparation of the common programme which Marshall had made a condition for American aid. Molotov refused this, insisting instead that each country should simply tell the Americans what it wanted. He said that a common programme would be an infringement of national sovereignty; it would in fact have been contrary to all the principles which then inspired Soviet foreign policy. The conference broke down; Russia not only refused to join the Marshall Plan herself, but also vetoed the participation of Czechoslovakia, which had indicated its wish to join.

I was deeply involved in organising support for the Marshall Plan among the European socialists, and wrote the Labour Party's memorandum on the subject. Besides emphasising the need for American aid, I stressed the value of the Marshall Plan as a step towards European unity.

My memorandum was accepted by the other parties on March 22nd, 1948. At this point, however, there began an argument which is still raging forty years later: what sort of unity should Europe seek? The French, Italian, German and Benelux parties all favoured the federal model, while the British and Scandinavian parties favoured functional cooperation between governments. The key figures in Washington supported a federal Europe, and exerted maximum pressure in the Continental capitals in favour of the federalistic proposals which began to emerge, notably the Schuman Plan for a European Coal and Steel Community, and the French proposal for a European Defence Community.

In fact, much of the European support for federalism was no more than lip-service. Churchill, who first put forward the idea of a European Army, finally had to admit he did not want Britain to join it; and in the end the French parliament itself rejected the European Defence Community. Germany could safely offer to renounce its national sovereignty since at that time it had none. There was more genuine support for federation in the Low Countries, particularly Holland; but I remember an Italian senator telling me that he would not believe in the sincerity of the Benelux federalists until they stopped growing tomatoes under glass. And Josef Luns had to admit that there was something in the charge that Holland's interest in European unity boiled down to the price of butter and landing rights in Hong Kong.

I now believe that Paris was worth a mass: Britain might have done better to pay the same lip-service as the others to the idea of European federation. Certainly, if we had gone to Messina in 1955, the Rome Treaty would have emerged in a form far more favourable to British interests than it had assumed when we finally signed it in 1973. The French are right to say: 'Les absents ont toujours tort'.

Nevertheless, I still think that the arguments I used against federation in my pamphlet *Feet on the Ground* in September 1948 are compelling. Federation was a good constitution for farming communities of common British stock in an empty continent, whether in eighteenth-century America or early twentieth-century Australia. But 'Europe's history of separate national existence has produced clearly defined interest groups. When such groups do exist no written constitution can by itself compel them to act against their perceived interests. More than most federal governments, a European federation would require forcible sanctions against secession. The prolonged and bloody American Civil War is not an encouraging precedent.' In fact the United States had more casualties in the Civil War than in all the wars which followed put together, including Vietnam; and its population was then only one seventh of what it is today.

The whole of my political experience has taught me that the complicated nexus of interdependent vested interests created by a modern industrial society is very resistant to change – especially change imposed from outside. Change or reorganisation in any institution can create disruptions which may take years to overcome. Thus the clinching argument against revolution in the modern world is that a revolution is bound to create an anarchy, in which an industrial society cannot be operated without a political dictatorship.

In modern Europe there are many other obvious difficulties in the federal approach – different languages, different cultures, and powerful nationalist traditions. The memoirs of Mussolini's Foreign Minister, Grandi, tell a story which illustrates the problem. He asked one of his intelligence agents in Vichy France to report on French feeling towards the British. The agent replied: 'The French feel about the British very much as we feel about the Germans.'

National character can change of course – and has, significantly, since the war. But the olive line remains as real a frontier as any in Europe. South of the line where olives grow, people have little respect for government and use personal discretion in paying their taxes. So a system which requires the Sicilian landowner to give the same respect to authority as the Dutch manufacturer is unlikely to work. Even today, the minimal military cooperation required to create a European pillar in NATO faces enormous difficulties, because Germany, France, and Britain each takes a different view of its relations with the United States, has a different approach to strategy, and protects the industrial interests of its own arms manufacturers.

My pamphlet was not well received by most of the European socialists, or by the small federalist group in the Labour Party, who said it should have been called 'Feet on the Table' or 'Heads in the Sand'. I admit it did contain one statement which I still blush to remember: 'Many of the dollars now spent on American cheese would be saved if Europe concentrated on producing cheap cheeses for mass consumption instead of luxury cheeses like Camembert and Gorgonzola'.

However, the row over *Feet on the Ground* was nothing to the storm created by the official Labour Party statement, *European Unity*, in May 1950. Though I had written the first draft, using most of my earlier arguments, Dalton got the National Executive to insert a number of passages which overemphasised the obstacles which the supranational approach would present to the economic programmes of a Labour Government. His press conference on the statement was even more aggressively sectarian. Moreover, we inadvertently published the statement at an excruciatingly inconvenient time – the day before the Government's White Paper on the Schuman Plan, which was noncommittal and far more emollient in tone.

Meanwhile the battle had shifted to the Consultative Assembly of the Council of Europe in Strasbourg, where Dalton led the Labour delegation. However, it was the head of the Conservative delegation who dominated the proceedings. He was Winston Churchill. When the leading European statesmen addressed a crowd of some hundred thousand in the Place Kleber, Churchill spoke last. His opening words were: 'Shitoyens et shitoyennes de Shtrasbourg, prenez garde.' A long pause. 'Je – vais – parler –Francais!' The roar of laughter must have been heard across the Rhine; continental audiences were not accustomed to hear statesmen making jokes. From that moment, of course, they were in the hollow of his hand.

I went to Strasbourg for two years as adviser to the Labour delegation, then for another two years as a delegate, after becoming an MP. The Council of Europe provided unrivalled opportunities for meeting leading politicians from all over Western Europe. Like the rest, I would goggle at the regular cross-talk between De Valera and an Ulster Unionist MP, Connolly Gage, about the Irish problem, little realising how deadly serious it would become. There were black MPs from the French Union territories in Africa. One of them failed to reappear the second year. We were told that during the recess he had been eaten by his constituents.

Since, however, the Assembly had absolutely no powers, it became frustrating after a time, and Strasbourg proved an unsuitable location, despite its links with both France and Germany. The food was excellent, but very rich; the wine was excellent, but very acid. Every meal would end with a glass of framboise, surely the driest and strongest liqueur in the world. So when delegates returned to the Assembly after luncheon, if they were capable of doing so, the milk of human kindness was not flowing strongly in their veins.

One of my jobs was to write speeches, if necessary, for our delegates to deliver. I wrote one for Billy Blyton, a Durham miner, on the Schuman Plan; he liked it so much that he repeated it many times both in Strasbourg and Westminster. Billy enjoyed the Alsatian food immensely, but only after taking out his false teeth and wrapping them carefully in an enormous spotted handkerchief.

In the weekends, Dalton used to take some of us for walks in the Vosges. He loved striding on the mountains 'where men have died for freedom'. On one memorable occasion he took Jim Callaghan, Tony Crosland, and myself, to climb the Haut Donon. We all got drunk that night, and, in hours of uninhibited conversation which continued even after breakfast, he told us more about himself than he had told anyone for many years. He records it as 'a wonderful trip, which I shall long remember, in most agreeable company, seasoned with wit and wisdom, walking and wine.' I believe our saturnalia released something in his psyche which badly needed freedom. A sad man.

These last years at Transport House were, however, dominated less by Europe than by the progressive strengthening of Britain's links with the United States – a process paralleled by my own deepening knowledge of America. As on the Marshall Plan, it was Bevin who took the initiative required to produce an American commitment. The putsch in Prague was followed by the Brussels Treaty and by talks with the United States on an Atlantic defence organisation. Progress was slow, partly because the State Department feared that Britain was trying to revive its wartime special relationship with America, instead of accepting its destiny in Europe. But the Soviet blockade of West Berlin brought the United States much closer together with Britain and France, and Schuman was an easier colleague than Bidault. The North Atlantic Treaty was signed in April, 1949. A month later Russia ended the blockade of Berlin.

I spent a week in Berlin just before the blockade ended, flying out from Schleswig in a Hastings aircraft loaded with coal, and back to Hamburg in a plane which had been carrying fish. I was redolent with the memory for some time afterwards. We had an impressive team in Berlin, led by General Robertson, under whom I had served in Italy, a man of calm common sense which served him well when he became the first chairman of the nationalised British railways. Robert Birley was his adviser on education, a slim, bright-eyed, lisping Balliol man. He next had a few years as headmaster of Eton, before showing great courage in opposing apartheid as a Professor at Witwatersrand.

The Socialdemocrats were the key to the strength of the Western position in Berlin. Ernst Reuter, the Lord Mayor, was a man of exceptional wisdom and experience, who knew the Communist strategy from first-hand experience. His link with the SPD in Hanover was Willy Brandt, who later succeeded him as Lord Mayor. Willy greatly impressed me with his pragmatism and decency. We were friends and colleagues for the next forty years.

In September that year I paid my first visit to America. Though I had by now many American friends, it is impossible to understand that continental superpower without exploring its variety in person; and even then it is not easy, since it is in constant flux. The occasion of my visit was a Commonwealth conference on world affairs in Canada, at which I was part of the delegation from Chatham House, the Royal Institute of International Affairs. I had joined the Chatham House Council just after the war, and remained an active member until I became a minister in 1964. It became a major source of my education in world affairs, since it enabled me to meet people with a knowledge and experience far removed from what was available to me in my work for the Labour Party.

For example, among my fellow Councillors was General Ian Jacob, a small shy scholarly man who had developed an unrivalled expertise in defence and diplomacy as Assistant Military Secretary to the War Cabinet. He also had an independent judgment, as he later proved as Chairman of the BBC, and in his official report on the reorganisation of defence. There were two merchant bankers and three outstanding economists, as well as a scattering of diplomats and politicians.

Standing rather apart from such members of the postwar establishment were men whose experience went back to Edwardian days – Lionel Curtis, a handsome old man with shaggy grey hair who had belonged to the group of young men surrounding Lord Milner in South Africa after the Boer War, – his so-called kindergarten, – Lord Brand, a courtly old merchant banker who had also been in that extraordinary kindergarten, and Arnold Toynbee, the father of my Oxford friend, Philip Toynbee, and son-in-law of Gilbert Murray. He was just emerging as a global intellectual superstar for his *Study of History*. I was not overly impressed by this type of Anglo-Spenglerism; like all attempts to trace historical patterns over the centuries, it became the slave of its author's theories; and I found it inaccurate on the few decades of Greek and Roman history which I had studied in detail at Balliol. Toynbee's judgment on contemporary history also had its flaws; in the thirties he met Hitler, and expressed confidence in the Führer's goodwill.

We travelled to Canada on a slow boat which took ten days to reach Montreal, so I had ample time to get to know my fellow delegates. They were led by Rab Butler. The real excitement began when I crossed the river into Detroit for my first taste of the United States. My four days in Detroit were spent with the labour unions, though I also managed to see the paintings of El Greco, Goya, and Georges de la Tour at the excellent

Institute of Art. There was a striking contrast between the Congress of Industrial Organisations, composed of the mass industrial unions, and the American Federation of Labour, which was largely craft unions. I felt quite at home in the CIO council meeting, which was discussing the defeat of its candidate in the mayoral primaries just as if it were the Leeds City Labour Party. At the headquarters of the mighty United Automobile Workers' Union, I met Guy Nunn, a friend from Oxford. He had been in the OSS during the war and after being captured in Hungary became a prisoner of war in Germany. Now he was running the UAW broadcasting station – an asset then unimaginable for a British union. The UAW was led by the remarkable brothers, Walter and Victor Reuther, who came from solid socialist stock in Württemberg. Walter could still address a mass meeting in Stuttgart in the local dialect. He was undoubtedly of presidential timber, and though he died young his union still carries his imprint. Victor, who succeeded him, was more of a backroom boy. He lost an eye when a bomb was thrown through his kitchen window. Industrial relations in the United States were still very violent. In the late thirties the UAW had had to fight pitched battles with gangsters hired by the Ford Motor Company before establishing itself in Detroit.

By contrast, the AFL Council which I attended was decorous to the point of tedium. Its members, all from craft unions, looked middle-class compared with the CIO. But racketeering was still endemic in its unions. One of its leaders showed me with pride the cupboard where they used to keep their tommy-guns. Years later Jimmy Hoffa of the Teamsters' Union kept millions of dollars stashed away in the sewers of Detroit.

For me, however, the greatest excitement of Detroit was not in its labour politics. It was in the fact that it was the sort of industrial city I had seen so often in American films. I loved the seedy bars, the drugstores where I could breakfast off a counter on coffee with a doughnut, the taxi-drivers who insisted on telling me the latest city scandals, and ordinary working people, black and white, who talked in the racy demotic argot of Clifford Odets. It was a far cry from the America of the Rhodes scholars I knew so well in Oxford.

The overnight train to Washington brought me into another world again, of spacious avenues flanked by dazzling white buildings. I spent a crowded day there with Dave Linebaugh, and met his friends in the State Department. His boss was Dean Rusk, a powerfully built thirty-nine-year-old with a round head, and an acutely intelligent face which reminded me of Spaak. From a poor home in Georgia he had become a professor at Mills College for women in California. The difference between academic life and government, he told me, was the difference between arguing to a conclusion and arguing to a decision – a distinction which many intellectuals in politics are slow to learn. He had served in military intelligence during the war and told me a story which he must have recalled many times in later life. As a Colonel in New Delhi, when the American troops took over from the defeated Japanese in Indochina, it was his task to inform them of American policy there. He cabled Washington for advice, and after anxious days of waiting, finally received a reply. It simply reported the following exchange from President Truman's press conference the previous day:

'Mr President, sir, what is America's policy in Indochina.'

'I just don't want to hear any more about Indochina.'

Prophetic words.

I saw a great deal of Dean Rusk in the following twenty years, and worked closely with him when he was Secretary of State and I was Defence Secretary. We often disagreed, particularly over Vietnam, but this never damaged our personal relations. He had immense dignity as an American, and served his country well both as an official and as a member of the Kennedy and Johnson Cabinets – though perhaps he drew too little distinction between bureaucracy and politics; he believed that the President had the right and duty to decide policy, while the Secretary of State's duty was simply to carry it out. He was never a member of the inner court of Camelot, and I felt that when the Democrats lost power in 1970 many of his old colleagues were too content that he should disappear to a minor academic post in Georgia, where they made no attempt to keep in contact with him.

This first visit to the United States ended with ten days of lecturing, divided between Boston, New York, and Yale. With Harvard College and Business School, the Massachusetts Institute of Technology, and the Fletcher School of Law and Diplomacy north of the river and Brandeis University just outside, Boston served as my intellectual paradise for many years. I managed to visit the area at least once on each of my annual lecture trips to the United States until I became Defence Secretary, and I still return when I can. None of the British universities has the same contact with the outside world as these great colleges. Many of the professors would spend years at a time working for their government in Washington or abroad, or fly down once a week as consultants. Yet even in the worst days of McCarthyism they preserved their independence of thought and expression. I always left wiser than I came, stimulated to think afresh about familiar problems.

Many of my diplomatic friends, from Europe and Asia as well as the United States, studied at the Fletcher School, including Dave Linebaugh. On this first visit to Harvard I made friends at the Littauer Center, such as the historian and political theorist Arthur Schlesinger, who had been at Cambridge before the war, Ken Galbraith, the Canadian liberal economist, and Sam Beer, the tall red-haired expert on the Labour Party, who was at Balliol just before me; they all remained friends for the rest of my life.

Yale, with its grey buildings in that warm autumn sun, reminded me very much of Oxford. I met there some of the leading American experts on world affairs, notably William Fox, whose book, *The Superpowers*, an exceptionally prescient study of postwar problems published in 1944, had already had a seminal influence on my thinking. For good or ill, I owe much of my understanding of the postwar world to such American academics, who combined the breadth and generosity of thought so typical of the United States in those days, with a scrupulous intellectual objectivity.

In New York I lectured to the Council on Foreign Relations, which was much more effective than its British counterpart, Chatham House, in engaging the interest of key figures from the city outside. It was regarded by the extreme Right in the United States as a sinister conspiracy of bankers who were soft on communism!

I loved New York – so many scenes from so many old familiar films, and so much new and totally unexpected. I have always found the city at its best in a crisp and sunny early fall, when Central Park is beginning to glow with autumn colour and even walking in the great stony canyons is a pleasure. New York at night from the top of the Empire State or the Rockefeller building is pure faery, as the darkness falls while the lights still shine in the office buildings. I got unfailing pleasure out of watching the skaters on the ice-rink in Rockefeller Plaza dance their beautiful ballets while Tchaikovsky echoed from the loudspeakers.

There were plenty of cakes and ale to add sparkle to my business in the United States, above all the magnificent art galleries in all the cities I visited – the Fogg Museum in Harvard, the National Gallery and Phillips in Washington, and in New York not only the Metropolitan and Museum of Modern Art, but that little renaissance jewel, the Frick Gallery, which is my favourite oasis in America.

That first visit to the United States in September, 1949 gave me a love for the country and its people which has survived many political dis-appointments; my love only deepened as I travelled the continent more widely and my knowledge increased.

The number of Americans who visited me in Transport House multi-plied in my last two years as International Secretary. They were usually liberal Democrats, curious about the lessons which Labour Britain might have to teach them. Irwin Ross, a gigantic young New Yorker, brought me his *Strategy for Liberals*, and Arthur Schlesinger his eloquent plea for a democracy which would be relevant to postwar industrial society, *The Vital Center*. There was also a clever young lawyer who worked for Hubert Humphrey, called Max Kampelman; I next met him nearly forty years later when he was guiding the talks on Intermediate Nuclear Forces to a successful conclusion.

One of my visitors had been a friend of Michael Young at Dart-ington Hall, the progressive school in Devon. He was a handsome young man called Michael Straight, who was editor of the liberal *New Republic*, which his parents had founded in 1914; Walter Lippmann was its first assistant editor. Michael's brother, Whitney, who won the Grand Prix as a racing driver, lived permanently in Britain; he had become the first managing director of the nationalised British Overseas Airways Corporation. Michael asked if I would write articles for the *New Republic*; I agreed, and began contributing pieces under the pseu-donym Blair Winston. Before long I was doing a weekly column under my own name; this continued until I became Defence Secretary in 1964, when my place was taken by a young writer on *The Economist* called Alastair Burnett.

When I knew him, Michael Straight was a good liberal Democrat who had fought the Communists in the American Veterans Committee, and fought McCarthyism no less fiercely. However, he had been a Communist himself at Cambridge in the thirties, where he was a close friend of Guy Burgess. When his hero, John Cornford, was killed in Spain, Anthony Blunt, a fellow Communist and member of the élite society of the Apostles, exploited his grief to recruit him as a spy for the Soviet Union. He seems to have given the Russians low grade political intelligence between 1938 and 1941, when he left government service and volunteered for the US Air Force. He broke with Russia and the Communist Party long before the war ended.

But he was haunted by his knowledge that Burgess was well placed in the Foreign Office and his belief that Blunt still maintained contact with the men he had recruited. When Burgess and Maclean defected to the

Soviet Union in 1950 he was tormented by the fear that he might know
of other British spies who had not been detected.

Yet it was not until 1963 that he finally told what he knew. President
Kennedy wanted him to chair an agency to encourage the arts in
America. Since this required a check by the FBI, Michael saw Arthur
Schlesinger, then the President's cultural adviser, and told him the whole
story. He was sent over to the FBI. The young man who took his
statement turned out to be the second son of his mother's head gardener,
to whom his cast-off clothes were given in the far-off days when he lived
as a little boy on the great family estate at Old Westbury. Oddly, he felt
this was his ultimate humiliation. Though British intelligence interrogated him in detail at that time about Anthony Blunt and other Soviet
agents, the story did not finally emerge in public until March 25th, 1981,
when Mrs Thatcher decided, against the advice of her security services,
to give Anthony Blunt's name to the House of Commons.

In 1983, Michael Straight published his own account in *After Long
Silence*. I find it honest and deeply moving. His description of Cambridge
in the years just before I was at Oxford rings completely true. A few
years ago, as I was leaving Dulles International Airport in Washington,
an old man with a ravaged face turned from collecting his baggage at the
carousel to call my name. It was Michael Straight. I had not seen him for
a quarter of a century. He was barely recognisable as the tall handsome
young man I first met in my office at Transport House – one more leaf
blown on the gale of the world.

Edna and I were on holiday with Jenny and Tim in an Italian farmhouse
at Bocca di Magra when the North Korean army invaded South Korea.
Tim was just a year old, so I had to carry him when we went on
mountain walks with an impressive group of young working men who
had been partisans during the war. Before we had a car, a foreign holiday
was a hazardous enterprise with our young family. We took the boat from
Calais, excited to find Rita Hayworth aboard, and changed trains and
buses several times. Edna carried Tim while I lugged a suitcase in each
hand, with an enormous army rucksack on my back. Since we had no
radio and rarely saw a newspaper, I did not realise the full gravity of the
Korean crisis until we got back to England.

Korea produced the first armed conflict of the Cold War and it taught
us some important political lessons which are still not fully understood.
Truman is rightly praised for the speed with which he organised the
United Nations' response to the North Korean invasion. But the invasion

would never have happened if the Americans had behaved more sensibly. When they decided to withdraw their own troops from South Korea, both Secretary Acheson and General MacArthur, the senior civilian and military spokesmen of the US Government, proclaimed that America had no strategic interest in South Korea. The North Koreans took that as the green light for their invasion. Mrs Thatcher's record on the Falklands was very similar.

However, this blunder had one useful consequence. Truman's immediate response to the North Korean challenge taught the lesson that a democratic government cannot be trusted in a crisis to act as it has indicated it will. A potential aggressor can never ignore America's military capacity; it cannot afford to rely on an estimate of America's intentions, even when that estimate is based on official American statements. This has become an important factor in maintaining the political stability of the strategic balance in the nuclear age. Korea also provided a text-book example of limited war: though tempted to use nuclear weapons, Truman decided that the political disadvantages would outweigh any potential military gain – and Attlee played a role in producing this decision.

Nevertheless, America made another massive error in its conduct of the campaign. China was not involved in the initial decision to invade South Korea, since North Korea at that time looked to Moscow, not Peking, for advice. Washington ignored China's warnings that it would not stand idly by if MacArthur crossed the thirty-eighth parallel. He did cross it, and the Chinese then entered Korea. So a war which might have ended with the successful landing at Inchon, six months after it began, lasted four more disastrous years. Besides the unnecessary human suffering, this produced a breach between the United States and China which lasted twenty years and contributed – again, partly through misunderstanding – to the tragedy of Vietnam. Yet – as General Marshall had reported at the time – only a few years before the Korean War, there had been a real chance that the new Communist regime in Peking would be prepared to break with the Soviet Union in order to have good relations with the United States. This series of blunders over Korea has always made me reluctant to give unqualified praise to Truman's presidency. Without them the history of the world in the last forty years might have been far happier. And if later presidents had studied the lessons of Korea, they might have avoided the historic catastrophe of Vietnam.

In 1951 I felt that my period at Transport House was approaching its end. Ernest Bevin died in April. I was deeply moved. By then I had come to regard him, as I still do, as one of the two greatest democratic politicians this century; the other is Franklin Roosevelt. The American patrician and the British trade unionist had two things in common – a powerful sense of direction which was rooted in moral principle, and a street-wise pragmatism in choosing the best route forward. Both men, too, had a constructive approach to politics. They were builders, not destroyers.

Bevin's successor, Herbert Morrison, was a poor Foreign Secretary, who made little attempt to master his brief. In June the Socialist International was finally established at Frankfurt. I felt that my work at Transport House was done. In December I put forward my name for nomination as Labour candidate in a by-election at South East Leeds.

PART TWO: Opposition

CHAPTER SIX

Member of Parliament

> How dreary to be Somebody!
> How public – like a Frog –
> To tell one's name the livelong June
> To an admiring Bog!
>
>   – 'I'm Nobody! Who are you?'
>   Emily Dickinson

MY DECISION TO RUN for Parliament in 1945 was not deeply considered; but I hesitated a long time before deciding to try again in 1951. Six years at Transport House had greatly increased my concern about the postwar world, and had given me a unique insight into some of its problems. I now wanted above all to find some way of helping to prevent a Third World War. On the other hand I had been neither excited nor impressed by what I had seen of party politics. Sitting at the bottom of the table in the Eighth Floor Board Room as the National Executive fought its internecine battles, I tended to see the worst of the great men who led the Labour Party. I was particularly repelled by the extent to which each of the most prominent figures had a clique of acolytes who never had a good word to say about the leader of a rival clique. In some cases the leader encouraged his clique through a back-bench MP who acted as his chief of staff – Morrison through Maurice Webb, for example, or Bevan through Michael Foot. In others a back-bench MP would organise the clique without the leader's authority; this was particularly true of George Brown's efforts for Ernest Bevin. It all made me determined never to encourage a personal clique to form round me; my reputation as a lone wolf goes back to those days.

Nor did my contacts with backbench MPs leave me with a passionate desire to join them. Some reminded me too much of Yeats' description of 'some typical elected man, emotional as a youthful chimpanzee, hot and vague, always disturbed, always hating something or other'. Even the best found it immensely frustrating to be backbenchers supporting a government with a large majority. The government wanted your votes, not your speeches; if you wanted to make a name for yourself you had to be a rebel. So you had to choose between silence, sycophancy and sectarian conspiracy. It was not an attractive prospect for a young man who wanted to save the world.

In my last two years at Transport House I became more involved with party policy outside my own area of foreign affairs. For example, I attended the joint meetings of Cabinet and National Executive to draw up the programmes for the general elections of 1950 and 1951. These too were not wholly edifying occasions. I recall a meeting at a hotel in Shanklin on the 1950 programme which was deeply divided on the wisdom of nationalising the insurance industry. A. V. Alexander, the Defence Minister, predicted that it would be opposed by the cooperative movement, which sold its own insurance policies. Jim Griffiths, the Minister for Social Security, warned that it would mobilise the whole corps of door-to-door insurance agents against us. As Chancellor of the Exchequer, Stafford Cripps said that it could only be profitable if it was a ramp. On the other side, Nye Bevan argued in favour of nationalisation on the grounds that the insurance companies were anti-social parasites, and Dalton on the grounds that they provided services so necessary to society that only the state should operate them. In the end the meeting decided to compromise on 'mutualising' insurance, without defining precisely what that meant.

The argument on nationalising ICI followed similar lines, with those who knew anything of the industry, or had members working in it, strongly opposed, and the ideologues in favour. Michael Foot argued that we must nationalise ICI because we must nationalise something. On this occasion, however, Attlee put his foot down, strongly supported by Bevin, Cripps and Morrison, and the idea was dropped. So we confined our nationalisation proposals to water and cement. I doubt whether any of our candidates made much of the issue, and our majority was too small to allow us to carry the proposals out. The Labour Party is not unique in the carelessness with which it sometimes compiles its election programmes, as any honest Conservative will admit, as he tries to make sense of the Poll Tax.

I was, however, impressed by the quality of some of the Cabinet ministers of whom I had seen little at Transport House. Herbert Morrison showed an exceptionally deep knowledge and understanding of domestic politics. Cripps had an incisive common sense, but was cautious in inflicting it on the National Executive; he still felt the bruises left by his expulsion from the Labour Party in the thirties. Shinwell was scarred by his early years as minister responsible for nationalising the coal industry, without any guidance whatever from the Party on how it should be done. He felt we should demonstrate success in the industries we had already nationalised, before looking for new industries to nationalise.

Bevin, as always, dominated every discussion with a powerful common sense which was rooted in his experience as a trade unionist. Within a week of his death on April 14th, 1951, Nye Bevan resigned from the Labour Government, taking Harold Wilson and John Freeman with him. He chose a moment for his gesture which was exceptionally damaging for his Party. The Gallup Polls were showing a swing to the Conservatives, who were harrying the Government relentlessly with wildcat votes. Attlee was ill, and Hugh Gaitskell, Cripps' successor as Chancellor, was defending his unpopular first budget. When Bevan broadened the issue on which he had resigned, from payment for teeth and spectacles supplied by the National Health Service, to the whole of Labour's foreign and defence policy, I began to play an active role in the campaign against him. I did so with some reluctance, since he had written an enthusiastic preface to my book on the destruction of the socialists in Eastern Europe, *The Curtain Falls*.

By then several of my possible alternatives to a parliamentary career had come to nothing. I had been approached to take E. H. Carr's chair at Aberystwyth University as Professor of International Relations; but they wanted a full-time academic to replace Carr, who had spent too much of his time writing editorials for *The Times*, and I thought Aberystwyth was too far from London. I had been asked to become Foreign Editor of the Labour newspaper, the *Daily Herald*, but was blocked by the notorious Catch 22 which the National Union of Journalists operated against outsiders; they would not let me take the job unless I was already a member of the union, and would not let me join the union unless I already had the job. So, once the 1951 general election was over, I decided after all to try for parliament.

My reluctance to enter politics directly had been rooted essentially in the fear that I was not cut out for public life, and that I would find it intolerable to make the compromises required of a party politician. On reflection, however, I came to realise that almost any alternative which met my desire to do something useful about the state of the world would have the same disadvantages, while offering less opportunity for effective action. The jungle warfare unleashed by competing ambitions is much the same in any profession – certainly in business and academic life, not to speak of the Church, as Trollope illustrates. Politics differs from those professions only in that most of its fighting takes place in public, rather than in the secrecy of common rooms or cathedrals; that is one reason why politicians are more prone to vanity.

However, publicity is inescapable in any profession which aims to influence the public directly. Some of the greatest poets were all too aware of this – notably Yeats, whose description of poetry as 'the struggle of the fly in marmalade' applies equally to politics. The choice I faced in 1951, he too had faced half a century earlier:

> The intellect of man is forced to choose
> Perfection of the life or of the work,
> And if it take the second must refuse
> A heavenly mansion, raging in the dark.
> When all that story's finished, what's the news?
> In luck or out the toil has left its mark:
> That old perplexity an empty purse,
> Or the day's vanity, the night's remorse.

Emily Dickinson, apparently the least political of poets, escaped that choice only by shutting herself up in her little house at Amherst for the last thirty years of her life, and refusing to publish her poems; she did not want to 'invest her snow'.

Short of that heroic, even saintly, abnegation, poets are subject, as are politicians, to 'the dirty devices of this world'. Auden understood the politician's problem because he too was a public figure:

> These public men who seem so to enjoy their dominion
> With their ruined faces and voices treble with hate,
> Are no less martyrs because unaware of their fetters.
> What would *you* be like, were you never allowed to create
> Or reflect, but compelled to give an immediate opinion,
> Condemned to destroy or distribute the work of your betters?

When I was finally resigned to my fate, I had a last fling of freedom in December 1951 on the way to the Council of Europe. During one glorious weekend, in Paris, Edna and I saw the incomparable Gerard Philipe in a school hall at Surêsnes giving his greatest performance as *Le Cid*, and watched the epicene Jean Louis Barrault with Madeleine Renaud in *Amphitryhon* and *Oedipe*. For films we chose Buñuel's first blockbuster *Los Olvidados* and De Sica's *Miracolo a Milano*. We went to *Le Lapin Agile* for its cabaret and basked once more in the Louvre and the Jeu de Paume.

A day later I had a phone call asking if I would accept nomination for a by-election in South East Leeds.

Chance plays a larger role in politics than in most walks of life. If I had not received that phone call in Strasbourg, I doubt whether I would have had another opportunity to fight a Labour seat for many years, particularly since at that time members of the staff at Transport House had to resign before putting their names on the candidates' list. So I would have had to take some other job, and that might well have trapped me in a different career.

Moreover, if the Attlee Cabinet had not been so tired – its key members had been in office since 1940 – they could have soldiered on at least until the economy turned for the better twelve months later. In that case, Labour might well have won the general election without me, and, like the Swedish Socialist Party, have remained in power for a generation. In fact, even in October 1951, the Labour Party got more votes than the Conservatives. Indeed it got more than any other party in British history, and a higher percentage of the national vote than in 1945 – 48.7 per cent – which was the highest share of the total vote received by any party since the war. Only a quirk in the way the votes were distributed between constituencies gave the Conservatives an overall majority of seventeen seats in Parliament. By this time, however, the Labour leaders were too tired even to complain. Exhaustion can sometimes play as important a role in politics as chance.

My by-election, too, was marked by a series of accidents which turned out lucky for me. The seat became vacant because the victorious Conservatives did not want the retiring Speaker to be replaced by his Deputy, Major Milner, the Labour MP for South East Leeds. So Milner was given a peerage in compensation, and gave up his seat in the Commons. The main claimant to the seat was a Labour councillor in Leeds, John Rafferty, who, as so often with local personalities, had as many enemies as friends. His enemies looked for an outsider to run against him. Solly Pearce, the editor of the *Leeds Weekly Citizen*, who had immense influence behind the scenes, liked the articles I had written for him from time to time, and knew I had done well in the nearby seat of Pudsey and Otley in 1945. Since I had no personal friends in the constituency, he got a member of my trade union, Councillor Cohen, to persuade the Leeds branch of the Jewish Labour Party, Poale Zion, to nominate me. The National Executive was furious that I was standing, and nominated a defeated Labour MP, Aidan Crawley, against me. Crawley sank without trace on the first ballot; he was unwise enough to boast to a Yorkshire audience that he had played cricket for Kent. He later found a seat as a Conservative.

In the final vote at the selection conference John Rafferty got twenty votes, while I and another man got ten votes each. The rules provide that a candidate must have an absolute majority of those voting. When successive ballots failed to break the deadlock, the selection conference was adjourned for a few weeks. At the second conference I had a comfortable majority.

The by-election itself was fairly tame, partly because of the appalling weather; snow and ice made canvassing unpleasant and even dangerous. When I called on the Bishop of Leeds, Joseph Heenan, he was able to tell me the date on which my grandfather had lapsed from the Roman Catholic church in Todmorden half a century before; I found this a little too reminiscent of the Communist Party. Nevertheless, although my Conservative opponent was a Catholic schoolmaster, the great majority of the Roman Catholics voted for me, since my name is Irish; in any case, Catholics in Britain vote according to their personal views. Though I have always supported the reform of the law which prohibited abortion, I have always had friendly relations with the Catholic priests in my constituency and with the hierarchy outside.

Otherwise my by-election was memorable only for two events which had nothing to do with it. I took an afternoon off to judge a speaking contest for young socialists, and chose as winner a bonny lass from Dewsbury who danced as a Tiller girl in the chorus of the local pantomimes: her name was Betty Boothroyd and she later became a Labour MP herself. She is now the Deputy Speaker of the House of Commons. The other event was even more historic. King George VI died two days before the poll, so our loudspeakers were silenced and we had to abandon our plans for the final burst of campaigning. It was inevitably a low poll; but I managed a small swing to Labour, and had a majority of 7,199.

I have held substantially the same seat ever since, despite boundary changes every few years, and the intervention of Liberal and Communist candidates from time to time. The only serious threat to my survival came with the redistribution of boundaries in 1955, only three years after my first election; I had to go through the whole procedure again, in even less auspicious circumstances.

The redistribution eliminated one of the Labour seats in Leeds altogether. Inside the Labour Party the Bevanite civil war was at its height. The Right wing of my local party was Bevanite, the Left wing was Trotskyite. The whole of the Left of the Labour Party in Leeds was determined to get rid of me as a right-wing anti-Bevanite. The selection conference in the new constituency of East Leeds took place a few days after the Parliamentary Labour Party had enraged constituency activists all over the country, by withdrawing the Whip from Nye Bevan. The first question put to me by a dour and grim-looking selection conference was how I had voted. I replied that they had no right to ask, but that in fact I had voted to withdraw the Whip. I told them that they would have done the same if any Labour councillor in Leeds had behaved as Bevan had in Westminster. They gave me a majority of two to one, and I have never had serious personal trouble with my constituency party since.

Of course we have frequently disagreed on policy. I have often had to quote the message sent to Frederick the Great by one of his generals, after being ordered to carry out a disastrous attack: 'Please tell his majesty that after the battle my head is at his disposal, but during the battle I propose to use it in his service.'

A member of Parliament who works hard in his constituency and is trusted as a human being by the active members of his local party can normally count on personal loyalty to override differences about policy. Yorkshire people are slow to accept outsiders. As an intellectual from London, and above all as a product of Transport House, which was then distrusted in the constituency parties as a citadel of reaction, it took time for me to win the confidence of my party activists. Edna's warm, outgoing personality made up for my own weaknesses. She worked hard in the constituency and spoke better than I at election meetings. At that time I could only make my audience think. She could make them laugh and cry.

Once I had established myself, however, I was invulnerable. I was particularly lucky in the character and quality of the key members of my local party. Douglas Gabb has been my agent ever since that first by-election, even when he was Lord Mayor of Leeds. We have grown up together with the constituency, and I have learned much from him. He was born in the poorest part of the city; his mother was an usher at the local theatre and he saw little of his father, who was a soldier. As a little boy during the recession he relied on a charity called 'Boots for the Bairns' for his footwear. He never forgot the humiliation of being made to stand in front of the class while his teacher described him as an object of charity, nor the pain of walking home in boots which would not bend at the ankle.

After selling theatre programmes for a while, he went at the age of fourteen to a stables in Newmarket to train as a jockey – he was small and wiry. His mother made him come home again after seeing Mickey Rooney beaten with a horsewhip during a race in some Hollywood film; so instead he trained as an engineer at the Yorkshire Copper Works. He remained an engineer the rest of his life, making aircraft during the war, tanks at the Royal Ordnance factory afterwards, and finally running the engineering laboratory at Leeds University.

The whole of his spare time was dedicated to unpaid work for the Labour Party, as a city councillor and as my agent. He refused to draw daily expenses as a councillor when they finally became available, and took only £50 at general elections as my agent, all of which he spent on his party work. For a time he earned a little extra as a milkman, getting up at five o'clock every morning, and his wife, Ivy, ran a small newsagents shop.

When we first met in 1952 Douglas was somewhat suspicious and prickly – and very left-wing. Today he is one of my closest friends. We disagree less on political matters than we used to, but he is as candid and direct as ever when we do disagree. He always thinks for himself, and once he has reached a conclusion, is totally dedicated to carrying it out. For example, he argued strongly for the sale of council houses long before it was acceptable in the Labour Party; he foresaw that pride in ownership would transform our council estates, and that Labour councils themselves would benefit financially from the change. In later years he somehow found time for other interests – ballroom dancing with his wife, playing an electric organ, gardening, and above all his family. Always trim and dapper, with sharp features, bright eyes and a wise smile, he symbolises for me everything that is best in the British Labour movement.

During the most difficult period in my own career, when many of my friends had deserted the Labour Party and I was forced into a divisive battle with Tony Benn to remain Deputy Leader, any thought of leaving was ruled out by my sense of loyalty to my friends in Leeds, like Douglas Gabb, who had been loyal to me and to the Labour Party over so many testing years. Ironically enough, after I had finally scraped home by an eyebrow, Dougie said to me: 'You know, Denis, if you'd been beaten I'd have left the Labour Party.'

My constituency was one of the handful first won by the newly formed Labour Party in 1906. In my early years there I had the privilege of working with several old men who had campaigned to make Jim O'Grady their MP almost half a century before. Jack Gallivan, a white-haired, craggy-featured Irishman, to whom Dougie Gabb had been apprenticed at the Yorkshire Copper Works, went back almost as far, and continued to work for the Party until his death at the age of ninety-two. Such pioneers set the tone of the local party as I first knew it.

Leeds at that time was much less familiar to me than Bradford, where I had been at school. As a boy in Keighley, like children all over the West Riding of Yorkshire, I saw Leeds as the metropolis – the great city where you could buy things which you could get nowhere else but in London. We went to Leeds to see plays before they opened in the West End, and to watch Yorkshire play cricket at Headingley; I once saw my hero, Don Bradman, caught out there. I remembered Roundhay Park for its great boating lake, where my small brother Terry alarmed us all by trying to walk on the water. I remembered the ancient mansion at Temple Newsam because it was the birthplace of Mary Queen of Scots' ill-fated husband, Darnley.

It was a city which had seen its share of history, from the Viking invasions, through the building of the beautiful Cistercian abbey at Kirkstall, to the civil wars. When Defoe travelled there in the early eighteenth century he found it a 'large, wealthy and populous town', and spent several pages of his journal on the cloth market, 'which is not to be equalled in the world' and exported cloth all over the globe, from St Petersburg to Virginia. Then the Industrial Revolution brought foundries, iron-works, engineering, and textile mills. The population exploded, from 15,000 to 207,000 in the hundred years to 1861, doubling again in the next fifty. Charles Dickens described Leeds as 'the beastliest place, one of the nastiest I know'. The housing was appalling, the dirt indescribable. Until the Clean Air Act in 1956 it was still one of the smokiest towns in Europe.

Leeds also produced some of the early campaigners against the conditions it represented. The Chartist, Fergus O'Connor, published the *Northern Star* in Leeds. 'King' Oastler got Parliament to pass the Ten Hours Act, which limited the working day of children who had previously got up at three thirty in the morning and worked till ten thirty at night, with only half an hour's break.

So when the Labour Party was formed, Leeds had a strong radical tradition for it to build on. Between the wars Labour's achievements, particularly in housing, were well-known throughout Europe; their guiding spirit was a Socialist parson, the Reverend Jenkinson. His memory was still fresh when I took the tram from City Station, past the Quarry Hill flats which were his main monument, to my first meeting with my local party.

The character of postwar Leeds was summed up by Tony Harrison, the city's best contemporary poet:

> Venus, Vulcan, Cupid stare
> out vacantly on City Square,
> and 'Deus iuvat impigros'
> above the bank where God helps those
> who help themselves, declares
> Leeds purposeful in its affairs.

My own constituency, East Leeds, was typical of a Labour seat in any provincial city. It had one middle-class ward on the edge of the lovely countryside surrounding Leeds, two solid working-class wards based on council housing estates, and one ward of uncertain allegiance, composed mainly of two-room back-to-back houses of red brick which were rented from private landlords; its tenants therefore felt a cut above the council tenants, although their living conditions were often much worse. In recent years one of the working-class wards fell to the Liberals, partly because the Labour council was held responsible for the bad housing, while the marginal ward swung towards Labour as immigrants from the sub-continent moved in. So East Leeds remains a Labour constituency, and my majority is still high.

Economic changes have transformed East Leeds like the rest of Britain. In 1952 it was the centre of the world's clothing industry. Burton was the world's biggest multiple tailor, with over six hundred outlets, and its biggest factory was in my constituency. My visits there at election time were a triumphal progress through rows of cheering women wearing red rosettes and red fancy garters, past machines festooned with red ribbons and 'Vote Healey' stickers, while my eyebrows glared down from enormous cartoons above every doorway.

Burton's was only one of several large clothing firms in East Leeds. Now all are closed. Burton itself failed to adapt to changes in men's fashion; it went on making three-piece suits long after people stopped wearing waistcoats, and failed to adapt to the growing taste for casual wear. The rest went under in the holocaust of Mrs Thatcher's first two years in office.

The other main source of local jobs in the fifties was engineering; that also went under in 1981, with so much else of manufacturing industry. Finally the Conservative Government sold off the Royal Ordnance factory at Barnbow to Vickers, thus creating a monopoly supplier of tanks for which it was itself the only customer – an odd decision for a Party which aimed to cut defence costs by enforcing competitive tendering. So unemployment on the council estates in East Leeds became exceptionally high; the service industries which took up some of the slack created by the decline of manufacturing did not require the old skills which the government had made redundant, and there was no provision for retraining.

Nevertheless, rising living standards brought social changes with them. By the mid-eighties nearly every home had fitted carpets and colour television, many had video recorders too, and foreign holidays were common; my local Labour Club sometimes found it cheaper to give its old-age pensioners a weekend in Benidorm than in Bridlington. The mass culture, now shared by the whole of the developed world, is weakening the old class barriers without destroying them; it has had a similar effect on regional differences. The popular television soap operas *Coronation Street* and *Eastenders* reflect the persistence of class as well as regional distinctions; indeed regional differences are more readily celebrated nowadays by television than they were after the war; in those days all radio announcers affected the same strangulated 'Oxford' English and regional accents were in England what a black face was in the United States – the sign of a comic inferiority. The only regional accents then accepted as normal on radio were Scottish and Canadian.

Despite all these economic and social changes the number and nature of the personal cases I have had to deal with has not greatly altered in nearly forty years. Like most MPs I have always represented over sixty thousand constituents. Their demands continue day in, day out, whether Parliament is sitting or not, like the problems which give rise to them.

Inadequate housing is still the biggest single cause of preventable human misery in Britain. Many broken marriages result from young couples being obliged to live with their parents while their families are growing, and from overcrowding in damp and filthy rooms. In 1952 the waiting list for council housing stretched out for twenty years. Despite herculanean programmes of house building by the local authority, it is still far too long. For many years the clearance of pre-war slums added to the list. Then defects in postwar housing created new problems – multi-storey flats totally unsuited to young families, houses which had to be pulled down because of defects in their design or construction, and above all, houses in which modern heating systems caused a horrific form of condensation, producing black mould on the walls and leaving clothes sopping wet in wardrobes. One visitor brought me some slugs in a jam jar from his kitchen. In the eighties, the great increase in the number of single-parent families and of people living alone added new problems, at a time when the Conservative Government was slashing finance for council housing.

My other main responsibility as a local MP was to compel government departments to carry out their own rules, particularly on questions of taxation and benefits. In one case out of every three or four I raised, the department had to admit its error. Since only a miniscule proportion of the population has the slightest idea what tax it should pay or what benefits it may draw, and very few of those who feel they have been unjustly treated bother to approach their MP, this suggests that the percentage of errors may be formidably high.

Indeed, when I was Chancellor I was told that if the Government introduced a certain change in benefits too quickly, a third of the cases might be mishandled for want of notice in the social security offices. The Cabinet ignored this warning and went ahead. Yet I never received one complaint on the issue as an MP in the following months. This may not, I fear, mean that the warning was unjustified – only that most of those affected were unaware of their rights.

There is almost nothing which happens in his constituency on which the MP may not be approached, and little on which it is absolutely impossible for him to help. With the rise in unemployment, the number of social security cases rose relative to housing; it rose again when the Government cut a series of benefits in 1988. Following cuts in the National Health Service, problems in the hospitals loomed larger than problems in the schools. In my early years, one Catholic school had to hold classes in the vestry of the church; more recently I found a mental hospital so overcrowded that there was no space between the beds. My admiration for the teachers and nurses who have to work in such conditions is unbounded. More recently, the problems of immigrants from the subcontinent added a new dimension to my work. Here again it was lightened by the dedication of those who worked for the immigrant communities, particularly in the Law Centres.

The most difficult problems of all were those on the fringe – of men or women who thought they had wrongly been committed to prison or to mental hospitals. There were the cases where I seemed powerless to help – the persistent criminal, the religious maniac, the addict who would rob to get the money for his drugs unless a friendly doctor would prescribe methadone, and a whole range of individuals who inhabited private hells.

Two well-spoken but deranged young sisters kept me chasing hares about their persecution by various public authorities for months; then by accident we discovered they had left their dead father in a chair in their council house sitting-room until he was almost mummified. Following up the case of a man who was organising robberies by young boys, we found him keeping hens and pigeons in the bedroom of his council house; the stench was unimaginable. Saddest of all was a handsome, distraught young woman who used to call on me with her little girl; she once threw a poem on my desk which described her misery all the better for its mistakes in spelling and prosody:

> Fourteen years ago you lost your baby, your husband and your pride
> You wanted to just sit in a dark room and hide.
> For that you where put in a padded cell
> That day started 'Fourteen years of HELL!'
> But god stayed by your side all the time. You realise that now!
> Yes he lead you, boy and how.
> He sent you an angle, your little girl who stands by you through thick
>   and thin
> She gives you the strength and courage you need to win.
> There's no adult who could, or will ever give what she has given
> A reason, yes a reason to go on living.
> She's only eight years old but her love and will power
> Give you strength to finish and to carry on, to do what you must do
>   and she makes you feel as tall as a TOWER!

People sometimes complain that since the war MPs have had to waste too much of their time as welfare officers. I profoundly disagree. Every MP should act as a Miss Lonelyhearts. The busier a politician is with national or international affairs, the more important is his constituency case work. It is that above all which keeps him in touch with the problems of those he is supposed to represent, and teaches him how legislation at Westminster actually affects real people on the ground – or how powerless it is to help them. Some of this case work could be done by others; many MPs leave it to their constituency secretaries. I believe this is a mistake; there are many cases where only the personal intervention of the MP himself can help. And this is perhaps the only part of his work where he may see concrete evidence that his existence is worthwhile. Since I first went to Leeds in 1952 I reckon I have dealt with at least twenty thousand individual cases; in perhaps six thousand I had some success. It was as worthwhile for me as it was for them.

My own constituency Labour Party was not immune to the changes taking place around it. At first it was dominated by members of the manual trade unions – engineers, garment workers, and railwaymen, with a sprinkling of miners. Now it is dominated by teachers, public employees, health and social service workers. In my early years our favourite meeting places were the Labour Clubs, most of which maintained fraternal relations with the Labour Party itself. Edna and I would spend many evenings sitting dazed and deafened below a pop group belting out the latest hits, through loudspeakers which must have been borrowed from the brainwashing cell in a North Korean prison camp. But we laughed as loud as the rest at the glorious breed of club comics, often as brilliant as any we had heard in the London music-halls, and much less inhibited. Few of the Labour Clubs now retain more than a vestigial interest in the Labour Party. Television, video, and the soaring cost of beer persuade more people to spend their evenings at home nowadays. Sometimes only striptease will entice them out.

My first headquarters in Leeds was a condemned terraced house of unimaginable squalor, with a lavatory outside which was full of filth and would not flush. I thought nothing could be worse until I fought my second election from another condemned property, which had sold pies and peas. When we opened the kitchen door we found ourselves submerged in a tide of rats which had grown fat on the leavings. Finally we got a loan from a brewery to build our own Labour Club, with our Party rooms attached. We now live in comfort, though we have to let out our meeting room as a day nursery to make ends meet; so a brightly coloured Mrs Mouse looks down on our deliberations – the only rats we meet are made of cotton-wool and flannel.

As a university city, Leeds had its quota of academics. Some of them were active in my local Party. Ashoke Banerjea, a Bengali lecturer in electrical engineering, was a brilliant inventor. He served for some time as my Party secretary; his restless energy and passion for organisation sometimes outstripped the human material available to him. His wife, Yvonne, was a teacher, and the daughter of a Durham miner; her common sense and wry humour nicely set off Ashoke's occasional over-enthusiasm.

Ashoke's successor as Party secretary was Doreen Hamilton, an energetic and dedicated educationalist, who as a councillor transformed nursery teaching in Leeds. Her husband, Max Hamilton, was Professor of Psychiatry at the University, and travelled the world to lecture on how to apply statistical analysis to the findings of case-work. He opened up new insights into the psychology of genius; all psychiatrists are now familiar with the Hamilton Scale for measuring depression.

My old tutor from Balliol, Charles Morris, was Vice-Chancellor of the University when I first came to Leeds. There he achieved his life-long ambition of marrying science with the arts in a single academic institution. However, I made most of my contacts with the University through Bernard and Rose Gillinson, with whom I have stayed on my visits to Leeds since first becoming an MP.

Each was an exceptional individual who made a major contribution to the cultural life of the city. Bernard was a natural academic who was compelled to spend his working life running a warehouse business started by his father, a Jewish immigrant from Eastern Europe. He dedicated his spare time to promoting the visual arts; Leeds was then surprisingly deficient in this field, though it had nurtured both Henry Moore and Barbara Hepworth, the two greatest British sculptors of our century. A discriminating collector, Bernard was a friend of Renato Guttuso and in 1955 David Hockney sold to Bernard his first painting – the excellent *Portrait of my Father*.

Hockney was then eighteen, and had just left Bradford Grammar School for the School of Art. He was amazed to be offered ten pounds for his work. 'It was a great deal of money,' he records, 'and as my father had bought the canvas I thought, it's really his painting, it's his canvas – I'd just done the marks on it. So I phoned him up and said There's a man who'd like to buy this picture, can I sell it? And he said Ooh, yes. He thought it was because of him you see, and he said You can do another.'

A Leeds businessman had just established annual fellowships at the University for a sculptor, a painter, and a poet. At Bernard's regular parties for these Gregory Fellows, I met some outstanding artists – particularly the sculptors Reg Butler and Kenneth Armitage, and the painter Terry Frost. They kindled my interest in non-figurative art; I fear that I found their sparkling vitality an agreeable contrast to the dull predictability of some of my political colleagues. But Terry Frost told me a story which shows how easy it is to misjudge politicians. He had been a prisoner of war in Germany with another working-class boy, Fred

Mulley. Terry used his captivity to learn painting, Fred to study economics. When the war was over Fred was given a grant to pursue his
studies at Oxford; he spent part of his grant to buy Terry's first
paintings, so that he too could follow his calling.

Bernard Gillinson's wife, Rose, came from a wealthy Jewish family in
St Petersburg, which had gone to Palestine after the revolution. She
maintained her Russian connections in Leeds as well, and was a close
friend of Prokofiev's wife and her son, an abstract painter. The efferves-
cent Russian conductor, Nikolai Malko, enlivened my weekends when he
was in Leeds. A great beauty of irresistible energy, Rose loved organising
art exhibitions, particularly from foreign countries. Between them,
Bernard and Rose Gillinson transformed the standing of art in Leeds.

Unlike Bradford, Leeds came late to the arts, but like Bradford, it
owed much of its artistic reputation to its Jewish citizens. Unlike the
German Jews who brought their wealth and culture to Bradford in the
mid-nineteenth century, the Jews who were driven out of Russia and
Eastern Europe by the pogroms at the end of the century were desperately
poor; they had little time for anything but making money. But the
children of men such as Simon Marks, who built up Marks and Spencer
from a penny-stall in Leeds Market, and Montagu Burton, who started
the greatest multiple tailoring industry in the world at Leeds, used their
creative talents in many directions. Among my friends, Stanley Burton
helped painters and musicians, while Fanny Waterman started the Leeds
International Piano Competition.

The large Jewish community in Leeds always had good relations with
the equally large community of Irish Catholics, who played a major role
in local politics though not in the arts. Many of the Irish lived in my
constituency. I often held my 'surgeries' in Catholic church halls while
children were practising Irish dances for their festival, the Feis. Among
my best friends were Councillor Joe Moynihan and his wife Mary, who
always gave me lunch in the middle of my surgeries on a Saturday. One
morning as I entered their room the daylight was suddenly blotted out, as
an incredible hulk rose in front of the window. It was Mary's brother,
Jimmy Moran, an all-in wrestler who fought all over Europe under the
name Gargantua, specialising in the role of the baddy; all-in wrestling is
choreographed as carefully as ballet, its music provided by carefully
timed grunts and groans. Jimmy had a husky, sepulchral voice and an
exceptionally gentle personality. I asked him how long he would go on in
his profession. 'As long as my voice holds out,' was his reply.

I had many friends among the Protestant clergy. The Vicar of Halton,

Ernest Southcott, exercised a powerful influence on me. A tall, gaunt Canadian with black hair, a dark-brown face, hooked nose, and an enchanting smile, he would walk or cycle round the council estates in a long black cassock. He held services regularly in his parishioners' homes, and for many years I adapted his 'house church' for my political meetings. Ernie's Christianity was numinous, and he impressed me more than any priest I have met. His genius was for pastoral work. When he was moved to the clerical politics of Southwark Cathedral as Provost, he was cut off from his natural roots and had a nervous breakdown. They gave him an undemanding parish in Lancashire, but he died a few years later.

I can well understand why many men and women enter politics just to be good constituency MPs. That was never my prime purpose. But anything I may have achieved in other fields would have been poorer if I had not been able to derive strength and understanding from the people of East Leeds.

CHAPTER SEVEN

Party Politician

We, who seven years ago
Talked of honour and of truth,
Shriek with pleasure if we show
The weasel's twist, the weasel's tooth.

– 'Nineteen Hundred and Nineteen'
W. B. Yeats

ON FEBRUARY 19TH, 1952 I shook hands with the policeman at St Stephen's entrance to the House of Commons and entered Parliament for the first time as an MP. I was then thirty-five years old. Parliament has been my base ever since. John Freeman, now deputy editor of the *New Statesman*, speculated on the wisdom of my move from Transport House; he wondered whether I had simply exchanged the shadow for the shadow. For a long time I shared his doubts. It is often said that Parliament is a place where you can neither work nor rest. That was even more true in the early fifties than it is today.

Despite the upheavals caused by the Labour landslide in 1945, the House of Commons was still run on the assumption that politics was something which wealthy gentlemen did in their spare time; Parliament was simply the best club in London. There were some MPs who never spoke in the chamber and never asked a question, turning up only to vote on three-line whips, if then. It was said that one or two never visited their constituencies between general elections.

My salary in 1952 was only £1,000 a year, and was intended to cover all my expenses as an MP. I had no allowance for a secretary and had to pay for all my letters and telephone calls. Until I became a Cabinet minister in 1964 I wrote all my letters by hand – something much appreciated by my constituents, who attributed it to principle rather than to penury. I did not even have a desk to myself; if I was not able to grab a seat at one of the tables in the library, I had to work on a bench in the corridor with my papers on my knees.

Many Conservative MPs were company directors; their firms provided them with secretaries, cars, and offices. Some Labour MPs got help from the trade unions which sponsored them. The rest, like me, had to earn enough extra to support their families by some means which did not require them to spend too much time outside Parliament; that is why so many MPs were lawyers or journalists. Even a legal practice became difficult as constituency burdens increased and there were more and more three-line whips. Writing, radio and television were then the most convenient sources of extra income; I used all three.

As the years passed, the number of wealthy people on the Conservative benches diminished, as did the number of trade unionists on the Labour side. So the backbenchers of both parties united in demanding fairer pay and conditions – often against the will of both Labour and Conservative governments. MPs are now treated financially like middle-ranking members of the civil service, which is probably the best compromise available for an occupation which accommodates the extremes of overwork and idleness. But we are still a good deal worse off than the members of most other parliaments. In the fifties the confrontation between Capital and Labour was reflected in the physical appearance of the opposing sides in the House of Commons. It is now far more difficult to distinguish members of the two parties by their looks – or indeed their background. The majority on both sides are obviously middle-class.

From Monday afternoon to Friday morning, particularly when the government had a small majority and the whips were strict, I was tied to the Parliament buildings. Though backbenchers now have offices as well as the library to work in, many still spend hours every day in exchanging political gossip. The Members' Tea Room is said to be the centre of conspiracy for the Labour Party; I am not sure, since it is well known that I am unique in going there only when I want a cup of tea. The Smoking Room, which serves alcoholic drink, is favoured by ambitious Tories; I never go there at all. There are other bars which serve more normal social functions. These unusual working conditions help to explain why some MPs have a drink problem, and others cause a commotion by leaving their wives for their secretaries; occasionally those who fail to leave their wives for their secretaries cause an even greater commotion.

I suppose the average man believes that MPs spend most of their time in the Chamber of the House of Commons, making speeches. In fact, as a backbencher, I was lucky to make four speeches a year in the Chamber – and often for only five minutes, after waiting to speak for two days. I found it almost equally difficult to ask a question of a minister; each minister answers questions only once a month, and there are often ten times more questions on the Order Paper than there is time for. The Prime Minister answers questions for a quarter of an hour twice a week, when the chance of a particular question being reached is even smaller.

In my early years, like most MPs, I nevertheless spent a lot of my time in the Chamber, listening to debates even when I had no intention of speaking myself. And there was much worth listening to, particularly in my own field of foreign affairs. It was normal to have four or five major foreign affairs debates a year, in which controversial issues were hotly contested by a crowded Chamber for two days at a time. And there were a few exceptionally brilliant speakers who could be relied on to fill the Chamber whatever the subject – not only party leaders, like Churchill and Bevan, but also backbenchers like Bob Boothby and Dick Crossman, then at his best. I think the greatest parliamentary speech I ever heard was by Enoch Powell in 1959, castigating the Macmillan Government over the murder of African prisoners at Hola camp in Kenya; it had all the moral passion and rhetorical force of Demosthenes.

Winston Churchill was Prime Minister my first three years in the House. That astonishing phenomenon was past his best, and failing rapidly. But he was still capable of flashes of insight, such as his call for a summit meeting with Malenkov immediately after Stalin's death; I opposed it at the time, but now regard it as a historic opportunity missed. Churchill's sense of humour was unimpaired. When he visited Athens at the end of the war to look over the Greek politicians, he was much impressed by an old gentleman with a white moustache and a military bearing. His aide pointed out the name of General Plastiras on the list in front of him. 'Plasterass, Plasterass,' he mused. 'I hope he hasn't got feet of clay too.'

He described one of his thrusting backbenchers as 'that rising young stench', and Albert Bossom as 'neither one thing nor the other'. A friend of mine was present when he met the Papal Nuncio at the European Congress of the Hague. They shook hands. Winston had forgotten his cigar was still alight and the Nuncio was badly stung. As he rubbed his palm Winston looked at him and chuckled, growling: 'I imagine this is the first time in European history that a Protestant has burnt a Catholic in the Low Countries.'

Churchill's sense of history gave him a special insight into the problems of his own time. When Eden went to Chartwell to tell him of his plans for attacking Suez, Winston immediately walked to the bookcase, pulled down an atlas, and showed him exactly where Napoleon had launched his assault on Egypt a century and a half earlier. As I have already mentioned, Churchill also had the artist's capacity to see a complicated issue as a whole. His little manual, *Painting as a Pastime*, is not only the best guide for any amateur who wants to paint; it also contains much wisdom for a budding politician. For example, he compares painting with the art of war:

'It is the same kind of problem as unfolding a long, sustained, interlocking argument. It is a proposition which, whether of few or numberless parts, is commanded by a single unity of conception.'

The same applies to politics and the arts. Among postwar British politicians, Bevin was perhaps the only one to share this understanding with Churchill. Schnabel was the supreme interpreter of Beethoven for the same reason; he kept the architecture of the whole sonata in his mind as he played each bar.

Churchill was also capable of extraordinary lapses of judgment. He had a brutal contempt for Gandhi as a 'malignant subversive fanatic'. He wrote in 1931, 'It is alarming and also nauseating to see Mr Gandhi, a seditious Middle Temple lawyer, now posing as a fakir of a type well known in the East, striding up the steps of the Vice-Regal Palace.' Less well-remembered are his views of fascism in the early thirties. 'I think of Germany,' he cried in 1933, 'with its splendid, clear-eyed youth demanding to be conscripted into an army burning to suffer and die for their Fatherland. I think of Italy, with her ardent Fascists, her renowned chief, and stern sense of national duty.' Even in 1943 he decided to protect Italian war criminals and to support the Italian king who had decorated them for their crimes, because he believed: 'There is nothing between the king and the patriots who have rallied around him, and rampant Bolshevism.'

Like many great men, including my own favourites, Bevin and Roosevelt, Churchill had defects on the same scale as his virtues. But his virtues made up for a lot. Not only in 1940, but again and again throughout the war, his contribution to victory was decisive. He added a vision and poetry to British politics which enriched the lives of all who had the luck to see and hear him in action.

When he returned as Prime Minister in 1951 he confined himself largely to foreign policy, leaving Rab Butler to bring the Conservative

Party into the second half of the twentieth century. They made an odd, but not unsuccessful, partnership, despite a long-standing mutual hostility. In 1940 Butler had lamented Churchill's arrival at No. 10 with the words: 'The good clean tradition of English politics of Pitt rather than Fox has been sold to the greatest adventurer in modern history . . . a half-breed American.'

Eden, by contrast, was never more than a good plain cook. Even his diplomatic expertise deserted him as Prime Minister; he saw Nasser simply as a second-rate Mussolini and betrayed an inexplicable insensitivity to the feelings not only of the Arabs, whom he regarded with disdain, but also of his American allies. When I made my first speech from the Labour Front Bench in 1954, he paid it an exceptionally generous tribute, which included the words: 'It was all the Foreign Office's best briefs rolled into one, and expressed much better than they are usually put before me.' No other politician would have regarded that as a compliment! Churchill once remarked on the draft of a speech which Eden had handed him for approval: 'Anthony, I think that oration contains every cliché in the English language except "Please adjust dress before leaving".'

Eden was succeeded by Macmillan, one of the great actor-managers. History will put him alongside Harold Wilson as a superlative politician, though his speech on the wind of change in Africa gives him some claim to a higher ranking. His taste for play-acting was sometimes misplaced. When he tried to repeat his triumph over President Kennedy on Polaris with a similar sentimental appeal to De Gaulle over the Common Market, the General was not impressed; he told his colleagues afterwards in Paris: 'The poor old fellow looked so woebegone, I felt like singing to him like Edith Piaf, "Ne Pleurez Pas, Milord".'

I had little personal contact with these Conservative leaders, but found myself seeing a good deal of some of the younger Tories, particularly Reggie Maudling, Julian Amery, Enoch Powell, and Ted Heath. Powell and I were often required to represent opposing views by the media. In 1954 he wrote an article for the *Twentieth Century*, to which I was a regular contributor; it started characteristically with the words 'Queen Anne is not dead', and ended by saying that Britain should leave NATO and concentrate its military efforts on helping France to stay in Indochina. My reply began with a point which remained true until Mrs Thatcher tore up the Conservative tradition by the roots and attempted to replant it in the soil tilled by Adam Smith and the Manchester Liberals:

'The owl of Minerva only flies abroad when the shades of night are gathering.' Speaking for Conservatism, Hegel was right. And nothing proves it better than the postwar crop of Tory intellectuals, sprouting like mushrooms in the damp cellars of Abbey House. Not until the stimuli which originally conditioned Conservative reflexes have finally disappeared, can the intellectual emerge to provide a rationale for Conservative behaviour. So Conservative theory must always base itself on some form of historical restorationism. The moderate seeks the world of Joseph Chamberlain – or if he is daring, of Disraeli. The really advanced radical looks still further back, to Prince Rupert, or the Middle Ages, particularly if he is a Catholic.

I was thinking here of Christopher Hollis and John Biggs-Davison.

Enoch Powell was unique in the absolutism of the intellectual and moral propositions on which he based his arguments. When he was Professor of Greek at Sydney his colleagues used to call him 'the textual pervert'. He built glass towers of dazzling logical integrity, whose foundations in the real world became more and more precarious as they rose higher and higher. In politics as in life, a logical conclusion is usually a reductio ad absurdum.

Not all the mushrooms from Abbey House were so abstract in their reasoning. Reggie Maudling was a brilliant pragmatist whose idleness was not wholly affected: like Asquith, he could think so much faster than most people that he always had plenty of spare time. In the end his carelessness was his undoing; but his retirement from politics was a loss to his country as well as his party. Ted Heath appeared to many as the Widmerpool of politics – a man for whom luck and application made up for a lack of natural distinction. I do not believe this does justice either to the depth of his commitment, particularly on the Common Market, or to the imagination he has shown on international affairs, particularly over Communist China. His party has suffered greatly from his inability to reconcile himself to his defeat by Mrs Thatcher. The British people will not tolerate a sulker.

Julian Amery, who, like Ted Heath, had been a friend of mine at Balliol, never realised his early promise. He could not adjust his thinking to the realities of the postwar world; his wartime experiences with the Albanian resistance had left him locked in the imperial dream which his father Leo, as Colonial Secretary, had implanted in him. He longed for the life of Richard Hannay, which he had once shared in the Balkans with many of his friends, such as Billy Maclean, the MP for Inverness.

My first ten years in Parliament, however, were dominated by the internal divisions of the Labour Party, which prevented it from mounting an effective attack on the Conservative Government until Harold Wilson became leader in 1962.

Even at the time, I recognised that Bevin's death in 1951 marked a watershed in the history of the Labour Party. In an obituary article for my Norwegian paper *Arbeiderbladet* I pointed out that in Bevin the trade unions had lost their last powerful representative in the Party's inner councils and that the leaders Labour had inherited from the thirties were all on the way out. While Attlee, Bevin, Morrison, Cripps, Dalton and Bevan dominated a Labour Government, little could grow in their shadow; rebellion or journalism were the only avenues to fame; all the newcomers to the constituency section of the National Executive were middle-class journalists who supported Nye Bevan's revolt against the Labour establishment – Michael Foot, Tom Driberg, Ian Mikardo and Barbara Castle.

> By his conduct of the campaign against the Labour Government Aneurin Bevan has destroyed a good chance of succeeding to the Party's leadership. Whereas Bevan's proletarian virility has always hypnotised many middle-class intellectuals, the trade unionists tend to see in him the familiar figure of the self-seeking agitator . . . Bevanism is essentially a flight from reality into dogma. But its opponents have had little to offer as a positive alternative. The Great Debate in British Socialism has so far consisted in one side talking nonsense and the other side keeping mum.
>
> The Labour Party may hope to carry the Welfare State and planning further than the Tories, but for a long time physical and psychological factors will fix rigid limits. Further 'soaking the rich' will no longer benefit the poor to any noticeable extent. Further nationalisation no longer attracts more than a tiny fringe of the Labour Party itself; it positively repels the electorate as a whole. Even among Labour economists there is a growing revolt against physical controls in favour of the price mechanism. A policy based on class war cannot have a wide appeal when the difference between classes is so small as Labour has made it.

I have quoted at length from my words in 1951, because they are just as true nearly forty years later. The real tragedy of Bevanism in the fifties, as of Bennery in the eighties, was that it distracted Labour from tackling the problems created by the social changes which the Attlee Government produced, and by the secular decline of Britain as a world power. Moreover, by posing the issues in terms of a theological disputation about the religion of Socialism, it cut the Labour Party off from its natural roots, not least among the working class itself. It was a reversion to the romantic Messianism which led to the defeat of the first Socialist movements in Europe in 1848.

Bevan himself was less guilty of 'odium theologicum' than his supporters, particularly those who wrote in the weekly, *Tribune*, which then abandoned the pragmatic idealism which distinguished it after the war for a spiteful sectarianism.

Even *In Place of Fear*, which Bevan wrote in the white heat of his resignation, exhibits a broad-minded tolerance and intellectual imagination quite foreign to many of his disciples. At the same time he was too impatient of reality. There was a temperamental incompatibility between him and some of his Cabinet colleagues which finally exploded when, having seen Morrison take Bevin's place as Foreign Secretary, he was once again passed over after Cripps' death in favour of Hugh Gaitskell, who seemed to him to have come from nowhere and to have no roots in the movement.

The two men might have been chosen by my schoolboy guru, Woelfflin, to embody the Romantic and the Classical as political types – like Fox and Pitt, or Lloyd George and Asquith. Yet the 'desiccated calculating machine', as Bevan called Gaitskell in a cruel phrase which lacked all understanding of the man, recognised Bevan's virtues no less than his faults. On February 15th, 1951 Bevan wound up the defence debate in Parliament with a speech in which, unlike Attlee and Gaitskell himself, he made a categorical public commitment to the full rearmament programme, against which he later resigned in protest. Gaitskell described it thus:

> Nye gave one of his most brilliant performances . . . glittering with
> striking phraseology . . . What a tragedy that a man with such wonderful
> talent as an orator and such an interesting mind and fertile imagination
> should be such a difficult team worker, and some would say even worse
> – a thoroughly unreliable and disloyal colleague.

Ernest Bevin has been less charitable. When another Cabinet minister described Bevan as his own worst enemy he muttered sourly: 'Not while I'm alive, he ain't.'

What most infuriated me at the time was what I saw as Bevan's irresponsibility about defence and his deliberate exploitation of the anti-Americanism always latent in the Labour Party. We fought a marathon duel on this one summer evening in 1952 in the presence of Helen Gahagan Douglas, the attractive wife of the film star Melvyn Douglas; she had recently lost her seat as a liberal senator for California to Richard Nixon; Nixon never lived down the reputation he then established in a campaign of dishonest and ferocious slander. Helen Douglas watched goggle-eyed as Nye and I slashed at one another, first at the home of our host from the American Embassy, then on the terrace of the House of Commons until well after midnight. He called me 'a red-faced boy from Transport House'; I doubt if I was more complimentary about him.

Our next major confrontation came at the Morecambe Conference of the Labour Party that autumn, which marked a high point in Bevan's campaign. Morrison and Dalton were swept off the Executive by the constituency parties; Jim Griffiths was the only non-Bevanite to keep his seat. The union delegates were overwhelmingly against Bevan, however; so tempers ran high throughout the week. I attacked Bevan's anti-Americanism as just 'jingoism with an inferiority complex. A man who can get up in 1952,' I cried, 'and say that men like those fifteen million American trade unionists are afraid of peace because it might mean unemployment is committing a crime against international socialism ... I ask you to throw away the stale mythology of these political Peter Pans ... We cannot solve the problems of foreign policy on a diet of rhetorical candy-floss.'

The Morecambe Conference produced a big swing against Bevan among Labour voters, as well as in the country at large. Gaitskell decided that the time had come for him to speak out. He did so the following weekend at Stalybridge, in a speech which he discussed only with Solly Pearce when he drafted it in the offices of the *Leeds Weekly Citizen*. It contained two phrases which, in my view, cast doubt on his suitability as a party leader. He seemed to endorse a ridiculous estimate by a journalist for the Liberal *News Chronicle* that about a sixth of the constituency party delegates appeared to be communists; and he said: 'It is time to end the attempt at mob rule by a group of frustrated journalists.' Yet it was the Stalybridge speech which won him the succession to Attlee; it persuaded Arthur Deakin, Bevin's successor as head of the Transport and General Workers' Union, and other powerful union leaders, that Gaitskell was the man to back. The Labour MPs who in those days elected the Party leader on their own, saw Gaitskell as by far the best man to lead them to victory in the next election. He won by 157 to 70 for Bevan; Morrison got only 40 votes.

Attlee scarcely played any role in the struggle against Bevanism. He saw it as his job to keep the party together while the others fought it out. He was an odd man, whom few, even of his closest colleagues, really understood. Wilfred Fienburgh used to say that a conversation with an ordinary man was like a game of tennis; a conversation with Attlee was like throwing biscuits to a dog – all you could get out of him was yup, yup, yup. Attlee's only interests outside politics were cricket and his public school, Haileybury. He favoured anyone who came from Haileybury, such as Chris Mayhew and Geoffrey de Freitas, rather as Ernest Bevin favoured people such as Oliver Franks and Bill Braine, because they came from Bristol.

One of Attlee's few general statements about politics was that the Labour Party should always be led from Left of Centre. That was one reason why he stayed on until it was clear in 1955 that Herbert Morrison would not succeed him. However, I doubt if he was altogether happy to see Hugh Gaitskell take his place. Edna happened to be standing next to Attlee at Hugh Gaitskell's New Year Party in Hampstead after Hugh had taken over. Attlee called for silence and raised his glass in a toast to the new leader of the Labour Party. Hugh rushed in from the next room, where he had been serving drinks, and stammered: 'Oh, Clem, thank you, I never expected this.'

'And you'd no right to,' muttered Clem under his breath, just loud enough for Edna to hear.

Like me, all the other Labour MPs from Leeds were firm supporters of Hugh Gaitskell throughout his leadership. Alice Bacon, the MP for South East Leeds after the 1955 redistribution, was immensely valuable to him since she was also a member of the women's section of the National Executive Committee. She was a miner's daughter from Normanton who became a schoolmistress. A bonny Yorkshire lass of immense common sense and strong character, she had more than a touch of Jane Eyre about her. No Rochester ever entered her life, but she had a personal devotion to Hugh Gaitskell which went beyond politics. As Chairman of the Party's organisation sub-committee, which was responsible for discipline, she and the National Agent, Sarah Barker, another Yorkshire woman, were the terror of the Trotskyites. They expelled some members of my own constituency party during Gaitskell's most difficult period; at that time he could not visit Leeds without being assaulted by a crowd of students and university lecturers – I recall one of them actually spitting at him as he entered his hotel.

Charlie Pannell, the member for West Leeds, was a cockney engineer who succeeded in establishing himself in that difficult Yorkshire constituency without ever holding a surgery there. The Amalgamated Engineering Union, at that time under the leadership of the right-wing Bill Carron, was totally committed to Gaitskell.

Hugh himself, though member for South Leeds, stayed mainly, like me, with the Gillinsons after he became leader; so I came to know him well. I was never a member of his inner circle, like Tony Crosland and Roy Jenkins; nor did I join the Campaign for Democratic Socialism set up later by Bill Rodgers and Brian Walden to promote what they thought should have been his cause. I was worried by a streak of intolerance in Gaitskell's nature; he tended to believe that no one could disagree with him unless they were either knaves or fools. Rejecting Dean Rusk's advice, he would insist on arguing to a conclusion rather than to a decision. Thus he would keep meetings of the Shadow Cabinet going, long after he had obtained its consent to his proposals, because he wanted to be certain that everyone understood precisely why he was right. In the political world a leader must often be content with acquiescence; he is sometimes wise to leave education to his juniors.

I myself was young enough to indulge in educational activities – speaking, writing articles, and broadcasting to spread my gospel. Gaitskell took my views on foreign policy seriously. I think I helped to form his position on Suez, the Common Market, Russia, and the atomic bomb. Most of his Godkin lecture on disengagement was written by me. If he had become Prime Minister I would probably have become his Foreign Secretary, after Harold Wilson had held the job for a year or two; and he told close friends that he thought I would be the best person to succeed him as Party leader. Nevertheless, I have always doubted whether the fierce puritanism of his intellectual convictions would have enabled him to run a Labour Government for long, without imposing intolerable strains on so anarchic a Labour movement.

Gaitskell's first sponsor in politics was Hugh Dalton – for many years they were referred to a Big Hugh and Little Hugh. Like Dalton, he had something undeveloped in his personality – a trace of the undergraduate. In his case it was expressed in a passion for the more frivolous social activities which used to be described as 'night life'. He loved dancing, and would go to immense efforts to indulge his appetite late at night, when his companions were dying of fatigue and wanted nothing more than a good sleep. I was once in Paris with him and going off to bed, when he suddenly decided to look up some mutual friends, then working at the Quai D'Orsay, in the hope they would join us for a night out. We reached their address at about half past eleven and could get no reply. So he threw pebbles up at their window until they finally appeared in their dressing gowns. They were glacially polite in declining his invitation to the waltz.

During a visit to Yugoslavia with Sam Watson, the Durham miner, and Edna, we found ourselves in the provincial town of Lubljana – a sort of Slovenian Stoke-on-Trent. Hugh nagged our interpreter for the address of a night-club. With reluctance he finally agreed to order our driver to the local skyscraper – a dingy building about seven storeys high. We took the lift to the top floor and were admitted after scrutiny through a spy-hole. It was a garish room like a small café, with a few women sitting listlessly at rickety tables while a three-piece band played Palm Court music in a corner. Hugh grabbed Edna and whirled her remorselessly round the floor. Sam and I sat yawning at our table until Sam turned to me and said; 'I don't know about you, Denis, but my pants are full of little flies.'

Our visit to the Soviet Union in 1959 with Nye Bevan presented us with a different problem. For the first and only time to my knowledge, Hugh Gaitskell got drunk. It was at the final banquet in a *kolkhoz* outside Moscow; the interminable toasts on these occasions are a strain on the most disciplined constitution. When we got back to our hotel we found that Macmillan had just announced a general election. The press wanted a statement immediately from Hugh. Try as we might, we could not wake him up, so Nye took the press conference. At no time during Hugh's life did Nye or anyone else reveal the secret – such magnanimity is not universal in politics.

In fact that trip to the Soviet Union was the first time Hugh had an easy relationship with Nye – and I myself then developed a warm friendship with Nye which lasted until his death the following year. In those last months his conversations had an autumnal, philosophical tone, which suggested he might already have had subconscious knowledge of his cancer. He performed one more great service to Hugh and to the Party when he rescued Hugh from disaster at the winter conference in Blackpool, which followed our defeat in the 1959 election. His speech on that occasion was a masterpiece of virtuoso rhetoric, almost without intellectual content; it was devoted solely to establishing his personal solidarity with the man who had been his victorious rival for so long.

Gaitskell himself died at the age of fifty-six, just over three years later. Politics is one of the most demanding professions. It tends to kill many of its most active leaders before they are sixty. Those who survive often live beyond ninety.

As so often with politicians, Hugh received an outburst of affection and respect in death which he rarely encountered while he was alive. Attlee went to his memorial service in Westminster Abbey. As we walked across from the House of Commons he told me he had expected Hugh to go to his.

Harold Wilson won the succession without great difficulty, against George Brown and Jim Callaghan. The one man who might have beaten him at that time was Alf Robens; but Robens had left politics in 1961 for a peerage and chairmanship of the Coal Board. Chance as so often played the winning hand.

We used to describe the period of Conservative government from 1951 to 1964 as 'Thirteen Wasted Years'. The first eleven of those years were wasted by the Labour Party. Our bitter internal wrangling at that time gave us a reputation for division and extremism from which we have not yet recovered. Many of our difficulties were inherent in the unique structure and constitution of the party, which was well analysed by Bob Mackenzie, my erstwhile comrade from the CCF. His seminal work, *British Political Parties* was written in 1955; it is still a good introduction to the subject, although the Conservatives as well as Labour have made some important changes in their constitutional arrangements since then.

I sometimes think that the critical difference between a democracy and a dictatorship is that in a dictatorship there are only two people out of every hundred who take a personal interest in politics; in a democracy there are three. The political parties must depend for their organisation largely on voluntary workers. But a man or woman who will give up night after night after working all day to argue politics in a draughty schoolroom, or to canvas from door to door in the wind and rain, is exceptionally rare, and is by that very fact untypical of the ordinary voter.

The average Conservative activist is usually prepared to forswear a direct influence on his party's policy, providing he is able once a year to applaud his leaders and vote for hanging and flogging at the annual jamboree of his party conference. Not so the average Labour activist. He has always demanded control of his party's policy, and has tended to distrust his leaders ever since 1931, when Ramsay Macdonald made common cause with the Tories.

As far back as 1930, while he was a member of the second Labour Government, Sidney Webb observed: 'the constituency parties are frequently unrepresentative groups of nonentities dominated by fanatics and cranks, and extremists; if the block vote of the Trade Unions were eliminated it would be impracticable to continue to vest the control of policy in Labour Party Conferences.'

This fear, as well as the need for trade union money, explains why the Labour Party clung for so long to a constitution which must be the weirdest in the world. In 1959, when the party lost its third general election in a row, it claimed under 900,000 individual members, though there were actually many fewer. These cast over a million votes at the conference (since each constituency's membership was rounded up to the nearest thousand), electing seven members to the constituency section of the National Executive. The trade unions affiliated over five and a half million members to the Labour Party, and elected twelve members to the Executive. An anomalous group of Socialist Societies, of which the most important then were the Fabians, the Royal Arsenal Cooperative Society and Poale Zion, the Jewish labour party, with under ten thousand members between them, elected one member. What guaranteed trade union domination on policy, is that five women were elected to the Executive by the conference as a whole, which meant effectively by the trade unions, since they outnumbered the rest by nearly six to one.

The oddity of these arrangements, which still persist, is compounded by what lies behind the voting in each section of the conference. Every trade union casts its vote as a block; thus the Transport and General Workers' Union casts over a million votes as one, however varied the views of its members. Moreover, the union leaders are under no obligation to consult their members on how their votes are cast. In practice the views of the union's national executive are usually decisive; so a change in one individual on the union's executive may shift over a million votes – and frequently has.

The constituency member's views may well be similarly ignored. The individual members in a constituency rarely number more than five hundred nowadays, or one for every thirty Labour voters; out of these it is rare to find more than fifty attending the management committee meetings which mandate delegates to conference. So twenty-six members may decide how a thousand votes are cast. These twenty-six are rarely typical of Labour voters, or even of Labour Party members. Compared with the days of Sidney Webb, there are nowadays innumerable other ways in which even people interested in politics may prefer to spend their time – above all, in watching television. I have often argued that on polling day Labour's real enemy is not the Tories but *Crossroads* or *Coronation Street*.

The passionate commitment required to tear men and women away from such distractions – and from their families – makes them impatient of the practical obstacles which lie between them and their ideals. They are also often ignorant of the issues and personalities on which they must decide. Tom Driberg was elected year after year by the constituency parties, largely on the strength of articles he wrote for *Reynolds News* during the war, when he was a member of the Communist or Commonwealth Parties, although he was a grossly promiscuous homosexual and gave the information he gained on the Executive both to MI5 and to the Russians.

The small attendance at constituency party meetings makes it easy for a tiny group who are well organised to capture the constituency as a whole, even when they belong to a body outside the Labour Party and hostile to its objectives. In my early years such groups were usually Communist, often from front organisations, such as the innumerable societies for peace and friendship with the Soviet Union or the satellite states. Following the Hungarian rising, various Trotskyite organisations took their place. However, Alice Bacon and Sarah Barker succeeded in getting rid of the external infiltrators – from my own constituency among several others.

In those days the trade union block votes at conference could usually be relied on to defeat extremist resolutions from the constituency parties. In any case a successful resolution was not regarded as party policy unless it got at least two thirds of the votes, and even then was not included in the election programme unless agreed at a joint meeting of the National Executive and Shadow Cabinet – the latter elected by the Labour MPs. But, of course, once the television cameras were admitted, what happened at conference tended to receive more publicity than the words in an election manifesto. Bitter attacks by the Left on the party leaders were always grist to the Tory mill. They reached a new level of ferocity at the Blackpool conference after our defeat in 1959.

When Benn Levy, who had lost the safe Conservative seat of Chelsea, publicly accused Gaitskell of moral ineptitude at best, and at worst of crass hypocrisy, Charlie Pannell rose to his defence:

> I had hoped to come to a great religious revival: instead of that, I find myself in the middle of the biggest belly-ache I have ever come across. They might not understand nationalisation in Chelsea, because there is none of it where Benn Levy comes from. But I represent a seat which is in the cradle of the industrial revolution, and where they understand

that 'where there's muck, there's money' . . . Wherever a candidate
faced the electorate where there was potential nationalisation, he
suffered.

I myself went to Blackpool with no intention of speaking, since there was
to be no debate on foreign policy – the only subject on which I had ever
addressed our conference till then. The frightening refusal of so many
delegates to face the reality of our defeat finally forced me to my feet.

I pointed to the growing gap between the Labour activist and the
voter:

> Hugh Gaitskell was absolutely right when he said yesterday that what
> gets cheers at this conference does not necessarily get votes at elections.
> If it did we would have won Devonport [the seat which Michael Foot
> had just lost]. There are far too many people who . . . want to luxuriate
> complacently in moral righteousness in Opposition. But who is going to
> pay the price for their complacency?
>
> You can take the view that it is better to give up half a loaf if you
> cannot get the whole loaf, but the point is that it is not we who are
> giving up the half loaf. In Britain it is the unemployed and old age
> pensioners, and outside Britain there are millions of people in Asia and
> Africa who desperately need a Labour Government in this country to
> help them. If you take the view that it is all right to stay in Opposition
> so long as your Socialist heart is pure, you will be 'all right, Jack'. You
> will have your TV set, your motor car and your summer holidays on
> the Continent and still keep your Socialist soul intact. The people who
> pay the price for your sense of moral satisfaction are the Africans,
> millions of them, being slowly forced into racial slavery; the Indians and
> the Indonesians dying of starvation.
>
> We are not just a debating society. We are not just a Socialist Sunday
> School. We are a great movement that wants to help real people living
> on this earth at the present time. We shall never be able to help them
> unless we get power. We shall never get power unless we close the gap
> between our active workers and the average voter in the country.

Thirty years later I am still making the same speech.

CHAPTER EIGHT

Shadow Spokesman

> Achilles replied: 'Do not speak soothingly to me of death,
> glorious Odysseus; I would rather live on earth as a bondsman
> to a poor peasant, than be king of all the shadows.'
>
> – *The Odyssey* Book 11, Homer

My PASSION FOR international affairs not only brought me into
Parliament; it was also responsible for my rise in the Labour Party
hierarchy once I got there.

During the fifties both the House of Commons and the Party spent far
more time on foreign policy than they do today, and the major issues
were highly contentious. German rearmament, Suez, the Common
Market, and the Hydrogen Bomb were fiercely debated inside each party,
as well as between Government and Opposition. I made my first speech
from the Opposition front bench in 1954 and was elected to the Parliamentary Committee of the Labour Party, or Shadow Cabinet, in 1959.
For the following twenty-eight years without a break I remained a
member of the Shadow Cabinet in Opposition, or of the real Cabinet in
Government.

There is, of course, no guarantee that because your fellow MPs elect
you to the Shadow Cabinet, the Prime Minister will choose you for the
real Cabinet once your Party wins power. Winston Churchill concluded
the final meeting of the Conservative Shadow Cabinet before the general
election of 1951 with the words: 'Well, gentlemen, this is the last time we
shall all meet together – some of us.'

As shadow spokesman of the official Opposition in Parliament I found
myself for the first time obliged to think and speak in terms of the

responsibilities I would carry if I were actually in power – a very different situation from that of a journalist or party official. This is not easy for someone who has never had government experience; but it does, at least, provide useful training for a future minister. It also reduces the temptation to oppose for the sake of opposition, or to exploit a government's difficulties purely for personal or party advantage; there is nothing which concentrates a politician's mind so powerfully as the knowledge he may be confronting the same problems himself tomorrow. By contrast, the members of a new administration in the United States may have no prior knowledge or experience of the responsibilities they have to face, and the Congress has no incentive to be responsible in criticising them.

The British system, of course, provides no guarantee of bi-partisanship in foreign policy or anything else; the government and opposition parties may genuinely disagree on how to handle the same problem. In my time as shadow spokesman, however, the disagreements on foreign policy, though deep and passionate, tended to cut across party lines.

I do not regret my long period in opposition as a shadow. It was an invaluable apprenticeship for my real work as Defence Secretary and Chancellor of the Exchequer. Many of the friends I made all over the world later represented their governments as ministers or officials; so I already knew them well when we had to work together in NATO, the European Community, or the IMF. I was able to learn lessons from the experience of others – the problems of diplomacy and defence tend to recur again and again in different contexts. Above all, I think I learned a little about the way the world is moving, in an age of unprecedented political, economic, and technological change.

As we enter the last decade of the twentieth century, the most formidable problems we still have to solve are those which I watched governments wrestling with in the first two decades after the war – the division of Europe and of Germany, the relationships of the Soviet Union and the United States with one another and with their allies, instability and poverty in the Third World, and, overriding all else, the need to create an international society capable of controlling the new military and civilian technologies. For without control, these technologies may plunge East and West, North and South, into a common catastrophe.

With a poet's prescience, Dylan Thomas defined the central problem of postwar Europe:

> The hand that signed the paper felled a city;
> Five sovereign fingers taxed the breath,
> Doubled the globe of dead and halved a country;
> These five kings did a king to death.

Inevitably, the first big issue I had to face was the role of the German Federal Republic in the Western alliance. Once again, I found myself translated into the universe of military and strategic discourse, which I thought I had escaped for good when I left the army in 1945. Hiroshima had transformed the nature of that universe for ever. I have spent much of my life in trying to understand the nature of this transformation, which reaches into every area of foreign as well as of defence policy.

NATO had been set up in 1949 as a means of deterring aggression by committing the United States to nuclear retaliation against the Soviet Union if Western Europe were invaded. Though Russia exploded its first atom bomb a few weeks after the treaty was signed, it had as yet no means of delivering nuclear weapons on American soil. America, on the other hand, had no means of delivering them on Soviet soil without bases in Western Europe. Britain's willingness to provide such bases was an important factor in persuading the USA to join Western Europe in NATO, thus entering into precisely that sort of 'entangling alliance' which its founding fathers had forsworn.

When Field Marshal Montgomery was NATO's first supremo, he used to say that he needed only two American soldiers under his command – one for the Russians to kill when they crossed the frontier, and the other for him to kill if the Russians missed the first one. That ungrateful complacency did not last long. The blockade of Berlin showed those who had eyes to see that a war in Europe might break out through accident or miscalculation. In 1953 the rising in East Berlin rammed this lesson home. In neither case did NATO contemplate using nuclear weapons. Moreover, soon after NATO was set up the United States was involved for three years in a bloody shooting war. It accepted over 142,000 casualties in Korea without even threatening nuclear retaliation; the only time Truman did consider using the atomic bomb, his European allies begged him not to do so. These practical experiences showed that it would be highly dangerous to base European security on the threat of American nuclear retaliation alone; NATO must have substantial conventional forces too. It was inconceivable that the rest of Europe should defend Western Germany without any contribution from the Germans themselves. So German rearmament in some form was inevitable.

Because I had no confidence in federal structures for Europe, I never believed that the French proposal for embodying German forces in a European Defence Community made sense. In the event, Churchill, who was thought to have inspired it, announced that Britain would not take part and the French parliament turned it down. The only answer then was for Germany to become a normal member of NATO.

The Labour Party was deeply divided on this issue. Our activists in the country were overwhelmingly against German rearmament on any terms. The Bevanites favoured accepting the Soviet offer of a united but neutral Germany. Among my political friends, Frank Pakenham wanted a national German army, Chris Mayhew was prepared to accept Stalin's offer if he would concede genuinely free elections in the Soviet zone, and Woodrow Wyatt supported the European Defence Community with Britain as a member. I disagreed with all of them. In my opinion, German membership of NATO was essential, for political as well as military reasons. I felt that Germany could not be expected to become a loyal member of the Western community unless she had the same rights and responsibilities as all the others; artificial constructions which depended on the Germans permanently renouncing their sovereignty were bound to break down, with consequences far worse than if they had never been tried.

I found it easier to reach this conclusion, because I never shared the strong anti-German feeling so widespread in Britain after the war. My cycling holiday in 1936 saved me both from the pre-war illusion of the British Left that there was strong popular opposition to Hitler, and from the depth of its subsequent disillusion. I had also learned during that holiday that whatever their political views, most Germans were friendly human beings. Moreover, the knowledge I had gained at Transport House of the leading Social Democrats gave me confidence in the genuine anti-Nazis, who were now actively engaged in building a democratic Germany.

The Anglo-German Conferences held every Easter in Königswinter helped many leaders of British opinion, besides me, to form a balanced view of postwar Germany. They were organised, with help from both Governments, by Lilo Milchsack, the handsome wife of the Mayor of Düsseldorf. Irresistible charm and inexhaustible energy enabled her to get the most important politicians, journalists, and industrialists from both countries to spend a weekend together every Easter, in far from luxurious conditions, discussing the most important issues which concerned Britain and Germany. I had last seen Königswinter in 1936;

nothing had changed there since I first climbed the Drachenfels, and watched the barges moving slowly up and down the Rhine past the steep vineyards of the Siebengebirge.

For nearly a decade each meeting at Königswinter was dominated by one single issue which preoccupied all the Germans present, irrespective of party. Reunification, rearmament, and European unity succeeded one another as the exclusive topic of concern until about 1960, when the discussion became more general and opinions more diverse, a sure sign that Western Germany had returned to normal.

The major interest, however, as in all unofficial conferences, was in the human contacts made after the day's work was over. One evening we found some twenty-year-old Saar wine in a local Gaststube. I drank three bottles that night; the wine was like liquid gold and I felt no tremor the next morning.

Apart from the politicians, some of my best friends at Königswinter were journalists; I learned from them something of what was going on beneath the surface of politics. Two in particular impressed me. Marion Dönhoff, who still writes for *Die Zeit* in Hamburg, was a Baroness from East Prussia. She had left Freiburg University in disgust when the Nazis expelled her Jewish professors, preferring to study in Switzerland. When the war came and her elder brother was fighting on the Russian front, the job of managing the family estates fell upon her. She stayed in East Prussia until the advancing Red Army was only a few miles away. Then she led a long caravan of refugees westward, riding on horseback. Weeks later she arrived in Hamburg, filthy and exhausted, in a coal wagon. She was a calm, pale woman, with a quiet precision of expression and great generosity of spirit.

Peter Pechel was a complete contrast – a robust, jolly, bespectacled radio commentator. His father, whom I also met at Königswinter, had been a prominent anti-Nazi, and was in a concentration camp when the war ended. Peter was then the Captain of a tank squadron. He took his squadron to the concentration camp and ordered his father to be released into his custody; few sons have such an opportunity to prove their filial piety.

Another friend at Königswinter was General von Senger und Etterlin, who had commanded the German Army at Cassino while I was a few miles north at Anzio. A tall, cadaverous man, he was a lay priest of the Dominican order, and had now become headmaster of Salem, the experimental school which Kurt Hahn started, before he came to Britain and founded Gordonstoun. Senger and I had long talks about the Italian campaign.

The effect of the war was then evident in more than the wrecked bridges and ruined buildings. Denazification, following the purges carried out by the Nazis themselves, had left Germany desperately short of trained men and women for its new civil service; I doubt if Germany would have entered the Common Market on such unequal terms if its officials had been a match for the French. The economic boom promoted by the currency reform produced a new industrial middle class, which wanted to get rich quick and wanted to spend its wealth quickly. The scandal of the prostitute, Rosemarie, who died in an orgy typical of the nouveaux riches, inspired an excellent Brechtian film; Bill Cavendish Bentinck, the CBI's ambassador to German industry, told me it gave a good picture of what went on in Düsseldorf and Frankfurt. I had no personal experience against which to check his judgment; but I saw many other gross examples of male chauvinism. After a reception at the exclusive 'Redoute' Club in Bad Godesberg, I watched in stupefaction while a German industrialist hit his wife several times in the face as they were getting into his limousine.

One sign of Germany's postwar recovery is the contrast between the raw social climate of those years and the civilised atmosphere today. Germany has awakened from the nightmares of Georg Grosz and Hitler; it is again recognisable as the country of Beethoven and Heine.

Bismarck and Hitler both tried to destroy the separate identities of the different parts of Germany. By insisting on a federal constitution, the Allies made it possible for them to rediscover their historic diversity. Hamburg and Bremen now look outwards across the sea, as much as inland towards Bonn and Berlin; they are Hanseatic ports once again. Baden and Württemberg are once more proudly attached to their old liberal traditions. Bavaria, as in the days of Wagner and King Ludwig, cherishes its independence no less than Texas. Incidentally, to call a Bavarian something between an Austrian and a man, as Bismarck did, seems to me as unfair to Bavaria as it is to Austria.

Germany was finally admitted to NATO on May 5th, 1955. On May 11th Russia put forward new disarmament proposals, accepting the main principles which the West had been vainly pressing on her for ten years. On May 15th Molotov signed the Austrian State Treaty, for which Crossman had been prepared to give up West Berlin. A few days later Krushchev and Bulganin made their pilgrimage to Tito, and apologised for the treatment Russia had given him since 1948. Then they invited Adenauer to Moscow. It cannot be proved that these welcome changes in Soviet policy were caused by Germany's entry into NATO; but they were certainly not prevented by it. And Western Germany has remained a loyal ally ever since.

My stand on German rearmament in NATO was much more popular with the Conservative government than with the Labour Party. The next big issue found me execrated by most of the Tories, and for the first time approved even by the Left wing of the Labour movement. It was, of course, Eden's decision to land British troops at Suez.

Yeats' prophetic poem, 'The Second Coming', stands as a permanent warning to those who are tempted to take the Middle East for granted:

> Somewhere in sands of the desert
> A shape with lion body and the head of a man,
> A gaze blank and pitiless as the sun,
> Is moving its slow thighs, while all about it
> Reel shadows of the indignant desert birds.
> The darkness drops again; but now I know
> That twenty centuries of stony sleep
> Were vexed to nightmare by a rocking cradle
> And what rough beast, its hour come round at last,
> Slouches towards Bethlehem to be born?

I paid my first visit to the Middle East in 1954, when I was invited to spend a fortnight in Israel by the Labour Party, Mapai. Israel was then only six years old. Half the country was a gigantic building site. New towns and villages were sprouting up everywhere to house the flood of immigrants, half of whom were from backward parts of Asia and Africa, particularly the Yemen. They spoke fifty-two different languages, spanning the whole range of the world's cultures and customs.

One evening I wandered through the lines of a youth camp, in which six thousand children between twelve and eighteen were holding the first mass rally of Gadna, the para-military youth organisation. The first group I came across were Jews from Calcutta, with dark brown faces, blue-black hair and large soft eyes, indistinguishable from any other Indians. Next came some boys from Morocco, French speaking, with fair complexions. Then, as I was talking to some Arabian looking youngsters from the Yemen, there was a scuffle in the tent beside me, and out crawled their leader, a girl whose mother came from Edinburgh!

As is now all too apparent, because the existing Establishment then failed to arrange for the so-called Oriental immigrants to obtain a fair share of political and economic power in the new state, the Israeli polity suffered a damaging split a generation later. Most of the leading politicians had come from Russia and Eastern Europe, the financial and economic leaders from Germany and Central Europe. Among the few born in Palestine – the *sabras*, or prickly pears – I was most impressed by a young man in the Defence Ministry called Shimon Peres. He reminded me very much of the young Gaullists I had met at Strasbourg, such as Michel Debré and Chaban-Delmas; this was not at all surprising, since Peres' main responsibility at that time was to secure arms supplies from France.

Mapai was then by far the biggest single party. It was supported by the all-powerful labour organisation, Histadruth, which dominated the whole economy, owning the heavy industries and public works. Thoughtful Israelis were already worried that the influence of Histadruth was creating dangerous economic rigidities and a tendency to wage inflation.

My old friend from Transport House days, Teddy Kollek, was now director of Ben Gurion's office. I found him, as always, charming and straightforward, and as objective as could reasonably be expected. The director of the Foreign Office was the small and dapper Walter Eytan, who had been a don at Queen's College, Oxford in my time, when his name was Ettinghausen. His colleague from Cambridge was Abba Eban. Despite my support for Ernest Bevin, my meeting with Prime Minister Ben Gurion went well, since I was able, as half an Irishman, to discuss our common struggles against British colonialism.

Despite Ernest Bevin's opposition to the creation of Israel, there was no general hostility against the British; we were judged as individuals. Moreover, the Labour Party was overwhelmingly Zionist, and had far closer relations with Israel than the Conservatives – apart from a small group of Tory Zionists such as Churchill himself, Julian Amery, and Hugh Fraser.

Mapai had arranged the usual tour of kibbutzim and factories, with visits to the Dead Sea, Galilee, Tel Aviv and Haifa, which still had an Arab mayor, Abba Koushi. Beersheba was then a frontier town with more than a hint of the Wild West. The Negev was almost uninhabited, and Eilat just a scattering of houses by the Red Sea. I spent Yom Kippur on a non-religious kibbutz, Gan Shlomo, where I had fascinating discussions with an old man from Russia who kept hand grenades in his living room; he explained how the Hebrew language had been expanded to include modern English words, simply by adding the appropriate prefix and suffix. While travelling the Negev with Arthur Lourie I added to my knowledge of Hebrew when our car went to the head of the queue at a road block. We were stopped by a furious Yemeni labourer with the words 'Ain le ha boosha?' (Have you no shame?) I fear I have had to use those words to my Israeli friends more often in recent years.

I was immensely impressed by the dedication and ability of the Israelis I met, and by the idealism in the kibbutzim. But it was already obvious that it would be difficult to maintain the ethical traditions of the early Zionist settlers as the population increased. Analogies with the United States abounded; but where America was a melting-pot, Israel was a pressure cooker. Moreover, the European settlers in America had been able to take the land from its Indian inhabitants without fear of external interference; Israel was surrounded and out-numbered by a hostile Arab world, which accepted a sacred duty to help the Palestinians. From the first moment, Israel was a beleaguered garrison in which defence must have priority.

On my return to Britain I warned that pressure in Israel for a preventive war was mounting dangerously. If such a war took place, though Israel might win the early battles, foreign intervention would see she did not win the war; and even if Israel did win such a war, a second humiliation would make peace with the Arabs quite impossible. Two years later my warnings were borne out.

The humiliation of the Egyptian Army by Israel in 1948 produced the officers' coup which got rid of King Farouk, and finally put Colonel Nasser in power as President of Egypt. A handsome and intelligent man of extraordinary charisma, Nasser soon became the idol of the Arab world. Indeed it can be argued that, before him, the idea of an Arab world had no political reality. The concept of an Arab nation with a mission to achieve statehood was previously almost unknown, outside a small group of Lebanese intellectuals, who were, ironically enough, mainly Christian Arabs. On later visits to the Middle East I discovered that the Egyptians themselves were not regarded as genuine Arabs by most of the peoples to the East of them; and they spoke a language which the Iraqis, for example, often had difficulty in understanding.

On the other hand, Egypt, unlike its neighbours, was a nation state with an ancient history. Nasser himself, with the help of Cairo radio, was worshipped as the greatest hero of his time from the Atlantic to the Indian Ocean. In a mud village outside the mighty Sassanid ruins at Ctesiphon, in Iraq, I heard bands of young men chanting his name to the sound of a drum and shouting: 'Long live Arabism.' As Defence Secretary I saw his coloured photograph among the spices and boiled sweets in the soukhs of the Hadramaut. The Arab governments, however, took a very different view. Nuri Said of Iraq was his sworn enemy. King Hussein of Jordan distrusted him deeply. He was feared and hated by the kings and princes of Saudi Arabia and the Gulf.

In his early years, Nasser's main objective was to rid Egypt itself of the remnants of British colonialism, and to strengthen Egypt's economy by building the great dam at Assuan to control the waters of the Nile. He was as interested in the Maghreb as in the Middle East, and saw Egypt as having a historic role in Africa as well. It was Winston Churchill, as Prime Minister, who agreed in 1954 to remove British troops from the Suez base. Even Eden was favourably impressed when he first met Nasser; he told the Tory 1922 Committee that Nasser was the 'best sort of Egyptian, and a great improvement on the Pashas of the past'. From that moment on, however, Eden's Middle East policy became more and more erratic. He reversed his attitude to Nasser twice a year – four times in the twelve months up to the nationalisation of the Canal, as I pointed out when the House debated the issue on August 2nd, 1956. By that time, he had decided that Nasser was a mixture of Hitler and Mussolini, and must be overthrown, if necessary by force.

The story of the Suez Affair has been told many times. New revelations have emerged every year, not least when most of the official records were made available in 1986. All the evidence reinforces the conclusion I reached at the time. In conception Suez was a demonstration of moral and intellectual bankruptcy. In execution it was a political, diplomatic and operational disgrace.

Suez divided the British people more deeply than anything since Munich. At first the country was split almost equally, but once the landings had begun there was a ten per cent swing to the Government. Eden saw himself as standing up to aggression by a dictator; in fact he was the aggressor, in defiance of the international law he had once espoused. The echoes of 1938 were startling. The meeting I addressed at Oxford Town Hall during the invasion of Suez was the largest ever seen there – except for the meeting I addressed after Eden's resignation from the Chamberlain Government. There was one moment of sheer insanity during the Suez campaign, when Eden was threatening to bomb Israel's airfields, during a panic over a presumed threat to Jordan. So we might have been fighting Israel and Egypt at the same time. It reminded me of Chamberlain's readiness to fight Russia and Germany at the same time in 1939.

In the whole of my political life I have never been so angry for so long as I was during the Suez affair. Reggie Maudling claimed that steam was actually coming out of my ears. On top of the crass stupidity and blatant immorality of the policy itself, there was the brass-faced attempt to deceive Parliament, not only on the conspiracy with Israel, but also on the lack of consultation with America; it was on the latter that I had to ask the Speaker on November 2nd if he 'could please tell me what is the Parliamentary expression which comes closest to expressing the meaning of the world "liar"'.

The final obscenity was the fact that Eden's invasion of Suez coincided with Russia's invasion of Hungary. Port Said fell to British and French troops on the same day as Budapest fell to the Red Army. I asked Eden if he had exchanged congratulations with Bulganin. While I was driving to a protest meeting in York against Suez, I heard on the car radio that last broken appeal from Hungary for help from the West. I had to pull into the side of the road until I had stopped weeping.

It may never be known whether the invasion of Suez turned the scales in the Soviet decision to invade Hungary. Russia had made a conciliatory offer to Hungary on October 30th – the same day as Eden announced his ultimatum to Nasser. Sir William Hayter, the British Ambassador in Moscow, later wrote that 'the Soviet decision to go all out in Hungary was caused by Nagy, and not by Suez, though the latter contributed something', but 'Suez was a Godsend to Russia'. This begs several questions, not least whether the West might have influenced the Kremlin against intervention, if Britain, France and the United States had not been preoccupied by their differences over Suez.

Incidentally Harold Macmillan chose this moment, when the socialist workers of Budapest were fighting Soviet tanks with their fingernails, to make a speech which broke even his own record for cynical fatuity. According to the *Daily Telegraph*, he referred to the spectacle of people trying to throw off the shackles of communism and added 'It would be strange if at the same moment we were to fasten the shackles on our own wrists. Make no mistake, communism and socialism are the same thing.'

Macmillan behaved with monumental irresponsibility throughout the Suez affair. He began as the most vociferous supporter of military action to overthrow Nasser, and was the first minister to suggest collusion with Israel. Yet as Chancellor of the Exchequer he was warned again and again by his own civil servants, as well as by emissaries from Eisenhower, that Britain's economy could not survive the inevitable interruption of oil supplies, and the certain withdrawal of American financial support. Then when Eisenhower carried out his threats, Macmillan became the leading advocate of unconditional surrender. A few weeks later he was rewarded for his opportunism by being chosen to succeed Eden as Prime Minister, over the head of Butler, who had opposed Suez all along.

Among the many mysteries of Suez is how the Cabinet could allow Eden to remain Prime Minister during the most serious crisis which had faced Britain since the war, although they knew he was physically ill and mentally unbalanced; an official friend of mine, who saw him regularly during the crisis, said he would respond to a question simply by gibbering. Many of his colleagues opposed military action, including Walter Monckton, who as Minister of Defence was responsible for the operation. Monckton retired shortly before the landing took place, but did not reveal his opposition in public even then.

Only two junior ministers resigned on the issue – Anthony Nutting, the Minister of State at the Foreign Office, and Edward Boyle, the Economic Minister at the Treasury. Eden got his private secretary to ask his Chief Information Officer, William Clark, to tell the press that Nutting was 'terribly under the influence of his American mistress and anyway was not quite himself nowadays'; at this, Clark resigned as well. Lord Mountbatten, then First Sea Lord, expressed his opposition to his political superiors in the defence ministry. He was told he had no right to give political advice. So he finally wrote a letter of warning to Eden himself, and offered to resign. His offer was refused.

I kept closely in touch with Conservative backbenchers who opposed Suez, such as Nigel Nicolson, a friend from Balliol days; he was later rejected as MP by his local Party association for his courage. Edward Boyle showed me his resignation letter before he published it; years afterwards he became a close friend as Vice-Chancellor of Leeds University. I also kept contact with the backbench Tories of the so-called Suez Group, such as Julian Amery, Hugh Fraser, and Billy Maclean, who had always wanted military action to get rid of Nasser, but could not bear Eden's hypocrisy and incompetence. 'You can't make war with church mice,' Billy would say.

Eden's continual changes of plan, and his unwillingness to permit effective military action for fear of exposing his political duplicity, were the despair of the Chiefs of Staff. Because the theoretical justification of the landing was to 'separate the combatants', and Eden was not supposed to know that Israel was going to invade Sinai, the Egyptians got ample notice of the landings, since it took some of the ships well over a week to reach Port Said from their base in Malta. It was said that the troops used to throw tram tickets into the water to make sure their landing craft was actually moving! Almost the only positive result of the whole fiasco was that the defence establishment realised they had become incapable of any type of fighting between the extremes of nuclear warfare and a police action in the colonies. So they took care afterwards to prepare forces for rapid intervention in limited war – as in the Falklands.

Otherwise the Suez Affair was a disaster for all concerned. Britain lost a political position in the Middle East which it had taken forty years to construct. Eden's equivocation, hypocrisy, and final surrender infuriated the French. What they saw as Albion's perfidy at Suez was a major factor in De Gaulle's refusal to allow Britain to join the Common Market. The French themselves gained nothing, least of all a reduction in pressure on their position in Algeria, which they wrongly attributed to Nasser. Israel was compelled to disgorge the territory it had gained in Sinai, which it might conceivably have been able to keep if it had not taken part in the tripartite conspiracy.

Suez was a historic signal to the world that European imperialism was finished, and that the United States was the only Western power which really counted. Yet it also cast doubt on the ability of the United States to fulfil that role. Dulles' bewildering shifts of position before Suez were a factor both in Nasser's decision to nationalise the Canal, and in his belief he could do so with impunity.

Eisenhower, on the other hand, emerges well from the affair, as from so many others in which he played a personal role. Indeed, like a distant mountain, his stature appears ever greater as time recedes. He was the only President who never allowed America's Middle East policy to be manipulated by the Zionist lobby on behalf of Israel. Eden counted on the Presidential election then taking place to prevent Eisenhower from doing anything of which Israel disapproved. He forgot that in 1953 Eisenhower had cut off American aid from Israel until it ceased trying to divert the waters of the Jordan river along the Syrian frontier. Eisenhower made his opposition to the Suez operation clear in public from the start; yet he nevertheless won the greatest majority of any American President in the middle of the crisis. Then, despite fierce opposition not only from the leading Democratic Senator, Lyndon Johnson, but also from the leading Republican, Senator Knowland, and from organised labour in the AFL–CIO, he used economic sanctions to force Israel out of Gaza and the Gulf of Akaba.

Suez was indeed the most striking example in history of economic sanctions achieving the desired effect – on Britain and France as well as Israel, and on issues which all three regarded as vital to their national interests. Suez was also the only case where the Soviet Union has tried nuclear blackmail – and it failed. At a time when Britain's own nuclear capability was much closer to that of the Soviet Union than it is today, Bulganin threatened Eden with nuclear retaliation unless he called the operation off. According to Chet Cooper, the CIA representative in Britain at the time, his British colleagues were 'ashen' at the threat. Eisenhower was so furious with Eden that he had ordered the American Sixth Fleet to harass the British and French task forces; yet he immediately offered Eden the support of America's massive nuclear armoury if Bulganin carried out his threat. There are lessons here too for the modern world.

Suez produced a degree of anti-American feeling among its supporters in Britain which took many years to die away. For example, though it converted Enoch Powell from imperialist to Little Englander, Suez gave him a life-long hatred of the United States. Sir Ivone Kirkpatrick, the Permanent Secretary of the Foreign Office, and one of Eden's few supporters there, broke off relations with the United States completely. Some weeks later I was rung up by a friend in our secret service with an odd request. Because the Foreign Office had been forbidden contact with its American counterparts, Washington had sent a leading member of the CIA, Kim Roosevelt, to try to re-establish some official relationship with Britain. Roosevelt was a good choice; he was exceptionally well regarded in Whitehall since he had played a key role in organising the overthrow of Mossadeq after the nationalisation of British oil companies in Iran. But Kirkpatrick ordered that no one was to see Roosevelt either. I was the only person my friend could think of who might be prepared to see Roosevelt and make his journey worthwhile! Whether my talk with Roosevelt really met his needs I doubt.

Suez also taught one other lesson worth remembering. The experts had all assured us that it was so difficult to navigate a ship through the Suez Canal that only a pilot trained by the Suez Canal Company could do the job. In the event a scratch team of pilots hastily assembled by Nasser did the job to perfection without any training at all. The Suez Canal Pilot Syndrome always enters my mind nowadays, when I am told that some group of experts has a special skill which no one else can replace.

The Suez affair had one useful consequence for me. For the first time I began to make a direct impact in the House of Commons with my speeches. Until then they made Eden's comparison of my maiden speech with a foreign office brief appear all too apt. They read well. But I delivered them in a leaden voice, with no variation of pace, and they were constructed like lectures rather than as a contribution to debate. The strength of my feelings over Suez led me at last to speak like a human being with emotions, rather than like a soulless automaton. I fear the effect was not permanent. It was not until I left the Treasury in 1979 and began to relax again in Opposition that my speeches in Parliament developed a consistently natural style.

CHAPTER NINE

Drawing Back the Curtain

Red granite and black diorite, with the blue
Of the labradorite crystals gleaming like precious stones
In the light reflected from the snow; and behind them
The eternal lightning of Lenin's bones.

– 'The Skeleton of the Future' Hugh MacDiarmid

THE FAILURE OF Western governments to lift a finger to help Hungary in 1956 led me and many others to consider whether there was some diplomatic initiative which might offer some prospect of greater freedom for the peoples of Eastern Europe. The risings in East Berlin and Budapest showed that the postwar settlement could not last for ever, and that justified attempts to change it might threaten peace in Europe, and indeed the world. The penetrating intellect of Emily Dickinson described the problem in what was almost her only poem to deal explicitly with a political theme:

Revolution is the Pod
Systems rattle from
When the Winds of Will are stirred.
Excellent is Bloom

But except its Russet Base
Every Summer be
The Entomber of itself,
So of Liberty

Left inactive on the Stalk,

All its Purple fled,
Revolution shakes it for
Test if it be dead.

I had watched with growing horror what was happening to the socialists
I had known in Eastern Europe after the war. Istvan Riesz, once Minister
of Justice and Hungarian representative to the International Socialist
Conference, was clubbed to death by the Security Police in 1950. Arpad
Szakasits, who had led the Social Democrats into fusion with the Communists, was tortured into signing a confession that he had spied for the
Gestapo and the British Labour Party. Paul Ignotus, a gentle intellectual,
whom I had known well as Press Attaché at the Hungarian Embassy in
London, was thrown into jail, tortured, and regularly beaten. Almost
anyone who had been abroad had to confess that they were spies. Since
they had no idea what they were supposed to have done or who had
recruited them, they made up any name which came into their heads.
Some who had been in France admitted spying for Voltaire or Arouet.
George Faludy, the poet, confessed to spying for two OSS officers
called Edgar Allan Poe and Walt Whitman.

Next the secret police all over Eastern Europe turned their attention to
their own comrades in the Communist Parties. Following Tito's break
with Stalin, Beria ordered them to find and punish Titoists. So there
were purges of anyone who could be plausibly accused of 'nationalist
tendencies' – Rajk and later Kadar in Hungary, Gomulka in Poland. In
Czechoslovakia the secret police mercilessly exploited anti-Semitism, by
concentrating on Jews in the leadership, who were accused of being
'bourgeois Jewish cosmopolitans' – a phrase which might have been
invented to describe Karl Marx himself. Eleven of the fourteen defendants
at the Slansky trial were identified as Jews and described as 'cynical men
of no national allegiance, deaf and blind to all sentiment, cunning men
who had sold themselves to the dollar.' One of the victims was Eduard
Goldstücker, the Czech Ambassador to Israel, who had been a friend of
mine and Edna's at Oxford, and was later to play an important role in the
Prague Spring of 1968.

In March 1953, after years of mounting mental instability, Stalin
choked to death in his villa outside Moscow. Three months later fifty
thousand workers rose in East Berlin and were crushed by Soviet tanks.
But the pods of revolution were bursting all over Eastern Europe. With
the death of Beria that summer, some of those Communist leaders who
had survived their imprisonment were set free, and inside the Communist

parties there was a serious attempt to understand what had gone wrong. The upheavals which followed in Poland and Hungary, as later in Czechoslovakia, were led by men who were dedicated communists; but they believed that the Soviet model, as it had petrified under Stalin, would not work in countries of a different, and as they saw it, a higher culture. Few of them, however, recognised, as did Djilas in Yugoslavia, that the sort of freedom their peoples wanted was incompatible with a single-party state, particularly if that party was based on the Leninist principle of 'democratic centralism'.

In February 1956 Krushchev made his secret speech to the Twentieth Congress of the Soviet Communist Party on the crimes of Stalin. When reports filtered through to Eastern Europe, the effect was electric. There was a ferment of argument in Poland, in which the writers and intellectuals took a leading part. In Poznan a workers' rising led to Gomulka taking over the leadership once again. The ex-Socialists, who had been forced to destroy their party, joined with thousands of anti-Stalinist communists who had been released from jail, and demanded free elections, first in the Communist Party, then in the state itself. When Krushchev descended on Warsaw to reverse the trend, Gomulka refused to budge. Krushchev threatened to intervene by force. Gomulka told him he would order the Polish Army to fight for its country's independence. Krushchev surrendered and Gomulka became a national hero. Once again Poland had demonstrated the character Daniel Defoe had described two centuries earlier:

> Uncommon monstrous virtues they possess,
> Strange odd prepost'rous Polish qualities;
> Mysterious contraries they reconcile,
> The pleasing frown and the destroying smile;
> Precisely gay, and most absurdly grave,
> Most humbly high, and barbarously brave;
> Debauch'dly civil and profanely good,
> And filled with gen'rous brave ingratitude.

Gomulka got away with it, because he was able to convince Krushchev that if Poland was allowed to take its own road to socialism, it would remain a loyal member of the Warsaw Pact. When Imre Nagy tried to follow his example in Hungary, he could offer no such guarantee. On the contrary, he was committed to negotiate the withdrawal of Soviet forces from Hungary, implying that he would leave the Warsaw Pact and adopt neutrality. Even so, Krushchev seemed to be looking for a compromise right up to the last moment, and there are some signs that Andropov, then Soviet Ambassador in Budapest, may have opposed military intervention. What is certain is that the Western powers, despite all the promises of American aid from Radio Free Europe in Munich, made no attempt whatever to influence the Soviet decision. They were totally preoccupied with their disagreements with one another over Suez.

What happened in Poland and Hungary that autumn taught me two lessons. First, so long as Eastern Europe was under Soviet control against its will, political unrest might lead to fighting; and such fighting might in some circumstances slop over into Western Europe. So the Western governments had a powerful interest, as well as a moral duty, to pursue policies which might offer the peoples of Eastern Europe a more tolerable future. Second, the strategy of NATO, which relied wholly on the threat of nuclear retaliation to prevent war in Europe, was both irrelevant and dangerous in the situations most likely to arise. The desperate men who might take to arms against a foreign dictatorship in Eastern Europe would not be influenced by calculations of what Washington might do to Moscow; and if their action did lead to fighting between Warsaw Pact and NATO forces somewhere in Central Europe, it would be impossible to control the situation by using strategic nuclear forces from the United States or Britain.

The first lesson led me to develop a detailed policy for disengagement in Central Europe. The second led to my search for some alternative to nuclear deterrence, at least for situations other than an all-out Soviet invasion of Western Europe.

I put forward my thoughts on disengagement in a private paper on the Diplomacy of Liberation at the end of 1956, and wrote one of Hugh Gaitskell's Godkin lectures on the subject the following summer. My first extended exposition of my views came in October 1957, when I gave a Fabian lecture, later published as a pamphlet entitled *A Neutral Belt in Europe?* The question mark was deliberate, since at that time I still had some doubts about the feasibility of the concept.

The essence of my proposal was that Soviet troops should be withdrawn from Eastern Europe in return for the withdrawal of foreign troops from Western Germany. The countries in the neutral area should be allowed sufficient conventional forces to deal with anything but a full-scale attack from outside, but no nuclear weapons. Such a disengagement in Central Europe should be followed by similar agreements between Russia and the

West in other areas of instability, notably the Middle East. It should be seen as the beginning of a process which would substitute disarmament and cooperation on mutual security for an endless arms race and military confrontation between East and West.

Meanwhile George Kennan had made similar proposals in his Reith Lectures for the BBC. More important, on almost the same day as I gave my Fabian lecture, Gomulka's Foreign Minister, Adam Rapacki, put forward an official Polish plan for nuclear disengagement in Central Europe, accompanied by cuts in conventional forces. Shortly afterwards I had a long talk with him on the subject. I was particularly anxious to know how far his proposal had Soviet agreement. Like many Poles, Rapacki had studied in Italy before the war; so we were able to talk freely in Italian, which his accompanying official did not understand. He left me with the impression that Moscow had not objected to him putting his plan forward, but had not committed itself to support it.

So I concentrated on spreading my gospel in the West. The following year I wrote three long articles on disengagement for the *New Republic* in the United States. They provoked a lengthy critique from Jim King, an old friend from Balliol, who had been working in Berlin with General Lucius D. Clay during the occupation, and was currently a military analyst in Washington. It also produced friendly comments from some leading academics. But I could not make much impression on policy-makers in the United States, though Henry Reuss had my articles put into the Congressional Record. When I described my ideas in Henry Kissinger's seminar at Harvard I had only one supporter – a pale young Pole called Zbigniew Brzezinski.

Although Eden had put forward a similar proposal in 1955, Whitehall was no more welcoming than Washington, apart from a friend of mine in the secret service, who had extensive personal experience of Eastern Europe since the war.

I believe the West missed an important opportunity in not following up the Rapacki Plan in 1957. Soviet foreign policy was then in the melting pot. Moscow had already withdrawn its troops from Austria in return for Vienna's commitment to non-alignment, and had accepted free elections there, even though it meant the local Communist Party being practically wiped out. Gomulka had persuaded Krushchev to allow Poland to pursue internal policies which were anathema in Moscow. Moreover Krushchev was determined to cut Soviet military spending. Between 1955 and the end of 1959 he cut Soviet troop strength from 5,763,000 to 3,623,000; then in January 1960 he demobilised another

1,200,000 men; this brought the size of Moscow's forces to less than half what it had been under Stalin.

Moreover, in order to maintain the loyalty of the East European Governments, Krushchev was obliged to allow their peoples higher living standards than the people of the Soviet Union itself; he complained that it cost twice as much to keep a division of the Red Army in Eastern Europe as in Russia. Russia was beginning to learn what Britain had already learned – that the economic cost of empire is higher than the economic gain.

The Western governments, however, having just expended enormous efforts to get Germany into NATO, were not prepared even to consider a policy which might seem to nullify those efforts – although disengagement might well have been presented as the reward of Western efforts, like the INF Treaty in 1987. And Krushchev himself sometimes behaved in ways which appeared to justify the worst suspicions of the anti-Soviet crusaders. He contrived the second Berlin crisis in 1958, compelling the West to concentrate on the military side of its relationship with Russia. In 1961 he built the Berlin Wall. The Cuban missile crisis followed in 1962. So the climate in which disengagement might have been possible disappeared for a quarter of a century. Perhaps Gorbachev is trying to bring it back today.

I paid my second visit to Poland in February 1959. Once again the country was gripped by winter. But the ruined cities I had seen eleven years earlier were restored to their pre-war grandeur. The old town in Warsaw itself had been meticulously reconstructed from old photographs and paintings. The Palace of Culture towered over all, an excrescence from the worst period of Stalinist architecture. The Poles would ask: 'Where do you get the best view of Warsaw?'

'From the top of the Palace of Culture.'

'Why?'

'Because it is the only place from which you cannot see the Palace of Culture.'

At that time, the hopes aroused when Gomulka came back in 1956 were already fading; he himself was becoming more conservative every week. But the explosion of cultural freedom triggered by 1956 was still reverberating everywhere. There was total freedom of speech, although the newspapers were liable to censorship. Polish films led the world in humanity and depth of meaning. Wajda's great triptych on the war years has an honesty and force which no other country has been able to match. *Ashes and Diamonds* in particular, with Cybulski playing the young anti-communist guerrilla like a Polish James Dean, still appears in style and content as one of the greatest films ever made.

I met Lesjek Kolakowski, a pale, thin youth, then regarded as the outstanding Marxist philosopher of his time. He is now a refugee in Oxford and the most perceptive theorist of democratic socialism; I have often quoted him in recent years. Mieczyslaw Rakowski was then the ebullient editor of *Politika*, the most outspoken political weekly; when I next met him, as Vice-Premier of Poland under Jaruzelski, his white face was seamed with the furrows etched by years of reluctant conformism. He used the casuistry of Dostoevsky's Grand Inquisitor with a skill and rationality which lacked all conviction. He was still using it when he became Prime Minister; but in legalising Solidarity perhaps he too was kissing Jesus Christ.

A short visit to Kraków, the ancient capital, gave me a far better feeling for Poland as a nation than was possible in the artificial antiquities of Warsaw. I went to a concert in the mediaeval castle of Wawel to celebrate the return of the Crown Jewels from Canada; this had been arranged by the pianist Malcuzynski, whose brother was press attaché in London. Under the tattered banners of forgotten wars sat the three aristocracies of modern Poland – the old nobility, the new Communist élite, and the Catholic hierarchy. They all dissolved in tears together as, hectic with influenza, Malcuzynski played Chopin's heroic Polonaises.

My most unforgettable experience in Poland, however, was my visit to the concentration camp at Auschwitz. Alone, except for my guide, I tramped through the frozen snow from one grey barracks to another, inside the double fencing of electrified barbed wire. The most harrowing sight was not the piles of human hair and teeth, carefully collected from the dead to serve the Nazi war effort; it was wall upon wall of small identity photographs of the men, women and children who had died there, Gentile as well as Jew, from every country in Europe, including Germany. Auschwitz is a monument of man's inhumanity to man. It far transcends even the searing horror of the historic situation which produced it. Years later I found it difficult to tell others what I had seen there without tears. Political activity needs no other justification if it can help to prevent Auschwitz from happening again.

In the early years after the war, when we first heard the truth of what Russia was doing in Eastern Europe, and began to look more objectively at the Soviet Union itself, my generation was powerfully influenced by George Orwell's *1984*, and by a flood of books which purported to analyse the nature of totalitarianism. We had a tendency to see the communist regimes as absolute evil and incapable of change – except through some external intervention.

My visits to Eastern Europe cured me of such illusions. No external power could destroy national traditions which were rooted in centuries of history. Moreover, these peoples yearned to return to the Europe in which Chopin and Bartok were part of a common civilisation with Bach and Verdi. Once Stalin died, it was clear that Soviet Communism already carried the seeds of its own destruction. The Russia of Tolstoy, Tchaikovsky and Herzen was still there beneath the surface. Stalin could no more expunge it from the consciousness of its people than Hitler could liquidate the Germany of Beethoven, Goethe, and Kant.

Nevertheless, Stalin was not Hitler. Soviet totalitarianism was different from the totalitarianism of the Nazis. The greatest danger to world peace after 1945 was not another Munich, but another Sarajevo. Besides creating dangerous tensions among the occupied peoples, the presence of the Red Army in Eastern Europe exerted enormous pressure on the narrow Western fringe of Eurasia where American troops now stood guard. I felt it essential to try to learn more about the nature of the Soviet colossus. Even Churchill had described it as 'a riddle wrapped in a mystery wrapped in an enigma'.

I had been fascinated by Russia since I read its great novelists as a schoolboy. My years in the Communist Party at Oxford had given me sufficient understanding of Stalinism to reject it, even while I still saw Russia as a socialist state and a necessary ally against Hitler. I was also impressed by much of pre-war Soviet culture. The great Soviet film-makers of those days – Eisenstein, Pudovkin, and Dovzhenko – seemed superior to their Western rivals. Though I loathed 'Socialist Realism', I admired the paintings of Deineka. They were in a book given me by a friend in Keighley whose sister married a professor in Tiflis; she also introduced me to Shostakovich's opera, *The Lady Macbeth of Mtensk*.

After the war I found that the sister had disappeared with her husband during the great purges, and that Stalin had banned *Lady Macbeth*. This helped to reinforce the bitter hostility I had developed for Soviet policies both at home and abroad while at Transport House. When Stalin died, I was at first deeply suspicious of the changes introduced by his successors.

There were ample grounds for my distrust. The new men were all products of the old system, and claimed loyalty to its principles. Krushchev had said: 'We are in favour of a *détente*, but if anyone thinks that for this reason we shall forget about Marx, Engels and Lenin, he is mistaken. This will happen when shrimps learn to whistle.' I pointed out that Stalin himself had launched the new line four years earlier, and that the previous period of 'co-existence' took place in the late thirties, at the same time as the great purges.

At the beginning of 1956 Malenkov came to Britain as Deputy Premier, shortly after losing the leadership to Krushchev. His visit was such a propaganda success that people wondered how the Politburo could ever have replaced him. I described it in words which might have been used thirty years later of Gorbachev:

> Malenkov mingled freely with the British people both at work and at play, performing all the rituals expected of a professional politician in an Anglo-Saxon democracy – kissing babies, patting children's heads, and distributing appropriate flatteries to all he met . . . Those who met Malenkov for private talks were no less impressed by his obviously quick intelligence and subtlety. At the long press conference held at the end of his visit, he answered or parried all questions with wit, moderation and adroitness. For example, when asked his opinion of British women, he replied with a twinkle that it was rather difficult to make love through an interpreter!

Bulganin and Krushchev followed Malenkov to Britain a few months later. Their visit was less successful. It was marred at the outset when a naval intelligence officer, Commander Crabbe, was found drowned in circumstances which suggested he had been investigating the hull of their cruiser. At a dinner with the Labour Party leaders Krushchev lost his temper; it was a scene worthy of Dostoevsky's comic genius.

George Brown subjected Krushchev to what was described as 'good humoured banter' – an experience which could try the patience even of his Labour colleagues. Krushchev replied with a bullying tirade which his hosts found shocking and offensive. In the stunned silence which followed, Gaitskell rose to bring the meeting to a close, with questions about Jews and socialists under Communist rule. Krushchev declared that Gaitskell would have to look elsewhere for 'agents who would protect the enemies of the working class'. At this point Bevan piled in with a heated defence of social democracy. The Soviet leaders finally beat a retreat long after they had intended, leaving their new Popular Front programme in ruins behind them.

Yet in fact Krushchev continued and extended the liberal programmes which Malenkov had introduced. The Foreign Office rightly saw him during that visit as a shrewd and cunning political leader, by comparison with the better educated and more courteous Bulganin. By 1958 I myself had come to the conclusion that Krushchev was 'one of the half-dozen greatest political leaders of this century. It is doubtful whether any other known figure could operate the Soviet system on a basis of persuasion and incentive as successfully as he. His outstanding personal character- istics are pragmatism and self-confidence ... Compared with Stalin he seems little interested in the theory of communism – his faith is all the more formidable because it is not overdogmatic. Both at home and abroad, he insists on seeing things for himself – no modern Prime Minister has travelled so widely. To this extent summit conferences may have a special value in dealing with the Russians today, providing the West can produce leaders of comparable ability.' I still maintain these views; they apply even more to Gorbachev.

It was now clear that the picture which the West had painted of the Soviet Union in the early post-war years needed drastic revision. I made my first visit to Russia the following year as part of a Labour Party delegation, with Hugh Gaitskell and Nye Bevan. Our meeting with Krushchev confirmed the views I had now formed of him. He was exceptionally well briefed, but was not ashamed to ask Gromyko to put him right if necessary. I was delighted to find that he treated Boris Ponomarev with contempt, since Ponomarev had been my bitterest opponent while I was at Transport House and he held the equivalent job as Secretary of the Soviet Communist Party's International Department; he still had the same job when Gorbachev took over a quarter of a century later.

Krushchev reminded me greatly of Ernest Bevin; he too had learned his political skills in what Bevin called 'the hedgerows of experience'. They belonged to the last generation of world leaders who could achieve supreme power without any formal education. Yet like Bevin, Krushchev never carried a chip on his shoulder about men born in more fortunate circumstances. He had a natural dignity and self-confidence which rejected class envy. Thus he was able to say of John Kennedy:

> As regards our backgrounds, he and I were poles apart. I was a miner, a metal fitter ... Kennedy was a millionaire and the son of a millionaire. Despite the irreconcilability of our class antagonism, however, Kennedy and I found common ground and a common language when it came to preventing a military conflict. I would like to pay my respects to Kennedy, my former opposite number in the serious conflict which arose between our two countries. He showed great flexibility, and together we avoided disaster. When he was assassinated I felt sincere regret. I went straight to the embassy and expressed my condolences.

The good impression I formed of Krushchev in Moscow was strengthened by Edna's meeting with his wife. As a normal courtesy, Dora Gaitskell had brought her a present from London; to everyone's surprise she and Edna were asked to have tea in the Krushchev's flat on the Lenin Hills overlooking Moscow, to deliver it in person. So far as I know, no foreign visitor had ever been invited to visit a Soviet leader's private home before. Mrs Gromyko took them there and acted as interpreter. It was an unpretentious room, with old-fashioned furniture, and an unkempt garden outside. Dora and Edna found Mrs Krushchev as charming and unaffected as the Americans were to discover a few months later – Krushchev was the first Soviet leader to take his wife with him on official visits abroad.

After talking for an hour or so, Mrs Gromyko asked if anyone had a camera. Edna admitted she had brought a little Pen-F half-frame of mine. So they all went into the garden while Edna and Mrs Gromyko immortalised the occasion on film. Or not quite. When I got back to London I rushed up to my darkroom to develop the film, and for the first and last time in my life, I poured in the fixer before the developer. So the film was wiped clean.

Most of our visit was spent in sightseeing. We were of course taken to schools, factories, and collective farms, but also to the great monuments of Tsarist times – the Kremlin, the Hermitage in Leningrad and the magnificent summer palace of Peter the Great overlooking the Gulf of Finland, its fountains sparkling in the autumn sun, its rococo buildings gleaming with white and gold; like most other palaces, it had been meticulously restored to its former glory after almost total destruction by the Nazis. In Leningrad we were given a concert at what had originally been the club where members of the first Russian Parliament, or Duma, used to meet. In those nineteenth-century surroundings, the concert itself was like a salon at the court of Queen Victoria, as sopranos and baritones in evening dress sang ballads and songs by 'Kompositori Verdi'.

By comparison with the eighteenth-century canals of Leningrad, which might have been part of Amsterdam or Bremen, the Kremlin brought us to the heart of old Russia. I had imagined it a building as grimly functional as the Party it housed, and was quite unprepared for the mediaeval splendour of its palaces and churches, scattered among copses of birch and lilac.

Many other Western visitors have since had a visit to Russia like ours in 1959. I believe it is an essential experience for anyone who wants to understand something of the Soviet enigma. It is a platitude nowadays to talk of the influence on Soviet Communism of its heritage from the Tsars. Even so, few political analysts recognise how many of the most disagreeable elements in the Soviet system were carried straight over from the past. In 1839 the Marquis de Custine, an aristocrat whose father and grandfather had been guillotined during the Reign of Terror, spent five months touring Russia in the belief it would provide a model of enlightened despotism for France to copy. He was sadly disillusioned, like so many later fellow-travellers. The Russia he describes is extraordinarily like the Soviet Union under Stalin.

We ourselves found parallels everywhere, not only in the brutal and secretive dictatorship, with its deep suspicion of all foreigners, but also in the structure of society itself. The Tsarist 'tchin', a 'military order applied to an entire society' had become the Soviet 'nomenklatura', as anyone who has attended an official reception in Moscow could testify. The privileged class wore civil or military uniform as it did in Tsarist days, and was no less remote from the mass of the people. The bureaucracy was as heartless, incompetent and corrupt as when Gogol and de Custine described it. But we also found the Russian people as attractive as in those days, with the same warmth, generosity – and scepticism.

De Custine's criticisms of the system were often made by Russian writers before the Revolution – though they sometimes paid for their honesty through imprisonment or exile. For the first time since 1917 the same devastating criticism is now being made by the leader of the Soviet Union himself. Even Krushchev never made *perestroika* or 'reconstruction' his objective, or insisted that *glasnost* or 'openness' was the precondition of reform. What is becoming all too clear, however, now that Gorbachev has pledged himself to a transformation of the system he inherited, is that some of his greatest difficulties come from long before the Communist Revolution. They are rooted in centuries of history.

The pressure for reform under Tsarism, led by liberal middle-class intellectuals, produced the revolution of 1905 and the beginnings of parliamentary democracy. It was Kerensky's failure to disengage Russia from the Great War which allowed another group of middle-class intellectuals to get enough support from the workers to carry through the revolution of 1917. What went wrong in the twenties is now just beginning to be debated inside the Soviet Union itself. If Stalin had not won the succession, despite Lenin's warnings, if the more liberal Communists like Bukharin had been able to continue the New Economic Policy of the early twenties, the history of the Soviet Union might have been very different. However, though Stalin's regime was mainly responsible for the domestic disasters which followed, I now believe that a failure of will and of imagination in the West has some responsibility both for Stalin's pact with Hitler before the war, and for the Cold War afterwards.

On April 18th, 1956, when Krushchev was dining with Eden at Claridges, he launched into a bitter attack on the failure of the Chamberlain government in 1939 to send someone of high standing to negotiate an agreement with the Soviet Union. He told Eden that the Russian leaders had interpreted the decision to send only a low-level military mission to Moscow as displaying Britain's intention to launch Germany against the USSR. So they felt obliged to make an agreement with Germany instead. If there had been an agreement between Russia and England, said Krushchev, the Second World War might not have taken place. Eden replied that he had opposed Chamberlain at the time, though he was no longer a member of his government. It may be significant, however, that in 1956 Eden suppressed all mention of this exchange. It came to light only thirty years later, when the relevant Cabinet papers were published for the first time.

It is still impossible to know whether an agreement between Russia and the West on disengagement might have been reached while Krushchev was in power. As I have said, much of his behaviour did not encourage the West to take the risks involved. But I also believe that the yawning political and cultural gulf which divided Western governments from the Soviet leaders led to failures on the Western side to appreciate opportunities when they arose.

The worn-out vocabulary of Marxism-Leninism was a major obstacle to understanding. Western diplomats were so deafened by the beating of Soviet ideological tom-toms, that they could not hear what the Russians were trying to say. Foreign ambassadors in Moscow were confined to ghettos which were continually bugged; they were subject to all sorts of petty harassment whenever they left their embassies, and they had to assume that their Russian servants were working for the secret police. One British ambassador had to be recalled after being seduced by his maidservant. It is not surprising that even the most intelligent and liberal diplomats in Moscow sometimes succumbed to a sort of persecution mania, which distorted their ability to see what was happening. I recall being told by one American ambassador that, in a speech we had both heard, Gorbachev had said exactly the opposite of what in fact he did say.

The enforced isolation of Western diplomatists in Moscow was paralleled by the self-imposed isolation of Soviet diplomatists abroad. Before the war, most of the Russians in regular contact with the West had had the same sort of education as those with whom they had to negotiate. Foreign Minister Litvinov had an English wife. Ambassador Maisky had spent some time before the revolution in Highgate, like Marx. Molotov's real name was Scriabin – he was related to the composer. After the war many of the top diplomatic posts began to be filled by men who came into the service from factories or mines, like Krushchev himself. Western diplomats often found it as difficult to make real contact with them as with miners and factory workers in their own country. It was much easier for them to understand Malenkov, with his middle-class origin and university education, than the unlettered Krushchev.

My visit to Russia in 1959 began to give me some sense of these cultural obstacles to understanding of the Soviet Union. Edna and I were immensely impressed, however, by the charm and quality of the young sixth formers we met in Leningrad, at a school which seemed to be drawn from children of the Nomenklatura. In manner and appearance they could have come from any of the upper-class families described by Turgenev or Tolstoy. Those youngsters are now just moving into the upper ranks of the Soviet system. Similarly, the colleges which taught foreign languages and international affairs were giving a rounded education to able young men and women from Eastern Europe as well as the Soviet Union, who are now in key positions in their state or party structure, where their knowledge of the outside world is invaluable.

Although Krushchev himself had little formal education, he took a far more relaxed attitude towards the intelligentsia than Stalin. He had good relations with Sakharov, despite Sakharov's strong opposition to testing the hydrogen bomb, and at the end of his life apologised to Kapitsa for not allowing him to leave the Soviet Union. 'The creative intelligentsia', as he called the writers, artists, and musicians gave him a 'more difficult and slippery problem'. But at least he recognised their need for creative freedom. He authorised the publication of Solzhenitsyn's exposé of life in a labour camp, *A Day in the Life of Ivan Denisovich*, and allowed Yevtushenko to publish his moving poem on anti-Semitism in the Soviet Union, *Babiy Yar*. We saw signs of the cultural thaw all around us. Though Krushchev himself disliked jazz, he did not use the power of the state to prevent it. But its public performance was then largely confined to the circus and music hall. In Leningrad we saw an ice-spectacular in which the girls were half-naked, in costumes reminiscent of the pre-war *Folies Bergères*.

The theatre and ballet had changed little since the revolution. The Moscow Arts Theatre performed Chekhov as Stanislavsky had produced it half a century earlier – as sad comedy rather than as tragedy with humour. The only ideological change I noticed was in *Uncle Vanya*; Astrov was presented as a handsome, vigorous young prophet of a better future, rather than as the wrinkled cynic of Olivier's interpretation at the Old Vic. We saw the aging Ulanova at the Bolshoi in a ballet based on a novel by Peter Abrahams about Apartheid in South Africa, which called on her to act rather than to dance. Nye Bevan was furious because the white man was portrayed with a red beard, pith-helmet and stockwhip, as a caricature of Simon Legree. On the other hand we saw Plisetskaya at her best as prima ballerina in Prokofiev's *The Stone Flower*. I shall never forget her rippling sinuosity. Twenty-five years later I saw her again, confined as Ulanova had been, to a largely acting role in *Carmen*.

We were always conscious of the omnipresent secret police. Our guide almost wept with anxiety, crying 'Mr Geeli!, Mr Geeli!' on the few occasions when I managed to slip away from the delegation. Returning unexpectedly to our hotel in Leningrad, we found two burly men in black suits doing something to the inside of the piano in our suite. They slipped away without apology or explanation. However, we got our own back. Our first night in Moscow we were awakened by the delivery of an enormous wicker basket at our door. It had been sent down to us by Hugh Gaitskell, who thought it was part of our baggage. In fact it was his own laundry, picked up by mistake when the taxi called at his home in Hampstead on the way to the airport. I like to think of some secret policeman painstakingly listing the dirty shirts and underclothes in a desperate attempt to unravel our secret code.

One thing which impressed us greatly on that visit was the number of young Chinese men and women in every factory and institute of learning. The Russians were deeply impressed, and not a little alarmed, not only by their intelligence, but also by how hard they worked.

In 1963, when I next visited Russia, there was not a Chinese to be seen. The break between Krushchev and Mao had taken place. There was then much speculation about how long Krushchev himself would last, and who would succeed him. Yet the general atmosphere was more liberal than on my first visit, and as I was not on an official delegation, but attending an informal conference between Soviet and Western politicians, I had a good deal more freedom.

One morning I went with George Thomson, a fellow Labour MP, to the open-air swimming pool in Moscow. George started his career editing the children's comics, *Dandy* and *Beano*, and, some would say, completed the circle by ending it as a peer and Chairman of the Independent Broadcasting Authority; he was a good friend and close colleague in all my battles inside the Labour Party. Since the temperature that day was twenty degrees below zero the air was full of steam; we were not encouraged by the news that a few days earlier a religious sect had been murdering swimmers in the pool, to be discovered only when the water turned red.

Our guide was a gentle young man called Kolya who had just got his degree in foreign languages; he did not expect to get a place in the foreign service, as he hoped, because his parents had no influence. He had been at the World Youth Congress that summer in Moscow, and greatly enjoyed reciting phrases of hair-raising obscenity which he had picked up from his American comrades. Jazz was now all the rage, and since imports of Western records had been stopped, a disc by Dave Brubeck was beyond price. Since then the international youth culture has swept the whole of Russia like a hurricane.

The conference itself was worthwhile mainly because I was able to have long talks with two of Russia's most distinguished 'bourgeois Jewish cosmopolitans'. Ilya Ehrenburg, the novelist, had been a member of the cultural avant-garde in the Paris of the twenties. Though he was often accused, with some justice, of trimming to Stalinism, he at least had the courage to refuse to sign a declaration that there was no anti-Semitism in the Soviet Union, though Kaganovitch had signed it; in spite of his prominence, he was not a member of the Communist Party. Ivan Maisky was a sad figure, with rheumy eyes, desperate for news of Britain, where he had greatly enjoyed his time as Ambassador; he was fascinated by anything I could tell him of Israel. Like several Russians I met on that visit, he thought that Kennedy had been murdered by the extreme Right in the United States, and that his death meant a return to the anti-Soviet crusade.

I learned much from these first two visits to Russia, restricted though they were, and was to learn more still from later visits. I do not accept the view that short visits to foreign countries are more likely to mislead than to educate. On the contrary, providing you have done your homework before you go, they not only enable you to check some of your views, but also provide you with a library of sense-impressions which give reality to any news you read later. However, for this purpose I think three days is better than three weeks. Anything over a week and less than three years is liable to confuse you. But a series of short visits, at intervals of over a year, can give you a sense of the underlying trends in a foreign country which no amount of reading can provide.

Since the Labour Party was then in opposition, there was little that I or my colleagues could do on these visits except to talk and learn. But they enabled me to follow the later evolution of the Soviet system with more understanding than some of the professional experts who knew nothing of Soviet reality. I did not find the emergence of Gorbachev surprising. Nor, like so many Russia-watchers, did I ever think that his early speeches were simply designed to take the West off its guard. When I later met men like Burlatsky, who had written speeches for Krushchev, I knew that his articles had to be taken seriously; he, like Gorbachev himself, represented something in Soviet society which had always been there, even in the darkest days of Stalinism.

Above all, I learned that the Russians, like us, were human beings, although they were not human beings like us.

CHAPTER TEN

Uniting the West

America is neither a land nor a people,
A word's shape it is, a wind's sweep –
America is alone many together,
Many of one mouth, of one breath,
Dressed as one – and none brothers among them:
Only the taught speech and the aped tongue.
America is alone and the gulls calling.

– 'American Letter: For Gerald Murphy'
Archibald Macleish

EVEN AS A member of the Shadow Cabinet, I often found Opposition immensely frustrating. In the heat of a Parliamentary battle on a major issue on which I felt strongly, like Suez or Hungary, I could feel I was making some contribution to what happened in the real world – particularly when the issue cut across party divisions, and there was some chance of my speeches influencing some votes. But there were also long periods when nothing in particular was happening in my own field, and my role seemed irrelevant: I felt that 'This pudding has no theme' as Churchill used to say.

My frustration was deepest when Macmillan took over as Prime Minister in 1957 after Eden's catastrophe at Suez, for which he had carried a major responsibility. Macmillan was an unscrupulous opportunist and a brilliant actor; his air of Edwardian langour enabled him to get away with innumerable deceptions and political somersaults without ever being detected. The world did not discover about his secret agreement with Eisenhower on Thor missiles, or about the scale of an unreported nuclear accident at Windscale, until the secret documents were released thirty years later. Despite his calculated pose of unflappability, he was often badly rattled by an unexpected setback. Though he publicly dismissed the resignation of his Chancellor, Peter Thorneycroft, with two other Treasury ministers as simply 'a little local difficulty', he wrote in his diary that there was a 'real risk of the complete disintegration of the Cabinet . . . and an election in which the Conservative Party would be in a hopeless and even ridiculous position, without policy or honour'.

After the Common Market was set up in 1958 he told his Foreign Secretary and his new Chancellor that they should tell de Gaulle and Adenauer that 'if Little Europe is formed without the parallel development of a Free Trade Area . . . we would take our troops out of Europe. We would withdraw from NATO. We would adopt a policy of isolationism.' In fact, however, he developed even closer ties with America, without realising that this would simply strengthen de Gaulle's fears that Britain would join the Common Market only as the agent of the United States. In the end the 'night of the long knives' and his mishandling of the Profumo affair, which followed it, led him to hand over No. 10 to Sir Alec Douglas-Home, thus robbing Rab Butler for the second time of his chance of becoming Prime Minister.

Macmillan's extraordinary skill in manipulating public opinion concealed his serious weaknesses as head of government for thirty years; at the time Hugh Gaitskell was no match for him either in the House or on the hustings. So the Labour Party languished in Opposition until it produced a Macmillan of its own in Harold Wilson.

When Aneurin Bevan died in 1960, Gaitskell made me Shadow Commonwealth and Colonial spokesman, just as the troubles of the Rhodesian Federation were beginning to explode. When Gaitskell died in 1963, Wilson made me his Shadow Defence Secretary. This suited me down to the ground. I took every opportunity of learning more about the responsibilities I would face in office. I had worked hard to win support for NATO ever since my postwar years at Transport House. Now I had to consider how to reconcile Britain's role as the United States' main partner in NATO with her need to come to terms with our European allies in the Common Market. Fortunately I had already accumulated a wide range of friends on both sides of the Atlantic.

The great pianist, Arthur Schnabel, used to say that when good Americans died, they formed a queue and took the road to Heaven. After a time they came to a fork in the road. The left arm of the signpost read: 'This way to Heaven.' The right arm read: 'This way to a lecture on Heaven.' Most of them turned right. Americans have been listening to lectures from Englishmen for well over a century. Oscar Wilde was flaunting his velvet knee-breeches in San José the very day that Jesse James was shot in St Joseph.

I did not allow a single year to pass after I first entered Parliament, without giving at least one lecture in the United States. At first I used to make lecture tours for the official British Information Services, visiting colleges and foreign policy associations in every part of the country. Oscar Wilde earned eight thousand dollars in 1882 for a fortnight's lecturing in California – about a hundred thousand dollars at today's prices. I rarely received a fee; my hosts simply paid my fare and expenses. This allowed me to make an annual visit to Washington as well, so as to catch up with developments in the political underworld.

My travels gave me a sense of the size and diversity of the United States, and of the obstacles its politicians faced in persuading their electors that there was a world outside. They found it difficult enough to convince their constituents that there was anything which mattered beyond the frontiers of Kansas, or Nevada, or Georgia. I found it much more difficult to explain the relevance of politics in Europe or the Middle East – except of course to members of an immigrant minority. However, these minorities tended to preserve in aspic the prejudices which they or their parents had brought from their original country, as it was when they left it. Because at that time the Democrats represented mainly such minorities, they were more interested in world affairs than the Republicans. But they were also far more prejudiced – in favour of the Irish, or the Jews, or the Poles, or indeed the British, whose descendants provided so many of their top advisers in those postwar years.

On the other hand, the Republicans reminded me very much of my own Labour Party in their behaviour patterns, though not in their policies. Because the mass of Labour Party members had shown comparatively little interest in the outside world until the rise of fascism in the thirties, when the war ended they tended to see international affairs as a continuation of the anti-fascist struggle, in terms of good and evil; they still saw Germany and Franco Spain as the main threat to peace. Since the Republicans had been mainly isolationist in the thirties, and woke up to world affairs only after the war, the Soviet Union played that role in their demonology. Politicians found that the easiest way of winning their support was to find Reds under their beds.

Some Republicans reminded me of the Labour Party in other ways as well. I was sitting next to a Republican millionaire at a dinner in San Francisco, just after the Democrats had won a stunning victory in the state elections. I asked him how he explained his party's defeat. 'Well,' he replied, 'the people of California like the Democratic policies better.'

'Then why don't you pinch some of the Democrats' policies? That's what the Tories would have done in Britain.'

'Because if we'd done that we would not have been Republicans,' was the reply. How often have I heard a similar response from Labour Party activists in similar circumstances.

Before long a benign providence developed another mechanism for assisting impecunious European socialists to learn something of the outside world – the international conference. Königswinter performed this function for Germany. The Council of Europe covered Western Europe as a whole. The NATO Parliamentarians Conference brought politicians from Europe, the United States, and Canada together once a year. Before long there was also an annual meeting in Bermuda of British MPs and members of Congress. Then the great American foundations of Ford and Rockefeller took a hand. There was a proliferation of cultural conferences in all parts of the world, including the Congress for Cultural Freedom, where I could meet people less directly involved in politics such as the poet Stephen Spender, the philosopher Raymond Aron, and the novelist Mary McCarthy. I later discovered that the Congress for Cultural Freedom, like *Encounter* magazine, was financed by the CIA; both nevertheless made a useful contribution to the quality of Western life at that time.

Of all these meetings, the most valuable to me while I was in opposition were the Bilderberg Conferences – so called after the Bilderberg Hotel near Arnhem, where the first was held in 1954. They were the brain-child of Joseph Retinger, a Pole who had settled in England after the Great War, married the daughter of the socialist intellectual, E. D. Morel, and worked for a time as secretary to Joseph Conrad, another Polish expatriate.

Retinger was a small wizened man, with a pince-nez on a wrinkled brown face. He was crippled by polio. During the war he had been an aide to General Sikorski, and despite his extreme physical disability was parachuted into Poland to make contact with the Home Army. After the war he organised the Congress of the Hague, which launched the European Movement. Convinced of the need for a similar forum to strengthen unity between Europe and North America, he approached Hugh Gaitskell, General Colin Gubbins, who had commanded SOE during the war, and several leading politicians and businessmen who were concerned to strengthen Atlantic cooperation. They asked Prince Bernhard of the Netherlands to act as Chairman, because they rightly thought it would be difficult to find a politician whose objectivity would be above suspicion, and who could call Cabinet ministers from any country to order without causing offence.

I was invited to the first meeting and later acted as convenor of the British who attended; Reggie Maudling and I were the British members of the Steering Committee. Retinger and his successor, the Dutch Socialist Ernst van Der Beughel, who later became chairman of KLM, were extraordinarily successful in persuading busy men to give up a weekend for private discussions, though they found it more difficult to attract ministers than politicians out of office.

The Bilderberg conferences inevitably aroused jealousy, because they were exclusive, and suspicion, because they were private. In America they were attacked as a left-wing plot to subvert the United States, in Europe as a capitalist plot to undermine socialism. They were neither. Immense care was taken to invite a fair balance from all political parties, and to include trade unionists as well as businessmen. Though the discussions were more carefully prepared than at many such meetings – I myself wrote a paper for most conferences – their real value, as always, was in the personal contacts outside the conference hall. Industrialists like Gianni Agnelli and Otto Wolf von Amerongen had to listen to socialists and trade unionists – and vice versa. Experience has taught me that lack of understanding is the main cause of all evil in public affairs – as in private life. Nothing is more likely to produce understanding than the sort of personal contact which involves people not just as officials or representatives, but also as human beings. That is why the Commonwealth Scholarships, which take British students to the United States, and the Rhodes Scholarships, which bring students from America and the Commonwealth to Britain, have made a contribution to good relations between the Anglo-Saxon democracies out of all proportion to their cost.

Lecturing in the United States, and attending conferences on both sides of the Atlantic, in addition to my work in Parliament and my constituency, left me all too little spare time; I preferred to spend what leisure I had with Edna and the children rather than with my political colleagues, thus reinforcing my reputation as a loner. A busy politician has to choose between his family life and his social life; I never hesitated to put the former first. And I was not prepared to cut down my work abroad. It offered me opportunities of learning to understand the people and problems I hoped to deal with as a minister, which are simply not available once you are in office.

The men who made the American Revolution represented all that was best in the culture of eighteenth-century England. Only Voltaire in the whole of Europe could then compare with Benjamin Franklin for wit, intelligence and breadth of understanding. Washington and Jefferson stand alongside Pericles as an inspiration to all democrats. Because theirs was essentially a revolution against colonial rule rather than against the tyranny of class, it left none of the social scars which tormented post-revolutionary France. When I first came to know America in the fifties, its foreign policy was largely in the hands of men of British extraction – White Anglo-Saxon Protestants, or Wasps – who were proud of their revolutionary forefathers, but whose families had changed from yeomen into patricians over the intervening years. Yet Tocqueville was still as good a guide to the United States as de Custine to the Soviet Union.

Outstanding among these patricians was Dean Acheson, Truman's brilliant Secretary of State, who continued to exert an important influence through the Kennedy years. To Americans he seemed more English than the English, with well-cut suits and a short military moustache which led to a caricature by Vicky showing him side by side with Eden over the caption: 'Which twin is the Tony?' In fact the two men could not have been more different. Acheson could not stand Eden's vanity and affectation. He was a lifelong member of the Democratic Party because it was 'the party of the many'. After Yale and Harvard Law School he had gone to Washington to work for Roosevelt in the New Deal. Despite his background he was a close friend and admirer of both Harry Truman and Ernest Bevin. Acheson was also a gentleman in the best sense. In 1950 when Alger Hiss was on trial for perjury as a Soviet spy, he was asked to comment, since Hiss had worked closely with him. He replied:

> I do not intend to turn my back on Alger Hiss. Every person who has known Alger Hiss has to decide what his attitude is in the light of his own standards and principles. For me there is very little doubt. They were stated on the Mount of Olives and you will find them in the twenty-fifth Chapter of the Gospel according to St Matthew beginning with verse thirty-four.

Acheson then offered his resignation. Truman of course refused it. But from that moment Acheson became 'the Red Dean of Fashion' and the main target of Senator Joe McCarthy's anti-Communist smear campaign. I came to know him personally after he left office. He was an enchanting companion, witty and civilised, though with a waspish tongue. He insisted on seeing me whenever I was in Washington, although in his later years he totally rejected my views on Africa; most surprisingly, he thought Britain should have stayed in Rhodesia.

George Kennan was the leading American expert on Russia. In 1947, while head of the Policy Planning Staff in the State Department, he wrote the famous article recommending 'containment' of the Soviet Union, which was published by *Foreign Affairs* under the pseudonym 'Mr X'. Although Kennan did not mean to imply that Russia should be contained by military force, his article has been used ever since to justify ringing the Soviet Union with foreign bases, not only in Europe but also in the Middle and Far East. He has since spent much of his life arguing against this approach.

A tall, slim, scholarly man, he was essentially a thinker, and perhaps too sensitive for politics. The sort of attack which Acheson could shrug off with a laugh would wound Kennan deeply. His greatest virtue as a political adviser was his sense of history. For example, he introduces his memoirs with a careful description of his ancestors:

> The fact is that in pioneer farming families such as ours, the eighteenth century lasted a half-century longer than its name suggests – down to the 1860s – just as it did in the American South, and in Russia. The eighteenth-century culture that lingered on in these families was not that of the *ancien régime* in France, nor that of London and the English establishment. It was the Puritan culture of Scotland and the northeast of England.

He once told me he was a conservative, because he thought that society should never change so fast that a grandson could not learn from the experience of his grandfather.

I first met his successor, Paul Nitze, while he was still Kennan's deputy at the State Department, and have known him well ever since – partly because of our common interest in strategic questions. He had worked in the war on the US Strategic Bomber Survey, with Ken Galbraith and George Ball among others, to rebut the Air Force's gross exaggeration of the value of mass bombing. I suspect this experience encouraged his later scepticism about nuclear weapons as the answer to every problem. He was of medium height and exceptionally handsome, with grey hair, blue eyes in a bronze face, and a smile of astonishing sweetness. Though originally a Republican, he joined the Democratic Party in disgust when the victorious Republicans refused to reappoint him, simply because he had worked for Truman.

Although Nitze and I have often disagreed, particularly when he fought Carter over SALT II as a member of the Committee on the Present Danger, I have always respected his intellectual integrity. There is a Teutonic remorselessness about his thinking which leaves no room for doubt. I have made only two serious bets in my life, since I abhor unnecessary gambling – politics provides too many occasions when gambling is unavoidable. The most profitable was with the many friends who actually believed that de Gaulle would not veto Britain's entry into the Common Market. The other was with Paul Nitze, who bet me that Krushchev had contrived the second Berlin crisis so as to provoke the West into a conventional battle which it would lose, after which NATO would collapse. I won that bet as well, of course.

When I once remarked that governments might disagree on an issue either through differences of interest, or through differences of judgment, he demurred; he could accept differences of interest, but not of judgment. Yet he developed great skill as a negotiator, not only with the Russians, but also with the power brokers in Washington. His success in marginalising his rival, General Rowny, during the disarmament negotiations in Reagan's later years, will long stand as a classic victory of bureaucratic in-fighting. It may also have marked a turning point in world affairs.

The other enduring friendship I made in those years was with George Ball. A great bear of a man, with curly fair hair, large features, and a quizzical smile, he was a voice of sanity in many Democratic administrations, and sometimes the only one. We crossed swords at many meetings over Britain's role in Europe. When the Strategic Bomber Survey was complete, George worked as legal counsellor to Jean Monnet at the French Supply Council in Washington; the devotion he then developed for Monnet and his European ideals remains undimmed. On all other issues including American politics, where George is an unashamed liberal, we have seen eye to eye. He was one of the first in Kennedy's team to argue against America's involvement in Vietnam, and stuck to his guns although it may have cost him promotion. He is almost unique among leading Democrats to have warned consistently against the way in which the Zionist lobby has been allowed to manipulate America's Middle Eastern policy – often against the interests, and sometimes against the wishes, of the Israelis themselves. Even at eighty, neither his energy nor his gusto ever seems to flag.

My friends in American politics were of course based in Washington, a clean aseptic city of broad boulevards and parkland. At that time it was totally absorbed by government in all its forms; until Jack Kennedy it had little time for culture. The black majority were seen by the visitor only as servants; their pent-up frustrations did not finally explode until the riots of 1968 set the city on fire.

New York, on the other hand, brought me into touch with the realities of urban America. That great metropolis of minorities, where even the language changed when you crossed the street, was as stimulating to me as any drug. My friends there were mainly Jewish journalists. I wrote a monthly article for the *New Leader*, then a journal of the non-Communist Left. Its editor, Sol Levitas, was a Russian Menshevik whose views had changed little over thirty years of exile. He paid me thirty dollars for each article – about twelve pounds in those days; I believe I was the only contributor he ever paid at all. Yet many of America's best journalists were proud to write for him, and he assembled round him the cream of New York's Jewish intelligentsia.

My closest friend among them was Daniel Bell, now one of the world's leading sociologists, whose first major work on *The Post-Industrial Society* produced an international buzz-word, like Michael Young's *The Rise of the Meritocracy*. A small, vigorous young man with horn-rimmed spectacles and a moustache, he was my guide both to New York and to the American labour movement. He took me once to an imperial meal at the Chinese Rathskeller – oddly named, since the food was Cantonese only, and it was on an upper floor of a skyscraper. When I looked for it on my next visit the whole block had been taken away. New York has always been an unreal city in a state of permanent flux. Through Danny I began to write also for *Commentary*, then acting both as a Jewish house journal and as an organ of the international intelligentsia.

These Jewish intellectuals in New York were an exceptionally brilliant group, which included some of the greatest American writers of their day. Their story began with the founding of *Partisan Review* in 1937, which attracted not only Jews such as Lionel and Diana Trilling, but also goys such as Mary McCarthy and Dwight Macdonald. Its second generation added Saul Bellow, Delmore Schwartz, Albert Kazin, and Leslie Fiedler; and yet a third generation brought Irving Kristol, Steven Marcus, Susan Sontag and Norman Podhoretz into the Family. Their writing was always taut and precise, with a tendency to exhibitionism. I was often reminded of remarks by John Butler Yeats, the poet's father:

> I think all American magazine writing is far too frightfully clever. It is as if a man had by mistake hired an acrobat for a footman, so that when he asked for a glass of water it was handed to him by a man standing on his head.

They started as anti-Communist Marxists, accepting their Jewishness simply as a matter of fact, but rejecting Zionism. At present their heirs tend to be hard-line Zionists of the radical right; they use a rabbinical rhetoric which is shrill with hatred of the unbeliever. I believe that the turning point was their sudden realisation that the state of Israel was obliged to fight for its life in a hostile Arab world in which Machtpolitik was king. One of their most effective champions, Midge Decter, expressed her position on Israel in 1987 with chilling clarity:

> For those of us whose hearts have turned to stone, love is utterly beside
> the point. We know ourselves to be bound by ties so deep, so essential,
> so unconditional, that they are beyond daylight examination. To be a
> Jew is not an act, it is a fate. The existence of Israel is absolutely
> central to that fate. The rest is mere details – knowable, unknowable, it
> makes no difference.

Norman Podhoretz and Irving Kristol seem to have travelled in the same direction. The philosopher Sidney Hook, who was the political guru of the group, did not; to the despair of many of his disciples, he remained a socialist to the end of his life. And Danny Bell has followed the path laid down by Sol Levitas, which he described as, 'steering to the right of the left, and to the left of the right, seeking always the road of freedom and intellectual decency'.

The evolution of this section of the Jewish intelligentsia in New York is a matter of more than parochial interest; they have had an influence on the political thinking of modern America out of all proportion to their numbers. Perhaps more important, they have been a seminal factor in the development of American Zionism as a pressure group which has exercised at least a negative control over Washington's Middle East policy for more than thirty years. However, the Palestinian 'intifada' in 1988 seems to have undervalued their influence over American Jewry.

New York, like Israel itself, is a pressure cooker rather than a melting pot. Its values did not survive for long in California, where I met another life-long Jewish friend, Paul Jacobs. Though brought up in New York, he had been a Trotskyite rather than a Stalinist as a student, so he had less to react against as he grew up. He, too, was a brilliant journalist, writing simultaneously for *The Economist* and *Playboy* magazine. His wife, Hannah, was a lawyer deeply involved in working for the release of the convicted murderer, Caryl Chessman. They lived in San Francisco, the

loveliest of all American cities, on Vallejo Street, with the island prison of
Alcatraz below.

Paul was small, bald, and ugly, but liked to imagine himself as tall and
handsome, with curly fair hair. When he stayed with us in Highgate he
would enchant our children, who of course adored him, by sleeping in a
strait-jacket from *Mad* comic, and wearing enormous footwear he described as space-boots. He had a fish tattooed on his ankle to save him
from drowning. When the U2 was shot down he happened to be in a boat
on the Volga, so he hung a notice round his neck saying in Russian: 'I am
an American, but I cannot fly an aeroplane'. While visiting a laboratory
in the Sierra Nevada with a group of other journalists, he was briefed by
a scientist with a strong German accent about the space programme.
'And ve are confident that vithin a year ve vill haf a man on the moon; ve
are carrying out the necessary experiments now,' he was told. 'Oh yes,'
said Paul, 'and what are you using for Jews?'

Yet he tended to reject his Jewish identity until he was sent to Israel to
cover the Eichmann trial. This disturbed him deeply. He was never so
flippant again. He called his autobiography *Is Curly Jewish?* – it is a
deeply moving book. He went on writing, more seriously now, on *The
State of the Unions* and on the race riots at Watts, contributing regularly
to *Mother Jones*, a journal of the labour Left. Finally his wife died of
cancer and he followed her within a few months. I found his mixture of
gaiety and seriousness most impressive. He had an extraordinary capacity
for penetrating the heart of any problem. His anarchic individualism was
a refreshing contrast to the conformism which so often saps creativity in
the United States.

California encourages such characters. The relaxed freedom of the life-
style, the eternal summer, the sense of earthly paradise outside the great
conurbations of San Francisco and Los Angeles, all combine to make the
state a magnet for the restless, not only from North America but
increasingly from Latin America and Asia. Men and women change their
partners as often as they change their cars. It was easier there to look
across the dazzling Pacific towards China and Japan than to imagine
Europe, six thousand miles away, far beyond the whole land mass of the
United States.

The pioneering past was not just a memory from the nineteenth
century, when the grandfather of my friend at Oxford had spread the
Gospel there on horseback. My daughter had a friend whose parents
drove there from Indiana during the great recession of the thirties, in a
battered car with no roof or lights, the wife holding a lantern out of the

side, the husband wiping the windscreen with his left hand while he steered with his right.

I much preferred the Nirvana of San Francisco to the smog-filled basin of Los Angeles – a hundred suburbs in search of a city. But I had good friends in the universities there, where the dazzling research facilities were irresistibly attractive to British scientists; one friend from Highgate went there, simply because the space programme meant he could get as many monkeys as he liked for his veterinary research, compared with one a year in London.

In the spring of 1956 Edna and I spent three weeks at Haverford College outside Philadelphia. It was one of two small colleges founded by the Quakers, near the women's college of Bryn Mawr, where they used to sing:

> Swarthmore boys are good as gold,
> Never fresh and never bold.
> Girls, if you are feeling bored,
> You can go to Haverford.

The Quaker tradition was still powerful. Prayer meetings were held regularly, though not always with great success. John Baker Evans, an old man who wore the traditional black Quaker uniform with no buttons, once lost his patience at the failure of anyone in the congregation to bear witness, and announced: 'As one skeleton said to another in the museum, if we had any guts we'd get out of here.' The students took us to meals, usually of jumbo lobster, in Philadelphia, and offered us a great evening out at the end of our stay; we chose to see a dull musical about the Amish people of Pennsylvania rather than the first performance ever of an unknown piece called *My Fair Lady*.

Politics in Philadelphia was anything but Quaker. Though we found the Mayor, Joe Clark, an impressive liberal, and heard the great Judge Bok giving his decisions in a typically informal courtroom, the body of a union leader was fished out of the river during our short stay, wearing concrete boots.

I made fewer visits to the South. In Little Rock I saw the house where General Douglas MacArthur was born, prompting the question: 'And where did the three wise men stay?' Shortly after Suez we had a Bilderberg conference on St Simon's Island in Georgia, among great avenues dripping with Spanish moss. The Anglophile Americans there complained only that Eden had not finished the job; they were astonished to find a languid British Air Marshal joining me in attacking the expedition. He told a story which had a special poignancy in Georgia: an Egyptian friend he had made during his service in the Canal Zone had come to visit him in London. When asked how he spent his afternoons, the Egyptian replied: 'I just sit in the window at Claridges and watch the natives passing by'.

On my way back to New York I stopped in Atlanta, still a citadel of white supremacy, and an economic backwater where the blacks lived in appalling slums. When I next came, after segregation had been ended, it was one of the most prosperous cities in the United States, under a black mayor.

The NATO Parliamentarians' Conference brought me two good friends on Capitol Hill. Congressman Stewart Udall from Arizona was a young Mormon, whose ponderous manner concealed a lively wit and great intelligence. He was a close friend of the poet Robert Frost, and later, as Kennedy's Secretary of the Interior, he did much to preserve the American environment. He named his son Denis, after me. After losing his seat he left politics to his Senator brother Mo, a craggy figure with the looks and wit of Lincoln, who stood unsuccessfully for the Democratic nomination in 1972. John Lindsay from New York was a tall, handsome, and immensely attractive liberal who also had Presidential ambitions; he had to settle for Mayor of New York just as its finances were collapsing. His own political career collapsed with them.

The most impressive Presidential candidate I knew was Adlai Stevenson, the choice of every thinking man. Grandson of Grover Cleveland's Vice-President, he proved his own worth in several federal posts before becoming an outstanding liberal Governor of Illinois. He was drafted as Democratic candidate for President in 1952 although he had not sought nomination. He lost. He lost again in 1956. There were just not enough thinking men around. In any case it was impossible to beat Eisenhower, since Americans like their President to be king as well as head of government.

Stevenson had the same self-deprecating sense of humour as Rab Butler in Britain; they both had the intellectual's distaste for the cruder elements in political life. While he was Ambassador at the United Nations, shortly before his sudden death, I brought him an early edition of the Cavalier poet, Cleveland, and drew his attention to my favourite, 'The Anti-Platonick', which is as relevant to politics as to sex:

> For shame, thou everlasting wooer,
> Still saying grace, and never falling to her.
> Love that's without ambition placed

Is Venus drawn but to the waist.
Unless thy flame confess its gender,
And thy parley cause surrender
Th'art salamanders of a cold desire
And live untouched amidst the hottest fire.

The Eden and Macmillan Governments got on badly in those days with Eisenhower, and even worse with his Secretary of State, Foster Dulles. I often found myself agreeing more with Washington than with Whitehall. In any case I had long since abandoned the idea that Britain might be able to organise a Third Force between the United States and the Soviet Union; this dream was still attractive to the Labour Left. Though it was difficult to live with the Americans, I was convinced it was impossible to live without them. For postwar America, isolationism was no longer an option; if she could not cooperate with allies, she would go it alone.

Above all, I felt that science had made it impossible to operate for long a diplomacy governed by the old rules of power politics; if we could not replace the anarchy of nation states with some sort of international order, humanity would end by committing suicide. Since the Soviet Union rejected the idea of a world society which included both communist and capitalist states, we must concentrate on building some sort of Atlantic Community.

But we Europeans would always find it difficult to work with an American democracy which was so resistant to authority. I had been struck during the war in Italy by the contrast between the cartoons in the *Eighth Army News* and those in the *Stars and Stripes*. The British troops loved Jon's 'Two Types' – a couple of young captains in the exotic uniforms Monty had made fashionable, who spoke in the slang of the officers' mess. The Americans adored Bill Maudlin's Willie and Joe, two unshaven GIs who had a total contempt for the officers who commanded them. The contrast survives to this day, between Commander James Bond and Rambo.

My early visits to America also showed me that the United States is at least five countries, not one. Apart from having English as a common language, the West, the South, the Mid-West, the North East, and New York City have little more in common as social and cultural entities than have Britain, the Mediterranean countries, Germany, France, and Scandinavia in Western Europe. It is not possible to understand California or Texas by applying the same rules as work for New York or Boston.

In the generation which has passed since my first visits to the United States, the cultural differences inside Western Europe, and between Western Europe and American Eastern Seaboard, have been reduced because both sides of the Atlantic watch the same television programmes, listen to the same pop music, and read magazines which are becoming indistinguishable in everything except language. However, the American people are now becoming more diverse, through a massive immigration of Hispanics and Asians, particularly in the South and West. And political power has followed economic power away from the north-eastern states on the Atlantic to the South and West.

Meanwhile the constitution established by America's founding fathers is beginning to creak. The way in which the parties choose their Presidential candidates – and even more their Vice-Presidents – can rarely be relied on to produce a suitable leader for the most powerful country in the world; and only a third of the adult population bothers to vote in Presidential elections. Administrations of both parties have found it increasingly difficult to get their policies through a Congress whose members have no direct personal obligation to consider their country's national or international needs. However, since any reform is bound to affect the federal structure itself, as well as powerful vested interests, all significant constitutional change is excluded from discussion.

The predominance of the United States in the Western world is nevertheless undisputed. It rests on an economy which, thanks to an enormous internal market, still produces twenty per cent of the world's output, and is able to sustain an enormous apparatus of military power. Increasingly since the war, thinking Europeans have had to consider whether they can develop a form of collective organisation which will enable them to cooperate with the United States on equal terms. Their aggregate economic strength in terms of output and manpower is now more than equal to that of their American partner. So long as that economic strength is fragmented among sixteen independent nation states, it cannot be reflected in a comparable military or diplomatic influence, unless new political institutions are established expressly for that purpose. To create a common market on the American model might bring economic benefits, but would not in itself create coherence in other areas of policy; indeed it might have the opposite effect.

Yet it is above all the American example which has created enthusiasm for a federal Europe. I have never believed that a federal constitution would be possible or desirable as a means of uniting Europe politically. In recent years my distrust of the federal model has been strengthened by the increasing difficulty of reconciling the American Constitution with the needs of modern government, and by the growing nationalist revolt against central government among the republics of the Soviet Union. Moreover, unless the postwar division of Europe is to be permanent, any machinery set up to create greater unity in Western Europe must be capable of accommodating the countries of Eastern Europe too.

Daniel Defoe described the underlying problem in 'The True-born Englishman', attributing it, reasonably enough, to Satan himself:

> The rest by deputies he rules as well,
> And plants the distant colonies of Hell.
> By them his secret power he maintains,
> And binds the world in his infernal chains.
> By zeal the Irish, and the Russ by folly,
> Fury the Dane, the Swedes by melancholy,
> Rage rules the Portuguese, and Fraud the Scotch;
> Revenge the Pole, and Avarice the Dutch.
> Satire, be kind, and draw a silent veil
> Thy native England's vices to conceal.

In multiplying my contacts with Western Europe during those years in opposition I discovered that Defoe had not exaggerated the diabolical diversity of our continent. I learned quite as much from our camping holidays every summer as from my political discussions in the European capitals. Once I bought my first car, at the age of thirty-five, we found that camping was by far the easiest and cheapest way to spend a holiday with a young family. We all enjoyed the fresh air and freedom, though for Edna camping involved housework in the most difficult conditions. Any wife who has spilled boiling fat over her bare feet in a thunderstorm will understand.

We made our first motoring expedition to the Continent for five weeks in 1955. Edna and I slept in a small pup-tent with Cressida. She was then just able to crawl; fortunately for much of the day and night she was content to lie gurgling in my army canvas bath. Tim and Jenny slept in the back of the car, a small Hillman Husky station wagon. Drenching rain forced its way in a misty drizzle through the roof of our tent every night on the long drive to Klagenfurt in southern Austria, where I had seen the war end ten years earlier. After a few blissful days at a farmhouse in the foothills of the Carinthian Alps, we crossed the Loibl Pass into Yugoslavia; Edna and the children had to walk as I nudged the steaming car up the steep mountain track. Then we spent a week camping by the sea near Senj, where the coastal road ended. I knew it well from the aerial photographs I had studied while planning my last abortive assault landing.

Despite the heavy rains, it was a superb holiday, and I learned a lot about the human realities underlying European politics. Round Klagenfurt I found there was a large Slovene minority which had provided partisans for the allies during the war. From our camp near Senj, I used to walk to the nearest farm every morning to buy milk and eggs for breakfast. The old man in the farmyard still wore his Austrian Army greatcoat; he told me that he had never been happier than when Slovenia was in the Austro-Hungarian empire.

From that year onwards we spent every summer holiday camping on the Continent. We would stay for a week by a lake in the Alps, usually near Annecy or Montreux, then have a week high in the mountains, and end with a week by the Mediterranean or by an Italian lake. In 1958 we saw the farm-buildings in France painted for the first time since the war; some great change was clearly under way. In fact de Gaulle took power a few months later.

The political anarchy under the Fourth Republic probably made de Gaulle's return inevitable. However, it was his promise to keep Algeria French which made the demand for his recall irresistible. Once President, he cut his losses and gave Algeria independence; this produced a backlash in the French armed forces which almost brought him down. I was at a Bilderberg meeting in Canada when we got news of the mutiny at the Maison Blanche in Algeria. Bets were laid on whether the French general with us would fly back to Paris or to Algeria; in fact he chose Paris.

De Gaulle had a pestilential effect on European and Atlantic unity, but he presided over an economic renaissance in France itself. His historic achievement was to make France safe for the Inspecteurs des Finances. These top civil servants, who provided most of his ministers, ran the country much better than the politicians who preceded them.

During the rising in Budapest there was a black joke in Eastern Europe that the Hungarians behaved like Poles, the Poles behaved like Czechs, and the Czechs behaved like pigs. I adapted it to Western Europe, saying that after the war the British behaved like Frenchmen, the French like Germans, and the Germans, thank God, like Belgians. That is still broadly true, though after de Gaulle had gone the French behaved rather less like Germans, while under Mrs Thatcher the British have behaved even more like Frenchmen.

People used to tell a story about the books written on the elephant by the different nationalities. The British book was entitled *Elephants I Have Shot*, the French *L'Elephant et l'Amour* and the German *Prolegomenon to a Future Metaphysic of Elephants*. The great comic journalist, Art Buchwald, whose jokes often convey more political insight than the editorials in his paper, extended the saying to Scandinavia: the Finn wrote a book called *Finland's Debt to the Elephant*, the Swede *What Sweden did for the Elephant during the Second World War*, and the Norwegian *Norway and the Norwegians*.

My visits to Scandinavia confirmed this. Norway was fiercely determined to protect the independence it won in 1905 from Swedish rule; it looked outwards across the Atlantic rather than to its eastern or southern neighbours, rather like Portugal in relation to Spain. The secretary of its Labour Party, Haakon Lie, used to tell me that if the Norwegians had had another hundred men at the battle of Stamford Bridge, half the world would now be speaking Norwegian. The Swedes were still a little guilty about the benefits they derived from their neutrality, and sought to atone by making a special contribution to world peace and prosperity. Denmark was always torn between the economic pull of Germany and the political pull of Britain. The foreign policy of all three countries was constrained by their affinity with a neutralised Finland, which tended to limit their cooperation with countries outside Scandinavia.

Norway has always appealed to me as a twentieth-century equivalent of the ancient Greek city-state. All the problems of the modern world are reproduced in Norway with crystal clarity, and are usually dealt with more neatly than elsewhere. For example, when its Finance Minister clashed with its Defence Minister in 1951, just at the time when Gaitskell and Bevan were at loggerheads in Britain, the Norwegian Prime Minister solved the problem immediately by sacking them both. Outside the region round Oslo, Norway is effectively an archipelago a thousand miles long, since half its people can reach one another only by sea. Yet even before North Sea oil, when its population of four million had few natural resources, Norway had one of the highest living standards in the world. It has also made a major contribution to modern culture. Ibsen is, with Chekhov, one of the two greatest playwrights since Shakespeare; he is also, with Shakespeare, one of the very few dramatists who can deal convincingly with politics, though he rarely strays beyond the confines of a parish. Even his treatment of the war between the sexes is essentially political; it is concerned with power rather than with love. The paintings and graphic works of Norway's greatest painter, Edvard Munch, explore the mysteries of life, love and death in a way which is equally independent of any particular time and place.

In general, I found Sweden less exciting than Norway; but it is even more impressive for the social and economic achievements of its Social Democratic governments for well over half a century. They have been in power for fifty-one years out of the last fifty-seven. The secret of their success is that they have cultivated social consensus among a people previously notorious for the violence of its class divisions. And their pragmatism has produced a comfortable symbiosis between a public sector which includes the basic industries and services, and a private sector which competes successfully in world markets with a minimum of government interference and support. I believe their brand of market socialism offers an example which Britain and other countries could follow with advantage. The great Swedish writer, August Strindberg, was the product of an earlier and less orderly society – which may explain some of his neuroses. He too had political insight. Per Jacobsson, the avuncular Swede who was Director of the International Monetary Fund, enjoyed quoting from Strindberg: 'Why does he hate me? I have never helped him.'

My admiration for Scandinavian socialism was one of many reasons why I thought Britain should not join the Common Market. I believed that the European Free Trade Association would provide a better international framework for Britain's economy, by linking us with Scandinavia, Austria, and Switzerland. The economic arguments then used to support our entry to the Common Market seemed to me the crudest nineteenth-century dogmatism. Tariffs were far less relevant to the flow of international trade than exchange rates, on which the Marketeers then had nothing to say. I was also very unfavourably impressed by the volte-face of my friends in the British civil service; their sudden conversion in the late fifties reflected a collapse of confidence in their own ability to solve Britain's problems, rather than an intellectual conviction that the Common Market would help us. I felt, on the other hand, that if we could not solve our problems on our own, we could scarcely hope to survive in the jungle of competition with European economies far more efficient than ours.

Loyalty to the Commonwealth, however, was the decisive factor in leading Hugh Gaitskell to oppose Britain joining the Common Market. He was immensely impressed by the unanimous opposition of Commonwealth Socialist leaders at a meeting we called in the autumn of 1962.

The Prime Minister of Singapore, Harry Lee, or Lee Kuan Yew, as he now prefers to be called, made a typically trenchant speech in which he appealed to Britain's imperial traditions. Hugh may also have been influenced by his brother Arthur, who had been in the élite Sudan Civil Service. It was after this meeting that Gaitskell made his first unequivocal statement against Britain's entry; it was actually drafted by Peter Shore, then head of the Party's Research Department. At the Party Conference in Brighton a few weeks later, Gaitskell made a passionate speech against the Common Market, in which he claimed that entry on any attainable terms would mean not only 'selling the Commonwealth down the river' but also 'the end of a thousand years of history'. To complete the offence, in the eyes of his closest friends such as Roy Jenkins and Tony Crosland, he looked back nearly half a century to the help the Dominions had given Britain in the Great War. 'We, at least,' he cried, 'do not intend to forget Vimy Ridge and Gallipoli.'

I myself had reached the same conclusions as Gaitskell. However, like Tony Crosland, who came down marginally on the other side, in favour of Britain's entry, I thought that both camps grossly exaggerated their case. The arguments which revolved round British sovereignty, in particular, seemed to me quite absurd. No country in the modern world enjoys absolute sovereignty in any case; but by the late fifties I already found it inconceivable that the Common Market would acquire supranational powers in any major area, still less become a federation. On the other hand, although I did not share Gaitskell's romantic chauvinism, in those days I overestimated the chances of the Commonwealth exerting a collective influence in world affairs, and of Britain playing the central role in the new Commonwealth.

Above all, at that time I saw the whole issue as a futile distraction, since it was certain that de Gaulle would veto Britain's entry. Apart from all other arguments, such as what every Frenchman regarded as Britain's cowardly duplicity at Suez, de Gaulle saw Britain as America's Trojan horse in Europe. His suspicions were confirmed when, after the failure of the Blue Streak missile, Macmillan abandoned the attempt to produce an independent British nuclear deterrent. He decided to seek an American delivery system instead, and continued to seek it even after, without even consulting him, Kennedy cancelled the Skybolt missile he had promised to sell him. Thereafter de Gaulle's veto on Britain's entry into the Common Market was inevitable.

Despite the rage in Whitehall, and the angry disappointment of most Europeans, I saw de Gaulle's veto as a blessing in disguise. 'The nation can no longer delude itself,' I wrote, 'into thinking that the painful changes in both domestic and external policy required to invigorate its flagging economy will automatically be imposed by entry into the EEC.' On the other hand, if we could meet this economic challenge, I foresaw another attempt by Britain to join the Common Market. This might come when de Gaulle had disappeared, after turning it into an organisation which might be more compatible with British interests, when Willy Brandt and the SPD held power in Western Germany, and when the other members might be ready to override opposition from Paris. So in fact it proved.

Meanwhile Britain faced more important problems overseas. She had still to liquidate the remnants of her colonial empire. She had to try to convert the United States to more realistic policies in the Middle East and Asia. Above all she had to persuade NATO as a whole to come to terms with the new strategic realities created by Russia's growing arsenal of nuclear weapons.

These three problems dominated my later years in opposition, when I was Shadow Spokesman for the Commonwealth and colonies, and when, after Hugh Gaitskell's death, Harold Wilson made me Shadow Secretary for Defence.

CHAPTER ELEVEN

Ending the Empire

Take up the White Man's burden –
And reap his old reward:
The blame of those ye better,
The hate of those ye guard –
The cry of hosts ye humour
(Ah, slowly!) toward the light:
'Why brought ye us from bondage,
'Our loved Egyptian night?'

Take up the White Man's burden –
Ye dare not stoop to less –
Nor call too loud on Freedom
To cloak your weariness;
By all ye cry or whisper,
By all ye leave or do,
The silent, sullen peoples
Shall weigh your Gods and you.

– 'The White Man's Burden (The United States
and the Philippine Islands)' Rudyard Kipling

THE SUEZ DEBACLE was a turning point in postwar history. It signified the end of Britain's imperial role outside Europe. It brought the biggest rift till now between the United States and its major European allies. It provoked Russia's first threat to use nuclear weapons against a Western power. Yet all this was brought about by the British and French Government's attempt to protect their ownership of a canal of which ownership proved to have no practical importance.

For me Suez had other lessons. It was final proof that the postwar Conservative leaders had no more understanding of the outside world than the men of Munich before the war. It also showed that the paramount interest of the West in the Middle East was not in military bases, but in political stability and access to the growing oil supplies in the Gulf. The final humiliation of Britain and France had been due as much to the Arab ban on oil supplies as to Eisenhower's financial sanctions. If the Middle East remained so unstable, and there was no peace between Israel and her Arab neighbours, further wars might threaten a direct confrontation between the Soviet Union and the West.

I set out all these conclusions at length in the American magazine, *Commentary* in October 1957; my article provided detailed estimates of the growing Western dependence on an increased output of Middle Eastern oil, and of the extent to which the sterling area depended on the dollars earned from sales of that oil. For example, the little oil sheikhdom of Kuwait alone was believed to provide the London capital market with a quarter of its funds.

I argued that pan-Arabism might not be a very effective ally, but that it could be a deadly enemy. This meant that the West must accept Arab neutrality in the Cold War, and encourage the conservative states round the Gulf to make some of their enormous dollar surplus available for investment in Egypt, Jordan, Syria, and Lebanon. I accepted that 'some of the revolutionary groups are more reactionary and obscurantist than the regimes they hope to supplant'. But there was an under-employed intelligentsia, often Palestinian, in most countries, and an officer class to supply it with physical backing; in combination they might soon displace many of the existing pro-Western monarchies.

Finally, I thought 'it would be reasonable to aim at an agreement with Russia to exclude certain forms of intervention by either side in the Cold War, and particularly to limit arms deliveries to all major countries in the area'. This would be in Israel's interest too, since 'nothing can do more to harm her prospects than for her to justify the Arab suspicion that she is essentially the spearhead of Western penetration in the Middle East'.

These views were much less acceptable thirty years ago than they have become today. Even the growing importance of Middle East oil seemed to play little part at that time in the foreign policies of Western governments; the American oil companies, though they controlled Washington's diplomacy in Saudi Arabia, had little impact on its policy towards Israel.

However, at this time I had no personal experience of the Arab world. My only visit to the Middle East had been to Israel in 1953. Fortunately my views came to the attention of Billy Fraser, the head of the Kuwait Oil Company – then still a British concern; he invited me as Labour's deputy spokesman on Foreign Affairs to make an extensive tour of the Arab countries and Iran in Easter 1960.

It was a stunning experience. After a few days in Cairo, where the political atmosphere was not all that different from what I had known in Greece or Italy, I flew to Kuwait. My reception party took place in a sandstorm which made it difficult to see across the room. In stifling heat I swallowed canapés covered with a thin film of sand, and drank gritty Martinis until the room swam round me. I arrived in Abu Dhabi as Geoffrey Stockwell was signing the agreement with Sheikh Shakhbut which gave British Petroleum the right to extend its drilling; till then it was confined to a desert island in the Gulf.

Shakhbut's palace was a *Beau Geste* fort in the desert, with a scattering of palm trees and wattle huts nearby. A few weeks earlier one of the sheikh's brothers had died of cancer in a tent outside the palace; he made the desert hideous with his screams as the witch doctors beat him with chains to exorcise the evil spirits. When I visited Prince Sultan in the palace, I sat on a low cushion and was served with fragrant tea by a negro slave. Then the prince leaned forward and asked me for the latest news of Nye Bevan's illness. The British Agent's house, in which I stayed, was one of the few concrete buildings in Abu Dhabi at the time. Now Abu Dhabi is like Miami – a jungle of white skyscrapers.

I spent that Easter holiday in Isfahan, a city as beautiful as Florence, in a landscape as lovely as Tuscany – the grass a vivid green, the apple trees foaming with blossom, and everything bursting into leaf. The air was icy clear under a brilliant sun, the blue sky patterned with fleecy clouds. The people were worthy of the landscape – above all the children, with great lustrous black eyes, cheeks the colour of a russet pippin and jet black hair; they wore tunics and trousers of multi-coloured cotton.

The climax of this expedition to Elysium was a journey from Shiraz to Persepolis through the middle of the Qashgai migration. The Qashgai were at that time a tribe of half a million people with three million camels, sheep, goats, donkeys and dogs; they travelled five hundred miles for pasture every spring, from the shores of the Gulf into the mountains of central Persia, and back again in the autumn. As my taxi climbed over the pass, we were engulfed in a vast sea of Qashgai, gorgeous in their gypsy raiment, striding or riding towards Persepolis.

All over the Middle East I found evidence of ancient civilisations. In Egypt the Pyramids and the great temples at Thebes gave added meaning to the treasures of Tutankhamun, surely the most remarkable collection in the world. The contrast between the lonely columns of Persepolis and the vulgar mediocrity of the Sassanid tombs nearby was an object lesson in cultural decline. A thousand years later the same area produced the great civilisation of the Muslim world, which stretched from Spain to the Moghul Empire of the Indian subcontinent. The mosques I visited, particularly Ibn Tulun in Cairo and the Friday Mosque in Isfahan, are among the greatest monuments of religious art. They reminded me that Islam is a more powerful and enduring force in world affairs than the concept of Arabism – a lesson which the Western world is beginning to learn again.

This first journey to the Middle East took place at a time when the magnetism of Nasser's personality made Arab unity appear irresistible. The sense of a common Arab destiny was a palpable reality among the Arabs, whether in the shadowy bazaars of Baghdad or in the dazzling casinos of Beirut. It seemed almost inconceivable that any Western statesman should have said, like Lord Salisbury after Suez: 'The Middle East is suffering from an unhealthily stimulated spirit of nationalism . . . That spirit is not a natural growth but one deliberately inculcated as an instrument of policy by the present leaders of Russia.'

The truth was that the Soviet Union, after its postwar withdrawal from Northern Persia, had been surprisingly inactive in the Middle East; it began to intervene only after Britain and the United States set up the so-called Northern Tier of anti-Soviet alliances with Turkey, Iran, and Pakistan, which led to the Baghdad Pact and in 1958 caused the downfall of Nuri Said's regime in Iraq. Nasser himself was riding the tide of Arab nationalism, rather than creating it. The cause, without doubt, was the creation of Israel. This not only established a common enemy for the Arab world to unite against, but also scattered able Palestinians in a diaspora to every corner of the Middle East. It was these Palestinians, who, as teachers, civil servants, or even government ministers in their countries of refuge, did most to fan the flames of Arab nationalism against Israel.

I met President Nasser twice in Cairo. He was a large, handsome man of immense charm and ability, whose reach always exceeded his grasp. Like the hero of Montherlant's novel, which I had so much enjoyed in my youth, he suffered from *le demon du bien*; he simply could not resist a flattering temptation. So when Syria invited him to bed, he set up the absurd United Arab Republic. When his admirers in Yemen appealed for help, he sent his soldiers there – to discover a people of almost prehistoric backwardness. He described his crusading mission in Yemen to me in terms which, I said, Lord Lugard had used of Britain's imperial mission in Nigeria. 'Ah,' he replied, 'but these are fellow Arabs.' Though he did much for his country, he never succeeded in mobilising the mass of the Egyptian people behind his work of national reconstruction. His party, the Arab Socialist Union, never became that 'transmission belt between the leaders and the masses' which he hoped to create following the example of Lenin.

Nasser's foreign adventures were no more successful. The United Arab Republic broke down in 1961 and the Baath Socialists, who then took over in Syria, became his deadly enemies. On my second visit to Cairo in 1963, Nasser nevertheless talked of building a federation with Syria and Iraq, where the Baath also dominated the government. But before long the Syrian Baath broke with the Baath in Iraq, and the two countries have remained deadly enemies ever since. Finally, when Nasser withdrew his troops from Yemen, the Yemenis turned to Saudi Arabia instead of to Egypt. When he died, his successor, Sadat, made a treaty with Israel which outraged the other Arab states. Of Nasser's ambition to make Egypt the leader of a united Arab world, nothing survived his death.

The fact is that the Ottoman Empire, which controlled the Arab world for five hundred years, left behind it an anarchy of warring tribes belonging to different Muslim sects. After Turkey's defeat in the Great War, the European Allies drew frontiers among these tribes and gave them national flags. The frontiers took little account of political or religious realities. For example, France separated Lebanon from Syria, and gave it a constitution designed to perpetuate rule by the Christian minorities. Britain was mainly concerned to secure its strategic positions in Egypt and Iraq, so as to protect its route to India.

After the Second World War India's independence destroyed the strategic rationale for Britain's Middle East policy. In most of the Arab world young officers deposed their monarchs and tried to modernise their military and civilian establishments – in that order. Their political principles were vague or non-existent. I tried hard to find something like a socialist movement, but without success. The Baath called itself socialist, but I could never discover why. In Lebanon the best known socialist was Kamal Jumblatt, the millionaire chieftain of the Druse community. He ruled his people from a mediaeval castle in the mountains, and told his friends he wanted to drink blood from Maronite skulls.

Military coups and mutinies were taking place all the time. In Baghdad

I was woken up one morning in my hotel by what I thought was a road drill. It was, in fact, machine-gun fire. When I met the young Baathist Foreign Minister later that morning, he was still excited by his narrow escape from a band of mutineers at Rashid Ali camp, who had not known who he was. Two days later, in Damascus, I found tanks rumbling down the streets to suppress another mutiny.

As Defence Secretary, I once delighted the sheikhs in the mountains surrounding Aden with the story of the frog and the scorpion. A frog was sunning himself on the banks of the Nile when a scorpion walked up and asked for a lift across the river.

'No fear,' said the frog, 'if you get on my back you'll sting me and I'll die.'

'Nonsense,' replied the scorpion, 'if you die, I'll drown.'

The frog thought it over, and agreed. The scorpion got on to his back and the frog plopped into the river. When they were exactly half way across, the frog felt an agonising pain between his shoulder-blades and realised he had been stung.

'Why did you do it,' he asked, as his limbs began to stiffen. 'You know you'll drown.'

'Yes, I know,' replied the scorpion. 'But after all, this is the Middle East.'

In January 1962 I found many of the problems of the Middle East reproduced in West Africa, which I visited after becoming Shadow Commonwealth and Colonial Secretary. I flew to Brazzaville in the French Congo and crossed the swollen Congo river into the newly independent Congo Republic, where the United Nations peace-keeping force was trying to cope with the civil war. Then I paid short visits to every country from Nigeria to Senegal. It was obvious that European colonialism had a lot to answer for.

During the nineteenth-century struggle for Africa, the rival European powers had drawn frontiers which bore little relationship to geographical or tribal realities. All was made worse by the fact that the countries of the French Union spoke French, while those of the British Empire spoke English. Thus Gambia was three hundred miles long, but only fifteen to thirty miles wide, with an English-speaking population of only 300,000, sticking like a finger into the middle of French-speaking Senegal, whose people were ten times as many and belonged to the same tribes. In the larger countries ancient tribal hostilities always threatened civil war, and were often fanned by European commercial interests. The Congo was already torn by tribal fighting, with the Great Union Mining Company financing Katanga's bid for secession. Before long Nigeria was to suffer civil war as well.

At that time, however, all looked set fair in British West Africa; it seemed to provide a model for the continent. The territories were well administered by Africans with British training, some of whom, like Chief Adebo in Nigeria, would have been a credit to any civil service. The Nigerian police and army units who worked for the United Nations in the Congo were popular and efficient. A brilliant young Ghanaian, Robert Gardiner, was taking over from a Swede as head of the UN operations in Leopoldville.

I was less impressed by the French territories because they gave less respect to African culture. Whether independent or not, they were largely run by Frenchmen or by Africans who had been totally assimilated to French culture. Today, after the tragedies and disappointments we have seen in Nigeria and Ghana, I am less sure about the superiority of Lord Lugard's policy of the 'Dual Mandate', which involved indirect rule through local Africans rather than the assimilation of Africans to a European model.

A long talk with the impressive but very conservative Houphuet-Boigny, President of the Côte d'Ivoire, left me incredulous that he could ever have been a Communist member of the French parliament. The secret was explained to me by his friend Laminguey, Speaker of the assembly in Senegal. When the war ended and the newly elected deputies from the French Union took their places in Paris, they decided that they would have little influence unless they were members of the French political parties. So they drew lots, and Houphuet-Boigny drew the Communist Party. Western leaders who are alarmed by the Communist past of some African politicians should bear this story in mind.

The Russians, though they tried hard enough, had little influence in Africa at that time. President Sekou Touré had recently expelled the whole of their mission from Guinée for conspiring against his government. When he finally agreed to accept a Soviet ambassador again, he kept him waiting for months in a small hotel without air-conditioning, before granting agrément. The Russian happened to be someone I had met at the Quaker summer school for diplomats in Vevey. When he saw me he greeted me as an old friend and poured out his soul. The Soviet Ambassador to the Congo was also expelled shortly after independence. Asked if he was sorry to be going, he roared with laughter:

'Not at all,' he said. 'They sent me here to create chaos, but when I got here I found chaos already existed.'

I had never been to black Africa before, and was quite unprepared for the dull skies and soggy damp of the Western coastlands. I was disappointed too, at the absence of big game, though while having tea with our minister in Leopoldville I saw a green mamba hanging from a branch above my seat; the American Consul had found a crocodile in his garage.

On the other hand I found the African people immensely impressive. The men I met were intelligent and dedicated to making independence work. The women were full of character. In Ghana they ran the country's commercial life. Their clothing differed according to their tribe or country far more than that of the men; in Nigeria the Yoruba women wore bright blue turbans and dresses, while the Wolof women in Dakar wore silks and gauze in styles of the French Second Empire. I paid a visit to a tribal chief, the Alafin of Oyo, near Ibadan in Western Nigeria. My arrival in his compound was heralded by tom-toms, and I sat on one of his many thrones as we talked; his favourite throne was a dentist's chair. Oyo had a custom which might well be copied in the West. When the elders feel that the Alafin is not up to his job, they send him a bowl of parrot's eggs, and he takes his own life.

Centuries of slavery have left little art in West Africa, with one outstanding exception – the bronzes of Benin. I saw many in the museum at Ife; they are of astonishing sensitivity, and reminded me of Buddhist sculpture in the Far East, though the technique of cire fondue used to produce them is thought to have been taught by the Portuguese.

Later that year Edna and I represented the Labour Party at the celebrations of independence in Uganda. I was surprised by the contrast with West Africa. Instead of lowering clouds over a tropical rain-forest, we found dazzling skies over rolling hills planted with tea and coffee, and a multitude of wild animals. We spent two days at the magnificent Queen Elizabeth game park, where the blue peaks of Ruwenzori hang over scrubland teeming with elephants, hippopotami, cheetahs, and every sort of deer, monkeys and tropical birds. I nearly terminated a promising career by going out alone the first evening, and wandering across the route taken by a herd of hippopotami on the way to their watering pool. Next day I just escaped a rampaging elephant.

The beauty of the landscape was not reflected in Uganda's political life. The frontiers, as usual, cut across tribal communities, and relations between the dominant tribes were exceptionally bad. The Prime Minister, Obote, was an Acholi from the north, a young man with a limp who had fought his way to the top by sheer ability. The President was the hereditary Kabaka of Buganda, in the middle of the country; he too was a young man, chosen as Kabaka because he was the senior son of his father's only Christian marriage. Born into autocracy, he did not hesitate to use his *droit de seigneur* over women of his tribe; he sometimes sent a car up to Makerere College for half a dozen girl students. He wanted the capital moved outside Kampala to tribal territory, where he would always take precedence. In another tribal kingdom, Toro, the king was drinking himself to death and the tribesmen in the mountains were waiting to take over. Yet another tribal area, Bunyoro, had been taken over by Buganda, and the Kabaka refused to give it up. To complete this ominous picture, trade and commerce were in the hands of immigrants from India and Pakistan. I stayed with one of them, a merchant of cotton and sisal; he was certain that after independence the Asians would be forced out of East Africa. Next time we met he was living comfortably in Golders Green.

After that short visit I was not surprised by the tragedies which have racked Uganda since independence. But whatever Obote's shortcomings, I was shocked when Sir Alec Douglas-Home gave official recognition to General Amin within hours of his military coup; it suggested a degree of foreknowledge, if not complicity, which Amin's subsequent behaviour did nothing to excuse.

Independence celebrations, like state funerals, provide good occasions for multinational diplomacy. I met in Uganda many of the friends I had made in West Africa earlier in the year, and many people I was to work with later. There was a large delegation of nationalists from Kenya, which still had two years to wait for independence. I found Jomo Kenyatta a man of great charisma and exceptional vision. He had once married an English schoolteacher, and I was later to appear on many television programmes produced by his son Peter, who worked for the BBC. Nothing could have been less true of Kenyatta than the description of him by a British Governor during the Mau Mau rising, as 'a leader to darkness and death'.

Kenyatta was one of the few African leaders to recognise that Africa must find a way of overcoming tribalism if it was to flourish after independence. So he used as his successor a brilliant young man of the Luo tribe, Tom Mboya, instead of a member of the dominant Kikuyu, to whom he himself belonged. And he went out of his way to keep Kenya attractive to the British expatriates. His Minister of Agriculture was the extraordinary Bruce Mackenzie, a moustachioed Scottish extrovert who knew Kenya better than most Africans; he was an invaluable adviser to Kenyatta on almost every aspect of policy. Mboya's murder in 1969, probably by a Kikuyu gang, and the death of Mackenzie in a mysterious plane crash, might well have upset the precarious stability of Kenya's politics. But Kenyatta had succeeded in building a multi-tribal state. His successor, Daniel Arap Moi, for whom, to my amazement, I had found my cousin Joan Holdsworth working as a secretary, carried on his tradition; but in recent years he seems to have relied on force rather than persuasion to maintain his rule.

Ten years earlier, when I had just entered Parliament, I had a long talk with Arthur Creech Jones, who had been a progressive Colonial Secretary in the Attlee Government, after spending the whole of his political career fighting for colonial freedom. He had helped to lead Ghana and Nigeria towards independence, although they did not achieve it until later. When I asked about the prospects in East Africa, he replied: 'Denis, Kenya will not be independent in my lifetime or in yours.'

At that time, what Macmillan was now calling 'the wind of change' in Africa was not yet even a gentle breeze. The colonial powers grossly underestimated the strength of nationalism in their empires overseas, preferring to see the hand of Moscow in any demand for their departure. Even the more liberal experts on Africa were too often blinded by the views they had formed before the war, in discussions with an earlier generation of African intellectuals; they underestimated the political skills, as well as the sincerity, of the younger men who now led the growing popular demand for independence. What had already happened in India, what was happening in Algeria, and what Nasser seemed to be achieving in the Arab world, gave a new urgency to this demand; but the European governments could not admit that their worthy ambition to train African élites, to which they could hand over power when they thought the time was ripe, no longer matched the political realities. Even today, white liberals in South Africa have similar illusions. The young 'comrades' in the townships are as different from the generation of Mandela as his generation was from that of Albert Luthuli.

The real tragedy of British Africa is that, once the British Government found that the colonies were beginning to cost more than could be got out of them, and that the new states would choose their own future in their own time, they saw no interest in providing the economic and social infrastructures which would be needed when independence came. France took a different view, and may prove to have shown more insight.

Yet, amazingly, Whitehall was prepared to spend millions on building military bases in Africa, which were bound to be useless after it had handed over power. There was a saying in the British Army that a base was certain to be handed over, once they had finished building its Anglican church. We learned that lesson in Kenya. I was to learn it myself, as Defence Secretary, in Aden. Before long it will be learned in Hong Kong – and perhaps the Falklands too

British governments were equally short-sighted in believing that by training and equipping African armies they would be able to maintain influence where it really mattered after independence. The Africans learned all too quickly that power grows out of the barrel of a gun. Most of the military coups which have proliferated in British Africa since independence were led by men trained in British military schools and staff colleges; but their regimes have not necessarily accepted British influence.

The problems Britain faced in West and East Africa were simple compared with those in the Central African Federation, where the rights of large white minorities were entrenched by law. One example of the postwar Labour government's failure to recognise the pace of change was that it encouraged and financed settlement in the Rhodesias by British ex-servicemen. The white population of Southern Rhodesia more than doubled after the war. The new immigrants were not only British; many came from other European countries, particularly Italy. However, the white Rhodesians had fought for Britian during the war, and had made friends in the British forces. Ian Smith, who led the battle against African rule and made Southern Rhodesia's unilateral declaration of independence, had been a fighter-pilot in the Battle of Britain. It was easy for opponents of independence in Britain to argue that we should not betray our 'kith and kin'. When British governments, under Macmillan as well as Wilson, considered the possibility of military intervention, they could not assume that the morale of Britain's forces would stand the strain. Indeed Douglas Hurd, who was later to become Home Secretary in Mrs Thatcher's government, wrote an excellent thriller based on the imagined mutiny of a Guards battalion when it was ordered to intervene in Rhodesia.

I myself had friends among the white settlers in Central Africa. I had come to know Winston Field, a tobacco farmer who became leader of the Rhodesian Front, while his battalion was stationed in Keighley; later we served together in Italy. Roy Welensky, the tough railwayman who sought some sort of partnership between the races in Northern Rhodesia, used to visit me at Transport House, and Michael Blundell, another key figure, was a Yorkshireman from Appletreewick, where I had spent every Whitsun camping as a schoolboy.

I had friends among the African leaders too; Oliver Tambo, now leading the African National Congress in exile, lived near us in North London. Kenneth Kaunda, now President of Zambia, sometimes stayed with us in Highgate when he was visiting Britain. He was a gentle man of high intelligence, yet I saw him rouse a mass audience in London to frenzy.

Though I was opposition spokesman for colonial policy at that time, the new Conservative Colonial Secretary, Iain Macleod, was moving as fast towards black majority rule as I thought possible. His real opponents were on his own backbenches, and among the Conservative peers, such as Lord Salisbury. The attacks of these Tory imperialists, by no means all of the older generation, were vicious enough to make up for my complaisance. Macleod was a man who had vision and imagination, as well as exceptional political ability. His early death was a loss to the nation no less than to his party.

I rounded off my long apprenticeship in the shadows with three weeks in Asia in April 1964, as the Labour Party's spokesman on defence. It proved invaluable to me when I finally entered office as Secretary for Defence a few months later, since I was able to visit the three theatres where Western forces were actually fighting – Vietnam, Borneo, and Aden.

My tour started in Tokyo. At that time Japan was little known in Britain, and most people found the memory of its wartime atrocities a real barrier to understanding how it had changed since 1945. Indeed the reaction to Prince Philip's attendance of the funeral of Emperor Hirohito shows that many still do. I found a country bursting with vitality. New roads and buildings were exploding everywhere through the middle of old ones. Tokyo trembled with the noise of drills and hammers. My dominant impression was of people swarming everywhere, as much in the temple gardens of Kyoto as in the city streets of Osaka; and the great majority were young. The gulf between the pre- and post-war generations was visible in the contrast between the older ladies, bowing low in their traditional robes and sandals, and the independent young women in Western clothes, with a body language which proclaimed their independence.

The emphasis on material success reminded me of Germany; but the successful lived in conditions of unostentatious modesty, which was much more Swiss than German. Conspicuous consumption was reserved for corporate boardrooms, where the status symbol might be a drawing by Rembrandt or an etching by Picasso.

I found the language a much more difficult barrier to understanding than the cultural differences, of which so much is made. Any Japanese who could speak English well seemed to talk very good sense, and showed fewer prejudices than I had encountered in some other countries. Above all, I found the Japanese supremely rational in tackling their problems, and determined to find a consensus before taking a decision. This, in my view, is the secret of their astonishing economic successes since the war.

I talked to many politicians, finding the Socialists too divided to make an impact, and the Liberal Democrats a collection of personal clienteles, rather like the Christian Democrats in Italy. Everyone was content with the 'low posture' in foreign policy; the militarism of the thirties seemed dead for good, not least because it had led Japan to catastrophe. China was seen as a potential market, not as a military rival. But the Soviet Union aroused real hostility because it had occupied the Kurile islands.

The Philippines was a sad contrast. In a shed just outside my luxury hotel, I found a trade unionist lying on a bier; he had been stabbed to death. A yacht had been boarded by pirates in the bay outside Manila just before my arrival. The local gangsters imposed a reign of terror by firing steel darts from powerful catapults at those who stood in their way. After five centuries in a Spanish convent and fifty years in Hollywood, as the saying went, the Philippines was a divided and corrupt society; violence came second only to tuberculosis as the main cause of death.

The politicians I met in the Philippines were mediocre. But I was greatly impressed by a number of Jesuit priests, who seemed to play an important role in the country's intellectual life, and spoke with knowledge and passion about its politics. After what they told me, the later fall and disgrace of President Marcos came as no surprise.

The landscape, however, was incredibly beautiful. I was taken to the extinct volcano of Tagaytay through fishing villages, rice fields, coconut groves, and rolling hills of mangoes; we ate delicious ice-cream from a young coconut shell as we looked down on the turquoise waters of Lake Tal.

My next stop was the scene of the greatest political tragedy and military debacle suffered by the United States in its whole history – Vietnam. I had watched the French cut their losses in 1954 through the Geneva Agreement, which Eden helped to negotiate but Dulles refused to endorse. In June that year, even before the meeting in Geneva, I had written that, if the West wished to contain communism in Asia by military force, it would need more ground troops than it was able or willing to provide:

The idea of entangling the Western countries in Asia by a policy of
creeping intervention involves gambling that once America has committed
a division to Indo-China, she will be compelled to reinforce failure by
committing a whole army. The further gamble that Britain and America's
other allies would be compelled to add their military weight is also
dangerous; it might do irreparable damage to the Western Alliance.

It would be foolish to underestimate the military importance of Indo-
China to the defence of Southern Asia, or to pretend that Western
prestige will not suffer by its loss. But a prize of infinitely more
importance than Indo-China could be thrown away if the West chose
the wrong methods for trying to save Indo-China from communism.

In the event, the United States got the worst of both worlds – the odium
which its military methods were bound to attract, plus the humiliation of
ultimate defeat. Yet, whatever the views of some of their military advisers,
neither Eisenhower, Kennedy, nor Johnson ever intended to entangle
America in Vietnam as in fact they did. Eisenhower's motto was 'Let Asians
fight Asians'; but when he left office there were eight hundred American
military personnel in Vietnam. Kennedy rejected the recommendation of
General Maxwell Taylor and Walt Rostow that he should send ten thousand
combat troops to Vietnam. Following his assassination, President Johnson
defeated Goldwater in the 1964 election after rejecting both the despatch of
'American boys to do the fighting for Asian boys', and the bombing of the
supply lines in the north. Yet by November 1963 there were already 15,500
American military personnel in Vietnam. Two years later they had risen to
184,000. They had reached half a million by early 1968.

When I landed in Saigon in April 1964 the Americans were everywhere
but in the front line. Besides the military 'advisers' there were thousands
of Americans from the CIA, the US Information Services, the Aid
Programme, and, of course, the Embassy. The US Army, Navy and Air
Force were engaged in fighting one another, and all three were at
loggerheads with the CIA and the State Department; the latter tended to
share the British view that the Vietnamese Government was heading for a
disaster from which no amount of military intervention by the United
States could rescue it.

I was fully briefed by the Americans, and taken in a helicopter gunship
to positions in the Mekong Delta, where the fighting was fiercest. On the
advice of a British policeman with intimate experience of the emergency
in Malaya, the Americans persuaded the Vietnam Government to herd
the peasants into 'strategic hamlets'. It was a disaster; peasants should

never be taken more than five miles from the land they farm. Instead of breaking the communist infrastructure, as intended, these hamlets were heavily infiltrated by the Viet Cong; of eight thousand only one thousand were judged secure. The mutinous despair of the peasants in the one I visited was worthy of the Gulag Archipelago.

In fact the analogy with the Malayan emergency was misguided. In Malaya the communists belonged almost wholly to the Chinese minority; they were easily identifiable and loathed by the Malays as trying to impose a Chinese dictatorship. The Viet Cong, on the other hand, were drawn from Vietnamese in the Delta; they had a long history of struggle against foreign domination, in which the Communist Party had played a leading role since the Japanese occupation in 1944. In the early years of American involvement, those Viet Cong who came down from the north were practically all refugees returning to their homes. The Viet Cong fought almost entirely with weapons captured from the government troops. There was no evidence of Chinese intervention whatever. Indeed the historic enmity between China and the Vietnamese ensured that the only Communist power which had good relations with the Viet Cong, or with the Communist Government in Hanoi, was the Soviet Union, not China. The main recruiting agent for the Viet Cong was indiscriminate bombing and shelling by the government forces, and the Viet Cong's main arsenal was the United States.

All this was explained to me not only by the excellent British military attaché, Major Henry Lee, but also by friends in the Commonwealth embassies, and even by the new Vietnamese leader, General Minh, a big melancholy man with the physique of Ernest Bevin but none of his character. The briefing from the American generals, however, was grossly overoptimistic about the military situation, and significantly reticent about the fighting qualities of the Vietnamese themselves.

General Stilwell, the American Chief of Staff, had been with me at a strategic seminar in Switzerland some years earlier, and I had met General Dupuy at the Imperial Defence College, where I had been lecturing for several years. There were other IDC 'graduates' in the British, Australian, and American embassies in Saigon, all of whom had been on the same course twelve months earlier. This confirmed my view that those British inter-service colleges which accepted foreign students could play an invaluable role in lubricating cooperation between the British Government and its allies, as well as between the different armed services and government departments inside Britain itself. As Defence Secretary I made a point of encouraging these colleges.

When the case against America's involvement was so compelling, and the unsuitability of America's strategy so obvious, it was difficult to understand how Washington had got itself so deeply involved – particularly after successive Presidents had argued so powerfully against it. The reasons were so deeply rooted in the psychology of America's postwar foreign policy that they are worth describing.

First, there was the feeling that the United States had a moral duty to promote its own concept of political freedom wherever it could project its power – a conviction which Kennedy held much more strongly than Eisenhower.

Second, most Americans believed that the enemy of freedom everywhere was the Soviet Union, which used the monolithic apparatus of international communism as its weapon. American leaders found it difficult to imagine that Communist governments could be hostile to one another, even after Tito's defection from the Cominform. Thus on May 18th, 1951, Dean Rusk could say of China as Assistant Secretary of State: 'The Peiping regime may be a colonial Russian government – a Slavic Manchukuo on a larger scale. It is not the Government of China. It does not pass the first test. It is not Chinese.' Yet hostility between the Soviet and Chinese Communist Parties went right back to 1926.

For these reasons, American governments found it difficult to appreciate that conflicts in the Third World might arise from local or regional factors which had deep historical roots. I was familiar with the syndrome; I had been arguing for years with British socialists who believed that capitalism was the only cause of war, as if there had been no wars before Hargreaves invented the spinning jenny. It did not surprise me that some American Presidents could believe that, as Reagan once said, if it wasn't for Communist Russia, 'there wouldn't be any hot-spots in the world' – as if there had been no wars or revolutions before the Bolsheviks stormed the Winter Palace.

Finally, Americans combined their Manichean view of world politics, as a struggle to the death between absolute good and absolute evil, with a failure to understand the psychology of America's allies; from this union the Domino Theory was born. This theory held that if the United States lost one battle, or failed to respond to one challenge, all its alliances would collapse like a row of dominoes; and every country in the world would turn for protection to the Soviet Union. Even the most sophisticated Americans, such as Henry Kissinger, often used this argument. Yet when the United States finally withdrew in humiliation from Vietnam, not one domino fell, even in Southeast Asia. The only consequence in the region was a gruelling war between the two victorious Communist states, Vietnam and Cambodia; each was supported by one of the Communist superpowers, Russia and China.

These psychological misperceptions continue to distort American foreign policy. Despite efforts by the State Department and the CIA to put a more balanced view, the White House regularly ignores their expert advice. The military leaders – particularly the generals, such as Marshall and 'Vinegar Joe' Stilwell – have often had a more realistic view of the political issues than their political Commander in Chief. But, as I first discovered on that visit to Vietnam, once American forces were actually engaged, the strategy and tactics they adopted were often the product of inter-service rivalries, and they had a tendency to rely far too much on sophisticated weaponry in situations to which it was wholly inappropriate.

It was an immense relief for me to leave Saigon for Malaysia. There I found British forces engaged in another jungle war – the so-called 'confrontation' with Indonesia. But they pursued a strategy totally different from that of the Americans in Vietnam; and they had every prospect of success.

After meeting the political and military leaders in Singapore and Kuala Lumpur, I flew to Borneo to see the fighting on the ground. It was a fascinating experience. My guide was General Walter Walker, a wiry energetic enthusiast with bright eyes and a clipped moustache. As a fighting general with long experience commanding Gurkhas in the jungles of Burma and Malaya, he was perfectly suited to his job as Director of Operations.

The political background to the Confrontation was not encouraging. Sabah and Sarawak, the British territories in Borneo, had been pushed into the Federation of Malaysia with Malaya and Singapore, four hundred miles away across the sea, with whom they had nothing in common except a disaffected Chinese minority. Embedded in Sarawak was the little sultanate of Brunei, which was under British protection, but not part of the Federation. In 1963 Indonesia's President Sukarno decided to make common cause with the communists among the Chinese in Borneo; he began to infiltrate his soldiers across the nine hundred mile frontier separating Malaysian Borneo from the much larger part of the island, Kalimantan, which was part of Indonesia. His aim was to establish Indonesian control of the whole southeastern corner of Asia by destabilising Malaysia. The Indonesian island of Sumatra lay only a hundred miles off the western coast of Malaya itself; so he also tried to infiltrate agents across the straits of Sumatra into Singapore and Malaya, but the Royal Navy made this much more difficult.

When Confrontation began, the Malayan troops sent over from the mainland behaved very badly towards the local people in Borneo, whom they despised as barbarous tribesmen. All this meant that the task of dealing with infiltration had to lie overwhelmingly with British forces, since Sabah and Sarawak had no forces of their own, and the local tribes had nothing to fight with except blowpipes and parangs – the latter were useful for cutting off heads, but little else. The frontier ran across mountains and marshes, in dense forest and jungle. There were no roads. The helicopter was king; a battalion with six helicopters was worth a brigade with none. But most useful of all were units of the Special Air Service and its marine equivalent, the Special Boat Service. It was on that visit to Borneo that I first came to appreciate the extraordinary qualities of these élite forces.

Walter Walker took me to the group of huts which served as headquarters to 22 SAS. I was met by its commander, Lieutenant-Colonel John Woodhouse, a diffident, unmilitary figure, in rumpled khaki, who might have been a botanist. He was, by common consent among the few who knew his record, the greatest guerrilla warrior yet produced by the West – a man to compare with Ho Chi Minh. When his job in Borneo was over, the British army marked its appreciation of his unique qualities by putting him in charge of rifle ranges in Germany.

The SAS in Borneo worked in sixteen patrols of four men each, carrying medical supplies, sophisticated signals equipment, explosives and a variety of other weapons. Both officers and NCOs could speak Malay, Thai, and Arabic. They had been attached to casualty wards in British hospitals to learn how to treat all types of injury, and made a point of treating the local people as well as themselves. The key to their success was good relations with the tribes on the frontier, who provided intelligence and scouts for the British forces; the SAS lived in the tribesmen's huts and ate the same, often revolting food. The British army had learned in many campaigns, and particularly under General Templer in Malaya, that winning what it called 'the hearts and minds' of the local population was the pre-condition of success in guerrilla warfare. Next to the SAS, the Gurkhas were most effective, since, in addition to their long experience of jungle fighting, their battalions were up to strength. The British infantry battalions were usually short of a quarter of their men, and took four months to become as good as Gurkhas, since they had to learn special jungle skills like tracking. Nevertheless, many later visits confirmed my first impressions – there is no army in the world which has men as disciplined, adaptable, and good humoured, with the ability to fight well in any environment, as the British professional soldier.

I met three old friends from Britain during that brief visit to Borneo. The *Observer* correspondent was Dennis Bloodworth, from my days in North Africa. The Governor's private secretary was Peter Ratcliffe, a debonaire schoolfriend from Keighley, who had ended a very irregular war by running an illegal radio station in Indonesia. The curator of the anthropological museum in Sarawak was Tom Harrison, the Cambridge man who had helped to start Mass Observation and irritated us at Oxford by that all too accurate study of our love lives entitled *Oxsex*; during the war he had organised the headhunters in Borneo against the Japanese.

My next stop was in Aden, where another misbegotten federation was in trouble. The Conservative government had forced the urbanised Arabs round the military base in the old Crown Colony, many of whom were from Somalia, into a federation controlled by the backward sheikhs from the protectorates in the surrounding mountains, whose main occupation was fighting one another. The federation as a whole had bad relations with all its neighbours – with Nasserite Yemen to the west, with the monarchy of Saudi Arabia to the north, and with the Sultan of Muscat to the east. Once again the British soldier had to clean up the mess his government had created.

The town of Aden was a concrete furnace built on the extinct volcano which gave its name to Crater, the most populous area. Though Britain established a coaling station there in the nineteenth century, Aden had no strategic importance until the RAF started building its largest base in the world at Khormakshar in the sixties; the word Aden does not appear once in Sir John Glubb's book *Britain and the Arabs*, published in 1959. Since Britain rarely obtained the right to overfly Arab countries after the Suez affair, Khormakshar was of limited value except as a staging post for military aircraft on their way to East Africa; even then they could reach it only after flying over Turkey and stopping at Bahrain in the Gulf.

However, this increase in Britain's military presence gave Nasser his chance to inflame the local people against Britain through his client state in Yemen. By putting Aden into a federation with the backward sheikhdoms of its hinterland, the Conservative government made both its political and military problems more difficult. Resistance to Britain among the Adenis was greatly increased by their forced marriage with people they regarded as barbarous brigands; and it was far more difficult for British forces to control the mountain tribes than to control Aden itself.

Just before I left Britain, there had been an uproar in the press because some SAS soldiers killed near the Yemeni frontier had had their heads cut off. When I landed from Singapore our infantry were fighting rebellious tribesmen in the mountains of Radfan. The British soldier was as resourceful in those barren mountains and deserts as in the tropical forests and jungles of Borneo. But once the troops moved out of an area, the rebels moved in again. The air force tried to control the region with its aging Hunters, as it used to control the north-west frontier of India; but their bombing and machine-gun fire did nothing to endear Britain to the local people.

I returned to Britain with my admiration for our armed services strengthened. Both in Borneo and in Aden I had learned that for this type of limited warfare we needed forces with light equipment and specialised training – exactly the opposite of the Americans in Vietnam. The key to success was to win 'the hearts and minds' of the local people. However, my dominant impression was that we had drifted into both these wars because we had adopted misguided expedients for dealing with short-term political problems, without considering Britain's real interests in the long term. I was determined that I would try to avoid this error if I ever became Defence Secretary myself.

I learned some other lessons from these visits to Africa, the Middle East and Asia before I entered office – above all that it is most unwise to generalise about the Third World. The phrase 'Third World' was first used at the height of the Cold War to distinguish the developing countries from the West and the Communist bloc; it is still useful for this purpose. But it covers such a variety of countries, with cultures and histories so diverse, and in economic and political situations so different, that it can be dangerously misleading. It is no more helpful to put all these countries together as 'non-aligned'; the group which met together at Bandoeng under this title included Japan as well as India and Yugoslavia but excluded Austria, which is non-aligned by treaty.

A government's foreign policy cannot afford to use so broad a brush; it must be based on far more discriminating criteria, which take account of each country's history, its relations with its neighbours, its social, economic, and political conditions. This applies as much in Europe, the American subcontinents, and the Communist world, as it does in the so-called Third World. The temptation to oversimplify for political or intellectual convenience should be resisted.

Oversimplification is no less dangerous in defining the foreign policy of one's own country. Dean Acheson misled a generation when he said:

'Britain has lost an empire, but not yet found a role.' Countries are not actors in a soap opera which must choose whether to play the *jeune premier*, the grandfather, the hero, or the villain. They are complex societies of individual human beings undergoing continual change. Their governments must try to understand the special needs and aspirations of their own peoples, and consider how the world outside their frontiers affects the fulfilment of their aims.

Every government also inherits a complex structure of prior commitments and interests abroad, which can be changed only slowly, if at all. And all governments may have to adapt to technological changes which affect not only their foreign policies, but their very chances of survival. This was the problem which exercised me most of all, since the development of nuclear weapons was shaking the world to its foundations.

CHAPTER TWELVE

Taming the Atom

Tyger! Tyger! burning bright
In the forests of the night,
What immortal hand or eye
Could frame thy fearful symmetry?

In what distant deeps or skies
Burnt the fire of thine eyes?
On what wings dare he aspire?
What the hand dare seize the fire?

When the stars threw down their spears,
And water'd heaven with their tears,
Did he smile his work to see?
Did he who made the Lamb make thee?

– 'The Tyger' William Blake

VERY SOON AFTER the end of the war I had become obsessed with the moral, political, and military implications of nuclear weapons. How could governments justify the threat to slaughter millions of innocent civilians as a means of deterring war, especially after the Nuremberg trials had sentenced political leaders to death for less? When Russia had acquired the capacity for nuclear retaliation, was the threat really credible in any case? And if it was credible as a deterrent against an attack on a country which possessed nuclear weapons, could it deter an attack on an ally who had no nuclear weapons of his own, and no control over their use? Had nuclear weapons, as de Gaulle used to claim, made alliances impossible? Or had Churchill been right in suggesting that nuclear weapons might make war itself impossible?

I have been wrestling with such questions for the last forty years. Changes in military technology, and better understanding of what the effect of using nuclear weapons might be, have had some impact on the nature of the problem. It is possible to draw a few conclusions by studying the many wars which have taken place over the period, some of which have directly involved countries which possess nuclear weapons. But it may be impossible to give final answers to all the political and military questions unless a nuclear war actually takes place – and there may then be no survivors to learn the lessons.

An answer to the moral question is no less difficult, unless you believe that the use or threat of force at any level is wrong in all circumstances. If, however, you believe, like me, that the moral acceptability of nuclear deterrence depends on whether it can in fact prevent a Third World War, then the answer becomes a matter of political rather than of moral judgment. A Third World War would be an unimaginable catastrophe even if nuclear weapons were not used, given the vast increase in the destructiveness of other weapons. Worse still, now that most sixth-formers know in principle how to make nuclear weapons, a world war which started even in a non-nuclear world would be unlikely to end without becoming nuclear; for one side or the other would produce and use nuclear weapons, either to avoid its defeat, or to accelerate its victory – like the United States in 1945.

That is why sensible governments are now coming to the conclusion that lasting peace cannot be achieved if the arms race continues. Peace in the nuclear age must depend on cooperation between at least the major powers, to establish a new international security system in which all weapons – and not just nuclear weapons – are subject to collective control.

This was an objective I had already embraced for many reasons in my *New Fabian Essay* in 1951. I have always defined socialism as the collective control of power in society, whether political, economic or physical. The crucial factor in slowly bringing governments to see that there must be control of military power by an international society, has been their failure to find any other means of coping with the problems posed by nuclear weapons.

As I have described, my first reaction to the news of Hiroshima was enormous relief; like millions of other servicemen, I was simply grateful that I would not have to fight in the Far East now that the war in Europe was over. Yet I was appalled when I heard suggestions that the West should use its nuclear monopoly to force Russia into political submission.

Fortunately, however tempting the military arguments, whenever responsible political leaders were presented with that option, they rightly
backed away. The American monopoly did not last long in any case;
Russia exploded its first hydrogen bomb only nine months after the
United States. I tried to explore the implications in November 1953:

> At present US planners estimate that seventy per cent of an attacking
> bomber force would penetrate America's air defences. Thus America's
> atomic deterrent has vanished in a night – indeed America may well be
> more vulnerable to atomic attack than the Soviet Union, since America's
> industrial strength is concentrated in known locations, largely around the
> American frontier, while Russian industry is dispersed throughout Asia.'

This was the point at which Washington began to look for alternatives to
an all-out nuclear exchange. Unfortunately, when Dulles redefined America's policy, as deterrence by the threat of 'massive retaliation at a time
and place of our own choosing', his words were taken as a restatement of
the old doctrine of all-out strategic attack on the Soviet Union, rather
than as a modification of it. Meanwhile the British government was
moving towards total reliance on the nuclear destruction of Soviet cities,
just as American thinking was moving in the opposite direction. In 1954
Prime Minister Churchill justified handing over the British base at Suez
on the grounds that the hydrogen bomb had made such bases irrelevant.
'If I were to portray to the House,' he stammered, choking with emotion,
'the first few weeks of a war as it would be under present conditions, I
would convince members of the obsolescence of the base.' He made this
speech just after the Korean war, in which Britain as well as the United
States suffered heavy casualties without using nuclear weapons. Ironically
enough, two years later Eden felt able to ignore Krushchev's nuclear
threats during a war over Suez.

Korea, Suez, Hungary and Vietnam all showed that the value of nuclear
deterrence had severe limitations. I did not believe that any of the
Western governments were devoting adequate attention to the imminent
prospect of the so-called 'nuclear stalemate'; so I spent much of my last
eight years in Opposition working on this problem, with friends in
Britain and the United States who shared my concern.

We were a mixed bunch. In Washington our most important associate
was Paul Nitze, while Jim King took a critical interest in our work.
Senator Ralph Flanders, the patrician Republican from Vermont who,
almost alone in the Congress, had fought Senator McCarthy's smear

campaign, was another supporter. There were also journalists, academics, and scientists all over the United States; for example Colonel Dick Leghorn was an expert on aerial photography who worked in Rochester for Eastman Kodak.

In Britain the core of our group was four people with very different backgrounds: Rear Admiral Sir Anthony Buzzard, Professor Patrick Blackett, Richard Goold-Adams, and myself. Tony Buzzard was a pale intellectual monomaniac – not an uncommon type in the British services – who wore a surgical collar round his neck; he had just retired as head of naval intelligence and was a committed Christian. Pat Blackett was a lean, dark and handsome scientist who had won the Nobel Prize for physics, after doing operational research for the navy during the war. He had already caused a stir by his scepticism about the feasibility of producing a hydrogen bomb small enough to fit on an aeroplane; he was not the only scientist whose technical judgment was sometimes distorted by his moral feelings. Dick Goold-Adams was an equable, level-headed Wykehamist who worked for *The Economist*; he made sure we did not stray too far from common sense.

We first came together after I wrote an article for *Encounter* in July 1955 entitled *The Bomb that Didn't Go Off*. The West's proven reluctance to employ nuclear weapons, I argued, cast doubt on the credibility of nuclear deterrence. Yet so long as the use of nuclear weapons was assumed to be inevitable in any European war, and the Europeans had no say in the decision to use them, there was little incentive for Europe to make the peacetime sacrifices required for any alternative strategy. I wrote:

> There are signs that Western Europe is slowly slipping into the sort
> of apathy about defence in which neutralism breeds. Is there any
> policy which does not entail the use of weapons which would be self-
> destructive? There is a strong case for basing NATO defence policy
> not on the H-bomb, but on so-called conventional forces with atomic
> arms. This policy would work, however, only if the West deliberately
> aimed at restricting war to the military targets in the theatre of the
> land fighting; otherwise it would be difficult to prevent a rapid
> transition to the indiscriminate use of thermonuclear weapons against
> enemy cities.

This theme was taken up by others, such as Alastair Buchan, son of the novelist and diplomat John Buchan; he was then political correspondent of *The Economist*, and had excellent connections in Washington. Meanwhile my friends and I were meeting almost weekly to produce a booklet on the subject for the Royal Institute of International Affairs. It was published in the autumn of 1956 with the title *On Limiting Atomic War*. This booklet was the first extended treatment of the doctrine which was becoming known as 'graduated deterrence'; it formed the basis of the strategy adopted ten years later by NATO as 'Flexible Response'.

Henry Kissinger had independently come to similar conclusions in his magisterial work on *Nuclear Weapons and Foreign Policy*, which was published almost simultaneously with ours, by the Council on Foreign Relations in New York. I had no personal contact with Kissinger at the time. When we first met a year later we both bitterly regretted we had committed ourselves to the concept of limited nuclear warfare. By then we knew the results of two NATO exercises which assumed the use of tactical nuclear weapons, 'Carte Blanche' and 'Sage Brush'; these demonstrated that, however carefully such weapons were targetted, their explosion would kill scores of millions of civilians, and render West Germany uninhabitable. Nevertheless, our general analysis of the impact of nuclear weapons both on strategy and on diplomacy remained valid, and is still the basis of our thinking, though we have often disagreed about its implications for policy.

Following the publication of the Chatham House booklet, others gathered round us, particularly attracted by the moral case for an alternative to the global nuclear holocaust. The outstanding Anglican intellectual, Bishop Bell of Chichester, the leading layman of the Church of England, Sir Kenneth Grubb, and Alan Booth, Secretary of the Methodist Conference, agreed to join us in convoking a meeting at Brighton in January 1957, to which we invited senior service officers who had recently retired, some leading politicians, and a handful of journalists with an interest in defence. George Ball came from the United States, where there was growing support for our views.

The Brighton Conference was a great success, and the members agreed they should form an association to keep in touch. We used the few hundred pounds left over to circulate roneoed copies of relevant articles from the American press which were difficult to obtain in Britain. On October 27th that year I was at a Bilderberg meeting at the Italian spa of Fiuggi, when we heard that the Russians had just launched their Sputnik. Among the Americans present were Paul Nitze, and General McCormack, who had recently retired as head of Air Force Research and Development, and was already sympathetic to our views. They were flabbergasted at the news, and deeply concerned at the superiority of Soviet missile technology which it implied. I took advantage of the situation to take Shep Stone, of the Ford Foundation, for a walk beneath the dripping plane trees outside the hotel. Would his foundation consider giving us a thousand pounds to continue the work of our Brighton Conference Association? He replied that they never considered applications for less than a hundred thousand dollars.

On my return we drafted an application for enough money to set up an Institute of Strategic Studies in London, which would do serious work on these problems. It would involve other Europeans besides the British, and develop contacts with similar bodies in the United States. The Ford Foundation agreed immediately, and we had the Institute running within a year, with Alastair Buchan as its first Director. It has remained the most respected independent authority on strategic problems ever since, and has now become the International Institute of Strategic Studies, at which leading members of the defence intelligentsia from all over the world are proud to spend a year or more.

For many reasons we focussed initially on the implications of nuclear weapons for the North Atlantic alliance. How could America's commitment to nuclear retaliation on behalf of its non-nuclear allies be made more credible? Could some way be found of sharing America's decision to use nuclear weapons with its allies, or at least with those on whose soil the weapons were based? Was there any strategy for the use of battlefield nuclear weapons in Europe which would be militarily advantageous and acceptable to the Europeans? Once nuclear weapons were used at any level, would it be possible to avoid escalation to global thermonuclear war? Was there any way to prevent the proliferation of nuclear weapons to any country with the capacity to produce them, not only inside the alliance, but also outside?

I produced innumerable speeches and articles on these problems, and was continually forced back to the conclusion I described in an international magazine called *Confluence*, in 1957: 'It is in seeking a new security settlement based on the international limitation and control of armaments in Central Europe that NATO might find the solution of its current military problems. The "shield" concept has already been found to make too heavy demands on its manpower. The "tripwire" concept which has replaced it will prove to make too heavy demands on its willpower.' If NATO failed to develop realistic policies for arms control in Europe it would become 'a symbol of old-fashioned thinking about the Cold War, increasingly remote from the desires and expectations of the peoples to which it is responsible – a millstone rather than a rock of strength.'

Whether or not they agreed with this conclusion, the military and diplomatic analysis on which I based it was well understood among the new breed of defence intellectuals which was then proliferating on both sides of the Atlantic. It was much more difficult for me to explain my thinking to the politicians in Britain. When, in 1957, I told the House of Commons there was a risk that if war broke out in Europe, Russia and the United States might confine their use of nuclear weapons to the territory of their allies, keeping their homelands as sanctuaries, the Conservative benches roared with laughter at the very idea. I met little more understanding among my Labour colleagues. They were immersed in theological disputations which were primarily designed to avoid the need for answering specific questions about what Britain should do in the real world. The gulf between 'unilateralism', the new fashion in which the pacifist tradition of the party now clothed itself, and 'multilateralism' was beginning to widen.

In December, 1957 I went to a meeting in the flat of Kingsley Martin, editor of the *New Statesman* to discuss whether it would make sense to launch a national campaign on these issues of nuclear strategy. Besides Kingsley and his partner, Dorothy Woodman, I found old friends there such as George Kennan and Pat Blackett, and some Labour colleagues such as Michael Foot, the Methodist parson Reg Sorenson, and the brilliant lawyer, Gerald Gardiner, who later became Wilson's Lord Chancellor. There were also more exotic types like Stephen King-Hall, a liberal publicist, the Old Bradfordian novelist, J. B. Priestley and his wife, the archaeologist Jacquetta Hawkes, the philosopher Bertrand Russell – who had once recommended the West to use its nuclear weapons against the Russians while it still had a monopoly – and Canon Collins, an Anglican cleric– who in manner very much resembled his namesake, the curate Mr Collins, in *Pride and Prejudice*, though I do not believe they were related.

Kennan, Blackett and I were not sufficiently impressed to attend a second meeting at Canon Collins' house, at which it was decided to support a Campaign for Nuclear Disarmament. We found the arguments of the others unrealistic, and distrusted some of their motives. Even so, at the initial rally which followed, the Executive Committee of the new Campaign did not want to commit itself either to unilateral nuclear disarmament by Britain, or to a mass movement carrying out public demonstrations like the Aldermaston march. It nevertheless surrendered to the demand for both, for fear that otherwise the unilateralists would set up a separate organisation of their own.

Such surrenders by the executive to the floor of the conference have characterised CND ever since. Broadly speaking, most of the executive committee has been sympathetic to the Labour Party, and sometimes to the Communist Party, while the conference has been controlled by the New Left – a mixture of Liberal utopians and leftist ex-Communists of every type; my old comrade from Oxford, Philip Toynbee, spoke at the first Aldermaston rally.

None the less, CND soon established itself as a powerful force inside the Labour Party. Its greatest triumph in the early years was to capture some of the major trade unions for unilateralism – the Transport and General Workers' Union, the railwaymen, the mineworkers, the engineers, and the shop-workers; in 1959 even the traditionally moderate General and Municipal Workers succumbed.

As a result, the arguments inside the Labour Party about defence became ever more Byzantine; Nye Bevan, who had already committed himself not to 'go naked into the conference chamber', performed prodigious acrobatics in a vain attempt to straddle the divide between unilateralist and multilateralist. At one point he told the left-wing leader of the transport workers, Frank Cousins, that he would rather get out than be told by the trade unions what to do in the Foreign Office. In any case, he reminded Cousins, the way union delegates voted at their conferences bore no relation to the way their members voted at general elections – a seminal truth too often disregarded.

Nowadays the political debate about the so-called 'independent British deterrent' is conducted as a sort of morality play between abstract ideas called Unilateralism and Multilateralism. It is easy to forget that in the fifties and sixties both sides were much more concerned with the political, economic and military arguments about the wisdom of diverting Britain's scarce defence resources to the maintenance of a strategic nuclear force. Leading Conservatives with relevant ministerial experience expressed doubts or outright opposition to a British deterrent; they included Anthony Head, who had been Eden's Defence Secretary at Suez, Peter Thorneycroft, who was to become Defence Secretary under Douglas-Home, Nigel Birch, my wartime colleague in Italy who had been the minister for the army, and Aubrey Jones, who as Minister of Supply had been intimately concerned with our nuclear weapons programme. George Jellicoe, while he was actually First Lord of the Admiralty and responsible for the Polaris programme, suggested in March 1964 that Britain might pool its nuclear deterrent with the rest of the alliance.

These days most people believe that when Gaitskell decided to 'fight,

fight, and fight again' against the decision of the 1960 Labour Party
Conference to reject 'any defence policy based on the threat of the use of
strategic nuclear weapons', he was fighting to maintain an independent
British nuclear deterrent. On the contrary, he was simply demanding that
Britain should remain in NATO, and that the alliance should continue
relying on American nuclear weapons unless there was an international
disarmament agreement to get rid of all nuclear weapons. The Campaign
for Democratic Socialism, which fought for Gaitskell at the grass roots of
the Labour Party, supported the unilateral renunciation of Britain's own
nuclear weapons. The statement, 'Policy for Peace', on which Gaitskell
finally won his battle at the 1961 Party Conference, explicitly stated:
'Britain should cease the attempt to remain an independent nuclear
power, since this neither strengthens the alliance, nor is it now a sensible
use of our limited resources.'

The Punch and Judy show between Multilateralism and Unilateralism
into which the argument has since degenerated is mainly the responsibility
of CND. That body has in recent years combined its demand that
Britain should give up its own nuclear weapons, with the demand that we
should expel all United States' nuclear forces from Britain; it is also
committed, although its spokesmen usually prefer to play this down, to get
Britain out of NATO altogether.

Conservative Governments have also distorted the argument by exploiting an atavistic jingoism to justify the 'independent deterrent'. As I said at
the time, they clutched at the nuclear missile as a virility symbol to
compensate for the exposure of their military impotence at Suez. Yet when
Douglas-Home made Polaris the central issue in the 1964 election campaign,
he lost by a narrow margin, although public opinion was with him on that
particular issue. It is possible, of course, that Labour would then have
had a larger majority if it had had a more popular defence policy.

By then, however, the strategic problems posed by nuclear weapons for
NATO were becoming inseparable from the general problem of nuclear
proliferation. On February 13th, 1960 France carried out its first nuclear
test in the Sahara. An American study of *The Nth Country Problem and
Arms Control* estimated that within five years a further eleven countries
would be able to produce atomic weapons at very low cost. A country
might produce its first two kiloton weapons from scratch for a total
expenditure of 150 million dollars, or for as little as ten million dollars if
it had already amassed twenty kilograms of plutonium 239 in its existing
industrial reactors – and for even less if it cut corners in arranging
protection against radiation. Heavy expenditure would be required only

for the delivery system, if the enemy had sophisticated defences. I pointed out that two Hiroshima-size bombs exploded in the holds of cargo vessels in Haifa and Tel Aviv might destroy Israel as a state.

Meanwhile the United States and the Soviet Union were each becoming concerned with the risk of an enemy first strike on its retaliatory forces. To make a surprise attack less effective, each decided to make enormous increases in the number and variety of its nuclear delivery systems, and to make them less vulnerable – by hardening missile sites, by putting bombers on airborne alert, and by putting missiles in submarines. The nuclear arms race was accelerating rapidly, and its cost was rocketing up. In March 1960, I explored the new universe of problems now emerging in a Fabian pamphlet entitled *The Race against the H-Bomb*.

I argued that neither of the superpowers could achieve security in such an arms race. The increasing cost and difficulty of achieving absolute security should direct attention to the likely intentions of a potential enemy, rather than to his military capability alone. The size of the superpowers' existing nuclear forces made it highly unlikely that either would deliberately take any risk of challenging the other directly; this had enormously reduced the degree of credibility needed to make nuclear deterrence effective in Europe. In the second Berlin crisis, Russia was taking fewer risks of war with America than a decade earlier, when its relative nuclear strength was much smaller; the European allies were worrying too much about the credibility of the American deterrent.

This led me later to formulate 'The Healey Theorem': it takes only five per cent credibility of American retaliation to deter the Russians, but ninety-five per cent credibility to reassure the Europeans. Most of the strategic argument inside NATO is concerned about narrowing the gap between the degree of credibility needed for deterrence and that needed for reassurance; and Europe's concern with the credibility of American deterrence is a function of its general confidence in the wisdom and consistency of American leadership, rather than of changes in the relative military power of the United States and the Soviet Union.

The Cuban missile crisis in October 1962 threw more light on the problem. There was at first a real and dangerous misunderstanding between Krushchev and Kennedy. Krushchev put his missiles into Cuba after the Bay of Pigs affair, because he could think of no other way of deterring another American attack on his Cuban client; he thought America would not react, because he himself had not reacted when America put missiles into Turkey on the Soviet border. Kennedy, still perhaps influenced by his own false election propaganda about 'the missile gap', thought the Soviet missiles were designed to take part in a surprise attack on the United States. He compelled Krushchev to reverse his plans – not, however, by threatening a nuclear attack on the Soviet Union, but by using his navy to impose a blockade of Cuba. Once Krushchev realised his own error, he took out the missiles already planted, and Kennedy removed his Jupiter and Thor missiles from Europe in return.

The Cuban missile crisis was in some ways the mirror image of the crisis twenty years later which led to the INF agreement. Kennedy might well have claimed, as Reagan did, that it was only his firm response to his opponent's deployment of missiles, which led to an agreement in which he had to give up less than his opponent. Like the INF agreement, the resolution of the Cuban missile crisis produced exceptionally good relations between the Soviet and American leaders in the short period before Kennedy's assassination. And despite the alarm the allies initially felt over Cuba, Kennedy's skilful handling of the crisis created a confidence among them which they had not felt for some time.

On the other hand, the Cuban crisis greatly strengthened the feeling among members of the Kennedy administration that they must abandon reliance on the nuclear tripwire for deterring an attack on Western Europe. The Defence Secretary, Bob McNamara, was convinced that no American President would ever actually authorise the use of nuclear weapons, unless the United States was under direct attack; he was equally convinced that no President would be justified in doing so. He was deeply worried that Britain or France might try to trigger off the thermonuclear holocaust by using their nuclear weapons first. Indeed some statements by leaders in London and Paris suggested that they saw their 'independent' deterrents as really intended for this catalytic role.

A year earlier Dean Acheson had chaired a committee for Kennedy, in which Paul Nitze and Albert Wohlstetter took part. This recommended a substantial improvement in NATO's conventional capability, sufficient to stop anything but an all-out invasion, together with central control by the United States of all allied nuclear forces, including those of Britain and France. Indeed, it claimed, 'over the long run it would be desirable if the British decided to phase out of the nuclear deterrent business. If the development of Skybolt is not warranted for US purposes alone, the United States should not prolong the life of the V-bomber force by this or other means'.

Kennedy and McNamara endorsed the Acheson Report. When the US Air Force decided that Skybolt would not meet its needs, they cancelled it in November 1962 without even informing Macmillan in advance. Since Macmillan had abandoned the attempt to produce a British strategic nuclear system, it looked as if his 'independent' deterrent was gone for good.

But Macmillan insisted on meeting Kennedy in Nassau in December, seeing this as his chance of getting Kennedy to let him have the far superior Polaris system. He exploited Kennedy's guilt over the way Skybolt was cancelled, and invoked the memory of his own American mother, in a tearful appeal to the Anglo-American heritage. To the chagrin of the American officials present, including McNamara, Kennedy gave in, and offered Britain Polaris. He thereby wrecked not only his own defence policy, but also a major objective of his foreign policy – to get Britain into the Common Market. For the Polaris deal made it certain de Gaulle would veto Britain's entry.

A key condition of the Nassau agreement was that Britain should put its Polaris submarines into a multilateral naval force to which all the NATO navies would contribute. This so-called MLF was a Heath Robinson contraption whose only purpose was political; it was designed to control the British and French strategic nuclear weapons and to give the non-nuclear Europeans the impression that somehow they would share in the decision to use America's nuclear deterrent. I used to call it 'artificial dissemination'. George Ball, however, then Under Secretary at the State Department, and Henry Owen, head of its Policy Planning Staff, saw the MLF as the grit in the oyster, round which the pearl of European unity would form. In fact it never got off the stocks; France opposed it in principle, of course, and no one had the slightest idea how it would work in practice.

The Labour Party gave the impression it would abandon Polaris if it won power, but committed itself only to 'renegotiate the Nassau agreement'. It was still deeply divided between unilateralists and multi-lateralists. However, I myself and most of the Labour defence experts in Parliament, were less concerned with Polaris than with getting a shift in the strategy of NATO as a whole; we wanted to move away from deterrence by the nuclear tripwire, towards defence by conventional forces which would be adequate to resist anything but an all-out attack by the Warsaw powers – which, in our view, was an almost inconceivable contingency.

In the course of all these discussions of nuclear policy I came to know many of the key figures in Western strategic thinking on both sides of the Atlantic. In the United States some of the administration's most important advisers had no direct experience of fighting in a real war. This was particularly true of the brilliant intellectuals at the RAND Corporation in California, which had established itself as the leading think-tank for Pentagon, and had access to all its secrets. They were mainly economists by training, and had developed a vocabulary for 'thinking about the unthinkable' which had all the weaknesses of economic jargon. The universe of nuclear strategy was so difficult to comprehend, and the horrors it contained were so repugnant to normal people, that its study required the same clinical detachment as the study of venereal disease. But that very detachment tended to blind the experts to the human realities, and to enslave them to abstract concepts, the validity of which had never been tested, and in many cases could never be tested. Moreover, many of these American concepts were quite foreign to the thinking of Soviet strategists on the other side.

Even the concepts of 'first-strike' and 'second-strike', 'counter-force' and 'counter-city' required assumptions about the enemy reaction which might be quite unfounded. I remember reviewing an American book on Soviet strategy which argued that, because Soviet missiles were heavier and more accurate than American, the Kremlin must be planning a first-strike against America's retaliatory power; it never occurred to the writer that the Russians might prefer as a matter of common sense to build heavier and more accurate missiles if they were able to do so. Similarly, the Russian leaders found it difficult to accept the concept of 'mutual assured destruction'. Krushchev started developing defences against nuclear attack simply because – like Reagan later – he thought defence was a good thing; he was baffled when the Americans claimed that such defences could have no rationale except as a part of a first-strike force.

The cleverest of these gurus from RAND was Tom Schelling, a young Harvard economist of Danish extraction who looked like a cross between the comedian Joe E. Brown, and Mr Noah in a child's toy-box. He had one of the most powerful intellects I have ever come across, with a remarkable capacity for the illuminating analogy. However, after his first visit to Vietnam, where he saw his abstract theory of 'compellence' put into bloody and senseless action, he expressed his resulting sense of guilt in a moving address to the annual ISS conference. RAND's most brilliant virtuoso, however, was the astonishing Herman Kahn, a fat ebullient oracle who talked with the same scintillating rapidity as Isaiah Berlin, but with none of the latter's pragmatic common sense. He was said to have had the highest IQ ever found in the American Army, and listed a Sears–Roebuck catalogue of nuclear options in his book *On Thermonuclear War*. I am glad to say that when he gave me a copy, he inscribed it to 'my most persuasive dissenter'. The most pragmatic intellectual from RAND was Albert Wohlstetter, a tall, red-haired German whose wife, Roberta, was a historian as clever as he; he has spent his life in a fruitless hunt for a way of using nuclear weapons without blowing up the world, for fear that Russia will find it first. I suspect that if anyone ever does find such a way, it will be an Israeli.

The British defence intelligentsia were refreshingly different. Strategic studies at that time had little appeal for the academic community, with the outstanding exception of Michael Howard, who had been wounded in the war. Most of my colleagues in this field were recently retired service officers who could apply the lessons of their own experience in war to the abstract theories of the American intellectuals. Two of my best friends were senior Air Marshals; Jack Slessor had organised the dropping of supplies to Warsaw as head of the Middle East Air Force, and Ralph Cochrane had commanded bomber groups during the war. Their fighting experience went right back to the Great War, when the British air force was founded.

I found such senior officers exceptionally objective and humane in their approach to nuclear problems. Ralph Cochrane shocked some Americans when asked whether he thought a British pilot would think twice about obeying an order to drop the atom bomb on Moscow. He replied: 'I hope so.' I have rarely found soldiers, sailors and airmen to be as bloody-minded as journalists and politicians.

In those days there was much less interest in strategic nuclear problems on the Continent. The outstanding German in the field was Helmut Schmidt, then a young senator from Hamburg, who wrote his first book on nuclear strategy, *Defence or Retaliation*, in 1961. He was my age, had fought in Russia while I was fighting in Italy, and had come to very similar conclusions. We became close friends, and worked together in and out of government for thirty years.

It was much more difficult to make contact with French experts on nuclear strategy. Raymond Aron, a wise political philosopher who worked for *Le Figaro*, had written an excellent general book on *The Century of Total War*, but had little influence on government policy. But I did come to know the leading exponent of de Gaulle's strategic thinking, General Gallois. He was an air force officer, with the piercing pale blue eyes of a fanatic, and argued with Cartesian logic that alliances were impossible in the nuclear age, and that every country should therefore have its own nuclear deterrent – except Germany, of course.

By the time I entered the unimpressive portals of Britain's Defence Ministry as Secretary of State I was well equipped at least for the strategic problems I would have to face.

PART THREE: Office

CHAPTER THIRTEEN

Defence Secretary

He fought like those who've nought to lose;
Bestowed himself to balls
As one who for a further life
Had not a further use!

His comrades shifted like the flakes
When gusts reverse the snow;
But he remained alive because
Of vehemence to die!

– Emily Dickinson

WHEN THE GENERAL ELECTION took place on October 15th, 1964, I had been working for the Labour Party, as an official at Transport House or as an MP in Opposition, for nineteen years, without once having the power to decide directly what should happen in Britain or the world. I had been deeply involved as a constituency MP in the consequences of domestic policies. I had helped to frame the Labour Party's programmes both through the National Executive Committee and the Shadow Cabinet. But my responsibilities and my interests at the national level had been overwhelmingly in foreign policy and defence.

This in itself led me to play an active role in the battles over Bevanism in the fifties, and in the Byzantine manoeuvres over nuclear policy in the early sixties. Though I spent many exhausting days in these internecine struggles, I have not described them here; they are reported and analysed at length in Philip Williams' excellent biography of Hugh Gaitskell, and in the diaries or memoirs of many participants. Necessary though they were, I did not find such arguments rewarding. They were too often confined to theological disputations about socialist doctrine. Instead of concentrating on the formidable realities we would face once we were in office, they were concerned too much with how to present our policies so as to cause least offence to the Party's power-brokers in the trade unions or the constituencies.

Nevertheless, if ever I felt my socialist faith was weakening, I could restore it in a few minutes simply by standing in the gangway by the Tory backbenchers, as they returned exuberant from a good dinner to hear the Government speaker wind up a debate. And in my own field my faith was reinforced by comparing the purposeful solidity of Ernest Bevin with the feverish vacillations of Eden and Macmillan.

Labour fought the 1964 election with every confidence of victory; but so we had in 1959. So I was immensely relieved when the first results showed an undeniable swing to Labour. It was an extraordinary day. I was touring the polling stations in East Leeds when I heard that Krushchev had been removed from power in Moscow. Robin Day interviewed me in Leeds Town Hall at one in the morning, after my re-election had been announced; he was more interested in Krushchev's fall than in my own good fortune or the Labour Party's return to power.

I went to bed at three o'clock. It then looked as if Labour would have an overall majority of about twenty seats. But when, after a few hours' sleep, Edna and I started the long drive back to London, we heard on the car radio our majority melting away, as the results came in from scattered rural constituencies. By the time we reached our home in Highgate, Labour's overall majority had shrunk to four. And China had just exploded its first atom bomb – using, as I heard later, a technique which none of the existing nuclear powers had adopted.

Krushchev's fall and China's bomb were a useful warning of the unpredictability which was to complicate my life as Defence Secretary over the next six years. But I had no leisure to reflect on these or any other issues that weekend. Indeed I was too busy even to luxuriate in the knowledge that Labour was back in power at last.

I scarcely had time to unpack before Harold Wilson called me to No. 10 Downing Street and offered me the Ministry of Defence, saying he had already told the Queen of my acceptance. There followed a weekend of pandemonium, in which only my excitement at my new job kept my post-election exhaustion at bay.

Colleagues telephoned to offer themselves for posts under me; one said that if I chose him he would be glad to go to the House of Lords so as to make his seat vacant for the new Foreign Secretary, Patrick Gordon Walker, who had just been defeated in the general election. My Permanent Secretary, Sir Henry Hardman, called for an hour and a half's background briefing; I won my essential first battle with the bureaucracy by refusing to accept a new Private Secretary in place of the able Arthur Hockaday, who had been working for my Conservative predecessor, Peter Thorneycroft.

My chauffeur took me in a resplendent limousine to the Privy Council Office to rehearse the swearing-in ceremony with four other new Cabinet ministers, before going to the Palace to kiss hands with the Queen and receive my seal of office. Jim Callaghan was sworn in after me, because as Chancellor of the Exchequer he was not a Secretary of State; he was very touchy about this, but got his own back by sneaking ahead of me in the Privy Council ceremony.

My first introduction to the world of Whitehall intrigue came from Solly Zuckerman, now the Ministry's Chief Scientific Adviser, whom I had scarcely seen since that lecture at Oxford before the war. He spent two hours on the Sunday morning giving me accurate though slightly malicious sketches of the main service and civilian chiefs with whom I would have to work, and described the main issues for early decision. It was a useful visit, intended partly, I suspect, for him to learn what he could about my intentions before a dinner in his Chelsea flat that evening; his other guest was Lord Mountbatten, who as the Chief of Defence Staff was the senior service officer in the Ministry.

This was my first substantial encounter with Mountbatten. His charm, self-confidence, and good looks enhanced a reputation for radical independence which had already impressed me. I found him a formidable personality to have as my senior service adviser as Secretary of State for Defence.

We ranged that evening over the whole field of defence policy, though Mountbatten was very sleepy by ten o'clock, and we were constantly interrupted by calls from the Prime Minister; Harold Wilson had failed to persuade Kenneth Younger to be his Minister of Disarmament and wanted Solly to take the job. We both strongly advised Solly against it, and he refused. It was midnight before I got home, totally exhausted.

Next morning I took possession of my room overlooking the Thames, on the sixth floor of an undistinguished office block in Whitehall which had just been made the headquarters of the Ministry of Defence.

I was forty-seven years old and had never held office before. Only

Harold Wilson himself and Patrick Gordon Walker had served in the Attlee Cabinet (Frank Soskice had been Attorney General for the few final months). Most of the other members of Wilson's Cabinet, however, had been junior ministers under Attlee. I still had everything to learn. I knew nothing about running a department, or about fighting my corner in the never-ending battles of Whitehall. It did not take me long to discover that, as Governor Cuomo once said, 'You campaign in poetry; you govern in prose'.

On the other hand, I had two advantages as Defence Secretary. Since the early fifties I had been working with men on both sides of the Atlantic, many with unique military experience, trying to understand the unprecedented problems created for strategy and diplomacy by nuclear weapons. And my service in the wartime army had given me insights into military realities which cannot be acquired by any other means. The same was true not only of my service advisers, but of many of my civil servants too. Ours was the last generation at the Ministry of Defence to have shared the knowledge which can only come from experience in war.

My own military service had another advantage. Many senior officers tended to believe that Labour politicians were pacifists or column-dodgers. My record cleared me of that suspicion. In fact several of the Generals who worked for me were friends from the war.

One hot summer afternoon in 1943, on the slow voyage from North Africa to Sicily, our landing craft let down its ramp so that we could bathe in the lukewarm Mediterranean. I found myself, naked and dripping wet, standing next to a skinny young Guards officer in the same condition. When we next met, General Miles Fitzalan Howard was my Director of Military Intelligence. A few years later, to his great surprise, he found himself Duke of Norfolk and the senior layman of the Roman Catholic Church in Britain. In that role he attracted interest by some soldierly reflections on the topic of contraception; but I suspect he may be better known as the father-in-law of David Frost.

Throughout my six years as Secretary of State for Defence, I worked harder than I had ever imagined I could. I toiled ten to twelve hours a day for five or six days a week, in my own office or in Cabinet committees; then I spent several hours every night across the road in Admiralty House on my despatch boxes. This routine was broken by regular visits to our forces at home and abroad, and occasional meetings with my colleagues in NATO or the Commonwealth. It was not easy to squeeze in my monthly weekends in Leeds, and more difficult still to find time with my family.

Yet I loved every minute of it. It was the most exhilarating period of my life. The work itself was challenging in the extreme, and stretched me to the limit; that is why I compare myself with Emily Dickinson's soldier. After nineteen years' apprenticeship at Transport House and in Opposition, I felt like a man who, after driving his Jaguar for hours behind a tractor on narrow country lanes, finally reaches the motorway. I was immensely impressed by the calibre of the officers and civil servants who advised me; many of them remained my friends for life. My visits to South Arabia and Borneo introduced me to peoples and cultures hitherto unknown except to explorers, and provided inexhaustible material for my camera. Above all I came to know and respect the exceptional human qualities of the men and women in our forces; it was a privilege to serve them.

For me it was the culmination of everything I had done since 1940. But for Edna and the children it meant a tremendous upheaval. After some months, we had to leave our home in Highgate, with its lovely garden overlooking London, for Admiralty House in Whitehall. This was a large Georgian mansion which formed the right wing of the original Admiralty building. Originally the residence of the First Lord of the Admiralty, it had been used by Harold Macmillan while No. 10 Downing Street was being refurbished. When we moved in, we found it highly inconvenient. The ground floor, with its magnificent paintings by Westall and Hodges, was used for Government hospitality – mainly for entertaining official foreign visitors. Edna and I lived on the first floor; I had an office there with a highly protected safe. The children lived on the top floor, where the Chief Whip, Ted Short, also had a pied-à-terre. They were separated from us by George Thomson, the Commonwealth and Colonial Secretary, with his wife, Grace, and their two daughters. Fortunately George and Grace were old friends, and our children got on well with theirs. But we could communicate with our children only up a winding back staircase. And they greatly disliked having to come and go past the hulking security guard at the front door.

Our younger daughter, Cressida, suffered appallingly from loneliness. She was only eleven years old when we first went to Admiralty House. Her school and all her friends were miles away in North London; Tim and Jenny, now sixteen and seventeen years old, were always out, and Edna was often abroad with me visiting the forces. Cressida's loneliness reached such a point that she actually considered asking if she could go away to a boarding school. Children are often the first casualty of successful political careers. Fortunately Edna was as good a mother as she was a wife, and the family survived.

We slept in a great bedroom facing a massive wardrobe in which Queen Mary used to keep row upon row of her toques. One bright summer morning when Edna was washing up, the woman who cleaned our flat rushed into the kitchen, her face as white as a sheet.

'There's a lady in your bed,' she gasped.

Edna calmed her down and said it was impossible.

'No, no, she has fair hair and blue eyes. I've never seen her before,' the maid insisted.

Edna went into the bedroom with her and found the bed empty and unwrinkled as she expected.

We never got to the bottom of the story. It has often provoked ribald comment from my friends. If it was a ghost, the most likely candidate would be Lady Diana Duff Cooper, who fitted the description when she slept there in pre-war days as the wife of the First Lord of the Admiralty. Her son, John Julius Norwich, thought it possible. But she was still alive. Can you have a ghost of a living person?

One night we were woken at three in the morning by Ted Short in his dressing gown, followed by a couple of police. He had seen shadowy figures walking past his window along the parapet outside. A thorough search revealed nothing unusual except a tramp, who had been sleeping undetected in the basement for several nights. My private theory is that the figures must have been soldiers from the Horse Guards, on their way to an assignation with Wrens in the Old Admiralty Building.

I had little spare time in Admiralty House, though I had a darkroom in the basement where I developed and printed the photographs I took on our tours. In fact I had little relaxation at all until we bought the small gatehouse of an Edwardian mansion near Withyham, on the border between Kent and Sussex. We had a few apple trees and a large field which took me a whole weekend to mow. I spent much of my spare time gardening; my proudest achievement was a large ornamental pool with a rockery in which I not only kept goldfish, but actually got them to breed. Above all, Windleshaw Lodge, as it was called, gave me the chance to spend time with the children, walking through the bluebell woods nearby, or striding over the heathland of Ashdown Forest.

We made local friends who helped to keep my mind off my work – Frank Giles, the deputy editor of the *Sunday Times*, who had once been Ernest Bevin's Private Secretary, and his spirited wife Kitty, Denys Lasdun, the architect of London's South Bank, and Pat Gibson, the publisher, who later became Chairman of the Arts Council and of the National Trust. He lived at Penns-in-the-Rocks, a beautiful old red-brick house, so-called because William Penn, the founder of Pennsylvania, had married the heiress of the property. My idol, William Yeats, used to visit the poet, Dorothy Wellesley, when she held literary court there in the thirties; before the Great War Yeats had himself lived nearby at Coleman's Hatch, with the young Ezra Pound as his secretary. It was there that Pound led him out of the Celtic mists into the hard light of a cold and passionate dawn. I felt surrounded by ghosts.

Through Pat Gibson I started going again to Glyndebourne and to Covent Garden. Opera became a passion for me, though in London I was often called back to vote in the House of Commons at ten o'clock; it was only on my fourth visit to *Eugene Onegin* that I succeeded in seeing the duel scene and hearing Lensky's great aria! I also took up the piano again in the weekends.

Without my rural oasis at Windleshaw Lodge I doubt if I could have survived the whole six years as Defence Secretary.

The Ministry of Defence is quite unlike any other department in Whitehall. When I took over, I became directly responsible for 458,000 servicemen and women and 406,000 civil servants, scattered all over the world from Washington to Oslo, from Malta to Hong Kong. In the sixties the government owned the military nuclear installations, the naval dockyards, and the ordnance factories; but the overwhelming majority of service weapons and equipment were produced for the Ministry by commercial firms. The manpower working on these defence contracts was probably another million. No other minister had management problems on this scale.

Ever since the war, defence had been under exceptional economic pressure, since technology increased the cost of new equipment much faster than the increase in the nation's wealth. In the fifties and sixties the cost of naval frigates doubled, the cost of much army equipment quadrupled, and the cost of military aircraft increased tenfold. Costs are rising even faster nowadays, with the introduction of electronics into every area of warfare. Indeed the extrapolation of current trends could mean that within a century the number of modern weapons which a country like Britain could afford would have fallen to single figures – a prospect which NATO refers to as 'structural disarmament'.

A major weapon may take ten years from research and development to entering service, and may be expected to remain in service for twenty years or longer. So defence planners must try to look thirty years ahead; they must guess which countries will then be potential enemies, and how their forces will then be equipped. In fact, of course, it is impossible to predict every change in international relations, or every scientific breakthrough. For example, Britain had to cancel the Blue Streak missile before its development was completed, because its liquid fuel required so long to prepare for firing, that it would have been vulnerable on its site to attack by the solid-fuelled missiles then entering the Soviet inventory.

These economic and intellectual problems required the Defence Ministry to spend money more efficiently than most other departments. Just before I took over, it had begun to adopt a range of techniques developed in the United States by Bob McNamara with the help of the RAND Corporation – Planning-Programming-Budgeting and functional costing, assisted by systems-analysis and cost-effectiveness studies. I was grateful for these innovations, and carried them further in several areas; they were invaluable in my running battles with the Treasury.

The Treasury, which sometimes seemed to know the price of everything and the value of nothing, was always pressing me for further cuts in defence spending. However, no government should cut a military capability without cutting the political commitment which made that capability necessary. And this the Foreign Office was usually reluctant to do; it seemed to regard every commitment as an invaluable pearl without price. So I had to fight a war on two fronts.

The decisions of a defence secretary often have important industrial implications which affect domestic politics. The cancellation of an aircraft or the closure of a dockyard may throw thousands of people out of work – perhaps in a marginal constituency of vital importance to the party in power. So I sometimes came under political or industrial pressures which had nothing to do with defence at all.

Finally, an operation of this nature on this scale means that there is always ten years' work in the pipeline. So I could not make major changes in equipment without wasting vast sums of money already spent, and incurring big cancellation charges. And changes in political commitments had to be negotiated with the governments concerned.

All these factors guarantee that the job of a defence secretary will be exceptionally difficult. It was even more difficult for me, because the preceding Conservative governments had left me a defence programme which it would have been financially impossible to carry out at the best of times. Moreover, our forces were overstretched and underequipped. Morale in the Ministry itself was bad, not only for these reasons, but also because of the way in which Duncan Sandys and Peter Thorneycroft had imposed fundamental changes of policy and organisation since 1957.

Conservative premiers had appointed nine different defence ministers over their thirteen years in office; they seemed to regard Defence as a convenient place to park colleagues temporarily, on their way up or down the government ladder. So there was little incentive for an ambitious politician to take difficult decisions during his months at the Ministry of Defence. The exception was Duncan Sandys, appointed by Macmillan when Anthony Head resigned after the Suez fiasco. Macmillan himself had spent seven months as Defence Minister in the middle fifties. He had concluded that nuclear weapons made conventional forces irrelevant; the failure of the Suez expedition, for which he had pressed so strongly, did not change his mind. When he succeeded Eden, he picked Sandys as Defence Minister and gave him a strict mandate – to abolish conscription and slash conventional weapons, in order to make room for a British nuclear deterrent.

Sandys was just the man for the job. He had a good war record. As a young officer, his attack on Chamberlain's mishandling of the Norwegian campaign in 1940 helped to bring his father-in-law, Winston Churchill, to power. While he was very slow to master a brief, he worked hard and long, with a ferocious dedication to the task in hand. He was totally unscrupulous in getting his way. Although the Hull Committee, which he set up, concluded the army would need at least 200,000 men to carry out its appointed tasks, he published instead the figure of 165,000, since this was the most it thought possible to recruit without conscription. According to Mountbatten, Sir Gerald Templer, the peppery Chief of the General Staff, was so infuriated to be told of this decision that he walked up to Sandys, clapped him on the back, and said: 'Duncan, you're so bloody crooked, that if you swallowed a nail, you'd shit a corkscrew!' (Ziegler claims that Templer addressed these words to Mountbatten himself.)

After a few quiet years under Harold Watkinson, the services got Peter Thorneycroft as Minister of Defence in 1962. His period of office saw the first serious effort to centralise the service ministries under the Ministry of Defence, along the lines favoured by Lord Mountbatten, the Chief of Defence Staff.

Mountbatten had been First Sea Lord – the head of the Royal Navy – for four years from 1955. During this period he had opposed the Suez operation, and joined Templer in resisting the sacrifice of Britain's conventional forces for the sake of an independent British nuclear force. He said a British nuclear force would be 'neither credible as a deterrent, nor necessary as part of the Western deterrent', though he strongly supported the American strategic forces as essential to NATO. As Chief of Defence Staff from 1959, he was obsessed by the need to destroy the independence of the separate service Chiefs of Staff. He persuaded Macmillan and Thorneycroft to move in this direction. In July 1963 the Government published a White Paper on Central Organisation for Defence, which raised the status of Defence Minister to Secretary of State and brought the top military and civilian staffs of the service ministries together with the central staffs, in the office block which was now my headquarters.

Unfortunately, Mountbatten pursued his objectives with a lack of scruple worthy of Duncan Sandys. On one occasion Sam Elworthy, the Chief of Air Staff, told him to his face that he was a liar and a cheat. Even Sir Ian Jacob, whose report was the foundation for these reforms, said that Mountbatten was 'universally mistrusted in spite of his great qualities'. Sam Way, the Permanent Secretary of the Army, told his Minister that Mountbatten was 'the most mistrusted of all senior officers in the three Services for his ambition and his motives'. At his worst he could be devious and dishonest, as well as inordinately vain. Philip Ziegler, his brilliant biographer, found it necessary to place on his desk a notice saying: '*Remember in spite of everything, he was a great man.*'

He was indeed a great man. His strong, handsome features added to a personal charm which could bowl over the unwary, when he chose to exploit it. He showed a unique energy and vision in his defence roles, with a sense of the wider political context, rare in service chiefs. I suspect, however, that his most important contribution to British history was not in defence, where his contempt for his colleagues often made him impossible to work with. It was in India, where as Viceroy he guided the subcontinent through the agonies of partition to independence. His personality, and that of his wife, fitted perfectly with that of Jawaharlal Nehru, another aristocratic radical. Without the ruthless clarity of Mountbatten's vision, I doubt whether Attlee would have found the strength to take the difficult decisions demanded of him during those traumatic months.

My most urgent task, on entering the Ministry, was to decide whether to renew Mountbatten's appointment as Chief of Defence Staff the following July. I spent many hours interviewing the top forty people in the Ministry on the subject. Only one favoured Mountbatten's reappointment – Sir Kenneth Strong, the Director General of Intelligence; but he had been a personal friend of Mountbatten for twenty years and was a key member of his personal court. When I told Dickie of my decision not to reappoint him, he slapped his thigh and roared with delight; but his eyes told a different story.

He was strongly opposed to the appointment of Dick Hull, the Chief of the General Staff, as his successor. I overruled him; and Hull softened the blow by making Dickie a Colonel in the Life Guards. He was like a little boy in his delight, since he could now wear the Life Guards' helmet and uniform when he took part in Trooping the Colour, while the band played the Preobrajansky March, which had been composed for one of his Russian ancestors.

We continued to work together in the Ministry for the next nine months. It was a fascinating experience for me, particularly since I was told that some of my penniless Irish relations – whom I had never met – lived in peat huts outside his castle at Classiebawn, and were delighted to know I was his boss. He was disappointed not to find me as malleable as Thorneycroft; when he tried to draft a minute for me I said: 'I am sorry, but I do not like taking other people's minutes as my own.' Yet, according to Ziegler, he found me 'brilliant, charming and nice'.

I could not always use the same words about him. Though he had many of Churchill's qualities, he had similar weaknesses too, plus some monarchical characteristics, including the need for a personal court. He was immensely proud of his royal birth. When he was standing in line with Edna and me at a reception for a thousand attachés and their wives in the Banqueting House, Edna turned to him after shaking several hundred hands and said that her wrist was feeling sore. Dickie looked down at her and pronounced: 'My Great aunt – the Empress of Russia – used to have a blister on the back of her hand – as big as an egg – at Easter – where the peasants had kissed it. She never wore gloves.' There was no answer to that.

I had already heard something of his royal arrogance from my brother. As a naval officer during the war, Terry had seen him ram another British warship, just after having the bows of his own destroyer, HMS *Kelly*, repaired. He had to have his own bows repaired all over again; but his birth saved him from the court martial any other officer would have faced.

On the other hand, his royal background made him quite indifferent to the rank or position of others; indeed, perhaps because London society had never properly accepted his wife, Edwina, or his father, Prince Louis of Battenberg, he was conspicuously anti-Establishment. It is said that he answered the door at his country seat, Broadlands, to a Tory canvasser during the 1945 general election. 'I don't have a vote because I'm a peer,' he told her. 'If I did, I'd vote Labour. But I think my butler's a Conservative.'

The only member of his personal court who could and would stand up to him was Solly Zuckerman, who never hesitated to tell him when he was wrong, and often succeeded in making him change his mind. Solly had worked with Dickie during the war at Combined Operations, and left an outstanding academic career to work with him again as Chief Scientist at the Ministry of Defence. He was intolerant of people he regarded as less clever than himself – a very large group – but could always be relied on to think outside the ruts in which the rest of us were too often stuck.

His scientific brilliance gave him special clout with the leading defence scientists in the United States, such as Isidore Rabi and Jerome Wiesner, who were Jewish like himself; he was one of the few foreigners – and indeed Americans – who could get on with Admiral Hyman Rickover, father of the Polaris submarine.

Solly was also Honorary Secretary of the Zoological Society, so was able to do little services for Dickie, such as providing him with elephants for the Buddhist Ceremony of the Tooth. Like Dickie, he had an active social life, and held glittering evening parties at the Zoo, always producing at least one film star among the guests; I once sat next to Merle Oberon at dinner there.

Unfortunately, Solly's mercurial nature did not make him an ideal Chief Scientific Adviser for me. He was liable to change his position without warning, and to reject advice which his own staff had given me weeks earlier. If I did not accept his views, he would go behind my back to other ministers for help. He admits in his autobiography that from my point of view his behaviour was intolerable. In the end I managed to persuade Harold Wilson to take him to No. 10. 'When I left Defence,' he recalls, 'Denis sent me a letter which, in the light of the difficulties that I had made for him, I did not deserve. It was as warm a letter of appreciation for my critical approach to defence policy as could ever have been written.'

In fact he did deserve it. In recent years we have found ourselves together again in the campaign for a more rational approach to nuclear weapons. But like Mountbatten himself, Solly was not a team player.

Mountbatten had something else in common with Solly; he liked film stars. Douglas Fairbanks Jr and Charlie Chaplin were his close friends. When Harold Wilson sent Derek Mitchell, his Private Secretary, to ask Dickie if he would lead the Commonwealth Mission on Immigration, Dickie was in Hollywood on his farewell tour of the forces as CDS – no doubt justifying the detour by his role as Chairman of the Army Kinema Corporation. Derek found himself at a party where the guests played a game in which they were physically tied together after dinner. He was lashed inextricably to Claudia Cardinale, while Dickie had the even greater pleasure of being roped to Shirley MacLaine – one of my own favourites, though I was not able to meet her until I was Chancellor.

The one issue on which Mountbatten and I were always at odds was his determination to get rid of the separate service Chiefs of Staff and establish single central organisations to carry out the administrative functions of the three services. I agreed to 'functionalise' intelligence and signals as he suggested, because I found the case compelling. The separate service intelligence organisations tended to distort their findings so as to support the interests of their own services, and the case for functionalising signals was demonstrated during the American landings in Grenada; I was told that the Ranger commander on one of the beaches there found it impossible to make direct contact with ships offshore, because his signals equipment was incompatible with theirs; in the end he had to use his credit card to ring up the Navy Headquarters in the United States from a call-box!

I also gave my deputies functions to look after, instead of services, and planned to abolish the Parliamentary Undersecretaries for the Army, Navy, and Air Force. However, I did not think that functionalism across the board made sense in operational terms, any more than in financial planning, where we costed in terms of outputs rather than functions. A gun in a ship is part of a ship, while a gun in a tank is part of a tank, though both are guns. It was sensible to have combined inter-service headquarters for British operations outside Europe, for example in Aden or Singapore; but in Europe each British service had to operate more closely with the same service in the allied forces, than with the other British services. Above all, the services were sick and tired of continual reorganisation. Throughout my six years as Defence Secretary, we were coping with massive reductions in our defence capability and commitments; I did not think it made sense to carry out an appendix operation on a man while he was lifting a grand piano.

I suspected, too, that behind Mountbatten's obsession with integrating the services was the desire to establish central control of defence policy and operations under himself as Chief of Defence Staff. In my opinion, it was the Secretary of State's job to control defence policy, as an elected member of the British Cabinet, and I was determined to carry it out. Experience in many fields has convinced me that abstract arguments for one form of organisation or another count for little compared with the personal qualities of the individuals available for the key jobs. I doubt if anyone else in my time could have met the requirements of a Chief of

Defence Staff as Mountbatten conceived the post; few other officers shared his confidence in his own qualifications for such a job.

The only officer who equalled Mountbatten in chutzpah and self-confidence was another wartime hero, Field Marshal Lord Montgomery of Alamein. Monty had retired from the British Army in 1958 after serving for seven years in NATO as Deputy Supreme Allied Commander, Europe. After appointing him to this post Churchill said of him: 'In defeat, indomitable; in victory insufferable; in NATO, thank God, invisible.'

When I took over Defence, Monty was living alone in Hampshire. He came to see me in my first month to complain against the possibility that I might make Jim Cassels Chief of the General Staff, when Dick Hull replaced Mountbatten as CDS. I had not met him since that afternoon in Hammamet over twenty years earlier, when he so offended us officers of the First Army. Apart from looking even more wizened and shrunken, he had changed very little since then. For the rest of my time at Defence he tended to drop in for lunch and a chat when he was visiting the House of Lords. He got on particularly well with our younger daughter, Cressida. With the percipience of childhood she told us afterwards: 'That is a very lonely old man.' So indeed he was.

He told Edna that one afternoon while driving back to Hampshire he had seen a little boy trudging home from school, and had offered him a lift. 'What do you do for a living?' asked the little boy. 'I'm a Field Marshal,' replied Monty. The little boy's face lit up.

'My father works in the fields too,' he said. 'He's a farmer. What do you do in the fields?'

'I kill people in the fields,' said Monty.

'I think I'd like to get out now,' said the little boy.

I think it was loneliness more than anything which brought Monty so often to see me and the family at Admiralty House. However, he had one professional concern – to end the tradition under which all the Chiefs of Staff were given the rank of Field Marshal for life when they retired. It was indeed an odd custom; the United States, with very much larger armed forces, had no one of that rank at all. But with all my other problems I did not regard it as a priority to change the tradition, simply because Monty felt he should be the only Field Marshal alive.

One day when he called on us, Monty was under press attack for something he had said about China. He stopped in front of the bust of Wellington in Admiralty House. 'Great mistake for that man to go into politics,' he snapped. 'A soldier should never go into politics.'

I believed it was essential for the defence secretary himself, as an elected politician, to control the administration of his department as well as its policy. It was a formidable task. The Permanent Secretary, on whom ministers normally depend for advice, often had little personal experience of defence problems. My first Permanent Secretary came from the Ministry of Agriculture, and had never served in a defence department before. So they, like most of the other civil servants in the ministry, tended to confine themselves to administration and finance rather than plunge into policy. Even so, I find it difficult to forgive Sir Edward Playfair for saying he was glad to leave Defence in 1961 after only one year as Permanent Secretary, because 'it lacked intellectual challenge'!

The intellectual challenge was in fact overpowering. My job as Defence Secretary was in some ways like that of the film director I would once have liked to have been – to control large bodies of men and women, each with his own field of expertise, so as to produce a coherent whole. However I had no chance of persuading my sponsors to put up more money – on the contrary, the Cabinet was continually cutting my money as I went along. But there were prima donnas in the services no less than in the acting profession. And the competition for money required the senior officers of all three services to develop all the skills of the politician and the trade unionist. I sometimes felt that I had learned nothing about politics until I met the Chiefs of Staff. Each felt his prime duty was to protect the interests and traditions of his own service.

The Royal Navy was proud of a history which went back to the Armada. Living as I did in Admiralty House, surrounded by paintings of Captain Cook's expeditions to the South Seas, eating under the marble eyes of Nelson and the great admirals of the eighteenth century, I was not likely to forget it. Even in my time the navy recruited many of its most successful officers from families scattered round the great naval ports on the south coast, which had provided Admirals for generations. It was convinced, with some excuse, that only naval officers could understand what the navy did, and had great difficulty in explaining to outsiders what it was for. It tended simply to fob off enquiries with whatever slogan best fitted the current fashion – 'broken-backed war', 'peace keeping East of Suez' or simply 'sinking the Soviet Navy'.

The army was similarly wedded to the memory of the great generals of the past, from Marlborough and Wellington to Montgomery and Alexander – the Crimean War and the Great War had fewer demigods to offer. In the infantry, regimental tradition was regarded as the cement of loyalty and discipline in war, though some younger officers realised that the inevitable contraction of the army would undermine it. As a student at the Imperial Defence College, Colin Mitchell wrote an eloquent thesis recommending the replacement of regimental names by numbers; he later surrendered to the call of duty and led the national campaign to 'Save the Argylls'.

The Royal Air Force, on the other hand, was not born until 1918. It recruited its officers far more widely than the other two services, and was much readier to promote officers from the ranks. One of my ablest Air Marshals, 'Tubby' Earle, started as an apprentice at Halton and finished as Director General of Intelligence. The father of Neil Cameron, who finished as Chief of Defence Staff, was a Sergeant in the Black Watch.

Each of the services tended to believe it could win a war on its own, and spent much of its time fighting the others. But each service had its internal divisions too. The submariners believed they could sink any aircraft carrier afloat – in an exercise in the Mediterranean shortly before I took over, a British submarine had sailed under the keel of a carrier for days without being detected. In the army, the gunners and sappers considered themselves superior to the infantry, the Royal Tank Corps despised the cavalry, while all tended to be suspicious of special forces like the paratroopers, the Gurkhas and the SAS. In the RAF there were similar rivalries between bomber and fighter pilots, and both were hostile to the missile forces which looked like threatening their existence; indeed Duncan Sandys had wrecked the military aircraft programme because he thought the days of the manned aircraft were over.

Service traditions and the rivalries they engendered may have contributed to fighting morale, but for more than a century they had been disastrous to defence planning. In the early nineteenth century the Admirals were so wedded to their wooden walls, that they fought for decades against steam vessels; later they fought to keep coal for firing their steamships, instead of the cheaper and more convenient oil. As late as 1916 Kitchener dismissed the tank as 'a pretty mechanical toy' and in 1925 Lord Haig attacked Liddell Hart's faith in armoured warfare with the words: 'I am all for using aeroplanes and tanks, but they are only accessories to the man and the horse.'

The RAF had fewer such blunders to record, because it had not existed so long and was more in tune with modern technology. But it was dominated by Trenchard's belief in victory by air power, and remained attached to the V-bombers as a strategic nuclear force, long after they had lost their ability to penetrate Soviet air space, and when they were vulnerable on the ground to missile attack from Soviet submarines. Led by ex-pilots, the RAF was often attracted to speed for its own sake, though in many situations outside Europe even the ancient Hunter fighter-bomber was far more suitable than the supersonic Lightning.

I saw it as my job to introduce more rationality into decision-making on defence, and I was prepared to stay on for as long as it took to achieve this. So apart from the Prime Minister himself, I was the only member of Wilson's first two governments to stay in the same post throughout the six years. Altogether, fourteen other ministers served under me, seven of whom later became my colleagues in the Cabinet. Since officers and civil servants rarely serve more than three years in the same post at the Ministry of Defence, in the second half of my time I had been longer in my job than any of my advisers in theirs; this gave me special authority.

Though I was determined to control my ministry, I had learned enough from the mistakes of my predecessors to insist on consulting all the senior officers who were affected by my decisions. So I never had to impose a policy against the will of all my advisers, though I was frequently compelled to override the objections of significant minorities – such as the navy when I cancelled the new carrier.

I knew that Whitehall committees tended to smother disagreements in a soggy compromise, and that the Chiefs of Staff were notorious for log-rolling – saying 'I'll support you on this if you support me on that'. So I was not prepared to take an important decision on the recommendation of a Chief of Staff, Permanent Secretary or Chief Scientist unless I knew what arguments had preceded his recommendation. Wherever possible I insisted on having more than one course of action put in front of me, and often held mass meetings of all who had something to contribute. Thus junior officers or officials were able to put their views to me directly in the presence of their seniors – a practice which some of the military found less agreeable than the civilians!

The quality of most senior officers was very high indeed. Many had experience of combined commands and had spent a year or more in study with members of the other services, with Commonwealth or American officers, and with civilians of other government departments, at the excellent Joint Services Staff College or the Imperial Defence College. So they had a breadth of vision and understanding unique in Whitehall. On the other hand, as they began to approach retirement in their fifties they sometimes paid undue deference to the Chief of Staff of their own service, on whom their final appointments would depend. In their last years they tended to worry about how they would answer questions from their predecessors in the Army, Navy, or Air Force clubs, about how they had protected their own service.

Such generalisations do not do justice to the extraordinary variety of the personalities I found among my service colleagues. Sam Elworthy, the RAF chief who succeeded Dick Hull as Chief of Defence Staff was a New Zealander who had studied law at Cambridge before the war; as a young barrister he made a friend for life of Leslie Scarman, the most liberal of recent judges. He was tall, slim and handsome, with fair hair, blue eyes, and a shining sense of honour – a modern chevalier Bayard.

Mike Lefanu, the Admiral who was appointed to succeed him, but died tragically of leukaemia before he could take over, was a ginger-haired practical joker, sometimes introducing himself as the Chinese Admiral Lee Fan Yew. He adored his wife Prudence; though she was confined by illness to a wheelchair, he would take her bathing inside the shark-nets at Aden. Blessed both with great intelligence and a sensitive understanding of human nature, he knew exactly, as Chief of Naval Staff, how to handle the brash but brilliant young Under-Secretary for the Navy I appointed in 1968 – David Owen.

The ablest intellectual in the Services – and one of the best brains I have ever encountered in public life – was Mike Carver, who became Chief of the General Staff just after my time. While still in his twenties he had commanded an armoured brigade in the Western Desert; after the war he wrote classic histories of El Alamein and Tobruk. In a sense he was an unwilling soldier; his father's bankruptcy in the Great Slump compelled him to forgo a university education, so he left Winchester for the army, characteristically choosing the Royal Tank Corps rather than a cavalry regiment. His mind could cut to the heart of any problem with surgical precision, but his dedication to the efficient truth prevented him from suffering fools gladly; he could deliver the most wounding judgment on a fellow-officer in public, without realising how much it hurt.

His rival throughout his later army career was 'Shan' Hackett, a cavalryman turned paratrooper with an equally distinguished war record, particularly at Arnhem. Like many small men, he fizzed with energy, and sometimes tried unsuccessfully to provoke me with acts of insubordination. Having left Australia to take a Double First at New College, he was never averse to an ostentatious display of intellectual superiority. At our first meeting he startled me by using the phrase 'Socratic elenchus'; I paid him back a few hours later by making a welcoming speech to the Italian Chief of Staff in Italian, one of the languages Shan did not understand. His brother officers sometimes failed to appreciate his qualities – in Northern Ireland they called him 'Deirdre of the Sorrows'. He was an exceptionally good Commander in Chief in Germany, where political skill was important. His wife was Austrian, so he spoke the language well; he worked successfully with the British Ambassador, Sir Frank Roberts, a man of similar physical and intellectual stature; I used to think of them as two waltzing electric mice with sharp teeth and powerful muscles.

Hackett and Carver jointly produced the proposals for remodelling the territorial army into a useable reserve force. It made them, and me, very unpopular at first with the retired officers in the existing territorial battalions; they felt their surnames were all too appropriate, and produced a tie with a crossed hatchet and carving knife to commemorate their work.

I had, of course, to deal with many officers of more traditional character. When I was staying with one of my Generals in Germany he thrust a *Reader's Digest* into my hands just as I was going to bed. 'Gather you like reading,' he said gruffly. 'Don't read much meself. Got this from my batman. Hope you like it.' My most bizarre experience was an interview with the Colonel of the Brigade of Guards, General Michael Fitzalan Howard, the brother of Miles. I asked him to see me in order to discuss the unduly small proportion of blacks in the Guards regiments. We had a deaf men's dialogue straight out of Monty Python. He simply could not understand what I was on about. He pointed out that there was once a black man who played the big drum in one of the Guards bands – no doubt he thought the leopard-skin made that appropriate. But he found the idea that black men should serve in a Guards fighting unit was so preposterous that his mind simply refused to encompass the idea. I had to give up in despair.

I soon discovered that, to run the ministry in the way I wanted, my most essential need was for a first-rate private secretary – a clever young man with experience of defence and a knowledge of the key civilian and military personalities which the permanent secretary could not be expected to have unless, as has more recently been the case, he has himself served recently in the Ministry of Defence. A minister's private secretary is not only his eyes and ears; it is he who must decide who and what actually reaches the minister personally out of the hundreds of men and thousands of documents always clamouring for his attention. Besides a first-class brain, he needs inexhaustible tact, demonic energy and an understanding wife – for he must arrive at the office an hour before his minister and leave an hour later. Small wonder that few private secretaries are expected to serve more than two years, and that they receive a special allowance.

Arthur Hockaday was an ideal man to help me through my early months, since he had been private secretary to Peter Thorneycroft before I arrived. When he went off to be Deputy Secretary General of NATO in 1965 I picked Pat Nairne to succeed him. He turned out to be the perfect choice for the most difficult two years of my service as Defence Secretary, when I was taking my most important decisions on equipment, commitments and strategy.

Pat had won the Military Cross as a Subaltern in the Seaforth Highlanders during the campaign in the Western Desert, and had served in the Admiralty after getting a First in modern history at Oxford after the war. He was a glutton for work; his one weakness was his desire to do everything himself, because he rightly thought he could do it better than anyone else. Unfailing courtesy and a pretty wit made him a joy to work with; he well described Sir John Grandy as 'a good-looking wild boar', and when I escaped his care for an hour in Hong Kong he asked innocently if I had been 'to see a fellow called Bunbury'. He also shared my pleasure in all the arts. His father, a retired army Colonel, had taught art at Winchester, and Pat was a good water-colour painter, rather in the style of Wilson Steer. He always took a paint-box when we travelled together. If I snatched a few minutes to take photographs in the Hadramaut or San Francisco, he would take out his paints and do a sketch, sometimes to be worked up into a larger picture later, perhaps while he was watching his sons rowing.

He ended his civil service career as Permanent Secretary at the Department of Health and Social Security, where the complexity of functions suited his talents perfectly. I shall always regard him as the very model of the best British civil servant, with a genius for administration bred of his early years wrestling with the Royal Navy. Indeed his devotion to government could carry him too far. As a member of the Franks Committee on the Falklands he joined in endorsing the final paragraphs which exonerated the Government of the blame which was heaped on it in the body of the report. When he left the Civil Service, instead of taking a lucrative job in business, like so many of his colleagues, he chose to succeed my old school friend, Alan Bullock, as Master of St Catherine's College, Oxford, where I was able to renew our friendship at least once a year.

As my work-load increased I decided to establish a body which would serve me as a minister in France is served by his 'cabinet'. I called it the Programme Evaluation Group, and made it formally responsible to the Chiefs of Staff, though this device did not deceive them for a moment. Essentially its job was to make sure that I asked the right questions of the ministry and got relevant answers in time, using my newly created Defence Operational Analysis Establishment to provide a technical input where necessary. PEG did invaluable work for me on service communications, on NATO strategy, on the navy's anti-submarine programme, and on the RAF's combat aircraft requirements. It consisted of officers from each of the three services, with a scientist, a civil servant and an economist.

Each of them was instructed to look at the problems in the interests of the country's defence as a whole, ignoring pressures from the individual services. They did so with conspicuous courage. In one case PEG nearly cost the RAF its ablest officer. I first met Neil Cameron as a Group Captain at the IDC when I was lecturing there in 1963. He was the Air Commodore responsible for training cadets at Cranwell when I asked him in September 1966 to join PEG. His father, an army Sergeant, had died when he was three weeks old and he was brought up in the Poor House in Perth, where his grandfather was Inspector. After doing badly at school, he joined the RAF just before war broke out, so he was able to fly Hurricanes in the Battle of Britain. Then he had spells in Russia, the Western Desert, and Burma, finishing the war with a DSO and DFC.

A tall, powerfully built man with wavy fair hair and the face of an eagle, he was the image of a fighter pilot. He was also an outspoken Christian, who thought deeply about the morality of nuclear deterrence. Outstanding even in an outstanding team at PEG, he followed every argument wherever it led. So he inevitably created enemies in the Air Staff; they felt that his objectivity was letting the Service down, particularly when he endorsed a report that the RAF had no operational requirement for a long-range strike aircraft. After two years I dissolved PEG and appointed Cameron as head of a new Defence Policy Staff under the CDS, hoping thereby to encourage the Chiefs of Staff themselves to treat defence policy with more objectivity. In this role Cameron established a first-rate policy machine, and played a major role in the development of NATO strategy and service education – until I left the ministry after Labour's defeat in 1970.

Then the Air Staff got its revenge. They gave him a succession of marginal appointments and refused to promote him. When I ran into him by accident one morning in Whitehall, he told me he was thinking of resigning from the RAF altogether. Fortunately, a day or two later I met Andrew Humphrey, who was shortly due to become Chief of Air Staff, and was able to warn him of Cameron's state of mind. Humphrey promoted Neil to the Air Force Board as the member responsible for personnel. Within two years Cameron had become Chief of Air Staff himself; after less than twelve months he was promoted again to become Chief of Defence Staff. He filled that job, too, with exceptional distinction, although he created a political furore by saying on a visit to Peking that China and Britain had a common enemy. When he finally retired from the service he was appointed Principal of King's College London – a post earlier held by Shan Hackett – but was struck down by cancer at the height of his powers. He and I spoke together just before his death at the IDC, now renamed the College of Defence Studies. He was grey and gaunt, leaning on a stick, and in great pain. It was a tragic end for a great public servant.

I had lectured regularly at most of the Service Colleges for years before I became Defence Secretary, and now found it an invaluable means of learning what the rising young men in the forces were thinking, and of explaining what I was trying to do. I used to compare myself with the Indian chief who called his braves together at the onset of winter and said: 'I have two bits of news for you – one bad, the other good. First the bad news. There's going to be nothing to eat this winter except buffalo shit. Now the good news. There's going to be plenty of buffalo shit around.' The story was always well received except on one occasion at the Army Staff College in Camberley, where it was met with only a nervous titter. I discovered that it had been told only an hour earlier by someone else.

It was essential that I should keep the services closely in touch with what I was doing, and that they should understand why. On top of all the inherent difficulties of running the Ministry of Defence, and of the additional problems I inherited from my predecessors. I represented a Government which was rightly convinced that Britain could not continue to spend twice as much of its national output on defence as its European allies.

So in addition to ending the overstretch in service manpower, providing the forces with the weapons they needed, and reorganising the existing programmes so as to eliminate forthcoming bulges in expenditure which no government would be able to accept, I was instructed to cut the spending planned by the Conservatives by £400 million at 1964 prices, or sixteen per cent, over the following five years. Continuing economic difficulties later led the Government to insist on further cuts. In the end I had to reduce defence spending from over seven per cent of the nation's output to five per cent – implying that the defence budget by the end of

1972 would be running a third below the level envisaged by Thorneycroft. The total saving over the period was some £5,000 million. When I left office, for the first time in its history, Britain was spending more on education than on defence.

I was often asked whether it was right to allow economic rather than military criteria to determine the total figure for defence spending. The answer is that no government in the world, including that of the United States, can acquire every military capability which is desirable on purely defence grounds. 'To govern is to choose' was a fundamental political truth long before Nye Bevan said that 'the language of priorities is the religion of socialism'. No government should ever risk the survival of its country for economic or party-political reasons, as Baldwin and Chamberlain did in the thirties. But in 1949 Britain decided that its survival should depend on NATO. How much one ally should contribute to NATO spending compared with another, and in what field, have been matters of controversy ever since. But there is no purely military criterion to determine the answers on how the NATO defence burden should be shared.

Outside the NATO area Britain's survival has never been at stake; but Britain has had important interests in many other parts of the world for the last two centuries. The extent to which those interests are best protected by military force, and what is their value compared with the cost of protecting them by force – these are the issues which only the government as a whole can decide. They were to dominate the second half of my time at Defence.

The first half was concerned more with questions of equipment. How could I hope to save the £400 million initially required by the Cabinet, and still provide the forces with the weapons they needed? Inevitably I had to focus on the RAF and the Royal Navy; the army equips men while the other two services man equipment.

My most urgent problem was the aircraft programme. *Flight International*, the official organ of the Royal Aero Club, rightly pointed out that Sandys' 'truly disastrous "no-more-manned-aircraft" decision deprived Britain's fighting services – and export effort – of supersonic successors to the best-selling Vampires, Meteors, Canberras and Hunters for a whole generation'. Guilt did not wholly lie with the politicians. The RAF continually changed its operational requirements, and the aircraft firms often submitted quite unrealistic estimates of the cost and delivery time for a new aircraft, so as to get the contract to produce it.

Moreover, the Ministry had no adequate machinery for controlling the development and production of the aircraft it ordered. It relied on civil servants and officers who would have come from a quite different field, and after three years on procurement would move on to another job. A man who had been commanding a fighter squadron in Cyprus would be made responsible in the Ministry for controlling the expenditure of millions of pounds, knowing that he would move on after three years to do intelligence work in Singapore; it would be a miracle if he had the ability or incentive to establish effective control over the full-time experts at the British Aircraft Corporation or Marconi.

As a result, in the thirteen years of Conservative rule, twenty-six major projects had to be cancelled at a cost of £300 million, with absolutely nothing to show for it. The Hunter and the Canberra would have had to stay in service for fifteen years if I had stuck to the Conservative programme; yet I had to disband the whole of the Valiant force after only nine years' service because of metal fatigue.

When I asked the air force if there was any alternative to the Conservative plans, they were only too glad to tell me. There was a cheaper American equivalent of all the three major British aircraft on order; in at least two cases they would be available much sooner, and of equal or superior performance. I decided to buy them instead, and met the Treasury's concern about their cost in dollars by negotiating an offset agreement, under which the United States would buy British goods to the same value.

The Hercules transport we bought under this arrangement cost only one third the price of the British alternative, came into service at least four years earlier, and is still doing yeoman work after over twenty years. Unfortunately, the Cabinet's insistence on putting a British engine and avionics into the Phantom fighter meant that each of these aircraft cost twice as much as it would have cost if we had bought the American model off the shelf; and because this meant redesigning the airframe, there was no saving in foreign exchange.

The Parliamentary debate on these purchases was a triumph for Roy Jenkins, the Minister of Aviation, and me, not least because Sir Roy Dobson, the chairman of Hawker-Siddeley, which lost work by our decision, gave a television interview which put all the blame on the Conservative 'twerps', as he called them. 'The Labour Government are implementing what the Conservative Government would have liked to have done,' he said. 'God only knows, I'm not a Socialist, but the Conservatives just would not make up their minds about anything – they just waffled . . . In the light of what has happened before, it is very difficult to quarrel with Jenkins and Healey.'

My decision to cancel the TSR2 strike-reconnaissance aircraft was more difficult. The original estimate of its cost in 1960 had tripled to £750 million in the four years before I became Minister. Though its original target date for delivery was 1965, in 1964 there was at least three years' development to go before the RAF got its first operational plane. The programme over ten years was likely to cost at least £250 million more than the American alternative, the swing-wing F111. However, Prime Minister, Harold Wilson, was worried about announcing its cancellation with the other decisions, on February 1st, 1965; he preferred to smuggle it into the Chancellor's Budget speech in April. So I had to keep development going for purely political reasons at a cost of over £1 million a week until April 6th; I was deeply conscious of what could have been done with that money for more useful purposes.

The Cabinet agreed that I should buy the F111 to replace the TSR2, against strong opposition from the Prime Minister and Roy Jenkins; the meeting went on after midnight and my final majority was only twelve to ten. From that moment on there was a powerful lobby in Cabinet for me to cancel the F111 purchase as well. I was finally compelled to do so three years later, in January 1968, as part of a further cut in defence spending – partly to save money, partly to avoid buying a third American plane. When the decision went against me, I was on the point of resignation, because I felt my honour was at stake: I had been able to persuade the air force to cancel the TSR2 only by guaranteeing them the F111 in its place.

I had already formed the view that a minister should never resign unless either he felt he could improve the situation by resigning, or he knew the situation was irreparable. On the other hand, if I did not resign, there was a danger Sam Elworthy would resign as CDS – he had got it into his head that I had done a deal with Wilson to scrap the F111 in return for becoming Foreign Secretary! What finally made up my mind not to resign was a story Anthony Head had told me about his resignation as Defence Minister after Suez. After telling Macmillan of his decision, he glanced down at Macmillan's daily list of engagements as he was leaving the room. To his horror he saw that the Prime Minister's next visitor was Duncan Sandys; he realised that he had made a horrible mistake. You should never resign without knowing the name of your successor. I feared my successor might be Dick Crossman. So I stayed put.

In fact I would have found it impossible to justify, either to the Party or the public, resigning over the cancellation of the F111. PEG had just concluded that, in the light of our pending withdrawal from the Middle and Far East, we had no operational requirement for such an aircraft, though I was not then aware of their conclusion. The real tragedy is that the TSR2 should ever have been begun; it would have been possible to develop the naval Buccaneer strike aircraft to meet the RAF's needs much faster and at far less cost. But under the conditions of internecine warfare which then ruled between the services, the RAF would never accept an aircraft originally designed for the navy – a syndrome described in the Ministry as NIH, or 'Not Invented Here'. Indeed Admiral Sir Varyl Begg, my outstanding Chief of Naval Staff, who was a paragon of inter-service objectivity, claimed that Mountbatten had allowed the RAF to go ahead with the TSR2 only to compensate them for losing the strategic deterrent to the navy's Polaris submarines – a typical example of 'log-rolling'.

Though my initial savings depended on the substitution of three American aircraft for three British, I was able to provide valuable work for the British aircraft industry by ordering the Nimrod maritime recon-naissance aircraft and the world's first jump-jet, the Harrier, which performed so well in the Falklands. But it was obvious that a country of Britain's size could not afford to order sufficient sophisticated combat aircraft to make their enormous cost worthwhile. So I developed a programme of cooperation with my French colleague, Pierre Messmer, who was responsible for the French aircraft industry as well as the French armed forces. After a disastrous start with the Anglo-French swing-wing project, from which France withdrew when it threatened to displace some of its own aircraft, we made a great success of the Jaguar and of a package of helicopters. I also launched the European project for a multi-role combat aircraft which, now called the Tornado, has been the backbone of the West European air forces for many years.

International cooperation on the procurement of weapons was one way of reducing their cost. It was, however, made very difficult not only by industrial and political vested interests in the countries concerned, but also by the difficulty the services found in reconciling their operational requirements; these were often dominated by quite irrelevant experiences in the Second World War. For example, the British tank forces had learned their tactics fighting in the Western Desert, where there was little natural cover and your survival depended primarily on the strength of your armour. The German and American tank generals had learned their trade mainly by fighting in Europe, where there was plenty of cover, and survival depended primarily on the speed with which you could move from one copse or valley to another. When the US Army came over to demonstrate its plans for a new NATO battle tank, Shan Hackett simply asked after the presentation: 'It looks nice, but will it keep out the rain?'

In the areas where I felt the services and the Ministry lacked the relevant expertise, I employed civilian experts to advise on changes in our organisation. For example Donald Stokes, then head of British Leyland, proposed a new organisation for selling our equipment abroad, to which I appointed the brash but shrewd Ray Brown, from Racal. Edward Pickering came from the Mirror group of newspapers to advise on improving our public relations staff; as a result I appointed as Chief of Public Relations Philip Moore, an exceptionally able young man I had met on my first visit to the Far East as Deputy High Commissioner in Singapore. Unfortunately at that time he had so impressed the Lord Chamberlain, that he was soon taken away to Buckingham Palace as Assistant Private Secretary to the Queen; he later served for years as her Private Secretary. I chose Henry Benson, the doyen of British accountants, to advise me on improving our financial organisation.

I believe that Government can gain substantially by using such outside experts to help improve its own organisation; but it is usually wiser to use such outsiders for temporary advice rather than to do the job permanently themselves. Civil service morale is damaged if, as in Washington, most of the top jobs are given to outsiders; and the outsiders are liable to assume the habits of the insiders soon after they are embodied in the bureaucratic machine.

By far my most difficult equipment decision was to cancel CVA-01, the new strike carrier planned by the navy. A country like the United States, which wants to project its naval power world-wide and can afford to maintain a force of fifteen carriers, as the US Navy then did, may find them a valuable investment. But quite apart from the cost, the Royal Navy was too short of manpower to envisage manning more than three carriers in the seventies; when I took over, the cruiser HMS *Blake* was in reserve because there were not enough technical personnel to man her.

The carrier had its primary role East of Suez, where it was thought Britain might have to operate a naval task force outside the range of friendly land-based aircraft. But, given the need for regular refits, a three-carrier force would have provided only one carrier permanently East of Suez, and for part of the time that carrier would have been *Hermes*, with only eight strike aircraft and twelve fighters. The cost of this limited capacity would have been around £170 million a year.

I commissioned innumerable studies to find out whether it was possible to perform the carrier's function with existing RAF aircraft. The answer was that, in most places which concerned us, we could support land operations more cheaply and effectively with land-based aircraft. Moreover, our political commitments would not be affected if we renounced the option of landing or withdrawing troops against sophisticated air opposition, outside the range of friendly land-based aircraft. I asked the navy to invent a plausible scenario in which the carrier would be essential. The only one they could conceive was a prolonged naval battle in the straits of Sumatra, in which the enemy had Russian MIGs on the adjoining coast, but we had given up our bases in the area; this seemed too unlikely to be worth preparing against.

Oddly enough, no one suggested the only relevant situation which has actually arisen, namely the landing and supply of British forces in the Falklands against opposition from Argentina. Fortunately, on that occasion the navy still had the small through-deck cruiser, HMS *Invincible*, with Harriers aboard, both of which I had ordered fourteen years earlier. Ironically enough, the Thatcher Government had already sold that ship to Australia, but it had not yet left Britain. As Lord Carrington admitted to the Franks Committee, he expected General Galtieri to wait until *Invincible* was in Australia at the end of 1982 before invading the islands; in that case Britain would have been rid of a commitment which the Foreign Office had been trying to slough off for years – but Galtieri might still be running his military dictatorship in Argentina.

The navy argued its case for the carrier badly; I had to keep sending its papers back to be made more persuasive. The air force, on the other hand, was represented by two able lawyers – Sam Elworthy himself, the Chief of Air Staff, and Peter Fletcher, the Air Marshal concerned with policy. They made rings round the navy, carrying the army and the Chief of Defence Staff, Dick Hull, with them.

The Navy Board inevitably took the decision to cancel CVA-01 very badly. It had fought hard to establish an air arm independent of the RAF, and was immensely proud of its young pilots, who had to demonstrate every day and night a skill and courage which was more rarely demanded of their air force rivals. I suspect that the ordinary sailor was less concerned; service on those great floating slums was not popular. The Chief of Naval Staff, gentle Sir David Luce, felt he had to resign, if only to ensure the other Admirals stayed at their posts. And the Navy Minister, my old friend from Oxford, Chris Mayhew, resigned as well. He had never reconciled himself to the junior status of the Service

Ministers on which I insisted, and based his case, not so much on the military grounds which he had argued in the Ministry, as on the Government's failure to cut its commitments East of Suez. These cuts, however, had already begun, and more were to follow. I imagine historians will best remember my six years at the Ministry of Defence for the liquidation of Britain's military role outside Europe, an anachronism which was essentially a legacy from our nineteenth-century empire.

CHAPTER FOURTEEN

East of Suez

They'll turn us out at Portsmouth wharf in cold and wet and rain,
All wearin' Injian cotton kit, but we will not complain,
They'll kill us of pneumonia – for that's their little way –
But damn the chills and fever, men, we're goin' 'ome today!
    We're goin' 'ome, we're goin' 'ome,
      Our ship is at the shore,
    An' you must pack your 'aversack,
      For we won't come back no more.
    Ho, don't you grieve for me,
      My lovely Mary-Ann!
    For I'll marry you yit on a fourp'ny bit
      As a time-expired man.

– 'Troopin'' (Old English Army in the East) Rudyard Kipling

WHEN I TOOK over the Defence Ministry in 1964 Britain had more troops East of Suez than in Germany. We had a major base for all three services in Singapore, from which to mount and control operations anywhere in South East Asia. We had a similar base on Aden for operations in the Middle East and Africa. We had smaller bases in the Gulf, at Bahrain, and in Borneo, at Labuan. We had air staging posts at Ascension Island in the Atlantic and at Gan in the Indian Ocean. We had garrisons in Hong Kong and Gibraltar for local defence. Our tri-service bases in Malta and Cyprus were mainly for NATO purposes, but were available for operations in North Africa or the Near East. And our troops were actually fighting in South Arabia and Borneo.

All these bases were necessary because of our political commitments – our responsibility for defending our dependent territories or our treaty obligations to other sovereign states such as Kuwait or Malaysia or Australia. We could not give them up until our colonies had become independent or we had renegotiated our treaties with our allies.

In my 1966 Defence White Paper, which caused Mayhew to resign, I warned that it would be impossible to save the £180 million still left out of the £400 target I had been set, after the cancellation of the carrier and the replacement of three aircraft, without relinquishing some of our present commitments overseas: 'We set out not only to decide which political commitments we must give up or share with others, but also to limit the scale of military tasks which may be imposed by the commitments which remain.'

It was not just a case of saving money: 'Although our political commitments have become fewer in recent years,' I said, 'larger military tasks have been imposed by those that remain, because the military power of certain countries has been increased over the same period, particularly by supplies of advanced equipment from abroad.' Julian Amery had put the point more offensively during the Suez debates, with his phrase 'Wogs have Migs'.

The White Paper pointed out that because we sometimes had no units of the strategic reserve in Britain, we had to withdraw troops from Germany. The consequent increase in the strain on the forces had led to falls in recruiting and re-engagement, further increasing the overstretch.

In fact the 1966 White Paper did announce our intention to withdraw from one of our bases overseas – Aden. Unfortunately, withdrawal from Aden was unlikely to save manpower so long as we retained our commitments in the Gulf. And so long as we were still engaged in the war of Confrontation in Borneo, we could not reduce our forces in the Far East.

At that time I myself believed that our contribution to stability in the Middle and Far East was more useful to world peace than our contribution to NATO in Europe. In 1961 our intervention in Kuwait had saved oil facilities vital to the West from falling into the hands of General Kassim, the half-crazed military dictator of Iraq – with no loss of life. In January 1964 British forces had helped to preserve civilian governments in the newly independent Commonwealth states of Kenya, Tanzania and Uganda from military take-overs – the first two countries still have civilian governments in consequence.

The Chiefs of Staff had learned the lessons of Suez and produced a versatile mix of forces admirably suited for such tasks. As Shadow spokesman for Defence I had already been most impressed by our sensitive and effective conduct of the operations in Borneo. My complaint about the fighting in South Arabia and Borneo – as later in the Falklands – was that more sensible policies would have made it unnecessary, not that it was wrong in principle to fulfil commitments outside Europe.

The ability of small bodies of British troops to maintain stability over vast areas East of Suez had been demonstrated in India before the war. On the other hand, India had also shown, after the war, that it is impossible for large bodies of troops to maintain order once the local population wants independence; even non-violent protest could defeat a whole army. And the humiliating surrender of the British forces in Singapore to Japan in 1942 showed that Britain could not resist a large power outside Europe if it was armed with modern weapons. Harold Wilson's claim that Britain's frontier was on the Himalaya was exposed as an embarrassing farce, when India and Pakistan chose the Soviet Union rather than their Commonwealth partner, Britain, as a mediator to end their war with one another in 1965. Later, when Wilson offered them nuclear protection, they simply ignored him.

The growth of nationalism outside Europe made it obvious that in some areas the presence of British troops was becoming an irritant rather than a stabilising factor. The scales fell from my eyes when I discovered that the Kuwaiti Government, with which Britain had a defence treaty, would not let us keep troops in Kuwait itself for fear of riots from the local population; we had to keep them hundreds of miles away in Bahrain. But the Kuwaiti Government was financing the Free Bahraini movement, which was trying to get us out of Bahrain as well!

The argument that our military presence East of Suez was needed to protect Britain's economic interests was the reverse of the truth. Recent American research has shown that as early as 1880, the British Empire was producing an economic return lower than investment in Britain itself, while to preserve it the British taxpayer was paying two and a half times more for defence than the citizens of other developed countries. If its military, administrative, and financial costs were added together, the empire was a bad economic bargain. The Soviet Union is now learning from its own experience in Eastern Europe and Central Asia that Lenin's theory of imperialism is contrary to the facts; the cost of holding colonies abroad is greater than the value of the markets or raw materials they may provide.

My problem was to extricate our forces from their commitments East of Suez with the least possible damage to Britain's influence in the world, and to the stability of the areas where they were present. The United States, after trying for thirty years to get Britain out of Asia, the Middle

East, and Africa, was now trying desperately to keep us in; during the Vietnam war it did not want to be the only country killing coloured people on their own soil. Moreover, it had at last come to realise that Britain had an experience and understanding of the Third World, which it did not possess itself. We were under Commonwealth pressure to remain in Asia – not only from Malaysia and Singapore, but also from the governments of Australia and New Zealand, which regarded it as their forward defence zone. Later, our attempts to withdraw our forces from Malta and Gibraltar were resisted by the colonial peoples themselves.

There was no substitute for seeing the problems on the spot. I paid the first of many visits East of Suez as Defence Secretary in June 1965. Edna came with me. Wives played an important part in the armed services, and maintaining morale among families serving abroad was vital to the morale of the fighting men themselves. Edna would visit the families while I visited the men.

We travelled in a Comet, specially adapted to the needs of the Defence Secretary and his staff, with comfortable bunk beds which were essential on longer journeys. My main purpose on that first visit was to look at what was happening in Aden. I found it no easier than on my earlier visit in opposition, to understand how the previous government could have planned to force the urbanised cosmopolitan Adenis into marriage with the backward tribesmen of the interior; it was like expecting Glasgow City Council to work smoothly with seventeenth-century Highland chiefs.

We flew up to see the fiercest of these chieftains, the Sherif of Beihan, in his whitewashed palace on the edge of the great desert which separates the coastal fringe from the heart of Saudi Arabia. He was a wiry, black-bearded buccaneer, notoriously fond both of fighting and of ladies; we were disappointed, however, to discover that the two beautiful women who waved at us from the parapet of his palace were British missionaries. We ate a meal of curry, maize, rice, goat, lamb and chicken, followed by fruit salad and custard, sitting cross-legged in excruciating discomfort on the floor. Then Edna went to visit the harem, while I tried in vain to engage the Sherif in political discussion. Edna gained more from the visit than I. As we were about to board our plane on the dusty airstrip, the Sherif with great gallantry presented her with a belt of beaten silver, largely made of Maria Theresa thalers. Trying it on, Edna found there was no spindle to fasten the clasp. The Sherif beckoned his camel driver, who provided a rusty nail for the purpose.

Unexpected gifts are a common problem in the Arab world. You can accept gifts only providing you give something of comparable value in return. After visiting Sheikh Isa of Bahrein I was given presents for the whole of my party. My staff received modest gold watches, and Edna a tiny lady's watch with a series of coloured straps. I got an Arab robe and head-dress, with a belt and dagger, together with an enormously expensive chunky gold Rolex. When I asked the Foreign Office what we should do with them, I heard with some chagrin that everyone could keep the other presents, provided I gave up the gold Rolex. At the next Cabinet meeting I noticed that Harold Wilson was wearing a gold Rolex identical with the one I had just surrendered. I am sure there was an innocent explanation!

After visiting the Federal Council and some of the other sheikhdoms we flew to the Hadhramaut, for two of the most enjoyable days of my life. The Hadhramaut is a beautiful sunken valley about a hundred miles from the coast of the Indian Ocean; it is given extraordinary fertility by an abundance of sweet water. As a young man I had been fascinated to read about it in books by Freya Stark, the latest in a long line of Englishwomen who fell in love with the Arab world. She first explored the Hadhramaut when it was still in a state of mediaeval barbarism. The British later established some sort of law and order there, and it was still effectively under colonial rule. There was some idea of putting it into the Federation, so I went to explore the idea.

As we drove from the airstrip the towers of Shibam rose above the horizon like the skyscrapers of Manhattan. We dined, cross-legged again, with the Sultan of Saiyun, beneath a velvet sky on the open terrace of his summer palace. Then we slept under the stars on the roof of the British Adviser's house, waking to see a cold dawn paint the cliffs of the valley rose-pink. Like many houses in the Hadhramaut, it had one room downstairs filled with four feet of cool water for bathing, which afterwards flowed out to irrigate the garden; this was an inestimable boon after hours inspecting the military levies and visiting officials.

I was not surprised to hear that they did not want to join the federation, so we dropped the idea. Like many of the peoples near the coast of the Indian Ocean, they tended to look, not inland to the Arab world, but across the sea to India and Indonesia. Many Hadhramis had brought brides home from Java or Sumatra, who found it difficult to exchange the lush jungles of their native land for this valley of sand and palm groves.

Back in the noise and stench of Aden's crowded slums it was impossible to imagine that its marriage with the sheikhdoms could survive. The

Adenis were overwhelmingly for Nasser and the Arab League. Even in the sheikhdoms most of the schoolteachers were Egyptian nationalists. One of them had married the local sheikh. Her first act was to get her headmaster executed.

Nevertheless, I was impressed by the top British officials in the area. Sir William Luce, the Resident in the Gulf, was the brother of the First Sea Lord who was to resign over the cancellation of the carrier, and the father of Richard Luce, who became a member of Mrs Thatcher's Government. A typical product of the élite Sudan Political Service, he was too pragmatic and experienced to imagine that the status quo would last; but he had the confidence both of the services in the area and of the local rulers.

The Governors of Aden in those final years were a remarkable quartet. Sir Charles Johnson was a languid cynic, married to Natasha Bagration, a descendant of the royal family which ruled Georgia before it was taken over by the Tsars; together they produced an excellent translation into Byronic stanzas of *Eugene Onegin*. Sir Kennedy Trevaskis had himself designed the ill-fated Federation. His successor, Sir Richard Turnbull, was from the colonial service in Africa; so he was familiar with the spectacle of Britain abandoning its military bases as soon as they were completed. He looked like a pernickety schoolmaster; but he was a tough administrator. He told me that when the British Empire finally sank beneath the waves of history, it would leave behind it only two monuments: one was the game of Association Football, the other was the expression 'Fuck off'.

The last Governor, who had the formidable task of supervising our withdrawal in 1968, was Sir Humphrey Trevelyan, one of the ablest of all British ambassadors, whom I had already met in Baghdad and Moscow. A small man, like a leprechaun with a twinkling brown face, he had started in the Indian Civil Service before the war. After joining the Foreign Office he had served his country well all over the world, in the most exciting posts at the most exciting times – Germany, the United Nations, China and the Soviet Union among them. His greatest expertise was in the Middle East; in Cairo he had managed to keep in touch with Nasser throughout the Suez affair; in Iraq he had enjoyed reasonable relations even with the mad dictator, Kassim. We brought him out of retirement for his last appointment in Aden; his calm intelligence made him ideal for a most difficult job.

Such men were the last of Britain's proconsuls, a remarkable breed, who brought a degree of order and justice to millions of people who had known much less, but ultimately wanted much more. They do not deserve less respect because the tides of history have washed away so much of their achievements.

The cost of trying to stay in Aden, with an increasingly hostile population armed and supported by Nasser's agents from neighbouring Yemen, was out of all proportion to the gain. The Conservatives had announced in 1962 that they intended to station British troops in Aden 'permanently'; but they agreed in 1964, before Labour took over, to give it independence in 1968. Since the population was hostile to Britain, and deeply riven by internal divisions, these two promises were obviously incompatible. We found it impossible to make any constitution work, and had to impose direct rule in 1965. So we decided to stick to the date for independence but to remove our troops at the same time. All alternatives would have been worse.

Our decision was published in the White Paper of February 1966. Trevelyan took over in May the following year and tried desperately to find someone to negotiate with, so that we could leave a viable government behind. But the nationalists in Aden were slaughtering one another, and the sheikhs of the interior were, as always, fighting among themselves. The Sherif of Beihan drove off across the desert to Saudi Arabia, and at one point threatened to send his tribesmen back across the frontier, to fight a relative who had taken over in his absence with the help of a battalion we were helping to pay and arm! The South Arabian Armed Police mutinied and killed nine British soldiers. Though our own troops showed immense courage and discipline, particularly when the Argylls re-established control of the Crater district under their colonel, Colin Mitchell, the anarchy grew worse.

When Trevelyan finally left on November 28th, 1968 the military band played 'Fings ain't wot they used to be'. As he wrote later, 'We left without glory but without disaster.' Ironically enough, Nasser was taking his troops out of Yemen at the same time. Since 1963, fifty-seven British servicemen had been killed to preserve an enterprise which should never have been undertaken. In this case, at least, Turnbull produced the right epitaph; they still play Association Football in Aden.

Britain's situation in South East Asia was very different. Malaya had won independence in 1957 after a prolonged emergency in which the Communist Party's attempt to take over was frustrated by a brilliant campaign under Gerald Templer. Singapore secured full self-government in 1959 and its young Chinese Prime Minister, Lee Kuan Yew, asked for a merger with Malaya. Fearing that the Chinese would have a majority in such a merger, Malaya asked Britain to include its colonies of Sabah and Sarawak, on the island of Borneo. Greatly to the concern of the Philippines and Indonesia, Britain agreed, largely because it had no better solution to the problem of those territories. The new state of Malaysia was born in September 1963, and almost immediately the dictator of Indonesia, General Sukarno, began infiltrating soldiers across the frontier in Borneo in a campaign of what he called 'Confrontation'. A year earlier Sukarno had supported a rebellion against the Sultan of Brunei, a little oil-rich enclave in Sarawak under British protection. So British forces were already engaged on the island.

The Federation of Malaysia was obviously an artificial construction. There was no historical connection between Malaya and the Borneo territories, which were four hundred miles away across the sea at their nearest point. The Malayans regarded the head-hunting tribes of Sabah and Sarawak as barbarians, and tended to behave with imperial arrogance towards them. But the threat from Indonesia, combined with sensible diplomacy from the British in the area, created a unity which has survived till now.

However, Singapore left the Federation in August 1965. Three quarters of its people were Chinese; it would never have been a comfortable partner for Malaya, which had six times the population, and had just defeated a rising by Communists, who were mainly from the Chinese minority. These ethnic differences were greatly aggravated by the personal incompatibility between the Prime Minister of Malaya, Tunku Abdul Rahman, and the Prime Minister of Singapore, Lee Kuan Yew. I came to know and like them both.

The Tunku had led Malaya to independence, and remained Prime Minister of the Federation till 1970. He was of royal blood – 'Tunku' means Prince – had studied Law in Britain, and worked as a civil servant under British rule, until he formed a political party to fight for independence. Relaxed, tolerant, and affable, he found Lee far too serious and intense. When he heard that Lee had been pushed into a deep drain by a mob he was trying to reason with, he laughed till the tears came to his eyes. He loved racing, and kept his own stable. His pride in one of his ancestors, who was said to have been a vampire, led him to finance a film, *The King with Fangs*, out of which he made $100,000. Despite appearances, he was an able and cunning politician. So far as defence and foreign policy were concerned, he told me his simple rule: 'If you have an enemy you can defeat on your own, fight. If you have an enemy you can defeat with allies, fight. If your enemy is China, surrender.'

Lee Kuan Yew was different in every way. An intellectual through and through, he had been the most brilliant schoolboy of his age in Singapore, as his wife, Choo, was the most brilliant schoolgirl. He took a Double First in Law at Cambridge. Choo also took a First there, after only two years' study; she managed his law firm while he was Prime Minister. Lee was brought up in English, which he speaks far better than most British politicians, and learned Mandarin as well as Malay only when he entered politics. Yet he is immensely proud that his Chinese ancestry makes him part of the oldest, and, as he would say, the greatest culture in the world. He is especially proud of being of the Hakka people, which originated in North China. The Hakka are the Prussians of China, and there is a lot of the Prussian in Lee Kuan Yew. He believes in discipline and hard work.

Though he was attracted by communism as a student in England, on his return he fought successfully to destroy communist influence among the Chinese in Singapore. Indeed, as Prime Minister, he would not allow young men from Singapore to visit China, in case they became infected. His combative nature often made him unnecessary enemies; he could indulge in a sarcasm no less wounding because it was so elegantly expressed. The Australians were often the object of his most bitter remarks, because he could never forget what, as a young student after the fall of Singapore, he had seen as their collapse of morale, compared with the discipline of the British soldiers.

The Japanese occupation made a lasting impression on him. Though he worked as a translator for their official news agency, he had to kowtow and have his face slapped like the rest. In my opinion, this sudden collapse of his whole world when he was a schoolboy gave him a lasting sense of political insecurity, which may help to explain his drift towards authoritarianism in later years. On one visit I had a long talk with him alone. It was shortly after his return from a conference in Lagos; on arriving in Singapore he was appalled to learn that the respected President of Nigeria, Abu Bakr, who had been his host a day or two earlier, had been deposed by a military coup, his body thrown in a ditch. The morning of the day we met there had been a minor scuffle at a recruiting office in Singapore. For the first time I had known him, Harry – he liked his friends to call him by the name in which he was brought up – was really shaken; he felt that a truckload of soldiers might drive up to his residence at any moment and subject him to the same fate as Abu Bakr. I suspect it was at this time that he decided his young son should join the Singapore Army and become its Commander in Chief.

I got news of the secession of Singapore from the Federation of

Malaysia during the summer recess in 1965, when I was one of the few ministers left in Whitehall. At first I was concerned that the split might undermine our operations in Borneo; there had been rumours that the Tunku was planning a coup against Lee. Later I came to believe that it was arranged amicably between them, though neither breathed a word to the British. In any case, it had no effect on our military campaign.

This was still going well. We had persuaded the Malay soldiers and officials to be less high-handed with the local peoples. There was now unity against the common enemy. Above all, as I had seen during my visit in Opposition, the British commanders knew that their success depended on winning the hearts and minds of the local population. Walter Walker, the brilliant jungle general, later wrote: 'It was indelibly inscribed on our minds that one civilian killed by us would do more harm than ten killed by the enemy.' I strongly agreed. When the RAF commander in Singapore asked me for permission to bomb the Indonesian ports of entry in Eastern Borneo, I refused; I suspect he did so only to satisfy the firebrands on his staff, and expected my refusal.

On the other hand, when Walker asked me to allow our forces to cross the border so as to ambush the enemy soldiers before they could enter Malaysian territory, I gave them permission, under strict control. A feature of campaigns East of Suez was the need for close and continuous control of military operations in the light of their political implications – sometimes from my own office in Whitehall. So I allowed the border crossings, first for small groups up to 5,000 yards, and later for up to 20,000 yards and with large bodies of men. These operations, code-named 'Claret', remained secret until long after the war was over. Our own forces never talked about them, and no doubt the Indonesians kept silent because they would have been humiliated to admit they could not prevent them. In any case they were doing the same to us; after all, that was what Confrontation meant.

Fighting in the jungle was dangerous and exhausting in the extreme. The Gurkhas and the Malays were used to it; we also had invaluable support from Australian and New Zealand battalions which had been based in Malaya. What most impressed me, however, was the ability of our own British soldiers to come straight from the stony mountains of South Arabia or the barren heaths of North Germany, and to fight with cheerful skill in jungles which had never before been penetrated by white men, except for the occasional explorer. Oddly enough, Eddie Shackleton, at that time my excellent Air Minister, was there on a Cambridge University expedition before the war; his father had been a famous explorer in the Antarctic.

I visited our troops in Borneo as often as I could. In July 1966 I was able to spend a whole fortnight in the Far East, and to see every aspect of the problem at first hand on the ground. In Kuching, the capital of Sarawak, I dined with the Governor under a superb portrait of the Byronic James Brooke, who founded the dynasty of White Rajahs there in 1841; it lasted a hundred years. Then I met the Paramount Chief of the Iban tribe, whose long ringlets were regarded by the Tunku with the same distaste as the headhunting, to which Confrontation had given a new impetus. We flew by helicopter to little wooden forts on the frontier, from which our troops organised their jungle patrols – high on the ridge of blue romantic mountains with names like Bukit Nukel, or by a muddy river surrounded by monkeys, iguanas, and crocodiles. We stayed in General Lea's lodge outside Brunei – he had just succeeded Walter Walker as Director of Operations. It was there that I first met the exceptional Nigel Bagnall, a pale-faced, ginger-haired officer who twenty years later was an outstanding commander of the British forces in Germany, and would have moved from Chief of the General Staff to CDS if Mrs Thatcher had any judgment of men.

One day we flew to a small long-house on the upper reaches of the Limbang river. There we drank 'tuak' – a potent mixture of cider with honey and gin. A rifle was fired and a cock waved over our libations before we embarked on long-boats, made of hollowed-out tree trunks and powered by outboard motors, for a two hour journey down the river and over the rapids. We disembarked at another long-house and were welcomed by the headman, who had fought with Tom Harrison against the Japanese. After drinking more tuak, we were made to join in the sword dancing; it was quite an ordeal after so much alcohol in the boiling heat.

Edna performed so well that the headman gestured for a large rope net to be lowered from the rafters. Out of it rolled a number of small wicker baskets about the size of small melons. The headman picked one out and presented it to Edna. It contained the head of a Japanese soldier, perfectly preserved by being hung in the smoke of a fire. Edna accepted it with every show of enthusiasm, and thought desperately what she might give in return. There was nothing for it but to take off the watch she had been given a year earlier by the ruler of Bahrain, and to present it to her host. On returning to London we declared the head to the Customs as an anthropological specimen. It lay in a plastic bag behind the sofa in our bedroom at Admiralty House until discovered by a woman cleaner. When she had returned to consciousness we sent it over to the Ministry of Defence, where I suppose it still lies.

A few days later I spent a day at sea with the Far East Fleet, travelling in everything from a rubber dinghy to an aircraft carrier – where I had to explain to a sceptical audience my decision to cancel CVA-01. The climax was being winched off the deck of a submarine at sea, into a hovering helicopter. Pat Nairne had some difficulty managing my camera bag during the process. Edna was not with me on this occasion. This was unfortunate, because she missed seeing the performance of a group of Marines from the Special Boat Service. They parachuted from an aircraft into the sea and swam to meet me on the submarine; one of them was a young officer called Paddy Ashdown.

A month after this visit, in August 1966, the Indonesians called off Confrontation. Sukarno was gone, and we have had good relations with Indonesia ever since. I regard the campaign as a textbook demonstration of how to apply economy of force, under political guidance for political ends. At a time when the United States was plastering Vietnam with bombs, napalm, and defoliant, no British aircraft ever dropped a bomb in Borneo. On the other hand, if we had not had aircraft and warships available, the Indonesians might have escalated the fighting. Though at the peak of Confrontation we deployed 17,000 servicemen on the island, our casualties were only 114 killed and 181 wounded – a high proportion were Gurkhas. The civilian casualties, almost all local people, were thirty-six killed, fifty-three wounded and four captured. After a campaign which lasted nearly four years, the toll was comparable with that on the British roads in a single Bank Holiday weekend. We estimated that the Indonesians lost 590 killed, 222 wounded and 771 captured.

At the same time, Confrontation was one of the most arduous campaigns which British soldiers had ever fought. Apart from the ordeal of jungle warfare, in territory where it would often take a day to move a hundred yards, our soldiers were fighting formidable enemies. As Field Marshal Slim has pointed out: 'The Asian fighting man is at least equally brave, usually more careless of death, less encumbered by mental doubts . . . He is better fitted to endure hardship uncomplainingly, and to look after himself when thrown on his own resources. He has a keen practised eye for country and the ability to move across it on his own feet.' The Americans learned this lesson the hard way in Vietnam. We had learned it in Burma and Malaya. But though many of our officers had invaluable experience from earlier campaigns, most of their men were meeting the jungle for the first time.

The Gurkha battalions played a critical role, and Walter Walker, our leading Gurkha general, showed not only military skill but also deep political insight throughout the fighting. However, once the campaign was over, he deeply offended Dick Hull, then CDS, by fighting as hard against the General Staff to keep the Gurkhas, as he had fought against the Indonesians. When I heard his future career was in danger, I intervened to save him. It was a mistake. All the political skills he had shown in the Far East deserted him in Europe. As the NATO Commander in Oslo, he had a series of public quarrels with the Norwegians. Back in England he got involved with a group of right-wing crackpots who appeared to be thinking seriously of subverting the government. Not for the first time I found that almost every important responsibility in life requires a special group of qualities, which are rarely transferable. A good fighting soldier may be a bad Staff Officer. A good battalion commander may be a bad General. And a good General may be an appalling politician, as MacArthur demonstrated. Eisenhower and de Gaulle were exceptions which proved this rule; their military careers were successful primarily because of their political skills.

With Confrontation over, we were free to look objectively at the future of our commitments East of Suez. We soon decided that we should withdraw from our base in Singapore during the seventies. When I told Lee Kuan Yew of our decision in April 1967, we were sailing on his ministerial yacht in the Straits of Johore. He was at first very cast down. After a few minutes he recovered, asking only that I should try to delay our departure until at least 1975. He thought he could count on the Tunku to change our mind. In fact the Tunku was unworried, asking only that we should put Brunei in the Federation first – which we refused. He told me that so long as there was one British soldier in the area he would feel safe.

We had in fact decided to maintain a military capability for action East of Suez after the bases in Singapore and Aden had gone, making it clear that we would expect those on whose behalf we might intervene to provide the necessary facilities. At this time we were thinking of a possible base in Australia; we wanted somewhere far from the mainland of Asia, where our colonial past would always risk creating local opposition. At that time we were formally linked with Australia and New Zealand in the Far East through the South East Asia Treaty Organisation, or SEATO, along with the United States and France; but SEATO had become a dead letter by 1964. Nevertheless, Australia and New Zealand had set up a Commonwealth Brigade in Malaya with Britain, and their troops gave us valuable assistance during Confrontation. They also had a small contingent with the Americans in Vietnam. We felt we should consult them about all our decisions on our role of East of Suez. So I spent three days in Canberra at the beginning of February 1966, six months before the ending of Confrontation, to explain the purpose of my Defence Review and the reasons for the decisions I was shortly to announce, on leaving Aden and changing the aircraft and aircraft carrier programmes.

My visit to Canberra came in the middle of a whirlwind journey round the world for consultations on the Defence Review. The journey took ten days, and since I was travelling from East to West, many days were twenty-eight hours long, and included only four hours' sleep. Every waking moment on my Comet was spent preparing for discussions and press conferences at the next stop. We flew via the Azores and Bermuda to Washington, where I briefed President Johnson, Dean Rusk, and the defence officials under Bob McNamara. Then we flew across the United States to San Francisco, where our Comet broke down. Instead of flying straight on across the Pacific, we had to spend the night at the San Francisco Hotel, where my frustration was relieved by seeing a poster which advertised the charms of a 'Mrs Spiegelbaum, the Only Topless Mother of Eight.'

Next morning we had to take a commercial flight via Hawaii to Fiji, crossing the international date line on the way. Then on to Canberra. It was my first visit to Australia, though I had many Australian friends at Oxford. Canberra was a new city, widely spread over low hills, with a large artificial lake in the middle – a sort of Milton Keynes with wallabies. I spent the best part of a day giving a seminar to the Prime Minister and those members of his Cabinet who were concerned with foreign affairs and defence. Apart from Paul Hasluck, the Foreign Minister, they were not over-impressive; many of the best Australian politicians preferred state to federal politics, and did not like living in Canberra. Harold Holt had become Prime Minister only a week before I arrived, and Gough Whitlam, the leader of the opposition Labour Party, overshadowed all the members of the Government.

On the other hand I found the top civil servants both able and attractive; they remained my friends for many years. Both as Defence Secretary and as Chancellor, I sometimes found it less worthwhile to talk to my ministerial colleagues, than to their advisers. The Permanent Secretary of the Defence Ministry, Harry Bland, was a feisty little man of immense energy; he never left an important detail unexplored. Jim Plimsoll of the external affairs department, who later became High Commissioner in London, was tall and quiet, with immense reserves of wisdom and experience. Even more impressive were the Australian academic experts on defence. From the middle fifties Australia has contributed far more to international understanding of defence problems than any country of similar size. The reputation of people like Hedley Bull, Coral Bell, and Larry Martin has been high for two decades on both sides of the Atlantic, and there is now a new generation of comparable stature, such as Des Ball and Andrew Mack. The climate of the Antipodes seems conducive to producing good defence intellectuals and Air Marshals, as well as great sopranos.

On this first visit to Canberra I still believed it was right and possible for us to stay East of Suez. I told the National Press Club: 'We intend to remain, and shall remain, fully capable of carrying out all the commitments we have at the present time, including those in the Far East, the Middle East, and in Africa and other parts of the world. We do intend to remain in the military sense a world power.' But even then I did not think we should plan on keeping our base in Singapore indefinitely. However, when I explored with the Australians the possibility of replacing it with a new base in their own country, they were unenthusiastic. They said that it would be difficult to find the necessary construction workers; in reality they did not want us to leave Singapore at all. Moreover, they would have found it difficult to explain to their electorate why they were building a base for Britain in Australia, while their own troops were fighting in Vietnam without British troops at their side.

In any case, though we planned to run on the existing carrier force until 1975, thereafter we would be unable to do so without CVA-01. It might then be impossible to reach any base in the Far East for a campaign in the area, unless we had airfields in the Indian Ocean through which we could stage our aircraft, without crossing territory whose government might refuse us overflying rights. We already had an airfield on the beautiful coral atoll of Gan, but could reach it only after flying over Arab countries which might refuse us permission in a crisis. So we decided to construct an airfield on the little island of Aldabra off Mozambique, which could be reached round the Cape or over friendly African countries. Since it was inhabited only by giant tortoises, frigate birds, and the great booby, we expected no political difficulties. We reckoned without the environmental lobby, which won its first great victory against us, aided by a brilliant campaign of parliamentary questions from the assiduous Tam Dalyell. We did not abandon the idea of a base on Aldabra until the further spending cuts which followed devaluation in November 1967. But I had already decided that it did not make military sense. Fortunately we had still spent no money on it.

As always, I was under pressure from the Treasury to cut spending, and from the Foreign and Commonwealth Offices not to cut commitments. Meanwhile each of the services saw our East of Suez role as an opportunity to get a greater share of the defence cake; besides, they much preferred fighting in the glamorous Orient to patrolling the North German plain or the East Atlantic. At the same time, there was a growing clamour among Labour MPs for us to abandon our East of Suez role immediately; in this chorus, the voices of the Common Marketeers provided a counterpoint to those of the anti-colonialist Left. Well before Confrontation was over, Michael Stewart as Foreign Secretary joined me in telling our Parliamentary colleagues that we were in a 'posture of withdrawal' – but to no avail. Meanwhile the United States and the Commonwealth were redoubling their efforts to get us to stay indefinitely. It was a difficult time for the Defence Secretary.

The end of Confrontation made it politically possible for us to reduce our commitments. A year later, devaluation made it economically essential. At that point the Chiefs of Staff reversed their position; they insisted that since their capability was to be further reduced, our commitments should be cut with them. I then faced only one obstacle in Whitehall – the Foreign Office, and the overseas governments it appeared to represent. Even this obstacle began to crumble when the Cabinet finally decided to apply for membership of the Common Market in May 1967. From that moment it was clear that we would leave Singapore and cut our remaining commitments in the Gulf. The only questions remaining were the specific dates of our withdrawals, when we should announce our intentions, and how we should handle our allies overseas – the issues I was discussing with Lee Kuan Yew and the Tunku on my visit in April 1968.

In July that year my White Paper announced that we would cut our forces in Singapore and Malaysia by half in 1970–1, and would withdraw altogether a few years later. In January 1969 we announced the end of our commitments in the Gulf, and set December 1971 as the date for our final withdrawal from Singapore. With typical foresight the persistent Lee Kuan Yew had persuaded us to fix a time after the last possible date for the general election in Britain. He believed that a Conservative Government would carry out the undertakings its spokesmen made in Opposition, to reverse our withdrawal from East of Suez. This was perhaps the only occasion in his career when he allowed his judgment to be corrupted by innocence and wishful thinking.

Besides Aden and Singapore, we also had a military base in Hong

Kong to which I paid regular visits. The problem for Britain in Hong Kong, however, was very different. If China had chosen to invade, Britain would have been no more able to defend the colony against her, than against Japan during the war. Indeed Peking could have brought Hong Kong to its knees at any time without using military force, simply by cutting off the supply of water from the Pearl River across the frontier. Moreover, we were bound by treaty to return the so-called New Territories of the peninsula to China in 1997; without them the island of Hong Kong itself would be unviable from every point of view. On the other hand, although Peking regarded the whole of the colony as rightfully part of China, it recognised its interest in maintaining the status quo; Hong Kong was its main channel of contact with the West, and a source of financial profit. So the West was able to use Hong Kong as a station for monitoring events on the mainland, and during the Vietnam War it provided rest and recreation for the American forces.

The main purpose of our military presence there was to prevent illegal immigration from the mainland, and to maintain internal security. Neither were easy. Although our navy could intercept boats which were suspected of smuggling immigrants, our British and Gurkha battalions were too few to cope with the hundreds of thousands of Chinese peasants who were liable to flood across the land frontier when there was a famine anywhere nearby. There had been such a tidal wave shortly before I became Defence Secretary. When the Japanese were defeated in 1945 the Chinese population was under a million. It had risen to four million by the time I left office in 1970, creating formidable housing problems.

The early post-war immigrants were often political refugees from Communist rule, but in my time most of the newcomers had left China largely for economic reasons; they still owed political allegiance to Peking. So there was a latent tension between supporters of Peking and supporters of Taiwan, organised through the Communist Party and the Kuo Min Tang respectively; it was liable to erupt in riots and street fighting, particularly during celebrations of the Chinese New Year. During the Cultural Revolution in China, which began in August 1966, such riots, and the accompanying strikes, threatened a total breakdown of law and order. However, both sides recognised that a prolonged conflict between them could have provoked a reluctant military intervention from China itself; so there was little local pressure in those days for free elections in the colony, except from a handful of British expatriates and Chinese lawyers.

Partly for this reason, Hong Kong was the last surviving outpost of the pre-war colonial tradition. The social customs at Government House on my first visit were pure Edwardian – one sherry only before dinner, then pairing off with the appropriate lady in long white gloves, followed by a meal which would have disgraced a minor prep school, consisting of boiled mutton with lumpy mashed potatoes, ending with suet pudding and custard – and this in the culinary capital of the world! I would escape whenever I could to eat the celestial food available in a Chinese restaurant.

Apart from visiting the British forces, the main purpose of my visits to Hong Kong was to negotiate more financial support for our military presence. As always, the British colonial officers there supported the local interest against Whitehall. I always retired hurt from my encounters with the redoubtable Financial Secretary, John Cowperthwaite. Hong Kong has been uniquely fortunate in being able to combine the intelligence, hard work and commercial genius of its Chinese population with the honesty and efficiency of its British administrators. This combination has produced an unparalleled concentration of economic and financial success which I believe China will not wish to jeopardise when 1997 comes.

Despite its shanty towns, clinging precariously to the hillsides outside Kowloon, and the harbours littered over with the floating villages in which a large part of its people still lived; Hong Kong was then a place of great beauty. The paddy-fields, where Hakka women planted rice in wide brimmed hats with fringes of black cloth, are now often replaced by shining new cities of skyscrapers. But the view over Hong Kong from the Peak remains one of the wonders of the world, especially at night.

I tried hard, on one of my visits, to arrange a quick trip to Angkor Vat in Cambodia; it had been my ambition to see it ever since reading of its beauty in an early novel of André Malraux, who spent some years of his youth searching for antiquities in the jungles nearby. Unfortunately the Foreign Office felt it would be improper for me to go to Angkor unless I also paid a courtesy visit on the Government in Vientiane, and I had not time to do both. But at least I saw the temples and floating markets of Bangkok. It meant getting up before five in the morning, since I was meeting the Prime Minister at eight. My determination not to miss anything worth seeing and photographing led Pat Nairne to call me 'maximum extraction Healey'; but I have never regretted it. The temples, or Wats, in Bangkok are exceptionally beautiful, like inverted bells or wine-glasses. As you walk round their terraces, among Buddhist priests in their saffron robes, past life-size gilt statues of legendary birds with the bodies of women, it is difficult to believe that most of them are only a century old and that their glittering multicoloured surfaces consist of millions of pieces of broken crockery.

Ever since I worked at Transport House I have tried to learn a few words in the language of the country I am visiting, so that I can begin my speeches with a sentence or two in Russian or Hungarian or whatever is appropriate, breaking into English only on the grounds that otherwise our Ambassador may not understand. Thai, however, defeated me. The meaning of every word depends on how it is inflected. The Thai intelligence colonel who took me round tried again and again to get me to pronounce the syllables correctly; but most of the time I could not detect any difference between the sounds I made and what he was trying to get me to say.

Unlike most of the countries I visited in Asia, Thailand was unique in never having been under colonial rule; so it suffered from none of the post-imperial neuroses. Its trading contacts gave Denmark a special place in its affections, but its leaders always met all Europeans on equal terms. The weight of the American presence during the Vietnam war, however, had an impact on Bangkok which Western and Japanese tourists have since deepened; the innocence celebrated in *The King and I* has disappeared for good.

For political purposes my role in Britain's disengagement from East of Suez ended in June 1969 at a conference in Canberra of the Commonwealth governments concerned. Prime Minister Harold Holt had disappeared while skin-diving, and his place was now occupied by John Gorton. It was an unhappy Government. Gorton was unpopular with many of his colleagues, and his senior civil servant, Len Hewitt, was even more unpopular with the permanent secretaries of the departments. Personally I found Gorton attractive, with the same type of charisma as Pierre Trudeau in Canada. A fighter pilot during the war, he had been badly disfigured when his aircraft crashed; he took pride in showing me his photograph from 1940 when he was exceptionally handsome.

Changes were taking place in Malaya too, where I stopped on my way home; a group of young Turks led by Musa Hitam were beginning to move up into the higher ranks of government, and some of the abler civil servants like Ghazali were now established in political roles. I got up at six-thirty one morning for a round of golf with the leading ministers in Malaysia. The golf course was well established in Eastern Asia as the best place for serious political or commercial discussion. It was already intensely hot, and sweat poured down our faces as we hooked and sliced our way to the final green. A large posse of security men accompanied us on our round; their main function was to recover our balls from the tropical vegetation which surrounded the course, picking leeches off their legs as they emerged with their trophies.

Throughout this long and difficult period I had to work in harness with the Foreign and Commonwealth Secretaries, who were normally my only reliable allies against the Treasury. On two occasions I was able to reward them with the physical support of my fists. During the Leyton by-election, in which Patrick Gordon Walker tried vainly to get back into Parliament after losing his seat in the general election, I was speaking for him at a noisy meeting attended by a strong contingent of the National Front. At a given signal, all the Fascists in the audience launched flour bombs at the platform. Suddenly their leader, a repulsive brute called Colin Jordan, emerged from behind the curtains where he had been hiding, and began to harangue the mob. I knocked him off the stage, on to an inoffensive reporter who took years to forgive me for his broken spectacles.

A year or so later I was speaking at a by-election in Walthamstow with Arthur Bottomley, who was Wilson's first Commonwealth Secretary. Again a group of Fascists began throwing flour bombs at the platform. When Arthur went to remonstrate with them, they knocked him to the floor and began to kick him. I jumped from the platform into the mêlée, and began to lay about me, until the police restored order. Since it was recorded by the television cameras, the incident did wonders for my image. The newspapers called me 'Hurricane Healey'; on my next visit to Washington I was solemnly congratulated by the formidable commander of the Marines for laying into those 'Commie bastards'!

My closest colleagues in the political departments were Michael Stewart, George Brown, and George Thomson. Michael, who succeeded Patrick Gordon Walker after he failed to win the by-election, served for eight months as Foreign Secretary, then after three years in economic departments went back to the Foreign Office when George Brown resigned. Michael was the ideal 'safe pair of hands'. A schoolmaster by profession, he had total moral and intellectual integrity, but perhaps lacked the drive and imagination the job needed at that time.

George Brown, my colleague during the most difficult period from 1965 to 1968, was very different. Like the immortal Jemima, when he was good he was very, very good, but when he was bad he was horrid. A working class Londoner, he became an official of the Transport and General Workers' Union after serving as a fur-salesman. He idolised its leader, Ernest Bevin. In 1947, as a young MP he conspired unsuccessfully to get Attlee replaced as Prime Minister by Bevin, greatly annoying Bevin himself, who had not been consulted. Brown had none of Bevin's magnanimity; he carried an enormous chip on his shoulder, which tended to make him jealous of anyone with a university education. Like many people with an inferiority complex, he could be an appalling bully. But he did not mind people standing up to him. After being subjected to a particularly tiresome tirade, his Private Secretary, a small man called Donald Maitland, pulled himself up to his full height, looked George in the kneecaps, and said: 'You do not imagine, Foreign Secretary, do you, that a person of my stature has got where he is today, by kow-towing to bullies?' George was suitably abashed.

He had a powerful mind allied with great energy, and could often get to the heart of a problem faster than anyone else. But he was quite unpredictable, and came to depend so much on drink that in the end I tried to avoid seeing him after midday. He was always resigning, some-times on the most trivial issues. When our troops in Aden were under particular strain, I decided to call up a few reservists who were being paid extra specifically for accepting such a liability – something my predecessors had never dared to do. George exploded. 'They'll never stand for it in Swadlincote,' he said. Swadlincote was a small village in his constituency, always quoted by George as a touchstone of public opinion. 'There'll be revolution. The Government will fall.' And he resigned. Next morning only one newspaper even mentioned the call-up, and that in a single paragraph. George withdrew his resignation.

In spite of everything, we managed to work quite well together. But the strain of acting as a psychiatric nurse to a patient who was often violent became intolerable. My patience was finally exhausted when George once again resigned one evening in March 1968, on the grounds that Wilson had not consulted him properly about the decision to close the gold market. I was touring RAF stations in the West country at the time. One of his friends rang me after midnight to say that George was in the House of Commons drinking heavily; he had given news of his resignation to a number of lobby correspondents as well as to any MP who would listen. Would I speak to him, as so often in the past, and ask him to withdraw his resignation? I said no, and went back to bed. Enough was enough. So the steady and reliable Michael Stewart was back in the Foreign Office for my last two years.

On the details of our commitments East of Suez, however, I worked more closely with George Thomson, both as Minister of State at the Foreign Office, and later as Commonwealth Secretary. We were old friends. His calm, reasonable approach to difficult problems had a core of steel, which made him an ideal diplomatist during the prolonged and painful renegotiations of our policy outside Europe.

There was some jealousy in the Foreign Office that the Ministry of Defence was making all the running on our commitments. I was told that the Foreign Office at that time was divided into two groups – those who thought I should be Foreign Secretary, and those who thought I was. But since the Foreign Office seemed quite incapable of setting priorities among our commitments overseas, I had no alternative but to take the lead.

I had invaluable support from Frank Cooper, as Deputy Under Secretary of Defence for Policy. He had been flying Spitfires during the war; Merlyn Rees, my air force minister, had served with him in Italy. For much of his career he and Pat Nairne, the other official on whom I most depended, had been rivals in the department. Frank was a very different type from Pat; he was relaxed where Pat was intense, and always preferred the wood to the trees. Though he sometimes gave a misleading impression of careless indolence, in fact he was immensely sharp and to the point; he liked to proceed by making broad hypotheses which he would drop the moment they appeared untenable, for political or other reasons. This led some to accuse him of opportunism. But he fully deserved his later promotion to Permanent Secretary of the department; the Ministry then benefited greatly from at last having an expert on defence in the engine room.

Even today the Wilson Government is often attacked from two sides for its handling of our commitments East of Suez. Many Americans, and some Conservatives, still tend to the view that we should have stayed to maintain stability and order. Retired governors like to quote Philip Larkin's melancholy verses:

> Next year we are to bring the soldiers home
> For lack of money, and it is all right.
> Places they guarded, or kept orderly,
> Must guard themselves, or keep themselves orderly.
> We want the money for ourselves at home
> Instead of working. And this is all right.

Initially I shared some of that feeling. But hard experience compelled me to recognise that the growth of nationalism would have made it politically unwise for Britain to maintain a military presence in the Middle East and South East Asia, even if our economic situation had permitted it.

In Britain itself, the more common criticism nowadays is that we were too slow to recognise the facts, and should have announced our intention to withdraw immediately we took office in 1964. That would have been impossible. Our troops were fighting both in South Arabia and Borneo. Four independent Commonwealth countries were fighting with us during Confrontation. Even if we had intended to go, we could not have revealed our intention without the consent of our partners. It is true, however, that Harold Wilson had illusions of grandeur about our post-imperial role in Asia and Africa; they endured even after his Cabinet had swung against it.

In an imperfect world, the Wilson Government's handling of the issue compares well with the Attlee Government's withdrawal from India, which produced millions of refugees and at least 200,000 dead; it compares better still with the tragic débâcle of America's military involvement in Vietnam. The skill of British troops in Borneo helped to preserve a stability which has already endured for twenty years after our withdrawal. South Arabia is a mess; but it was already an irredeemable mess when the Wilson Government took over. The lower Gulf is at least as stable as it was while Britain maintained its military presence there. The agony created in the upper Gulf by the war between Iraq and Iran could not have been prevented by British troops. Indeed it can be argued that by involving the Shah in an alliance against the Soviet Union, by supporting his secular dictatorship against the mullahs, and by organising the overthrow of Mossadeq in 1953, Britain and the United States made it inevitable that anti-Western Muslim fundamentalists would ultimately take over in Iran. Similarly, by joining with Israel and France in the attack on Nasser's Egypt in 1956, Eden made it impossible for Arab rulers thereafter to rely openly on British troops for their protection.

With hindsight, it is not difficult to see that the withdrawal from India meant that Britain's military role in Asia was bound to end before long. By historical standards, the Wilson Government handled the inevitable with reasonable speed and skill.

Meanwhile, both economic and political pressures were compelling Britain to concentrate its military efforts in Europe. Here, NATO was well established as the necessary framework for its defence policy, and the role of nuclear weapons in NATO strategy was under fundamental review. This was a complex of problems with which I had already been wrestling for at least a decade.

CHAPTER FIFTEEN

NATO and Nuclear Strategy

That civilisation may not sink,
Its great battle lost,
Quiet the dog, tether the pony
Our master Caesar is in the tent
To a distant post;
Where the maps are spread,
His eyes fixed upon nothing,
A hand under his head.
Like a long-legged fly upon the stream
His mind moves upon silence.

– 'Long-legged fly' W. B. Yeats

I DOUBT IF ANY General or defence minister has ever enjoyed the luxury of developing his strategy in the silence Yeats imagines for Caesar. I certainly did not. Fortunately my years of argument and reflection in Opposition helped me to cope with the torrent of nuclear decisions I was called to make over six years, in the midst of all my other work.

In my first week of office I had a top-secret presentation on the Polaris programme, and began discussions with United States ministers and Chiefs of Staff about the need to revise NATO strategy. The fall of Krushchev and the Chinese nuclear explosion were fresh in our minds. It was clear that Lyndon Johnson would be elected President in a few weeks' time, and that he was rapidly losing whatever enthusiasm he had ever had for Kennedy's proposal of a Multilateral Force, or MLF, as the solution to NATO's nuclear problems. A visit a few days later from the German Chief of Staff convinced me that Adenauer had initially supported the MLF only as a political gimmick to make his rapprochement

with de Gaulle more acceptable to Washington – the military in Bonn
were hostile to the MLF, in so far as they could make any sense of the
idea.

For me, however, the first question was whether Britain should
continue the Polaris programme at all, since Macmillan had agreed at
Nassau in 1962 to support the MLF and put his Polaris submarines in
it, only because Kennedy had made this a condition of letting him have
Polaris.

The navy told me that, though the hulls of two Polaris submarines
were already laid down and long-lead items had been ordered for two
more, it would still be possible to convert them into hunter-killer
submarines at no additional cost. Moreover most of the senior admirals
were reluctant to take on the Polaris force within their existing budget at
the expense of other ships, and were uncertain whether they could find the
additional skilled personnel to operate and service Polaris. When I gave
Wilson and Gordon Walker this unexpected news they asked me not to
let other members of the Cabinet know; Wilson wanted to justify
continuing the Polaris programme on the grounds that it was 'past the
point of no return'. I did not demur.

On February 26th that year, while I was still in Opposition, I had told
Parliament that a Labour Government would not necessarily cancel
Polaris. I now thought that in the uncertain world into which we were
moving, a few Polaris submarines would be worth more than the same
number of hunter-killers, both because they would give Britain more
influence, particularly in Washington, during the coming revision of
NATO strategy, and because they would tend to reinforce the credibility
of the American deterrent. Moreover, their running costs would be only
£4 million a year – about two per cent of the defence budget.

The overwhelming majority of the Cabinet took the same view, as did
Mountbatten. The only consistent opposition to Polaris came from
George Wigg, to whom Wilson had given mysterious responsibilities in
the field of security as Paymaster General, and Alun Chalfont, who had
been appointed Minister for Disarmament on Wigg's advice – after
Wilson had failed to persuade a series of other candidates, including Solly
Zuckerman, to take the job.

Wigg was an extraordinary phenomenon. He had first been drawn to
my attention during the war by the aging and eccentric Erica Lindsay,
wife of the Master of Balliol, who greatly admired his work as a Colonel
in the Army Bureau of Current Education. The admiration was reciprocated. After ten years as a Corporal in the Tank Corps, mainly in the

Middle East, George had purchased his discharge in 1931, and became an active Socialist. As a tutor for the Workers' Educational Association, he came to know and love the Lindsays. It was they who encouraged him to stand for Parliament when the war ended.

He had a good but undisciplined mind, and was passionately concerned for the reputation and welfare of the British Army. When Shinwell was Minister of Defence, George was his Parliamentary Private Secretary. After Labour lost the 1951 election, besides playing a major role in Opposition in revising the Army Act, George became an expert on Parliamentary procedure. Because he was both anti-Communist and anti-Establishment, he became an ideal conduit through which MI5 could exert pressure on the Tory Government over the Philby and Profumo affairs. However, his first passion remained defence. Since he had fiercely opposed Sandys for abandoning national service and relying totally on nuclear weapons, he also opposed Labour continuing the Polaris programme. His honesty and sincerity were never in doubt, but his arguments were often incoherent. Moreover, his interest in security made him both see and organise conspiracies everywhere. I cannot say my heart always rose when his long ant-eater's proboscis began to quiver, and his mouth began its gobbling splutter. In the end Wilson lost patience, and George was able to pursue his other life-long passion, as Chairman of the Horserace Betting Levy Board.

Lord Chalfont was a very different kettle of fish. Born Alun Gwynne-Jones, he left the Regular Army as a Lieutenant-Colonel in the South Wales Borderers, to become Defence Correspondent of *The Times* in 1961. He was a brilliant journalist, far better informed than most of his colleagues. His attacks on the defence policy of the Conservative Government made him a natural friend and ally of George Wigg; as a result he was appointed Minister of Disarmament with a Labour seat in the Lords, despite being a life-long Liberal. Though charming, handsome, and immensely articulate, he had no personal base in politics, except the Prime Minister. So Wilson could always rely on his support in case of need. Later he was to show the same loyalty to the Shah of Persia, and to defend the independent British nuclear deterrent as eloquently as he had opposed it while a Minister.

A more formidable dissenter was George Brown. He was at first inclined to cancel the Polaris programme altogether, but later maintained that we should limit the number of submarines to three. He argued that since this would not allow Britain to maintain at least one submarine permanently on station, a force of three submarines could not be regarded as an independent British deterrent. Michael Stewart drily remarked that this reminded him of a debate he attended in the Fulham Cooperative Society during the thirties: they had been discussing whether for the first time the Coop should sell wine – an idea which shocked the good Methodists on the Committee. It was finally agreed that they should sell wine, on the strict condition that it should not be good wine.

In the end the Cabinet accepted my recommendation that we should cancel the fifth submarine planned by the Conservatives, but produce the other four. Four was much more cost-effective than three; it was also the minimum required if we should need to keep one submarine permanently East of Suez. This was at a time when Wilson wanted to offer nuclear protection to India, in case she was under nuclear threat from China, though India ignored Wilson's offer.

Having decided in principle to continue the Polaris programme, the major question which faced us, at a Chequers weekend in November 1964, was how to get rid of Macmillan's commitment to put the submarines into the MLF, since we were to meet President Johnson in Washington a fortnight later.

The MLF, in which the non-nuclear Europeans would provide crews of never less than three nationalities for each ship, was a military monstrosity; one German Admiral told me he would rather swim than sail in it. It offered no answer to the European demand for more influence on the American decision to use nuclear weapons, since its nuclear component would always be under physical control by Americans, and Washington would retain its veto over the use of the force as a whole. Any attempt to provide a collective European voice in the decision to use the force would require years of divisive argument, and was likely to fail. France was determined not to take part. Germany now saw it as an obstacle to better relations both with France and Russia. Macmillan had become increasingly uneasy about his surrender to Kennedy on the MLF at Nassau. Because it would cut across their special relationships with the US Navy and Air Force, the British Naval and Air Staffs were deeply hostile to the MLF. Essentially an American recipe for 'artificial dissemination', it was bound to create far more problems than it would solve.

We therefore decided at Chequers to oppose the mixed-manned surface fleet which was the core of the MLF, and to oppose any suggestion for a bilateral arrangement between the United States and Germany which might emerge as an alternative. Instead we would propose the establishment of an Atlantic Nuclear Force to which we would commit all our strategic nuclear weapons, providing we were free to use the V-bombers in a conventional role outside Europe. We also decided to seek a reduction in the British conventional contribution to NATO, so that we could fulfil our commitments East of Suez – to which Washington also gave higher priority at that time – and to press for negotiations on conventional disarmament in Europe.

Our meeting in Washington went smoothly enough. I described it as 'Ball's last stand', since, in spite of George Ball's desperate pleading, Johnson agreed to drop the MLF in favour of the ANF. Within a year the ANF had also sunk without trace, because nobody wanted it. As Franz Josef Strauss put it, ANF was the only fleet in history which had not been created, yet torpedoed another fleet which had never sailed. Their experience with the MLF should have taught both the European and American governments a lesson of seminal importance – that there can be no hardware solution to the quintessentially political problem of nuclear sharing.

Unfortunately the whole episode left Bonn with the feeling that Washington had led it up to the top of the hill and then down again, thus humiliating those German leaders who had argued publicly in favour of the MLF. Its memory, therefore, playing a damaging role when Carter treated Helmut Schmidt in the same way over the neutron bomb, and contributed to the bad feeling among some German politicians about Reagan's withdrawal of the Cruise and Pershing missiles after the INF agreement. On the other hand, the initial deployment of Cruise and Pershing itself stemmed from a failure to remember the lessons of the MLF – that the credibility of the American deterrent cannot be increased simply by deploying new weapons.

I had defined what I saw as the real problem in a speech to Parliament on March 4th, 1963, well before I became Defence Secretary:

> The only answer is to bring America's allies into much more intimate
> consultation on the organisation of America's nuclear forces and the use
> to which they will be put. In return for America giving us a greater
> share in the control of her nuclear force, we on our side of the Atlantic
> must be prepared to reduce America's liability by raising the threshold
> at which NATO is compelled to use atomic weapons in response to a
> conventional attack, and also by withdrawing atomic weapons back from
> the front, where their use would be inevitable in any conflict . . . Is there
> not everything in the world to be said for trying to make such unilateral
> action bilateral through negotiating an agreement with the Warsaw Pact
> powers, to control arms and forces on both sides of the Iron Curtain?

Nowadays there is wider agreement on such an agenda. As Defence Secretary in the sixties, I tried to pursue it in my talks with my alliance colleagues on both sides of the Atlantic once the MLF was out of the way.

The American Secretary of Defence, Bob McNamara, saw some of these issues very much as I did. In May 1962 he had laid out his views on the shrinking utility of nuclear deterrence in a carefully argued speech to the NATO Council in Athens. His main purpose was to dissuade his European allies from over-reliance on nuclear weapons, and to get them to build up their conventional forces. However, he insisted in effect that the United States alone should plan and control the use of nuclear weapons by the alliance; later he went on to claim that the nuclear forces of other allies were 'dangerous, and lacked credibility as a deterrent'. So he infuriated the French and British governments.

Moreover, though he offered the allies consultation on America's nuclear policies, and on its decision to use nuclear weapons, in practice neither he nor President Kennedy consulted them. For example, McNamara had announced the cancellation of Skybolt in a press conference at London Airport, without telling Macmillan in advance; a few weeks later when Kennedy offered Britain Polaris instead, he failed to consult any of his other allies – thus giving de Gaulle the excuse he wanted to veto Britain's entry into the Common Market.

McNamara himself was a man whose exceptional qualities were offset by some weaknesses. Wiry to the point of emaciation, with rimless spectacles, hair plastered flat on his skull, and the vocabulary of a management consultant, he gave the impression of being a desiccated calculating machine far more than had Hugh Gaitskell. He was in fact a passionate, if puritanical, humanist, deeply devoted to his wife and children. While at Berkeley he had chosen to study art history; at our first meeting we discussed a new book on Picasso by the painter's mistress and I noticed a Rouault on the wall of his office. But when he left Berkeley for the Harvard Business School, he entered a world where numbers were more important than shapes and colours; he never escaped it. We used to have breakfast together in Brussels before every meeting of NATO Defence Ministers. He usually flew there overnight from Vietnam, in a bomber with no windows so that he could sleep. I once asked him how things were going in Vietnam. 'Just fine,' he replied. 'Next month we'll be dropping twice the tonnage of bombs we are dropping this month.'

McNamara, like the American whizz-kids who had so much influence on his strategic thinking, demonstrated what I call the 'lamp-post fallacy' in its purest form. Late one night a policeman found a man on his knees under a lamp-post. 'What are you doing?' he asked.

'I dropped my keys at the bottom of the street,' was the reply.

'But that is a hundred yards away. Why are you looking here?'

'Because there's no light at the bottom of the street.'

As I had decided long ago at Oxford, what you do not know, indeed what you cannot know, is often more important than what you know. The darkness does not destroy what it conceals. Adjectives and adverbs are often far more important than numbers, even if far less precise. And as I was to discover at the Treasury, the precision of numbers often bears no relation to the facts.

One reason why I decided we should after all keep Polaris, was that there was little chance of influencing McNamara's nuclear strategy if we had renounced nuclear weapons ourselves; he opposed smaller countries having nuclear weapons essentially because he wanted to centralise all nuclear decisions in Washington. I did not think it was wise to entrust the future of the human race to the mathematicians in the Pentagon, who seemed to assume human characteristics only when they thought their institutional interests were at risk.

Despite our differences of temperament and experience, McNamara and I worked well together and become friends for life. Once he took me to the room where the so-called 'hot line' linking the White House with the Kremlin, was under constant test. I was fascinated to find that while the American typed passages from the *Encyclopaedia Britannica*, the Russian used *A Sportsman's Sketches* by Turgenev.

We were both anxious to find some way of organising more effective consultation between America and her allies on nuclear policy, and finally established a Nuclear Planning Group. McNamara was determined that the defence ministers themselves should understand the problems, rather than leave them to their officials; he insisted on designing a table just large enough for the ministers to sit around elbow to elbow, with no more than two officials behind each. It worked well enough so long as at least one European minister was prepared to take on the American on equal terms. Unfortunately, as in Britain under the Conservatives, most Continental governments regarded the defence ministry as unworthy of an able politician, and tended to appoint figures of little political influence. So I had to carry a disproportionate share of the European burden. But though the fine points of nuclear strategy may have eluded some of my colleagues, the central disagreements on the nature and purpose of the alliance emerged clearly enough.

For most of the Europeans, NATO was worthless unless it could prevent another war; they were not interested in fighting one. They thought that for Europe, at least, a conventional conflict would be as bad as a nuclear one; they also believed that nuclear weapons could deter any sort of war, while conventional weapons could not, at least in Europe. They could scarcely fail to be aware that as the Soviet Union approached nuclear parity with the United States, America's readiness to use nuclear weapons on their behalf would become less certain – Secretary Herter had already told them that, and McNamara had continually repeated it. The Hungarian rising and two Berlin crises had shown that the Europeans themselves would be as reluctant as the Americans to use nuclear weapons in practice. But they espoused the 'Healey Theorem' without knowing it: so long as there were American troops in Germany, and plenty of American nuclear weapons with them, the Kremlin would never deliberately risk an attack which might lead, however irrationally, to the use of those weapons.

The Americans were equally convinced that they could no longer accept an unlimited liability for the nuclear defence of Europe, and that nuclear deterrence was no protection against a conflict which might start by accident – as could have happened over Cuba or Berlin. So the stage was set for a period of transatlantic bargaining, in which Washington would implicitly threaten to remove its nuclear umbrella, perhaps by withdrawing some of its troops so as to reduce its stake in Europe's security, while Europe would increase its conventional contribution to the alliance, so as to raise the nuclear threshold and thus reduce America's nuclear liability.

In my time the Americans presented their case as a process of theoretical logic, using the vocabulary developed by the schoolmen from RAND, in which arithmetical equations played an important role. I was unimpressed by this approach. My personal experience of war had taught me that battles never go as expected, and that the most rational man can behave irrationally once the bombs start falling. To get some sense of how the decision to use nuclear weapons would present itself in practice, I chose to be the first European defence minister to play his own role in the annual NATO exercise to test procedures for a crisis which might escalate to the use of nuclear weapons; the part of defence minister and prime minister was normally played by a civil servant. This was a revelation; it showed me that a responsible politician would go to any lengths to avoid triggering a process which might lead within minutes to the death of his family, and perhaps the extinction of the human race.

On the other hand, everything I had seen and read of the pitiful inadequacy of alliance diplomacy as practised between the wars convinced me that NATO could not hope to guarantee the security of its members unless it maintained and strengthened the new type of unity which it had developed since 1949; this meant, above all, the deployment of national forces side by side along the threatened front in peacetime, under an integrated command structure. Providing this integration was maintained, the alliance was likely to deter aggression even if its strategy was intellectually flawed.

In any case, I had never believed that the Soviet Union was bent on the military conquest of Western Europe since it had failed to challenge the Western airlift to West Berlin in 1948–9. And I was impressed by the fact that Russia became more, not less, cautious in challenging the West as its own nuclear forces increased. On the other hand, the risings in East Berlin and Hungary, like that which was to come in Czechoslovakia, showed that Russia might use force to maintain its control of Eastern Europe; once fighting started there, it might conceivably slop over the Iron Curtain and involve the West. So NATO did need conventional forces at least large enough to control such incidents.

De Gaulle, like all his successors in France, took a different view. He thought that nuclear weapons had made alliances impossible, since no country would risk its own destruction for the sake of another; however, even a small, invulnerable nuclear force could deter direct attack, even by a superpower, because it could inflict damage out of proportion to any benefit the superpower could hope to gain. De Gaulle also believed that his national nuclear force might trigger off the much larger American force if there was a general Soviet attack on Western Europe; he may have thought, too, that it could enable France to keep out of a war between Russia and the United States of which he did not approve; that was the only sensible meaning of his Chief of Staff's definition of French strategy as '*défense à tous azimuths*'. The plausibility of the Gaullist position depended on convincing the enemy that you would blow yourself up rather than surrender – but so, after all, did the plausibility of the American and British positions. But the idea that any country could keep out of a nuclear war between the superpowers, either by possessing its own nuclear weapons or by renouncing them, disappeared for ever with Chernobyl and the concept of Nuclear Winter.

On March 7th, 1966 de Gaulle took France out of NATO and expelled all NATO's forces and headquarters from France, while remaining a member of the alliance for political purposes. From this moment on, I saw it as my role to act as a bridge between McNamara, who, as he now admits, really wanted NATO to abandon the first use of nuclear weapons altogether, and the Germans, who really wanted to go back to the strategy of massive nuclear retaliation, triggered by a tripwire on their Eastern frontier. We reached the necessary compromise on May 9th, 1967; on January 16th, 1968 NATO formally replaced the strategy of Massive Retaliation with the strategy of Flexible Response. Flexible Response has been NATO's official strategy ever since.

Like most compromises, Flexible Response had obvious weaknesses and did not fully satisfy either side. It envisaged using NATO's conventional forces alone against minor incursions; if the conventional forces proved inadequate, NATO would then take the first step on a ladder of nuclear escalation, moving steadily further up the ladder as necessary, with a full-scale strategic nuclear exchange as the ultimate sanction.

McNamara had appeared to endorse such a ladder of nuclear escalation in 1962 when he said in his Athens speech: 'The United States has developed its plans in order to permit a variety of strategic choices. We have *also* instituted a number of programmes which will enable the alliance to engage in a controlled and flexible nuclear response in the event that deterrence should fail.' But his real aim was to dispense with the need for using nuclear weapons in Europe altogether, if the enemy did not use them. It was already becoming clear that there was little chance of controlling a nuclear war once it started at any level. After all, the enemy might not choose to play by your rules. War is unpredictable. Moreover, the electronic pulses emitted by the first nuclear explosions might black out telecommunications over a wide area, making it impossible to command and control the military operations.

Unfortunately McNamara's actions too often cast doubt on the views he expressed in our meetings. Although he was immensely sceptical that tactical nuclear weapons could be used for military purposes – a scepticism shared by most Generals throughout NATO – during his period of office he increased the number of tactical nuclear weapons in Europe from 2,500 to over 7,000, often without telling the allies concerned. And he had infuriated Macmillan by trying to foist the American 'Sergeant' tactical nuclear weapon on him, at the same time as he was pouring scorn on Britain's own nuclear forces.

For all its weaknesses, Flexible Response marked an important advance on the tripwire theory it supplanted. The European countries began to build up their conventional forces to a level which many experts now believe could deal with anything but a large-scale deliberate invasion.

And as the European Defence Ministers in the Nuclear Planning Group got down to the problem of defining specific steps on the ladder of escalation, they discovered that nuclear warfare was not as simple as they had imagined. In my time they never got beyond listing a series of possible options in very general terms, with no attempt to define which might be appropriate in what circumstances; I doubt if they have got much further in the following twenty years. For example, when we considered how to use nuclear land-mines in practice, it turned out that no minister would allow them to be used on his territory – even the Turks would not consider their use to block their uninhabited mountain passes. Twenty years later NATO finally decided to get rid of nuclear land-mines altogether. I took every opportunity of persuading the elected politicians to consider in detail the implications of decisions which they had taken in principle without any thought of their practical consequences.

My first success in this area was to get NATO to instruct its military to base their plans on the forces which were actually available to them, rather than on the forces which ministers promised to contribute at their annual meeting, but never actually provided. It seemed to me a reasonable proposal; but I had great difficulty in getting my ministerial colleagues to agree, since it meant admitting that they were either unwilling or unable to meet the annual force goals which they endorsed so happily each December.

Then as now, the central problem in devising a sensible strategy for NATO was to get its governments to take the issue seriously. Most of them preferred to leave strategy to their military advisers. But in the nuclear age, when the wrong military decision may mean the end of civilisation, Clemenceau's dictum is a thousand times more valid – war is far too serious a matter to be left to the Generals. The Generals are the first to recognise this fact. Again and again, NATO's Supreme Allied Commander in Europe has had to complain that the decision to use nuclear weapons must be taken, not by himself, but by governments, in full knowledge of the consequences. Yet governments are unwilling to try to understand the formidable problems posed by nuclear weapons. Even the defence ministers are often too much engaged in fighting for their share of their national budget to spare time for the psycho-political mysteries of nuclear deterrence; and their military advisers are usually more concerned to get the biggest possible share of the defence spending for their own individual service, than to produce a coherent strategy for the use of their resources.

For example, in my time the NATO navies sought to justify their size on the grounds that they would have to protect Atlantic convoys of men and equipment for a period of months or years. Yet the NATO armies assumed that conventional fighting could not last for more than a few days; and once the fighting turned nuclear there would be no ports left through which to land supplies. Even so, they wanted to stockpile arms and ammunition sufficient to last for thirty days of intensive fighting.

Given this jungle warfare between the services, governments tended to abdicate their responsibility for NATO strategy to a tiny group of middle ranking civil servants and staff officers in the defence ministries, who had little contact with their own ministers and none with public opinion; in fact they had little contact with anyone outside their own charmed circle. Moreover, as 1945 receded, fewer and fewer of these men had any practical knowledge of what war is really like. Yet the views of this minuscule Mafia were often represented to parliaments as 'public opinion'. When I was told that 'the Germans will never stand for it', my informant was usually referring to three or four junior officials in the Defence Ministry in Bonn.

The most dramatic illustration of this gap between public opinion and the defence Mafia came twenty years later, when Gorbachev accepted the Western proposal for abolishing all intermediate-range missiles. All the Western members of the Mafia, both at NATO itself and in the national defence ministries, including the Pentagon, briefed their ministers to oppose the so-called 'zero option' which they had themselves proposed. Almost without exception, the European governments expressed their concern; but when Reagan persisted, they found that in fact their own peoples strongly supported him; so they reversed their stance – Mrs Thatcher and Chancellor Kohl leading the reluctant retreat to sanity.

McNamara was a shining exception to the general rule. Like me, he took an intense personal interest in NATO strategy. But, as shown by the contradiction between his words and deeds on tactical nuclear weapons, his position was not always as coherent as it appeared in his speeches. He was also vulnerable to political pressure from President Johnson, who took less interest in nuclear strategy than in electoral politics.

With my strong support, McNamara persuaded the Nuclear Planning Group to oppose Anti Ballistic Missile systems, on the ground that they would tend to destabilise the nuclear balance between the United States and the Soviet Union. Yet in September 1967, on the very day before a meeting of the NPG in Turkey, without consulting me or any of his allies, McNamara made a speech in San Francisco which used the existence of the tiny Chinese nuclear forces as an excuse for going ahead with an American ABM system. This was particularly surprising from a man who had always treated third-party deterrents as worthless. When we met privately in Ankara the next day, I was not moderate in my rebuke. Oddly enough, this incident was later echoed by President Reagan. When he made his initial speech in favour of the Strategic Defence Initiative in 1983, the NPG was actually meeting in Lisbon; even Richard Perle, the most formidable of all the Mafiosi, had been given no warning of what he was about to say.

The fact that both the United States and the Soviet Union were engaged in the late sixties in building defences against ballistic missiles, even though they were unlikely to be effective for many years, compelled me to consider what, if anything, should be done to enable our Polaris missiles to penetrate such defences. Washington was planning to replace some of its Polaris submarines with larger Poseidon submarines which would carry missiles with penetration aids and a bigger number of warheads called MIRVs, each capable of hitting targets far apart. We ruled out asking the Americans for the right to adopt the same programme, partly because of its immense cost, and partly because we would be responsible, as with Polaris, for producing the nuclear warheads, and we could not expect to master the MIRV technology except at a disproportionate cost in our scarce scientific manpower. So instead we started research into possible ways of improving the penetration capability of our Polaris missiles. At one stage in our discussions Harold Wilson got so discouraged that he suggested selling our Polaris submarines back to the United States; no one else supported this proposal. It was left to the next Conservative Government in 1971 to order the development of a system to penetrate the Soviet ABMs – they ultimately gave it the code-name 'Chevaline'. I regard it as one of my mistakes as Chancellor not to get Chevaline cancelled after 1974 when the following Labour Government found that its costs had escalated beyond control, and Russia had meanwhile agreed in the ABM Treaty not to extend its ABM system beyond Moscow. Perhaps Wilson's suggestion was not so bizarre as it seemed at the time.

In December 1967, McNamara left the Pentagon to become head of the World Bank. Though he had not gone as far as he wished, with the adoption of Flexible Response he had achieved his major objective inside NATO. He was increasingly depressed by the growing catastrophe in Vietnam, and by the divisions created in American society and in his own family by the war. His place was taken by Clark Clifford, a man as different in style and temperament as it was possible to conceive.

Clifford was tall and handsome with wavy silver hair like a millionaire patriarch in *Dallas*. His urbane courtesy failed to conceal the sharpest and most experienced political mind in Washington. The wealth he had acquired as one of America's most successful lawyers enabled him, in his own words, to live like a Republican. But he had been a liberal Democrat ever since leaving college, and had the same ability to identify with ordinary Americans as that other patrician, Franklin D. Roosevelt. He was famous as the architect of Truman's surprise victory in 1948, and though since then he had played little part in public affairs, he knew where every body in American politics was buried. I used to describe him as the only Whig Duke alive and living in Washington.

The moment he entered the Pentagon, Clifford asked to see all the papers on the Vietnam war. He concluded immediately that America should get out as fast as possible, and started the process which led to withdrawal under Nixon. He was less interested in NATO problems than McNamara, but had an excellent team of advisers, led by his young law partner Paul Warnke, a dedicated supporter of arms control, who later became President Carter's expert on disarmament.

I found Clifford and Warnke congenial colleagues in the elaboration of more rational strategies for NATO. However, now that France had gone, NATO's survival depended primarily on maintaining the support of Germany. Just before my time, when Franz Josef Strauss was Defence Minister, he was pressing for Germany to have its own nuclear weapons, a posture encouraged by de Gaulle's rhetoric and by Macmillan's 'grouse-moor Gaullism'. That this demand has never since been revived owes much, I think, to the involvement of German ministers in the discussion of nuclear strategy through the Nuclear Planning Group. Though Washington claimed that the British deterrent would provoke German demands for parity, Defence Minister von Hassel told me that he hoped Britain would maintain its nuclear forces, because he did not want France to be the only European country with a nuclear deterrent; the same point was put to me with great force by Paul Henri Spaak, who had been NATO's Secretary General from 1957 to 1961. Since those days no important German leader has wanted Germany to have its own nuclear weapons.

Throughout the late fifties and early sixties, expert discussion of nuclear problems was greatly influenced by concern that most of the countries which had the ability to produce nuclear weapons would actually do so. It was feared that the arguments used by Macmillan, Douglas-Home, and de Gaulle to justify their nuclear deterrents would provoke others to follow suit. Our work in NATO steadily reduced the danger of nuclear proliferation, at least in Europe. In 1968 the Wilson Government helped to produce the Non-Proliferation Treaty, which reflected the new mood. But outside Europe such arguments, put forward by powers which already had their own nuclear weapons, carried little moral or political weight. The Chinese bomb in 1964 was followed by an Indian nuclear explosion a few years later; this still threatens to produce a chain reaction on the subcontinent. The Israeli bomb may do the same in the Middle East. It is still unclear whether the assistance which Israel received from the United States in developing its nuclear weapons programme, was obtained with the consent of the authorities in Washington. But they made clear to me at the time that they knew what was happening, whether or not they approved it. This is not the only issue in which America's commitments to Israel have contradicted its broader objectives.

I spent as much time as I could afford in Germany, visiting the German forces as well as the British. At first I found it more rewarding to talk to the Chief of Staff, General de Maiziere, a music-lover of Huguenot extraction, than with my political colleagues. My links with Bonn were greatly strengthened when Willy Brandt won power in 1969 and appointed my old friend, Helmut Schmidt, as his Defence Minister. We immensely enjoyed working together again as ministers with practical responsibility, on the problems we had argued out over so many years in theory. Schmidt had extraordinary intellectual energy and political drive; in those days he showed no sign of the tendency to Wagnerian melancholia which sometimes overcame him in his later years. I suspect that it was largely due to Helmut that I saw my services to closer defence cooperation between Britain and Germany finally rewarded in 1970 by being made a Knight of the Order Against Pomposity – *Wider den Tierischen Ernst*.

This was an Order established by the Aachen Carnival to honour people in public life who did not take themselves too seriously. It is said that a German joke is no laughing matter. So it proved. I turned up in Aachen at four o'clock one afternoon after a gruelling day with the Rhine Army. For the next four hours I had to exchange witticisms in German over schnapps and a type of champagne called *Kalte Ente* – 'cold duck'. At eight o'clock we went to a banquet with about two thousand guests. After another four hours' drinking, this time with food as well, I had to enter a golden cage with a jester's hat on my head and make a speech on television in German, finishing with a song in the Aachen dialect. There was an audience of about thirty million people, in the Low Countries as well as Germany. Drinking continued until four in the morning. At eleven next day we all met for a *Kater-Frühstück*, or 'hangover breakfast', of salt herring and beer. When I resumed my visit to the British forces that afternoon my hosts found me untypically subdued.

In 1969 I spoke at the annual conference in Munich on defence, called the 'Wehrkunde'. That beautiful city, so like Venice in spirit and appearance, was enjoying the carnival. Young men and women in fancy dress walked hand in hand through the colonnades or made love in the porticos. After two gruelling days discussing nuclear strategy I went, appropriately enough, to hear Birgit Nilsson singing Brunnhilde in *Götterdämmerung*. It was a stupendous performance, and quite reconciled me to Wagner after my wartime revulsion against his anti-Semitism. At the long interval I had supper with Peter von Siemens, of the great electrical company, and was fascinated to discover that he never missed a single performance of the Ring while it was playing in Munich.

'You must be a passionate music-lover,' I ventured.

'Not really,' he replied, 'but I adore the philosophy.'

Next morning I glimpsed another facet of the German character when I had breakfast with the uncrowned king of Bavaria, Franz Josef Strauss. He was suffering from a heavy hangover, but talked with his usual brilliance and wit. Only his undisciplined personality prevented him from being one of the great European statesmen of our time.

Helmut Schmidt was particularly useful in helping me to create a closer sense of European identity inside NATO through the Eurogroup which I set up in 1968. For some time I had been organising informal dinners of the European Defence Ministers to discuss issues which we were to tackle next day at formal meetings of the NATO Council, along with the Americans and Canadians. I took advantage of a chance encounter with Henry Kissinger during Eisenhower's funeral to suggest that we should recognise these informal discussions among the Europeans as an official part of the NATO machinery. He got Nixon's consent, and the Eurogroup has functioned formally ever since, with France as an observer. Differences on strategic policy have prevented it from providing that European pillar inside NATO for which I originally hoped; but it has been of some value in developing common European projects for arms and equipment.

The election of Nixon as President in November 1968 had brought Kissinger into the centre of Atlantic policy-making as National Security Adviser in the White House. By then we had been friends for a decade. Shortly before that election we met during the annual conference of the

Institute of Strategic Studies at Oxford. Squeezed together in the bus which was taking us back from Alastair Buchan's country home, he told me that he had been approached by a member of Nixon's campaign team to see if he would take a job in a possible Nixon administration. Henry told me he was deeply uncertain. He had supported Nelson Rockefeller in the primaries and felt that to switch to Nixon might be seen as a betrayal. More important, though he had done a little work over the years for various administrations as a consultant, he was fundamentally an academic, and did not know if he could survive in the Washington environment!

He turned out, of course, to be the great survivor, brilliant at handling the politicians and bureaucrats alike. As National Security Advisor he succeeded in centralising all major decisions on foreign policy and defence at the White House; this gave a coherence to American leadership which it never had before – or since. In my opinion, his White House years, with Hal Sonnenfeldt to advise him on the Soviet Union, and Al Haig as his military deputy, saw the peak of his achievement. When he moved to Foggy Bottom, he failed to make use of the talent available in the State Department, and displayed little of the sensitivity to European feelings which he had shown to be so important in his academic writings. His so-called 'Year of Europe' was a disaster. Moreover, when international economic policy became critically important, he found himself at sea, allowing John Connally as Secretary of the Treasury to plunge the Western world into a maelstrom from which it has not yet escaped.

His most disappointing performance was over Vietnam, where the Johnson Administration had put the ball at his feet by committing the United States to disengagement. Determined to withdraw with honour, he made the best the enemy of the good. By invading Cambodia he prolonged the war unnecessarily, imposed unnecessary death and suffering on a horrific scale, conjured up the appalling Pol Pot and the killing fields, yet still failed to spare the United States the ultimate humiliation.

Nevertheless, history may forgive him that because he shifted American policy towards an accommodation with the Communist powers. He persuaded Nixon to recognise the Communist Government in Peking, and ushered in a period of détente with the Soviet Union through the first treaty on limiting strategic nuclear weapons – SALT I. The so-called 'back channel' he established with the Soviet Ambassador, Dobrynin, though it infuriated the official negotiators, broke bureaucratic deadlocks again and again. If he had not been born in Bavaria – where I had cycled through the little town of Kissinger in 1936 – he might well have been elected President. But ironically, his achievement of détente with

Russia made the extreme Right believe he was soft on Communism. This
prevented him from playing a role worthy of his powers in the Reagan
Administration.

In that sense only, you could argue that Kissinger did not survive the
Washington environment after all. The real survivor was another old
friend, Paul Nitze, with whom I had been constantly in touch since I
spent a weekend on the rolling hills of his farm in Maryland overlooking
the Potomac, while he was Director of the State Department's Policy
Planning Staff under Harry Truman. We had attended innumerable
conferences on defence during my years in Opposition; I worked with
him again when he was Deputy Secretary of Defence under Johnson. In
1987 we discussed the negotiations on intermediate nuclear forces, just
before he clinched the agreement with Russia in 1987. No doubt we shall
continue our discussions in the Elysian fields.

It was through Henry Kissinger that I had my first meeting with
President Nixon. Nixon was paying a visit to London shortly after taking
office, and Henry asked if I would have breakfast with him at Claridges
before his official engagements began. I was immensely prejudiced against
Nixon, having followed his political career ever since his disgraceful
campaign against Helen Gahagan Douglas way back in 1950. So I
entered his suite with very mixed feelings – distaste for the man who had
risen on a tide of McCarthyism, combined with some awe at meeting the
new President of the United States. In fact Nixon was sweating with
anxiety when we met; he was more lacking in self-confidence than any
leading politician I have known. Once we started talking, however, I
found him intelligent and well-informed, an impression he made on the
whole Cabinet later that morning, when Wilson invited him to attend it.

That was an odd occasion, since of course we did not discuss the real
business of Cabinet. Wilson simply invited us to tell Nixon something of
what we were doing. Tony Benn made a most eloquent contribution,
echoing Wilson's famous speech about 'the white heat of the technological
revolution'. When, however, Benn asserted that the younger generation
in Britain were interested in nothing except the latest developments in
modern science, it was too much for me. I turned to my neighbour, Tony
Crosland, and muttered under my breath: 'Balls!' My judgment was duly
published in the following week's *Private Eye*, one of the few occasions
when I have been honoured with a mention in that journal of record.

I met Nixon thereafter several times in Washington with the other
NATO Defence Ministers. It was clear that he took his responsibility for
pressing the nuclear button very seriously; he knew the problems inside

out, and discussed them with us in detail with great frankness and courtesy. In this he was a marked contrast with President Johnson, one of the few politicians with whom I found it uncomfortable to be in the same room. Johnson exuded a brutal lust for power which I found most disagreeable. When he said 'I never trust a man unless I have his pecker in my pocket' he really meant it. He boasted acting on the principle 'Give me a man's balls, and his heart and mind will follow.' I could never forgive him for the way he destroyed Hubert Humphrey's personality while Hubert was Vice-President, thus costing the United States the best President it never had. Lyndon Johnson was a monster.

Nixon and Johnson both had great flaws as human beings; yet in spite of all, they left office with achievements other Presidents might have envied. Johnson succeeded in leading the United States towards his Great Society, where Kennedy would probably have failed; and in the end he was persuaded by Clark Clifford to begin disengaging America from Vietnam. Nixon recognised Communist China and took the first essential strides towards a constructive relationship with the Soviet Union; he started a process which the more upright Carter almost derailed. Politics is all too open to the contradictions which Yeats found in poetry when he wrote of the choice between perfection of the life and of the work.

Finding that many of my ministerial colleagues were incurious transients in the field of strategy, I found it more worthwhile to cultivate their civil servants or members of NATO's permanent staff. Manlio Brosio had been a friend since he was a Senator of the small liberal Republican Party in Italy after the war. He had been an excellent Ambassador in London, and was Secretary General of NATO throughout my period as Defence Secretary. Tall and lean, with a close cropped eagle's head, he was a skilful diplomatist with great common sense – qualities of special value during our troubles with de Gaulle, and the Soviet invasion of Czechoslovakia. His Directeur du Cabinet was another old friend from Italy, Fausto Bacchetti, and his assistant for defence planning and policy, Arthur Hockaday, had been my Private Secretary in London. So I had plenty of friends at court.

Since the ministers met only a few times a year, NATO depended greatly on the quality of its central staffs, and on the ambassadors who were the permanent representatives of their governments in Brussels. The doyen of these ambassadors was the indestructible Belgian, André de Staerck; his great-grandmother had heard bells pealing for the first time when the Concordat with the Vatican was signed; she remembered the fields of Waterloo as being covered with snow in June 1815 – in fact it was wadding from the muskets. The American Ambassador, Harlan Cleveland, had been a candidate to succeed me as chairman of the Oxford Labour Club in 1939 and was an active supporter of Hubert Humphrey. His British colleague, Sir Bernard Burrows, was a gentle proconsul with a beaked nose and a clipped military moustache who had been chairman of the Joint Intelligence Committee in London. His remarkable wife, Ines, smoked cigars in a cigarette holder; they had married in Cairo, where she was said to have inspired the character of Justine in Lawrence Durrell's *Alexandria Quartet*. An enthusiastic amateur of the arts, Bernard took me to a private house in Brussels where the walls were covered with Surrealist frescoes by Paul Delvaux – perhaps his most striking work.

In 1969 there were several attempts to draft me as Secretary General to succeed Brosio. The job did not appeal to me; an international civil servant has even less power to make policy than a national civil servant and in any case I wanted to stay in politics. An unsuitable Secretary General can damage the functioning of NATO, as I think Josef Luns did in his later years, by being far too rigid. But even the best Secretary General, like Peter Carrington, can do no more than keep the alliance running smoothly if governments allow it; he has little power to influence decisions on the central problems of foreign policy and military strategy. If the national ministers would not take an active interest in NATO's problems, the arteries of its international bureaucracy were bound to harden, however vigorous and imaginative the Secretary General himself. Thus in the last twenty years the strategy of Flexible Response has remained unaltered, despite all the changes in weaponry and a far greater understanding that it would be impossible to control nuclear war. NATO's military and civilian staffs have continued to disagree widely about the relative capability of NATO and Warsaw Pact forces. Worst of all, NATO has been quite incapable of responding sensibly and in time to the successive initiatives of Gorbachev on disarmament.

As Britain's Defence Secretary I was able to influence NATO's position on the important issues far more than any official. My role in the formulation of Flexible Response was one example. The Czech crisis in 1968 was another. I had to rush back from a much-needed holiday with my family in Switzerland, so as to warn the Soviet Union that the alliance would not stand idly by if Brezhnev tried to extend his intervention to Yugoslavia, even though Yugoslavia was outside NATO.

I was also in a position to influence America's policy on disarmament, though my influence here was not decisive. Elliot Richardson, then one

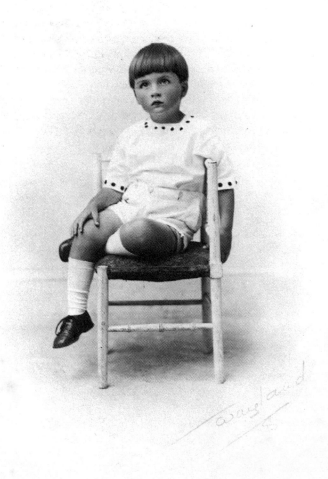

1. Denis Healey when five years old.

2. With his brother Terry.

3. Denis and Terry with their parents.

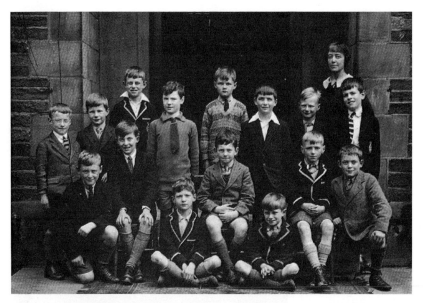

4. The first year at Bradford Grammar school. (Back row, third from right.)

5. With Mary and Gordon Griffiths in the Lake District, 1937.

6. Peter Beach at Anzio a few hours after the assault landing on January 22nd 1944. German prisoners on the right.

7. Captain in the Sappers, 1944.

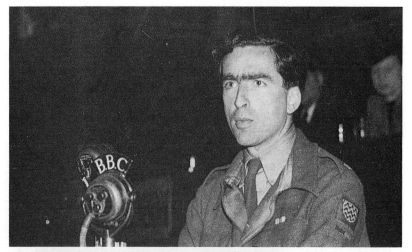

8. At the 1945 Labour
Party Conference at
Blackpool.

9. Wedding day,
December 21st 1945 at
the Marylebone Parish
Church of St Peter with
St Thomas.

10. The staff at Labour Party HQ, 1947. From left to right: Morgan Phillips, Arthur Bax, Wilfred Fienburgh, Denis Healey, Mary Sutherland, Len Williams and Hilda Finch.

11. Campaigning in Leeds, 1952.

12. The Leeds MPs in 1954. Denis Healey with Alice Bacon, Hugh Gaitskell and
Charlie Pannell.

13. Edna in 1956.

14. Earl Mountbatten, Edna and Denis Healey at a reception at the Banqueting House in 1964.

15. With the Tunku of Malaysia.

16. Aden. Denis Healey with C. in C. Sir Charles Harington, Brigadier 'Monkey' Blacker and Lieutenant-Colonel Jack Dye.

17. The Secretary of State for Defence leaving HMS *Anchorite*.

18. Receiving the Order Against Political Pomposity, 1969.

19. The family camping at Grindelwald – Edna's leg in plaster.

20. With Helmut Schmidt when they were both defence ministers.

21. Denis, Jenny and Cressida at Television Centre with Ernie Wise and Eric Morecambe, 1970.

22. The campaign launch, 1974.

23. At the Labour Party Conference, 1974.

24. Denis Healey and Edna at No. 11.

25. The Chancellor of the Exchequer on his way to the House, 1977.

26. Sermon on Nuclear Disarmament, election campaign, 1987. St James's Piccadilly.

27. With Derek Mitchell, Alan Lord, Sir Douglas Wass, Sir Brian Hopkin, Leo Pliatzky and Joel Barnett.

28. With the Lord Mayor of London and Gordon Richardson.

29. At the NEDC meeting, 1976.

30. David Owen, Roy Mason and Peter Shore at the Labour Party Conference, 1977.

31. The team in Leeds: Douglas Gabb, Leslie Rosen, George Mudie and Len Worth.

32. Denis' secretary Harriet Shackman with Mike Yarwood as his 'sister' Denise.

33. At the Bonn Summit in 1978 with Giscard d'Estaing, Jean Chrétien, James Callaghan, Helmut Schmidt, Jimmy Carter, Count Lambsdorff and Edmund Dell at the Palais Schaumberg.

34. Fritz Mondale, Denis Healey and Jimmy Carter at the White House, 1978.

35. Denis Healey, Michael Foot and President Brezhnev in 1981.

36. With Neil Kinnock and Willy Brandt in Bonn, 1984.

37. 'Nice to see you, Mr Ambassador.' Ronald Reagan and Neil Kinnock, 1987.

38. Denis Healey, Neil and Glenys Kinnock with a newly married couple in Leningrad, November 1984.

39. Denis Healey and George Bush as Vice President in 1987.

40. Denis Healey and Edna with Claudio Abbado and John Tooley at Covent Garden during the visit of La Scala.

41. This will save us a few bob on defence.

42. 'He's watching from next door again, dear – I just saw the eyes move.'

43.

44.

45. Denis Healey and Edna at Alfriston, 1988.

46. Edna at Alfriston.

47. Lake Como from the Healeys' bedroom at Bellagio.

48. Campaigning at
Huddersfield in 1987.

49. Opening a children's
playground at Seacroft
in 1986.

50. The Barry Humphries Show, Xmas 1988, with Dame Edna Everage, Roger Moore and Lulu.

51. Denis Healey at Alfriston.

52. Father Christmas at the Epping by-election, 1988.

of Kissinger's deputies at the State Department, came to consult me about the wisdom of excluding MIRVs from the SALT Treaty then under negotiation. MIRVs had just been developed by American scientists; they were small nuclear bombs of which several could be fitted into the nose-cone of a single missile, but could be guided to separate targets. I argued strongly, with Richardson's agreement, that though America might be ahead in this technology at the moment, the Russians were bound to catch up, and since their missiles were much more powerful, would then be able to pack more MIRVs into a single nose-cone. We proved right, and Kissinger later admitted that his failure to include MIRVs in SALT I was a serious mistake. Washington looks like making the same mistake by refusing to include sea-launched cruise-missiles in the START talks. Here too, Russia is bound to catch up with the United States, which would be far more vulnerable to such missiles, since most of its population and industry lie close to its Atlantic and Pacific coasts.

My role in NATO was not confined to these great issues. Britain was one of the few allies which maintained forces for action on the northern and southern flanks of NATO, in Norway and the Mediterranean. In fact my first official invitation abroad was from Gubbe Harlem, the Labour Defence Minister of Norway, a handsome Viking with blue eyes and fair hair who was a doctor by profession; his daughter, Gru, became Norway's Prime Minister in the eighties. So Edna and I flew one Friday in April 1965 for a weekend in the Arctic Circle. We started in Tromso, where we dined in the home of a local councillor. It was like straying on to the set of a play by Ibsen – the claustrophobic nineteenth-century furniture with aspidistras and heavy curtains, the mayor with his pretty young wife, the bishop and the army officers. You expected Hedda Gabler to enter with her pistols any moment; unfortunately we did not even see the mayor's wife break into Nora's dance. Next morning we flew up the coast, scaring herds of reindeer over the snowy tundra, to visit airfields, underground headquarters and artillery positions in the far north, where British forces made regular use of the winter warfare training school.

On NATO's southern flank Britain's responsibilities were primarily to help in the naval control of the Mediterranean, and to maintain our position in Cyprus, Malta, and Gibraltar, where the desire for national independence was tempered by economic dependence on the jobs our bases provided; any attempt to reduce our military presence was fiercely resisted by the local leaders; at least one of them, Archbishop Makarios, knew that his survival as President of Cyprus would have been at risk if we left. He was a most engaging personality – far more than 'a wily Oriental prelate', as Churchill had described him. Younger than his long black beard suggested, he was exceptionally energetic in mind and body. Like most Orthodox priests, he was quite as much the political leader of his flock as their spiritual instructor. Indeed when he went to Boston after the war he had considered leaving the Church altogether. Though he used the demand for union with Greece as a means of winning power, once he became President of Cyprus he did his best to reconcile the Turkish population to the concept of an independent binational state; but as so often in history, he was undermined in office by his allies in opposition. His earlier cooperation with the Greek resistance fighters under General Grivas in the struggle for enosis had created a Frankenstein's monster which he was unable to control. It provoked a response from the Turkish Government which finally led to the invasion of Cyprus in 1974. Even during my visits in the sixties this beautiful little island, the legendary birthplace of Aphrodite, was divided by military checkpoints operated by local Turkish and Greek soldiers. A United Nations force under a raffish British Commander, General Mike Harbottle, managed to keep the tension between the communities from boiling over, while Britain's own forces were confined to their tasks in their Sovereign Base Areas – an extraordinary anomaly which has persisted to this day because it suits no one to disturb it.

I also paid several visits to Libya, which under King Idris had good relations with Britain, and depended on us for military equipment. It was obvious that the monarchy was likely to fall at any moment to an army coup, and I tried to guess which of the young colonels I met was most likely to lead it. In the end I decided it would probably be Colonel Shelhi, an intelligent young man who was said to be influenced by Nasser. I was wrong – but not very wrong. Shortly after Colonel Qadaffi had taken over, I was told by our Ambassador, Donald Maitland – whom I had first known as George Brown's courageous Private Secretary – that Shelhi had been woken by his batman on the morning of the coup with the words: 'Excuse me sir, the Revolution has begun.'

'Don't be silly,' was the reply. 'It's tomorrow.'

This was not the first or last time that Western observers have failed to identify the leaders of a revolution which was obviously inevitable. The British and American governments made a much more serious mistake over Iran ten years later.

Even as we were liquidating our commitments East of Suez, we found ourselves continually entangled in situations outside Europe which might have involved British troops. A few weeks after becoming Defence Secretary I had to get Wilson to withdraw an unconditional offer by the Foreign Office to help the Belgians in Stanleyville. Developments in Southern Rhodesia were constantly raising the possible need for military intervention, as I shall describe later. And we had a nagging anxiety lest British forces should be required to defend one of the hundred or so little territories in the Caribbean or the Pacific which were too small to defend themselves if they became independent; in many cases they did not want independence for that reason. Moreover, these little colonies were often islands which got on too badly with their neighbours to join them in a single viable state.

Only one such situation in fact required our intervention, and that was pure musical comedy. We had set up an 'Associated State' in the West Indies, comprised of St Kitts, Nevis, and Anguilla; but the local leaders of the six thousand inhabitants of Anguilla refused to accept the link with the other islands. There were rumours that the Mafia was planning to turn Anguilla into a gambling centre like Cuba under Trujillo. On March 12th, 1969 a junior minister from the Foreign Office was chased off the island. The ponderous machinery of Cabinet Government swung into action to consider what we should do – accompanied by an avalanche of press leaks which brought ribald comments from the public. In the end we decided to send a tiny force of troops, supported by Metropolitan policemen, to restore order. They were instructed not to force Anguilla back into association with its neighbours; so it had to be put back under colonial rule. The operation caused hilarity throughout the world – it reminded too many people of the Peter Sellers comedy, *The Mouse that Roared*. Yet it taught lessons from which the United States could have benefited in Grenada. No government should ever carry out such an operation unless it has good intelligence of the local situation, has first consulted all governments which may feel themselves concerned, has clear political objectives, and has made careful psychological preparations.

All my experience as Defence Secretary rammed home the lesson that Britain must depend in future on professional services, capable of operating as a united force with skill and discipline in every conceivable environment – from riot control in Belfast, to winter warfare in the Arctic Circle and to a potentially nuclear battlefield in Germany. I was determined that those forces should be paid the rate for the job, and be led by men with a far wider understanding of British society and world affairs than the traditional officer.

For this reason I remodelled the old Imperial Defence College, too often regarded by its students simply as an opportunity to have a year off in London; it became the Royal College of Defence Studies, with a university-type curriculum, and examinations to match. With great difficulty I persuaded the Chiefs of Staff to appoint as its first Director Alastair Buchan, a civilian from outside Government with a world-wide reputation as a defence journalist and intellectual. I also encouraged the Joint Services Staff College, which trained younger officers of exceptional ability, to move in the same direction.

To establish a proper rate of pay, I had the jobs of the main ranks in every service evaluated so that they could be paid as well as civilians with similar skills. As a result we discovered, for example, that an infantry Corporal now required abilities as a driver and signaller as well as the traditional competence in handling his weapons, which put him well up the ladder of skilled workers.

I was greatly assisted in these tasks by Gerry Reynolds, my Minister for Defence Administration, who had worked with me at Transport House as Local Government Officer and knew how much modern society depends on the quality of those who protect it as soldiers or policemen. His early death from cancer was a major loss to the Labour Party and to the nation.

My six years at the Ministry of Defence were the most rewarding of my political career. I liked the work, and I liked the people I worked with. Regular visits to exotic places in the Middle and Far East added a spice to my life which few other ministers had the chance to enjoy. I was able in my NATO role to work constructively with friends old and new, on what had been my underlying objective in politics ever since my student days – the prevention of world war.

I was fortunate in taking office at a time when overdue changes in the planning and organisation of defence were already under way. However, my predecessors had failed to make use of these new tools to bring our commitments into line with what we could afford to spend. Their continuing failure to take necessary decisions had left our forces over-stretched, underequipped, and underpaid.

Every important decision I took to remedy this situation was bitterly opposed by the Conservatives in Opposition. None of them was reversed when they finally took office themselves. It would have been quite possible in 1970 for them to order a new aircraft carrier, to increase the number of Polaris submarines to five, as planned by Macmillan, to build up our forces in the Gulf and Singapore, and to restore the Territorial

Army in its original form. Despite their statements in Opposition, they chose to do none of these things. On the contrary, Lord Carrington paid a generous tribute to my work when he succeeded me. As Neil Cameron wrote in his autobiography, which was published after his death, that testimony, and the acceptance of ninety-five per cent of my other reforms, was evidence enough that my labours had not been wasted.

The decisions I had taken under increasing economic pressure during the years of the Defence Review gave the services a decade of stability. Unfortunately Mrs Thatcher reverted to the bad old practice of changing her defence secretary every year or two. Under her, only John Nott attempted that general review of defence which had again become necessary; the Falklands campaign compelled him to abandon his efforts. The inevitable adjustments of Britain's forces and commitments have been made no easier by the delay. But the prospect which Gorbachev now offers of a new international framework for global security should make the next Defence Review quite as exciting as the one I carried out in the sixties.

CHAPTER SIXTEEN

Cabinet Minister

Come let us mock at the great
That had such burdens on the mind
And toiled so hard and late
To leave some monument behind,
Nor thought of the levelling wind.

Come let us mock at the wise;
With all those calendars whereon
They fixed old aching eyes,
They never saw how seasons run,
And now but gape at the sun.

Mock mockers after that
That would not lift a hand maybe
To help good, wise or great
To bar that foul storm out, for we
Traffic in mockery.

– 'Nineteen Hundred and Nineteen'
– W. B. Yeats

FOR MY FIRST YEAR or two as a Cabinet Minister I found my work as
Defence Secretary all-consuming. Before long I was being described
as essentially a technocrat rather than a politician. This did not worry
me; technocratic seemed simply a pejorative word for competent, an
adjective which not all my fellow-ministers invited. I was said to dominate
my colleagues rather than to persuade them. But they were content in the
main to let me get on with my job, so long as I did not interfere

with theirs. So for some time I played little part in Cabinet discussions about the domestic issues in which my department was not directly concerned.

Though I deeply resented having to make new cuts in defence spending every time our economic performance fell short of expectations, I accepted the sacrifices required of me, providing my colleagues in the other spending departments also made their due contribution; so I usually supported the Chancellor in Cabinet discussions, however much I argued with him in private about my own programmes.

I also tended to form an alliance with the Foreign, Commonwealth and Colonial Secretaries against ministers who did not take the world outside Britain as seriously as we did. The arithmetic of Cabinet worked strongly against us, however, once the necessary departmental amalgamations had been carried through. For most of the post-war period the external departments had had seven representatives in Cabinet – since, besides the three separate Foreign, Commonwealth and Colonial Secretaries, there were three separate Secretaries of State for the Navy, Army and Air Force, as well as the Defence Secretary himself. The end of the colonial empire, and the increasing independence of the new Commonwealth, combined with the integration of the service ministries, meant that by 1970 there were only two Cabinet Ministers to cover all Britain's external policies – the Defence Secretary and a single Foreign and Commonwealth Secretary. So by then the external departments had little prospect of winning their case unless the Prime Minister himself threw his weight behind them. Membership of this oppressed minority was a good preparation for the even lonelier position I was later to occupy as Chancellor of the Exchequer.

Nevertheless I could usually count on a few friends outside the external departments. Charlie Pannell, my fellow Leeds MP, was Minister of Works, and normally supported me, perhaps because I allowed his department to continue carrying out all the construction work for the Ministry of Defence. And I quickly developed good relations with the Minister of Aviation, Roy Jenkins, although he fought his departmental corner against me on the cancellation of the TSR2 and the purchase of the F111A in its place.

The project to build the supersonic Concorde airliner divided us less, since he agreed it had no chance of recovering its costs. However, the lawyers advised us that it would be impossible for us to save money by cancelling it, since the contract Julian Amery had drafted would have compelled us to continue paying our share if the French Government wished to continue the project. Ironically enough, Pierre Messmer later told me that if we had stuck to our guns ten days longer the French would have agreed to cancellation; in Paris as in London the Finance Minister and the national airline wanted to abandon Concorde. In Washington, McNamara was equally hostile to the supersonic transport aircraft which Boeing and the Congress were pressing on him. At one point he offered me an SST disarmament pact – Washington would not support the Boeing SST if we cancelled Concorde. I told him that such a pact would be meaningless; Britain could not get out of its agreement with France, and if Congress wanted an SST the United States would build one, whatever McNamara promised. In fact, after twenty years America is still not convinced that an SST is worth the money.

Concorde is a good example of how a government can find itself supporting a glamorous scientific breakthrough which does not make commercial sense. Modern space programmes are full of others. Worst of all is the tendency for scientists at defence establishments to dream up new weapons for which there is no military requirement; once they have excited the imagination of politicians, they become not only a drain on scarce resources but also a major factor in accelerating the arms race. Reagan's Strategic Defence Initiative is a classic case.

My relations with Roy Jenkins have undergone many vicissitudes since we first met at Balliol. At Oxford, since he was even then a Social Democrat, while I was a Communist, we were not particularly friendly. However, we met several times as young officers during the war, and saw a lot of one another in the early postwar years when I was at Transport House and Roy entered Parliament in a by-election. Our relations strengthened during the thirteen years when we were both fighting for Hugh Gaitskell against Nye Bevan, as Labour MPs in Opposition. In those days Roy took less interest in the cut and thrust of party politics, than in issues like the laws on obscenity and homosexuality, on which I shared his views. He showed exceptional skill and courage in helping to get these laws changed, both as a backbencher and as Home Secretary.

When Labour won the General Election in 1964 Roy was still somewhat on the fringe of Westminster. He was much better known as the author of books on Edwardian politicians like Balfour, Dilke, and Asquith, than as a politician himself. If he had not been given a place in the government he might well have left politics altogether to become, for example, Editor of *The Times*.

However, fate intervened in the unlikely shape of George Wigg, who had also played fairy godmother to Alun Chalfont. Wilson was very uncertain whom he should appoint as Minister of Aviation, until Wigg remembered that Roy had written an article on Concorde some months earlier for the *Observer*. Wilson read it, was impressed, and rang Roy to offer him the job. This was quite late in the weekend following the election. Tired of waiting hour after hour by the telephone, Roy had gone out for a walk. His young son answered the call instead, and forgot to tell Roy on his return. Fortunately, when he did remember, it was not too late.

In my view, Roy's best period in office was as Home Secretary in the Cabinet of 1966; he then succeeded in stamping his liberal humanism on a department not notorious for that quality. He was not well suited to the politics of class and ideology which played so large a role in the Labour Party. His natural environment was the Edwardian age on which he wrote so well. He saw politics very much like Trollope, as the interplay of personalities seeking preferment, rather than, like me, as a conflict of principles and programmes about social and economic change.

Though his father had been a miners' agent in South Wales, who served as Attlee's Parliamentary Private Secretary, Roy's drawling voice, his pronunciation of 'r' as 'w', and his sometimes lackadaisical manner limited his appeal to the Party activists. Yet he was a brilliant Parliamentary debater, and could rouse enthusiasm even in the Labour Party Conference when he spoke on a subject like the Common Market, on which he was passionately committed. He had the same capacity as Nye Bevan and Hugh Gaitskell to inspire a deep and personal devotion among his disciples.

His appearance had the sleek pomposity of Mr Podsnap; behind it there was a sharp and unsentimental mind. He once told me: 'I will never be caught with a dagger in my hand unless it is already smoking with my enemy's blood.' Above all, he was never satisfied with second place in any field; he always wanted to be top. I believe this explains much in his career after his poor showing in the election for the Labour Party leadership in 1976.

With hindsight, I regret that, though we often worked closely together, an element of mutual jealousy which went right back to our undergraduate days prevented us from cooperating more effectively. A more intense sibling rivalry separated Roy from Tony Crosland, with whom at Oxford he had been as close as Castor with Pollux.

Neither Tony nor I ever shared Roy's dedication to the Common Market – an issue which had also strained his relations with Hugh Gaitskell. Both of us found the arguments of the Euro-fanatics intellectually disreputable. Unlike Tony, I supported Douglas Jay's

determined campaign against making a second application for membership
in 1966, not least because I was certain that Wilson would be no more
successful than Macmillan, so long as de Gaulle was alive. But, like
Tony, I found the extremism of many anti-Europeans equally distasteful.
Our agnosticism on the Common Market won us no friends in either
camp. On issues which arouse strong feelings, like nuclear weapons or the
Common Market, politics awards no prizes to pragmatists.

My old antagonist, Dick Crossman, was tucked away in the Ministry
of Housing and did not often cross my path. Though he and George
Wigg hankered occasionally after a return to conscription, they had no
support in Cabinet. Dick was still capable, however, of exasperating me
with his perverse and capricious cynicism. For example, the day after the
Red Army invaded Czechoslovakia, he told Cabinet this was a good
thing, since if Dubcek were allowed to succeed the East Germans might
get out of hand. Perhaps it was not so much cynicism as a total lack of
political judgment. Crossman was genuinely surprised when his announcement of an increase in charges on teeth and spectacles three days before
the local elections in 1969 produced an explosion of anger in the Party. A
Macchiavelli without judgment is a dangerous colleague.

Before long my main problem, and that of the Cabinet as a whole, had
become the Prime Minister himself. Vaguely Liberal at Oxford, and a
civil servant during the war, Harold Wilson had won fame as Attlee's
President of the Board of Trade, by promising 'a bonfire of controls'. He
applied himself seriously to Labour Party politics for the first time when
he threw in his lot with Bevanism in 1951, as 'Nye's little dog', to use
Dalton's words. Then, as Bevan's star faded, he moved far enough towards the centre to be elected leader of the Labour Party when Gaitskell
died in 1962. By now he had become an accomplished speaker; he roused
the Party Conference to wild enthusiasm by talking of 'the white heat of
the technological revolution'. In the General Election of 1964 he made
rings round the skeletal inadequacy of Sir Alec Douglas-Home.

Just before the election he talked frankly to the Harvard Professor,
Dick Neustadt, about how he planned to behave as Prime Minister.
Neustadt, who was enquiring into British attitudes on the MLF for
President Johnson, reported:

> He means to take all decisions into his own hands. He wants not only
> to make ultimate decisions but to pass issues through his own mind
> early, sitting at the centre of a brains-trust, with himself as the first
> brains-truster, on the model, he says, of J. F. K. . . . Also, more

importantly, he has to keep one step ahead of all his colleagues in the precedent-making first encounters and arrangements which set tone and style for their relationships. 'I shall be Chairman of the Board, not President,' he says, but 'Managing Director too, and very active at it'.

This was all too true. No prime minister ever interfered so much in the work of his colleagues as Wilson did in his first six years – though I am glad to say that he gave me a pretty free hand on defence, except when there was a crisis. Unfortunately, since he had neither political principle nor much government experience to guide him, he did not give Cabinet the degree of leadership which even a less ambitious prime minister should provide. He had no sense of direction, and rarely looked more than a few months ahead. His short-term opportunism, allied with a capacity for self-delusion which made Walter Mitty appear unimaginative, often plunged the government into chaos. Worse still, when things went wrong he imagined everyone was conspiring against him. He believed in demons, and saw most of his colleagues in this role at one time or another. I was no exception. Fearing that if he left a minister too long in the same department he might develop a power-base from which to challenge him, he shifted his ministers around far too often. He was always offering me another job – the Commonwealth Office, the Board of Trade, Housing, Power, Technology, Industry, First Secretary, indeed everything except the one job which might have tempted me away from Defence. He told Dick Crossman that if I were Foreign Secretary, then, in combination with my permanent officials, I would be impregnable against influence from No. 10.

Yet he was curiously reluctant to lay down the law in Cabinet by openly overriding opposition from the majority, as every prime minister should from time to time. Even a prime minister as weak and sick as Eden was during the Suez affair can do so if he wishes. So, to make sure he always had his own built-in majority in Cabinet, Wilson packed his Cabinet with yes-men – or yes-women; this seriously diluted the quality of his Government in its later years.

He was at his best during his first period of office, when for the final months he had a majority of only one; he enjoyed living from hand to mouth and was exceptionally quick on his feet. In those days he was always brilliant in debate, both in the House of Commons and at the Labour Party Conference. Though his careless overoptimism attracted criticism after the event, he showed great tactical skill in handling the early stages of the long drawn-out crisis over Southern Rhodesia.

Once it became clear in March 1965 that Ian Smith was bent on breaking away from Britain altogether if he could not get a free hand to maintain rule by the white minority, Wilson looked for a compromise which might salvage something from the wreckage. As Defence Secretary I was directly concerned, since both the Party and the Commonwealth wanted Britain to overthrow Smith by military force. It was far too risky an enterprise to be seriously considered. In a similar situation in Northern Rhodesia, when we still had a base nearby in Kenya, Roy Welensky had made it impossible for Britain to fly troops in, simply by rolling barrels on to the runway. Southern Rhodesia would have been a much harder nut to crack. Our nearest base was now Aden – as far from Salisbury as London is from Cairo. Southern Rhodesia had powerful armed forces and we had no reason to believe they would not fight us if we attempted to intervene. So we could not count on a rapid victory.

Wilson rightly believed that he would not get political support at home if he got involved in a long campaign to suppress 'our kith and kin'. The white Rhodesians had fought side by side with British soldiers during the war; Smith himself had been badly wounded as a fighter pilot in the Battle of Britain. Indeed at one point I heard there had been some mutinous muttering among senior army officers about our policy on Rhodesia, and I had to give the Chief of the General Staff a severe warning about it.

On the other hand, though we had to rule out an invasion of Southern Rhodesia, we had a clear moral responsibility to protect the newly independent Commonwealth countries against the reprisals which Smith might take against them, if we applied economic sanctions against him. So we flew supplies into Lusaka, sent soldiers to guard the Kariba Dam, and stationed fighter aircraft in Zambia, supported by an aircraft carrier in the Indian Ocean. Even then we had serious difficulty in getting overflying rights from some of the other African countries.

However, Wilson did commit one classic strategic blunder. On October 29th, 1965 he announced that he would not intervene with military force even if Smith unilaterally broke away from Britain. Thus given the green light, Smith had only to pick his date. He cleverly chose Armistice Day – November 11th, 1965 – for his Unilateral Declaration of Independence. Thereafter Wilson did his best to persuade him to return to legality by offering him constitutional independence, but only on condition he first established rule by the African majority. It was a hopeless task, as both he and Smith must have known.

Wilson was rightly criticised for claiming that his economic sanctions would bring Smith down in 'weeks not months'. There was no chance whatever of sanctions having a significant effect on Southern Rhodesia, so long as Smith could get everything he needed directly from neighbouring South Africa. The well-publicised Beira patrol, which blockaded supplies through Portuguese Mozambique, was a waste of time. Yet Wilson's illusions about sanctions were shared and encouraged by officials who should have known better. When I told the Cabinet Secretary that a niece of mine travelling by land to Australia had found Salisbury swarming with large motor cars, he simply refused to believe me.

As Conservative leader, Edward Heath moved from initial support for Wilson's policy on Rhodesia to carping criticism; but his party was split three ways on the matter. He made the negotiations with Smith a central issue in the General Election campaign in March 1966 and was heavily defeated. Wilson won an overall majority of ninety-seven. He was now free from Parliamentary anxieties.

This was small comfort, since he soon found himself buffetted by economic storms from which his political agility could not rescue him. The first major sterling crisis hit the new Government in July that summer, bringing as usual more cuts in defence spending. Union opposition to his prices and incomes policy compelled Wilson to introduce a total freeze on wages for six months. It was never bright confident morning again.

Wilson sought refuge through talks on joining the Common Market; but de Gaulle was no more disposed to compromise than Ian Smith. Like so many other prime ministers, as his domestic worries increased, Wilson found that dabbling in foreign affairs was a distraction no less enjoyable for being futile. His attempt to mediate in the Vietnam War infuriated Johnson without achieving anything constructive. He was no more successful in the Middle East. King Feisal of Saudi Arabia was actually with him in London when Nasser closed the straits of Tiran to Israeli shipping. A fortnight later, on June 5th, 1967, Israel attacked Egypt, and Nasser closed the Suez Canal. Iraq, Kuwait, Syria, Algeria and the Lebanon cut off their oil supplies to Britain. There were threats by Arab countries to withdraw their sterling balances. Within weeks the Nigerian civil war cut off all our supplies of oil from Nigeria as well.

The effect of the Middle East war on our balance of payments was compounded by dock strikes in London and Liverpool. The consequent weakness of the pound was aggravated by French attacks on the international role of sterling and some bad by-election results. Despite desperate attempts to shore up sterling through a loan from the IMF Wilson had to devalue the pound by forty cents to $2.40 on November 18th, 1967.

Nowadays exchange rates can swing to and fro continually by amounts greater than that, without attracting much attention outside the City columns of the newspapers. It may be difficult to understand how great a political humiliation this devaluation appeared at the time – above all to Wilson and his Chancellor, Jim Callaghan, who felt he must resign over it. Callaghan's personal distress was increased by a careless answer he gave to a backbencher's question two days before the formal devaluation, which cost Britain several hundred million pounds.

Wilson himself regarded the sanctity of sterling as so absolute that he allowed Cabinet to discuss the issue only once, on July 19th, 1966; and he refused to circulate the minutes of that meeting, even to the Cabinet ministers who attended it. Thereafter he vetoed all attempts to discuss the exchange rate in Cabinet, or even in any of the Cabinet committees on economic affairs. After the 1966 election Wilson had set up a small committee of key ministers to consider the major issues of economic policy – SEP; but every time we tried to raise the subject of devaluation, it was evaded. Michael Stewart, Dick Crossman and I soon joined a lobby for devaluation led by Roy Jenkins, Tony Crosland and George Brown, who had forced the abortive Cabinet meeting on devaluation in 1966. But Wilson continued to veto any formal discussion of the matter until the last moment, when he had already agreed with Callaghan that devaluation was inevitable. It was not until four days before the date fixed for the change in parity, that he set up a small group of ministers to supervise the details; he made me a member, I suspect, only because he wanted to commit me to yet another cut in defence spending as part of the accompanying economic measures.

From the moment devaluation took place, the Government was shaken by crisis after crisis, and Wilson's behaviour became steadily more bizarre. He was thrown off balance by the ridicule he provoked with his television statement that devaluation would not affect 'the pound in your pocket'.

On November 28th de Gaulle vetoed our entry into the Common Market. Next day Callaghan finally resigned as Chancellor, to become Home Secretary, while Roy Jenkins took over the Treasury. It looked for a moment as if we might have a period of quiet over Christmas to adjust to all these changes. No such luck. In the second week of December, Jim Callaghan sparked off a new crisis by suggesting at a private meeting of Labour MPs that the Government might modify its ban on supplying arms to South Africa. The Wilson Government never really recovered its balance or its unity, after the ensuing crisis over South African arms.

On December 8th there had already been a meeting of the Defence and Overseas Policy Committee of the Cabinet, of which Jim was no longer a member, to reconsider the arms embargo. George Brown and I recommended that, in the difficult economic situation following devaluation, we should accept a year-old application from South Africa for naval weapons – which could not be used to enforce Apartheid – while refusing spares for Centurion tanks; the Prime Minister had already asked George in July to find out if the South Africans were still interested in the purchase. The Committee's discussion was inconclusive; Roy and Tony supported us, while Barbara Castle was strongly opposed. Wilson summed up by saying that the Committee was prepared in principle to sanction the sale, but that there should be a short delay before a final decision was made; if the decision was positive, it should be presented together with a package of cuts in public spending, as part of our response to devaluation.

When I returned a few days later from a NATO meeting in Brussels, I found that Jim's comments had produced an explosion against South African arms sales in the Parliamentary Labour Party. Worse still, the Chief Whip appeared to be orchestrating the backbenchers against George Brown and me, on the instructions of the Prime Minister himself. I saw Wilson at midnight to protest. George Brown himself was now abroad for his part of the NATO meeting, and unable to attend the Cabinet next day. Harold agreed to postpone a decision for twenty-four hours, until Brown returned. Nevertheless he put the blame on George when he answered questions in the House that afternoon. Meanwhile Roy told me at lunch that sterling had come under very heavy pressure and that we must make big new cuts in public spending. He also informed me that my loyalty to George had made me the Prime Minister's Public Enemy Number One. We agreed to stand together.

The resumed Cabinet took place on Friday December 15th. It was the most unpleasant meeting I have ever attended. George Brown was thunderous in denouncing Wilson's campaign of character assassination, and his manipulation of the press. Besides Brown and me, Jim Callaghan, Tony Crosland, Gordon Walker, and Ray Gunter proposed selling the arms immediately. Roy Jenkins, George Thomson, Dick Crossman, Fred Peart, Willie Ross, Dick Marsh and Frank Longford also favoured selling the arms, but after some delay. This made a total of thirteen. The Prime Minister's opposition was supported only by Michael Stewart, Barbara

Castle, Peter Shore, Tony Benn, Tony Greenwood, Gerald Gardner and
Cledwyn Hughes – a total of eight. George Brown threatened to read out
the letter the Prime Minister had sent him in July, asking that he should
raise the matter with South Africa. I did read out the Prime Minister's
summing up of the committee meeting a week earlier, which agreed in
principle to sell the arms. In fact a good time was had by all.

After the weekend the Cabinet met yet again. Roy and Tony still
insisted we should stick to Friday's decision. But, with Jim and Patrick
Gordon Walker leading the rout, Cabinet reversed its position; that
afternoon the Prime Minister informed the House that the ban on arms
for South Africa would stay.

It was a deplorable episode, yet characteristic of any government in
serious trouble. Five years earlier Macmillan had sacked a third of his
Cabinet in his 'night of the long knives' – an episode which caused
Jeremy Thorpe to say: 'Greater love hath no man than he who lays
down his friends for his life.' Two decades later Mrs Thatcher followed
the example set by Wilson over South African arms, in her handling
of the Westland affair, notably by using her officials to mislead the
press and undermine a Cabinet colleague. This was not the only respect
in which Macmillan, Wilson and Thatcher shared the same political
style.

I now think, however, that in supporting George Brown I showed
gross insensitivity to the hatred of Apartheid both in my party and in
the Commonwealth. My personal experiences in South Africa after we
lost the election in 1970 completely changed my attitude towards its
problems. The crisis in December 1967, however, was about far more
than South African arms; it was about Harold Wilson's style of government. The steady deterioration of the economy following his victory in
1966 led him to see enemies in every corner; at worst he began to
behave, in the words of an uncharitable journalist, like 'a demented
coypu'. Inevitably, his persecution mania finally turned his nightmares
into reality. There was increasing talk both inside the Labour Party
and outside about trying to find another leader.

Much of this talk was reflected and magnified in the changing attitudes
of Cecil King, the chairman of the International Publishing Corporation,
which owned the Mirror group of newspapers – the only part of Fleet
Street to support the Labour Party. King was an outsized man, both in
physique, ambition and in self-esteem. His mother was the sister of Lord
Northcliffe and Lord Rothermere, and he was determined to exert the
same political influence as his uncles; but his reach far exceeded his

grasp. Though immensely vain, he lacked self-confidence in public, and eschewed the limelight. So he would invite leading politicians and civil servants to lunch alone with him in the Mirror building. Most of them, including the Cabinet Secretary, talked to him with appalling indiscretion, little knowing that he planned shortly to publish a diary in which he recorded all they said. I am glad to say that I told him nothing which caused me embarrassment later, although with hindsight I might have been wiser to tell him nothing at all.

From the moment we first met in 1966, King tried repeatedly to get me to conspire against Wilson, and to promote me as leader of the Labour Party or of a Coalition Government. He finally accepted that I was not interested, and turned his attention instead to Mountbatten. In May 1968 he invited Mountbatten to meet him with Hugh Cudlipp and Solly Zuckerman. At this extraordinary meeting, recorded separately by all four who were present, King forecast that the Labour Government's loss of authority would lead to bloodshed in the streets, and military intervention; he asked Mountbatten if he would be prepared to take over as head of a Government of National Unity. The bait was rejected. A few weeks later King used the columns of his newspapers to call openly for Wilson's replacement. Instead, his colleagues on the board of IFC gave King himself the sack.

In fact the Labour Cabinet had already survived its worst crisis over the previous Christmas and New Year, when Roy Jenkins was fighting for the cuts in spending which were needed to make devaluation work. As Defence Secretary, I myself was under particularly heavy pressure, since I could now rely on no protection from the Prime Minister. The Chiefs of Staff were threatening to resign *en bloc* unless we cut our commitments before agreeing further cuts in defence. My junior ministers told me that if I did resign they would all go with me. In the light of my experience over South African arms, I decided that for the first time I should lobby the Party and the press for support. I invited a large group of sympathetic backbenchers to Admiralty House for a briefing on the situation, and with some difficulty persuaded Wilson to let me do an interview with David Frost – on the strict condition that he did not raise the question of South African arms.

The Frost interview, on December 28th, 1967, was a triumph – for me. For years afterwards people would come up to me in the street and congratulate me on defrosting Frost. I invited the studio audience to agree with me that Frost's researcher had not briefed him properly – a ploy doubly disagreeable to Frost, who liked people to imagine that he did all his own homework, and habitually enlisted the support of the studio audience against his guests. He was so upset at this humiliation that he asked me to come back after the interval following the planned interview; then he spent fifteen minutes vainly trying to needle me over South African arms, which he had promised not to raise. But I at least had the pleasure of hearing him tell the world that it was the Prime Minister who had been leaking Cabinet secrets. I also did an interview on *Panorama* with Robin Day, who was, as always, formidably tough but scrupulously fair. Unlike David Frost, Robin Day did his homework thoroughly; he is still a model to his profession. Television interviews have now become an essential part of a politician's stock-in-trade; it is important to know how to deal with the personal style of the different interviewers.

After a month of almost continuous Cabinet meetings, we finally settled the public expenditure package. I won my case for the timing of our withdrawals from the Gulf and Singapore, but my defeat on the F111 tempted me to resign, as I have already described. The Government had its greatest difficulties, however, over its decision to delay two years before raising the school-leaving age to sixteen; this produced moving protests from Jim Callaghan, George Brown, and Ray Gunter, all of whom had been denied a university education by having to leave school too early to take the necessary examinations. But the only minister to resign over the delay was an Etonian, Frank Longford. The reintroduction of prescription charges was almost equally difficult, and roused the Party to fury. Twenty-six backbenchers abstained when the House voted on the issue.

These cuts in public spending did not do much to relieve the pressure on sterling, since, contrary to my advice, they were not accompanied by measures to reduce private consumption. Roy had been asked by Harold to wait until his spring budget for this. In any case, Roy's orderly mind preferred dealing with one problem at a time, a luxury which chancellors can rarely afford. One result was the gold crisis in March, which led to the resignation of George Brown. Morale in the Party was still deteriorating, and there was a swing of eighteen per cent against Labour in three by-elections. So Harold Wilson resorted to another expedient popular with prime ministers in trouble – a Cabinet reshuffle.

The reshuffle took nine days to complete, in the full glare of press publicity, triggered off by Dick Crossman at the Prime Minister's behest. It was a difficult time for me, since the newspapers were full of stories that Wilson would either sack me, or provoke me into resigning. After at first refusing to see me about these rumours, Wilson finally offered me the Department of Economic Affairs, with responsibility for coordinating the whole of the domestic economy. However, so far as I could discover, I would be given no powers over the other ministers concerned; so I turned him down and stayed at Defence, as I wished.

The only important casualty of the reshuffle was Patrick Gordon Walker, who had been no more successful as Education Secretary than at the Foreign Office. There were a number of changes in departmental responsibilities, none of which proved particularly useful; tampering with the machinery of government is another hobby of prime ministers in trouble. The Committee on Strategic Economic Policy was replaced by a Parliamentary Committee which was to function as an Inner Cabinet; I was made a member.

The new Cabinet was no happier than the old. Although he could now normally depend on a built-in majority, Wilson remained neurotically suspicious of conspiracies to overthrow him. The local election results in May were appalling – for the first time ever, we lost solid Labour wards on working-class housing estates in my own constituency. In a typically manic moment, Wilson fell for a story in *Private Eye* that the correspondent of a Sunday newspaper was regularly going to bed with five named Labour backbenchers; the story carried little credibility with anyone who knew the lady in question. The Parliamentary Party was seething with discontent. In June Ray Gunter resigned. I was lucky to be able to escape occasionally from the Byzantine intrigues of Westminster to the pristine purity of politics in Cyprus, Malta, or Tripoli.

In such times I found my weekends at our cottage in Withyham an indispensable solace. I would spend them walking in Ashdown Forest with the children, especially Cressida, talking with friends about anything except politics, and playing the piano – with an occasional visit to Glyndebourne. Hard physical work in the garden also helped. I made a large pool with a rockery and a waterfall in our meadow, and built steps and retaining walls. I even took up carpentry, making bookcases and a large chest for the family's muddy shoes and wellingtons; this 'welly box' thoroughly deserved Edna's description as 'Bodger's Best'.

Nineteen sixty-eight was a difficult year throughout the Western world. The trauma of Vietnam sent a tidal wave of student revolt flooding over Europe from the campuses of the United States. Vietnam, however, was simply the occasion, not the cause. The convulsions which shook Western universities in 1968 echoed the student unrest which had shaken Europe a hundred and twenty years earlier. Indeed Chekhov

records in one of his letters a series of demands then made by the
students of St Petersburg, which exactly foreshadows those made at the
LSE and the Sorbonne. One cause was the great increase in both
the numbers and living standards of students throughout the West since
the end of the war. This had created an inchoate demand for unlimited
freedom from all the constraints imposed by older generations; unfortunately this demand was not accompanied by any knowledge or experience of
the political or economic realities in the outside world. A newly privileged
section of the middle class was protesting against the facts which were
bound to circumscribe its privileges. The looming threat of a nuclear
holocaust gave the protest additional urgency. Yet the student revolt had
little following among the working people it professed to represent. In
August that year its self-indulgence was cruelly exposed when the students
of Prague led a genuine national uprising against real injustices. The only
practical consequence of the demonstrations of 1968 was to entrench the
conservative forces wherever they held power – above all in France.

My son Tim gave me some insight into the feelings of his generation,
since he himself was a student in Paris for much of the year. To my
immense pride, he had won an Exhibition to Balliol at seventeen, a
year younger than I was when I won mine; so he decided to spend
the interval studying at the Alliance Française. Though he shared in the
passion and excitement of *les évenements*, he was always able to preserve
a certain detachment. So he recovered faster than many of his contemporaries; after twenty years, some of them still find it difficult to come to
terms with the modern world, without having the slightest idea of how
they would like to change it.

As Defence Secretary, the student radicals called me 'Hitler Healey',
and attacked me with particular venom. On one visit to Cambridge, after
a meeting at which I had won over a substantial majority of my audience,
a raging mob set upon my car and tried to overturn it. We managed to
get through, but not before I had put two fingers up against the hate-
distorted features of a demented theological student; this incident oc-
casioned my second appearance in *Private Eye*.

Meanwhile Britain's economic troubles continued. Harold Wilson infuriated the Bonn Government by calling in the German Ambassador
late one night, to insist that the Deutschmark should be revalued. He was
rebuffed, and de Gaulle refused to devalue the franc, so the pound was
left alone to face the full force of international speculation. By the end of
November 1968 Roy told me that, if the pound collapsed again, Britain's
only hope would be a partnership between me and Reggie Maudling! He

introduced import deposits, increased excise duties, and asked for another series of spending cuts.

I told my colleagues I would resign rather than cut defence yet again. This time even Wilson supported me. He was now looking for allies against Jim Callaghan, his latest demon; indeed he threatened to reshuffle the Cabinet again if Jim did not stop attacking him. Jim told me he wanted desperately to take Harold's place when the next crisis came. I was unimpressed, since his only ideas for improving our economy were to sack Michael Stewart, abolish the Department of Economic Affairs, and abandon a fixed rate for sterling in favour of floating.

Nevertheless, the following year seemed to offer Callaghan the opening he wanted. In January 1969 Barbara Castle, now First Secretary, put forward proposals for tightening control of the trade unions. Harold told me when we were lunching alone in his ultimate sanctuary, the little flat at the top of No. 10, that he had decided on union reform because he had given up hope of making his incomes policy work. Barbara's proposals were published under the title *In Place of Strife*; in fact they produced six months of civil war throughout the Labour movement, splitting both the Cabinet and the Party, and nearly bringing the Government down. Callaghan campaigned publicly against them in the hope of winning enough trade union support to force Wilson out and take his place. Wilson reconstructed his Inner Cabinet without including Callaghan. By now I had become the Prime Minister's favourite. In April he asked me to become Party Manager without Portfolio, and was mortified when I once again refused to leave Defence.

Plotting against Wilson reached a crescendo in the Parliamentary Party. Ministerial meetings grew more and more bad-tempered, until on May 8th Wilson told the Cabinet flatly that he would not get out and leave the choice of his successor open, since he was certain no one else could form a government. The tension temporarily abated. Roy signed the Letters of Intent which fixed the conditions of a British loan from the IMF. He told me he now wanted to leave the Treasury for the Foreign Office, providing I would replace him as Chancellor. In June, while I was away in the Far East for a fortnight, Wilson and Barbara Castle finally accepted defeat on trade union reform.

The Government had wasted six months on a hopeless fight, which had caused permanent damage to our relations with the trade unions, without making them any less necessary to our survival. *In Place of Strife* did for Wilson what the hopeless attempt to delete Clause Four from the Party Constitution had done for Hugh Gaitskell.

Once again Wilson toyed with the idea of reshuffling the Cabinet and making further changes in the machinery of government; he wanted to punish his erstwhile sycophants for their disloyalty during the battle for trade union reform. But this time reality intruded.

Although violence had been increasing in Northern Ireland since the previous October, the Government still hoped that political reforms would restore tranquillity. In mid-August rioting caused the army chiefs to see me about the threat to law and order, which was increased by the grossly anti-Catholic bias of the B-Specials, the Protestant auxiliary police. We invited the leading Unionist politicians to Downing Street and offered to put all security under the British General in the province, on condition that we were able to reform the local police forces, so as to purge them of sectarianism. On the recommendation of Lord Hunt, the conqueror of Everest, we appointed a new Inspector General for the Royal Ulster Constabulary, seconded members of the English police to assist it, and replaced the B-Specials with a new Ulster Defence Regiment under army control.

The immediate effect was to reassure the Catholics and give us a period of calm. When I flew over to Northern Ireland a few weeks later, I was greeted by crowds of cheering Catholics as I walked down the Falls and Crumlin Roads – accompanied, without knowing it, by two leaders of the IRA. It was, surprisingly, my first visit to the land of my fathers. I was appalled by the squalor of the mean streets in Belfast and Derry, and even more by the atavistic sectarianism of both communities. In one long row of red-brick back-to-backs in Derry, every window carried a picture of 'King Billy' – William of Orange, the Protestant victor at the Battle of the Boyne. For the Catholics the massacre at Drogheda happened yesterday, not in the sixteenth century.

To me, Catholics and Protestants were physically indistinguishable – indeed when I first entered Parliament there was a young Unionist MP, James Harden, whom Edna sometimes mistook for me when she was up in the gallery. But every Catholic and Protestant in Northern Ireland could identify a member of the opposing community at a glance. The conflict was expressed in terms of religious differences; but it was best understood as a form of tribalism. Many of my socialist friends in England tried to see it as a sort of class war, or as a struggle for colonial freedom. They were soon to discover that the hard core of uncompromising opposition to the unity of Ireland was the working class of the Protestant majority in the North. Again and again I recalled the under-graduate debate on Ulster which I had heard at Balliol, and my fatal ignorance when my father stumped me by asking for the Labour Party's policy on Irish unity in the 1945 election campaign.

I warned my Cabinet colleagues from the beginning that, once we committed the army to keeping law and order in Northern Ireland, we would find it difficult to end, or even to limit, our commitment. But like them, I could see no alternative, nor can I see one now. The young British soldiers, who have had to bear the burden of the politicians' inability to find a political solution, have shown unique self-discipline in the dangerous and unpleasant task of maintaining internal security, in the face of violence from both communities. I do not believe that any other army in the world could have performed so well, nor could the British Army have done so if it had still relied on conscripts.

The crisis in Ulster created a new unity in the Wilson Government. As Home Secretary, Jim Callaghan handled the situation with incomparable skill and understanding, both on the spot and in Westminster. I myself was in hospital for a hernia operation for a few weeks from the end of July, so I was out of action when the crisis first hit us. However, Roy Hattersley, who had recently taken over as my deputy after the tragic death of Gerry Reynolds, showed exceptional flair in dealing with it; I had no qualms in leaving the defence aspects to him for the rest of our period in office. The Labour Government was seriously hampered throughout by the absence of adequate intelligence about the illegal organisations in Northern Ireland, Protestant no less than Catholic, and by lamentably poor communications between Whitehall and Stormont. Both these weaknesses resulted from generations of inexcusable neglect.

From the autumn of 1969 even Northern Ireland receded into the background, as the Government became increasingly preoccupied with the need to face the electorate again. Wilson put me on the Campaign Committee, composed of ministers and members of the National Executive, to consider the programme and organisation for a general election. I began touring the country to make political speeches – something I had managed to avoid in my first five years as a minister, except for the short General Election campaign in 1966. On November 20th I went to South Wales to speak at the farewell dinner of the retiring MP for Bedwellty, Harold Finch. I was met at Newport station by the new candidate, a red-haired young WEA lecturer with a pretty wife who was pregnant. He made a rousing speech over the cold ham and salad in the Miners' Institute, with excellent and unfamiliar jokes which I wrote down in my diary along with his name – Neil Kinnock.

In January 1970 Ted Heath called his Conservative Party colleagues to a pre-election conference at Selsdon Park and committed it to a policy of what would now be called 'Thatcherism'. The Conservative lead in the opinion polls began to shrink, but it was still seven per cent when Harold Wilson called a special meeting of the Inner Cabinet at Chequers to consider the date of the election. Though we still had over a year to go, it is never wise to wait until the last moment, nor to dissolve Parliament after less than three years if you have a reliable majority; the British people do not like unnecessary elections. As a rule, a prime minister does not consult more than a handful of colleagues before picking the date; but on this occasion Harold wanted to be sure that the blame would be widely shared if he took the wrong decision.

Wilson put the considerations clearly before us at Chequers. In June the England football team would be defending its possession of the World Cup in Mexico. Wilson was worried that, if it were defeated just before polling day, the Government would suffer; but on learning that the match would be shown on television very late at night he decided to ignore it. Other factors were more compelling. It would be foolhardy to call a general election before we knew the result of the local elections in early May. After the third week of June we ran into the Wakes Weeks in the North of England, when the working population in many Labour constituencies went on holiday *en masse*. Hoping to get a majority of Jewish votes, Wilson excluded Yom Kippur. So we faced a choice between June and some time after late September, which would severely restrict our room for manoeuvre. Harold was at his best in this type of calculation.

Though Dick Crossman and Barbara Castle favoured October, because the new social benefits would then be in people's pockets, the majority favoured June, when we would have a fresh voting register. But we all agreed we needed more evidence from the polls before taking a final decision. In April Roy produced a cautious Budget which provided for a small fiscal surplus. The borough elections in May nevertheless produced a big swing to Labour. So Wilson decided to call the general election for June 18th.

The early days of the campaign were darkened for me by the collapse of my dear friend, Ernie Southcott. Overwork and, I think, the frustrations of his role as Provost of Southwark had given him a nervous breakdown; when I saw him in Guy's Hospital he was like a light bulb which has burned out.

It was my first election campaign as a national leader. I held press conferences in London every morning and travelled all over the country for the rest of the day. Somehow I managed to squeeze in quick visits to Rome and Venice for meetings of NATO and the Nuclear Planning Group. On the Sunday before the poll our lead in the opinion polls varied from 2.5 per cent to 12.4 per cent. So our defeat four days later was as big a surprise for the Conservatives as it was for us; even George Brown lost his seat at Belper.

It is not easy even now to say what brought about this last minute reversal of public opinion. The newspaper polls were certainly unreliable, as the wide variety of their findings suggested. Moreover, as public opinion becomes steadily more volatile, impulsive decisions to change one's vote, or to abstain, become more common; even the more sophisticated techniques used nowadays cannot track such movements of opinion, which may be occurring in millions every day. Bad trade figures in the last week may have given credibility to Heath's final attack on Labour's handling of the economy.

In any case, there is no doubt that the 1970 general election was lost by the Government rather than won by the Opposition. The Wilson Government of 1966 to 1970 was not regarded as a success even by the Labour movement. It can now be seen as the turning point which started a long decline in the Labour Party's fortunes.

As a newcomer to office, I was both surprised and depressed by the amount of Cabinet in-fighting. But a hundred political memoirs can testify that it has been all too common in governments of all parties at many times. In terms of intellectual ability, the Wilson Government was exceptionally well equipped; eight of the Cabinet in 1966 had First Class degrees from Oxford, including the Prime Minister himself. Harold Wilson, however, failed to give the Government that sense of direction which only a prime minister can impart, and which the public looks for in its leaders. Thus it never appeared as the master of events, but always as their victim.

It is easy in retrospect to see that the Government as a whole, like all British governments since the war, failed to appreciate the size and nature of the adjustments in our foreign, defence, and economic policies which had been made necessary by the end of the empire, the rise of the superpowers, and the recovery of Western Europe. We knew in our hearts that Acheson had put his finger on something important when he said that Britain had lost an empire, and not yet found a role. But we could ignore his underlying message because his metaphor was highly inappropriate; international politics is not a stage on which actors can choose their parts. And the problems faced by modern industrial democracies will not yield to simple prescriptions, however skilfully promoted and aggressively administered.

In domestic politics the Labour Party had still failed to adapt its thinking to the profound social changes it had itself initiated through the Attlee Government after the war. Television and the press were diffusing the same new cultural values throughout the population – and those values were often American as much as British – a trend little affected by what was probably Wilson's greatest personal achievement, the creation of the Open University. Class feeling was receding. Living standards had risen substantially and most of the British people now felt that they had something to conserve; so self-interest was no longer sufficient by itself to promote greater equality. The trade unions were now emerging as an obstacle both to the election of a Labour Government and to its success once it was in power.

I was to spend the next twenty years wrestling with these new political realities.

CHAPTER SEVENTEEN

Entr'acte

'Tis a strange place, this Limbo! – not a Place,
Yet name it so; – where Time and weary Space
Fettered from flight, with night-mare sense of fleeing,
Strive for their last crepuscular half-being; –
Lank Space, and scytheless Time with branny hands
Barren and soundless as the measuring sands,
Not mark'd by flit of Shades, – unmeaning they
As moonlight on the dial of the day!

– 'Limbo' S. T. Coleridge

AFTER SIX YEARS of hard work on something worth doing, it came as a bewildering shock to be thrown again into the Limbo of opposition. In Britain, unlike the United States, there is no transition period to cushion the change. The moment I heard that Harold Wilson had gone to the Palace to tender his resignation, I picked up the telephone to arrange for my furniture to be removed from Admiralty House. Since it was late on Friday night, I could find no one available at short notice. In the end my piano shop at Kentish Town agreed to take what was needed to our house in Highgate, and I hired a Hertz van for the rest. Our daughters helped in the loading, and I drove the van myself to our cottage in Withyham. When I had negotiated it through the gate without an inch to spare on either side, I felt I qualified for membership of the Transport and General Workers' Union!

I now had nothing to do but talk and write – and learn – with little prospect of influencing events in the world outside Westminster until Labour won power again. Offers of work came in immediately. I agreed to write ten articles a year for the *Sunday Times*, and to produce a book on defence as a problem of government, something which no one had yet done – nor have they even now, so far as I am aware.

I stopped writing for the *Sunday Times* three years later. In June 1973 the features editor refused to publish an article of mine because he found the argument so preposterous as to be embarrassing; I actually dared to predict that there might be an international oil crisis that autumn because the OPEC countries might restrict their output to force up the price, unless the consumer countries negotiated a long-term agreement with them, and the West ceased to support Israel against the Arabs. It was not the first or last time I made myself unpopular with untimely predictions. When I told the Bilderberg conference that de Gaulle would veto Britain's entry into the Common Market, they had attacked me as fiercely as if I had been the General himself. On the eve of the IMF General Meeting in September 1982, I warned the Anglo-Italian Chamber of Commerce that Mexico's inability to service its debts might trigger off an international debt crisis, which could threaten the Western financial system; I was lambasted as the cause of the crisis when it came.

My book on defence suffered a worse fate than my articles for the *Sunday Times*. I managed to write about a third in the interstices of a busy political life during my first two years in opposition, and then went to the Rockfeller Study Centre at the Villa Serbelloni in Bellagio for a month, in the hope of making faster progress. Besides attending a seminar on reductionism in biology, in which my favourite living philosopher, Karl Popper, saw fair play between four Nobel prize-winners, I managed to write another third of my book in four weeks at that earthly paradise. When we returned to London paradise was lost with a vengeance; my suitcase was stolen at the air terminal, with all three copies of the first third inside it – a catastrophic blunder which I shall never make again. I never got them back. Though I rewrote about half of what was missing, my heart had gone out of the project. It was no comfort that Carlyle and Lawrence of Arabia had suffered similar misfortunes.

Although you have much less real work in opposition than in office, it is likely to take you longer. You have to do so many things yourself which others do for you when you are a minister. In 1970 an MP's secretarial allowance was nothing like enough for a full-time secretary, and there was no allowance whatever for assistance in research. Like most ex-ministers, however, I missed my official car most of all. Driving oneself around in London is no fun, and parking was already becoming almost impossible.

This led to one of my few serious brushes with the law. Driving home after a vote one night I ran into the back of a parked car at Cambridge Circus. Swelling with pride in my sense of civic duty, I drove up to the police station in Tottenham Court Road to report the accident. As I opened my offside door, another car ran into it. I was trembling with fury when I spoke to the Sergeant on duty. He wrote down my report and as I turned to go, a taxi-driver who was also at the desk said: ''Ere, this fellow's drunk.'

The breath test showed a positive result. Next morning my mishap was the first item on the news; I later discovered that a press informer at the police station had tipped off his paymasters. Within the day I was cleared of being drunk; the urine test showed me far below the danger limit. This fact, of course, got no publicity. Still, as a result, I can claim to be one of the few people in the world who has been certified by separate processes of law to be both sober and non-Communist – during the McCarthy Red scare I had to be certified by Congress as no longer a member of the Communist Party in order to be allowed entry to the United States.

My official driver at the Ministry of Defence, Jim McCaul, also suffered a misfortune. During the election campaign he discovered from other drivers in the car-pool – by far the best source of government intelligence – that if Labour won, I would be Chancellor of the Exchequer. He arranged to be transferred to the Chancellor's car. Labour lost; so he drove Iain Macleod and Tony Barber for four years before getting me back again.

Though the need to do everything for myself left me with even less spare time than I had as Defence Secretary, I was able to enjoy my leisure more, since I was less tired when it came. I began to take up the piano more seriously, and bought several second-hand instruments for the cottage. The first was full of woodworm; when I got tired of finding little pyramids of dust on the carpet, I paid thirty pounds for an 1870 Erard grand piano instead. This was a magnificent instrument, eight feet long, with a bass register as sonorous as an orchestra, though its upper register went pink-a-pink. Unfortunately it had been mercilessly hammered at the ballet school from which I bought it, and the pegs kept slipping; so it needed continual tuning. Since the pegs were rectangular, not square, like those in modern pianos, I had to get an expert in antiques to tune it. But it gave me a lasting addiction to grand pianos; I now have a Bechstein.

I began doing music programmes on radio and television, which I found a refreshing change from *Any Questions* and *Panorama*, and was even able to exploit my secret taste for thrillers. The Crime Writers' Association invited me to present their Golden Dagger Awards in 1971, because I had helped to rescue John Franklin Bardin from his postwar obscurity; he had written two surrealistic masterpieces, *Devil Take the Blue Tail Fly*, and *The Deadly Percheron*. Their re-publication in a Penguin Omnibus is one of my few unambiguous services to the human race.

Edna and I saw Emrys James in the performance of a lifetime, as Brecht rehearsing *Coriolanus* during the workers' revolt in East Berlin, in Günther Grass's brilliant play *The Plebeians Rehearse the Uprising*. This is one of the most penetrating studies of modern politics I know, though its dramatic structure falls apart at the end. I had a long talk with Grass afterwards. Apart from H. G. Wells in *The New Machiavelli* he is the only writer I know who has made poetry out of social democracy. Asked why he supported Willy Brandt, he replied: 'Because he shortens the legs of lies.' His account of his work during Brandt's election campaign in *From the Diary of a Snail* is full of political insight, not least in the concluding essay, 'Variations on Melencolia', which treats Dürer's engraving as a symbol of man in contemporary society. I found it all too relevant:

> Our Melencolia sits brooding between ideologies and stunted reforms, impoverished amid inertia. Tired, disgusted by long-drawn-out snail processes, dejected amid timetables, she, too, like Dürer's *Melencolia*, props up her head and clenches her fist, because in hermaphrodite fashion stasis in progress begets and gives birth to progress from stasis. In a moment she will rise to her feet, reform some bungled reform, appoint a provisional goal, set some important deadlines and – on the sly – plan a simon-pure utopia, in which cheerfulness will be compulsory and melancholy strictly forbidden.

I needed all the political insight I could get, since I was now personally involved for the first time in every aspect of the Labour Party's work.

The first job facing us after the election was to choose the Parliamentary leadership. Though initially reluctant, Roy Jenkins became Deputy Leader under Harold Wilson, whose position seemed now more secure than for many years, even though he had led us to defeat. In fact he now had no rivals; George Brown had left active politics for the House of Lords, and Jim Callaghan, now sixty years old, was losing his taste for the arena. He even allowed Harold to suggest him as a candidate for Managing Director of the IMF.

I came second to Jim Callaghan in the Shadow Cabinet elections, and Harold made me Shadow Foreign Secretary, opposite Alec Douglas-Home. Much more surprisingly, I was elected for the first time to the National Executive Committee by the constituency parties, which had never elected a right-winger since the Bevanite split in 1952. Indeed Jim Griffiths and Jim Callaghan, who were regarded as from the Centre rather than the Right, had been the only constituency representatives not from the Bevanite Left, and each had survived on the Executive only by becoming Deputy Leader and Treasurer respectively after a few years. I survived as a constituency representative for five years, until my second year as Chancellor; there were, after all, some limits to the tolerance of our activists.

The Labour Party tended to regard the Ministry of Defence as the grave of ambition. In fact, it was my performance there which gave me a national political status for the first time. Though more than fifty left-wing backbenchers regularly voted against my Defence White Papers, they did not seem to hold my policies against me. I was also lucky in my Tory opponents. Enoch Powell rejected both Britain's role East of Suez and our reliance on nuclear deterrence, so he was an odd spokesman for the Conservative Party, which complained only that I was not keen enough on either. The other Tory spokesmen were poor Parliamentary performers.

Though there had been regular debates at the Party Conference about the foreign policy of the Wilson Government, these tended to centre on Vietnam and our relations with the United States rather than on defence, where the complaint, not confined to the left wing, was about our slowness in withdrawing from East of Suez. Surprising as it must seem nowadays, our decision to keep a British nuclear deterrent was never contested; opposition focussed on our agreement to host the American Polaris submarines at Holy Loch. I had never hesitated to justify our policy on nuclear weapons, and had explained NATO's nuclear strategy in detail in the House of Commons. Edna herself had launched our second Polaris submarine, *Renown*. Yet none of this then counted seriously against me in the Party.

Membership of the NEC brought me an enormous amount of additional Party work – not only meetings of the committee and its subcommittees at least once a month, but also speaking all over the country in by-elections, regional conferences, and constituency meetings. I began to work with leading trade unionists such as Hugh Scanlon and Jack Jones, and saw a lot of the General Secretary of the TUC, Vic

Feather; he was a Bradford man, whose Yorkshire humour and common sense made us good friends.

The Party in the country had changed a great deal since I had last known it well, during my postwar days at Transport House. I had watched the changes in my own constituency. In 1952 my Party was dominated by trade unionists from local manufacturing industry, many of whom had worked in the constituency from the early twenties, and had suffered unemployment and deprivation during the Great Slump of the thirties. In 1970 they were giving way to active young men and women from the public services, whose work had often brought them to Leeds from other parts of Britain. Among them was a small group of Trotskyites from the so-called Militant Tendency, sometimes described as the 'bed-sit brigade', because they chose to move to constituencies where they could cause maximum trouble for the Labour Party. The Communist Party was no longer a serious problem except in a few trade union branches.

Many of the younger radicals from the expanding middle class found it difficult to accept the Labour Party's attitudes and policies as a package. They saw no reason why, for example, because they believed in helping the underprivileged, they should support the nationalisation of industry, or oppose the Common Market. The seventies saw the rise of single-issue organisations like the Child Poverty Action Group, Age Concern, and Shelter, as well as a number of environmental lobbies interested only in saving the whale or stopping the fur trade. Many of these organisations took potential members away from the Labour Party. Others encouraged their supporters to join the Labour Party, but only in order to capture it for their own purposes. This was particularly true of the Campaign for Nuclear Disarmament, which was also active in the trade unions; it finally succeeded in capturing the whole of the Labour movement for unilateralism, against the wishes of the inactive majority both of Labour voters and of trade union members. Feminism was growing, particularly among young women, who found sexual discrimination or harassment at their place of work. Homosexuals also sought solutions to their social difficulties through political action.

As the Labour Party found its traditional support declining with the erosion of manufacturing industry and the spread of middle-class values, some of its leaders, particularly on the Left, felt that it should seek a new constituency by creating a 'Rainbow Coalition' among these single-issue groups. They sought to overcome the conservatism of the Labour leadership by changing the party constitution; their aim was to make MPs more accountable to the constituency activists, and to diminish the influence of the Parliamentary Labour Party as a whole, by giving the constituency parties and the trade unions the decisive voice both in deciding Party policy and in choosing the leadership. By the end of the decade the organisations they set up inside the Party had become strong enough to achieve most of their objectives.

The Democratic Party in the United States was then moving even faster in the same direction. The abolition of the seniority rule for committee chairmanships had already undermined the power of the party managers in the Congress. The so-called Charter Movement made similar changes in the Democratic Party's organisation in the country, and won its greatest victory by getting George McGovern nominated as the Democratic Presidential candidate against Nixon in 1972. The scale of McGovern's subsequent defeat should have been a warning to the Labour Party in Britain. But the Labour Party has never been prepared to learn anything from the experience of foreigners.

Meanwhile the Conservative Party was having its own problems in confronting change. They were made more, not less, difficult by its experience in office under Ted Heath. In many ways Heath played Kerensky to Mrs Thatcher's Lenin. Perhaps he would prefer to say that he played Lenin to her Stalin since she rejected his New Economic Policy as soon as she replaced him.

The Selsdon Park declaration of January 1970 was what we would now call pure Thatcherism. It asserted an absolute confidence in the efficiency of the market economy as against government intervention, promised no more rescues of industrial lame ducks, and utterly rejected the philosophy of compulsory wage control. As if to underline the end of the bipartisan approach to social and economic policy which had come to be called Butskellism, Heath then chose to replace the liberal Edward Boyle as Shadow Education Minister with a young MP hitherto unknown except for her very right-wing views – Margaret Thatcher.

He showed some of Mrs Thatcher's personal characteristics too, not least in regarding the Foreign Office as hopelessly 'wet'. When one of its most experienced officials gently suggested while he was in opposition that he would be unwise to reverse Labour's decision to leave the Gulf, Heath exploded with anger, accusing the Foreign Office of feebleness and bad faith. He was no less contemptuous of the Foreign Office when he became Prime Minister. He simply brushed it aside when it warned him that he could destroy the Commonwealth by selling arms to South Africa, and later when it suggested that, by offering cooperation with

France on nuclear weapons, he would damage relations with Germany and undermine NATO. By his unnecessary aggressiveness towards the media, Heath disturbed Conservative Central Office in the seventies no less than Mrs Thatcher in the eighties.

According to Douglas Hurd, who, after working for Heath in Opposition, succeeded Marcia Falkender as the Political Secretary at No. 10, Heath saw himself as a latter-day Robert Peel, creating a new Conservative Party to fit the new social realities of which he was himself the product. It was a good analogy. Heath was the first Conservative leader from the lower middle class, as Peel was the first leader to represent the new rich who had made their money out of manufacturing industry. They had similar personalities too. Peel was described by contemporaries as 'an iceberg with a slight thaw on the surface', his smile 'like the gleam of the silver plate on a coffin lid'. Both men had to make up in vigour and industry what they lacked in more human and exciting qualities.

It could be said of Heath, as it was of Peel, that he ended up like 'the Turkish Admiral, who steered his fleet into the enemy's port'. He finally came under heavy attack from inside his own Party for lack of Conservative principle. In taking Britain into the Common Market, like Peel in repealing the Corn Laws, he never won the general consent of his Party. Heath was also a confirmed pragmatist, though he has always been reluctant to admit that he ever changes his mind.

In fact no Prime Minister has ever reversed the whole thrust of his policies as fast and completely as Heath. He abandoned his Thatcherism lock, stock, and barrel when he discovered it was causing mass unemployment. Contrary to his declared intentions, he baled out Rolls-Royce and Upper Clyde Shipyards, abandoned the market economy in favour of industrial interventionism, embraced the control of prices and incomes, and condemned the Lonrho affair as 'the unacceptable face of capitalism'.

His New Economic Policy was no more successful than his 'Thatcherism', partly because he was no more willing to take advice from the Treasury than from the Foreign Office; and Tony Barber, who took over as Chancellor after Iain MacLeod's premature death, had neither the courage nor the experience to stand up to him. Yet, once he had decided he must work with the trade unions rather than against them, Heath came within an inch of persuading them to accept an incomes policy, which might have saved him from defeat in 1974. He established particularly good relations with Len Murray, who had then succeeded Vic Feather as General Secretary of the TUC. Unfortunately this was the one issue on which Tony Barber did stand firm; he wrecked the chance of agreement on an incomes policy in December 1973, thus making the miners' strike inevitable. Heath's defeat in the election two months later appeared to many Conservatives as a blessed release rather than a disaster.

As Shadow Foreign Secretary, my first task was to expiate my own crime, by opposing Heath's abortive attempt to sell arms to South Africa. I spent a week in South Africa myself in September 1970 as guest of the National Union of South African Students, which was strongly opposed to Apartheid. Direct contact with the Africans in the black townships, and with the Asians and 'coloureds', who often lived in scarcely more tolerable conditions, convinced me, as it was to convince the Commonwealth Eminent Persons Group sixteen years later, that rule by the black majority was inevitable; and also that it would not come without appalling bloodshed, unless the outside world imposed heavy pressure on the white minority.

Robert Birley, a friend from Königswinter, had spent some years at Witwatersrand University in the sixties after retiring as Headmaster of Eton. He told me that you could then divide the whites into two groups – those who believed in the Thousand Year Reich, and those whose motto was *Après moi la deluge*. The first group was already shrinking fast in 1970; it had completely disappeared on my second visit in 1986. But there was also a large number of whites who were working to overthrow Apartheid, either within their own community, like most of the Progressive Party, or in more or less active cooperation with the non-whites. Since their congregations were overwhelmingly black, most of the Christian clergy in the South African Council of Churches found themselves working with the blacks. Their most outstanding representative was Beyers Naude, an obstinate Afrikaner who had once been a member of the racist Broederbond, and was now fighting Apartheid with unflinching courage.

My hosts from NUSAS were all young men and women of exceptional quality. Their Secretary, Horst Kleinschmidt, stood out among them for political wisdom and dedication to his cause. His fair hair and good looks revealed his origin. Five generations earlier his family had landed from Germany in South West Africa, now Namibia, as the first white missionaries in the area. In 1936, at the age of seventeen, his father had been picked out by the Hitler Jugend to tour the Reich – I must have been there at the same time. He returned an ardent Nazi. However, Horst himself was educated at Windhoek after the war by left-wing German refugees and went to Witwatersrand, where he came under the influence of Ernie Southcott's ex-curate, John Davies, now working there as a missionary. Horst refused the Government's invitation to spy on his fellow-students, and became an active campaigner against Apartheid. His Nazi father accepted Horst's right to choose his own path, and even made no trouble when Horst married a pretty Jewish girl; however, she was never forgiven by her parents for marrying a goy.

When Horst later left South Africa to work for the resistance abroad, he sometimes stayed with us in London; his wife soon found the life of a political exile too much for her and returned home. Horst Kleinschmidt and Beyers Naude stand as warnings against the tendency to judge people by their origins or background. Like many Afrikaners and Germans in South Africa, they have dedicated their lives to fight against the principles in which they were brought up. The struggle against Apartheid depends critically on men and women like them.

I flew from London straight to Durban, and dumped my luggage at the University hostel, where the warden turned out to have been the best friend of my first sweetheart, Pat, at Bradford Girls Grammar School. I decided that Paul Jacobs was right in saying that there are only a hundred real people in the world, and you come across them wherever you go!

By eleven-thirty on the morning of my arrival, after travelling all night, I was off on a journey of 550 miles by car into the heart of Zululand. Besides Horst, my companion was a young black student who looked rather like the film actor Sidney Poitier. His name was Steve Biko.

Steve's brother had been arrested as a member of the People's African Congress, and Steve himself had developed his political conscience when taking food to him in prison. He broke with NUSAS because it was largely run by whites, and acquiesced in a degree of segregation. When I met him he had just formed the all-black South African Students' Organisation. But he was nevertheless a close friend of Horst Kleinschmidt. I was impressed throughout this short visit to South Africa by the good personal relations between members of the different anti-Apartheid groups, and of the different Christian churches. Outside the Afrikaner church, there was none of the sectarian bigotry so common in Britain.

A few years later, I heard that Steve Biko had been arrested, and savagely beaten in jail. He was thrown handcuffed, bleeding, and unconscious into the back of a truck for a hundred mile journey to hospital, jolting over rough tracks most of the way. He never recovered consciousness. The news of his death came as a personal blow to me. It was a tragic loss for Africa and the world.

After picnicking on the grass in a small town – blacks were not allowed to eat in the same café as whites – we went to see Bishop Zulu, the head of the Anglican Church in Zululand. He insisted that we walk in his garden as we talked, so as to escape the eavesdropping devices in his office – the law prevented him from living in the official bishop's residence. He told me that there was unlikely to be progress towards ending Apartheid without some violence, and that if the opponents of Apartheid showed excessive faith in the white liberals they might produce a black backlash; the situation was already polarising, with the mirror-image of Powellism growing among the blacks.

Like many of the Africans I met, Bishop Zulu preferred the Afrikaners to the English: 'They call you a dog and you know where you are. The Englishman smiles and betrays you.' I began to realise that the gulf between the English and the Afrikaners was only a little less deep than that between the whites and the blacks. The memory of the British concentration camps in the Boer War, and persistent discrimination against the Afrikaners since then, had destroyed any chance of understanding between the two white tribes. Even the most intelligent English professional people would boast complete ignorance of what their Afrikaner colleagues were thinking.

After leaving Bishop Zulu, we drove up into the mountains to visit Chief Gatsha Buthelezi in his kraal. As a hereditary chief of the Zulus, he was obliged to serve as Chief Executive Officer of the African Authority in Zululand. He was then a nervous but able young man of forty-two, deeply resentful that there was already insufficient land for his people, still less for the two million more Zulus scheduled to come when the so-called Zulu homeland was established. At this time, and for many years afterwards, he was closely in touch with the banned African National Congress, and cherished his friendship with Nelson Mandela. Indeed Oliver Tambo, the ANC leader in exile, later told me that it was he who advised Buthelezi to revive the traditional Zulu organisation, Inkatha – advice which he came bitterly to regret.

Because I had been Defence Secretary and could be expected to value the Royal Navy's base at Simonstown – and no doubt remembering my ill-starred role in the Labour Government's crisis over arms for South Africa – the government in Pretoria accepted my request that I should be allowed to visit Nelson Mandela in prison on Robben Island. I was able to spend an hour in conversation with him in one corner of the Governor's office while a member of the British High Commission kept the Governor busy in the opposite corner. Nevertheless, neither I nor Mandela could assume that our talk was not being taped, so we felt unable to talk about South African politics.

I had met Mandela only once before, when my friend of army days in Italy, Mary Benson, introduced us during one of his clandestine visits to London. In London he had worn a beard, and was dark with sunburn. On Robben Island he was clean-shaven, close-cropped, and pale. His moral authority, even over his warders, was immense, and he kept himself in good physical condition by playing tenniquoit. He and the other thirty-one political prisoners were not allowed to mix with the ordinary criminals, but they were now permitted to meet with one another. Mandela himself could receive only two visitors a month, and two letters, with two replies. Yet his morale was high, and he was far better informed about events in the outside world than I expected.

He had no chance of escape. The island was surrounded by rocks and seaweed; the water was very cold, and the currents strong enough to sweep any swimmer out to sea. I walked round the island, which was uninhabited outside the prison, while waiting for the aircraft to take me back. It was like a tiny Garden of Eden, in which rabbits and guinea fowl which had never seen a man played unfrightened among arum lilies, wattle and a profusion of spring flowers. When I saw him in September 1970, Nelson Mandela was fifty-two, a few months younger than I. He had already been a prisoner for over eight years. He is still a prisoner.

When I next visited South Africa in the summer of 1986, the Botha regime had just declared a State of Emergency; its purpose was to destroy the social and political tissue of the black community by putting its leaders into jail without charge or trial. Archbishop Desmond Tutu of the Anglican Church, the Methodist Reverend Alan Boesak, and the Roman Catholic Archbishop Hurley were working together against Apartheid, and were too prominent to be imprisoned. So was Winnie Mandela, who had been separated from her husband almost since the day they were married; she had become an international symbol of black resistance. I was distressed, but not altogether surprised by the tragedy which later befell her, when accusations of murder were made against some of her bodyguard; she was a passionate woman whose emotions were liable to betray her when there was no possibility of directing them to constructive ends.

The Commonwealth soon compelled Heath to drop his plans to sell arms to South Africa. Then the overriding issue for British foreign and economic policy became his negotiations for British entry into the European Economic Community. De Gaulle had frustrated earlier attempts by Macmillan and Harold Wilson; but Pompidou was now the President of France, and his attitude was unknown. Moreover, with Willy Brandt as Chancellor of the Federal Republic, the climate was more favourable both for the diplomatic negotiations and for subsequent endorsement of an agreement by the House of Commons. The Labour Party, however, was more deeply divided on the issue in Opposition than it had been in office. So far as Britain's domestic interests were concerned, I found both the pragmatic and the doctrinal arguments finely balanced. The external factors were now a little more favourable, since the Commonwealth was slowly coming to terms with the idea of British entry. But the other EFTA countries would still face difficulties if Britain joined without them, and most of them had governments friendly to the Labour Party.

I spent many hours discussing the problem with my European friends. All the French representatives of the Community itself, such as Commissioner Deniau and Ambassador Berthoin, wanted Britain to join. Jean Monnet, the originator of the idea, was particularly enthusiastic; but much of the Labour Party still took seriously the old joke that Monnet was the root of all evil. However, Brandt and Helmut Schmidt were actively pressing Europe's cause; and Brandt's Ostpolitik had made him one of the Labour Party's heroes. The photograph of that massive figure, kneeling in contrition at the memorial to the Warsaw ghetto, had already become one of the great symbolic images of our time. Even the Labour Left found it difficult to criticise Willy Brandt.

Unfortunately, as tends to happen to all parties in Opposition, the argument on the Common Market was increasingly presented as one of fundamental political principle. My attempts to direct attention to the real issues were regarded by the zealots on both sides as opportunism. When I signed a statement on the Community which was intended for our socialist colleagues abroad, my closest friend in Leeds, Douglas Gabb, who was also my constituency party agent, denounced me in public. An article I wrote for the *Daily Mirror*, which put the arguments on each side, and was described by the *Manchester Guardian* as 'far from euphoric', was treated by both camps as indicating unconditional support for entry. In fact my main point was: 'If our economy is strong when we go in we should reap a splendid harvest. If it is weak, the shock could be fatal.' In any case, everything would depend on the terms.

Wilson made himself equally unpopular over the Common Market. He showed great courage in refusing absolutely to reject British entry in principle. He argued instead that if Heath's application did succeed, the result should be judged exclusively on the terms he obtained. He also insisted that whatever decision the Labour Party finally reached, there should be no victimisation of the minority, if it voted against the majority decision.

He managed to carry the 1972 Party Conference for this position. A week later he persuaded the Parliamentary Party to oppose the terms which Heath had now negotiated with Pompidou – mainly because the Common Agricultural Policy was a nonsense which imposed a grossly unfair burden on Britain. There followed a tense period in which the main issue was whether Labour should allow a free vote on the issue; Heath had wisely chosen to allow the Conservatives a free vote, knowing that there would be more support for him on the Labour benches than opposition on his own. Wilson nevertheless imposed a three-line whip, believing that a free vote would be inconsistent with his undertaking to the Party Conference. In the event Heath had a majority of 112; sixty-nine Labour MPs voted with the Government and twenty abstained.

The whole affair was extremely demoralising for the Labour Party, and feelings on both sides remained bitter. I had more sympathy for Harold Wilson's conduct on this issue than on some others. As Attlee had demonstrated during the Bevanite challenge in the fifties, in Opposition the overriding duty of the Leader is to keep the Party together. Wilson was fully aware of the ignoble role which circumstances imposed on him over the Common Market. At one meeting of the Shadow Cabinet, his real feelings erupted; he told his colleagues: 'I've been wading in shit for three months to allow others to indulge their conscience'.

When the Shadow Cabinet elections took place I paid the price for my pragmatism, just scraping on in the bottom place. The Labour MPs were now split into three equal groups, to none of which I belonged – the Tribunite Left, the Marketeers, and the anti-Marketeers. However, the order of precedence in Shadow Cabinet elections is an unreliable guide to one's future in the Party; Reg Prentice came top a few years before he joined the Tories.

Roy Jenkins now came under increasing pressure from his young acolytes, such as Bill Rodgers and Dick Taverne, to leave the Shadow Cabinet. He finally surrendered to them, resigning as Deputy Leader and Shadow Chancellor in April 1972, just after Tony Barber published his Budget. Wilson appointed me Shadow Chancellor in his place. For the first time in my life I was launched on the stormy and shark-ridden seas of economic policy.

My domestic life was changing too, since all our children had left home. Edna and I were now alone together. Jenny had married Derek, who had been a friend of Tim's at their primary school at Gospel Oak. She was now teaching there herself, and proved to have a genius for her vocation. Under an exceptional headmaster, the school had become a magnet for the intelligentsia of North London. So, Jenny found herself teaching the children of Jonathan Miller, the philosopher Freddie Ayer, the film-maker Ken Loach, and Nick Monck, who was later to be my Private Secretary at the Treasury.

Tim had just married Jo, a girl he had met in Oxford, and was writing for a living. His first novel was, like so many, a thinly disguised autobiography. It has not been published – a pity, since it has a compelling title; for some reason he called it *Son of Kong*. Cressida, to my delight, was studying the social sciences at Leeds University, so I was able to see her during weekends in my constituency. She fell in love with Leeds, and worked in a Citizens Advice Bureau there for a year after getting her degree.

For some years, Edna had been lecturing to Literary Societies and women's clubs, attracting audiences of a size and enthusiasm I could never command as an MP. Now she was able to begin a new career as an author. She started work on a biography of Angela Burdett-Coutts, the Victorian philanthropist who had lived at Holly Lodge, the site of our home in Highgate. *Lady Unknown* was an instant success when it finally came out in 1978.

My new career as Shadow Chancellor was interrupted soon after it began, by a visit to China with Edna in the autumn of 1972. The Chinese had wanted us to go in the spring, before Kissinger's first visit, since they knew he was an old friend; but I was snatched away by Roy's resignation to speak in the budget debates. So in the end I acted instead as John the Baptist to Sir Alec Douglas-Home, who arrived in Peking the week after me, as Foreign Secretary.

China had fascinated me ever since I had been bowled over as a boy by the exhibition of Chinese art at Burlington House. I had read Edgar Snow's classic account of the Long March, *Red Star over China*, as an undergraduate. Malraux's novel about the suppression of the communists in Shanghai, *La Condition Humaine*, had made a lasting impression on me during the war. I had done my best as International Secretary to support Kenneth Younger in trying to get Bevin to recognise the Communist regime before the Korean war. So when Britain finally established limited relations with Peking, I made a point of getting to know the Chinese chargé-d'affaires. My standing with the Chinese diplomats greatly improved when they discovered that Jenny was teaching some of their children at Gospel Oak, and even more when they decided that her husband was a genuine member of the British proletariat; the Cultural Revolution was exceptionally snobbish in this respect. They were also grateful when I put their military attaché in touch with British experts on the Soviet armed forces, such as Malcolm Mackintosh and John Ericsson.

We flew to Peking through the Soviet Union, stopping at Moscow, Omsk and Irkutsk. Even on the short stops en route I could see that living standards had improved remarkably under Brezhnev. We drove into Moscow for a few hours through great new housing estates; in the city itself we found modern boulevards flanked by big stores with fronts of glass and steel, where in Krushchev's time wooden houses crowded the narrow streets. People were better dressed and looked more prosperous; at the airports the women officials wore angora hats over Western hair-styles. When I described this to my Chinese hosts, they took it as just more evidence that Brezhnev was a revisionist and Russia was becoming a bourgeois state. They were half right. Later visits to Moscow confirmed my impression that ordinary Russians had seen substantial increases in their standard of living during the Brezhnev years. I suspect Gorbachev may come to regret the record of unrelieved failure he has attributed to his predecessor, particularly if *perestroika* fails to produce similar improvements for the average citizen.

However, hatred of the Soviet Union was then universal in China, with Krushchev rather than Brezhnev as the arch-villain, since it was Krushchev who had broken with Mao for being too Stalinist. Indeed Krushchev had behaved to Mao Tse-tung after their break, like de Gaulle to Sekou Touré after Guinée left the French Union. He not only withdrew all the Soviet experts who were helping to rebuild the Chinese economy; he made them take all their plans with them, and cut off all supplies, for example the special steels essential for the great bridge over the Yangtse river. While Krushchev's picture was nowhere to be seen, it was odd for a European in 1972 to see a giant portrait of Stalin taking its place alongside Marx, Engels, and Lenin in the great square in front of the Imperial Palace.

We found the Chinese attractive and intelligent as individuals, with a very English sense of humour. There was no sense of an omnipresent secret police, which was so oppressive in the Soviet Union. Nor was there much sign of the armed forces, so common in Moscow; the few we did see all wore the same cotton uniforms, without insignia of rank, and were treated with no special respect by the crowds of civilians.

Nevertheless, the system at that time was still totalitarian in the strictest sense, allowing not the slightest divergence from the official line in any field. Once the initial deportations, imprisonments and dismissals had been carried out the Communist Party maintained absolute discipline mainly by psychological and social pressure, rather than by physical force. It seemed to need its special demons to blame for all mistakes. Lin Piao was cast in that role while we were there; later he was replaced by the Gang of Four. Conversation was normally relaxed and easy; but the moment it approached dangerous areas, the shutters came down and we were treated to blasts of official propaganda, couched in the same standard phrases. Ultimately the uniformity became depressing, since it extended far beyond politics to literature, painting, the theatre, and even music. There was the same uniformity of dress. Everyone wore the same drab cotton uniforms, men and women alike, though I noticed that the uniforms of senior officials were better cut and made of superior material.

We followed the usual route for foreign visitors – political discussions in Peking, short trips to Shanghai, Hangchow, and Nanking, visits to schools, factories and collective farms, sightseeing at the Great Wall and the Ming Tombs, evenings at the theatre to see acrobats or Chinese operas on propaganda themes.

Every moment was fascinating to us, from our first walk in the gardens outside the Imperial Palace the warm autumn afternoon when we arrived, to our final visit to a hospital, where we saw acupuncture anaesthesia used for operations of thyroidectomy, removal of a cartilage, female sterilisation, and dentistry. The whole population had gone mad on photography, snapping one another at all the tourist attractions; a camera had become the fourth consumer durable for families which could afford it, after a bicycle, a radio, and a sewing machine. Peking was a city of bicycles; there were very few cars. For the first time the regime was beginning to worry about environmental pollution, planting trees to control the omnipresent dust which blew in from the surrounding countryside. Dust was the reason why so many people wore gauze face-masks in the streets. It did not prevent them from spitting; this seemed to be the great national pastime, as it was for Americans in the nineteenth century. We had one alarming experience walking through unlit alleys back to our hotel at night, followed by the Phantom Spitter, an invisible presence which drew nearer and nearer in the dark, hawking ever greater yockers every moment. In the hope of limiting the growth of China's population, marriages were discouraged before the age of twenty-five, and young men and women were not allowed even to hold hands in public.

The Cultural Revolution was then coming to an end. It was difficult to believe that one of our most intelligent guides had threatened the London police with an axe while he was serving at the Chinese mission a year or two before. The only time we saw Mao's famous Little Red Book was at the end of a political opera in Shanghai, when the whole cast advanced towards the audience waving it. Moreover, there was little sign of the cult of Mao. Though the lounges of the hotels and airports carried great silk banners inscribed with verses from Mao in his own calligraphy, our guides claimed they could not read them. Mao Tse-tung was then in mental and physical decline, rarely appearing in public or greeting foreign visitors. The country was being run by the redoubtable civil service, as it had been for thousands of years, under the direction of Mao's formidable chief of staff, Premier Chou En Lai.

Chou was the most impressive political leader I have ever met. As was normal, though I had asked to see him, no time for our meeting appeared on my programme. But one evening in Peking I was advised that it would be worthwhile staying in my hotel. At eleven o'clock precisely, a car called for us and took us to the Prime Minister's reception room, where the British Ambassador was already waiting. Chou entered with his interpreter, the famous Nancy T'ang, who had been born in Brooklyn, and a few officials. He was small and wiry, with a dark, intelligent face, urbane and dignified. When we shook hands I found he had difficulty in using his right arm – it had been badly damaged during the fighting in the civil war. He was beginning to feel his age, and kept referring to my youth. This was not altogether agreeable, since, like Wilson Mizner, I hate careless flattery – the kind that exhausts you in your effort to believe it.

I was then fifty-five. He was seventy-four years old, had been in the Politburo of the Chinese Communist Party since 1927, and Prime Minister since the end of the civil war in 1949. The whole of his adult life had been spent at the highest level of politics and administration. Most of the time he had been fighting as well, against the Kuo Min Tang and the Japanese. I was quite tired after only six years as Defence Secretary in peacetime Britain; so I could forgive him for stressing his age.

While Mao Tse-tung was of peasant stock, Chou was the son of a mandarin. He had learned English at a school financed by American missionaries, picked up Japanese as a student in Tokyo, and spoke good French and German since he had become the head of the European branch of the Chinese Communist Party, after joining it while working in France. In 1924, when Sun Yat Sen insisted that the Kuo Min Tang and the Communist Party should work together in the national cause, he became Chief Political Instructor at the élite Whampoa Military Academy, where he first met Chiang Kai-shek. Three years later, when Chiang turned his troops against the communists in Shanghai, he became Mao's right hand man in a civil war which lasted for more than two decades. No other Chinese leader, except Mao himself, could match his knowledge and experience.

His English was good enough to allow him to correct his interpreter on occasion; it interested me that she showed no embarrassment in admitting her mistakes or asking him for a word. There seemed to be none of the subservience to rank so normal in the West – and in the Soviet Union.

We talked for four hours, with five minutes break at midnight. No one else said a word. Foreign Minister as well as Premier, he was exceptionally well informed about what was happening all over the world. China was at that time genuinely worried about the possibility of a Soviet nuclear attack, although it claimed that its vast territory and enormous population would allow it to survive. When the Japanese Prime Minister visited Peking a few months earlier, Chou had taken a grim satisfaction in telling him that, though the bombs might explode in China, the fall-out would come to earth in Japan.

My American friend from Leeds University, Owen Lattimore, was staying at our hotel. Chou told me he had been severely criticised for inviting Owen to China; his colleagues thought that, as the world's leading expert on Mongolia, Lattimore must be a Soviet spy. In fact the two men had been friends since the war, when Owen was with the American mission in Nanking and Chou was the Communist representative in the Chinese government. I doubt whether anyone but Chou would have felt himself able to flout the security police at that time for the sake of a friend. No one except Mao himself could challenge Chou's authority. Meanwhile Chou's personal loyalty to Mao, and his admiration for the man whose leadership had been essential to the revolution's survival and ultimate success, prevented Chou from attempting to replace him, even when Mao was leading China to disaster. Nevertheless, it was thanks above all to Chou that China survived the Cultural Revolution, which ruined its economy and inflicted untold suffering on the managers and intellectuals on whom China's future was bound to depend.

When we visited the University in Peking, it still had only a third of its student complement, having re-opened two years earlier after being closed for most of the Cultural Revolution. We met an old professor who had studied at the London School of Economics before the war; he had been transported for six years to work as a peasant on a collective farm a thousand miles away, because as an intellectual he belonged to the 'stinking Ninth Category'. The Cultural Revolution was by no means ended, as we discovered when we visited a 'May 7th Cadre School' near Peking. Government servants were sent there for brainwashing – three months for the bureaucrats, six months for the teachers. It was possible to sympathise with the concept, which was closely linked with Mao's theory of permanent revolution; he argued 'if you don't constantly sharpen your knife, it will rust' – a maxim Mrs Thatcher would endorse. To prevent officials from losing contact with the realities of peasant life, they were made to perform the most menial tasks available on a collective farm, while studying communist theory in the evenings. We watched a headmistress trying to call her hens to order with her school whistle.

Typical of the thrust of the course was a systematic demonstration that ordure was a precious gift to agriculture, and not something dirty to be despised. One after another the students got up and recited to us how they had been made to clean out the latrines on their first day, and how awful the smell was as they plunged about in the muck, splashing the stuff all over their clothes. It would have been more impressive if they had not all spoken in the same lugubrious tones and used exactly the same words to describe their ordeal. I must confess that by the end Edna and I had the greatest difficulty in keeping our faces straight. Nevertheless my memory of that 'May 7th Cadre School' appeared in a rosier light later, when, as Chancellor, I had to listen to officials who had never done a day's manual labour in their life pontificating on the pay scales appropriate for dustmen and miners.

Our last evening brought us a surrealistic experience. Three elderly gentlewomen from Boston were dining at the next table, dressed in old-fashioned dimity dresses, with lace cuffs and collars; they looked as if they had strayed in from *Arsenic and Old Lace*. We discovered that they had all been missionaries in China before the Revolution. Only one had stayed behind, to become the target of Senator McCarthy's wrath and a leading propagandist for the Communist regime. Her name was Tabitha Gerlach; her friends, Ida Pruitt and Doris Russell, had at last come to visit her and see again the country they loved. The American missionary connection remains as powerful in China as is the Scottish missionary connection in Africa; it is probably one of the factors which made it possible for Nixon to recognise Peking without destroying his credibility as an anti-Communist.

Fourteen years later I spent a few days in Peking again. There had been a social and economic revolution so complete that I felt a little nervous whether perhaps it had gone too far too fast. The new men in power, unlike those whom Gorbachev was just appointing in Moscow, were not the products of the previous system, but its victims. But politically there was the same uniformity as before; no one was allowed to say a good word about the old days. And though I was delighted to find that young lovers could at last hold hands in the public parks, and that China was no longer a cultural desert, there were worrying signs that the new market economy was bringing corruption in its wake.

My visit to China in 1972, however was only a happy diversion from my new responsibilities as Shadow Chancellor. I spent the second half of the Heath Government locked in combat with the real Chancellor of the Exchequer, Tony Barber, over the whole field of economic policy. Though I had played some role in the economic arguments of the Wilson Cabinet's later years, I had no ministerial experience in the field. Moreover, I had no more knowledge of economics than the average newspaper reader – and I had never bothered to look at the City pages. Now I had to engage the Government over every aspect of finance, taxation, industrial and economic policy. I was thrown in at the deep end, by having to speak on the 1972 Budget the moment I was appointed, and to deal with an exceptionally complicated Finance Bill.

Fortunately I had an excellent team to support me. Joel Barnett, a feisty Manchester accountant and his close friend Bob Sheldon were later to join me in the Treasury. Brian Walden, a brilliant Parliamentary debater who had played an active part in the Campaign for Democratic Socialism in the days of Hugh Gaitskell, was already growing restive in Parliament and soon decided that television was more rewarding. With their help, I survived the Finance Bill with only one minor wound; predicting that the Government would have to devalue the pound just as it was about to do so, I enabled Barber to blame me for what his own mismanagement had made inevitable.

Visits to Washington kept me in touch with the international dimension of economic policy. George Shultz, then Secretary of the Treasury, was always ready to see me. On one occasion, however, when he was due to meet me just after giving evidence to a Congressional Committee, he mysteriously cancelled both engagements at short notice. When we did meet the next day, he told me he had been playing golf in Florida with George Meany, the all-powerful czar of the American labour unions; he certainly had his priorities right!

I myself was no less careful to see a great deal of the British union leaders, particularly Len Murray and David Lea of the TUC, Jack Jones of the massive Transport and General Workers and Hugh Scanlon of the engineering union. So I was able to keep in touch with their negotiations on Heath's incomes policy, which were frustrated within an inch of success by Tony Barber in December 1973.

There was no shortage of professional economists willing to help me. Pre-eminent were the terrible twins from Hungary, Nicky Kaldor and Tommy Balogh, whom Hugh Dalton used to describe with some justice as Buddha and Pest. Nicky had worked for Jim Callaghan in the Treasury, and was best known for inventing the Selective Employment Tax. By restricting it to the service industries, he hoped SET would move labour into manufacturing industry; it worked so well that overmanning became a crippling burden on manufacturing for many years. Nicky was the most brilliant economist of his generation in Britain, but he was typically insensitive to the political and social implications of his proposals; his advice to governments in the Third World was notorious for provoking revolution. Like all good academics, he was always ready to get back to the old drawing board when one of his theories failed; the ministerial victims of his advice usually found that their drawing boards were taken away, and sometimes their heads as well. Tommy Balogh had worked for the Prime Minister himself in the Wilson Governments. The years had soured him since we first met at Balliol. Suspicious and conspiratorial where Nicky was genial and expansive, I found him a less stimulating tutor.

For Opposition purposes in the House of Commons, I found it sufficient to concentrate on attacking the contradictions and inequities in Barber's policy; this became an easier task as 1973 advanced, when the crisis produced by OPEC hit an economy which had already stalled through overheating. But I was still too unsure of my subject to react quickly when the situation changed; my response to Barber's package of spending cuts in December 1973 was so stumbling and inadequate that many of my colleagues wondered whether I was up to the job. I was much better when I had time to reflect, and made a devastating attack on the Government's record just when it mattered most, the day before Heath called the election in 1974.

It was more difficult to exercise the necessary influence on the Labour Party's programme for the election. I lectured the Party Conference in 1972 on the need for realism and caution in making our election promises, warning the delegates that our central problem would be inflation, and that inflation had proved to be a cause of unemployment and not its cure.

To the dismay of some of my colleagues, I made it clear that the next Labour Government would need a policy for pay and prices, and that this would require a redistribution of both incomes and wealth. I pointed to Austria and Sweden as countries which had been able to operate an incomes policy successfully, because their governments were in continuous and friendly contact with both the trade unions and the employers, over the whole range of economic problems.

In the 1973 Conference I used words about the Barber crisis which I might well have applied to Nigel Lawson fifteen years later:

> The main reason for this enormous foreign deficit is that he gave away
> four thousand million pounds in the last three years in tax reliefs,
> mainly to the rich, without cutting expenditure to scale and without
> making any attempt to be sure that British industry had the capacity to
> meet the consequent increase in demand, so we have had a steady
> increase in imports of manufactured goods, a yawning trade gap, and
> continual runs on sterling.

I warned Conference that we would have to raise taxes:

> But before you cheer too loudly, let me warn you that a lot of you will
> pay extra taxes, too. That will go for every Member of Parliament in
> this hall, including me . . . There are going to be howls of anguish from
> the eighty thousand people who are rich enough to pay over seventy-five
> per cent on the last slice of their income. But how much do we hear
> from them today of the eighty-five thousand families at the bottom of
> the earnings scale who have to pay over seventy-five per cent on the
> last slice of their income – and thirty thousand of them actually
> lose twenty-five new pence or more, when their wages go up a
> pound?

This reference to the so-called 'Poverty Trap' was the origin of the belief that I said my main aim was to make the rich howl with anguish – which still hangs round my neck like Wilson's phrase 'the pound in your pocket', and Heath's election promise to cut prices 'at a stroke'. I never said either that I would 'squeeze the rich until the pips squeak', though I did quote Tony Crosland using this phrase of Lloyd George's in reference to property speculators, not to the rich in general. This type of misrepresentation is an occupational hazard for politicians.

The Party Conference received my lectures with adequate enthusiasm.

Not so my colleagues on the National Executive; Tony Benn was now moving to the Left at a speed which already made Michael Foot look conservative. He was beginning to play a spoiling role in the Labour Party similar to that of Enoch Powell in the Conservative Party, though he was not yet aligned with Powell on the Common Market. My insistence that we should cost every spending proposal so that we knew its tax implications in advance was generally regarded as somewhat pedantic. But the most difficult issue was the determination of the Left that the Labour Party should commit itself to take a controlling stake in the twenty-five biggest private companies in Britain. No reason was offered to justify this proposal. It was regarded as very bad taste when I enquired whether we wanted Marks and Spencer to be as efficient as the Co-op. In the end Wilson and the Shadow Cabinet had to veto the proposal in the final meeting with the Executive before the election.

Meanwhile Heath was running into ever heavier weather, with little obvious benefit to the Labour Party. We won our last by-election at Bromsgrove in 1971; thereafter it was the Liberal Party which gained from the Government's unpopularity, winning even safe Conservative seats like Ripon, which I had nearly won in 1945, when it formed the bulk of the Pudsey and Otley constituency. In the autumn of 1973 Heath was punished by the oil producers for his friendship with Israel during the Yom Kippur war, even harder than Wilson had been in 1966. Next, the miners voted for a ban on overtime. Heath was determined not to cave in, as he had in 1972. He decided to fight both the oil crisis and the coal crisis at the same time, and imposed a three-day working week; but he did not impose petrol rationing, though he had already printed the necessary coupons.

Throughout January 1974 Heath was dithering over whether or not to call a general election. I told the House: 'There is an element of stony rigidity in his make-up which tends to petrify his whole personality in a crisis. He should never have allowed himself to be manipulated into this dead end by an oddly assorted quartet of his colleagues, who are now trundling him like a great marble statue towards the precipice.' On February 7th he toppled over, and called the election. On February 10th, fortified by an enormous majority in their ballot, the miners called a full-scale strike.

Inevitably the election was fought on the issue 'Who Governs Britain?' On that basis it seemed impossible for the Government to lose – but lose it did. As in 1970, the Opposition did not win the election; the Government lost it. Heath was already an unpopular Prime Minister; the public blamed him rather than the miners for their privations during the three-day week. In fact the result was the mirror image of 1951; this time it was the Conservatives who won the most votes, while Labour won four more seats. The growing strength of the other parties, Nationalist as well as Liberal, helped Labour more than the Conservatives. But we were still thirty-four short of an absolute majority in the House. In another general election eight months later the result was very similar, although this time Labour won an absolute majority of seats with less than forty per cent of the vote and the Conservatives won the lowest share of the poll in their history. For the second time in a year a government was formed with three out of five voters preferring its opponents.

In this sense at least, 1974 was a watershed in British politics. The electorate was trying to tell us something. But was anybody listening?

CHAPTER EIGHTEEN

Chancellor of the Exchequer

> In the bad old days it was not so bad:
>> The top of the ladder
> Was quite an amusing place to sit . . . Honours
> Are not so physical or jolly now,
>> For the species of Powers
> We are used to are not like that. Could one of them
>> Be said to resemble
> The Tragic Hero, the Platonic Saint?
>> Or would any painter
> Portray one rising triumphant from a lake
>> On a dolphin, naked,
> Protected by an umbrella of cherubs? . . .
> The last word on how we may live or die
>> Rests today with such quiet
> Men, working too hard in rooms that are too big,
>> Reducing to figures
> What is the matter, what is to be done.

> — 'The Managers' W. H. Auden

IT WAS AN immense relief for me to be released at last from Limbo. After my six years as Defence Secretary I appreciated all too well the accuracy of Coleridge's description of a shadow – 'unmeaning as moonlight on the dial of the day'. Nevertheless, I entered on my new life as Chancellor of the Exchequer with less confidence than I had brought to my first Cabinet post.

Hector Berlioz, like me, had found it necessary for much of his life to earn a little extra by writing weekly articles as a *feuilletoniste*. He hated it, saying that there could be nothing worse – except being Finance Minister in a Republic; in nineteenth-century France that was the exact equivalent of Chancellor of the Exchequer in a Labour Government.

My five years at the Treasury gave me no cause to disagree with Berlioz. It was exceptionally hard and frustrating work, with few of the diversions which made my six years at Defence so exciting and enjoyable. At first it seemed by no means certain I would get the job. Ted Heath tried hard to persuade the Queen to invite him to form a Government, infuriating the Palace with his assumption that the monarchy was the property of the Conservative Party. And when Wilson was finally appointed Prime Minister, Roy Jenkins made a last-ditch attempt to return to the Treasury, rather than descend to his earlier job as Home Secretary.

I finally heard that I was Chancellor of the Exchequer at 9.30 p.m. on Monday March 4th, 1974 in a telephone call from the Permanent Secretary, Sir Douglas Allen; my predecessor, Tony Barber, had already congratulated me before No. 10 formally confirmed my appointment. Next morning I was picked up by my old driver from Defence, Jim McCaul, very relieved that his prescience was finally rewarded, and took possession of the old Air Force Board Room at the Treasury which was to be my office for the next five years.

I was soon to discover that Defence and the Treasury had more in common than the Air Force Board Room and Jim McCaul. As at Defence, I had to preside over four separate institutions, each offering its own advice and proud of its special traditions and responsibilities. The Bank of England, the Inland Revenue, and the Customs and Excise felt themselves to be at least as independent of the Treasury as the three armed services of the Ministry of Defence. I saw this as an advantage. As at Defence, it left me free to choose the advice I found most convincing; as a rule, however, I again preferred to have issues argued out in front of me in large meetings, at which junior officials were encouraged to disagree if necessary with their superiors.

The Inland Revenue and the Customs and Excise, though both concerned with taxes, were very different in style and character. The Revenue saw themselves strictly as laying down the law to a nation of natural tax-dodgers; it was said of one of my favourite Board Members that he never saw a joke except by appointment! They produced men and women of outstanding quality. Some were distinguished by the most penetrating tunnel vision, like Arthur Cockfield, who later brought his remorseless and unwavering integrity to the Price Commission and to Brussels, where it was not fully appreciated by Mrs Thatcher. Others, like Alan Lord, had great breadth of understanding allied with a dynamic practical energy, which made him my natural choice to run my Industrial Strategy unit before he went into private industry himself. The best Revenue men were often poached by the Treasury, which also infiltrated its own men into the tax departments from time to time – my last Private Secretary at the Treasury, Tony Battishill, had been a Revenue man and finally returned there as its chief.

The Customs and Excise, on the other hand, was always in direct contact with ordinary men and women at every level, from the holiday tourist or the local shopkeeper to the chairman of a multinational corporation. One of the first Controllers of the Customs was Geoffrey Chaucer in the fourteenth century. Compared with the Inland Revenue, the Customs and Excise drew its wisdom from *The Canterbury Tales* rather than from Euclid's Theorems. They knew well enough that 'the gretteste clerkes been noght wisest men', and that human frailty is often rooted in lack of understanding rather than in deliberate dishonesty. Indeed, at best, their relationship with the public was like that of the copper on the beat. The Value Added Tax, which the previous Conservative government had introduced, vastly expanded their area of responsibility, since it covered services as well as goods; I believe they coped well with the myriad problems it created, and in the end were trusted even by their victims. In recent years controlling the drug smugglers has given them more formidable problems.

The Bank of England stood at the opposite end of the democratic spectrum. It still attempted to maintain the cabbalistic secrecy of its most famous Governor, Montague Norman, seeing itself as the guardian of mysteries which no ordinary mortal should be allowed to understand. In its attitude towards outsiders there was more than a little of the 'Suez Canal pilot syndrome', which I had identified in 1956. But in 1974 its reputation had been badly damaged. The previous Governor's handling of the White Paper on Competition and Credit Control, which encouraged the banks to compete more vigorously with one another for lending, had led to an explosion of uncontrolled credit like the deregulation of the eighties. This had been a major factor in bringing Barber's dash for growth to a full stop; it also helped to produce the crisis of the secondary banking system which rumbled on through my period at the Treasury, right up to the troubles of Johnson Matthey when Geoffrey Howe was Chancellor.

The job of a central banker is not easy at the best of times. It has been said that he must always exude confidence, without actually lying. On the other hand he must take the punchbowl away just as the party is getting merry. These duties are not always easy to reconcile. But a central banker's fundamental responsibility is to protect the value of the currency both at home and abroad. The only instrument under his direct control is his power to change the price of money by raising or lowering interest rates; as the Thatcher Government has discovered, this is an instrument of limited and uncertain effectiveness. So a central banker cannot on his own control inflation, or keep the exchange rate stable. He must work with the Treasury and with the elected Government, both of whom may quite legitimately have different priorities from him.

In Britain relations between the Governor of the Bank of England and Labour Governments have sometimes been very bad, especially when, as in the case of Lord Cromer, the Governor was a committed Conservative.

I was luckier than Jim Callaghan in this respect. Throughout my period at the Treasury the Governor of the Bank of England was Gordon Richardson, a highly intelligent and cultured barrister who had spent ten years as chairman of a leading merchant bank, Schroder Wagg. Fair haired and good-looking, with immense charm, he appeared typical of the gilded upper class which in those days slid effortlessly into most of the plum jobs in the City. In fact he had been at Nottingham High School, like his younger counterpart at the Treasury, Douglas Wass, who was to become Permanent Secretary soon after I arrived there. As a young officer at the beginning of the war, Gordon had married Peggy, the daughter of the progressive parson, Dick Sheppard, who was famous in the thirties for his work for the under-privileged. Theirs was an exceptionally happy marriage, a fact which made them particularly attractive to Edna and me. I never detected any Party prejudice in him.

Gordon and I had a relationship of creative tension. I sometimes disappointed Douglas Wass by taking the side of the Bank rather than the Treasury when I thought Gordon had the better of the argument. On the other hand, I upset Gordon by insisting on making my own personal contacts with the financial institutions in the City; the Bank traditionally regards itself as the only authorised channel of contact between the City and the Treasury. At one point, when I wanted to meet the leading private bankers to discuss investment in industry, I could mollify Gordon only by accepting the presence of a spy from the Bank of England.

Gordon Richardson was ably assisted as Governor by the robust Jasper Hollom, who bore the brunt of clearing up the crisis in the secondary banks, and the Australian economist, Kit McMahon, who had recently left academic life to run the international policy of the Bank, a job he performed with exceptional flair. Both were able to give and take hard knocks. When I asked Jasper whether it would make sense to publish the Treasury's monetary targets, he replied: 'You would simply be redesigning your cross.' Besides giving me invaluable advice on the international issues which took an increasing amount of my time as Chancellor, Kit McMahon played the central role in unfreezing Iranian assets in 1980, thus making it possible for the Ayatollah to release the American hostages just before President Carter left office. We shared the same taste for George V. Higgins; Kit used to bring me his latest novel whenever he returned from the United States. I believe Mrs Thatcher made a great mistake in not promoting McMahon to Governor when Gordon Richardson retired; but the Bank of England's loss was the Midland Bank's gain, since McMahon finally left public service to rescue the Midland Bank from its troubles.

Though the Bank, the Revenue, and the Excise had important and semi-independent responsibilities within my field, it was of course the Treasury on which I mainly relied, both for advice and for information. Like the Bank, it had lost prestige during the Barber years. It had been at least as deeply implicated in the fiasco of Competition and Credit Control, and was not known to have resisted the policies which led to the whole economy seizing up in 1973. Yet the most severe critics have to admit that the Treasury commands most of the best brains in a civil service which has no intellectual superior in the world. Perhaps it illustrates the familiar problem of the Rolls-Royce in a market dominated by the Volkswagen and the Honda. In an increasingly complex and interdependent world, in which Britain's industrial performance had been in relative decline for over a hundred years, Whitehall's obsession with procedure rather than policy has left it poorly equipped to handle change.

I doubt whether any other country has so fully developed a committee system as Britain. Because no decision can be taken until every departmental interest has had its say, this system has a natural tendency to produce a soggy compromise. The Treasury lies at its heart; it is represented on every committee which might conceivably take a decision leading to the spending of money. Its central role, however, is to control the existing apparatus of government rather than to initiate change. Precisely because its representatives are so often the ablest on any committee, they find it too easy to stifle the initiative of others. As Defence Secretary I had felt that the Treasury knew the price of everything and the value of nothing. Though I was now poacher turned gamekeeper, this suspicion remained at the back of my mind.

While the job of Chancellor had more institutional similarities with that of Defence Secretary than I expected, they were totally different in one vital respect. When I was responsible for the nation's defence, I had the power to see that my decisions were carried out by nearly a million military and civilian personnel under my direct control. When I was responsible for the nation's economy, the success of my policies depended largely on people over whom I had no direct control whatever, and over whom no one had any central control – the workers and managers in British industry, and the men and women who bought what they produced, both at home and abroad. My central problem was to discover which of the decisions open to me as Chancellor were most likely to get these people to behave as I wanted.

The study of economics is supposed to provide the answers to this problem. I am often asked whether I did not find it a disadvantage as Chancellor to have studied Latin and Greek, philosophy and ancient history, rather than economics. My answer is always no. In my experience, a minister who has studied economics at university usually has at best only a general recollection of what he was taught at least twenty years earlier, by academics who had studied the economy at least twenty years earlier still. Economics is not a science. It is a branch of social psychology, which makes the absurd assumption that you can understand how people behave when they are making, buying, and selling things, without studying the society in which they live, and all the other ways in which they spend their time.

The study of political economy, on the other hand, can help a Chancellor. I learned a lot of lasting value from that seminal treatise, *Capitalism, Socialism, and Democracy*, by Joseph Schumpeter. He had been a right-wing Finance Minister in Austria before devoting his life to the academic study of economics in its political and social context. It was not his only interest. Shortly before he died, he said that he had always had three ambitions – to be the world's greatest economist, the world's greatest horseman and the world's greatest lover. He had failed, he said, in one of those ambitions – because there were no horses at Harvard. Men as different as Kenneth Galbraith, the liberal economist, and Arthur Burns, the conservative Chairman of the United States Federal Reserve, have paid tribute to Schumpeter's brilliance as a teacher.

The central thesis of his masterwork *Capitalism, Socialism and Democracy* was that Marx and Adam Smith were both wrong, since they failed to allow for the ways in which political democracy would enable people to create institutions to protect themselves from the operation of market economics – for example, through trade unions, political parties, and cartels. Though published in Harvard in 1942 it gave an uncannily accurate forecast of the Labour Party's postwar election victory, and of the policies the Labour Government in Britain would then follow, in the 'transition from a war economy to a peace economy under conditions of suppressed inflation.'

In 1946 he published a new edition in which he warned that:

> the real problem is labor . . . Unless socialisation is to spell economic breakdown, a socialising government cannot possibly tolerate present trade union practice . . . As things actually are, labor is of all things the most difficult to socialise. Not that the problem is insoluble. In England, the chances for successful solution by the political method of democracy are greater than they are anywhere else. But the road to solution may be tortuous and long.

I spent my five years as Chancellor discovering how right he was. Nor have we yet reached the end of that road.

In 1936 Maynard Keynes had issued his famous warning: 'Practical men, who believe themselves to be quite exempt from any intellectual influences, are usually the slaves of some defunct economist. Madmen in authority, who hear voices in the air, are distilling their frenzy from some academic scribbler of a few years back.'

In 1974 the Treasury was the slave of the greatest of all academic scribblers, Maynard Keynes himself. America's recovery from the Great Depression under the New Deal had rightly been attributed in large part to Keynes' influence. He had played a key role in managing Britain's economic relations with the United States during the war, and had helped to set up the International Monetary Fund. Though he died in 1946, his influence was still dominant, particularly in his own university, Cambridge, which produced many of Britain's leading economists after the war, including my own advisers, Nicky Kaldor and Douglas Wass; it now harboured the New Cambridge School of economists, led by another attractive Bloomsbury intellectual, Wynne Godley, who was to become my severest critic when I abandoned Keynesianism in 1975.

As many of Keynes' disciples would now admit, his theories had two important weaknesses when applied in postwar Britain. They ignored the economic impact of social institutions, particularly the trade unions; in fact Keynesian policies were unlikely to work in Britain without strict control of incomes, a point of which the Treasury was already well aware. And they ignored the outside world. This mattered little in the great continental economy of the United States, which, particularly in the thirties, was comparatively self-sufficient. It was of crucial importance in the Britain of the seventies.

In my time exports represented over thirty per cent of our gross domestic product, compared with only twelve per cent of Japan's; a difference of one day in the date of payment for our imports and exports made a difference of £250 million in currency flows. Changes in the value of sterling fed through quickly into our prices and into our trading performance. For example, by the end of 1974, the increase in oil prices which took place just before I took over had added £2.5 billion to our current account deficit, increased the cost of living by nearly ten per cent and reduced our Gross Domestic Product (the total value of the goods and services produced in Britain) by five per cent.

Wrestling with such problems, which were generated by foreigners over whom I could have no control, consumed an increasing share of my time at the Treasury, and Keynes had little help to offer here. I was more concerned to find that the fundamental Keynesian concept of demand management had become unreliable. Keynes believed that a government could maintain full employment of a country's productive capacity without creating inflation, by increasing or reducing the demand for its output, through adjusting taxes or government spending. But it had become impossible to discover with any accuracy how much additional demand the government should inject into the economy so as to produce full employment. It was equally impossible to know how people would use the money you did inject by cutting taxes or increasing public spending. It might go into higher wages or profits, creating more inflation rather than more jobs. It might be used to buy foreign rather than British goods, so worsening the balance of payments and creating jobs abroad instead of in Britain. Or it might be saved instead of spent. To the surprise of all economists, the increase in inflation led to an enormous increase in saving, rather than the reverse. A rise of one per cent in the savings ratio was equivalent to a cut in demand of £2,000 million.

Economics has acquired a spurious respectability through the use of numbers, which appear to many people, like my old friend McNamara, much more meaningful than mere adjectives or adverbs, because they appear to be precise and unambiguous. Unfortunately I soon discovered that the most important numbers were nearly always wrong. This applied not only to the economic forecasts, which usually admitted a sizeable range of error; that is why an economist is often defined as a man who, when you ask him for a telephone number, gives you an estimate. It applied also to the statistics about what was actually happening in the economy at the time. It even applied to what had happened in the previous twelve months. As Defence Secretary I had found it possible to get fairly accurate figures for the Russian armed forces, or for the range and payload of a Soviet missile, which the Kremlin tried its best to keep secret. As Chancellor I found it impossible to get accurate figures of our national output the previous year, or of our imports and exports; yet all the data appeared to be readily available. Recalling my personal experience as a railway checker at Swindon station, I was not altogether surprised.

Figures for the nation's gross domestic product are compiled in three different ways – by adding up separately the figures for income, spending, and output. In theory they should all give the same result. Yet in practice their results are always widely different; but the differences are not consistent, so they cannot be allowed for. The trade statistics are even more unreliable; the current balance is usually underestimated, but again not consistently so. Worst of all are the estimates of next year's Public Sector Borrowing Requirement, which, under the Treasury's version of Keynesian theory, should help to indicate the amount of demand the Chancellor should put into or take out of the economy in his Budget.

When I entered the Treasury, the PSBR was defined specifically as the amount which the government would have to borrow by selling gilt-edged stock, in order to finance the deficits incurred by the central government itself, by the local authorities, and by the nationalised industries. This was a far wider definition of the fiscal deficit than is used in any other country – most of them exclude both local spending and the nationalised industries. The PSBR represents the difference between enormous flows of revenues and expenditure; and these flows are in part determined by unpredictable factors like the pattern of personal spending and the propensity to save – even the weather can affect them. So it is impossible to get the PSBR right. Yet it was the estimate of the PSBR which lay at the heart of the so-called 'budget judgment', which in turn determined the extent to which taxes or spending should be raised or lowered.

For my first budget, three weeks after I took office, the Treasury gave me an estimate of the PSBR in 1974/5 which – leaving aside all the fiscal changes later in the year – turned out to be £4,000 million too low. This was the equivalent of 5.4 per cent of that year's GDP. The magnitude of that one forecasting error was greater than that of any fiscal change made by any Chancellor in British history. Two years later, in 1976, the Budget estimate of the PSBR was £2,000 million too high; and in November that year I handed an estimate to the IMF which turned out to be twice as high as it should have been. Moreover, long before any of the measures imposed by the IMF had any chance to take effect, our balance of payments in 1977 was in equilibrium, compared with the heavy deficit originally forecast. If I had been given accurate forecasts in 1976, I would never have needed to go to the IMF at all.

I found it difficult to blame the Treasury for these mistakes, though others did. None of the independent forecasting bodies had a better record. Nor is it easy to blame the markets for taking the forecasts seriously; they had nothing else to go on. In the seventies all the major Western countries suffered from a combination of inflation and stagnation, which traditional economics regarded as a contradiction in terms. This so-called stagflation had an impact on economic behaviour which even now is not fully understood. The traditional assumptions about economic relationships – between saving and consumption, between interest rates, borrowing, and economic activity, between output and employment, between the exchange rate and trade performance, for example – were breaking down. Perhaps that is why the main decision makers in the economy, from the heads of great corporations to the average housewife, had become much more sluggish in reacting to changes in their economic environment, and why inflationary pressures tended to increase at much lower levels of economic activity.

After only eight months in the Treasury, I decided to do for forecasters what the Boston Strangler did for door-to-door salesmen – to make them distrusted for ever. So I summed up my misgivings about economic forecasts in my November statement:

> Like long-term weather forecasts they are better than nothing . . . But
> their origin lies in the extrapolation from a partially known past, through
> an unknown present, to an unknowable future according to theories
> about the causal relationships between certain economic variables which
> are hotly disputed by academic economists, and may in fact change from
> country to country or from decade to decade.

The most fashionable reaction to these uncertainties, which had made it so difficult to follow Keynesian prescriptions in managing demand, was to drop Keynes in favour of Milton Friedman, and rely simply on controlling the money supply. However, no one has yet found an adequate definition of money, no one knows how to control it, and no one except Friedman himself is certain exactly how the control of money supply will influence inflation, which is supposed to be its only purpose. Moreover, the monetary statistics are as unreliable as all the others. In 1976 I found the arch-conservative Arthur Burns, as Chairman of the Fed, telling the Congress: 'Let me go to the month of February. We published a figure of 6.5 per cent [for the growth of money supply]. It might have been, using a different seasonal correction, 0 per cent, or it might have been 10.6 per cent. And that is not the end of the story. These figures are revised.'

My own reaction, therefore, was a deep scepticism about all systematic economic theories. I never went quite as far as President Johnson, who once ruminated characteristically to Ken Galbraith: 'Did y'ever think, Ken, that making a speech on ee-conomics is a lot like pissing down your leg? It seems hot to you, but it never does to anyone else.' For me, the main effect of these disappointments with economic theory was to stimulate an intense curiosity about how the economy actually worked in practice.

I took every opportunity to meet the boards of industrial companies and of the financial institutions – the Stock Exchange, the building societies and the insurance companies, as well as the banks. I talked to trade unionists at their conferences. I had a rowdy but rewarding meeting with two hundred young dealers in foreign exchange – there were no old foreign exchange dealers, since the pressures of exchange dealing burnt you out by the middle thirties. In addition I had meetings, sometimes more often than once a week, with leaders of the TUC and CBI, as well as my regular monthly meetings with them as Chairman of the National Economic Development Council. Finding that the CBI was not always the best guide to industrial opinion, since it was heavily weighted towards the big international companies, I made a point of meeting chambers of commerce as well, because they better represented the broad range of small and middle-sized firms.

My visits to my constituency were particularly revealing, since in Leeds I could meet rank and file trade unionists and junior managers, who would talk to me frankly, with a very different perspective from the grandees at Congress House or Centre Point. I also met at my surgeries ordinary men and women in their vital economic roles as consumers and taxpayers – a species too often neglected by my advisers, who seemed interested only in people as producers. Sometimes their views were a useful corrective to the official orthodoxies, of the Labour Party as well as of the Treasury. My own constituency party, which I had found far to the Left of me on almost everything, voted by a large majority in favour of lower taxes rather than higher spending; on another occasion I was warned by an impeccably left-wing supporter in Glasgow that inflation was politically far more dangerous than unemployment. I made a point of touring the Labour Clubs in East Leeds on the Friday following each of my budgets, to find that the popular reaction was often quite different from that of the press and parliament.

The main conclusion I drew from all these investigations, as from my experience as Chancellor in general, was not that economics is bunk, any more than history is bunk. I decided instead that, while economic theory can give you valuable insights into what is happening, it can rarely offer clear prescriptions for government action, since economic behaviour can change from year to year and is different in one country from another. Keynes was right in saying that adequate demand is a necessary condition for full employment; but, given the inadequacy of the information available and the uncertainty about how people will use their money, fine tuning of demand is not possible. However, if demand is grossly above or below productive capacity, the economy will be in trouble.

Fine tuning of the money supply is even less possible, as my Conservative successors soon discovered. But if the supply of money is allowed grossly to exceed the capacity of the economy to meet demand for any length of time, as it did under my Conservative predecessor, the result is bound to be overheating and inflation. So I became an eclectic pragmatist. Karl Popper played a far more important role in my thinking than Karl Marx – or Maynard Keynes, or Milton Friedman.

The last word on the subject was also the first – at least the first to be printed in Britain. Round about AD 1170, a certain Richard, Son of Nigel, was Treasurer of England and Bishop of London – God and Mammon had closer links in those days. He wrote a Latin dialogue about how to run the Exchequer which included the following words:

'Non enim in ratiociniis sed in multiplicibus iudiciis excellens scaccarii scientia consistit' – or in English, 'For the highest skill at the Exchequer does not lie in calculations, but in judgments of all kinds.'

I had ample opportunity to exercise my judgment, since I sat on more government committees than any other minister, and took the chair at the most important. As a member of the Labour Party's National Executive Committee for my first eighteen months, I attended all its meetings and many of its subcommittees. I was throughout a member of the Liaison Committee which linked the Cabinet, the National Executive, and the

General Council of the TUC. The key members of the General Council who attended NEDC – the so-called Neddy Six – sometimes seemed to be squatting in my official residence at No. 11 Downing Street; at the height of the annual pay talks which began in 1975 we met there several times a week, often till after midnight. And I had regular weekly meetings with the Prime Minister to discuss not only economic questions, but anything else on which he wanted to hear my views.

In addition to all these meetings in Whitehall, and innumerable discussions inside the Treasury itself, I went at least once a month to the Council of Finance Ministers of the European Community in Brussels, and to meetings of the International Monetary Fund on both sides of the Atlantic, not to speak of the private meetings of leading finance ministers in Europe or the United States. I worked far harder and longer even than I had as Defence Secretary. Nearly all the work was intellectually demanding, and often strained me to the limit. Re-reading the scanty diaries I kept at the time, I am shocked to find how often each day's record ends with the words 'To bed dog-tired'.

The mental fatigue took its physical toll. I had constant trouble with my teeth; when the revolution comes I shall abolish teeth. I contracted colds or influenza more often than ever before, developed arthritis in a shoulder, deafness in an ear. I had to prepare one of my budgets when I was bruised all over after slipping on the stairs, another when I had an attack of shingles. When I had my routine medical check-up, the doctor and nurse together found it impossible to get any blood out of me, confirming all the popular myths about chancellors.

However, I have the useful though sometimes dangerous capacity to shut physical or personal troubles out of my mind when something has to be done; I do not believe I ever took a day off in the whole five years. Nevertheless physical and mental exhaustion is not an ideal condition in which to take difficult decisions. My work shut out my family more than was good for me, or them; even Edna was usually quite unaware of problems which caused my fatigue. There must be better ways to run the Treasury than the way I felt compelled to follow. Fortunately, after two years I was able to hand over my responsibility for the gilts market to Harold Lever, and in my last year Roy Hattersley took over the time-consuming task of ruling on specific pay claims.

I often envied my foreign colleagues the comparative lightness of their load. Many of them had no constituency duties. In several countries an MP had to give up his seat when he became a minister; in the United States the Treasury Secretary, like most members of the administration, was usually drawn from outside the Congress altogether. No other finance minister carried so wide a range of responsibilities as the British Chancellor of the Exchequer. In most governments, economic policy was under a different minister from financial policy, as it had been in Britain when George Brown ran the Department of Economic Affairs. In the United States the secretary for finance was not responsible for government spending, which came under a separate Bureau of the Budget. But my responsibilities also gave me powers which the American Finance Secretary could only envy. Moreover, my decisions were nearly always certain to be endorsed by Parliament, since in Britain the Government can normally count on a majority.

In Washington the Congress invariably changes the Administration's proposals for tax and spending, even when the ruling Party has a majority there. Congress is under no obligation to ensure that its decisions are compatible with one another, or meet the needs of the nation as a whole. The only public authority in the United States economy, which can normally rely on its decisions being carried out, is the Federal Reserve Board, which is independent of both the Administration and the Congress. But practically the only decision it can take is on the level of interest rates. Paul Volcker used to complain bitterly as Chairman of the Fed that he was expected to drive the economic automobile with no instrument except the throttle – the steering wheel and the brakes were in other, less responsible hands. In Germany too, the central bank in Frankfurt is constitutionally independent of the Government in Bonn. Even the head of the Government has to ask for special permission to address it – a privilege only once requested in my lifetime.

Harold Wilson retired in 1976. When Jim Callaghan took his place, he was well aware from his own experience how heavy a burden I had to carry. Indeed he told me he did not think any man should be Chancellor of the Exchequer for more than two and a half years. In the event I stayed for five; he did not want to move me, and I did not want to be moved. So instead he suggested that the Treasury should be split, perhaps by putting public spending under another minister.

I disagreed, arguing that this would only add to my burdens, since I would be locked in permanent negotiation with the minister responsible for spending, without in the last resort being able to impose my views on him. In fact Joel Barnett was so reliable in controlling the details of public expenditure that he took much of that burden from me, especially when the Prime Minister finally accepted my argument that Joel should himself be a member of the Cabinet. However, whatever the ministerial organisation, no one except the Chancellor can set the appropriate level for spending as a whole in any particular year. It was the argument about this level, which sometimes had to be changed more than once in the course of a year, which I found most exhausting.

I could not have survived my five-year ordeal without the love and support of Edna and the children – and particularly Edna, since Jenny and Tim were now married and starting their own families, while Cressida was away in Leeds. Whenever possible, I escaped for the weekends to our cottage at Withyham, where I purged my frustrations by hard work in the garden, which gave me no time to think about my weekday worries. Even though Jim McCaul often called twice in a weekend with several boxes of Government papers, I found it much less tiring to read them under the apple trees among the daffodils. On a Saturday I would drive the few miles into Tunbridge Wells, and return with a haul of second-hand books from Hall's Bookshop. Before long I had collected so many that we had to think of finding a larger house.

It was the need for book-space, and for a room large enough to take a grand piano, which led us finally to buy a large family house in four acres of downland at Alfriston, where the Cuckmere valley winds down to the sea. The newspapers, of course, insisted on calling it my 'farm'. In fact it was my earthly paradise. My political ambition, such as it was, has fought a losing battle ever since.

Thanks to Pat Gibson and Jack Donaldson, I went as often as possible to the opera both in London and the country. I was a regular visitor to Glyndebourne, where George and Mary Christie became good friends. On one occasion I was able to use my influence as Chancellor to repay a little of my debt to opera. Covent Garden was organising an exchange visit with La Scala in Milan, but it looked like falling through because the Italian Government would not put up its share of the money. Emilio Colombo, the Italian Finance Minister, was a friend and colleague in Brussels; I had given him some of my Neapolitan swear-words in exchange for some Roman swear-words of which he was aware, but never used; he was a very religious Christian Democrat. I suggested that we really should extend this exchange to the field of opera. He finally surrendered, and the Scala brought to London some of the best productions Covent Garden had ever seen.

I managed to get away to see Ponnelle's uproarious *Cenerentola* with Teresa Berganza, Alva, and Montarsolo, and the following night saw Giorgio Strehler's historic production of *Simon Boccanegra* with Abbado conducting and Capuccilli, Freni, and Raimondi in the main roles. I met them all at the final party which followed. Flown with music and champagne, I bade them welcome in Italian as *scaligeri* to the home of the *giardinieri* – I will snatch at any excuse for showing off my Italian. In return I was presented with a facsimile of Verdi's manuscript of his final masterpiece *Falstaff*, which has become one of my half-dozen favourite operas. I doubt, however, whether the whole episode did much for my reputation in the City, which seems to regard its visits to the opera as requiring maximum visibility with minimum audibility.

Edna's biography of Angela Burdett-Coutts, *Lady Unknown*, was published at the beginning of 1978, and was exceptionally well-received by the critics. She was asked to act as a judge in a competition organised by the Spastics Society, and was immensely impressed by an extraordinary piece of writing by an eleven-year-old spastic Irish boy, called Christy Nolan. In Edna's words, 'both luminous and obscure', it combined the vocabulary of Dylan Thomas with the vision of a young Rimbaud. She insisted on giving it a special prize. Christy's mother, Bernadette, who had taught him to type with a peg fastened to his forehead, since he had no physical control of his body, brought him to London for the ceremony. Afterwards Edna invited them to No. 11 and showed them round the whole building, including No. 10 next door. Christy has described the visit in his first book, *Dam-Burst of Dreams*, and wrote to thank her:

> All mans platonic sallies certify the measure men may possibly leap in
> search of beautiful literature. Only you may make testimony of a poor
> lonely cripple, locked mightily, ostensibly in lasting silence. Much loving
> memories stem magically from your judgment of my art. London indeed
> looked lovely, I loved every moment spent there. My crowning glory
> came when I visited you in 11 Downing Street. Thank you most humbly,
> manfully, sweetly, for making a young man deliriously happy.

I was able to spend a little time with them myself, and was unutterably moved and humbled by the experience. It was difficult to decide who was more impressive – the bright-eyed little boy lolling and grunting in a wheel-chair, his exploding imagination searching for self-expression, or his quiet mother, whose love and patience had finally unlocked his prison door. I gave him Gerard Manley Hopkins' poems, which seemed to me best suited to his needs.

It is all too easy for a minister to lose contact with the human tragedies and triumphs which in the end are the only justification for his existence. I shall always be grateful to Christy and Bernadette Nolan for reminding me of those realities.

CHAPTER NINETEEN

Managing the British Economy

Bullfight critics ranked in rows
Crowd the enormous plaza full.
But only one man's there who really knows,
And he's the man who fights the Bull.

– Domingo Ortega (tr. Robert Graves)

THE CHANCELLOR OF THE EXCHEQUER'S is a lonely job, particularly in a period like mine, when he is obliged to disappoint the hopes of his Party and the aspirations of his colleagues – not to speak of his own. Without the support of the prime minister it is impossible. Fortunately Harold Wilson took a much more relaxed view of his responsibilities when he returned to Downing Street in 1974. He interfered much less in the work of his ministers, and was no longer plagued by the demons of jealousy and suspicion which had tormented him in his first two Governments. The prospect of early retirement helped; he had told me during a journey to Helsinki in 1972 that he did not plan to serve for more than three years next time he was Prime Minister.

I took care to keep him closely in touch with what I was doing, not only at our private meetings every week, but also by dropping in to see him whenever it seemed useful. The chancellor is the only minister who can do this without alerting the press-men who hang around Downing Street; his residence is connected with No. 10 by an internal door on the ground floor. It has normally been kept unlocked, except when Ramsay MacDonald was Prime Minister; Ramsay and his chancellor could not stand one another.

However, Wilson also had an independent source of information about economic and financial matters in Harold Lever, whom he appointed

Chancellor of the Duchy of Lancaster with an office in No. 10. Harold
Lever continued in this role under Jim Callaghan, though by the end he
had become something of a double agent, helping me as much as the
Prime Minister. Harold Lever had an intellectual brilliance with many
facets. He and his elder brother Leslie, also a Labour MP, came from a
typical Jewish family in Manchester and went to Manchester Grammar
School. Leslie made his career mainly in local government and became
Lord Mayor of Manchester; his service to the city's large Roman Catholic
community led many to call him Leslie O'Lever. Harold became a
barrister and had an outstanding career in business and finance.

Though he became a Labour MP in 1950, Harold was at first notoriously relaxed about his Parliamentary duties; on the rare occasions
when he made a speech, it was often against the Labour Party's official
line. Everything changed, however, in 1962 when he married an exceptionally beautiful Lebanese girl called Diane. She had the large eyes
and fine features of the French actress Jeanne Moreau, while Harold
could have doubled for the Hollywood film-star Walter Matthau, except
that he was totally incapable of looking grumpy. Diane was also extremely wealthy. When people said Harold had married her only because she had two million dollars, Harold replied that he would have
married her if she had only had one million. In fact Harold was by
then very wealthy himself; he is the sort of man who can make a
million in ten minutes any afternoon simply by lifting up the telephone.
They were an exceptionally happy and well-matched couple. It was
Diane who persuaded Harold that he should take his political duties
seriously. So in the first Wilson Governments he accepted several ministerial jobs, including two at the Treasury. If he had not had a bad
stroke during the Heath years, which left one side of his body paralysed, I am sure he would have become the head of a major department.

At first I resented Harold's privileged access to the Prime Minister,
and his tendency to second-guess my decisions without having any
responsibility for carrying them out. When I felt more at ease in my job I
found his understanding of the financial markets invaluable, and I
normally accepted about one out of four of his suggestions – a high
average for any external consultant. However, he had certain prejudices
which I found it necessary to discount. The most important was that
Harold would never have the Government spend its own money if it
could borrow someone else's; I had been brought up to regard borrowing
as sinful. On the other hand, he had an inexhaustible supply of what I

used to call 'Leverettes' or 'Lever's ripping wheezes', with which to bamboozle the financial markets; this I regarded as a legitimate objective.

Three of my four junior ministers were also from Manchester, where they had been close friends in the local Labour movement. Joel Barnett and Bob Sheldon had been on my Treasury team in Opposition. Joel remained in charge of the vital negotiations on public spending throughout my five years as Chancellor – a role played by another Jewish accountant from the North, Jack Diamond, in the first two Wilson Governments. Inexhaustible energy and immense good humour are indispensable in that most demanding job. Joel had both. He was well assisted for much of the time by my Oxford friend, Leo Pliatzky, also from Manchester, who had left the Fabian Society for the civil service in 1947 and was promoted from the Treasury to become Permanent Secretary at the Department of Trade in 1977.

Yet another Mancunian, Edmund Dell, was effectively Deputy Chancellor for my first three years, as Paymaster General. I had known him slightly in the Communist Party at Oxford, though his elder brother Sidney, now at the United Nations, was a closer friend. Quiet and slow-speaking, he combined a rigid integrity with the most powerful mind. While on an official visit to Canada he was asked by our High Commissioner, John Ford, to comment on an interesting anecdote. As a young officer at the end of the war, Ford had called at the British mess in a ruined German town, to find another officer sitting alone and playing chess with himself. Ford asked whether he could have a game. 'Yes,' said the other, 'but only if you let me play you blindfold.' Ford agreed, and lost three games in a row. Edmund had to confess that he was indeed the other officer. When in 1977 Edmund became Secretary for Trade, with Leo as his Permanent Secretary, he was my most formidable ally in the Cabinet. Unfortunately he had been losing interest in politics and in the Labour Party for some time. He soon resigned for a job in the City, in which his abilities were never fully used.

Finding an appropriate chief economic adviser gave me immense difficulty. The Treasury itself had an economic section staffed by able young men and women whose most important job was to prepare the official forecasts – a task which, as I have shown, was of limited value. It was customary to put them under a chief economic adviser from outside the Treasury; I inherited a professor from Cambridge, Ken Berrill, in this role. Unfortunately there was a long history of academic hostility between him and Nicky Kaldor, whom I had made my personal adviser.

Odium academicum is quite as virulent a disease as odium theologicum; political rivalries pale in comparison. So in the end I had to move Berrill across Downing Street to become head of the Central Policy Review Staff following Victor Rothschild's retirement – as I had moved Solly Zuckerman to the Prime Minister's office for similar reasons when I was Defence Secretary.

Oddly enough, Nicky himself came increasingly to remind me in some respects of Solly's master, Lord Mountbatten. He found it difficult to work with the Treasury, and was disappointed that Douglas Wass, who had been his friend at Cambridge, was less sympathetic than he had expected. His political judgment was bizarre, and his economic judgment was too often distorted by his changing theories. After years of enthusiasm for devaluation as an economic panacea, he had now switched his affection to import controls. He would nag me as persistently about them as Mountbatten had nagged me about integrating the services. In the end I did not discourage him from going back to academic life. I still regard Kaldor as the most brilliant economist of his generation in Europe. But government was not his *métier*. The role of the outside expert in Whitehall is a difficult one; if he cannot get on with the civil service he can do more harm than good. Either he will isolate his Minister from what should be his main source of advice, or he will kick his heels with frustration and become a source of continual friction. The same is true of an outside political adviser; my first had a reciprocated mistrust of all permanent officials, while the second, Derek Scott, did me yeoman service because he could argue with the Treasury without losing its confidence.

At one point, in despair of finding a really first-class British economist as chief adviser, Douglas Wass and I seriously considered asking the brilliant American liberal, Arthur Okun, to leave the Brookings Institute in Washington and work for me. In the end I decided that his appointment would be too unpopular with his British rivals and with both sides of Parliament; whatever the economic advantages, politically it would be a self-inflicted wound I simply could not afford.

My problem, after all, was not advice, of which I had plenty already available. My Permanent Secretary, Douglas Wass, was a Senior Wrangler and as able an economist as any; he also possessed great personal charm and administrative skill. What I needed was judgment – and this was something I had to develop for myself by practical experience.

Most people would agree that the first responsibility of any chancellor is to manage the economy so as to produce the best possible combination of high growth and low inflation. A Labour chancellor has the further duty – to maximise social welfare by producing a fairer distribution of the nation's wealth. Both these responsibilities were particularly daunting in my time. My predecessor left me an economy on the brink of catastrophe; my task was continually obstructed by events outside Britain over which I had no control. Moreover, the trade unions' unwillingness to limit their wage increases to what the nation could afford not only damaged the prospect of combining growth with low inflation, but also took the distribution of the nation's wealth out of my hands. Added to this were all the uncertainties about economic behaviour which I have already described. It sometimes seemed as if the phrase 'economic management' might be a contradiction in terms – an oxymoron like the 'crisis management' I had been supposed to master as Defence Secretary.

In 1970 Tony Barber had inherited from Roy Jenkins an economy in better shape than any incoming Chancellor since the war; there was no balance of payments problem and no industrial trouble, public spending was under firm control, and the PSBR was in surplus. Four years later the situation I inherited from Barber was described as practically beyond repair, both by the monetarist London Business School and by the Keynesian National Institute of Economic and Social Research. It was like the Augean Stables. The country was racked by the miners' strike. Retail prices were rising at thirteen per cent a year and the money supply at twice that rate. The balance of payments had been in deficit in the second half of 1973 by over £1 billion, and the PSBR was well over £4 billion in that fiscal year. Because Barber had crammed more tax cuts and spending increases into an economy already growing much too fast, growth had come to a halt by the middle of 1973. In the first two months of 1974 output fell sharply because Heath had imposed the three-day week.

Finally, on top of the monetary profligacy of the previous two years, I had to cope with Heath's so-called 'threshold' agreements, which indexed wages monthly to a cost of living which was just beginning to feel the impact of the increase in oil prices; these 'threshold' agreements were triggered six times by the end of July. The first words the Permanent Secretary addressed to Edna were that I was not to be congratulated on my new responsibilities, nor she on having to witness my martyrdom!

Since the tax year was almost at an end, I decided to produce my first budget in three weeks, and to wait until the autumn for any major reforms. Ted Heath congratulated me when I sat down after introducing it in a speech lasting two hours and twenty minutes; he said I had presented 'one of the most complicated and wide-ranging budgets of modern times with clarity and lucidity'. It was received with rapture by the Labour movement as representing the first step in that 'irreversible transfer of wealth and power to working people and their families' which we had promised in the election; the right-wing press attacked it, of course, on the same grounds. However, it attracted little criticism for failing to meet the nation's economic needs. Yet in fact it had three major flaws as an instrument of economic management. One, I believe, was venial in the circumstances of the time. The other two were due to gross forecasting errors by the Treasury.

I had accepted the sensible view of both the IMF and OECD, that the industrial countries should not add to the deflationary impact of the increase in oil prices, by trying to eliminate the resulting deficit on their balance of payments too quickly. Effectively, they were making much the same point as they were to make in 1987, when they advised Western governments to offset the contractionary effect of the stock exchange crash by feeding more money into their economies; the monetary squeeze after the Crash of 1929 had produced the Great Slump of the thirties. In 1974, however, Western governments made a mistake almost as damaging as in 1929, and thus produced an unnecessary recession; they cut their spending heavily so as to reduce their imports. Britain and Italy were alone in following the advice of the international institutions, and in fulfilling the promises made earlier to the IMF; we both kept our spending up. This was a mistake, since my first budget made Britain's balance of payments worse; we exported less than we expected because world trade was shrinking. It is not possible for a country like Britain to grow alone when the rest of the world is contracting.

This error was greatly aggravated by the Treasury's £4 billion under-estimate of the PSBR; thus a Budget I intended to be roughly neutral turned out to be reflationary. Finally, the Treasury grossly overestimated company liquidity, so that the increases I made in corporate taxes brought many companies close to bankruptcy. However, in my November budget that year I introduced tax relief on stock appreciation, which left British companies the most lightly taxed in the developed world; in fact no manufacturing company which re-invested its profits paid any tax at all thereafter. This tax relief was Nicky Kaldor's invention, and his most valuable contribution to my work at the Treasury; it led to a volume increase in manufacturing investment of fourteen per cent a year in both 1977 and 1978 – far more than in most other countries.

In my two 1974 budgets I tried to deal with the inflation caused by the

Heath Government and the increase in oil prices by cutting VAT, introducing rates relief, lending money cheap to the building societies so that they could keep mortgage rates down, and subsidising food and housing. I hoped that in return the trade unions would respond by limiting their wage increases to what was needed to compensate for price increases in the previous year, after taking account of what they had received already through threshold agreements; they had agreed to do this in their so-called Social Contract with the Government. Tony Barber's policies and the oil price increase had raised inflation to seventeen per cent by the time of my second budget in autumn 1974 and would have raised it higher in the following year. But if the unions had kept their promise, inflation would have been back to single figures by autumn 1975.

They did not. When I introduced my third budget in April 1975, I pointed out that the Government had carried out its side of the Social Contract by repealing Heath's anti-union legislation, by starting on the redistribution of wealth and income through its tax changes, and by increasing old-age pensions and other benefits. In fact the value of services provided by the Government, which we tried to get people to see as their 'social wage' amounted to about £1,000 a year for every member of the working population. But the unions defaulted on their part of the contract. Len Murray, the General Secretary of the TUC, had warned me in February that the going rate for wage increases was already thirty per cent, although inflation was still only twenty per cent. Because earnings were rising so much faster than prices, at a time when the increased price of oil and other commodities had cut our real national income by about four per cent, our balance of payments deficit had swollen to £3.8 billion, some five per cent of GDP. By June inflation had risen to twenty-six per cent and basic hourly wage rates were up thirty-two per cent on the year. A more effective policy for controlling wage increases was now an absolute precondition for saving the economy as a whole.

Harold Wilson had told me earlier in the year that he would support me on anything I wanted – except a statutory incomes policy. He was determined not to repeat the humiliating fiasco of Heath's attempt to use legal sanctions against the dockers in 1972. On Monday June 30th he made a somewhat complacent speech at an agricultural show which was seen as rejecting an incomes policy. But in fact he was already drifting in my wake. When I saw him later that day he said he would after all support a statutory pay policy, providing the legal sanctions were directed only against employers who conceded too much, and not against workers who demanded too much. Then I persuaded the relevant ministerial committee to put such a statutory pay policy to the full Cabinet. I immediately warned Len Murray, who took it quite well. Michael Foot, however, the Employment Secretary, threatened to resign.

Next morning, July 1st, I had a big majority in Cabinet; besides the Left, the minority included Jim Callaghan, Eric Varley and Elwyn Jones, with Shirley Williams and Bob Mellish on the fence. I had just enough time to dictate my statement for Parliament over lunch; it said that the Government would not allow the increase in wages, salaries, and dividends to exceed ten per cent in the next pay round, starting in August. We would fix cash limits for pay increases in the public sector, and support the ten per cent limit in the private sector, if necessary by legal sanctions against employers. This would imply an average cut in living standards of 2.5 per cent over the year; but the distribution of the cut would depend on the precise way in which the pay policy was structured.

I spent the next eight days in continual discussions with TUC leaders on the details; most of them were very helpful. I accepted their proposal of a flat £6 a week increase for everyone earning up to £8,500 a year, which was then two and a half time average earnings. Jack Jones said he would do his best to discourage Michael Foot from resigning over legal sanctions. In the end we embodied the sanctions as reserve powers in the legislation. Michael did not resign. On the contrary, he became an indispensable supporter in the negotiations with the TUC over pay, which took up so much of my last three years as Chancellor.

Although I sometimes addressed the whole of the TUC General Council, and often talked to its Economic Committee, my detailed negotiations about pay were with the so-called Neddy Six, of whom by far the most important were Len Murray and the 'terrible twins' – Jack Jones of the Transport and General Workers' Union, and Hugh Scanlon, of the Amalgamated Engineering Union, representing the biggest groups of unskilled and skilled workers respectively. All three were determined to make the pay policy work, and equally determined, as professional negotiators, to get the best deal possible from the Government.

I had known Len Murray for many years; he had been working at Transport House in the TUC Economic Department while I had been there as the Labour Party's International Secretary. This period had given us both a certain scepticism about the infallibility of our masters. We had much else in common. We were both grammar school boys – he from rural Shropshire, I from industrial Yorkshire. Len, like

me, and many leading trade unionists at the time, had spent a few years
in the Communist Party as a young man. After his war service in the
army he had got a degree at Oxford. Quiet in style, cautious in temperament, and somewhat lugubrious in manner, he was an active and practising Christian; yet he was also capable of very rough language on occasion.
But he was essentially an intellectual civil servant, while Jack and Hugh
had battled their way up to the top of their unions from the shop-floor.

Jack Jones had great self-confidence, and a hot temper; his second
name was Larkin, after the Irish revolutionary trade unionist. He had
been a docker and engineer in Liverpool before the war, and had fought
with the International Brigade in Spain. During and after the war he
worked in the Midlands, and came to know the motor car industry
particularly well. He was essentially a product of the shop-stewards'
revolt against the traditional national leadership of the trade unions; yet
though, in a sense, he represented the rejection of much which Ernest
Bevin had stood for as the creator of his union, he was one of the few
union leaders I have met who shared something of Bevin's political
vision. He devoted his retirement to campaigning for old-age pensioners.
Hugh Scanlon was the cleverest negotiator of the three, and to me the
most human. He had a wiry figure with a bird-like head and an
expression of cynical good humour. His hobbies were golf and gardening;
but unlike me he could never get his goldfish to breed – this was a source
of continual banter between us. He had been an instrument-maker in
Manchester and was also a product of the shop-stewards' movement. I
led the Government side in our talks, with support from Michael Foot as
Leader of the House and 'prisoner's friend' for the unions, Albert Booth,
who had just succeeded him as Employment Secretary, Eric Varley as
Secretary for Industry, and Shirley Williams as Secretary for Prices and
Consumer Protection. Shirley's role was particularly important, since the
unions insisted that we should keep prices as low as possible in return for
their pay restraint, and our main sanction against breaches of the pay
code was to refuse price increases to the offending firm.

We normally met for dinner in the exquisite eighteenth-century Soane
Room at No. 11 Downing Street. Instead of the traditional beer and
sandwiches I provided good food and drink. Hugh Scanlon usually
insisted that the fish should be '*goujons de sole*'.

My hospitality was well worth it. In its first year the pay policy was a
resounding success. The rate of inflation was halved, from 26.9 per cent
in August 1975 to 12.9 per cent in July 1976. The flat increase of £6 a
week was easy to administer, and gave low-paid workers more than they

could ever have expected to negotiate in free collective bargaining. This did not prevent Alan Fisher as head of the public employees union from violently opposing the policy, although he represented the lowest-paid in local government and the health service. However, it was obvious that the second round of pay policy would have to make some allowance for restoring the differentials for superior skills, which had been compressed in the first round.

In my 1976 Budget Speech I told the TUC that if they accepted a pay package which would halve inflation again by the end of 1977, but only if they did, I would raise tax allowances so as to increase take-home pay still further, without adding to industrial costs and thus to prices. They were stunned by being made formally responsible for the level of income tax in this way, although they could not dispute that the economic facts of life saddled them with this responsibility in practice, whatever the Government might say. The negotiations which followed were extremely difficult. At our first meeting the TUC representatives actually refused to say a word for several minutes – which seemed an eternity to me. We had a month of long and exhausting meetings, including four in the last week; I had continually to threaten the withdrawal of my promised tax cuts. We finally reached agreement that the limit would be five per cent for those earning between £50 and £80 a week, £4 for those earning more, and £2.50 for those earning less – representing an average increase of 4.5 per cent.

Michael Foot sent me a typically generous letter of congratulations, which, for once, I shall untypically quote. He described the settlement as 'a herculean feat on your part, a sustained piece of intellectual argument with people who are born arguers themselves ... Only those who actually saw it,' he wrote, 'can have the remotest idea of what it involved and what combined persistence and intelligence were required to secure it. Quite possibly it has changed the whole prospect for the country and the Government; at least it has given us the chance to survive. And the achievement was overwhelmingly yours.' Jim Callaghan, now Prime Minister, sent me an equally flattering letter. Yet both had initially had the deepest misgivings about embarking on the pay policy at all.

The second round of pay policy, however, was not quite so successful as the first. When we approached the third round in 1977, the TUC was unable to promise more than that no union would seek more than one increase within twelve months. I made it clear that I wanted to limit the increase in earnings to ten per cent, implying settlements at seven or eight per cent. The sanctions against offending employers remained in place, and the Government remained involved in all major settlements. In January 1978 inflation was below ten per cent for the first time since October 1973. It had fallen to eight per cent by midsummer. In the meantime I had had to cope with Heath's threshold agreements, the rise in oil and commodity prices, and the runaway wage increases of my first year, which had brought inflation to peak at 26.9 per cent.

This achievement was due above all to our pay policy. But our success in the third round, when we had only minimal support from the TUC, blinded us to the growing anomalies which it had created, and to the groundswell of opposition from the shop-floor. Some of the productivity agreements we were asked to sanction, so as to justify pay increases above the norm, were bizarre in the extreme. I recall an attempt by Fleet Street to define a newspaper's productivity as the percentage of editorial matter compared with the amount of advertising! In summer 1978 Jack Jones, then retiring as General Secretary of the TGWU, was howled down at his own union conference when he asked for wage restraint. This spectacle led his successor, Moss Evans, to decide that discretion would always be the better point of valour; he was in any case much less concerned than Jack to help the Labour Government. I was warned during a visit to Leeds by his union's regional officer, one of the wisest and most upright men I have known, that it would be simply impossible to operate a national incomes policy for another year.

We were blind to these warnings – I as much as any member of the Cabinet, except perhaps the Prime Minister. Jim had become obsessed by inflation; he would have preferred a zero norm, and actually proposed three per cent at one meeting. He told me privately he was so disenchanted with the behaviour of the unions that he was contemplating legislation to control them. Only half in jest, I said that in that case I would 'do a Callaghan' on him; my reference to his role during the arguments over Barbara Castle's proposals, *In Place of Strife*, was not lost.

The Cabinet finally settled for a pay norm of five per cent. It was typical of the hubris which can overcome a successful government towards the end of its term. If we had agreed on a formula such as 'single figures' we would probably have achieved an earnings increase much smaller than we got; and we would certainly have been able to avoid the 'winter of discontent' which lost us the general election in 1979. Political history is full of cases where governments become 'dizzy with success', in Lenin's phrase, and 'overload the circuit', to quote Al Haig; hubris knows no frontiers of time or space – or party, as Mrs Thatcher was to demonstrate.

Despite its ultimate failure, our pay policy made an essential contribution to Britain's economic survival in the seventies. Whatever governments may claim, none can avoid having some sort of pay policy, if only because they themselves employ millions of men and women. They are bound to face industrial troubles if they pay their employees significantly less than people doing similar jobs can get in the private sector; the next Conservative Government was to learn this lesson, above all in the National Health Service. So controlling pay in the private sector is the real problem. Without union cooperation any government will be compelled to find some way of disciplining the employers. We sought to do so through controlling their prices, and by refusing them government contracts. Mrs Thatcher used more indiscriminate weapons – high unemployment to discipline the workers, a high exchange rate and high interest rates to discipline the employers; none of them had a chance of cutting the pay increases firms were prepared to offer when they were enjoying exceptionally high profits. Her draconian curbs on union freedoms have been no more effective in curbing excessive pay.

In Britain it is difficult to operate a pay policy even with the cooperation of the union leaders. For the real power lies not in the union headquarters but with the local shop-stewards, who tend to see a rational incomes policy as robbing them of their functions. Moreover, the TUC has no real power over its constituent unions, unlike its equivalents in Scandinavia, Germany and Austria; in those countries governments have normally been able to rely on the annual agreements made at national level between centralised organisations of unions and employers, without direct government intervention. This is even more true of Japan, where the recognised need for a national consensus on all major economic issues has made possible forty years of high growth, full employment, rapidly rising living standards and exceptionally low inflation.

No one in the world knows better than I the difficulties and disadvantages of trying to run an incomes policy. I spent the best part of six months each year trying to negotiate a viable policy for the next pay round, not only with the leaders of the TUC, but also with the CBI For the whole twelve months of each year I spent up to twelve hours a week as Chairman of the Cabinet committee on pay, examining the smallest details of the individual negotiations in progress at the time.

It is fair to say that in this area of my work I spent two-thirds of my time dealing with the disastrous consequences of free collective bargaining, and the other third dealing with the distortions and anomalies caused by my own pay policy. Adopting a pay policy is rather like jumping out of a second-floor window: no one in his senses would do it unless the stairs were on fire. But in postwar Britain the stairs have always been on fire.

In the United States, the combination of weak trade unions and a continuing flow of poor immigrants with a wide variety of skills reduces the pressure for excessive pay increases; I suspect that the inexhaustible supply of cheap consumer credit has also helped. Yet Arthur Okun was wise to remark: 'P. T. Barnum once noted that keeping a lamb in a cage with a lion requires a large reserve supply of lambs. Similarly, society may need a large reserve supply of incomes policies.' In that case, it will need a reserve supply of chancellors of the exchequer, too.

However, once the pay policy was in place in 1975, my overriding concern was to restore a healthy financial balance both at home and abroad. It had become customary among Keynesians – who had usually read no more of Keynes than most Marxists had read of Marx – to claim that there was no need to worry about a fiscal deficit when the economy was working below capacity, nor about a deficit on the current balance of payments when foreign capital was pouring into Britain. In 1975 unemployment was rising, and the Arab countries were parking their surplus oil revenues in British banks for the time being. So in theory there was no harm in running substantial deficits both at home and abroad.

However, the trouble with deficits is that they have to be financed by borrowing; and in the negotiation for a loan it is the lender who decides the interest rate and sets the conditions. It was obvious that before long the Arab countries would start diversifying their surpluses more widely round the world; and in any case their surpluses would shrink as their own development plans got under way. If we were not to become dependent on borrowing from other foreigners and from the IMF, we must try to eliminate our current account deficit within a few years. And we would be unable to reduce our external deficit if our internal fiscal deficit was still growing.

So I decided to reduce the PSBR by raising taxes and cutting public spending, so that firms would be compelled to export what they could not sell at home. It was a Herculean task. The enormous interest payments Britain had incurred by borrowing to finance its twin deficits since the Barber boom started in 1971, meant that we had to run very fast even to stand still. Yet we managed to complete the most important part of our task in just three years. In fact the latest statistics show that we had eliminated our balance of payments deficit in 1977. By the middle of

1978 our GDP was growing over three per cent a year, as against a fall of one per cent in 1975/6. Unemployment, which rose very fast in my first three years, had been falling for nine months; and inflation was below eight per cent. It was one of the few periods in postwar British history in which unemployment and inflation were both falling at the same time.

All this was achieved at a time when we were getting little benefit from North Sea oil. The capital investment required made it a net drain on our balance of payments in my early years. Even in 1978, North Sea oil was making good only half the impact of the OPEC price increase on our balance of payments, and was not yet producing any revenue for the Government.

Politically, by far the most difficult part of my ordeal was the continual reduction of public spending; almost all of the spending cuts ran against the Labour Party's principles, and many also ran against our campaign promises. Here again, my task was complicated by the Treasury's inability either to know exactly what was happening, or to control it. In November 1975 Wynne Godley, who had himself served in the Treasury as an economist, showed that public spending in 1974/5 was some £5 billion higher in real terms than had been planned by Barber in 1971. This was one of the reasons why I decided to fix cash limits on spending as well as pay, since departments tended to use inflation as a cover for increasing their spending in real terms. Cash limits worked all too well in holding spending down. Departments were so frightened of exceeding their limits that they tended to underspend, sometimes dramatically so. In 1976/7 public spending was £2.2 billion less than planned.

Consistent in its sado-masochism, the Treasury chose the most unfavourable definition of public spending, as it did of the fiscal deficit. I changed both before I left. The White Paper on public spending in February 1976 stated: 'The ratio of total public expenditure to GDP at factor cost has grown from 50 per cent in 1971/2 to about 60 per cent in 1975/6'. If true, Wynne Godley must have grossly underestimated the Treasury's incompetence. But it was unforgiveably misleading. Later that year, when we defined public spending in the same way as did other countries, our spending was reduced by some £7.7 billion at a stroke. And when we also costed GDP, like public spending, at market prices, the ratio of public spending to GDP fell from sixty per cent to forty-six per cent. By 1978/9 my successive cuts had brought it down to about forty-two per cent – about the same as West Germany but far below Scandinavia and the Netherlands.

This long overdue redefinition of public spending along the lines used by OECD was largely the work of Leo Pliatzky, who also made other valuable improvements in the presentation of our public accounts. I could find it in me to forgive the Treasury for the inaccuracy of its forecasts, since none of the outside organisations did any better. But I cannot forgive it, or those politicians who preceded me as Chancellor, for misleading the Government, the country and the world for so many years about the true state of public spending in Britain. Indeed I suspect that Treasury officials were content to overstate public spending in order to put pressure on governments which were reluctant to cut it. Government departments are liable to present the facts so as to favour their institutional interests in the Whitehall jungle, as I had found as Defence Secretary.

On the revenue side of the equation I was mainly concerned to make the tax system fairer. I closed some tax loopholes, increased income tax on the rich, and introduced a higher rate of VAT on less necessary goods; whenever I could afford to, I concentrated tax cuts on the poor by raising tax thresholds. In 1978 I introduced a lower rate band for the poorest tax payers. The only way of helping those who were too poor to pay income tax was by increasing their benefits. I can fairly claim that I personally suffered more than most taxpayers by these changes. Those of my colleagues who, like me, lived in Government residences, were not pleased when I taxed them for the privilege. As a result of my tax changes and my determination to prevent ministerial salaries from rising as fast as the pay norm, my own real take-home pay as Chancellor fell to only half what I had been earning as Defence Secretary, although I was working harder and longer.

There will always be controversy about taxation, and, since it directly affects the interests of every individual, the argument is unlikely to be very objective. My own experience as Chancellor led me to certain general conclusions which I am still ready to modify in the light of new evidence. First, it is impossible to combine elegance with equity in any tax system which tries to accommodate the wide variety of need and circumstance in any population. Second, any substantial attempt to improve the lot of the poorest section of the population must now be at the expense of the average man and woman, since the very rich do not collectively earn enough to make much difference, and the average man does not nowadays want to punish those who earn a little more than he, since he hopes ultimately to join them.

Third, in a prosperous society the balance between direct and indirect taxation is likely to continue shifting towards indirect taxation, providing that the most essential goods, like food and clothing, are not taxed. But in any given year the Chancellor will have to consider whether the effect of increasing indirect taxation will have a continuing inflationary effect. I still believe I was right in my first budget to cut the basic rate of VAT, since we then had no incomes policy, and any increase in the cost of living would have been reflected in wage increases, and more price increases, and so on. Geoffrey Howe's biggest mistake in this area was to double the rate of VAT in his first budget in the mistaken belief it would produce only a once-for-all increase in the cost of living; in fact it produced a chain reaction on pay and prices which lasted many years, doubling the rate of inflation in the first twelve months. It was not until 1977, when our pay policy had been working for two years, that I felt it safe to finance a cut of £2 billion in income tax by increases in indirect taxes. And then the Liberals, on whom we now depended for our majority in Parliament, compelled us to drop our planned increase in the tax on petrol – which was desirable in any case to save energy.

In 1978, on the other hand, the Liberals took the opposite line. They were not satisfied with a further cut of £2 billion in income tax, and insisted on more, demanding increases in indirect taxation to pay for it. So they sabotaged the budget by voting with the Tories to cut one penny off the basic rate of tax, though by that time we were linked by a formal pact in Parliament. It was never easy working with the Liberals, since David Steel was unable to control his tiny flock. I found it particularly difficult working with their economic spokesman, John Pardoe; he was robust and intelligent enough, but sometimes I felt he was simply Denis Healey with no redeeming features. More than once Joel Barnett had to pick up the pieces after we had sent the crockery flying.

Every special interest group in the country would make a point of lobbying the Treasury before each budget. I rarely bothered to meet these lobbies myself, unless I had some personal interest in the subject or the people concerned. It was a pleasure to be able to assure Peggy Ashcroft, Margot Fonteyn, Dorothy Tutin, and Danny la Rue that I had no intention of putting VAT on theatre tickets, and to give similar assurances to a sports lobby led by Colin Cowdrey, Mary Peters and Charlie Magri. When I agreed to meet a lobby from the College of Heralds I was surprised to find it led by my old friend Miles Fitzalan Howard, now the Duke of Norfolk; in this case I gave nothing away.

Wrestling with tax problems taught me several lessons. First, the frictional cost of any fundamental change in taxation may often outweigh the benefit to the economy. However bad an existing tax, those affected will adapt their behaviour to it in myriads of ways of which no government is aware until the change takes place; then the chancellor may have to amend the tax so widely that it emerges from the process as a different animal. I replaced the Estate Duty, which had become a laughing stock, since no one who could afford an accountant ever paid it, with a Capital Transfer Tax which covered gifts made before death as well. From the start I excluded money inherited by a man's widow from the tax. This piece of natural justice was long overdue; I still meet people who thank me for it. But in the end, I had to accept so many other special cases for exclusion that when I left office four years later, the CTT was still raising less revenue than the avoidable Estate Duty it replaced.

Another lesson was that you should never commit yourself in Opposition to new taxes unless you have a very good idea how they will operate in practice. We had committed ourselves to a Wealth Tax; but in five years I found it impossible to draft one which would yield enough revenue to be worth the administrative cost and political hassle. I suspect the Conservative Party is even more unhappy that Mrs Thatcher promised to abolish the rates without having the slightest idea what to put in their place.

I also learned to distrust confident assertions about the effect of taxation on the incentive to work. In my experience most people set themselves a target living standard for their family early in their married life; if they have to pay more tax, they will simply work harder to reach their target. On the other hand, once a man has achieved a living standard which satisfies him, he is as likely to exploit a cut in taxation by taking more leisure as by working harder. There are of course exceptions to this, as to any other generalisation about human behaviour; but it is relevant that Sweden and Japan both have far higher income taxes than Britain, and both have a far superior economic performance.

Even before I entered the Treasury, I had felt that Britain's poor industrial performance was the root cause of our economic troubles. Once there, I set up a small industrial unit to work on the problem. Though Britain led the world for a century after the Industrial Revolution, our growth rate went into decline from about 1860 to 1937, averaging only 1.1 per cent a year during the last quarter century of that period. By comparison with our dismal record between the wars, we had quite a respectable growth rate of about 2.5 per cent after the war, until the Barber boom brought the economy to a halt in 1973. But we were still doing badly compared with our main competitors in Europe and Japan.

I soon realised that, contrary to the views of right-wing economists, Britain's poor record was not due to excessive public spending, high taxation, the trade unions, or the welfare state; a glance at the figures I have quoted makes this clear. It was due to inadequate investment, leading to low productivity, and an innate conservatism which made us reluctant to move out of declining industries or to adopt new techniques of production. Another factor affected the United States no less than Britain, though America rested on a higher plateau because it had a far better record up to about 1950; both countries have a financial system which discourages long-term borrowing from the banks, and often makes it more profitable to invest abroad than in Britain.

Under the first Wilson Governments, we tried to improve our industrial performance through George Brown's National Plan. This failed because it was organised from Whitehall downwards, and we had no clear idea how to deal with the weaknesses in particular industries which frustrated the Government's plans. In 1974, like many of my colleagues, I was at first attracted by the French example. France since 1950 had achieved a growth rate double that of Britain by using the state to stimulate the necessary changes; it operated mainly through indicative planning of investment in the major industries, and also the centralisation of credit control.

However, France had a tradition of state control, or *dirigisme*, which went back to Louis XIV and Colbert. More important, postwar French governments had built on the prewar *Grandes Ecoles* to establish a National School of Administration (ENA); this provided their senior civil servants with management and administrative training far superior to anything available in Britain, where the job of a civil servant was still seen essentially as to advise his minister on policy. The omnicompetence of these so-called 'Enarchs' was legendary. My friend Felix Baumgartner, for example, moved without difficulty from being Governor of the Central Bank to Finance Minister to head of the great chemical company, Rhone Poulenc, without abandoning his wide range of cultural interests, which included a close friendship with Sophia Loren and her husband, the film producer Carlo Ponti. Since de Gaulle, the 'Enarchs' have also provided many of the political leaders in all parties. I have always regretted that I did not take advantage of the report of the Fulton Commission to press for similar training of British civil servants; but as Defence Secretary I had more urgent problems at the time. In fact, however, much of the success of the French National Plans was due to a once-for-all shift of the rural population into industry. After 1970 growth in France fell well short of planned targets; in the 1980s it was down to British levels and even below.

Inside the Treasury, many of my advisers believed that the key to France's postwar performance lay in her deliberate policy of keeping the franc undervalued. I did not believe that such a policy would suit Britain in the seventies. Undervaluation may have had advantages in the world of fixed exchange rates; but since the collapse of Bretton Woods allowed currencies to float, one depreciation may well be followed by another before the commercial advantage of the first is felt – in other words, what economists call the J-Curve becomes a W-Curve slanting downwards. It is notable that, although the value of sterling has fallen many times since 1966, Britain's share of world trade in manufactures has fallen with it.

Japan, on the other hand, has treated the rise in the yen as a spur to industrial innovation; so it has difficulty in reducing its share of world trade however high the yen may soar. Quality and reliability are nowadays as important as price in determining competitivity. In any case, in Britain the trade unions ensure that the inflation caused by devaluation is reflected in subsequent wage increases, which often wipe out any temporary gains in price competitivity.

I therefore concluded that the key to Britain's industrial performance lay in the efficiency of individual firms. The scope for Government intervention here was limited, since so much of our industrial output depended on small firms. Moreover, the large firms were often vulnerable to industrial action by a trade union movement which was at once stronger and more fragmented than elsewhere, and increasingly in the hands of local shop-stewards. However, the central problem lay with management. I noticed that foreign managers were often more successful in Britain than British managers in the same industry, while British managers were often more successful abroad than in Britain. This I attributed, as did many of my foreign friends, such as Helmut Schmidt, to the uniquely persistent class divisions in British society; they made confrontation rather than cooperation the natural relationship between management and the shop-floor, and were deeply rooted in many aspects of our culture, particularly in our educational system.

However, the failure of British industry to spend enough on research and development, its lackadaisical attitude towards identifying potential markets and in selling to them, had deeper roots. The existence of a captive market in the Commonwealth and Empire was one. I had been constantly depressed on my journeys to the former colonies, to find the Italians, Germans and Japanese far more active in marketing their goods than the British. More important still, the amateur tradition made production engineers very rare on the boards of British firms compared with their competitors; far too many companies still regard industrial training as the first thing to be cut when times are hard. Our studies showed that while many British firms were more efficient than the world average, and about twenty per cent were at least as good, three quarters of British firms, operating in the same environment, were less efficient than their international competitors.

I suspect that all these weaknesses in Britain's economic performance derive from the same historical fact as explains the unique stability of British society. Britain has not had to endure enemy occupation for nearly a thousand years, and has not known revolution or civil war for almost three hundred. Our national psychology rejects radical change. Our devotion to individual freedom limits our readiness to give central government the power to override our traditional power structures – except when our society as a whole is threatened by a foreign state. For this reason our Labour movement is the most conservative in the world, to the despair of Continental Socialists from Marx and Engels, through Lenin and Trotsky, to Mitterrand and Schmidt. Barbara Castle records Jack Jones telling the Labour Cabinet during the arguments over *In Place of Strife*: 'Let us face the reality. The question isn't whether our scheme works or your scheme works. It is the fact that our people won't accept government intervention.'

So there was no scope for any industrial policy which was not based on cooperation by consent between the Government and both sides of industry. By the end of 1975 I had begun to discuss an Industrial Strategy for Britain with the employers, trade unionists, and Ministers on NEDC. The word, however, was a misnomer; it was not a strategy but a methodology, based on forty tripartite working parties which covered just under half of the various sectors of manufacturing industry. Their main purpose was to ensure that the practices of the most efficient firms in each sector were followed by the rest. These Sector Working Parties were beginning to show results before I left; then the whole experiment was swept away by Mrs Thatcher. However, for most of the time my only tool for securing better industrial performance was public spending, which proved to be a very blunt instrument indeed.

In the first of its many U-turns, in 1971, the Heath Government had spent large sums of money rescuing Rolls-Royce and Upper Clyde Shipyards. By 1979 Conservative and Labour Governments had spent nearly £10 billion on such subsidies to private industry. Germany and France had been spending about the same. But far too much of Britain's aid was spent on inefficient firms in declining industries, particularly in areas of high unemployment; Germany and France spent most of theirs on firms with a promising future, in a market which had been carefully researched. We spent as much as many of our competitors on assisting research and development in private firms. But seventy per cent went to defence-related industries with a comparatively small commercial spin-off, while our competitors concentrated on areas of R and D which would have a direct impact on the efficiency and trade of their civil industry.

Our worst cases were inevitably in the motor car industry. Harold Wilson joined Benn in overriding the Treasury and rescuing the Chrysler company in Britain, only to see it taken over by Peugeot a few years later. We hived off British Leyland into the ownership of the new National Enterprise Board; this proved no more successful. On all matters concerning the motor car industry, the employers and unions made common cause against the Government. I had to go easy on the taxation of large company cars, because the British industry was kept afloat mainly by this enormous captive market. I had to forego saving energy by taxing diesel much less heavily than petrol, because the British industry did not produce enough diesel-fuelled cars. Worst of all, I had to abandon my plan to abolish the unpopular and widely avoided Vehicle Excise Duty; I proposed to recover the lost revenue by increasing the price of petrol, thus penalising people with large and expensive cars. The industry told me this would lead to a flood of imported small cars, since we did not produce enough small cars in Britain. Yet my sacrifices to the motor car industry were poorly rewarded. In August 1977, for example, we had negotiated a 'voluntary' agreement with the Japanese car industry to restrict its imports to Britain; yet bad management and industrial trouble prevented more than a handful of Rovers leaving the assembly line to take advantage of the opportunity.

Concorde was another disaster for economic common sense. The cost of the aircraft had escalated enormously since we had tried to abort it back in 1964. If we continued the project, there was no chance of recovering in sales or traffic even the money still to be spent; indeed BOAC did not think it could fly except at a loss, even if the whole capital cost was written off. As in 1964, the French Government was slowly moving towards the same conclusion. On the other hand, considerations of national prestige influenced both governments. Once again I did my best to persuade my colleagues to grit their teeth and cancel the project. I was frustrated, as was my colleague in the French Treasury, by the extraordinary coincidence that Tony Benn was not only the minister responsible for Concorde, but also the Member of

Parliament for Bristol, while the French minister responsible was the Deputy for Toulouse. Concorde was built in Bristol and Toulouse.

So in the end Concorde went ahead, to play its part in destroying the ozone layer and undermining government finances in both France and Britain. It is without doubt an impressive technological achievement, and of great convenience to businessmen and officials. But it is significant that no other country has bought it, or has tried to produce its own supersonic transport aircraft. Even Britain and France, after writing off the £1,000 million they had spent on developing Concorde, produced only seven aircraft each as against the hundred and fifty originally planned; each aircraft cost ten times the original estimate.

It is ironic that Tony Benn's ministerial career should have left only two monuments behind – the uranium mine in Namibia he authorised as Energy Secretary, which helps to support Apartheid and is in territory illegally occupied by South Africa, and an aircraft which is used by wealthy people on their expense accounts, whose fares are subsidised by much poorer taxpayers. When he left office the only Planning Agreement which existed was one established years before he entered Parliament – the annual Farm Price Review, chaired in my time by the Duke of Northumberland.

Our work in NEDC led us to give much greater weight to the impact on industry of our other policies. Shirley Williams, when she became Secretary for Education, began to shift the curriculum in our schools towards the needs of industry. Peter Shore, as Environment Secretary, started reducing some of the planning controls which inhibited and delayed new investment. I myself as Chancellor provided extra money for training schemes, aimed at reducing shortages of skilled manpower. We improved the range of government facilities for export finance, and supported sixteen special schemes to encourage investment in particular sectors, such as the technology of the silicon chip. We exercised eternal vigilance to make sure that new laws or regulations, which were attractive for other reasons, did not inflict unnecessary handicaps on industry. In a world growing more and more uncertain, industry's paramount demand of government was for the greatest possible stability in its fiscal environment. More than once I abandoned tax changes, such as a shift from the imputation system for corporation tax, which, though desirable in principle, would have imposed a damaging frictional cost on industry.

Sometimes, however, government action which is deeply resented by business may contribute towards improving its performance in unexpected ways. I believe, for example, that, by limiting the profit margin on domestic sales in order to control prices, I helped to persuade British companies to seek markets overseas where there was no limit on their profits. This was a vital factor in eliminating our balance of payments deficit.

All this helped, and would have helped much more, given more time. But I do not believe it would have been enough on its own to make British industry fully competitive in the late eighties and nineties, when our firms increasingly face the challenge, not just of foreign firms, but of foreign industrial strategies. Above all, it would not have enabled us to meet the challenge from a Japan in which government, finance and both sides of industry work together to fulfil a coherent long-term strategy. The careful cultivation of consensus between all the groups which make up their economy has enabled the Japanese to adapt their behaviour collectively to any external shock; so they have survived in turn the increase in oil prices, the soaring value of the yen, and the ferocious competition from the newly industrialised economies of their Asian neighbours.

Britain's economy too, was continually buffeted by shocks from the outside world, which were felt most severely by our financial system. They produced lurches in our exchange rate of a size and frequency which would have been inconceivable before the seventies. So I was increasingly preoccupied with trying to stabilise the pound within a more stable financial system in the world as a whole.

CHAPTER TWENTY

Stabilising World Markets

The mosquito knows full well, small as he is
he's a beast of prey.
But after all
he only takes his bellyful,
he doesn't put my blood in the bank.

– 'The Mosquito Knows –' D. H. Lawrence

BECAUSE BRITAIN DEPENDS so much on world trade, we have always been more vulnerable to external events than most other Western countries. A change in the value of sterling is reflected in our inflation rate almost immediately, because it changes the price of our imports; at least in the short run it has a double effect on our balance of payments, because it also changes the price we get for our exports. As I have said, the first OPEC increase in the oil price added £2.5 billion to the current account deficit of £1 billion I inherited from the Heath Government. Successive falls in the value of the pound made it more difficult to eliminate that deficit. In the circumstances we did well to eliminate our deficit altogether over three years, and to increase our visible exports from seventy-five per cent of our imports in 1974 to ninety-six per cent in 1978.

In 1974 sterling was still the world's second reserve currency, after the dollar; so changes of sentiment in the foreign exchange markets were often greatly exaggerated by the movement of reserves into or out of Britain. Britain had also been making an exceptionally high contribution to the defence of the Western world, in ways which imposed a heavy strain on her resources of skilled manpower and of foreign exchange. By comparison, Germany did not begin defence spending until well into the 1950s, and has always spent a much smaller proportion of its national income on defence; unlike Britain, it also derives great foreign exchange benefits from membership of NATO, because so many allied troops are stationed on its soil, while no German forces are stationed abroad. We calculated that the size of Germany's reserves in 1978 was almost exactly equal to Germany's net gain in foreign exchange since 1959, from the stationing of British and American troops on its territory. The cost of Britain's defence effort in foreign exchange alone amounted to £1 billion a year. In 1977 Germany was spending 3.1 per cent of its GDP on defence and 11.5 per cent on social security; Britain was spending 4.9 per cent on defence and only 8.9 per cent on social security.

In addition to this unequal defence burden, the Common Agricultural Policy of the European Community imposed an even more disproportionate burden on Britain; in 1979 we were the largest single contributor to the Community Budget, although seventh out of nine in per capita income. Finally, Britain was spending fifty per cent more of her GDP on foreign aid than Germany, and nearly twice as much as the United States and Japan. Much of the foreign exchange benefit the Labour Government ultimately got from North Sea oil was wiped out by all these expenditures abroad.

It would have been impossible for Britain to adjust to all the changes in the world economy during my period as Chancellor without the new international currency regime of floating exchange rates. The rest of the world found floating no less indispensable, if only because the impact of the oil price on inflation and the balance of payments differed so much from country to country. But floating brought the world a new set of problems, which grew steadily more intractable as the increasing globalisation of the financial markets made exchange rates ever more volatile.

In 1974 the Treasury, like most economists, believed that exchange rates were mainly determined by a country's rate of inflation and balance of payments relative to those of other countries. By the time I left office they were determined by the faceless men who managed the growing atomic cloud of footloose funds, which had accumulated in the Euromarkets to evade control by national governments. These money managers were at first mainly influenced by interest rates, which determined the income they could gain by putting their funds in one currency rather than another. They were also influenced by their expectation of whether a currency would move up or down, thus bringing them a capital gain or loss; however, their expectations about currency movements depended largely on the economic fashions of the time, which were largely monetarist in the later seventies. Since the markets moved money around in accordance with their prejudices, their expectations were largely self-fulfilling. Capital movements thus became by far the most important single influence on exchange rates, and seemed to defy all the earlier laws of economics; thus there was a period in which the dollar was continually moving up, while America's inflation was growing and its balance of payments was deteriorating. None of this was foreseen either by Keynes or by the monetarists.

The number, size, and speed of these capital movements increased as the new information technology produced a single global capital market open twenty-four hours a day. By 1988 the amount of money crossing the exchanges in search of short-term speculative profit was up to fifty times more than what was needed to finance the whole of world trade, in both goods and services. This again was totally unforeseen by all economists. I shall deal later with some of the consequences of the recent financial revolution, of which globalisation was only one part. In my time as Chancellor the revolution was already under way, and I was immediately concerned with some of its consequences. No previous Chancellor had faced such problems.

From the moment I entered the Treasury, I found myself more and more involved with the impact of floating on the value of the pound, and with the search for greater stability in the international financial system. In October 1976 the strain of dealing with these problems was almost too much for me.

However, my postwar experience of international politics, and the friendships I had made on both sides of the Atlantic, proved immensely valuable in this part of my work. My official advisers on world finance, both from the Treasury and the Bank of England, had few contacts abroad except among the exclusive mafia of officials who dealt with these problems in other finance ministries and central banks; this financial mafia sometimes reminded me in its intellectual arrogance and isolation of the mafia of nuclear strategists I had known as Defence Secretary. Their institutional responsibilities often made them insensitive not only to the political implications of their proposals, but also to many of the economic implications which concerned other parts of the government machine, including the Treasury itself. They seemed to have no ears except for the music of the financial markets. I often echoed the prayer of Winston

Churchill when he was Chancellor of the Exchequer: 'I would wish to see finance less proud and industry more content'.

During the years of crisis, my main Treasury adviser on international finance was Derek Mitchell, who had been Harold Wilson's Principal Private Secretary before 1970. He was a small man with a face of mobile white marble, a Greek in the Whitehall Empire. His cynicism about all politicians was spiced with a nice sense of humour: he insisted on pronouncing the name of my Japanese colleague, Fukuda, in a way which would justify describing him as 'the Welsh voluptuary'. At the Bank of England Kit McMahon was the international specialist; he was the sort of insubordinate intellectual I find most agreeable. Douglas Wass and Gordon Richardson were, of course, always at hand on the more important occasions.

The Treasury in general was surprisingly ignorant of the broader diplomatic context in which all these issues had to be resolved. On one occasion they asked me to see the German Ambassador at short notice. I agreed, since Karl-Günther von Hase was a close friend, who had introduced me into the Order Against Political Pomposity in Aachen several years earlier. When the door to my sanctum opened, it was the East German Ambassador who walked in; my staff still did not recognise the difference. Fortunately I knew him as well, and tried to disguise my astonishment.

Von Hase was immensely helpful to me as Chancellor in my relations with the Federal Republic. My problems with Washington were eased by the United States Ambassador, Elliot Richardson, with whom I had also worked before, particularly on the MIRV issue; his Minister, Phil Kaiser, had been a close friend since I succeeded him and Ted Heath as Chairman of the Balliol JCR in 1939. My years at the Bilderberg meetings also brought me many contacts in the financial world which now proved of great value. David Rockefeller, whom I had known since the very first Bilderberg meeting at Arnhem, was now head of the Chase Manhattan Bank, and particularly active in the international field; his brother Nelson was for many years Governor of New York State, and had run against Nixon for the Republican nomination in 1968.

On one visit to New York I stayed with Edna at David Rockefeller's house in New York. We were stupefied, on entering the front door, to see on the stairs facing us Picasso's *Young Girl with Flowers*, which had been one of my favourite paintings since I first saw it at Oxford in Gertrude Stein's book on Picasso. Above our bed was a good Vuillard, with a

Lautrec facing it. David told me that when Gertrude Stein died, he and Jock Whitney, another millionaire banker, decided to club together and buy her collection. Then they drew lots to decide who should have which picture, and David got the Picasso. Ah well!

I still managed to get to several Bilderberg meetings as Chancellor. At Mégève in April 1974 I met Helmut Schmidt, who was now once again my colleague, as Germany's Finance Minister. On the drive through the Alps from Geneva he asked me anxiously whether I thought any country could survive the current German inflation rate of 7.5 per cent; since ours was already twice as high, I was able to reassure him. Memories of the Weimar inflation, when people had to shop with prams full of banknotes, were still very much alive in Germany, as they are even today. Bonn will always give priority to reducing inflation rather than increasing growth. Helmut was at that time in one of his depressed moods; he had offered his resignation three weeks earlier to Willy Brandt, seeing him as weak and lazy, always giving in to the militant Young Socialists. His relations with Brandt did not improve; in their case prose and poetry could not live together. Though Helmut later became Chancellor himself when Brandt had to resign over a spy scandal, Brandt stayed on as Party Chairman. In spite of their difficulties with one another, I was later to feel there was something to be said for splitting the role of Prime Minister from that of Party Leader; but we never seriously contemplated it in the Labour Party.

Currencies were then in turmoil and Germany, like Britain and all the other oil-consuming countries, had an enormous balance of payments deficit to be financed. The immediate preoccupation of all Western finance ministers was the role of gold in official reserves. The question was whether the world's central banks should fix a new official price for gold or leave the price to the markets, or whether we should demonetise gold altogether by refusing to count it in the reserves, and try to establish the IMF Special Drawing Right, or SDR, as the main reserve currency. We British were all for demonetisation since the Bank of England had imprudently sold off most of our gold stock several years earlier; as I told my French colleagues, my motto was '*merde à l'or*'. The United States thought their dollar should be the only reserve currency in the world, and saw their gold in Fort Knox as invaluable support for its reserve role. In the Common Market the Germans and Dutch supported us against the French and Italians, who had vulnerable currencies but large gold stocks. In the end the most we could agree on was that central banks should be free to buy and sell gold among themselves, providing they did not increase the total stock of gold in the world's official reserves. Even then we had the utmost difficulty in getting Washington to stick to the agreement.

This introduction to international finance taught me useful lessons. Apart from the regrettable fact that in most situations every country would pursue its narrow national interest rather than seek a common international interest, no change could be made in the structure of world finance without the consent of the United States; and the United States would see no interest but its own, though its view of its interest might differ from person to person, or from administration to administration.

The ultimate forum for all these arguments was the International Monetary Fund, which normally held its annual meeting in late September at its headquarters in Washington. This was a large high building with an enormous inner atrium. It was said that the previous Managing Director, a world-weary Frenchman called Schweitzer, had kept a parrot in the atrium which he trained to say 'SDRs – up your ass'. Its words are still echoing there.

The annual meeting rarely did serious business, apart from ratifying agreements already reached in its committees. It was a great international jamboree, at which bankers, ministers, and financial journalists could gossip and do private deals during a hectic week of partying. Their gossip often produced rumours which created chaos on the foreign exchange markets. The real work of the IMF was done in its committees, of which the more important had no official existence. Their inner core was a group of the five leading finance ministers from the United States, Britain, Germany, France and Japan – the G-5. It met irregularly and in secret in various parts of the world.

Secrecy was difficult to achieve. On one occasion President Carter was giving his weekly press conference with his Secretary of Finance, Mike Blumenthal at his side. Blumenthal had just returned from a secret G-5 meeting in Paris. While the journalists were assembling, the President asked Blumenthal how the G-5 had gone. 'Oh, the French were bloody as usual,' was the reply. Unfortunately the microphones were already switched on. Worse still, their exchange was included in the official transcript of the press conference.

Surrounding the G-5 was a Group of Ten, which brought in the five next most important industrial countries too, and did not attempt secrecy. Resentful at their exclusion, the developing countries set up their own Group of Twenty-Four, to formulate their demands on the wealthy. The only recognised official committee of the IMF was the Interim Committee, which served as a sort of executive body; it is called Interim because agreement has never been reached on a permanent committee structure for the organisation. Parallel with these IMF bodies, the European Community had its own Council of Finance Ministers, which met monthly, and tried to reach agreement on major IMF issues before meetings of the Interim Committee. In addition, the Commonwealth Finance Ministers also held an annual Conference in some Commonwealth country immediately before every annual meeting of the IMF. Thus at the end of September my time was always pre-empted by a series of international meetings – the European Council of Finance Ministers, the Commonwealth Finance Ministers, the G-5, the G-10, the Interim Committee and finally the annual meeting of the IMF itself. My life was not made easier by the fact that the IMF's annual meeting in Washington usually coincided with the annual conference of the Labour Party in Blackpool or Brighton.

At the Commonwealth Finance Ministers' Conference we were always accompanied by our wives, who then came with us to Washington. It was the only occasion on which Edna was allowed to join me. Finance in those days was the last bastion of male chauvinism. Edna had always been able to travel with me all over the world while I was Defence Secretary, and had an RAF Comet at my disposal; so she was able to share something of my ministerial life, and to learn from the wives of our servicemen about the problems faced by their families. When I was Chancellor, she could not even have an official meal with me in London. In the whole five years she joined us at a meal in the Soane dining room at No. 11 Downing Street only three times. When I gave my major annual speech to the City in the Mansion House, she was forbidden to eat with the rest of us, and listened to the speech with the Lady Mayoress of London from a gallery above, like a mediaeval leper listening to a sermon from his squint. Her enforced isolation from the world in which I worked played a large part in her decision to start a new career as a writer, when our children left home.

Nevertheless, my exhausting routine of meetings abroad had some compensations. Art galleries were always a solace – an exquisite exhibition of Terborch at the Mauritshuis in the Hague, the superb Van Gogh Museum in Amsterdam, the Breughels in Brussels, and of course regular visits to the Phillips and National Galleries in Washington. Bob McNamara, now head of the World Bank, took me to see Ravel's *Enfant et les Sortileges* at America's nearest equivalent to Glyndebourne, the Wolf Trap in the wooded hills outside Washington; it was a reward for the help I tried to give him every year in persuading the American Government to contribute towards replenishing the funds for International Development Aid.

The Commonwealth Finance Ministers' Conferences took me and Edna to exotic places we might otherwise never have seen – the dazzling white beaches of Barbados, Dunn's Falls in Jamaica, where cool fresh water fans over a series of mighty boulders on to the sand and sea – the setting for a hundred advertisements – and Montreal in winter, which then became an underground city like a colony on the moon. I was fascinated by Guyana; the capital, Georgetown, had been laid out by the methodical Dutch in neat squares separated by canals, now choked by giant waterlilies. The beautiful parks had large ponds among the palm-trees in which you could see the weird sea creatures called manatees, which sailors used to mistake for mermaids. We tried to fly to the highest waterfalls in the world at Gaietur, but were frustrated by a violent thunderstorm which tossed our rickety biplane among the clouds like a ping-pong ball. As was customary, on the last night the Prime Minister gave us all a great party in the grounds of Government House. After plunging around the lush, dew-dripping lawns in the dark to the sound of steel bands, we were invited to a short trip on a river boat. Edna and I were so tired that we declined – perhaps wisely, since the boat returned at dawn minus two Canadian journalists who had fallen in the water, overcome by Guyanese hospitality.

I found the main value of these conferences of Commonwealth Finance Ministers, as of the IMF annual meetings, in the contacts I made outside the formal sessions – not just with my ministerial colleagues, but also with ordinary men and women wherever we met. They brought me into touch directly with the problems of the developing countries, and gave force to my arguments when I tried to get my Western colleagues to take the Third World more seriously.

At all my international meetings I found that the best business was done over food and drink, with no more than two advisers present for each minister – usually the governor of the central bank and the senior civil servant from the finance ministry. Human relationships played an important role. It was always easier to deal with a colleague I had known for some time, and I tried to create a social momentum over the meal which made it easier to move to constructive decisions. When Raymond Barre was the Prime Minister of France he was also its Finance Minister; so the G-5 often met at his official country residence in the grounds of the Palace of Versailles, a modest villa called 'La Lanterne'. At one meeting there I taught my colleagues to sing a Popular Front version of the French Revolutionary song, '*La Carmagnole*', which I had learnt as a student; the refrain ended with the words: '*Ça ira, ça ira, ça ira, tous les fascistes à la lanterne.*' It went with an appropriate swing. At another meeting I compared our discussion to a jam session, and discovered that almost all of my colleagues had at one time or another played a jazz instrument.

The only exception to my rule that difficult decisions were best taken with food, was the first G-5 dinner over which Mike Blumenthal presided in Washington. Because President Carter was still puritanically opposed to anything which might be regarded as luxurious living, we dined that night in a dark and cavernous room at the top of the State Department building with no central heating; we shivered with cold as the waiters brought in one atrocious course after another. My Treasury adviser said it was the first time he had ever seen me push my plate away uneaten. Mike was new to the job; he did not yet know his colleagues, or how to guide such a meeting to a decision. So one after another we simply recited our positions; the last speaker was another newcomer, the Japanese Finance Minister, who rejoiced in the name of Hideo Bo. He read out a prepared statement in Japanese for a whole hour. After another hour for the English translation, we departed without a further word to bed, well after midnight, chilled to the marrow, and with acute indigestion.

Japanese translation often posed special problems. I once tried to illustrate a point by telling of the Oozlem bird, which flies round and round in ever decreasing circles until it disappears up its own black hole; the young Japanese girl who had to translate pestered me for days to discover what might be the equivalent bird in Japan.

As Finance Ministers, we often disagreed with one another both in theory and practice. But, belonging as we did to the most depressed and unpopular caste in the political life of all our countries, as untouchables we developed a friendly freemasonry which transcended our economic differences. Bill Simon, for example, who was the American Secretary of the Treasury during my most difficult year, had made his million as a bond salesman in New York before he was thirty. Tall, frighteningly fit, with horn rimmed spectacles, he was far to the right of Genghis Khan and was totally devoted to the freedom of the financial markets. At one time he wanted to be President, though, as one of his friends told me, 'he couldn't even make President of his New Jersey Golf Club'. Nevertheless I found him a good colleague; in negotiation he was always fair and sometimes flexible. Ed Yeo, his international deputy during my ordeal with the IMF, was a slow-speaking, slow moving ex-Marine, with a dog-like devotion to his master; he could always enliven a difficult meeting with a ponderous but pointed joke.

Raymond Barre also came from the opposite end of the political spectrum from me, but I found him always helpful in looking for common ground. Notoriously a bon viveur, when he became Prime Minister he used to be pestered by autograph hunters at his favourite restaurants. Finally, in despair, he asked his son, who worked as a make-up man for television, to provide him with a suitable disguise; his son responded by making him up to look like a famous French comedian, so he was pestered more than ever.

Helmut Schmidt kept a close interest in economic policy, even after becoming Chancellor of the Federal Republic. One summer he invited Edna and me to his Sommerfest, a great annual equivalent of the Buckingham Palace garden party, held in the grounds of his official residence, the Palais Schaumburg by the Rhine. We left London for Bonn in a Luftwaffe aircraft at six that evening following a hard day's work. After we had spent several hours touring the sideshows – each Ministry had to provide one – watching the couples on five dance floors, and drinking enormous mugs of beer with film stars such as Curt Jurgens, Helmut took us to his private bungalow in the grounds. There we went on drinking with his personal friends, nearly all from his home town of Hamburg, until four in the morning, to be flown back at eight o'clock for another hard day's work in the Treasury. My experience at Aachen had trained me to take such parties in my stride.

As when I was Defence Secretary, I made a point of getting to know my colleagues' official advisers as well, in this case the central bankers and permanent secretaries. The head of the Federal Reserve in Washington was Arthur Burns, a grey haired economics professor full of cracker-barrel philosophy, who preached the old-time religion; it was said that he regarded Adam Smith's invisible hand as an unwarrantable interference with the freedom of the market. Appearances were misleading. In spite of his folksy personality, which seemed as Middle Western as Will Rogers, he was a Jewish immigrant from Galicia, born under the Austro-Hungarian Empire. He was notorious for having relaxed Fed control of the American economy to help Nixon in the presidential elections. So when he accused me of being the best Conservative finance minister he had ever known, I responded by saying he was like a Lutheran pastor running a whore-house. Such amenities did not impair our good relations.

In Germany the first Bundesbank chief I knew was a courtly old Social Democrat, Karl Klasen. He was succeeded by Ottmar Emminger, a lively and outspoken intellectual who was proud of having studied at the London School of Economics; he was never content with conventional wisdom, and showed an independence of officialdom unique among central bankers. The German Permanent Secretary was Karl-Otto Pöhl, an urbane and relaxed ex-journalist and Social Democrat, who always seemed to be on holiday. I used to wonder how the Germans could run their Finance Ministry with so much less effort than we British. The answer was, of course, that they had a separate Ministry of Economics, the Bundesbank was totally independent of the Government, and above all their pay policy ran smoothly without government intervention, through cooperation between a centralised employers' organisation and a centralised trade union movement. So half the work I had to do in the Treasury was outside the Finance Ministry in Bonn. In addition, German industry was far more efficient than ours, partly thanks to a more constructive relationship with the banks which financed it, and Government policies were not confused by the conflict between opposing economic theories which was already disturbing the Treasury.

When Pöhl became head of the Bundesbank he was replaced as Permanent Secretary by another Social Democrat, Manfred Lahnstein, who became a good friend of mine for life. A tall, red-headed footballer who played the trombone in a jazz-band, he had worked at the European Commission in Brussels and combined a brilliant intelligence with immense energy. He was also, like me, a passionate photographer, specialising in still-life.

In France the Permanent Secretary was a typical *Inspecteur des Finances*, Jacques de la Rosière, precise and Cartesian in style, and formidable in negotiation. He later succeeded Johannes Witteveen as Managing Director of the IMF Witteveen himself became a good friend, both as an antagonist during my negotiations for a British loan in 1976, and later when I myself became Chairman of the IMF's Interim Committee. He had been Finance Minister in the Netherlands, so he knew something of the political environment in which I had to take my decisions. Though not without the stubbornness for which the Dutch are famous, he always took the long view, and was, somewhat surprisingly, an adherent of the Persian religion of Sufism. My old friend and colleague, Bob McNamara, was head of the World Bank, and passionately devoted to helping the Third World, although he suffered badly from the failure of the Republican Administration to give him the financial and political support he needed. William Clark, who had resigned as Eden's press officer over Suez, was now Director of Public Relations for McNamara.

At the Common Market headquarters in Brussels we had a series of excellent British Ambassadors, who had mastered all the intricacies of the difficult economic issues I had to resolve. Michael Palliser was the best type of British diplomatist, married to the daughter of Paul-Henri Spaak, firm and skilful in negotiation, a very parfit gentyl knight. He later became Permanent Secretary of the Foreign Office, and played a central role during the Falklands affair. I have never forgiven Mrs Thatcher for failing to give him the traditional peerage when he retired; none of his predecessors deserved it more. He was succeeded in Brussels by the indefatigable Donald Maitland, who had found Colonel Qadaffi child's play after working for George Brown.

My main contact on the Commission was François-Xavier Ortoli, a good looking Corsican, who had served as a paratrooper during the war. He too was an *Inspecteur*, and had been Finance Minister before going to Brussels. Dining once with him and his successor as Minister, Pierre Fourçade, in the magnificent apartments of the Palais du Louvre which are the French equivalent of No. 11 Downing Street, I listened in fascination as Ortoli complained how much the cooking had deteriorated since he was there. As the aristocracy of the Enarchs, the *Inspecteurs des Finances* nowadays provide leaders for all the main French political parties as well as civil servants, bankers, and businessmen. Their common background and training make them a far tighter and more powerful mafia than the Establishment in Britain. They have now dominated most aspects of French domestic affairs for more than thirty years.

Apart from Takeo Fukuda, who had served as a diplomat in London before the war, I found it difficult to make human contact with the Japanese ministers, none of whom spoke English. But I developed a great respect and liking for their officials, particularly those from the Central Bank, who spoke English well and usually talked very good sense.

These, then, were the leading actors with whom I had to perform on the international stage – mainly, I am glad to say, in private. The first act of our drama was concerned with financing the deficits created all over the world by the five-fold increase in oil prices. In January 1974, before I became Chancellor, the leading oil consumers had agreed at the IMF's Committee of Twenty – the precursor of the Interim Committee – that they would accept their oil deficits and avoid policies which would simply shift the payments problems among themselves, at the expense of world trade and growth. As I have described, Britain and Italy were the only countries to fulfil this undertaking. The United States, Japan and West Germany did the opposite; they deflated their economies so as to reduce their deficits at our expense; within twelve months the industrialised countries as a whole had turned their collective deficit of $10 billion into a surplus of $19 billion. Because, within the whole, Britain and Italy still had big deficits, their currencies were vulnerable to pressure, though sterling was still buoyed up by the presence of surplus funds from the Arab countries in OPEC. However, the developing countries were still running enormous deficits – $53 billion in 1975 – although their deficits allowed them to grow faster than the industrialised countries, so long as they could be financed.

At this time I had no difficulty in financing the British deficit by borrowing from the commercial banks, and from Iran and Saudi Arabia, which were only too happy to lend us some of their surplus oil money. I believed that the only sensible solution to the international problem was along similar lines; we should organise an official mechanism through the IMF which would recycle at least $25 billion of the OPEC oil surpluses to countries which suffered from oil-induced deficits. If we had done so, the world would have maintained steady growth. Moreover, it would not have suffered from the international debt crisis, which exploded in 1982 and still threatens to overwhelm the Western financial system. I put my idea to the IMF annual meeting in October 1974, and persuaded Saudi Arabia to support it. But the Americans were bitterly opposed, because it would have meant interfering with the freedom of the financial markets – and with the freedom of the American commercial banks to make enormous profits out of lending to the Third World. When I discussed the problem with Henry Kissinger just before the IMF meeting he talked about setting up some sort of mutual insurance scheme to tide us over until the power of OPEC had been broken, either by energy conservation or by tanks. He could perhaps have been forgiven for underestimating the power of OPEC, since economics was never his strong point; even Milton Friedman predicted that OPEC would collapse long before oil reached $10 a barrel. Fortunately the Americans did not use tanks, or we might have had no oil at all. Unfortunately it did not practise conservation either; the United States went on using twice as much energy per head as Britain, at half the price.

Meanwhile the private banks were licking their lips at the thought of the money they would make out of lending to the developing countries. They thought that loans to governments carried no risk. Walter Wriston, the head of Citibank, the most aggressive of all the New York lenders, proclaimed 'Governments can't go bust'. On their side, most of the developing countries were happy to borrow from the private banks rather than from the IMF, because they could do so without limit and without conditions. It was the beginning of a series of miscalculations as disastrous as those which produced the Great Slump of the thirties; it could still end in a similar catastrophe.

In the absence of agreement on a comprehensive recycling scheme, I concentrated on organising similar arrangements on a smaller scale. The European Finance Ministers agreed to borrow from OPEC, and I mobilised their support for a limited IMF borrowing mechanism, to be called the Second Witteveen Oil Facility, or Witteveen II. My campaign for Witteveen II took me for the first time in my life to Saudi Arabia. The Saudis were still somewhat bemused by the circumstances which had turned them in a few years from a desert kingdom of bedouin tribesmen into one of the richest countries in the world. One of the wooden doors to the royal palace still carried the tip of Ibn Saud's sword, broken off when he stormed Riyadh in 1902. It was another thirty years before Ibn Saud was able to create the Kingdom of Saudi Arabia in 1932. Though he signed his first oil agreement a year later, it was only just beginning to bring him significant revenues when he died in 1953. Yet another twenty years was to pass before OPEC made the Kingdom a major power in world finance.

Contrary to many Western predictions, the Saudis have so far proved immensely skilful both in managing their sudden wealth and in adjusting to the social and political strains it was bound to bring with it. Their success is due above all to the young Western-educated technocrats who ran the largely untrained bureaucracy which administered the country. Sheikh Yamani was soon well-known in the West as their first oil minister. At least as impressive were the three others I came to know on my visit. Muhammed Abu al-Khail, then formally only the deputy Finance Minister, has now been running the country's finances for the last fifteen years; he is a small, gentle man with a quiet sense of humour. Abdul-Aziz al Quraishi, a similar personality, took over the central bank just before my arrival, and Hisham Nazir, a sardonic intellectual, ran the Ministry of Planning which was the key to the country's development; he has since taken Yamani's place as Oil Minister. All three had been friends since student days. They lived modestly in Riyadh and remained good Muslims, unlike so many Westernised Arabs who found the seductions of Western culture too much for them.

We had one embarrassing crisis during my visit. Yamani, who tended to treat his ministry as an independent satrapy, had told the major American oil company, Aramco, to pay in future in dollars instead of sterling. When the news hit the Western markets, I was woken up in the middle of the night with the news that there was a serious run on the pound. My hosts knew nothing of Yamani's decision; when I told them, they bought £200 million of gilts in the next two days, so the trouble died down. They were men of honour and integrity, to whom their country will always be indebted. They are still my personal friends.

My visit to Tehran was somewhat less inspiring. Corruption was rife, and all too visible. The Shah had surrounded himself with sycophants, and believed all they told him about his superhuman qualities. I was deeply embarrassed when at our interview I sat at his side, while his Finance Minister, Ansari, had to squat like a toad on a footstool below him. At the last minute Ansari tried unsuccessfully to wriggle out of the agreement he had made with me. I was not surprised some years later, when I heard that the Shah was overthrown, and that Ansari had managed to get to the United States with a Japanese passport.

The traditional beauty of Iran had been corrupted too. I found the lonely ruins of Persepolis desecrated by a vulgar group of pavilions left over from the Shah's anniversary celebrations. The magnificent Qashgais, whom I had seen striding in their thousands towards Persepolis on my first visit, had been denied their nomadic life and their annual migration; they could now be seen only rarely as individuals in the soukhs of Shiraz, still resplendent in their savage finery.

Though the Saudis and the European Community supported Witteveen II, Washington publicly denounced it as a sell-out to OPEC; it proposed instead a so-called OECD Support Fund, in which OPEC would have no role – I suspect this was what Kissinger had meant by his mutual insurance society. So I invited all my European colleagues to London to establish a mandate for insisting on Witteveen II. Armed with total solidarity from the Community, we flew to Washington on January 12th, 1975 for the show-down. I dined that night with Kissinger and Nelson Rockefeller, and Kissinger promised to help. The dinner lasted until well after midnight, and I finally went to bed at six in the morning, British time. I had sworn never to accept a serious engagement the night of arriving in the United States, but beggars cannot be choosers.

Our official meetings next day were extremely difficult. Finally we drove late at night through a blizzard to Bill Simon's house. He and Arthur Burns said that the President was personally committed to make it the OECD Support Fund or nothing. In that case, I said, we must insist on seeing the President ourselves. Bill wobbled, and after several angry hours he at last agreed to a Witteveen facility of $6 billion, on condition that we would support the OECD Support Fund as well. He absolutely refused to consider making the money available in the IMF's Special Drawing Rights, as we would have preferred.

I tried hard to contact Kissinger for help, but he was in an aircraft between New York and Washington; and the bad weather made it impossible for us to have an intelligible conversation. Next morning he said he had heard I had been 'terrorising his associates', but promised to do his best; this produced no more than a promise to renew or review the facility under certain conditions. In the event the $6 billion was soon used up, and not extended. But the OECD Support Fund never came into existence at all; though we Europeans all supported it as we had promised, the American Congress refused to ratify the agreement. It was fortunate that we persuaded Washington to agree to Witteveen II, even on a reduced scale; otherwise there would have been nothing at all.

I drew another lesson from this episode. I had already learned that it is almost impossible to get anything done through an international body without American agreement. But now I knew that it may be possible for the Europeans to secure a change in a fixed American position, providing they are united, determined, and well briefed. That is as true in the diplomatic field as I have personally shown it to be in the fields of both defence and economics. The tragedy is that the Europeans have so rarely organised that unity or demonstrated that determination.

Before long it was the financing of Britain's national deficit which took most of my time. It was inevitable that the OPEC countries would soon start placing their petro-dollar surplus in a number of other financial centres besides Britain, and would also want to invest it in hard assets like property in many parts of the world. Indeed they were being advised to do so by their British bankers, with that impartiality which our competitors so admire. In any case the Treasury was beginning to think that all these foreign funds were keeping our exchange rate too high for our commercial good, and that a gentle and controlled depreciation was in order. What we got in fact was a rout.

The Bank of England made two major mistakes. On March 4th, 1976 it sold sterling when the pound was already under pressure, so the markets thought it was trying to push the pound down. Next day it lowered interest rates instead of raising them, thus appearing to confirm the market's suspicions. In ten days the pound fell nearly ten cents below its level of March 3rd. Yet at that time our real economy was steadily improving. Our current account deficit was under £1 billion that year, compared with over £1.5 billion in 1975 and over £3.3 billion in 1974. Inflation was falling steadily. But the financial markets were now obsessed by their conviction that we were determined to contrive a big fall in the pound, so of course they did not want to hold sterling. It took us eighteen months of continuing struggle to restore their confidence. To a nervous man, everything rustles. When a currency is felt to be weak, the markets will put the worst possible construction on any piece of news which might affect it – economic, political, or even industrial.

I soon learned that there is not much point in complaining when the financial markets behave like hysterical schoolgirls. You can not buck the markets. But you can move them in your direction if you try to understand their psychology. And you can sometimes outwit them. That, after all, is a major responsibility of all central banks – a responsibility in which the Bank of England failed dismally in March 1976. It has since learned from that failure, although in recent times public disagreements between the Prime Minister and her Chancellor have made its task more difficult.

This was a very difficult time for me. So I was delighted and surprised to get a letter of encouragement from, of all people, Dickie Mountbatten, about a television interview I had made. 'Your performance was so outstanding,' he wrote, 'that I felt I had to write and congratulate you. This is what the country wants to hear. Well done.' That was just what I wanted to hear, as well.

Sterling came under heavy pressure again in the summer of 1976, until I announced a standby credit of $5.3 billion; it was provided by the Bank of International Settlements, Switzerland, and most of the G-10 – France and Italy opted out because they had similar problems themselves. I got the credit without difficulty because all the contributors shared my view that the pound was then undervalued. However, by this time the Conservative press was screaming for cuts in public expenditure; its frenzy was not discouraged by the Treasury's own misleading statement that public spending was taking sixty per cent of Britain's GDP and by the official Treasury forecast, which overestimated that year's PSBR by over £2 billion. In fact it later turned out that public spending actually fell by nearly two per cent in 1976/7, its first fall since 1969/70, when Roy Jenkins was Chancellor. Such major errors in the official forecasts were to play a major role in the IMF crisis which followed.

The PSBR forecast for 1977/8 also turned out to be much too high, but it was all I had to go on, and it was worrying the markets. I was determined not to go to the IMF for a conditional loan if I could possibly avoid it. So in July 1976, after an appallingly difficult series of meetings with my Cabinet colleagues, I announced spending cuts of just over £1 billion, together with a two per cent increase in the employers' National Insurance contributions, which brought in another £1 billion. Sterling seemed safe at last when Edna and I set off in August for a motoring holiday in Scotland.

It was one of the loveliest summers for years, with not a drop of rain even in the Highlands until the very end of our tour. We drove through Wales and the Lake District to Ardnamurchan, then on to Skye, and up the west coast to Ullapool, where we stopped at a little hotel on the quay. There followed a night of French farce. After a pleasant supper of Loch Broom smokies, we went to bed, to be woken up by a series of telephone calls. Each time I had to plod downstairs with my pyjamas covered by a raincoat, since the only telephone was in the hall, where the front door was wide open. First, a call from the police to say that there had been a bomb threat against me, and that Special Branch men were driving down from Inverness to protect me in the morning. Then a series of calls which I had to take more seriously, from Derek Mitchell and Gordon Richardson. They told me that sterling was under pressure; I agreed they should spend up to $150 million on intervention, but then let the pound fall. Finally I got back to bed for a few hours' sleep. Next day the flurry was over.

On the way home I spent a couple of days at the Edinburgh Festival meeting actors and singers, including Teresa Berganza, who had been an impeccable Cherubino in *Figaro*, and Peter Vaughan, Russell Hunter, and Alan Rickman after their brilliant production of *The Devil is an Ass* in the Assembly Hall. It was the first of several visits to the Edinburgh Festival, one of which rewarded me with the best production of *Carmen* I have ever seen, again with Berganza.

It was fortunate I had that holiday; the next four months were to be the worst of my life. Sterling came under pressure yet again in early September because there was industrial trouble at British Leyland, and the seamen were threatening a strike. There had already been a big outflow of sterling balances in the second quarter. I had to raise interest rates by 1.5 per cent to 13 per cent so as to get gilt sales moving. After a short respite the pound fell below $1.70 on Monday September 27th. We spent another $100 million on intervention, but to no effect. Next morning the pound was still falling fast. We drove with the Governor to Heathrow for my flight to the Commonwealth Finance Ministers' Conference in Hong Kong which preceded the annual IMF meeting in Manila. If I took the plane, I would be cut off from all contact with London for seventeen hours. I decided not to risk it, and drove back to London, still planning to go to Manila as soon as I had sorted things out. It took us three hours to agree that our best course was to announce that we were applying to the IMF for a conditional loan. I told Jim Callaghan, who was at the Labour Party Conference in Blackpool, and he agreed. Next morning the Ford workers went on strike. It was the lowest point of my period at the Treasury. For the first and last time in my life, for about twelve hours I was close to demoralisation.

On Thursday September 30th the Party Conference was to debate the economy. I rang Jim at breakfast, saying I would like to fly up to Blackpool and make my case. Jim asked me not to; he thought it would give an impression of panic, and in any case I would not be allowed to speak from the platform, since I was no longer a member of the Executive. I reluctantly agreed. To take advantage of my spare time I went to see Michael Levey at the National Gallery to choose an Ostade and a Wouwerman for my office at the Treasury, and a Van den Neer for No. 11. At 11.30 I had a message from the Prime Minister. He thought I should come to Blackpool after all. I raced out to Northolt, where the RAF had a plane waiting, only to find the runways flooded by a sudden storm. We finally took off just in time to reach Blackpool airport at 2.30 in the afternoon; a motor cycle escort got me to the Conference by 3 p.m.

The debate was already in full swing, and the mood was ugly. I got up to make my five minute speech at 4.30. A rumble of booing was mixed with some modest cheers. 'I do not come with a Treasury view,' I cried, 'I come from the battlefront.' I told them that a siege economy, which some of the speakers demanded, would be a recipe for a world trade war, and would bring the Tories to power with policies of mass unemployment. 'If you do not want those alternatives, then we have got to stick to the policy we have got. I am going to negotiate with the IMF on the basis of our existing policies . . . I mean things we do not like as well as things we do like. It means sticking to the very painful cuts in public expenditure . . . It means sticking to the pay policy . . . It means seeing that the increase in our output which has now begun goes not into public or private spending, but into exports or investment.' When I sat down the cheers were much louder. So were the boos.

The rest of the year was dominated by a series of negotiations around our application to the IMF. I had to negotiate on two main fronts – to persuade the IMF to accept the smallest possible package of spending

cuts, and to persuade the Cabinet to accept that package. Both negotiations were complicated by divisions among all the parties to them. Press
leaks suggested that some IMF officials wanted a much lower exchange
rate for sterling than the governments for whom they were supposed to
speak. Johannes Witteveen was under constant pressure from the leading
US Treasury officials to squeeze us harder than he wanted. In the
British Cabinet, at first only Roy Jenkins and Edmund Dell were
prepared to support any cuts at all. Inside the Treasury there was a
group, mainly surrounding Derek Mitchell, who wanted very large cuts
indeed; some press stories suggested that they were briefing the IMF
against me. At the other extreme, there were some Treasury officials who
thought it was wrong to make any more cuts when unemployment was so
high. I had the impression that Douglas Wass himself was often worried
that he might not be able to keep his own department under control.

Above all, Jim Callaghan's position remained uncertain until the very
end. He had been badly bruised by the Party Conference, and seemed
uncertain whether it was economically right or politically possible to
make more cuts in public spending. So for some weeks he cast about for
alternatives. He tried hard to persuade Helmut Schmidt and President
Ford to offer unconditional assistance. Neither was willing, and Ford was
soon a lame duck, since Jimmy Carter won the election in November.
From his own experience as Chancellor, Jim Callaghan distrusted the
Treasury, and had come to believe that our only real problem was the
sterling balances. Harold Lever did his best to persuade the Americans
and Germans to provide Britain with a 'safety net' to tide us over until
we could set up some arrangement for getting rid of these balances. But,
though I think Schmidt tried hard to convince his German colleagues, in
the end both governments said they would not be prepared to make such
arrangements before we had reached agreement with the IMF. When
Alan Whittome, an objective and personable Briton who had worked in
the Bank of England, brought his IMF negotiating team to London on
November 1st, it was almost a fortnight before the Prime Minister would
allow my Treasury officials even to talk to them.

At this time my own relations with Jim were shaken by an incident
just after the Party Conference. On October 6th I had asked him to let
me raise interest rates by another two per cent to the then unprecedented
level of fifteen per cent, in order to recover control of our money supply.
He refused. I said I wanted to take the matter to Cabinet that morning.
'All right,' he replied, 'but I will not support you.' Nevertheless I
insisted on taking it to Cabinet. I knew I had no chance of persuading

my colleagues without Jim's support. We both knew that I would have to resign if I was defeated.

I walked through to my office in No. 11 and fixed a meeting with Edmund Dell, the only member of Cabinet on whom I could count. Edmund had just arrived when the door opened and in came the Prime Minister's Private Secretary, Ken Stowe. 'Excuse me, Chancellor,' he said, 'the Prime Minister has asked me to tell you that he was only testing the strength of your conviction. Of course he will support you.' This was the only time I have ever used the threat of resignation to get my way, though I had made it clear to Jim that I would not remain Chancellor if he insisted on splitting the Treasury.

The fifteen per cent interest rate achieved its purpose. It began to decline almost immediately after we had sold the necessary gilts. The following year, when the IMF loan was in place, we were unable to prevent interest rates from falling much too fast. When Paul Volcker as Chairman of the Fed took similar draconic steps a year or two later, he was immensely relieved to hear of my experience, and asked me to send him a detailed account.

Alan Whittome was always helpful and flexible; he was rightly convinced that the Treasury's forecast for the PSBR was far too high. But his master, Johannes Witteveen, may have thought he was being too flexible; he flew over to see us. When he asked me for another £2 billion spending cuts next year, I told him it was out of the question. I took him to see the Prime Minister. Jim reinforced the message, but for the first time said he would support me on cuts of £1 billion.

In fact, once Jim was convinced there was no alternative to the IMF loan, he gave me unstinting support. The consummate skill with which he handled the Cabinet was an object lesson for all prime ministers. His technique was to allow his colleagues to talk themselves to a standstill in a long series of meetings, and then to invite the dissenters to put forward their alternative. The only alternative was to move towards a siege economy with import controls. But Peter Shore, its spokesman, lost all chance of support when he had to admit that this would require at least as much unemployment and as many spending cuts as the IMF would demand. Tony Crosland was a more formidable opponent; he argued persuasively that the situation was already under control. So in fact it was, but the markets would not believe it. Even Harold Lever, who had hoped to find other sources of borrowing, but also understood the markets best, finally had to admit that we must make a deal. In the end, Jim persuaded Tony to withdraw his opposition. My main problem now was to reach an agreement with the IMF on a cut of no more than £1 billion.

I finally got Whittome to accept this limit, and thought Witteveen had agreed. But Witteveen rang Wittome from Washington and asked for yet another billion. I told Whittome he should tell the Managing Director to 'take a running jump'. He smiled and said, 'We seem to have reached an impasse.' I told him to warn Witteveen that if he persisted, we would call a general election on the issue of the IMF versus the people. Witteveen surrendered. I suspect he had put forward his demand only because he had been got at by Ed Yeo, who was trying to mastermind the whole negotiation from the US Treasury.

The last big problem which now remained was to get Cabinet to agree how the cuts should be made up. This was extremely difficult. In the end Jim had to force the issue by appearing to lose his temper and saying that he and I would simply dictate the final package to the Cabinet. On December 15th I was able to announce an agreed package to the House. The Conservatives did not know whether to attack me for giving in to the IMF or for not doing enough. The Tory press had no doubts: I had not done anything like enough. 'Chicken Chancellor' screamed the *Daily Mail*. 'Britain's Shame', shrieked the *Sun*. The *Financial Times* was kinder: 'The first thing to be said . . . is that it can in no way justly be called, as Sir Geoffrey Howe called it, an IMF Budget.'

The outside world, however, was unanimously convinced that I had now turned the economy round. Within weeks we got the agreement Jim wanted on the sterling balances. The pound grew stronger month by month. Interest rates began to fall even faster than we wanted – they were only five per cent in October 1977. When I attended the annual meeting of the IMF that month, even the British correspondents described me as 'walking on water'. The Labour Party Conference which followed gave me a standing ovation. The leading American financial monthly, *Institutional Investor*, produced a cover story showing me as first among the six best finance ministers of the day. Since none of the other five had to operate in a democracy, I took this as high praise; it is much easier to manage an economy if you can use electrodes on the most sensitive parts of those who refuse to cooperate.

Yet, in a sense, the whole affair was unnecessary. The Treasury had grossly overestimated the PSBR, which would have fallen within the IMF's limit without any of the measures they prescribed. Later figures showed that we also managed to eliminate our current account deficit in 1977, before the IMF package had had time to influence it. Thus I was able to introduce a reflationary budget in 1978 to undo the damage done by excessive deflation in 1977; I had room to increase demand by £2.8 billion without infringing any of my undertakings to the IMF.

Moreover, I drew only half of the loan offered in return by the IMF, and had repaid it all – or the equivalent – by the time I left office. Similarly, over half of the standby credit remained untouched; I made no drawing on it after August 1977. During the long agony of the IMF negotiations I used to talk longingly of 'Sod off Day' – the moment when I would at last be free of IMF control. 'Sod off Day' came much earlier than anyone expected.

In practice, however, we could have done without the IMF loan only if we – and the world – had known the real facts at the time. But in 1976 our forecasts were far too pessimistic, and we were still describing our public expenditure in a way which was immensely damaging to our standing in the financial markets.

Another major factor in the impression of muddle we created was a fundamental disagreement, inside both the Treasury and the Bank of England, about economics in both theory and practice. This disagreement existed in many countries. It reflected the uncertainties created by the breakdown of the international economic order which had been created at the end of the war, largely by American and British experts under the influence of Keynes.

The core of this disagreement concerned the role of exchange rates, and the techniques for controlling them. The Bretton Woods Treaty required all governments to keep the value of their currencies fixed in relation to the dollar, changing their exchange rates rarely, and only by mutual agreement; agreement was given only when a change was believed necessary to bring their external accounts into balance, through what was then thought to be an 'automatic adjustment process'. Bretton Woods broke down when the Johnson Government refused to continue carrying the special responsibilities it imposed on the United States. A few years later, the increase in oil prices made a regime of floating currencies inevitable. In such a regime the value of a currency depended on the demand for it in the financial markets, which were not subject to control by any government.

Because at that time the markets distrusted governments which were significantly in debt either at home or abroad, the deficits which Keynesian theory recommended when demand was insufficient tended to reduce the value of the currency concerned; this fuelled inflation and made it even more difficult to borrow the money needed to finance the deficits.

The Time of My Life

The financial markets were advised by clever young men who were particularly susceptible to changes in academic fashion – 'teenage scribblers', as Nigel Lawson was to call them after he had ceased to be one himself. These advisers were mainly converts to the monetarist theories popularised by Milton Friedman; they began worrying about the monetary statistics, believing that inflation depended wholly on the money supply.

I have never met a private or central banker who believed the monetarist mumbo-jumbo. But no banker could afford to ignore monetarism so long as the markets took it seriously. So a conflict developed in Whitehall between unreconstructed Keynesians and unbelieving monetarists. Each theory had its partisans in both the Treasury and the Bank of England; institutional interest led the Bank to want a high pound so as to keep inflation down, while the Treasury often wanted a lower pound to make British industry more competitive, and to reduce the balance of payments deficit through the 'automatic adjustment process' – though floating had made such adjustment far from 'automatic'.

The theoretical conflict existed even inside the IMF itself. On Sunday October 24th, a week before the IMF team arrived in London, the *Sunday Times* reported a story that the IMF would demand that 'sterling should be let down to about $1.50 to the £ (against today's $1.64)'. The pound lost seven cents the next morning, even though the story was unequivocally denied both by Bill Simon and the IMF. It was patent nonsense as reported, since both the US Treasury and the IMF Board thought the pound was undervalued at that time; an agreement with the IMF was bound to send the pound up, not down, in any case. But I suspect it reflected the views of some IMF official who still believed that depreciation would engender an 'automatic adjustment process'.

In order to satisfy the markets, I began to publish the monetary forecasts we had always made in private, and then described them as targets, although I knew as well as Jasper Hollom that I was 'simply redesigning my cross'. Nevertheless, because I managed to keep the growth of £M3 (then the favoured measure of money) averaging ten per cent throughout my five years, I kept the markets quiet; later I took a grim satisfaction that Geoffrey Howe, who unlike me was a believing monetarist, let the money supply expand twice as fast as I had, and overshot his monetary targets by 100 per cent in his first two and a half years.

The doctrinal conflict continued however, in the Bank and the Treasury, reaching its climax in late 1977. There had been massive flows of foreign money into sterling, which threatened to push the exchange rate up well above $2, thus pricing many British exports out of their markets. So we intervened in the markets to keep sterling down, in ways which the monetarists thought would send our money supply well above its target. In theory, the way to escape an awkward choice between a deteriorating balance of payments and rising inflation would have been to relax exchange controls so that British citizens could invest their sterling abroad. The Cabinet ruled this out on October 24th; so we decided on October 28th to stop intervening for the time being. This was one of the few major issues on which I rejected Douglas Wass's advice, although some of his officials agreed with me, and some of the Bank's officials agreed with him.

In the event, I think I was proved right. Though the pound was about twelve cents higher in 1978, and rose above $2 once or twice, the balance of payments remained in surplus, and I achieved what was then a record: for most of my last year in office unemployment and inflation were falling at the same time. Yet the doctrinal conflict remains unresolved. To this day it continues to confuse Britain's financial policy. It lay at the heart of the argument about interest rates between Mrs Thatcher and her Chancellor, Nigel Lawson, in 1988.

Despite the fact that we used only half of the IMF loan, and might have managed without it altogether, it marked the turning point in our affairs. An agreement with the IMF is like the Seal of Good Housekeeping: it is regarded by the markets as a guarantee of responsible economic management. In the two following years international concern shifted from Britain to the United States, where the Carter Administration was running into serious economic difficulties.

Jimmy Carter was the most extraordinary President the United States had had since the war, though his successor, Ronald Reagan, proved no less extraordinary. Clark Clifford had described Carter to me as socially liberal and fiscally conservative. In fact he proved a moral puritan and an economic profligate. The puritanism came home to us when his Vice-President, Fritz Mondale, called on us shortly after the election. Jim gave him a riotous dinner at No. 10, at which we joined Fritz in singing old labour union songs until well after midnight. Next morning we discovered that one of his staff had taken the wine list back to his hotel and priced it. Then he told the press that the Labour Government lived in a state of decadent luxury which President Carter would never permit in Washington. The President's puritanism also perplexed his Cabinet colleagues; Mike Blumenthal told me that Carter had agonised for hours on whether unmarried men and women or homosexuals should be allowed to live together in public housing; he finally decided against it.

Carter was a man of great intelligence, who had won the esteem of the formidable Admiral Rickover as a young naval officer in the Polaris programme. In private meetings he was always courteous and well-briefed. But he could make appalling errors of policy through failing to consult his own experts. He took disarmament very seriously. Yet his first initiative simply ignored an agreement already reached at Vladivostok by the Republicans; so he infuriated Brezhnev and derailed the arms talks for many months. His Secretary of State, the able and dedicated Cy Vance, resigned when, against his advice, Carter went ahead with his disastrous attempt to rescue the American hostages in Tehran. And Carter made a major Presidential statement on inflation without clearing it with his own Treasury Secretary, Mike Blumenthal.

Jimmy Carter went to Washington from Georgia determined to break with all its political traditions, and to reject the wheeling and dealing without which the American constitution cannot work. So he ultimately gave the impression of wanting to be President, but not wanting to govern the country. As the columnist Dave Broder was to write, he finished up less like the captain of the ship of state than a frantic white-water canoeist.

Mike Blumenthal had already had government experience as a trade negotiator under Kennedy before Carter made him Secretary of the Treasury. Blumenthal too was an extraordinary man, but in ways very different from Carter. Small, pale, and taut in appearance, he was born in Germany of Jewish parents, who fled East to escape from Hitler, and ended up in Shanghai. As a boy, Mike had to make money for the family by selling newspapers on the Bund; he still speaks demotic Chinese. Then he came to the United States, and entered academic life as a professor of economics at Princeton. During the Nixon years he was head of the Bendix Corporation. He was a passionate Democrat, with an ideological commitment to liberalism which is rare even in that Party.

It took him some time to settle down to his ministerial role. To his surprise, he found he had no real power, compared with what he had commanded as a business executive; he also had far too little influence on his President. Before long the American economy was in deep trouble and the dollar was under heavy pressure. In the end Blumenthal resigned, saying: 'When the falling curve of the President's popularity intersects with the rising curve of interest rates, it is time for the Treasury

Secretary to go.' His successor, Bill Miller, was even less suited to that job than he had been to his previous job as Chairman of the Fed.

However, Paul Volcker then moved into the Fed and took the economy by the scruff of the neck. He restored stability by raising interest rates, the only instrument at his disposal, and a very inadequate one, as he was the first to admit. The price in unemployment was very much higher than it would have been if he had been able to use fiscal policy as well.

Meanwhile my own international reputation was secure. I realised I had won the battle for sterling as early as September 1977, when the Reuters correspondent at the Commonwealth Finance Ministers' Conference in Barbados came up to me, his face ashen. 'Look at this, Denis,' he said, thrusting a telegram into my hand. It told him that owing to the strength of the pound, henceforward he would be paid in dollars!

A few days later my colleagues elected me as Chairman of the IMF's Interim Committee. In 1975 I had refused this position because I was then too busy. I used my new authority to try to persuade the Western members of the Committee to show more sympathy and understanding for the Third World, which was the innocent victim of their failure to maintain adequate growth, and was suffering badly from the rapacity of their banks. I managed to get the IMF to subsidise interest rates for the less developed countries and to give them five thousand million Special Drawing Rights. Germany was now the main culprit in restricting growth; it was fearful of stimulating its economy in case inflation took off. But Japan and Switzerland were also at fault. In 1974 the OPEC surpluses had reduced world demand by $65 billion. By 1978 the combined surpluses of Germany, Japan, and Switzerland were many times greater than the OPEC surplus.

I took my first meeting of the Interim Committee as Chairman in Mexico in April 1978. The Mexican Government wanted it held in Acapulco, to boost its tourist trade. Carter thought this would give a bad impression to his Baptist supporters, so we held it in the noise and smog of Mexico City. Personally I thought it a much more suitable location in the circumstances, since my colleagues could not ignore the problems of the Third World when they were surrounded by unemployed peasants, who had crowded into the city slums with their families from an even poorer countryside. Banditry was so common that the Mexican central bank had to distribute its currency round the country in its own fleet of aircraft. One of them flew us after the meeting to the stupendous Maya city of Chichen Itza; on the terraces of its mighty pyramids I found the reclining figures of the Rain God 'Chacmool', which had inspired the young Henry Moore. In Mexico City itself, the Anthropological Museum's collection of ancient Mexican art rivals the treasures of Tutankhamun in Cairo.

During the rest of 1978 I was approached several times to see if I would be prepared to take Witteveen's place as Managing Director of the IMF when he retired the following year. If I had shown the slightest interest, I could have had it, 'no questions asked', as the *Financial Times* reported. I refused, as I had refused to be Secretary General of NATO because I did not want to be a civil servant, certainly not in an international organisation, and least of all in one which was so dominated by the whims of Washington. For anyone who wants to change the world there is no alternative to politics. So I remained chained to the oars of the Treasury galley as we drifted inexorably towards the Winter of Discontent.

The international financial scene during my last year as Chancellor was dominated by negotiations on the proposal for a European Monetary System, or EMS. Roy Jenkins had floated the idea when he was President of the European Commission, without arousing much interest. Then Chancellor Helmut Schmidt and his close friend Valéry Giscard d'Estaing, the President of France, committed their personal prestige to the concept, although neither had any clear idea how it would work financially. They saw it, however, primarily in political terms, as leading to a European Monetary Union which would in turn lead to some sort of European integration across the board.

Scarcely anyone else in authority was in favour. Ortoli, the European Commissioner concerned, was hostile, since he had lived through the ill-starred experiment of the 'European snake', a machinery for keeping the continental currencies closely aligned; France had twice been obliged to leave it in humiliation. The French central banker, Raymond Clappier, was opposed for similar reasons. The German central banker, Ottmar Emminger, thought it was dangerous nonsense. The only important supporters I came across in European financial circles were the Italian central banker, Paolo Baffi, and Manfred Lahnstein. Baffi thought that if Italy were given a little more latitude than the others, it might provide a means by which the lira could crawl downwards without too much drama. Manfred Lahnstein supported it on grounds of Germany's national interest. His argument was, as always, simple and powerful: the mechanism would require the weaker countries to intervene on the currency markets to keep the stronger currencies down, and vice versa; this meant that France and Italy would have to pay to keep the

Deutschmark lower than it would have been in a free market, thus keeping Germany more competitive, and other countries less so. That is exactly how it has worked – and disastrously so at times like the late eighties. When the dollar fell in 1987, making the United States more competitive, its trade deficit with Europe also began to fall. But it fell not, as was hoped, at the expense of the surplus country, Germany, but at the expense of other deficit countries, including Britain. The reason, as Lahnstein had predicted, was that the EMS had prevented the markets from pushing the Deutschmark up, once Germany had absorbed the reluctant three per cent revaluation forced on it in January 1987.

In Britain Edmund Dell was strongly against the EMS in principle from the beginning, as was the Treasury, while Harold Lever was strongly in favour. The Bank of England was mildly in favour, since they thought it would exert a useful discipline on British governments. The Foreign Office was strongly in favour; it is in favour of anything which includes the word 'European'. I was fairly agnostic until I realised, from long discussions with Lahnstein and others, how it was likely to work in practice; then I turned against it.

The EMS would never have come into existence without the remorseless pressure of Schmidt and Giscard; it is an undeniable example of the power of political leaders to triumph over their advisers when they know what they want. Nevertheless, despite surges of optimism from time to time, the EMS has not so far produced any significant movement towards a European Monetary Union. Nor has it achieved the more modest objectives its supporters set themselves. Fluctuations between its member currencies for many years were greater than fluctuations between the EMS as a whole and the dollar. It has not produced significant convergence between its member countries in growth or inflation, unless you believe that it has infected all its members with the so-called Eurosclerosis from which Germany suffered in the mid-eighties.

Britain's decision to stay out of the Exchange Rate Mechanism, which governs currency intervention in the EMS, was certainly justified in the first four years, when it had to accept seven realignments of its currencies. If we had joined the ERM at the outset, the intervention we would have been required to make in 1979 to keep sterling down would have raised our monetary growth to an annual rate of thirty per cent, while the weaker countries would have had to intervene on a massive scale to keep Britain more competitive. Far from paying a price to get Britain in, the other members of the European Community would have paid a lot to keep us out.

Like other international organisations, the European Monetary System
suffers from a crucial defect. It can impose agreed disciplines only on its
weaker members; the strong are able to reject them. On several occasions
when parity realignments took place within the EMS, essentially because the Deutschmark was too strong, the weaker countries were
obliged to reduce the value of their currencies so as to allow Germany to
limit the appreciation of the Deutschmark.

Similarly, the IMF has never been able to impose conditions on the
United States, even when the American economy was grossly out of
balance. In November 1978 Washington organised a collective support
arrangement for the dollar, without accepting surveillance by the IMF,
or carrying out the changes in domestic policy which were needed to
stabilise the dollar over a period of years.

In the 1980s the IMF compelled the debtor countries in the Third
World to accept draconian conditions, in return for financing their
deficits. But it was unable to persuade the Western world and Japan to
reverse their policies of inadequate growth and import restriction, which
were in part responsible for creating the Third World deficits in the first
place.

Worst of all, President Reagan was allowed to run enormous fiscal and
trade deficits which threatened to make the United States the world's
mega-debtor, owing more money than all the other countries put together.
Europe and Japan were obliged in their own interest to finance these
deficits, without any assurance that Washington would take the actions
necessary to reduce them.

Despite all the postwar efforts to create a world society based on the
democratic principles of justice and equality, international financial cooperation, like international cooperation in political and security matters, is
still liable in the end to yield to the country with the greatest power.

In the financial field this now presents immense dangers. During a
period when the private markets can operate world-wide without any
effective control by governments, Western leaders have consistently
failed to organise cooperation among themselves on the economic issues
on which their prosperity, and that of the world, depends. The Soviet
threat has tended to monopolise their attention for nearly half a century.
It now looks as if their societies will be proved far more vulnerable to the
threat of economic disorder and financial anarchy.

CHAPTER TWENTY-ONE

Minority Government

I think the Whigs are wicked knaves –
(And very like the Tories) –
Who doubt that Britain rules the waves,
And ask the price of glories:
I think that many fret and fume
At what their friends are planning,
And Mr Hume hates Mr Brougham
As much as Mr Canning.

– 'The Chaunt of the Brazen Head'
Winthrop Mackworth Praed

M Y WORK AT THE Treasury turned me from a mere politician into a celebrity, and from a specialist in foreign affairs and defence into a Party leader in the broader sense. As Defence Secretary I was isolated from the major issues of domestic policy, and took an active part in discussing them only in my later years. As Chancellor I was directly concerned in every Government decision the whole time, meeting the Prime Minister and Foreign Secretary regularly every week to discuss the problems ahead, both at home and abroad.

At Defence I was dealing with issues which rarely excited public opinion; I did not need to expend much effort in winning popular support. At the Exchequer I could achieve nothing without the understanding of the British people in general, and of the Labour movement in particular. In this sense, good public relations were fundamental to my hopes of success. Besides doing all I could to explain my decisions personally, I also encouraged my officials to speak their mind in public. This sometimes got me, as well as them, into trouble with Parliament.

Although I had to take many decisions which were deeply unpopular, I rarely encountered personal animosity from ordinary men and women. Some would gaze stonily ahead as they passed me by. The majority would smile when they recognised me – perhaps because the television mimic, Mike Yarwood, had made me a familiar figure of fun. I took over from him the phrase 'silly billy', which I had never used before he attributed it to me; it was less offensive than the expressions I found coming more naturally to my lips. If people in the street went beyond a smile, it was almost always to say either 'Stick to it, Denis, you're doing a grand job', or 'I wouldn't have your job for a thousand pounds'.

I had an exceptionally able head of public relations in Peter Middleton. Although a Treasury civil servant – untypically with a degree in economics – he had a genius for dealing with the media, who liked and trusted him as much as I did. He fully deserved his later promotion to Permanent Secretary over the heads of older men. One of the few things Mrs Thatcher and I have in common is a taste for a little lively insubordination in those who work for us – though in her case it does not seem to extend beyond her civil servants to her Cabinet colleagues.

On Peter's advice, I regularly invited the top editorial staff of the leading newspapers to dinner, and accepted their invitations in return. I would discuss my problems frankly with them, and never had a confidence betrayed. As a result, at least they understood what I was trying to do, even if they did not approve of it. However much I deplored their criticisms, I rarely felt it was unfair. This was true at least of the so-called 'quality press', including newspapers which supported the Conservatives. Not so the 'popular press' which, apart from the *Daily Mirror*, tended to react to whatever I did with the same knee-jerk vituperation. However, this did not worry me overmuch; the British people were already getting most of their information from radio and television, which were far more balanced in their reporting; they relied on the popular press for nudes rather than news. Between general elections, I doubt whether more than one out of a hundred who pored over the sports pages ever read the editorials.

I found that by far the best way of influencing opinion directly was in a television interview or discussion. A talk straight to camera, as in the old-fashioned party political broadcast, was usually an excuse to make a pot of tea, or get another can of beer out of the fridge. Politicians rarely look natural when they talk to camera. Their eyes usually glaze over as they try to read the teleprompter without their glasses, and their viewers' eyes glaze over too. A discussion, however, under a good chairman who insists that the question is not evaded, can make a real impact on the viewer, providing there are only two or three points of view in the argument; more tends to confusion.

Personally, I have always preferred an interview with a really tough professional who has done his homework properly. Robin Day is still in a league of his own here – remorseless but always fair in his pursuit of a straight answer. Thanks to a first-rate research team, Brian Walden was an effective expositor, but he used to irritate me by summing up my argument so as to suit his own case rather than to remind the viewer of what I had actually said. Peter Jay, who had worked in the Treasury himself, had the most powerful mind of all; but he was sometimes more anxious to demonstrate that fact than to explore my views.

I was able to get my own back on Peter some years later, when he chaired a discussion on monetarism between Milton Friedman, Geoffrey Howe, and myself. Friedman tried to refute me by quoting a notorious passage from Jim Callaghan's speech to the Labour Party Conference in 1976, in which Jim appeared to reject the very concept of Keynesian demand management, in principle and at all times. 'What do you have to say about that?' demanded Friedman. 'It just shows that you should not let your son-in-law write your speeches,' was my reply. As the son-in-law in question, Peter did not know whether to look pleased or offended.

The Budget was always the centre of a massive public relations exercise. It would start on the Sunday with a photo-call at our country cottage. Dozens of photographers would take pictures of me in wellington boots and a roll-neck sweater, performing some rural ritual like picking apples or mowing the grass while my adoring family looked on. This was supposed to prove that I was a human being after all. Next morning I had to reveal the secrets of my Budget to the Cabinet, many of whom would already have discussed with me any measures which affected their own departments. In the afternoon I would drive to Windsor to explain the Budget to the Queen, who was always briefed to ask the appropriate questions, after which we could turn to more agreeable subjects.

Tuesday was Budget Day. Much of the morning had to be spent on another photo-call; Edna and I would walk down the steps from Downing Street into St James's Park to see the pelicans, pretending to ignore the surrounding cameras and flashguns. On one occasion, as we crossed the road a great cavalcade of black Cadillacs swept down from Admiralty

Arch and stopped. Out jumped Senator Teddy Kennedy to press my flesh. He at least never felt faintly factitious at a photo-call.

Then, after a light lunch, I would sit down and go through my budget speech, underlining the key words with a red pencil. I normally speak from pencil notes; I find it difficult to recite a typescript without sending people to sleep, unless I mark it in advance for emphasis, like an actor. It was fortunate I did so, since in one budget speech I found that the penultimate page was missing, five minutes before I was due to hold up Gladstone's despatch box outside the door of No. 11, on my way to Parliament.

It was only after making my speech, and listening to the Leader of the Opposition's comments — often as late as seven o'clock in the evening — that I would sit down to prepare my Budget broadcast for television at nine o'clock. On Wednesday I would meet the Parliamentary Labour Party, the TUC and the CBI, appear on the Jimmy Young show, and broadcast to foreign audiences, as well as listening to the considered response of the Opposition's Shadow Chancellor, Sir Geoffrey Howe. He found this role as difficult as I had, although he was usually able to make some telling points. Fortunately for me, their effect was often blunted by his mumbling diction.

In one debate he had raised some difficult questions in his opening speech. I did not want to be distracted from my own argument by answering them, so I dismissed them by saying that I found his attack 'rather like being savaged by a dead sheep'. The phrase came to me while I was actually on my feet; it was an adaptation of Churchill's remark that an attack by Attlee was 'like being savaged by a pet lamb'. Some years later, I found myself again facing Geoffrey, but as his Shadow from the Opposition benches. I congratulated him on his appointment as Foreign Secretary. He responded by saying it 'was like being nuzzled by an old ram'. I got up immediately and said it would be the end of a beautiful friendship if he accused me of necrophilia. Such banter can often enliven a dull afternoon. It has never prevented me from having good personal relations with an opponent like Geoffrey, whom I like and respect.

On the other hand, my careless tongue often caused me difficulties inside my own Party — and sometimes beyond. At a meeting of the PLP I accused Ian Mikardo of being 'out of his tiny Chinese mind' — a phrase of the comedienne, Hermione Gingold, with which I thought everyone was familiar. On the contrary, when he leaked it to the press, the Chinese Embassy took it as an insult to the People's Republic.

Worse still was an exchange I had with some Labour rebels whose abstention in a vital vote on public expenditure enabled the Tories to defeat the Government. All our spending cuts were inevitably unpopular in the Party, but the dissenting MPs usually took care to avoid threatening the Government's majority. This demonstration went beyond all bounds; feelings were at boiling point on both sides. As I returned to the Chamber from the voting lobby one of the rebels used demotic language to cast aspersions on my paternity, so I praised his virility in similar language, several times. I do not think my words upset the left-wingers concerned, who are used to such terms of endearment. But it certainly cost me some votes from the soft Centre of the Party in the leadership election which started the following week, after Harold Wilson's surprise resignation as Prime Minister on March 16th 1976.

Similarly, I made a blistering attack on the trade union leader, Clive Jenkins, at the Party Conference in 1974, which was all the more effective for relying on ridicule rather than abuse. It won me a standing ovation at the time; but another trade union leader warned me that I might live to regret it. I remembered his words in 1980, when Clive Jenkins persuaded David Basnett to support a new system for electing the Party Leader, and later pushed Michael Foot into a premature resignation just after the 1983 General Election, so helping to stitch up the succession for Neil Kinnock. Just so, I recalled, in the concluding pages of *Le Rouge et le Noir*, Valenod had his revenge of Julien Sorel for a slight suffered many years earlier, by sentencing him to death. Stendhal understood this side of politics, and many others, better than any other novelist.

Although I lost my seat on the National Executive Committee of the Labour Party at its Annual Conference in 1975, they gave me a standing ovation when I spoke from the floor rather than the platform the following morning. And despite a very mixed reception at the 1976 Conference after I had applied to the IMF, I returned to favour the following year. But in October 1978, although my own speech was again well received, Conference passed a motion rejecting our pay policy by two to one; it was moved by the new right-wing leader of the engineering union, Terry Duffy – the clearest possible proof that we were heading for trouble that winter.

Nevertheless, we always commanded a massive majority for our economic policy among the Labour MPs. It was only when the Liberals or our own left wing made common cause with the Conservatives that our Parliamentary majority was at risk. However, our opponents inside the Party usually concentrated on trying to defeat us at Conference, using the Tribune meeting there as their rallying point. In 1975, Mikardo's attack on the Government so enraged Jack Jones that he jumped up on to the platform, 'jabbing an accusing finger at Mik like an Old Testament prophet', to quote Barbara Castle's account. Before long such behaviour had deeply divided the Left of the Party; meanwhile Tony Benn was moving cautiously to take Michael Foot's place as keeper of the Party's conscience.

Wilson himself had long since abandoned the position which led him to resign from the Attlee Government with Nye Bevan. He had now also abandoned many of the positions he had occupied during his first spell as Prime Minister. For example, on March 20th, 1975 he threatened to resign, if other Cabinet ministers who were also on the NEC did not use their influence to soften its hostility to the Common Market. At times his hatred of Tony Benn became almost hysterical. Though I much preferred the way Wilson now handled his role as head of the Government, I thought he was losing his taste for politics; he had told me in 1972 that he did not intend to serve another full term as Prime Minister. His failure to repeat his triumph of 1966 in the election of October 1974 shook his self-confidence. In December 1975 Harold Lever told me he thought Wilson would soon announce his resignation. Unknown to me, Lever gave the same message to Jim Callaghan, but much more specifically: Wilson would resign in March, and Jim must prepare himself to take over.

Wilson himself told Callaghan after his sixtieth birthday party on March 11th – the very evening of my row with the Left over their abstention in the debate on public expenditure. He told me in the lavatory outside the Cabinet room just before informing the whole of the Cabinet on March 16th; so I was as flabbergasted as nearly all the rest of my colleagues. In fact he had told Bernard Donoughue and Joe Haines, his Press Secretary, of his precise intentions much earlier – Donoughue as far back as March 1974. His inexplicable resignation honours list gave rise to rumours that there was some personal scandal behind his resignation. There is now too much evidence that he had planned it years earlier, to make that credible.

My work as Chancellor had led many people to see me as a possible Party Leader. But Wilson's resignation could not have come at a more inconvenient time for my chances of succeeding him. For some days I was determined not to run at all, rightly believing that my row with my left-wing colleagues, now widely publicised, would reduce my support to a derisory level. In the end pressure from my fellow ministers in the Treasury and from a range of backbench MPs, combined with a distaste for appearing to run away from the contest, led me to change my mind. Michael Foot was the main left-wing challenger, though Tony Benn was put up by the extreme Left. Jim Callaghan was the clear favourite from the Right; but besides myself, Roy Jenkins and Tony Crosland were also standing.

In the first ballot Foot got ninety votes, Jim eighty-four, Roy fifty-six, Benn thirty-seven, I thirty and Tony Crosland seventeen. Roy, Benn, and Crosland immediately dropped out, but I stayed in; as Barbara Castle wrote, I was a pugilist, not a patrician. In the second ballot Jim was already eight votes ahead of Michael, and I had picked up only another eight votes, so I dropped out automatically. Finally Jim was elected leader by 176 votes to Michael Foot's 137. He kissed hands with the Queen as Prime Minister on Monday April 5th, 1976. I too saw the Queen that day – to give her the outline of my fourth budget.

I presented my budget the next day, and spent most of the week explaining it to the leading newspapers, and meeting the disgruntled 'Neddy Six' on the second round of our incomes policy. As always, I went to my constituency for the weekend, to explore the impact of my budget at the grass roots. Meanwhile Jim was reconstructing his Cabinet. Despite anguished pleas from Michael Foot, he sacked Barbara Castle, along with Bob Mellish and Willie Ross. Barbara took her dismissal badly; she was still in shock from the death of her deputy and close friend, Brian O'Malley. Edmund Dell moved to the Department of Trade, and I decided not to replace him at the Treasury. I had told Jim, greatly to his relief, that I wanted to carry on as Chancellor, so Tony Crosland took Jim's place at the Foreign Office; Jim told the Lobby I would switch with Tony later. Michael Foot became Leader of the House of Commons, a job of particular importance when the Government had such a fragile majority. Roy Jenkins was left at the Home Office. I was not surprised a fortnight later when he decided to go to Brussels, as President of the Commission of the European Community. My old friend and fellow Leeds MP, Merlyn Rees, took his place as Home Secretary.

The firm decisiveness of that first reshuffle gave a foretaste of Jim's quality as Prime Minister. In my opinion, Jim Callaghan was, for most of his time, the best of Britain's postwar prime ministers after Attlee. Historians, basing their views on the partisan instant history served up by contemporary journalists, and with little understanding of his daunting inheritance, may never appreciate his true achievement. He took over at a moment when the British economy was battered by continual crises over sterling and pay policy, and with the agony of Northern Ireland at its worst. Moreover, he never had a reliable majority in Parliament. Despite all these handicaps, he never lost his sense of direction, until at the end the overconfidence created by his very success combined with physical exhaustion to cloud his judgment.

His earlier career gave little hint of his later quality. In Opposition he was seen as an opportunist, a reputation which his behaviour over *In Place of Strife* did nothing to modify. He was not particularly distinguished as Chancellor, as Home Secretary (except over Northern Ireland) or even as Foreign Secretary. When Heath was in power, Jim seriously thought of leaving politics altogether; he had undergone a major operation, and wanted time to enjoy his farm and his family. When Wilson returned to No. 10, the Foreign Office introduced Jim to a new world, in which the British Labour Party's troubles must have seemed very small beer. He used to say to me in those days that the three major Cabinet posts he had already held were more than enough to justify his life in politics.

Yet when Wilson's resignation offered him the unexpected opportunity, Callaghan pursued it with resolution. Once Prime Minister, he had no ambition except to serve his country well. The political skills he had perfected in his unregenerate days were now just what his office needed. Without them the Government would never have survived the negotiations with the IMF, or preserved its fragile hold on Parliament. He was never content simply to preside over a Cabinet committee. He would read his briefs carefully, decide what outcome was required, and then steer the committee to accept it. Sometimes he made his view clear at the outset so as to shorten discussion. In the more difficult cases he would allow his colleagues to exhaust themselves in argument before forcing a decision. During the IMF discussions he often did both.

He was always determined to give working people and their families a fairer share of wealth and opportunity; that is why he had fought so bitterly against the Wilson Government's decision to delay raising the school leaving age. But he had none of the middle-class socialist's illusions about how working people think. On social issues he was as conservative as the trade union movement which provided his political base. Many of the new freedoms demanded by the student intellectuals of the sixties found him perplexed and even innocent.

It was he who first realised that the Child Benefit, which had figured so long in Labour Party programmes, might cost us male votes because it would mean a switch from the wallet to the handbag; it would be paid to the wife at the cost of withdrawing a tax allowance from the husband.

Eric Varley, Shirley Williams and I were deputed to raise the matter with the TUC, so as to find out how they thought it would affect our pay policy. They recommended delay – though this did not prevent them from attacking me for betraying our commitment, when the delay was announced. We finally introduced Child Benefit in 1978. I believe it had the effect Jim feared; although that year saw the biggest increase in real family income for a long time, the Labour Party failed to reap the full political benefit, since working men did not find the increase fully reflected in their own weekly pay packets.

We had a similar argument over the perennial problem of tax relief on mortgages. Peter Shore, the minister responsible for housing, joined me in putting a paper to Cabinet which recommended the withdrawal, over six years, of relief for the 165,000 taxpayers who earned over two and a half times the average. The existing provision was grossly regressive; it distorted the housing market, and meant that a tiny minority of wealthier people paid far less interest on their mortgages than the rest of the population. Jim was strongly against our proposal because he thought it would lose us votes. It attracted hardly any support from the rest of the Cabinet; even left-wing ministers kept their mouths shut. So the rich are still able to pay far less interest than the poor in borrowing for their houses.

Jim's innate conservatism emerged very clearly when we discussed amending the Official Secrets Act, which made it a criminal offence even to publish the name of a Cabinet committee. So wide-ranging a definition of an official secret was so ridiculous that juries were often unwilling to convict people who were prosecuted under the Act. Both I and Douglas Wass, my Permanent Secretary, wanted to remove economic information from the scope of the act. We believed that in Britain, as in nearly all other democratic countries, an official who improperly revealed secret economic information should be subject only to discipline by his department. But Jim and most other ministers did not want any change in the Official Secrets Act, so it remained on the statute book, to give legal authority for idiocies like the handling of the *Spycatcher* case, which have made Britain the despair of her friends and the laughing stock of her enemies all over the world.

Jim could also be curmudgeonly on occasion. He was unfairly grudging in his thanks to Gordon Richardson for his skill in getting the agreement to run down the sterling balances once we had made our deal with the IMF. But such infrequent lapses were as nothing, compared with the consistent support he gave me as Chancellor during the most difficult period of Britain's postwar history. Nevertheless, he remained somewhat distrustful both of the Treasury civil servants and of the Bank of England throughout his time at No. 10; he too often attributed to political disloyalty opinions which were honestly held and forecasts which were sometimes as inaccurate as they were inconvenient.

Partly for this reason, in 1977 he set up an informal 'Seminar' to discuss interest rates and exchange rates, on which prime ministers and chancellors so often disagree. This consisted of Jim and me, Gordon Richardson, Harold Lever, and a handful of our officials. It proved useful at least in keeping No. 10 informed on what I was doing. We never had the sort of public argument between prime minister and chancellor which proved so damaging to market confidence during the Thatcher Government.

Our cooperation proved invaluable in preparing the annual Economic Summits which became a useful instrument of international cooperation in my later years at the Treasury. In November 1975, while Wilson was still Prime Minister and Jim Foreign Secretary, Giscard d'Estaing, the President of France, invited the heads of government from the United States, Britain, Germany, Italy and Japan to the castle of Rambouillet outside Paris. His main purpose was to get President Ford's cooperation on international financial issues, where America's conservatism was blocking cooperation on exchange rates and the oil surpluses. The Finance and Foreign Ministers of the six countries were also invited, although there was no room at Rambouillet for them to stay. So Jim and I had to travel to and from the British Embassy each day. Some of the other ministers were wiser; they stayed at three-star hotels nearby.

Giscard had a personal affection for Rambouillet, but it was exceptionally ill-adapted for our meeting. The British officials had to work in Napoleon's bathroom, trying to find their way to me or Jim along narrow twisting passages, up and down spiral stone staircases, with no plan to guide them. The officials were not allowed to attend the plenary meetings of the eighteen ministers, nor would there have been room for them in any case. Heavy iron gates barred out the press, who gathered with ordinary tourists in the village square outside. Anxious, as always, to take some photographs, I managed to escape for a few minutes, to be accosted by a journalist with the question: 'Aren't you Denis Healey?' 'Cosa dice?' I replied. 'Sono turista Italiano.' The newspapers duly reported next day that they had come across an Italian tourist who looked just like Denis Healey.

The only specific outcome of the meeting had already been agreed by us Finance Ministers – to limit currency intervention to what we called 'erratic fluctuations'. Derek Mitchell, of course, insisted on calling them 'erotic fluctuations' instead. But Rambouillet was useful in allowing heads of government to meet in private, without their officials, to discuss anything which was on their minds. It turned out to be the first of the annual Economic Summits which continue to this day.

The following year President Ford invited us all to Puerto Rico, adding Pierre Trudeau from Canada, who had failed to persuade Giscard to invite him to Rambouillet. At Puerto Rico we met in a millionaires' holiday camp on a palm fringed beach, and stayed in luxurious bungalows, travelling from one to another in electric buggies. This summit, too, produced little of concrete importance, but it did further strengthen the personal understanding between heads of government. It was Jim Callaghan's first summit as Prime Minister; he was able to make better use of those which followed in London and Bonn. By that time the European and Japanese heads of government were men who had all worked together previously as Finance Ministers, and had personal experience of the economic problems they had to discuss. Our old friend Fukuda was Prime Minister of Japan, and spoke English fluently, like Giscard and Helmut Schmidt. So translation was rarely necessary.

We British had one minor triumph at Puerto Rico. Jim decided we should fly there in Concorde, which had only recently entered service. We covered the whole 4,500 miles without a stop in four hours, greatly to the chagrin of Giscard, who had chosen to fly in an ordinary aircraft, and took almost twenty-four hours. Even this did not reconcile me to the money we had wasted on Concorde; I was glad to find that Giscard was as unhappy about its cost as I. Puerto Rico was also one of Tony Crosland's first meetings with Henry Kissinger, who found it difficult at first to understand Tony's sense of humour, and the somewhat patronising arrogance of his style.

The London Summit in 1977 gave Jim a chance of showing Jimmy Carter, the new American President, something of Britain's industrial heartland. So Carter was coached to begin his speech on the steps of Newcastle Town Hall with the traditional Geordie rallying cry: 'Hawa' the lads'; the applause was deafening. He handled himself no less impressively in the summit meetings themselves, though his relations with Helmut Schmidt had already begun to deteriorate over the conditions Carter wanted to impose on American supplies of nuclear fuel to Germany. They reached rock bottom later, when Carter decided to drop his proposal for putting neutron bombs in Europe, after Schmidt had expended a dangerous amount of his political capital in persuading his German colleagues to accept them. Schmidt's blistering comments on Carter at this time were of course relayed to Washington. They played an important role in the unnecessary wrangling over the appropriate Western response to the Soviet SS-20s, which did more to undermine support for the alliance than anything since Suez, as I shall later describe.

Nevertheless, by far the most successful and important summit held till then was that called in Bonn by Helmut Schmidt in 1978, which at first Carter had been unwilling to attend. The growing weakness of the dollar was threatening the stability of the Western financial system; meanwhile Germany's refusal to expand its domestic demand was holding back growth in the rest of the world, thereby facing the poorer countries with the temptation to default on their debts. Jim Callaghan put forward our proposals for a transatlantic bargain: its most important features were that the United States should take steps to cut its energy consumption in return for reflationary measures in Germany; each of the other five countries should make its appropriate contribution. At the Bonn Summit Carter agreed to cut America's oil imports and to raise the price of oil in the United States to the world level by the end of 1980. In return Schmidt, with much misgiving, agreed to stimulate demand in Germany by one per cent of GDP – a measure which certainly helped to get him re-elected the following year.

Economists still argue about the long-term effectiveness of the decisions taken at the Bonn Summit, since the second big increase in oil prices, which started in 1979, makes it difficult to disentangle the results of Bonn from everything else which then affected the world economy. No one, however, can dispute that Bonn marked the first serious attempt in history by the world's leading governments to adapt their domestic policies to the needs of the world economy as a whole. Later summits did not even make the attempt.

As Chancellor I was deeply involved in preparing each of these Summit Conferences. My officials worked hard with their opposite numbers in the other six countries. As always, I found it useful to get to know the civil servants who coordinated all this work for their heads of government; we called them 'sherpas', after the Nepalese who guide climbers to the summits of the Himalaya. Carter's sherpa, Bob Hormats, became a friend for life. The summit meetings also brought me close to the heads of government themselves.

In my opinion, Gerald Ford has been underestimated. I always found him decisive, shrewd and helpful in the private meetings, as well as an exceptionally nice and decent man. It was only in public that he could get into a tangle over words, provoking the cruel jibe that he could not walk and chew gum at the same time. The Italian Prime Minister, Aldo Moro was a sad and gentle figure, whose manner at Puerto Rico seemed to suggest foreknowledge of his capture and murder by terrorists a few months later. His successor, Giulio Andreotti, was the most professional politician in Italy, and had held all the senior ministries, some of them several times. It was said that when he left the Ministry of the Interior he was followed by several lorries, containing the secret police files on all his colleagues.

Pierre Trudeau was one of the most attractive and enigmatic public figures I have met. He had exceptional charisma, and could suddenly illuminate the most boring and predictable discussion with a refreshing flash of insight. Later his much publicised marital difficulties gave him a tragic melancholy.

Valéry Giscard d'Estaing had that air of effortless superiority once attributed to Balliol men. Yet another Inspecteur des Finances, he had worked as a Treasury official and as Finance Minister before becoming President. His high forehead and sensitive features told of his passionate interest in the arts. He once told me how much he had enjoyed reading Harold Pinter's script for a film Joseph Losey was making of Proust. We became involved in a long discussion of novels and politics; as a result I sent him several of Douglas Hurd's early thrillers, which gave a better picture of Whitehall politics than any academic work I know. *Yes, Minister* was yet to come.

Helmut Schmidt, of course, had been a close friend and loyal colleague for many years; our special relationship continued when he was Chancellor of the Federal Republic. In his later years he was increasingly impatient of the constraints imposed by party politics, and deeply concerned about the future of Europe and the world. Though he was liable to moods of black depression, they rarely lasted long. I recall one meeting at Chequers when he told me at lunch that he was on the point of giving up politics altogether; I had never seen him so exhausted. As we were leaving the table, his private secretary came to tell him that there was a television team from *Panorama* already set up to record a long interview. Within seconds his whole appearance changed. His slumping body grew taut again, his weary eyes began to flash, and he strode into the television room with exuberant self-confidence to give yet another brilliant interview in flawless English.

In December 1974 he had addressed a suspicious Labour Party

Conference on the Common Market, to which he knew it was profoundly hostile. Within ten minutes he had won them round with one of the most effective Conference speeches I have ever heard – again in perfect English. It was not the last time a foreign Socialist was to overcome the prejudices of a xenophobic British labour movement. In September 1988 Jacques Delors had a similar triumph at the Annual Congress of the TUC. However much we distrust Europe, we still like Europeans – when they speak our language!

I saw another example of Helmut Schmidt's sudden changes of mood when Jim Callaghan and I flew over to see him in Bonn, the morning after the rescue of the German hostages at Mogadishu, in which advice and technical assistance from our SAS had played a role. Helmut was cock-a-hoop, and bubbling with excitement. In the middle of the morning an aide brought in a message reporting that some German terrorists had committed suicide in prison though under continuous surveillance, as a demonstration against the rescue at Mogadishu. Helmut fell into the depths of despair; he was still drowning in misery when we flew back that afternoon.

My last ministerial encounter with him was over a far more important issue, in which I became deeply involved as a member of a small secret committee on which Jim had put me, not so much as Chancellor but as a former Defence Secretary – the Soviet SS-20s. Helmut had a dangerous habit of occasionally thinking aloud about an important issue without thinking it through. In October 1977 he gave a speech in London at the IISS, in which he reflected his growing distrust of Carter. He said that the current Soviet–American talks on limiting strategic nuclear weapons – SALT II – if they ended by neutralising the intercontinental nuclear capabilities of the superpowers, would magnify the importance of the disparities between East and West in shorter-range nuclear and conventional weapons. So, parallel with SALT II, there should be an agreement to eliminate the Soviet superiority in these other weapons. Behind this statement lay Schmidt's vague feeling – it was no more than that – that American Cruise missiles in Europe might be the best response to the Soviet deployment of new SS-20 missiles; he feared that Carter might give up this option as part of SALT II.

Schmidt's speech set in motion a train of events which nearly split the alliance and is still disturbing Western unity. For some time the other Western governments ignored the issues raised in Schmidt's London speech, and he did not follow it up himself. But about a year later the course of the SALT II negotiations compelled Carter to raise the same issues. He and Brezhnev were at loggerheads over how to handle what came to be called the 'Grey Area' – the intermediate range nuclear delivery systems based in Western Europe or the seas round it, and the similar Soviet systems based in Western Russia. The Russians, naturally enough, regarded as 'strategic' any systems which could drop nuclear weapons on the Soviet Union, wherever they were based – including, of course, those of Britain and France. The Europeans, for the same reason, wanted to include Soviet systems, like the SS-20 missiles now being deployed by Russia, which could hit them although not the United States. Carter knew he would not get Senate support for ratifying the SALT II treaty without help from his European allies. So he insisted that they should join him in finding a common position on the 'Grey Area'.

There followed a tragi-comedy which continued until well after Labour lost power in Britain. In October 1979 it produced the so-called 'Dual Track' decision, in which NATO undertook to deploy Cruise and Pershing II missiles in Western Europe unless the Soviet Union removed its SS-20s. Callaghan's small committee included the Foreign and Defence Secretaries and me. The crucial meetings of this committee took place in the early months of 1979, during the Winter of Discontent, when our main preoccupation was with Britain's escalating industrial troubles and the possibility of being forced into a premature general election.

Nevertheless, I believe we came to the right conclusions on all but one of the issues we discussed. We decided that Britain should put its Polaris force into the SALT III negotiations which were to start immediately after SALT II had been ratified – but only on condition that Britain took a direct part in the negotiations, preferably representing all the European members of NATO. I argued strongly against the concept of a 'Euro-strategic nuclear balance', which I thought would lead the United States to withdraw its intercontinental nuclear forces from their role in deterring attack on Western Europe; in the end I persuaded the committee to accept this view.

Our one mistake was not to cancel the Chevaline programme, which was intended to enable the Polaris force to penetrate the ABM system the Russians were building to protect Moscow. Chevaline was running far behind schedule and even further above its planned costs. David Owen and I did not believe that it was necessary for a British deterrent force to be able to guarantee the destruction of Moscow. We thought that the certain ability to threaten the destruction of the dozen next largest Soviet cities would be more than enough to deter an attack on Britain if the alliance had disintegrated – a contingency which was almost inconceivable in any case. Officials were instructed to present a paper on the so-called 'Moscow Criterion'; they produced a recommendation in favour of it, without any serious argument except that to cancel Chevaline would damage our prestige in both Moscow and Washington. I regard it as one of my major mistakes not to have insisted on the cancellation of Chevaline in my first years as Chancellor.

On the other hand we did not, as has sometimes been alleged, agree on the deployment of Cruise and Pershing as a counter to the SS-20. In fact, though Carter tried again and again to get Schmidt to say exactly what he wanted to do about the threat of the SS-20, Schmidt made no proposals on the issue before we left office. The other European governments in NATO were quite happy to continue relying on the allocation of Poseidon missiles to SACEUR; this had been agreed when America withdrew all its land-based missiles from Europe after the Cuban crisis. Jim rightly told the press at Guadeloupe that it made little difference to the citizens of Manchester or Frankfurt whether they were obliterated by an intercontinental missile or a mere medium range missile sited across the North Sea.

Nor did we tackle the problem of a possible successor to the Polaris force. Jim Callaghan was determined that we should stick to our election pledge not to move into a new generation of nuclear missiles. However, when Carter called the British, German, and French heads of government to discuss all these problems with him in Guadeloupe, we agreed that Jim should, without commitment, find out whether he might agree to let Britain have the proposed Trident C4 system, should a British government decide to ask for it. Carter's response was favourable. We noted it, again without commitment; David Owen had in any case been persuaded by Solly Zuckerman that a Cruise system would be as effective and far cheaper.

Jim Callaghan has given a full account of the Guadeloupe meeting in his memoirs, as he gave it to our committee when he returned. It is fully consistent with the account given by President Carter, and by Zbig Brzezinski, who was also present as Carter's National Security Adviser. However, some European journalists have claimed the authority of Schmidt or Giscard to say that the Guadeloupe Summit agreed to deploy Cruise and Pershing. I cannot believe this story; if it were true it is remarkable that Schmidt refused to clarify his views officially for months after the summit.

I suspect that there was no bad faith involved. Summit meetings are notoriously dangerous when the great men, or women, meet informally without anyone present to take notes. Mrs Thatcher and President Mitterrand had a public argument about what had been agreed at a later Economic Summit. I recall that after Wilson's first meeting with President Johnson, the State Department had to send an official to the British Embassy in Washington to find out what their own President had said. Jim Callaghan was always scrupulously careful to note down the course of every discussion in pencil on a grubby postcard immediately it was over, for the official minutes. There is something to be said for the traditions of British staff-work.

The SS-20 problem was not the only issue on which my experience at Defence served me well as Chancellor. I was familiar with all the tricks used by my old department to bamboozle the Treasury. Nevertheless, I was deeply offended when the head of Service Intelligence gave a briefing to the assembled Cabinet on the relative strengths of the two alliances. Despite my presence he tried to get away with excluding all the French armed forces from the Western side, while including the Poles and even the Rumanians on the Eastern side. I am glad to say that he was suitably abashed when I pointed this out.

Nineteen seventy-seven was my victory year as Chancellor, but it was marred by personal loss. My father fell dangerously ill in January, and died six weeks later at the age of ninety-two. I used to drive out every few days to see him in hospital at Whipps Cross, working on my budget in the car. Will raged against the dying of the light; he felt that somehow or other he had failed to realise his true potential, and to express his true feelings to his family. He never established that warm and natural relationship with his children, or even his wife, which he achieved effortlessly with his students. Too often he found it necessary to conceal his emotions behind a brutal facetiousness. But I still get letters from men and women whom he helped at Keighley Technical College, or at the end of his life, when he was teaching West Indians at Walthamstow. I chose the haunting beauty of the 'Pie Jesu' from Fauré's *Requiem* for his cremation.

While my father was dying at Whipps Cross, Tony Crosland had a brain haemorrhage; he died six days later. Tony had been a close friend since Oxford. Always gay and debonair, he was the most attractive character in the Labour Cabinet. In intellectual and imaginative power I thought he surpassed his close friend and rival, Roy Jenkins. But he lacked Roy's determination, and, rather like my father, sometimes used an offhand flippancy as a means of disguising his views or evading responsibility. He finally found the love and stability he needed in his second marriage, to the American journalist Susan Barnes, who was no less intelligent and attractive than he.

Jim was again relieved when I told him I would prefer to stay at the Treasury for the time being; I had broken my back in planting the tree, and I wanted to be there to gather the fruit. So he chose David Owen to replace Tony as Foreign Secretary, warning him, and the Lobby, that he might have to give it up when I was ready to leave the Treasury. It was probably a premature promotion for David. He began to mask his insecurity with an arrogance which was found offensive by many of those who worked for him, from his Permanent Secretary to his messenger or driver. Yet he got on well with his American counterpart, Cy Vance, as he had got on with Mike Le Fanu as First Sea Lord. Both were older men, who could forgive David's occasional spikiness for the sake of his vitality and enthusiasm.

The Labour Government's problems were complicated by the disappearance of its fragile majority in Parliament soon after Jim took over. For almost three years we had to live from hand to mouth, never certain that we would survive the next vote in the House of Commons. Some of our own backbenchers did not scruple to exploit the situation, by threatening to withdraw their vote on specific issues unless they got their way. Not only the Liberals, but the Ulster Unionists and the small nationalist parties from Scotland and Wales also found this an ideal situation for political blackmail.

Michael Foot was indefatigable in scraping up the odd votes when needed, sometimes by concessions of which none of us could be proud. In fact we had to operate more like a United States administration with the Congress, or like a French government under the Fourth Republic, assembling different coalitions in Parliament according to the subject in hand. No one who lived through that period can believe that proportional representation would necessarily produce better government than the traditional British voting system; nor could anyone imagine that the compromises imposed by the need for support from smaller parties would produce policies which better reflected the views of the majority of the British people.

Partly because of our weakness in Parliament, we had to spend a great deal of time and effort on issues which were marginal to our real problems; so it was difficult to give the Government a coherent theme. Wilson found that the only way to deal with the opponents of the Common Market in the Labour Party was to accept Tony Benn's long-standing proposal for a national referendum on the subject. By the time the referendum took place in 1975, Tony Benn's initial enthusiasm for the Common Market had turned to bitter hostility; but the British people produced a majority of more than two to one in favour. It was not the first time Tony's constitutional innovations produced a result he neither liked nor expected. By changing the law to allow himself to renounce his peerage and sit in the House of Commons, he made it possible for Alec Douglas-Home to become Prime Minister – after renouncing his peerage in turn.

The proposal for direct elections to the Assembly of the European Community produced another constitutional change with results which proved opposite to those intended. Many of my colleagues feared that direct elections would give the so-called Euro-MPs the political authority to assume powers to override the British Parliament. In fact, as I predicted at the time, the Euro-MPs now have less influence on events than before. Elected by a small proportion of the electorate from very large constituencies, they lack political authority; and because they are cut off from their national parliaments they lack influence where it really matters.

Another issue on which the Government spent an inordinate amount of time, unfortunately to no effect, was the report of a commission chaired by my school-friend Alan Bullock on industrial democracy. This aimed at introducing into Britain a system not unlike the German *Mitbestimmungsrecht*. Bullock proposed that workers should have the right to be represented on company boards, provided that at least one third of all the eligible workers had voted in favour. Unfortunately the trade union leaders insisted that they should represent the workers concerned, through their existing union structures, which could not be relied on to operate democratically. So the proposal ran into the sand. Genuine industrial democracy would in fact have undermined the power of the trade unions at national level. The employers were typically short-sighted in opposing it root-and-branch.

The issue which caused us the greatest trouble, however, was that of devolution. There had always been pressure in Scotland and Wales for greater devolution of power over their affairs from Westminster to their national capitals in Edinburgh and Cardiff. The development of North Sea oil greatly increased this pressure in Scotland, although cynics pointed out that the oilfields themselves were closer to the Shetland islands than to the Scottish mainland. What was particularly galling to both the Scots and the Welsh was that the Labour Party in England seemed to be in historical decline, while Scotland and Wales had permanent majorities of Labour MPs; so government from Westminster looked like overruling the political views as well as the national sentiments of the Scots and Welsh.

I had a lot of sympathy with these views, particularly in Scotland. During my years as Chancellor I had spent much more time in Scotland both at work and on holiday. There was no denying that it had a national identity quite separate from England. Much of what happened in Scotland found the English both ignorant and indifferent. The Labour Party's failure to take account of Scottish feeling had already produced a Scottish Nationalist Party which was winning Labour as well as Conservative seats there.

During one holiday in Scotland I was glimpsed through the window of my hotel by the Colonel of a Scottish regiment. He rang my wartime Brigadier, Reggie Fellowes, who had retired to a beautiful Adam farm-house near Dalmally. Reggie asked Edna and me to lunch the next day. It was a pleasure to meet the old man again. He had fought in France during the First World War, and returned to the army in the Second, when I served under him in North Africa and Italy. After we had exchanged reminiscences, he told me to my amazement that he had become an ardent supporter of the Scottish Nationalist Party. He was typical of many traditional Conservatives in Scotland at that time.

I was also immensely impressed by the quality of the Labour Party and trade union leaders in Scotland; though many of the latter were Communists, they were level-headed and dedicated to the welfare of those they represented. Helen Liddell, the Secretary of the Labour Party in Scotland, was a brilliant and attractive young woman who would have risen to the top in any other walk of life. Some of the young Scottish MPs were no less admirable. John Smith, a barrister from Edinburgh, was the youngest member of the Cabinet when he became Secretary for Trade at thirty-nine, after Edmund Dell left politics for the City. Donald Dewar was equally brilliant. George Robertson, who won the Hamilton by-election at the age of thirty-one, had already been Chairman of the Labour Party in Scotland and Scottish organiser of the General and Municipal Workers' Union; he was an excellent deputy for me as Shadow Foreign Secretary in the eighties. Robin Cook was an able debater. Scotland continues to send exceptional young men to Parliament at every election; Gordon Brown is one of the latest.

Yet our attempt to provide devolution for Scotland and Wales proved a disastrous failure, like so many other attempts to reform the British Constitution before it; in 1968 Dick Crossman's attempt to reform the

House of Lords was swallowed up in the quicksands of Parliamentary procedure, owing to joint manoeuvres by Michael Foot and Enoch Powell. Our attempts to achieve devolution also foundered, again because opponents on our own benches combined with the Tories to defeat it. Some Scottish and Welsh MPs, notably Tam Dalyell and Neil Kinnock, opposed it as the thin end of a wedge which would end by splitting both the Labour Party and the country into fragments; indeed the leaders of the Labour Party in Scotland were initially hostile to devolution for the same reasons. There were also many Labour MPs, particularly in north-east England and Merseyside, who thought that devolution in Scotland and Wales would divert resources from their own regions, and create a disruptive demand for devolution elsewhere.

Our first attempt to introduce devolution in December 1976 failed in the House of Commons a few months later. One consequence was that we were compelled to make a Parliamentary alliance with the Liberals. We launched a second attempt in November 1977. This survived in Parliament, but only at the price of amendments which ensured its defeat in the consultative referenda in Scotland and Wales on March 1st, 1979. The referenda were held when the Government's popularity was at its lowest, immediately following the Winter of Discontent. The Welsh rejected our proposals by the enormous majority of four to one, fully justifying Neil Kinnock's opposition. There was a slim majority in Scotland, but it did not amount to forty per cent of the total electorate – the minimum laid down in the amendment which had been forced on us. It was a shattering blow for the Labour Government. We still had seven months of our term to run. But the Scottish Nationalists put down a motion of censure against us, which the Conservatives decided to support. We lost by one vote. Jim decided to call a general election for May 3rd.

Most people had expected us to call a general election the previous autumn, when the economy was booming, family incomes had had their biggest boost for many years, and it was still possible that we might succeed in controlling pay increases without the formal support of the trade unions. In June 1978 inflation was down to only 7.4 per cent; if we had used the tax-price index later introduced by the Conservatives, and taken my tax cuts also into account, the cost of living had increased only 1.5 per cent. Jim and Audrey Callaghan had come to see us at our Sussex home, a few miles from their farm, on August 18th. He was minded to go through the winter if we could survive the votes on the Queen's Speech. Both the Labour Party's organisers in the country and all but two of the Labour Whips in Parliament preferred delay. I warned him that the growth of output and living standards would be slower during the winter; but Jim thought that by the spring the longer experience of improving living standards would count for more with the voters. Neither of us foresaw the industrial troubles which lay ahead, or our defeat on devolution, which was in part their consequence. What weighed most heavily with Jim was the general view of our organisers that we could not expect more than another hung Parliament if we held the election in the autumn. He was sick to death of the continual compromises required for our survival as a minority government; I think he would rather have lost than be condemned to a repetition of the previous three years.

Unfortunately, when he met the TUC leaders during their annual Congress he did not reveal his intention. When he made his speech to the Congress he sang the old music-hall song 'There was I, waiting at the church', which ends with the words 'I can't – marry you today – my wife – won't let me.' To me, this should have been a clear indication that he was planning to delay the election; but for some reason the TUC interpreted it in exactly the opposite sense. When it became clear that he was in fact going to run through the winter, they felt he had deliberately deceived them.

Our hubris in fixing a pay norm of five per cent without any support from the TUC met its nemesis, as inevitably as in a Greek tragedy. Ironically enough, the opinion polls, which had put us four per cent behind the Tories in August, gave us a seven per cent lead in October, with Jim far more popular than Mrs Thatcher. But the unions at Ford and British Oxygen then demanded pay increases of fifteen per cent – twice the rate of inflation – and the public sector unions wanted even more. On November 14th the TUC General Council split evenly on a helpful statement of guidance on pay which I had spent five weeks negotiating with the Neddy Six. The TUC Chairman, Tom Jackson, though he favoured the document himself, was obliged by convention to give his casting vote against it. Moss Evans, who had helped to draft the document, was abroad on holiday and had left no instructions for the other two delegates from his union. One of them voted for, the other against. This shambles was of course a triumph for Mrs Thatcher. The cowardice and irresponsibility of some union leaders in abdicating responsibility at this time guaranteed her election; it left them with no grounds for complaining about her subsequent actions against them. On the other hand we in the Cabinet should have realised that our five per cent norm would be provocative as well as unattainable. If we had been content with a formula like 'single figures', we would have had lower settlements, have avoided the winter of discontent, and probably have won the election too.

By December, although half a million workers had already settled within the Government guidelines, most of the other unions were steadily increasing their demands – the local authority manual workers claimed forty per cent. Worse still, many workers were going on strike to enforce their claims. Just before Christmas, the Ford Motor Company settled for seventeen per cent; and five Labour left-wingers abstained so that the Tories could defeat the Government's attempt to impose sanctions against the company. The road haulage and oil tanker drivers went on strike, with Moss Evans' encouragement, to support claims for increases of twenty-five to thirty per cent. Each night the television screens carried film of bearded men in duffle coats huddled around braziers. Nervous viewers thought the Revolution had already begun.

January was even worse. Rubbish was piling up in the streets because the dustbin men were on strike. In some cities the grave-diggers refused to bury the dead. Their union leader, Alan Fisher, refused to ask them to go back to work. The TUC General Council finally joined the Government in drafting a sensible guide on negotiating procedures and the conduct of disputes; but it was now as impotent as the Government to influence the strikers. Meanwhile Jim Callaghan was at his summit meeting in Guadeloupe. Pictures of him in the tropical sun did not improve the temper of ordinary men and women suffering from trade union action in the British winter. For once in his life, Jim himself was badly out of touch with popular feeling. Some careless remarks at the airport on his return led the popular press to mispresent him as saying 'Crisis? What crisis?' This phrase, which he never used, has now entered popular folklore along with Wilson's 'Pound in your pocket', Heath's 'Bring down prices at a stroke' and my own alleged promise to 'Squeeze the rich till the pips squeak'. No reference to the truth will ever dislodge them from the public mind.

By March Jim was exhausted and dispirited. I believe that if we had struggled on a little longer we might have cut Mrs Thatcher's majority by a few seats for each week we moved further away from the Winter of Discontent. But exhaustion is sometimes a decisive factor in politics; it had also led the Attlee Government to defeat in 1951. Even so, the Tories fell from an initial lead of thirteen per cent as low as two per cent at one stage in the campaign; but we never overtook them. Mrs Thatcher finished with sixty-nine more seats than Labour, and an overall majority of forty-one.

My five years at the Treasury were over. I had already accomplished most of the Labours of Hercules. The Augean Stables I had inherited from Tony Barber were cleansed. The Golden Apples of the Hesperides were now stored at the IMF. I hoped I might still be able to take the Girdle of Hippolyta. Instead I was to find myself wearing the Shirt of Nessus.

PART FOUR: New Challenges

CHAPTER TWENTY-TWO

Labour in Travail

Run out the boat, my broken comrades;
Let the old seaweed crack, the surge
Burgeon oblivious of the last
Embarkation of feckless men,
Let every adverse force converge –
Here we must needs embark again.

Run up the sail, my heartsick comrades;
Let each horizon tilt and lurch –
You know the worst: your wills are fickle,
Your values blurred, your hearts impure
And your past life a ruined church –
But let your poison be your cure.

Put out to sea, ignoble comrades,
Whose record shall be noble yet;
Butting through scarps of moving marble
The narwhal dares us to be free;
By a high star our course is set,
Our end is Life. Put out to sea.

> – 'Thalassa' Louis MacNeice

AFTER THE 1935 ELECTION, Churchill was excluded from the Conservative Government. He wrote that he was lucky to have been spared responsibility during the years that followed: 'And I had agreeable consolation. I set out with my paintbox for more genial climes without waiting for the meeting of Parliament.'

I was not quite so fortunate. Jim Callaghan told me within a week of the election that he planned to stay on as Leader of the Labour Party for eighteen months – 'to take the shine off the ball' for me. I did not complain, nor would I have changed Jim's mind if I had. My five years at the Treasury had left me exhausted. If we had won, I hoped I might have a chance of succeeding Jim as Prime Minister after a year or two. I did not look forward to the idea of succeeding him as Leader of the Labour Party in Opposition; I had seen that there is no more difficult job in British politics. Of course, I would not resist it if it came my way; and I would fight hard for it if I thought the alternative candidate was unacceptable. But I was glad for the chance to take things a little more easily until the ordeal became inescapable.

I did not follow Winston's example with my paintbox. Except for one or two watercolours during the summer holidays, I had practically given up painting for photography, although after leaving Defence I never had time to do my own processing. But I followed Churchill at least to the extent that I decided to write a photographic memoir, to be called *Healey's Eye*, and took advantage of visits to Japan and Greece to increase my collection of colour slides.

Long before the book was published, however, I was up to the neck in an exhausting struggle for the survival of the Labour Party. Jim's last eighteen months as Leader not only took the shine off the ball, but ripped away the leather as well. There followed ten years of internal fighting which was quite as damaging to the Party as the decade of struggle with Bevanism after Attlee lost power.

Within days of the election, the Party began an inquest into our defeat. Labour's share of the vote had been 36.9 per cent – our lowest since 1935. The Tory share had risen to 43.9 per cent, from 35.7 per cent in October 1974. This was partly at the expense of the Liberals, who had lost over two million votes from a larger electorate, but also because the turnout was over three per cent higher. The increase in the turnout went overwhelmingly to the advantage of the Conservatives. In my own constituency eighty per cent of the electorate voted in the Tory ward, compared with just over sixty-two per cent in the Labour wards. Worst of all, Labour won only half of the trade unionists' vote, while the Tories won nearly a third. Labour's vote fell furthest among skilled and unskilled workers; it actually rose five per cent among white collar workers, and eight per cent among the professional middle class.

The Labour Left used these figures to argue that the Callaghan Government had sacrificed the workers for the sake of middle-class votes, and that we could recover our position only by moving Left. They never explained how this would persuade workers who had just voted Tory to vote Labour next time, or how people who had not bothered to vote at all could be inspired to man the barricades of the class war. They often reminded me of Brecht's poem:

> After the uprising of the 17th June
> The Secretary of the Writers' Union
> Had leaflets distributed in the Stalinallee
> Stating that the people had forfeited the confidence of the government
> And could win it back only
> By redoubled efforts. Would it not be easier
> In that case for the government
> To dissolve the people
> And elect another?

All the evidence suggested that we had lost the election mainly because the Winter of Discontent had destroyed the nation's confidence in the Labour Party's ability to work with the unions; it had also turned large numbers of working people against their own trade union representatives.

The Winter of Discontent was not caused by the frustration of ordinary workers after a long period of wage restraint. It was caused by institutional pressures from local trade union activists who had found their roles severely limited by three years of incomes policies agreed by their national leaders; they felt, like Othello when he had to give up soldiering, that their occupation was gone. Ironically enough, workers' real income rose less as a result of the settlements achieved in the Winter of Discontent than they had in the previous wage round. And once she was Prime Minister, Mrs Thatcher saw to it that the trade unions paid a heavy price for their irresponsibility, though it had won her the election.

Unfortunately the Labour Party's financial and constitutional links with the unions made it difficult for us to draw too much attention to their role in our defeat. Jim Callaghan belonged to the generation of Labour leaders which had come to depend on the trade union block vote for protection against extremism in the constituencies; moreover, the trade unions had provided his main political base in the previous decade.

That base was now crumbling. Again and again in the critical years after the 1979 election, incoherence or incompetence in the trade union leadership led us to disaster. With the retirement of Jack Jones and Hugh Scanlon, the Party had lost its ablest supporters in the TUC. Their mantle should have fallen on David Basnett, the leader of the mighty General and Municipal Workers' Union. But Basnett seemed to find the mantle uncomfortable and embarrassing; it was in any case too heavy for him. He proved weak and vacillating in our years of travail, and was too much influenced by Clive Jenkins, the maverick left-wing leader of a professional union whose members mainly voted Tory. There were some tough and able trade union leaders, such as Bryan Stanley of the Post Office Engineers, Roy Grantham of my own professional union, APEX, Frank Chappell of the electricians, and Sid Weighell of the railwaymen. But their unions were too small to carry much weight, and their outspoken common sense only alarmed most of the other leaders. Terry Duffy, who had succeeded Scanlon as the engineers leader, was a right-wing Roman Catholic of immense courage; but his tactical judgment was not always reliable – it was to prove catastrophic at the crucial Wembley Conference in 1981. Moss Evans was a very inadequate substitute for Jack Jones as leader of the Transport and General Workers; he had no leadership qualities and little loyalty to the Labour Party.

Meanwhile Labour's defeat in 1979 provided the opportunity for a number of small groups inside the movement to extend their influence, both in the constituency parties and in the trade unions. Their aim was to change the Party constitution so as to give the Conference alone the power to choose the Party Leader, who would automatically become Prime Minister when Labour won an election, and to fix a programme of policies which a Labour Government would be compelled to follow. The first step in this process was to compel Labour MPs to follow the instructions of their constituency parties, by enabling the latter to replace them if they disobeyed.

The first and most important of these little groups had been set up in 1973 by a handful of rank and file Party members, who were unknown to the general public, and indeed to the overwhelming majority in the Labour Party itself. They called themselves the Campaign for Labour Party Democracy (CLPD), and were later joined by a number of other left-wing groups, notably the Labour Coordinating Committee (LCC) and the Militant Tendency. Unlike the other groups, the Militant Tendency was a splinter from the Trotskyite movement. Though believing that socialism could ultimately be achieved only by violent revolution, it had broken away from other Trotskyite bodies such as the International Marxist Group (IMG) and the Socialist Workers Party (SWP) because it believed that the first step towards revolution must be to capture the Labour Party from within, a tactic known as 'entryism'. Labour's National Agent, Reg Underhill, had produced a damning report on the Militant Tendency in 1977; but the National Executive refused even to allow it to be published.

It was all too easy for the Labour Party leadership to dismiss these little groups as no more than alphabet soup. Yet they succeeded in achieving most of their constitutional objectives within two years of our defeat in 1979. Thereby they condemned the Labour Party to defeat in the next two general elections as well.

Inspired by their single-minded dedication to three specific constitutional changes, they showed immense skill in organising support in the trade unions, as well as the constituency parties. By 1979, CLPD was already getting financial support not only from left-wing unions, but from sections of the most right-wing unions, including my own. Even so, they would not have been able to succeed if the Labour Party's official organisation had been strong and vigilant. In fact our individual membership had fallen to about a quarter of a million; many constituencies had under fifty active members, and were easy prey to penetration and capture by a handful of conspirators who knew what they wanted. The Labour Party had protected itself in the past by proscribing bodies which aimed only to undermine it – in those days mainly the Communist Party and its innumerable 'front' organisations. The NEC abolished the proscribed list in the early seventies. In any case most of the new left-wing organisations were hostile to the Communist Party; they could usually rely for protection on the traditional Left in the Labour Party, particularly the Tribune Group of MPs, who provided nearly all of the constituency representatives on the National Executives.

Though the trade unions had an enormous membership, of which over six million were then affiliated to the Labour Party, most of them were badly prepared for their political role. The number of members they affiliated to the Labour Party depended on the whim of their executive committees rather than the views of the members concerned. One union, a majority of whose members probably voted Conservative, affiliated the whole of those who paid the political levy – and sometimes more, it was alleged. The mighty Transport and General Workers' Union always affiliated a million and a quarter of its members, over a period in which the total membership of the union fluctuated between 2,200,000 and

1,348,712. The National Union of Public Employees increased its affiliation to the Labour Party by 100,000 just before the Party Conference in 1980, at which the leadership lost the crucial vote by 98,000.

The political line of a trade union was liable to change the moment it got a new general secretary, although there was no reason to believe that the views of its members changed the same day. Thus the engineering union was seen as right-wing under Bill Carron, left-wing under Hugh Scanlon, and right-wing under Terry Duffy. But sometimes a general secretary could lose control of his executive committee – or of his delegation to the Party Conference. In 1980, a single delegate of the engineering union switched his vote towards the left; this was sufficient to reverse the position approved by the union leadership.

As militancy inside the trade unions increased under repeated hammer blows from the Thatcher Government, many of the union leaders found it more and more difficult to control their members on the industrial issues which were their prime concern. So they became less inclined to fight the Left inside their unions on political questions which mainly concerned the Labour Party. First they gave way on the constitutional issues raised by CLPD, and later on major issues of policy like unilateral nuclear disarmament. Those union leaders who were more committed to the Labour Party formed the Trade Union Campaign for Labour Victory (TULV). Yet, although it was initially set up to support Jim Callaghan, even TULV sometimes served as a vehicle through which CLPD could impose its will on the Parliamentary leadership.

Nevertheless, for all their skill and dedication, the CLPD and its allies would have been unable to exploit the weaknesses in the constituency parties and the trade unions without some charismatic figure as a rallying point. Once Nye Bevan was gone, the Left ceased to exert a major influence on the Party for twenty years. After the defeat of 1979 Tony Benn emerged as at once the leader and the tool of the new Left. Until then his political position had been difficult to define. In his early days he appeared simply as an engaging and harmless eccentric. When Attlee and Gaitskell led the Party, he often reminded me in his earnest but destructive innocence of Gregers Werle in Ibsen's *The Wild Duck*, who ruins a happy family in his pursuit of the ideal. His destiny was indeed to be the thirteenth man at the table, as Ibsen put it. However, his gift for words and for television led Harold Wilson to choose him for a key role as propagandist in the 1964 general election.

After Wilson's victory Benn became Postmaster General; he served in all the Labour Governments which followed. Though he came to oppose many of their policies, he never chose to resign his office. But the moment we went into Opposition he launched an all-out attack on his former colleagues for betraying the Party, and became the spearhead of the movement for constitutional change. Yet he remained personally courteous at all times. Besides a silver tongue, he had a pretty wit, and was quite prepared to laugh at himself. Although I had more cause then most to dislike him, I did not share the general view of his opponents that he was an unprincipled careerist. He was much more in the mould of another upper-class radical, Stafford Cripps, who oddly enough was also a Labour MP for Bristol. In the thirties, Cripps had been not only one of Britain's leading barristers, but also a political ninny of the most superior quality. Besides his revolutionary political rhetoric on domestic issues, he had idiosyncratic views on the threat from Hitler.

'I think it is likely,' he judiciously informed the Party Conference in 1936, 'that if Great Britain were conquered by Germany, Socialism would be suppressed, though that is not certain. Do not forget that Ludendorff sent Lenin into Russia and that Germany entertained the Irish rebels during the war.' He told the people of Stockport that he did not believe that 'war would be a bad thing for the British working class; it would be a disaster for the profit-makers and the capitalists, but not necessarily for the working class.'

Benn was a worthy successor to the Cripps of the thirties. The phenomenon they represent has something in common with that feudal socialism which Marx and Engels described in the Communist Manifesto as far back as 1848: 'Half lamentation and half lampoon; half echo of the past, half menace of the future; at times, by its bitter, witty, and incisive criticism, striking the bourgeoisie to the very heart's core, but always ludicrous in its effect, through total incapacity to comprehend the march of modern history. The aristocracy, in order to rally the people to them, waved the proletarian alms-bag in front for a banner. But the people, as often as it joined them, saw on their hindquarters the old feudal coat of arms, and deserted with loud and irreverent laughter.' It was Tony Benn's 'total incapacity to understand the march of modern history' which ensured that, when he came close to capturing the Party machine, he came close to destroying the Labour Party as a force in twentieth-century British politics.

The main battlefield in the war for the Labour Party's survival was its National Executive Committee, which in 1979 was solidly dominated by the Left. I had lost my place there in 1975. So in the first, most critical years, I could play my part only as a member of the Shadow Cabinet; in the summer of 1979 I was elected to the Shadow Cabinet top of the list. I set out my views comprehensively in a Memorial Lecture for Sara Barker, a close friend since the end of the war; she had worked the whole of her life as a paid official of the Labour Party, starting as secretary-agent in Halifax, and finishing as National Agent, in charge of the Party organisation throughout the country. I started by quoting Aneurin Bevan's epitaph on our defeat in 1959: 'Working people voted against the consequences of their own irresponsibility.' Then I described what I saw as the central problem:

> It arises from the fact that men and women who will give up night after night, weekend after weekend, to work for a political party are bound to differ in their views and the fire of their enthusiasm from the great mass of the British people, for whom politics is something to think about once every year at most, more often once every four or five years. Only three out of every hundred Labour voters bother to join the Labour Party as individual members. Only about three in a thousand actually turn up to work for the Party between general elections. Fewer still turn up regularly at General Management Committees . . .

I then tried to explain the lessons for Labour's economic policy of my own experience as Chancellor: we had to combine the management of demand with control of the money supply, and to improve our industrial performance by reducing our unit costs, both through raising output per head and through keeping wage increases in line with increases in productivity. And I ended this message, which was none too popular in the climate of the time, with the words of Lesjek Kolakowski, whom I had met as a young Marxist philosopher in Poland twenty years earlier, and who was now an exile in England:

> The trouble with the social democratic idea is that it does not stock and does not sell any of the exciting ideological commodities which various totalitarian movements – Communist, Fascist, or Leftist – offer dream-hungry youth. It has no prescription for the total salvation of mankind . . . Democratic Socialism requires, in addition to commitment to a number of basic values, hard knowledge and rational calculation . . . It is an obstinate will to erode by inches the conditions which produce avoidable suffering, oppression, hunger, wars, racial and national hatred, insatiable greed and vindictive envy.

'This is not an ignoble vision,' I concluded. 'It will do far more to help real people living in the real world today and tomorrow than all the cloudy rhetoric of systematic ideologies, or the tidy blueprints of academic theorists.'

True enough. But it was not a very attractive vision for the shrinking band of constituency activists, who were offered much more exciting fantasies by the drug-peddlers of the Broad Left. The problem in any case was to defeat the CLPD strategy on the ground by organising better than they did; for the time being, they were deliberately ignoring the issues of policy in order to achieve their objectives of constitutional change.

So I had to spend two years exploring an arid wasteland in which hollow men went round and round the prickly pears of constitutional amendments. I fear it may be as tedious to read about as it was to endure in real life – 'shape without form, shade without colour, paralysed force, gesture without motion'. But on the outcome of these arcane rituals depended the future of the Labour Party as a force in British politics.

Just before the Party Conference in 1978 the National Executive had set up a working party on the reselection of Labour MPs. The working party recommended that constituency parties should be compelled to consider the fitness of all sitting MPs to remain as candidates for the next elections, in the light of their behaviour in Parliament. This was the CLPD's first objective. It was intended to give local Labour Parties total control of their MPs, who in British constitutional theory were supposed to use their judgment in the interests of their electorates as a whole, rather than to obey the dictates of a local party caucus. By a majority of four to three the Party Conference in 1979 endorsed this proposal, as well as a proposal to give the National Executive the final decision on the Party's general election manifesto. By the same majority it rejected a proposal to set up an electoral college to choose the Party Leader (and future Prime Minister).

So, within four months of our 1979 election defeat, CLPD had achieved two of its three constitutional objectives. In all probability it would have failed completely, if the AUEW delegation had voted as the union membership wanted. However, the weekend meeting of the delegation was a shambles; one of those present was not a member of the union at all, but a visitor at the hotel who was simply waiting for a friend, and a key delegate was absent through a heart attack.

In the weekend before this Conference, at the request of TULV, the National Executive had set up a Committee of Enquiry to recommend constitutional changes to the Conference in the following year. I led the attack on the way the National Executive had rigged this Committee of Enquiry. It had appointed seven left-wingers to represent itself, while the trade unions chose a balanced team of five, picked from all the main currents of opinion, and the Labour MPs were allowed only two representatives, Jim Callaghan and Michael Foot; so the National Executive had a built-in left-wing majority. The Parliamentary Labour Party appointed me to put its case against the composition of the Committee of Enquiry to the National Executive. They simply ignored my arguments. Having won two of the CLPD's three objectives at the previous Conference, they were determined to win an electoral college at the next.

On June 15th, 1980 the Committee of Enquiry held its final meeting at Bishop's Stortford; since I was not a member, I could not be present. It agreed by seven votes to six to recommend an electoral college; fifty per cent should be Labour MPs, twenty-five per cent trade unionsts, twenty per cent from the constituency parties, and five per cent from other affiliated bodies such as the Fabian Society. This college would not only choose the Party Leader, but also have the final say on the Party Manifesto. Terry Duffy, the AUEW leader, now said that he would oppose the mandatory reselection of MPs, although his union had voted for it at the 1979 Conference.

The Bishop's Stortford proposals were bitterly attacked from both Left and Right. The Left thought that an electoral college so composed would support the Right; most right-wing MPs thought that the college would destroy the traditional independence of Labour MPs, and put them at the mercy of the block vote of a single union. At the next meeting of the Shadow Cabinet David Owen and Bill Rodgers launched a violent attack on Jim Callaghan for betraying the Parliamentary Party. He responded by accusing them of complicity in a speech just made by Roy Jenkins, recommending the creation of a new Centre Party in Britain. Jim was mistaken. It was Bishop's Stortford which caused the conception of the Social Democratic Party, although its birth took place, appropriately enough, nine months later. Its period of gestation was particularly painful for me.

Surprising as it may seem in retrospect, the Labour Party was then running over ten per cent ahead of the Conservatives in the opinion polls, and Jim Callaghan even further ahead of Mrs Thatcher. In July 1980 I myself was running six per cent ahead of Mrs Thatcher as a potential Prime Minister. The Labour Party's internal troubles did not wipe out its lead in the opinion polls until the autumn of 1981, when the split which created the SDP, and the long battle over the Deputy Leadership, finally sealed our fate.

Our strength in the country was one of several reasons why I rejected pressure from the right-wing Manifesto Group to break with Jim Callaghan and lead an all-out attack on the Bishop's Stortford formula for an electoral college. Over half the intending Labour voters wanted Jim to lead the Party in the next election. Only a quarter wanted him to resign immediately – probably the same quarter as wanted a new Centre Party to be formed after a Labour Party split. Of the eighty MPs in the Manifesto Group, twenty-nine were in the end to join the SDP. A battle against the Bishop's Stortford agreement would have meant a break, not only with Jim, but with the majority of trade union leaders who had supported it, believing that it would at least protect the Party from a takeover by the Left. The fight I was being asked to lead would have had no prospect of victory. It would have meant splitting the Party and throwing away the clear majority Labour had in the electorate, thus guaranteeing Mrs Thatcher's victory at the next election.

Moreover, although I thought Jim had made some mistakes in handling the situation, mainly through sheer exhaustion, I had great sympathy for him in his predicament. He had stuck to his central position despite a barrage of the most offensive personal abuse both in public speeches, and perhaps even more wounding, in the private meetings of the National Executive, where he was almost alone; there were few with both the guts and ability to defend him. He was, as someone said, in limbo and in purgatory at the same time. If the 1980 Conference had accepted the Bishop's Stortford formula, we might have had at least the best of all possible worlds, and kept the Party together. In the event, a series of hair-raising blunders by the unions gave us almost the worst of all worlds.

In 1980 the million block votes of the AUEW were swung to the Left by the unsuspected defection of a single eccentric delegate from Dorset. So the Conference added one more leftist to the National Executive, and reaffirmed its support for the mandatory reselection of Labour MPs by under half a million votes. However, it rejected the National Executive's proposal to rob the Parliamentary Party of its veto over the Manifesto. It accepted the principle of an electoral college, but by under 100,000 votes out of seven million. Then it went on to reject, by narrow majorities, both the proposals put forward for implementing it.

Anyone with a spark of common sense would have left it at that. Both the Labour Party and the TUC occasionally passed resolutions which contradicted one another or had no practical meaning. Indeed the very next day the Conference passed resolutions in favour of both multilateral and unilateral disarmament, while rejecting by nearly eight to one a demand that Britain should leave NATO. That type of confusion is perhaps one of the necessary conditions for operating the type of popular democracy favoured by the British labour movement. But David Basnett and Clive Jenkins thought otherwise.

Basnett proposed that the Party should hold a Special Conference in January to decide how to implement the principle of an electoral college; he also asked that no leadership election should be held before it had taken its decision. His proposal won overwhelming support; under a million opposed it. But Jim Callaghan warned the Conference that if he retired before the Special Conference, the Parliamentary Party would have to choose a new leader under the old rules.

Earlier that day my old friend Jack Gallivan, who had given me his indispensable wisdom and support for twenty-eight years in my own constituency of East Leeds, was given the Labour Party's Merit Award at the age of ninety-one. It was a fitting memorial to the end of an epoch in the history of the Labour Party.

David Basnett and Clive Jenkins made it clear that one of their purposes was to prevent me from succeeding Jim as Leader. They tried hard to dissuade Jim from retiring until after the special conference had set up the new electoral college. Jim was not playing their game. He announced his retirement on October 15th. The campaign for his successor was on – and confined to the Parliamentary Labour Party. But everyone knew that a new system of choosing the Leader would be adopted in a few months' time. Moreover, since mandatory reselection had been imposed by the Conference, every Labour MP knew that he might soon have to account for his vote to his constituency activists, and risk losing his seat if he displeased them.

I was obviously the front runner, and no one else from the Right or Centre of the Party challenged me. Tony Benn was reluctantly persuaded by the extreme Left not to run, on the grounds that an election by Labour MPs alone was now illegal; he would have been heavily defeated in any case. Peter Shore and John Silkin stood from the moderate Left, while Michael Foot let it be known he did not intend to stand at all. However, the election soon became a 'Stop Healey' campaign. Silkin had no chance of defeating me, and though my own friends thought that in the new situation Shore might have a good prospect of victory, some trade union leaders joined the far Left in Parliament in pressing Michael to change his mind. Peter still fancied his own chances and tried to dissuade him. I would hear him plodding up and down the Shadow Cabinet corridor between his room and Michael's for anguished discussions. The carpet was worn bare by the time Michael finally decided to run. Peter was bitterly disappointed, particularly since Michael made it clear that he would run not, as most people assumed, as a caretaker until the electoral college was in place, but to lead the Party into the next general election.

Meanwhile David Owen, Shirley Williams and Bill Rodgers were already making contingency plans for setting up a new Party. They had issued a long statement of their views, so I spent several hours in a private discussion with them in September. On the one hand, I told them that a new centre party was most unlikely to establish itself as a serious competitor with the Labour Party; on the other, that the moderates had a good chance of winning a majority on the National Executive and thus transforming the situation – but this was bound to take several years. I did not impress them, although I was proved right on both counts. For the next six months I spent a lot of time as a psychiatric social counsellor to MPs who wanted to leave the Labour Party. Though I believe most of the MPs who ultimately joined the SDP voted for me in the Leadership election, I am certain that several voted for Michael Foot in order to be able to justify their later defection; their few votes alone were sufficient to explain my defeat.

The main battle, however, was for the votes of MPs who had no strong political alignment, but were torn between their desire for a quiet life and their desire at least to hold their own seats at the next election. I had never cultivated a clique of acolytes, but I doubt if that damaged my prospects. I had a large group of active campaigners, led by Eric Varley, Giles Radice, and Roy Hattersley, although Roy had justly complained of my insensitivity towards my own supporters: ''E bites yer legs.' The lynch-pin of my whole campaign was Barry Jones, a young Welsh MP who had been the best of all my Parliamentary private secretaries. He was totally honest, loyal, and indefatigable. Our canvassing was a little overoptimistic, like that of all the other candidates. We expected 120 votes on the first ballot, but got only 112, as against eighty-three for Michael Foot, thirty-eight for Silkin, and thirty-two for Shore.

On the afternoon of November 10th I was warned, five minutes before the official announcement, that I had lost to Michael by 129 to 139. I composed my features into a cheerful grin as I walked past the assembled

Lobby correspondents to Committee Room Fourteen for the Party Meeting, Michael was looking nervous and unhappy, so they assumed that I had won. The moment the result was announced I rose to congratulate Michael, and announced that I would be proud to serve under him as Deputy Leader if the Party wished, as I knew he would have served under me if I had won. There was a great storm of cheering and banging of desks. I glanced at Tony Benn. His face was ashen. So I knew I had done at least one thing right.

I was deluged with messages of commiseration on my defeat; indeed I still continue to receive them. My favourite was a quotation from Sam Weller sent by a second-hand bookseller in Hastings: 'It's all over and can't be helped, and that's one consolation, as they always say in Turkey ven they cuts the wrong man's head off.' My usual reply was in the words of an unsuccessful American candidate: 'I would rather that people wonder why I am not President than why I am.'

There has been much speculation on the reasons for my defeat, some of it fed by MPs who wanted to find a respectable excuse for what was essentially their cowardice. The contest would never have been a walk-over. Michael Foot had won 133 votes against Jim Callaghan's 176 less than four years earlier, and the general election of 1979 had shifted the composition of the Parliamentary Labour Party some degrees to the left. Apart from the future defectors who voted for Michael, there were a few mavericks, including Harold Wilson. He told me later that he had voted for me on the first ballot and for Michael on the second; I suppose this was an existentialist *acte gratuite* – he did not explain.

An important factor in my defeat was the number of enemies I had made by the many unpopular measures I had been obliged to take as Chancellor. Some Labour MPs could not forgive me for blighting their cherished aspirations in the course of my spending cuts. Many union leaders, particularly David Basnett, had been offended by my handling of our incomes policy. They exercised some influence on the votes of the MPs they sponsored. When I was a student Communist one of our favourite topics for discussion was 'Who will do the dirty work under socialism?' In later life I discovered that the answer was 'Denis Healey'.

The Defence Ministry and the Treasury were regarded by Labour politicians as the graves of ambition. Nevertheless, I do not regret the political price I may have paid for my work as Defence Secretary and Chancellor; I have always been in politics in order to do something rather than to be something.

Without doubt the desire for a quiet life cost me the votes of some

MPs who might otherwise have supported me; they feared that as Leader I would have split the Party. The Party split in any case, but from the Right rather than the Left. And no Labour MP has had a quiet life ever since.

Our next ordeal was the Special Conference of the Party at Wembley in February 1981, which was an even bigger shambles than its predecessor. This time the Conference was confronted with five separate ways of composing an electoral college. Basnett proposed the original Bishop's Stortford formula, which gave fifty per cent to the Labour MPs. It would have been carried easily but for the fatal purism of the AUEW; Terry Duffy wanted the Labour MPs to have seventy-five per cent and had decided not to support any motion which gave them less than fifty-one per cent. So his union abstained. Clive Jenkins acted as the catspaw of CLPD, by swinging his union behind a motion which gave the Labour MPs only thirty per cent, as against forty per cent for the unions and thirty per cent for the constituency parties. Jon Lansman, a twenty-three-year-old unemployed graduate, was a key organiser for CLPD. He put it in a nutshell: 'The only reason we won was because the AUEW did not vote against us.'

This was the last straw for David Owen, Shirley Williams, and Bill Rodgers, who had just been joined by Roy Jenkins, to make the so-called Gang of Four. Six months earlier Owen had dismissed Roy Jenkins' call for a new Centre Party with the words: 'We will not be tempted by siren voices from outside, from those who have given up the fight from within'; he said he was prepared for 'ten years hard slog' inside the Labour Party if necessary. Shirley Williams said that she was not interested in a third party; it would have 'no roots, no principles, no philosophy and no values'. They changed their mind because they thought the Wembley Conference destroyed their last hopes of fighting their cause successfully inside the Labour Party, now that its new constitution had so weakened the power of its MPs.

Some of them have since said that they would not have left the Party if I had been elected Leader instead of Michael Foot. David Owen himself identified my defeat as the decisive factor. Certainly the Wembley Conference would have taken a different course if I had been Party Leader; and the immediate concern of David Owen and Shirley Williams at that time was essentially with the leadership and structure of the Labour Party rather than its policies, much as they disliked some of them. The 1980 Conference's rejection of the Common Market played an important role, but not Labour's defence policy. Owen, like me, had opposed the concept of a Eurostrategic balance, which was the justification for putting Cruise missiles into Britain; he had opposed modernising Polaris, and continued to oppose replacing Polaris with Trident as militarily unnecessary, accelerating the arms race, and far too expensive. The Labour Party did not commit itself unequivocally to a policy of unilateral nuclear disarmament for Britain until the Conference of October 1983 – two years and a general election after the SDP was set up.

Even after the split, Owen and Williams were still hoping to construct a Mark II Labour Party. So they were desperately anxious to persuade the largest possible number of Labour MPs to join them. Apart from Bill Rodgers, only a dozen others joined the Social Democratic Party when it was first formed on March 26th, 1981. They managed to attract another fourteen in the following year. Roy Jenkins, however, was already planning, with David Steel's approval, to turn the SDP's loose alliance with the Liberals into an entirely new Party of the Centre. They ultimately outmanoeuvred Owen, who in 1988 found himself leading only a tiny rump of the SDP. Meanwhile, of the twenty-nine former Labour MPs who represented the SDP at its peak, only three survived the General Election of 1983. In 1987, though the SDP won five seats, two of its MPs defected to the new Social and Liberal Democratic Party as soon as it was formed the following year.

The lamentable history of the SDP bore out all the warnings I had given. Its most important effect was to delay the Labour Party's recovery by nearly ten years, and to guarantee Mrs Thatcher two more terms in office. Another effect was to weaken and fragment the centre in British politics, though this was largely due to David Owen's rebarbative personality; as Roy Jenkins once remarked, Owen was like the fabulous Upas tree, which destroys all life for miles around it. Like all right-wing breakaways from left-wing parties, the SDP achieved nothing significant on its own account, but did grievous damage to those who shared many of its views in the party it deserted. The departure of twenty-nine opponents of the extreme Left shifted the balance of power inside the Parliamentary Labour Party. Any MP who expressed opinions similar to those of the SDP was now accused of preparing to defect himself. I was in a particularly difficult position, because I was now Deputy Leader to Michael Foot; I had been elected unanimously by the Labour MPs, but was liable to challenge in the new electoral college later in the year.

The Deputy Leader of the Labour Party is like the Vice-President of the United States. If he is bad, he can do much damage; if he is good, he can do nothing. When Fritz Mondale was elected Vice-President, his ex-colleagues in the Senate gave him a brass spittoon, to remind him of the saying that the Vice-Presidency is not worth a barrel of warm spit. I felt myself compelled to agree with Michael in public on all issues at all times. Though at first I argued strongly with him in the privacy of the Shadow Cabinet, my other colleagues begged me to desist. So my arguments thereafter were confined to our personal encounters tête-à-tête. When we disagreed, I think he tried hard to meet me half way – as on defence policy in the 1983 election. However, he was distrusted both on the Right and the Left of the Party, and lacked both the personal authority and the political grip to impose his will. He was a natural rebel, and found leadership uncongenial; moreover, though a brilliant orator, he had no administrative experience or executive ability. For all these reasons he was unable to give the Party a sense of direction, either in Parliament or outside.

As Deputy Leader, I was now ex-officio a member of the National Executive and of the Liaison Committee with the TUC, as well as of the Shadow Cabinet. I was also Shadow Foreign Secretary. In fact, from the Leadership election in October 1980 to the General Election in June 1983 I was as busy as I had been at the Treasury – but with far less to show for it.

On April Fool's Day 1981 I was speaking in Hamburg on the Common Market when I heard the long awaited news: Tony Benn had decided to fight me for the Deputy Leadership in the electoral college, which would take its decision at the Party Conference at the end of September. A day later I was once again approached officially in Bonn to see if I would accept nomination as Secretary General of NATO. Some might have seen this as a tempting avenue of escape from our political troubles. Not I. For the second time I refused the offer, and for the same reasons as before, although the contest would have been far less demanding than that for Deputy Leader of the Labour Party. To go to NATO was no more attractive to me then than it had been twelve years earlier. As in 1981 it was not a lonely impulse of delight which kept me in politics; it was a dogged determination to do my duty. I happened to run into my wartime colleague, David Hunt, at about this time. He had just become famous as 'Mastermind', and warned me that I must now practise the Stoic virtues. He was right.

The next six months were the busiest and least agreeable of my life. I had two or three radio or television broadcasts almost every day, three or four meetings with trade unions or constituency parties every week, on top of all my other work in Parliament, the Shadow Cabinet, and

National Executive. And it was all for the sake of a job which I found disagreeable and which in itself was not worth having. I felt, however, that it was essential to deny it to Tony Benn. If he had become Deputy Leader there would have been a haemorrhage of Labour defections to the SDP both in Parliament and in the country. I do not believe the Labour Party could have recovered.

I had powerful and dedicated supporters inside the trade unions, including some unions whose national leadership was committed to oppose me. Indeed I learned more about the inner workings of the trade union movement in those six months than in my previous thirty-seven years of Party work. My strength was greatest in the industrial areas of Northern England, Wales, and Scotland, where the Labour Party was still winning seats. Tony was strongest in London and the South, where Labour was weakest, and growing weaker every day.

There was one moment in April when it appeared briefly that Tony might have to retire through illness. The news brought me a letter which appeared at first to have been written by that great New York immigrant, Hyman Kaplan:

> Ja Poppa!
>   Vot you dun to dat Mr Benn vid der leedle pointy needle; maybe you bin creep creep up vun darg night? Nixt thign we kno his ligs fall off compledely. Larf? I koffed borcht all ober de newtspaper.
>
> > Yr frind
> > Tim
>
> PS Here's anudder comtribution to Clayfoot Riserch Foundatiun. Und rimember to schpend it visely heh heh. Lige the newtspapers say, don kick the man vile he's down (just sit on him, mage sure he don get up agane).

It was from my son who was repaying a loan I had made him. I was uncharitable enough to laugh like a drain.

It was not all roses, however. Wherever I went, a group of Militant supporters followed me round to heckle. In Cardiff there was an orchestrated attempt to howl me down by extremist mobs of Trotskyites and anarchists, whom Tony Benn did nothing to discourage or condemn. He had made a point of inviting groups outside the Labour Party to join his cause, including even the Posadists. The Posadists believed that socialism would be brought to Earth by extra-terrestrial creatures from outer space, because they would have a high technology and therefore must be socialists; I suppose they provided a natural link between the Anthony Wedgwood Benn who had lectured Nixon on the wonders of technology and Tony Benn, the people's friend.

In my rally at Birmingham such groups were joined by a mass of IRA supporters who made it quite impossible for me to be heard. All these scenes were transmitted by television into ordinary homes throughout the country. They gave the Labour Party a reputation for extremism, violence, hatred and division from which it has not yet recovered. Yet Benn still insists on describing such election campaigns as 'a healing process'.

The electoral college finally met in the Conference Hall at Brighton on Sunday September 28th, 1981. No one could be sure how the votes would go. Tony was bound to get a big majority of the thirty per cent cast by the constituencies; despite threats from Benn's supporters, a majority of the thirty per cent cast by the MPs were likely to go to me. The trade unions cast their forty per cent in a single block for each union. But there was no uniformity in the way they reached their decision how to vote. Some had consulted all their individual members. Others had organised soundings of opinion through their regional headquarters. Some delegations voted as their national executive committees instructed, some ignored consultations and instructions alike.

In the first ballot I won 45.37 per cent of the college, Benn 36.3 per cent, and John Silkin 18 per cent. Silkin had been put up by Moss Evans of the Transport and General Workers Union (TGWU) so as to avoid having to vote for Benn; there was no way he would allow his union to vote for me, although the regional soundings inside his union had given me an overwhelming majority. When Silkin was defeated, Alec Kitson, the union's representative on the National Executive, let it be known that it would now abstain. But the union's delegation decided on the floor of the conference, how and by what majority is unknown, to vote for Benn. So I scraped in to victory by a hair of my eyebrow – 50.426 per cent against 49.574 per cent for Benn. If even that one union's delegation had voted as it knew its members wanted it to vote, I would have had a majority of two and a half million.

The union of public employees, NUPE, was more honest. It had carried out a consultation of individual members in their branches. This showed a majority for me, although the union leadership wanted Benn; so I got the 600,000 votes of NUPE. I discovered to my surprise that even Reg Race's branch had voted for me. Since Reg belonged to the extreme Left, I took pleasure in thanking him that evening. 'Huh,' he grunted, 'lot of fucking IMG!' The International Marxist Group certainly hated Reg's guts, but not enough to vote for me.

My victory was a turning point. Giles Radice wrote in his diary that evening: 'By beating Benn, however narrowly, Denis Healey has saved the Labour Party.' Two days later my success was reinforced. Our hard work in the unions was rewarded, as I had told Shirley Williams and her friends it would be, given time. We broke the stranglehold of the extreme Left on the Party by winning five more seats on the National Executive. We won two more the following year. The extreme Left has been an impotent minority on the Executive ever since.

Although I had just survived Benn's challenge, the nature of the campaign, and the shameless ballot rigging by the trade unions were fully covered on press and television. They did the Labour Party enormous and lasting damage. We dropped from a majority of ten per cent in the opinion polls in March, to level pegging with the Conservatives in October. Then the Social Democrats took off. Shirley Williams won the by-election at Crosby from the Tories because two-thirds of the previous Labour voters switched to her, and Roy Jenkins nearly won the Warrington by-election from Labour because he got two-thirds of the previous Tory votes. On December 18th Gallup gave the alliance of Liberals and Social Democrats 50.5 per cent as against only 23.5 per cent for Labour and 23 per cent for the Conservatives. Tactical voting seemed here to stay. For a moment it looked as if Roy Jenkins was right, and that the new centre grouping had broken the mould of British politics.

It was an illusion. Though in January unemployment passed three million for the first time since 1933, by March Gallup showed the Alliance and Labour level, with the Tories only a fraction behind. In April General Galtieri invaded the Falklands. In July, after his forces had surrendered, Gallup showed the Tories at 46.5 per cent, Labour at 27.5 per cent, and the Alliance at 24 per cent. By August Michael Foot's popularity had sunk to 15 per cent. The Tories kept their lead in the opinion polls. On May 12th, 1983, after a tax-cutting budget, Gallup gave the Conservatives 49 per cent, Labour 31.5 per cent and the Alliance only 17.5 per cent. Mrs Thatcher dissolved Parliament and called a general election.

CHAPTER TWENTY-THREE

Mrs Thatcher in Power

Where is the world of eight years past! 'Twas there –
   I look for it – 'tis gone, a globe of glass,
Cracked, shivered, vanished, scarcely gazed on, ere
   A silent change dissolves the glittering mass.
Statesmen, chiefs, orators, queens, patriots, kings,
And dandies, all are gone on the wind's wings.

Talk not of seventy years of age. In seven
   I have seen more changes, down from monarchs to
The humblest individual under heaven,
   Than might suffice a moderate century through.
I knew that nought was lasting, but now even
   Change grows too changeable without being new.
Nought's permanent among the human race,
Except the Whigs *not* getting into place.

               'Don Juan, Canto XI' Lord Byron

'THE IRON LADY', 'Attila the Hen', 'Britain's de Gaulle', 'Rambona', 'Rhoda the Rhino', 'The New Elizabeth', 'The Great She-Elephant', 'Virago Intacta'. These are only a handful of the epithets with which lesser mortals, including myself, have tried to capture some aspect of Mrs Thatcher. Her French colleague, President Mitterrand, once said that she had 'the eyes of Caligula and the mouth of Marilyn Monroe'.

No politician since Churchill has evoked such strong feelings among admirers and detractors alike. Churchill, however, did not give his name to a political concept. Mrs Thatcher did; so did Aneurin Bevan. Bevanism, like Thatcherism, was inextricable from the personality of its author. Whether Thatcherism will disappear like Bevanism when its author disappears, remains to be seen.

Mrs Thatcher did not create what is now called Thatcherism out of the blue. She gave expression to feelings which were already colouring public opinion on both sides of the Atlantic; the attitudes she rejected had already begun to lose their appeal. Underlying all these changes was a reaction throughout the developed world against the permissiveness of the sixties, which had found its most extreme form in the culture of the Hippy generation. Ordinary people longed for a return to order, to the family values which used to provide a moral framework for individual behaviour. They were not prepared to believe patriotism was evil, that all authority was bad, that every leader was bound to betray his cause, that the pursuit of excellence was what the New Left regarded as the worst of all possible vices – 'élitism'. Ronald Reagan represented this backlash in the United States, as Margaret Thatcher did in Britain; in this sense their victories were a triumph for traditional bourgeois values. Yet neither of them succeeded in reversing the trends in society against which they were campaigning. Violent crime and parental irresponsibility continued to increase in Britain as in the United States.

Combined with this backlash against the permissive society – and in some ways at odds with it – was a widespread desire to reduce the role of the government in economic and social affairs. There was a longing to make people more self-reliant, and less dependent on state assistance which was granted unconditionally to anyone in need. Too many people were seen as 'scrounging' on the welfare state. As confidence in the government diminished, faith in the magic of the market-place increased. The pursuit of personal gain was seen once again as the most reliable motive force not only in economic life, but in many other areas of society. In Britain even more than the United States, the trade unions were viewed as responsible for the weaknesses of the old system; they did little to discourage their unpopularity.

The Labour Party in Britain, like the liberal Democrats in the United States, for a long time refused to recognise this secular shift in public opinion. When at last they found it impossible to ignore, they would not admit how far it was justified, partly because it was nourished by their own shortcomings both in government and opposition. So while the Labour Parties in Australia and New Zealand, and the Socialist Parties in France, Italy and Spain came to terms with the new political mood – and won electoral support by doing so – the British

Labour Party allowed Mrs Thatcher to monopolise the opportunities it presented.

Essentially, Mrs Thatcher believed in the sort of Victorian values which were represented by the Whig manufacturers in the early nineteenth century and which Dickens immortalised in Mr Gradgrind. So her first task was finally to destroy the power of the landed gentry inside the Tory Party, and to give due influence to the expanding urban middle classes. Once she had hijacked the Conservative Party from the landowners and given it to the estate agents the tradition of 'noblesse oblige' soon withered and died. Harold Macmillan expressed his distaste for this aspect of her revolution by saying she had taken his Party away from the Etonians and given it to the Estonians.

In fact this reconstruction of the Tory Party had begun with Ted Heath, who came from a background similar to Mrs Thatcher's. But Heath still carried traces of Balliol and the Oxford Union, which limited his appeal to men and women who could easily identify with Mrs Thatcher and Norman Tebbit. Such people came as much from the working class as from the middle classes who now formed the backbone of Conservative support in the country. If only for this reason, British politics will never be the same again. For the Tory Party at least, Thatcherism has already meant a reconstruction as radical as Gorbachev's *perestroika* for the Soviet Communist Party.

It was Charlie Pannell, my fellow Labour MP in Leeds, who first drew Margaret Thatcher to my attention in 1960; she had just won her seat in Finchley at the age of thirty-four. For some reason Charlie had taken her under his wing. He told me to watch her, saying that she was exceptionally able, and also a very nice woman. This was quite a compliment coming from a Cockney engineer who was famous for his rough tongue.

I did watch her, but found little to excite my interest until she joined Geoffrey Howe as one of the Conservative Shadow Chancellor's team when I went to the Treasury. Then she did indeed prove herself exceptionally able; as a former tax lawyer she was a formidable opponent in our discussions on my first Finance Bill. I thought she had a more powerful brain than Ted Heath, and was equally assiduous in mastering a brief. But at that time I failed to detect either her vaulting ambition or her iron determination. Within twelve months these qualities enabled her to challenge Heath successfully for leadership of the Conservative Party; they then led her to victory at three general elections in a row.

If Heath had chosen to resign immediately after his two defeats in

1974, one of his more prominent colleagues would have succeeded him – probably Willie Whitelaw. But personal loyalty prevented them all from trying to force him out. Keith Joseph, who had led the intellectual attack on Heath's policies, was too bizarre a character to win the leadership of the British Conservative Party. I had come to know Joseph well, and to like him personally; he held the next seat to mine in Leeds. A Fellow of All Souls, he could easily hold his own in academic circles; but politically he was a mixture of Hamlet, Rasputin, and Tommy Cooper. So, almost by default, Mrs Thatcher became the standard bearer for all those Tory backbenchers who could not forgive Heath for being cold and arrogant – and above all, a two-time loser.

It was their Peasants' Revolt she led to victory. Once leader, she proved more like Mao Tse-tung than Jack Cade; she articulated and organised the instincts of the average Tory voter as successfully as Mao those of the Chinese peasantry. Her sayings will no doubt be collected some time in a Little Blue Book, perhaps by those Young Conservatives who share a faith in her Cultural Revolution as fervent as that which inspired Mao's Red Guards.

It was not, however, Mrs Thatcher's ideology which brought her victory over Ted Heath, or later over Jim Callaghan, Michael Foot and Neil Kinnock. In all cases it was her opponent who lost the election, rather than she who won it. Nor was the strength of her ideology at first apparent. In those days I used to call her 'Ted Heath in drag'. Her first Cabinet in 1979 included all of Heath's most prominent supporters. Some, such as Ian Gilmour, strongly attacked not only the new doctrines which she and Joseph had adopted, but also the very idea that the Conservatives should have a doctrine at all. Of course, they knew that if she consolidated her leadership, they were unlikely to survive; Jim Prior told me that if her majority had been more than sixty in 1979, she would never have included him in her Government at all. But the Heathites at first believed that if they stuck together they could control her wilder excesses until, like Heath, she finally made the U-turn they were certain would come. In December 1980 Michael Heseltine told me that there was a group in Cabinet, with Christopher Soames, Peter Carrington, Peter Thorneycroft and Quintin Hailsham as its core, which could always impose an effective veto on her wilfulness.

He was wrong; and his overconfidence was later to cost him his own place in her Cabinet. Even before the 1979 election Mrs Thatcher had expressed her views with typical frankness to the *Observer*: her way of constructing a government was 'to have in it only the people who want to go in the direction in which the Prime Minister wishes to go . . . It must be a conviction government. As Prime Minister I could not waste time having any internal arguments.' She saw consensus as a dirty word, because it meant a compromise between different interests or points of view. 'To me,' she said, 'consensus seems to be the process of abandoning all beliefs, principles, values and policies. So it is something in which no one believes and to which no one objects.' She told the diplomatist Tony Parsons while she was still in opposition that she regarded people who believed in consensus as 'quislings and traitors'. But, though she insisted again and again that she stood for conviction against consensus, it has never been clear whether by conviction she means anything more than her current state of mind; the content of her conviction is simply the opinion she happens to hold on a particular issue at any particular time.

Although her rhetoric projects an image of unwavering resolution, she was at first cautious and equivocal in applying her populist maxims. Her tendency to shoot from the hip in public, and to lay down the law in Cabinet discussions, often led her into an impossible position; so she was compelled to reverse her policy and to accept defeat by her colleagues more often than a prime minister like Callaghan, who would usually aim at producing a consensus before committing his personal prestige on a controversial issue. However, her U-turns often go unnoticed; once she realises she has made a mistake she is capable of reversing her position in a flash, without explanation or apology.

Her long battle over the miners' strike in 1984 is well remembered. In early 1981, however, she reversed her decision to close certain pits within two days of a miners' walkout; her short, low-key statement to the House of Commons was forgotten almost as soon as made. Least noticed of all her U-turns was her total abandonment of monetarism in her second term. Most visible was her U-turn on Rhodesia. She entered office with commitments on Rhodesia which were quite incompatible with a negotiated settlement; these commitments were simply ignored when she faced reality at the Commonwealth Conference in Lusaka a few months later. This was one of several issues on which Peter Carrington succeeded in persuading her to test her prejudice against the facts.

Carrington was one of her few colleagues who could get her to change her mind. His exceptional diplomatic skills were as useful in Downing Street as in the wider world; he was unscrupulous in exploiting a certain sexual chemistry to which she was always vulnerable. Most important of all, since he was a member of the House of Lords, he posed no threat to her position as Prime Minister. I made use of a report that Schmidt and

Giscard d'Estaing liked to refer to Mrs Thatcher as a rhinoceros, to describe Peter's relationship with her:

> The Foreign Secretary seems to be her zookeeper. He is dragged continually away from the delicate diplomatic task of feeding the marmosets by the news that Rhoda the Rhino is on the rampage again. The poor fellow has to put down his pipette, or whatever it is that one uses to feed marmosets, and follow a trail of wrecked cars, shattered shop windows and bent lamp posts, until he finally tracks her down in the middle of some great store, where the counters are overturned, the goods are strewn all over the floor, and sales staff are clinging to the tops of the pillars . . . By some magic, or pitchfork, he manages to lead her back to her pen, past the flamingo pool where the Lord Privy Seal [Ian Gilmour] is standing immobile, elegant and elongated, his long leg in the water, pink and wet.

After Carrington resigned over the Falklands, and his immediate successor, Francis Pym, was sacked following the 1983 election, Geoffrey Howe became Foreign Secretary. Though he lacked Carrington's glamour, his country solicitor's manner helped him to correct some of her more damaging mistakes without offence. For example, she declared in Peking, just before the negotiations on Hong Kong began, that she would never surrender sovereignty over the island; within twenty-four hours Geoffrey had persuaded her to reverse that position. In 1988 she reversed her opposition to Spain's membership of the Western European Union just as fast. However, in the end Howe found it impossible to control her verbal ferocity over South African sanctions and the Common Market. When she finally lost patience with his continual nagging on these subjects, she told the press that, while she used to regard Geoffrey as a comfortable slipper, he was beginning to feel like a very hard boot. Yet, in the face of all her insults and sabotage, he continued doggedly to speak and work for common sense in British foreign policy.

After the 1979 election, Mrs Thatcher had made Geoffrey Howe her Chancellor of the Exchequer; as his predecessor I spent my first eighteen months in opposition as his Shadow. So I was able to watch from close quarters Mrs Thatcher's calamitous love affair with monetarism. It was Keith Joseph who excited her interest in the theories of Milton Friedman. Heath's disastrous economic record had led many Conservative thinkers to lose faith in demand management altogether, particularly since in Britain it seemed to require some sort of incomes policy. They wanted something simple to put in its place. Friedman offered the patent medicine they were looking for.

He argued that governments had no power to influence any element in a country's economic behaviour except inflation, and that inflation was affected only by the supply of money available. So controlling the money supply was the only economic function which a government could usefully perform. Wages had nothing to do with inflation; if the money supply was under control, they would automatically fall into line. Finally, the demand for money could be controlled only by adjusting its price, through raising or lowering interest rates.

At first I used to describe these comic-strip syllogisms as 'punk monetarism'. Later, when my children told me this was unfair to the youth culture, I used the phrase 'sado-monetarism' instead. My years at the Treasury had taught me that the neo-Keynesians were wrong in paying so little attention to the monetary dimension of economic policy, though both Bank and Treasury had been working to undisclosed monetary targets since 1973. In 1976, before the IMF negotiations, I decided to publish these monetary targets, largely to placate the financial markets. But I never accepted Friedman's theories. Nor did I ever meet any private or central banker who took them seriously. After all, they spent their whole lives dealing with money, and knew something about it.

Walt Wriston, the head of Citibank in New York and the most formidable private banker of my time, was vexed beyond endurance by the hysterical market reactions to the monetary statistics, which were published weekly in the United States. He suggested they should be published daily, because then 'it would be like going into a topless bar – after ten minutes you might take a drink.' Fritz Leutwiler, the Swiss central banker and chairman of the central bankers' trade union, the Bank of International Settlements, abandoned monetary control altogether for a period of months, when he found that, by raising the exchange rate, it was throwing Swiss citizens out of work, as well as forcing immigrants to go home. Western Germany has consistently overshot its monetary targets since it first introduced them in 1975, yet has consistently enjoyed the lowest inflation and strongest currency of all the major countries – other than Japan, which has never even paid lip-service to monetarism.

Mrs Thatcher, however, has always believed in miracle cures. She seized on sado-monetarism as the answer to all her prayers. She ignored the advice of Friederich Hayek, hitherto one of her gurus, that monetarism was unlikely to work in Britain. Before long she was being criticised by

Friedman himself for an over-enthusiasm which was creating unnecessary unemployment. How far Geoffrey Howe really shared her monetarist fanaticism I could never discover; he rarely discussed the theoretical basis for his policies in public, or indeed with the Treasury officials. John Biffen, his Chief Secretary, seemed at first to be a committed monetarist; he certainly held the odd view that you could control wages by controlling the money supply.

The one genuine missionary for monetarism in Mrs Thatcher's first Treasury team was a recent convert from Keynesianism – Nigel Lawson, then Economic Secretary. During a visit to Washington in 1980 I dined at the Embassy with him and Paul Volcker, who had recently become Chairman of the Fed; we had a fierce argument about monetarism. Nigel was both surprised and discomfited to find Volcker citing his own experience to support my position; he warned Lawson against putting too much weight on monetary control and interest rates. Witteveen, as Managing Director of the IMF, took the same view; he often told me that if you wanted to control the money supply, you could be confident of doing so only through direct control of credit, as he had done in Holland.

It was Nigel who tried to convince the markets that the Government was serious about monetarism by publishing annually a Medium Term Financial Strategy, or MTFS, which set monetary targets for several years ahead. The irreverent claimed that the MTFS stood for 'Mrs Thatcher's Final Solution' or 'Muddling Through with Firm Sterling'. Intended to set a reliable framework of government policy within which the markets could form 'rational expectations' – another buzz phrase in those days – it simply demonstrated that no one should take seriously anything a Conservative Chancellor said. The Government never came close to meeting the monetary targets it laid down in the MTFS. In Mrs Thatcher's first two and a half years her chosen measure of money, sterling M3, rose as much as in my whole five years as Chancellor.

Far more serious, unemployment rose above three million for the first time since 1933, and twenty per cent of Britain's manufacturing industry was destroyed for ever. There was no fall in inflation to offset this disaster. On the contrary, thanks in part to Howe's belief that a doubling of the Value Added Tax would have only a once-for-all effect on inflation, the retail price index more than doubled, to 21.9 per cent, in the twelve months following Howe's first Budget. When inflation finally began to decline, this was due, not to his monetary policy, which had failed miserably, but to a dramatic fall in oil and commodity prices.

Yet, although support for the Conservatives plummeted over the period, the Labour Party gained nothing from the Government's cata-strophic management of the economy. British voters could see only the iron mask of division and extremism which Tony Benn and the CLPD had riveted round our neck. The opinion polls showed us as unpopular as the Tories, with fewer than a quarter of the electorate prepared to vote for us. Only the Alliance of the Liberal and Social Democratic Parties benefited; half the electorate was behind them for a few dizzy months.

At the end of 1980, when Michael Foot became Leader of the Labour Party with me as his Deputy, he asked me to leave the Shadow Treasury portfolio and take Foreign Policy and Defence together. Feeling that such a chalice would contain too much poison even for me, I declined the dual role. So I was simply Shadow Foreign Secretary when General Galtieri invaded the Falklands, transformed Mrs Thatcher into the Iron Lady, and restored the fortunes of the Conservative Government.

The Falklands was a war which need never have happened. It would not have happened if the Government had shown a spark of the courage and competence before April 2nd 1982 which brought it to victory afterwards. The islands had been a bone of contention between Britain, Spain and France since Lord Byron's grandfather established a tiny settlement there in the eighteenth century. When the Spanish Governor in Buenos Aires expelled this settlement, that great man, Dr Samuel Johnson, produced a pamphlet saying that the Falklands were not worth fighting for – 'an island thrown aside from human use, stormy in winter, barren in summer, an island which not even the southern savages have dignified with habitation, where a garrison must be kept in a state which contemplates with envy the exiles of Siberia.'

Argentina was a Spanish colony when Britain first put a settlement on the Falklands; when it achieved independence from Spain it claimed sovereignty over the islands, which it called the Malvinas. Two centuries after the first British settlement, the Falklands were still a British colony; but they had under 2,000 inhabitants, fewer than the average parish in rural England, and fewer even than those inhabitants of Kent who are threatened with losing their homes by the rail link to the Channel Tunnel. In fact there were far more British citizens in Argentina itself; and a sizeable proportion of the Argentine people were of British descent. However, the role of the Falklands in the First and Second World Wars had given them a significance in public opinion out of all proportion to their size.

When Perón became President of Argentina in 1946 he revived the Argentine claim to the Falklands, and his successors persuaded the

United Nations to bring Britain and Argentina into negotiations on the problem. Successive British governments recognised that it would be difficult for the Falkland islanders to prosper without access to the mainland, so they agreed to improve communications with Argentina, and even permitted Argentine workmen and technicians to build an airstrip at Port Stanley. In 1977, when Jim Callaghan heard threats of an Argentine invasion, he ordered a small naval task force to the area, including a nuclear powered submarine, and allowed the Argentine Government to discover this through secret channels. This deterrent was sufficient. There was no invasion.

When Mrs Thatcher took over, she was at first prepared to surrender sovereignty altogether. Lord Trefgarne, one of her Foreign Office ministers, told the House in July 1981, 'The fact remains that the Falklands are not and never have been part of the United Kingdom.' The Minister of State at the Foreign Office, Nicholas Ridley, proposed the so-called 'lease-back option', under which Britain would hand over sovereignty to Argentina, providing Argentina would immediately lease the islands back for Britain to administer. There was a storm of protest from the islanders and from backbenchers in Britain; against my advice, the official Labour Opposition joined in. The following year General Galtieri seized power in Buenos Aires.

It had been obvious from the moment Galtieri took over in December 1981 that he might launch an invasion of the Falklands. However, Lord Carrington believed that he would wait until late in 1982, when Britain would have lost the capacity for a military response. Against strong protests from myself and others, the Government had announced in 1981 that it would withdraw the only naval vessel permanently stationed in the area, in order to save £2 million a year. It had decided to scrap the aircraft carrier *Hermes* and the assault ships *Fearless* and *Intrepid*. Moreover, it was selling the mini-carrier *Invincible* to the Australian Navy, which was completing preparations to take it over when Galtieri invaded. These ships formed the heart of the task force with which Britain finally reconquered the Falklands. If Galtieri had waited, as Carrington expected, until they were no longer available, Britain would have had no practical alternative but to accept the *fait accompli*. Perhaps that is what the Foreign Office subconsciously wanted.

On the other hand, if Mrs Thatcher had begun to assemble these ships into a task force as soon as the Joint Intelligence Committee reported in 1981 that there was a risk of invasion, and had made the task force's existence known when firm intelligence of Galtieri's intention began to accumulate from the beginning of 1982, the invasion would not have taken place. Indeed, it appears from evidence given later by Galtieri himself and some of his officials that even as late as the end of March, when his task force was already at sea, he would have ordered it back, if Mrs Thatcher had given an unequivocal warning direct to Buenos Aires that she would fight to recover the islands.

Yet although she was already assembling the necessary task force in the North Atlantic, she made no direct contact whatever with the Argentine Government. Instead she telephoned President Reagan, asking him to state 'forcefully that action against the Falklands would be regarded by the British as a casus belli.' It was perhaps unwise to entrust President Reagan with such a phrase. In any case, the message was not transmitted until the very night before the Argentines landed on the islands.

Mrs Thatcher's utter fecklessness, in the face of mounting evidence that Galtieri was planning an invasion, was paralleled by military incompetence before it took place. Though the possibility of an invasion had been obvious for months, there were only two officers and some sixty fighting men on the islands when the Argentines landed; most of the men were without their weapons. There were no explosives available to make the airfield unusable; so the Argentinians were able to land supplies there at night throughout the war. The Governor was not warned that an invasion was imminent until sixteen hours before it took place, although Mrs Thatcher had already been assembling her task force for three days. Lord Hill-Norton had served as Naval Attaché in Buenos Aires some years before becoming Chief of Defence Staff, so he knew all aspects of the problem at first hand. He told the House of Lords on January 17th, 1983:

> Leaving aside the tragic loss of two hundred and fifty-five lives and nearly eight hundred wounded on our side, while it might have cost possibly ten million pounds to deter that aggression, it has cost two thousand to three thousand million to defeat it.

I brought out all these points in the course of our debates on the Falklands. But once the fighting started few were interested in how it had come about. Britain was swept by a tide of patriotic feeling which some of the tabloid press perverted into a mindless jingoism. Just as Reagan used the invasion of Grenada to purge America of the trauma left by Vietnam, so Mrs Thatcher exploited the victory of our forces in the Falklands to create the feeling, both at home and abroad, that Britain was great again; she portrayed herself as the greatest national leader since Churchill, if not since Elizabeth the Virgin Queen.

The tone was set by an emergency debate in the House of Commons on the Saturday morning immediately after the invasion took place. Michael Foot saw it as a repetition of the Nazi challenge which Britain had failed to meet in the thirties: it was an act of naked, unqualified aggression by a brutal military dictatorship, which Britain had an absolute duty to defeat on behalf of the Falkland Islanders, 'who have built their whole lives on the basis of association with this country. We have a moral duty, a political duty and every other kind of duty to ensure that that is sustained.'

I was cut off on the island of Rhodes when this debate took place, or I would have tried to moderate some of Michael's rhetoric; his words came back to haunt him when Alfonsin took power and tried to resume negotiations for a peaceful settlement of the Falklands dispute. Like Carrington, who was in Brussels and planning to fly to Israel that weekend, I had assumed that Galtieri would not dare to invade while we still had the capacity to respond. So I accepted an invitation to a conference in Rhodes, and was literally boarding the aircraft in Athens when my host told me there was a rumour that the Argentines had landed. I flew back to London on the Sunday, and took part in the second Falklands debate three days later. I then made most of the points to which I was to return again and again in the following months; the speech still reads well, but an attack of influenza led me to deliver it so badly that some of my audience thought I was on the point of collapse.

The Labour Party was deeply divided on Mrs Thatcher's decision to send a task force to recover the Falklands; most of the Left saw it as a colonial war in which Britain should have no part. I remember some Militant supporters in my own constituency arguing that, if the British and Argentine working classes would unite against the war, they could overthrow both their governments; in fact, of course, the Argentine trade unions were Peronist, and it was the working class on both sides who were most determined on fighting to a finish.

On the other hand, the Conservatives were by no means as united behind Mrs Thatcher as might have been expected. Some of them shared my own private concern that we might end up 'knee-deep in dead marines', as one defence expert put it; such a tragedy would have had catastrophic consequences for the Government as well as for the country. Moreover, they rightly feared that even if it succeeded, Britain would be saddled with an expensive long-term defence commitment to maintain the Falklands as a permanent fortress against a renewal of the Argentine attack. Most of the Cabinet were sufficiently aware of these dangers to insist that the Government should do its utmost to achieve a peaceful settlement of the dispute. Frances Pym, who had just become Foreign Secretary when Carrington resigned over the invasion, worked tirelessly for a compromise solution.

The American Administration was publicly divided on whether it should support Britain or Argentina; Galtieri had given military help to Reagan in El Salvador, but since both Al Haig, the Secretary of State, and 'Cap' Weinberger, the Secretary of Defence, strongly supported Britain, Reagan followed their advice rather than that of the pro-Argentine faction, led by Jean Kirkpatrick, his Ambassador at the United Nations. Although Haig had just endured a triple by-pass operation on his heart, he covered 33,000 miles in twelve days shuttling between Washington and Buenos Aires in search of a settlement. On one occasion he thought he had reached agreement with Galtieri, only to be told as he boarded his plane that other members of the military junta had refused to accept it.

Meanwhile Tony Parsons, as our Ambassador at the United Nations, was patiently mobilising support in the Third World for Britain's case. I flew to New York myself at the end of April to discuss the prospects of a role for the United Nations with the Secretary General, Perez de Cuellar, and his experienced British adviser on peacekeeping, Brian Urquhart. Then I saw Haig in Washington – I had known him since he was Kissinger's military expert on the National Security Council. Though worried about Mrs Thatcher's inflexibility, they were all doing everything possible both in New York and Washington to reach an agreement with Argentina before our task force reached the Falklands. I argued the British case as strongly as I could on American television and at public meetings in Philadelphia. The Cunard liner *Queen Elizabeth II* was anchored by the quayside as a floating hotel for any group of Philadelphians who chose to hold a meeting or party aboard; when I warned the captain that she would be sent to the Falklands as soon as she got back to Britain, both he and I thought I was joking – but she was.

I do not believe that diplomacy could have done more to reach a settlement, despite a tabloid press in Britain which, with the exception of the *Daily Mirror*, was screaming for war at any price. However, Mrs Thatcher herself was increasingly impatient of what she saw as Haig's continual compromises and Pym's readiness to negotiate through the United Nations.

On May 2nd the *Belgrano* was sunk, outside Britain's announced 'exclusion zone' and with a heavy loss of life. World opinion began to shift against Britain. Meanwhile Haig had persuaded the Peruvian Government to put a proposal to Galtieri which he had already rejected when put by Haig himself. On May 4th the Argentines sank the British destroyer, *Sheffield*. The Cabinet decided to support the Peruvian plan, and Pym told the House of Commons that my suggestion of a United Nations trusteeship for the Falklands 'might in the end prove highly suitable'.

Tony Parsons was called to a war cabinet at Chequers; he succeeded in persuading Mrs Thatcher to make a last effort for peace, along the lines of the Peruvian plan. At one point she asked him: 'Why are you smiling, Tony?'

'Because you amuse me, Prime Minister,' he replied. Only a civil servant whom she found personally attractive could ever get away with a remark like that. None of her ministers, except perhaps Lord Carrington, would have dared.

The Argentines turned down this last attempt to negotiate a settlement. It was now too late to abort the landing of British forces. Mrs Thatcher published an account of the negotiations, and publicly withdrew all the concessions she had offered in them. Our landing followed and Britain recovered the islands. Galtieri was overthrown and a democratic government was installed in Buenos Aires. That was the one indisputable benefit of the whole affair. The Falklands problem has remained to haunt both Britain and Argentina, more costly and less soluble than ever.

I do not believe there is the slightest truth in the idea that, by ordering the sinking of the *Belgrano*, Mrs Thatcher prevented Argentina from accepting the Peruvian plan, still less that this was her intention. There is no evidence that the junta would ever have accepted the Peruvian plan. In any case, the British Government wanted desperately to avoid a battle for the Falklands; it could have no confidence whatever of success, and failure would have been a catastrophe. It is true, however, that if the junta had accepted the Peruvian plan, or the final British variant of it, Mrs Thatcher would have faced a very difficult situation in her own party, once the plan came to be implemented, and the tabloid press bayed for her blood in revenge for being denied its war.

In my opinion, the one real mistake in those final days was not to have disabled the *Belgrano* instead of sinking it outright. But I understand that the captain of the submarine did not trust his new torpedoes, which were fitted with a proximity fuse so that they could disable a ship without sinking it; he decided instead to use his older torpedoes, which could explode only when they hit their target. If the new torpedoes had been reliable, the *Belgrano* affair would never have excited so much misplaced political speculation. On the other hand, eleven of the twenty-five bombs which hit our ships failed to explode because the Argentine pilots flew in so low; otherwise we might have lost the war.

The skill and courage of Britain's fighting men, and the dedication of the civilians who helped to get the task force on its way, brought us victory in the Falklands, against all the odds. However, Mrs Thatcher presented what she called the Falklands Factor as the natural consequence of her personal approach to politics and economics. 'We have ceased to be a nation in retreat,' she cried at Cheltenham race-course. 'We have instead a new-found confidence – born in the economic battles at home and tested and found true eight thousand miles away ... Printing money is no more. Rightly this Government has abjured it. Increasingly this nation won't have it ... That too is part of the Falklands Factor.'

It was the Falklands War which first established Mrs Thatcher both at home and abroad as a powerful national leader who must command respect, if not affection. In its current mood, the British people was longing to find that sort of authority at the helm. It would be churlish to deny that she deserved respect, not least because she knew that her conduct often inspired in a large minority of the British people the sort of personal hatred which most politicians find it difficult to bear. Though the so-called 'Falklands Factor' soon wore off, Mrs Thatcher continued to command respect for her single-minded determination to have her way – even among her colleagues in the Common Market, whom she so often exasperated by her obstinacy.

Her political dividend at home was a sudden jump in the Government's popularity to nearly fifty per cent, and a collapse in support for the Alliance, which never recovered. In January 1983 the polls showed the Conservatives beginning to slip back, but their fortunes were restored by a popular budget and the lowest inflation rate for fifteen years. Mrs Thatcher called a general election on May 9th; a week later, Gallup showed her with 49 per cent, well above the level with which she had won power in 1979.

Labour started the election with enormous handicaps. Michael Foot was a kindly and cultured man, as well as a brilliant orator, but he simply did not look like a potential Prime Minister; he had failed to command public respect as Leader of the Opposition. He did briefly contemplate resigning so that I could lead the Labour Party in the election campaign; a similar last minute change in the leadership had just swept Labour to power in Australia. The opinion polls showed that 49 per cent of the electorate would be more likely to vote Labour if I were Leader. But if Michael stood down now, although as Deputy I would automatically replace him for the time being, the new party constitution would require me to stand in the electoral college in October to have my leadership confirmed. In 1981 Andrew McIntosh had been displaced as leader of the Greater London Council by Ken Livingstone immediately after winning the local elections for Labour; this was a precedent the Conservatives were bound to exploit. So, though Neil Kinnock had floated the idea and Jeff Rooker had strongly recommended Michael to retire in my favour the previous November, he decided against it. It was not for me as Deputy Leader to plead my own cause. Only Gerald Kaufman did so once the election had been called, and by then Michael had made up his mind to stay.

Our second handicap was an election manifesto which Gerald Kaufman rightly described as 'the longest suicide note in history'. Though it was stuffed with detailed proposals in every conceivable field of policy, the section on defence was deliberately ambiguous. It was intended to accommodate both the unilateralists, who had won a two to one majority at the Party Conference the previous year, and the majority of the Shadow Cabinet, which thought like me that it would be politically wrong and electorally disastrous to give up our existing Polaris force for nothing. I learned how right I was on the very first day of my election campaign, at Allerton Bywater colliery outside Leeds. Again and again I was lectured by these Yorkshire miners, who were militant followers of Arthur Scargill on industrial issues, that neither they nor the voters would put up with unilateral nuclear disarmament.

In fact our manifesto said that, though we favoured getting rid of Britain's nuclear weapons, we would seek a bilateral agreement with the Soviet Union to eliminate an equivalent number of Russian nuclear weapons at the same time; Brezhnev had indicated to Michael and me during our visit to Moscow in 1981 that this would be possible. But of course we were continually asked what we would do if Russia refused such an agreement. Michael and I had agreed to answer that this would be a new situation, to be considered if and when it arose. There was no chance of getting away with such a formula when the manifesto also committed us to unilateralism. When a caller on a radio phone-in programme suggested that we should keep Polaris if Russia refused reciprocal disarmament, I had to admit that 'that seems sensible'. I never went beyond this feeble statement of my real views. However, Jim

Callaghan made a major speech expounding Labour's traditional support for multilateralism. It was impossible to conceal our deep divisions on defence any longer. Our defence policy certainly cost us the votes of many traditional Labour supporters.

Finally, our election campaign was worse organised than any I have ever known. The Party Secretary, Jim Mortimer, had been chosen, effectively by Michael Foot, instead of the excellent Scottish trade unionist who was the other candidate. Mortimer was an attractive personality. He had impressed everyone with a reasoned and powerful attack on the Militant Tendency at our Conference; few in his audience realised that he objected to them primarily because they were neo-Trotskyites, while he represented an older Marxist tradition. However, he had been a research worker in the trade union movement for most of his career; he had no experience in organisation or administration, and no feel for electoral politics.

Michael Foot and I were given ridiculously heavy programmes, and were foolish enough to accept them without protest. For almost four weeks we would start the morning at seven, with a meeting of our Campaign Committee in London, followed by a press conference which relieve lazy journalists of the need to follow us around. Then we would leave London for a series of meetings and walkabouts all over the country from ten in the morning until ten at night, returning to London after midnight for a few hours' sleep before the next day began. Many of our meetings were a complete waste of time; on one housing estate in the Midlands I was made to visit three old people's homes in succession, on the grounds that if I visited only one, jealousy from the others would cost us votes.

While Mrs Thatcher was allowed to restrict herself to one or two carefully stage-managed 'photo-opportunities', Michael was almost literally thrown to the wolves; the television cameras showed him practically torn limb from limb by a pack of hounds at a demonstration in favour of blood-sports. Our only compensation was to hear the television recording Denis Thatcher when he said to his wife as she gingerly nursed a calf at an agricultural show: 'If you don't look out, we'll have a dead calf on our hands.'

I had one unsolicited testimonial. The American actor, Lee Marvin, tough guy in so many Hollywood films, was making *Gorky Park* in Helsinki. We had met on some television programme and discovered that we had both specialised in assault landings during the war. He was also impressed to find me admitting I had been in the Communist Party before the war, since his favourite teacher at school had served in the Lincoln Brigade in Spain. 'Denis was the beachmaster at Anzio,' he told the press, in his gravelly voice. 'Those guys were really something, I can tell you.'

Even Lee Marvin's approval was unable to help me when I made one of the greatest bloomers of the campaign. At the end of a particularly exhausting day, I referred to Mrs Thatcher's exploitation of the Falklands Factor, and said that she 'gloried in slaughter'. The Tory press had been following me around for three weeks in the hope I would make myself vulnerable. Their patience was finally rewarded by this incautious phrase. For three days my words and the reaction to them got banner headlines. Edna happened to be reviewing the newspapers on breakfast television the morning after my speech; she explained immediately that I meant to say 'conflict' instead of 'slaughter'. It was too late. That evening, when I was doing the television programme, *Question Time*, with Robin Day, I apologised unreservedly for what I had said. My Tory opponent, Cecil Parkinson, failed to press his advantage, and then cut a poor figure in defending a particularly dishonest Conservative election poster. Weeks later I realised that our broadcast must have taken place at a time when he was agonising about whether to confess his relationship with Sarah Keays to the Prime Minister. He must have been under at least as much psychological pressure as I.

Perhaps the most depressing moment of the campaign for me was when Michael Foot's wife, Jill, told the press that 'even if the Party wins, I shouldn't think he would stay long (as Prime Minister).' The fact is that if Michael had gone well before the election, we might have won. We had no chance whatever so long as he was Leader.

In the event Mrs Thatcher got 42.5 per cent of the total vote – less than in 1979 – Labour 27.6 per cent, and the Alliance 25.3 per cent, of which the SDP got under half; so we would have lost even if we had received all the votes which went to the SDP. The scale of our defeat was devastating. Besides winning fewer seats than at any time since 1935, we came third or worse in 292 constituencies, and polled over three million votes fewer than in 1979. It was a just retribution for the years of in-fighting; that Tony Benn lost his seat in Bristol was small compensation. I put my views in a report to the National Executive:

> The election was not lost in the three weeks of the campaign but in the three years which preceded it. In that period Labour managed to lose about twenty percentage points in the opinion polls. In that period the Party itself acquired a highly unfavourable public image, based on disunity, extremism, crankiness and general unfitness to govern.

Nevertheless, we also lost eight points, or a quarter of our support, during the campaign itself. A modern election is fought essentially on television. Only one voter out of a hundred ever attends an election meeting, and he or she is nearly always already committed to one party or the other. Michael Foot and I, like most of the other Labour leaders, never had the slightest idea what was happening in the one campaign which mattered, on television; we were speaking every night at public meetings to people whose minds were already made up. We did not monitor our opponents' activities; they never missed the smallest detail of ours. And they were able to orchestrate the bulk of the press to make a concerted attack on one particular theme each day. Although between elections the press has only a limited political impact, banner headlines carrying the same message in all the Tory tabloids can have a devastating effect during the election campaign itself; I learned this to my cost over my Falklands bloomer.

Michael Foot had made it clear to his friends that if we lost he would not run again for Leader. But before he could announce his decision in public, his hand was forced by Clive Jenkins, who organised a group of union leaders to declare their support for Neil Kinnock almost as soon as the general election results were known. It was in fact no disappointment to me. The bulk of the movement wanted a younger man, and I had shared the blame for our election failure. I decided not to run for Leader or Deputy again, and supported Roy Hattersley in the leadership campaign which followed. Neil won a handsome victory in October; he had gained great credit by resisting all pressures from the Left to support Benn as Deputy Leader in 1981. Hattersley now took my place as Deputy Leader, automatically replacing me on the National Executive Committee of the Labour Party as well.

Almost as soon as Parliament returned from the summer recess, I was invited to leave politics for business. Arnold Weinstock, whom I had met a good deal as Chancellor, asked me to take Peter Carrington's place as chairman of his company, GEC. Peter had gone to GEC after resigning as Foreign Secretary over the Falklands; he had now been asked to become Secretary General of NATO when Josef Luns retired though Shultz and Weinberger opposed his appointment. It took me only thirty seconds to refuse Weinstock's invitation. A full-time career in business was even less appealing to me than being an international civil servant in charge of NATO or the IMF. Despite all my recent disappointments, I wanted to stay in politics. There was much I wanted to learn about the revolutions which were beginning to convulse the world, both in diplomacy and in finance. I looked forward to being able to concentrate on these aspects of international affairs, as well as having a little more spare time.

Neil asked me to run for the Shadow Cabinet. I came top, and stayed on as Shadow Foreign Secretary, as I had hoped. It was a relief to be released from the National Executive Committee, which continued to waste its time in exhausting wrangles. The extreme Left, which had just lost us two elections, seemed determined to lose a third. They were as offensive in their insults to Neil Kinnock as they had been to Jim Callaghan and Michael Foot.

Before Kinnock's first year was up he found himself engulfed in the miners' strike. As a miner's son representing a mining constituency it put him in a particularly difficult position, at a time when he had not yet had a chance to establish his authority as Party Leader. The whole affair was a godsend for Mrs Thatcher. She described it as fighting 'the enemy within' after defeating 'the enemy without' in the Falklands. The miners' President, Arthur Scargill, was probably the only public figure in Britain more disliked than the Prime Minister, and he commanded far less respect. Neil Kinnock compared him to one of the generals in the First World War, when lions were led by donkeys. Scargill made every tactical and strategic error in the book. He called the strike when coal stocks were high and the demand for coal was at its lowest. Then, when the strike was only a few months old, he turned down a compromise which even the Communist Vice-President of the Union regarded as a victory. In the end Mrs Thatcher was able to impose an unconditional surrender on the hapless miners. It was regarded as a triumph of Falklands dimensions by the majority of the public.

The Labour Party and the trade union movement inevitably suffered from their support for the miners, and from their inability during the strike to say what they really felt about Scargill's behaviour – although both Neil Kinnock and Norman Willis, the new General Secretary of the TUC, were howled down more than once for attacking the violence of some of the miners' pickets.

Her second election victory had already made Mrs Thatcher's self-confidence impregnable. She had sacked Pym immediately, and moved Prior to Northern Ireland, despite his public rejection of the office. Peter Walker was demoted to Energy, while Lawson, Brittan and Parkinson got promotion – the last only for the few months until October, when the Keays affair compelled him to resign during the Tory Party Conference.

The miners' strike further reinforced Mrs Thatcher's self-confidence. Yet within twelve months of her victory over Scargill she was faced by a rebellion in her own ranks, led by Michael Heseltine, which almost brought her government down. During the Westland affair, panic at the prospect of being driven out of office drove her into a ruthless conspiracy for self-preservation worthy of Macmillan or Harold Wilson at their worst. It ended with the resignation not only of Heseltine himself, but also of Leon Brittan, who had acted as her catspaw on the instructions of Bernard Ingham and Charles Powell, the most powerful members of her personal staff.

Though her vindictiveness towards her enemies was unrelenting, Mrs Thatcher was as capricious as Catherine the Great in picking up and dropping her favourites. By the end of her second term her sun had ceased to shine on Tebbit, Brittan, and Biffen. Within a year of her third election victory Whitelaw and Hailsham were gone as well, she had fallen out with both her Foreign Secretary and her Chancellor, and had told the press that there was no one in the next generation worthy of succeeding her. Her contempt for her colleagues went back a long way. In 1943, when as Margaret Roberts, 'a plump, solemn grammar school girl of nineteen', she had just gone to Somerville, another grammar school girl, Nina Bawden, asked why she was not joining the Labour Club. She tells how Margaret 'smiled her pretty china-doll's smile and replied that she was not playing at politics. She meant to get into Parliament, and there was more chance of being noticed in the Conservative Club, just because most of the members were a bit dull and stodgy.'

More and more she came to depend for advice and support on her kitchen cabinet at No. 10. Her press secretary, Bernard Ingham, who had once run for a Labour council seat in Leeds, and had previously worked for Tony Benn, became her favoured channel for telling the world what she dare not say for herself. This mattered less when he was blackguarding her Cabinet colleagues than when he was putting her views on major issues of economic or foreign policy. He caused a sterling crisis more than once; after his statement that she 'would help Kohl to screw Genscher' Kohl helped Genscher to perform that indelicate operation on her.

There was always something odd about her working relationships with her male colleagues in the real Cabinet. At a press conference with President Mitterrand she said: 'Men – I don't think I shall ever understand them.' She once told President Reagan: 'Oh, women know when men are being childish.' She told a dinner party, 'The cocks may crow, but it's the hen that lays the egg.' Such remarks were sometimes chosen for political effect. Sir John Hoskyns, who headed her policy unit for three years, pointed out: 'She was deliberately unreasonable, emotional and excitable – instead of being calm and consensus-seeking. She used the fact that she was a woman very powerfully to get her way.'

On the other hand, as her arrogance increased she became more careless about expressing her real feelings. Thus the woman who first entered No. 10 Downing Street quoting a prayer from St Francis could accuse her critics eight years later of 'drooling and drivelling about caring'.

Her speeches in Parliament became increasingly strident. As I watched the numb rows of Tory backbenchers while she was speaking I was often reminded of Yeats' words:

> And now we stare astonished at the sea
> And a miraculous strange bird shrieks at us.

I have always regretted that recent Parliamentary convention forbids any Opposition frontbencher except the Leader to take on the Prime Minister directly in the House of Commons. Thus I was never able to debate with her across the dispatch box when I was Shadow Foreign Secretary, although I often criticised her calamitous interventions into British foreign policy, starting with the Falklands. My best opportunity came in a speech on the Foreign Secretary's announcement that members of GCHQ, the Government's organisation for collecting signals intelligence, should no longer be members of trade unions.

> I have not wasted time on the Foreign Secretary this afternoon, although I am bound to say that I feel some of his colleagues must be a bit tired by now of his hobbling around from one of their doorsteps to another, with a bleeding hole in his foot and a smoking gun in his hand, telling them that he did not know it was loaded.
>
> The Foreign Secretary, however, is not the real villain in this case; he is the fall-guy . . . Who is the Mephistopheles behind this shabby Faust? The handling of this decision by – I quote her own backbenchers – the Great She-Elephant, She-who-must-be-Obeyed, the Catherine the Great of Finchley – the Prime Minister herself, has drawn sympathetic trade unionists, such as Len Murray, into open revolt. Her pig-headed bigotry has prevented her closest colleagues and Sir Robert Armstrong from offering and accepting a compromise.
>
> The Right Honourable Lady, for whom I have great personal affection, has formidable qualities – a powerful intelligence and great courage – but those qualities can turn into horrendous vices, unless they

are moderated by colleagues who have more experience, understanding, and sensitivity . . . I put it to the Government Front Bench, that to allow the Right Honourable Lady to commit Britain to another four years of capricious autocracy would be to do fearful damage not just to the Conservative Party but to the state.

There was plenty of laughter on the Government benches at my words. Her Cabinet colleagues joined in, and even the Prime Minister permitted herself a wan smile. But Edna has never forgiven me for suggesting a personal affection for Mrs Thatcher. How could I permit myself even a flicker of feeling, she asked, for someone so lacking in common humanity. It was Edna who pointed out to me one of the most disturbing features of Mrs Thatcher's personality: she has no hinterland; in particular she has no sense of history.

Perhaps my moment of careless charity was due to the fact that I had to leave Parliament within minutes of making that speech to speak for Tony Benn in Chesterfield, where he was fighting a by-election in the seat vacated by Eric Varley, who had decided to leave politics for business. As a frontbencher I did not think I could refuse Tony's invitation, but I was at a loss how I could praise him. I finally found the solution by referring to my long friendship with Eric Varley and then saying: 'And as for Tony, he and I for many years have been inseparable – like Torvill and Dean.' This reference to the famous pair of ice-skaters went down well, as did the scarlet banner on the wall behind us. It sank slowly to the floor in embarrassment at my predicament, making wonderful television.

It was often difficult for me as Shadow Foreign Secretary to disagree strongly with Geoffrey Howe. On some issues, like the Bill giving Canada total independence from Britain, and the negotiations with China on the future of Hong Kong, I did my best to help the Government, since it was doing what Labour would have done. On others, however, I felt that Mrs Thatcher was betraying British interests through excessive subservience to President Reagan, and that Geoffrey was too weak in conniving at her servility.

Mrs Thatcher's loyalty to the President had some excuse at first. It would have been impossible for Britain to win the battle of the Falklands without help from the United States. American facilities on the island of Ascension provided the essential mounting base for the operation. Intelligence from American spy satellites kept our forces fully informed of Argentine movements; and the United States Navy worked hand in glove with the Royal Navy throughout. 'Cap' Weinberger, the US Secretary for Defence, later received a knighthood as a reward for his services to Britain at that time.

President Reagan, however, received his recompense in Mrs Thatcher's unwavering public support through every twist and turn of his policies over eight years, from Central America through Libya to the Gulf, and from Star Wars through Reykjavik to the agreement on Intermediate Nuclear Forces.

The bitterest test of her loyalty came with the American invasion of Grenada, a small island in the Caribbean which had fallen under the control of a left-wing dictatorship some time after achieving independence from Britain. What irked Mrs Thatcher most was not so much the overthrow of the dictatorship, which she disliked as much as President Reagan, as the fact that he deliberately and successfully deceived her on his intentions, though he had often told her she was his personal friend and closest ally; moreover he did so as part of a conspiracy with certain Commonwealth governments in the Caribbean, which also kept Mrs Thatcher in the dark.

On October 24th, 1983, Geoffrey Howe answered a question from me in the House of Commons by saying that the new dictatorship in Grenada posed no imminent danger to British citizens on the island, or to the Governor General, who represented the Queen as Head of the Commonwealth. He knew of no American intention to invade the island. 'Grenada is an independent country,' he said. 'Our concern and what we are prepared to do about it must be determined by recognition of that fact.'

Within hours of that statement, without any warning to the British Government, President Reagan was landing 3,000 of America's élite forces in Grenada – Marines, Rangers, and paratroopers, supported by a powerful naval task force complete with aircraft carriers and helicopter gunships. All this was regarded necessary to defeat a tiny Grenadan Army which had no aircraft or missiles, and forty-three Cuban soldiers supported by a few hundred middle-aged Cuban construction workers, who had once had military training as conscripts. The Cubans did not have a single tank or any artillery. Even so, the operation was a military shambles. By the end, eighteen American servicemen had been killed and 116 wounded, many by accident or by their own forces. Forty-five Grenadan soldiers were killed in action, along with twenty-four Cubans. There were many civilian casualties.

Yet President Reagan presented Grenada as one of the greatest triumphs of American arms. It was in fact designed partly to wipe out the memory of the military disaster in Beirut which had just preceded it. On October 23rd, the American commander's failure to take elementary security precautions enabled terrorist bombs to kill 160 US Marines and thirty-four French troops in their barracks. In Lebanon too, Mrs Thatcher gave President Reagan automatic support; yet he never consulted her on his many disastrous decisions there, although she had put British troops in to help him. He finally ordered the unilateral withdrawal of the American forces; they had never been given a clear political or military role.

America's intervention in Grenada and in Lebanon, however, underlined a growing tendency for President Reagan to indulge in what was coming to be called 'global unilateralism'; he was liable to intervene with armed force anywhere in the world where he thought international Communism was threatening American interests, without consulting his allies, and sometimes in defiance of international law.

Central America was the main theatre for such intervention, and Nicaragua the worst case. When large-scale assistance to the Contra terrorists failed to overthrow the Sandinista regime, which Washington formally recognised as the government of an independent sovereign state, Reagan authorised the mining of Nicaraguan ports by the CIA. The International Court of Justice found him guilty of violating the United Nations Charter; Nicaragua was represented at the hearing by a distinguished American lawyer who had held office under the Carter Administration. Reagan refused to accept the Court's jurisdiction. He justified his action by arguing that Nicaragua was in the United States' backyard. In fact Nicaragua is as far from the United States as Britain from the Soviet Union; when I gave this information to 'Cap' Weinberger in a television discussion, he seemed genuinely surprised. On Reagan's argument, Russia would be justified in military intervention anywhere in the Middle East or Western Europe, and the KGB would have the right to plant mines in the Port of London. Yet, though most of the European governments did their best to restrain Reagan, Mrs Thatcher never uttered a word of criticism.

Even worse was to follow. Reagan subcontracted American foreign policy in the two most precarious parts of the world, the Middle East and Central America, to a Marine Colonel with a history of mental instability – Oliver North. North in turn subcontracted some of his responsibilities to private individuals from several countries, some of whom had a criminal record. The main purpose of the so-called Iran-Contra affair was to secure the release of American hostages by offering American arms to the Iranian regime, which Reagan had rightly accused of sponsoring terrorism. This in itself was contrary to undertakings which Reagan had just exchanged with the heads of the allied governments, on no account ever to pay ransom to terrorists. It was particularly inexcusable at a time when Reagan was pestering his European allies to support him in military action against Libya, on the grounds that Libya had been involved in terrorism.

The occasion of Reagan's decision to bomb Libya in April 1986 was a terrorist attack on American servicemen in Berlin; yet the West German police responsible for investigating the affair did not believe the Libyan Government was responsible. Reagan wanted to carry out a 'surgical strike' with F111-A bombers on Tripoli, of which the main purpose appeared to be to kill Colonel Qadaffi; this has never been publicly admitted, since the assassination of a foreign political leader is expressly forbidden by American law.

All the other European allies refused to have any part in Reagan's plan; the French and Spanish Governments even refused overflying rights. Mrs Thatcher, however, agreed, without consulting her Cabinet, that Reagan should use bases in Britain for the attack. In the event the operation was a disastrous failure. Qadaffi escaped unharmed, but there were substantial civilian casualties in Tripoli. Two British schoolteachers who had been kidnapped in Syria were murdered a day or two later, presumably in retaliation; in fact Syria is now believed to have been responsible for the attack in Berlin. Mrs Thatcher had little support from her Cabinet colleagues for her part in the raid; even Norman Tebbit protested. Two thirds of the British people also thought she was wrong.

Again and again Reagan rode roughshod over Britain's national interests and ignored his personal commitments to Mrs Thatcher herself. She took his most appalling behaviour without a murmur of protest in public. I was less inhibited. My criticisms of American policy, and of Mrs Thatcher's supine acquiescence in it, suddenly transformed me in the eyes of the Labour Left from a dollar imperialist into a champion of socialism and liberty. Some of their most prominent spokesmen would come up to me in the corridors of the House of Commons, and say that I should have been Leader of the Labour Party. I reminded them without rancour that they were mainly responsible for the fact that I was not. And I had no illusions that they would have behaved any differently to me than to Jim Callaghan, Michael Foot, and Neil Kinnock, if I had in fact been Leader.

By the end of 1986, however, it was clear that the whole world was undergoing a historic transformation, which with luck and good management could bring the end of the Cold War. Gorbachev was bringing an entirely new approach to Soviet policy both at home and abroad. Reagan was beginning to respond. These changes were partly the result of a better understanding on both sides of the diplomatic revolution imposed by nuclear weapons. They were also the product of economic difficulties in the United States as well as the Soviet Union, which had been exacerbated in each country by another revolution – the impact of electronic technologies on both industry and finance.

These developments played a major part both in Mrs Thatcher's third election victory in 1987, and in the difficulties in which she found herself thereafter. However, I was primarily concerned with their international implications. Not for the first time in my political life, I found unexpected changes in the outside world a refreshing challenge compared with the domestic scene.

CHAPTER TWENTY-FOUR

Russia Ends the Cold War

What does this sudden uneasiness mean,
and this confusion? (How grave the faces have become!)
Why are the streets and squares rapidly emptying,
and why is everyone going back home so lost in thought?

Because it is night and the barbarians have not come.
And some men have arrived from the frontiers
and they say that barbarians don't exist any longer.

And now, what will become of us without barbarians?
They were a kind of solution.

      – 'Waiting for the Barbarians' C. P. Cavafy, 1906

IT IS EASY to forget at the end of the eighties that when the decade began, the prospects for world peace seemed worse than at any time since 1945. Brezhnev's invasion of Afghanistan had already led President Carter to break off negotiations with the Soviet Union: he withdrew the SALT II Treaty from the Senate, where it was certain to be rejected, and started a massive rearmament programme. Ronald Reagan won the Presidential election in November 1980 on a platform which called for 'overall military and technological superiority over the Soviet Union'. Earlier that year he had told the *Wall Street Journal*: 'The Soviet Union underlies all the unrest that is going on. If they weren't engaged in this game of dominoes, there wouldn't be any hot spots in the world.' Throughout his first term this was his constant theme: 'They are the focus of evil in the modern world,' he told the National Association of Evangelicals in 1983. Mrs Thatcher was only too happy to echo this kind of fulmination, though Lord Carrington later deplored her 'megaphone diplomacy'.

At the same time, Reagan showed none of his predecessors' interest in nuclear strategy. When I asked Richard Burt, whom he had put in charge of alliance and security issues at the State Department, how Reagan would decide whether or not to use nuclear weapons in a crisis, he replied: 'Well, I guess he'd consult some of his cronies' – presumably Don Regan, Ed Meese, and Mike Deaver. Reagan alarmed his own people as much as the Russians by talking of his belief in the inevitability of the Biblical holocaust; on one occasion he solemnly announced on television – as a joke – that he had ordered a nuclear attack on the Soviet Union. His ignorance of nuclear weapons was legendary; for example he thought it was possible to recall a missile in flight. The man he put in charge of his civil defence programme achieved fame by saying that all that was needed to protect the American people in a thermonuclear war was three feet of earth: 'With more shovels we'll be OK.'

Yet, though Reagan increased America's defence spending by fifty per cent in his first term, he was not at first attracted by the idea of putting Cruise and Pershing II missiles in Europe, which was the first track of the Dual Track decision taken by NATO in October 1979; the second track was talks with the Soviet Union to get the SS-20s removed. His civilian experts in the Pentagon thought it a waste of money; indeed Richard Perle told the press that Cruise missiles had no military utility. Nevertheless, Reagan reluctantly agreed to uphold the decision when the British and German Governments protested that they would be politically damaged if he cancelled it, after they had spent so much effort in trying to get public support for it.

On the other hand, the European members of the NATO strategic mafia in the so-called High Level Group objected to the Dual Track decision for the opposite reason from Perle; they had recommended the deployment of Cruise and Pershing as a necessary step on the ladder of nuclear deterrence assumed by Flexible Response, and wanted to keep these intermediate range missiles in Europe, even if Russia dismantled the SS-20 missiles to which they were supposed to be the response. So they opposed the disarmament part of the Dual Track decision; indeed General Rogers at SACEUR said it gave him gas-pains.

For the first twelve months after his election, Reagan made no move to resume talks on arms control with the Soviet Union. However, although he did not formally consider himself bound by the provisions of SALT II and ultimately denounced it, he took care at first not to contravene any of its provisions during his arms build-up. Meanwhile the European governments were warning him that they would not be able to win parliamentary support for Cruise and Pershing unless he gave substance to the other part of the Dual Track decision by negotiating at least on intermediate range missiles.

This was the situation when Michael Foot and I flew to Moscow on September 15th, 1981, with a delegation of Labour MPs. I found it made a welcome break from my wearing campaign against Benn for the Deputy Leadership, which was then nearing its climax. Apart from the few hours on my journey to China in 1972, it was my first sight of Moscow for eighteen years; I had no occasion to visit Russia when I was involved in defence or economic policy.

We spent two crowded days entirely in political discussion. Of our six hours with members of the Central Committee, we wasted two whole hours listening to a counter-productive propaganda tirade against the United States from the International Secretary, my old antagonist Ponomarev, a veteran of the pre-war Comintern. I concentrated on the implications of the Dual Track decision, arguing strongly for the so-called zero-option: the Soviet Union should dismantle all its SS-20s in return for NATO not deploying Cruise or Pershing. I insisted that, though the existing nuclear balance was insensitive to substantial variations in the relative capability of the two sides, new types of weapon could destabilise that balance; the key to stopping the arms race was mutual agreement not to modernise existing weapons.

I was impressed by the calm and pragmatic way in which Vadim Zagladin responded to these arguments. He was one of Ponomarev's deputies, a large, fresh-faced man of middle-age, exceptionally well-informed on all the details of defence and disarmament. I have made a point of meeting him on my later visits to Moscow; he has so far survived all the changes since Brezhnev's death.

We met other pragmatic experts of his type at the Institute of World Economy, IMEMO; this was one of several new paragovernmental think-tanks which provided the Soviet leaders with policy research during the eighties. I found the comparative objectivity of these experts a refreshing change from the dogmatism of the diplomats and parliamentarians we met. Equally striking was the contrast between the rigid conservatism of the over-seventies and the lively frankness of the under-sixties: the war and Stalin's purges seemed to have wiped out the whole decade between.

As on my brief earlier visit, the increase in living standards under

Brezhnev was unmistakable. Parts of Moscow had been completely rebuilt, and for the first time since the Revolution it was possible to get stuck in a traffic jam during the rush hour. Moreover, there had been some revival of freedom in the arts. Lyubimov and Tarkovsky had brought a new creative imagination to the Soviet theatre and film. The Rustaveli company in Georgia was unsurpassed in the world; its exciting production of *Richard the Third* had been a sensation at the Edinburgh Festival.

Michael and I met Brezhnev himself at his office in the Kremlin; the Politburo was leaving just as we arrived. A slight slurring in Brezhnev's speech and a hint of paralysis on one side suggested a recent stroke; otherwise he appeared fit and had a good colour. In the official photograph his bulky frame and bushy eyebrows made me appear as if I were his son. After some banter, in which he seemed interested that I too had served in the war, he read us an impressive speech on disarmament – which Zagladin had written for him – in a strong, deep, crackling voice.

Although much of the anti-American rhetoric we heard in Moscow was a familiar repetition of the standard Soviet propaganda I had been hearing ever since the war, it was clear that Russian leaders were genuinely disturbed and puzzled by the attitude of the Reagan Administration. In the past they had always got on better with Republican than with Democratic Presidents. They had expected Reagan to take up the search for a lasting détente where Nixon left it. When I said that the Nixon–Kissinger regime had brought in a golden age of cooperation between Washington and Moscow, the whole of the Central Committee smiled and applauded.

Though they might have discounted Reagan's speeches as a sop for the Republican Right, they could not be so complacent about his massive arms build-up. Moreover, reports began to multiply that his advisers believed the United States could survive a nuclear war, and that some American generals were planning for a first strike against the Soviet Union. The Russians were particularly disturbed when Weinberger told his first press conference that, contrary to Carter's decision, the United States would 'probably want to make use of' its neutron warheads, and advocated deploying them in Europe. They saw the neutron bomb as the ideal capitalist weapon, since it could kill people without destroying property; so it would undermine many of the arguments then growing in the West against NATO using nuclear weapons first in a European war.

Thus, although the Russians recognised the goodwill behind the proposal for the zero-option when it was made by us and by the German Social Democrats, they were far more sceptical of Reagan's motives when, exactly two months after Michael Foot and I left Moscow, he himself proposed the zero-option on November 18th, 1981. Their scepticism had some justification. The President had been persuaded to put forward the zero-option mainly as a device for 'alliance management' – to make the Europeans think that he genuinely wanted disarmament. Alexander Haig and the State Department had opposed it, while Perle and the Pentagon supported it only because they thought it would be unacceptable to the Russians.

The negotiations on intermediate nuclear forces which followed were continually disrupted by Byzantine struggles between the rival bureaucracies in Washington. Paul Nitze, at the age of seventy-four, was put in overall charge of the negotiations, partly because he had opposed SALT II and had been a key member of the right-wing 'Committee against the Present Danger'. However, Nitze was an inveterate 'problem solver'. Drawing on a lifetime's experience in foreign affairs and negotiations on arms control, he worked tirelessly for an agreement, despite deliberate sabotage by his fellow-negotiator, the ineffable General Ed Rowny. In a typical piece of macabre clowning Rowny chose 'I'm forever blowing bubbles' as his theme song for the American team.

Richard Perle at the Pentagon was at daggers drawn with Richard Burt at the State Department, as well as with Nitze. In the summer of 1982 Perle sabotaged the formula agreed between Nitze and the Soviet negotiator, Kvitskinky, during their famous 'walk in the woods'. This gave the hard-liners in the Kremlin their chance to sabotage Kvitsinsky. The Russians began to talk of walking out of the negotiations altogether. When Brezhnev died in November 1982, his successor, Andropov, showed no greater flexibility. The zero-option seemed to be dead for the time being. Both sides were now talking of an 'interim solution'; NATO wanted at all costs to deploy some Cruise and Pershing missiles, while the Soviet Union wanted to keep some SS-20s – at least as many as the missiles owned by Britain and France. Agreement was clearly impossible. On November 23rd, 1983 the first American missiles reached the United States Army in Germany, and the Russians finally walked out.

Later, in justifying their walk-out, Russian spokesmen suggested that Reagan had broken an agreement between Kennedy and Krushchev during the Cuban crisis not to place land-based missiles anywhere in Europe, if Russia withdrew its missiles from Cuba. The Americans claimed, however, that they had been planning to withdraw their Thor and Jupiter missiles from Europe in the early sixties in any case, before the Cuban crisis. There is still some mystery about the truth.

However, I believe the main reason for the distrust which led to the Soviet walk-out was Reagan's enormous arms build-up, and the apocalyptic anti-Soviet rhetoric which accompanied it. In June 1982 Reagan had toured Europe and invited Mrs Thatcher and the other NATO leaders to join him in what he called a crusade against Soviet Communism. The Russians were genuinely frightened. In early November 1983, just before the Russian walk-out from Geneva, Western intelligence reported that a NATO military exercise had produced a wave of panic in Moscow; this was later confirmed by the Russian defector Oleg Gordievski, who had run the KGB mission in London. In fact the Russians were now obsessed by the fear that President Reagan was planning to launch a nuclear attack against them.

The biggest single cause for the Kremlin's fear at that time was the speech in which Reagan launched his Strategic Defence Initiative in March 1983, and the arguments used to support it. Reagan set as his objective to deploy a weapons system in space which would guarantee immunity for the American people against any nuclear attack, by shooting down all enemy missiles before they could reach their target. This would, in his words, make nuclear weapons 'impotent and obsolete'. He himself offered to share such a system with the Soviet Union, though no one believed he would ever do so.

However, his Defence Secretary, 'Cap' Weinberger, suggested that the real purpose of 'Star Wars', as it became known, was very different: 'If we can get a system which is effective, and which we know can render their weapons impotent, we could be back in a situation we were in, for example, when we were the only nation with a nuclear weapon.' The Russians were not impressed when Weinberger added that America had never used its nuclear monopoly against them after the war; it was known by then that both Truman and Eisenhower had considered a nuclear strike against the Soviet Union, even though they had finally decided against it. Thus there was a real danger that if Washington ever looked like deploying an effective strategic defence system, Moscow would feel it had no alternative but to get its blow in first, by attacking America's missile bases while they could still do so.

This argument had persuaded all Reagan's predecessors not to pursue such a system. After Reagan's speech, every previous president and defence secretary who was still alive, of both parties, expressed open opposition to his proposal. I discussed it myself with General Jim Abrahamson, who was in charge of the Star Wars programme, and with the leading officials concerned. It was obvious that Reagan's original concept of an 'astrodome' covering the whole of the United States was technologically impracticable, even if America could have afforded it. What did appear just feasible, though still appallingly expensive, was a system which would protect America's land-based intercontinental missiles against attack by Soviet ballistic missiles – though probably not against attack by aircraft or by cruise missiles launched from submarines close to the American coast.

As I told the House of Commons, many American experts were beginning to worry that the Russians might justifiably fear that such a system was intended to protect America's remaining ICBMs against a ragged response by the Soviet missiles which survived an American first strike. This fear was spelt out by the widely respected General Scowcroft, who had been Ford's National Security Adviser, and had produced an impressive report for the Reagan Administration on America's nuclear forces. Scowcroft had rightly stressed the importance of stability and predictability in the strategy of both sides; this point was later to form the foundation of Gorbachev's approach to military problems.

The European governments were no less alarmed by Reagan's obsession with Star Wars, partly because it might divert American resources away from the defence of Western Europe; they also feared that if it succeeded, it might cause America to retreat for good from Europe into its national sanctuary across the Atlantic. Geoffrey Howe made a careful speech in which he expressed such fears as politely as possible, drawing on similar arguments already used in the United States by Paul Nitze; he was rewarded by a torrent of personal abuse from Richard Perle during a visit to London; and Mrs Thatcher privately apologised to Reagan for Howe's impertinence! Mrs Thatcher then led the allied governments in making an agreement for British participation in the Star Wars programme, which her Defence Secretary, Michael Heseltine, predicted might lead to contracts worth fifteen thousand million dollars; so far it has produced contracts worth only a few hundred million.

Star Wars continued to present an insuperable obstacle to effective negotiations between Moscow and Washington on arms control for several years, particularly since Reagan announced that he would carry out certain experiments in space which had been forbidden by the Anti Ballistic Missile Treaty between Brezhnev and Nixon. However, the American Congress progressively cut the funds Reagan demanded for the programme, and it lost public support in the United States when it became clear that it could not offer the American people the protection Reagan originally promised them. And the whole situation was transformed when Mikhail Gorbachev became the leader of the Soviet Union.

Against the background of the appalling relations between Washington and Moscow during Reagan's first term, Gorbachev's achievement was stupendous. Within the four years of Reagan's second term he had set the whole of international affairs on a new course, which went far beyond simply ending the Cold War. Indeed it looked forward to the sort of cooperation between the world's governments which the United Nations had been set up to achieve, not only in the field of security, but on all aspects of human welfare. Ironically enough, Gorbachev achieved this transformation by adopting the strategy which Kennan had advised America to adopt towards the Soviet Union forty years earlier. Kennan had told the old story of the traveller, who simply wrapped his coat more closely around him when the cold wind blew, but took it off when the warm sun came out. Apart from his insight into the revolution which nuclear weapons implied for diplomacy and strategy, Gorbachev showed an extraordinary sensitivity to the personalities of the individual Western leaders, notably those of President Reagan and Mrs Thatcher. Both of them learned to trust him to a degree which seemed inconceivable in the light of their earlier rhetoric.

In just two years Gorbachev transformed President Reagan and Prime Minister Thatcher from fanatical anti-Soviet crusaders into champions of détente and disarmament. Even if the sincerity of Mrs Thatcher's conversion remains open to doubt, the practical consequences of their change of posture are irreversible. God moves in a mysterious way His wonders to perform, and sometimes chooses unexpected vessels for His grace. The alchemy of history can change the basest metals into gold.

I was able to watch the unfolding of this miracle at close quarters, since I visited the Soviet Union five times in the thirty months following Andropov's death, and had some twelve hours conversation with Gorbachev himself, starting with his visit to London before he took power.

In February 1984 I travelled to Moscow for Andropov's funeral with Mrs Thatcher, David Steel, and David Owen, representing the main British political parties. Andropov had been regarded by the liberal intelligentsia in the Soviet Union as a force for reform. It was he who had brought Gorbachev into the Politburo; and it was he, as Soviet Ambassador in Budapest, who had chosen a comparative liberal, Janos

Kadar, to replace Nagy after the Hungarian rising in 1956. In the West he inevitably had a sinister reputation as former head of the KGB; however, Averill Harriman, who had forty years' experience of negotiating with the Russians, had been much impressed by Andropov's goodwill and common sense at their meeting just before he died. It is possible that the KGB had by then become a force for reform in the Soviet system, since it knew better than any other organisation in the Soviet state how close the country was to economic and social breakdown; it was also the only organisation which had free access to foreign newspapers, and could express its views without fear of the KGB. None the less, there was little sign of *glasnost* under Andropov. The first time the outside world even knew he had a wife, was when she flung herself on his coffin as he was being buried under the Kremlin wall.

I had little chance to talk to Russians during that visit. Like all such state ceremonies, it was a working funeral. All the heads of government in the world were present, and wanted diplomatic discussions with the Russians, as well as with one another. As we walked in the crowded procession up one side of the great staircase in the old Imperial Palace to shake hands with Chernenko, I saw Yasser Arafat and Fidel Castro, each wearing his usual uniform, in animated conversation as they walked down the other side. Chernenko was old, frail, and obviously ill. He fluffed his memorial tribute several times when he spoke from the dais above Lenin's mausoleum, while we shivered on the frozen granite below.

When we returned to the Embassy to change out of our winter clothing, I opened a door to find David Owen and David Steel clinging to one another in their long-johns as they tried to take off their boots. I made a rapid departure, murmuring: 'I've heard of the Alliance, but this is going too far.' The only political benefit I derived from that visit to Moscow was a long and serious talk with Mrs Thatcher about the Gulf. I had been expressing some concern in the House about the risk that the United States and Soviet Union might stumble by accident into a dangerous confrontation over the Straits of Hormuz. Mrs Thatcher asked me to sit with her and her Private Secretary on the return journey to discuss the problem. She listened carefully to what I had to say, and even allowed me to rebuke her for failing to give Michael Palliser a peerage without losing her temper; for the first time I got some idea of how differently she could behave when she was not in an adversarial posture with her colleagues or political opponents. It was this delicate moment in the Gulf War which led to the first real discussion between Shultz and

Gromyko on what are nowadays called 'regional problems' – the sort of issues in the Third World where Russia and the United States have a common interest in avoiding unnecessary confrontation, and if possible jointly managing a crisis.

In November 1984 Neil Kinnock and I paid an official visit to the Soviet Union with our wives, as representatives of the Labour Party. In the course of a crowded week of political discussions, in Leningrad as well as Moscow, we were able also to see something of the Russian people, and to get some feeling of how the Soviet Union had changed since my last lengthy visit in 1959 with Gaitskell and Bevan.

The priority which the Soviet Union had given after the war to educating its children was already transforming the system. As late as 1939, 93 per cent of the Soviet people had had only an elementary education or less. Forty years later, in 1979, 42 per cent of them had had a high school education or more. The handsome, intelligent and sensitive sixth formers, who had reminded Edna and me during our visit in 1959 of youngsters from a novel by Turgenev, were now in their forties and occupying the middle ranks of the Soviet state and Party. When Gorbachev took power he was the first General Secretary since Lenin to have had a university education.

Neil and I were unable to see Gorbachev during our visit, since he was away on one of those long holidays in the South which he seems to use for recharging his intellectual batteries: on a later such holiday he wrote his book on *perestroika*. But we met many of the men who were to become his personal advisers. At IMEMO Aleksandr Yakovlev was now the Director. His somewhat mournful appearance may have come from his years of exile as Ambassador in Canada, when he was out of favour: it was he who had arranged for Gorbachev's first visit to the Western world, to tour Canada as Minister of Agriculture. IMEMO had a powerful group working on arms control: its thinking about the world economy was still distorted both by Marxist doctrine and plain ignorance. For example, we were told that the Soviet Union could not join the IMF because it would lose more than it gained, since its subscription would have to be paid in gold and oil, both of which earned vital hard currency.

Our visit to the other major think-tank, the Institute for America and Canada, was more worthwhile. Its Director, Georgy Arbatov, was already well-known in the West as the most persuasive and flexible advocate of Soviet foreign policy. Its young researchers were indistinguishable in their style and appearance from post-graduate students at Harvard or

Princeton, where some of them had studied. I was most interested, however, to meet General Milstein, a veteran of the Great Patriotic War and one of the few Jews to have served in the Soviet high command. His dry humour went well with the ageless cunning of his wrinkled brown face. We agreed that the opposing alliances in Europe should adopt non-provocative defensive strategies, using conventional weapons only.

'In that case,' I asked him, 'why are you so hostile to General Rogers' proposal that NATO should lay explosive pipelines on its own territory in peacetime, which could be used in case of war to create formidable barriers to the advance of Soviet tanks.' He replied without hesitation: 'Because that would be the conventional equivalent of Star Wars; it would give NATO an impregnable sanctuary from which to launch an attack on Eastern Europe.' The Russians were deeply alarmed at that time by the American concepts of Follow-on-Force-Attack, or FOFA, and of Air-Land Battle; the latter had already been adopted by the US Army in Germany, and involved deep strikes into the heart of Eastern Europe. I told Milstein that, much as I also opposed the concepts of FOFA and Air-Land Battle, if Rogers' buried pipelines could indeed make Western Europe into an invulnerable sanctuary, NATO should spare no effort to deploy them.

I had another long private talk with Zagladin about the state of the disarmament negotiations, in which he spoke with his usual honesty and frankness. He referred from time to time to a little printed manual which contained details of the performance of all Soviet and American weapons; I did not succeed in persuading him to give me his copy.

The meeting with Chernenko himself was of little value; he read a prepared statement in a low, husky voice, pausing from time to time for breath, and left his advisers, Ponomarev and Alexandrov, to answer the difficult questions.

More worthwhile were the informal conversations I had over food or drink with some of the newly liberated intelligentsia – particularly Fyodr Burlatsky, who as a young man had written speeches for Krushchev and was now producing a very liberal political commentary for *New Literature*. An ebullient and pugnacious conversationalist, his speech was as lively as his thought; he wrote an immensely popular play about the Cuban missile crisis in which Kennedy was portrayed as a tragic hero. It was through him that I was later able to meet some of the Soviet film-directors such as Efrem Klimov, whose films were shown for the first time, years after they were made, as part of Gorbachev's *glasnost*.

In Leningrad we visited the sombre and impressive memorial to the

640,000 who died during the siege; few in the West even now realise the full scale of Soviet losses in the last World War. The twenty million dead included one out of every three human beings in many parts of Western Russia. I remember Herman Kahn, whose baroque brilliance stood out even among the defence intellectuals at the RAND Corporation, arguing that if Russia could accept losses of twenty million in the last war, she would consider twenty million dead a small price to pay for victory in the next. No one who has actually visited the Soviet Union could make a remark so criminally stupid. Just before Neil and I arrived in Moscow, the American Ambassador had invited Soviet leaders to a concert by John Denver in his Embassy; he told me there was not a dry eye in the house when Denver sang songs of peace to commemorate the first meeting of American and Soviet troops in 1945.

Yet there were still plenty of relics of Stalinism around. When Glenys Kinnock and Edna visited the headquarters of the Soviet peace movement they were treated to a long tirade of abuse against Mary Kaldor and E. P. Thompson, the leaders of the movement for European Nuclear Disarmament – because they dared to seek converts to unilateral disarmament and the dissolution of alliances inside the Communist countries themselves, and had already made contact with sympathisers in Eastern Europe.

We were taken from Leningrad to see Catherine the Great's palace at Tsarskoye Seloe; it had been deliberately destroyed by the Germans, but was now restored in all its rococo glory. Its walls shone emerald and white under their golden cupolas above the winter snow; one lovely room was exquisitely decorated by the Scottish architect, Cameron. The Soviet leaders took as much care to restore the monuments of Russian imperial glory as the relics of the Revolution, such as the room in the Smolny school for girls where Lenin planned the storming of the Winter Palace. But many of the most beautiful church buildings, like the Donskoi monastery, had been turned into museums. Next to the monastery compound of Novo Dievichi, where Boris Godunov had been a monk before he became Tsar, there was a cemetery where Krushchev and his wife were buried; they had been excluded from the usual burial place of Soviet leaders under the Kremlin wall. I had to get special permission to visit it. I found the modest grave of Nina and Nikita covered with snow; unlike its neighbours, it had been strewn with fresh flowers and branches of fir.

Russia was visibly in transition. For the first time Zagladin brought his attractive young wife, a psychiatric social worker, to dinner at our Embassy. The enchanting old conductor, Gennady Rozhdestvensky, chatted to us about the ordeals of musicians under Stalin. I saw the ravishing ballerina, Plisetskaya, in *Carmen* and *The Spectre of the Rose*; now over sixty, she could still act brilliantly and move her arms with incomparable grace, but she was no longer capable of the leaps I had so admired nearly a quarter of a century before. In Leningrad the Kirov performed a new ballet which interpreted the life of Pushkin partly in dance, partly in oratorio, as a choir sang his poetry. Much more than on my visit with Gaitskell, I felt that Russia was now rediscovering its past as part of its future. The great nineteenth-century paintings of Repin shared the Tretiakov Gallery with the magnificent ikons of Rublev to emphasise the continuity of Russian history.

It was already obvious that Chernenko would not last much longer and that his successor would be Gorbachev. A few weeks after our return to Britain, Gorbachev arrived in London as leader of a Parliamentary delegation which included some of the men who were soon to be his closest advisers in the Kremlin. Besides Yakovlev, he brought the leading scientist, Velikhov, who was his expert on space research; though he looked like Roy Kinnear he talked like Solly Zuckerman, and had the same irreverence about politicians. General Chervov was his expert on disarmament; we had an argument about the British and French nuclear forces, which the Russians still wanted to include in the talks about intermediate nuclear weapons, although they had already been counted as part of the American strategic forces in the SALT I agreement.

I had long talks with Gorbachev himself both at dinners and at his meeting with the Labour Party leadership. He was something entirely new to all experts on the Soviet Union. The whole world is now familiar with his personal charm and intellectual flexibility; I had never before met such humanity and frankness in a Soviet leader, and not often in Western leaders either. He had loved his short visit to Italy for the funeral of the Communist leader, Berlinguer; 'bella, bella', he kept saying about it. His exceptional sensitivity and nervous energy were displayed by constant shifts of expression and a restless movement of his body. All other Soviet leaders would stand on the dais in the Red Square as motionless as statues on Easter Island; Gorbachev constantly shifted from one foot to the other as he was watching the parade. The charm and style of his wife Raisa conquered all who met her – except certain members of the Soviet Embassy, who thought her prominence quite improper. When Gorbachev finally flew home he left me puzzling over a mystery I still find insoluble: how could so nice a man have risen to the top in the Soviet system, and how would he be able to survive when he became leader?

Gromyko explained the contradiction simply by saying that Gorbachev had a nice smile, but steel teeth. Certainly no previous Soviet leader consolidated his position so fast, or got rid of so many enemies so quickly. The change of mood in the Soviet Union was everywhere apparent the next time I visited Moscow in May 1985 with my deputy George Robertson, for the celebrations to mark the fortieth anniversary of victory in Europe.

Gorbachev had then been in power for barely two months, but his impact was already being felt in every area of Soviet policy. All the other Western Governments from the wartime alliance sent prominent representatives, except the United States and Britain; Reagan would not even allow his Ambassador to attend. In a typical compromise, Mrs Thatcher refused to send a minister, but permitted her Ambassador to lay a wreath only slightly smaller than a soup-plate. The British Legion sent a delegation to support him at the second ceremony at the tomb of the Unknown Soldier, which I joined after laying a wreath for the Labour Party, with the other foreign delegates, at the mausoleum in the Red Square.

This led me to an interesting brush with Soviet security. After the ceremony at the tomb of the Unknown Soldier I had to rejoin the other foreign delegates for another ceremony inside the Kremlin. George and I made our way through the Alexandrov gardens to the gates in the Kremlin wall where hundreds of guests were queuing. Again and again I tried to persuade the young Red Army soldier to let me in, saying '*delegatsiya, delegatsiya*'. He continued to bar my way. Finally in desperation I pulled out my wallet and showed him my old age pensioner's bus pass from the Greater London Council. He let me in immediately. Perhaps 'Red' Ken Livingstone was more powerful than he knew.

The ceremony inside the Kremlin Palace was a jolly affair, with military bands marching down the aisles, a ballet about the war to music by Shostakovich, children from all over the Soviet Union wearing their national dress, and speeches from Gorbachev himself and national figures like the astronaut, Valentina Tereshkova.

Next day, after the military parade in the Red Square, I watched hordes of children climbing over the stationary tanks, and went to an enormous reception in the Kremlin for the whole of the Soviet nomenklatura; resplendent in their military and civilian uniforms, they gorged themselves on caviar and smoked sturgeon, washed down with copious draughts of vodka. It was in fact the last official function in the Soviet Union at which Gorbachev allowed hard liquor to be served.

Then I had a wonderful couple of hours to myself in Gorky Park to see how the ordinary Russians were celebrating. The lawns and glades were packed with veterans and their families, the children carrying balloons, the old men bowed down with medals; there were soft drinks and sausages instead of caviar and vodka. Though there had been rain the previous day, the sun was now shining; Zagladin told me that they had spent millions of roubles scattering chemicals to disperse the clouds, so as to make sure there was good weather during the military parade.

Ever since then I have made a point of spending a few hours in Gorky Park whenever I visit Moscow; the common humanity of the Russian people emerges better there than anywhere. Nowadays it could as easily be Roundhay Park in Leeds – the same family picnics, the same loving couples, the teenagers in jerseys and jeans, some with ghetto-blasters and punk haircuts, the little children screaming with delight on the roundabouts and model space-rockets.

The international youth culture is one of many factors which in my opinion make the Gorbachev revolution irreversible. The first time I went to Moscow in 1959, I had the familiar experience of being approached in the Red Square by a young man who said: 'I am Rooshan, Rooshan business man. I would like to buy your suit.' Nowadays you may be asked if you will sell a Sony Walkman or a video tape. In Leningrad and the Baltic Republics people watch Finnish or Swedish television regularly. Yet there is still no public telephone directory in Moscow; access to copying machines was first permitted in 1989, under careful control. The electronic revolution in communications is already transforming Soviet culture; it cannot begin to transform the Soviet economy unless the Soviet leaders are prepared to accept the political changes which must go with it.

We met Gorbachev and all the other members of the Politburo during the big reception in the Kremlin. I noticed that Gorbachev's main rival, Romanov, slipped away early from the receiving line; he seemed flushed with drink. Soon afterwards he was removed from power. It was during that reception that the American Ambassador, an old friend, told me he had been shocked the day before by the aggressive statements made by Gorbachev in his speech in the Kremlin Palace. He refused to believe me when I quoted Gorbachev's actual words about the creation of a new collective security system; later he admitted that he had been mistaken. The isolation of foreign diplomatists in Moscow is liable to produce that sort of paranoia.

The extent of the change in the Communist world was brought home to me even more sharply when I paid short visits to Hungary and East Germany in 1986. I had been deeply moved by the rise of the Solidarity movement in Poland in 1982, and somewhat encouraged that the Russians were prepared to ignore the Communist Party; they allowed a nationalist Polish General to take over, rather than send in the Red Army. Jaruzelski refused to come to terms with Solidarity until 1989, and partly for that reason failed to improve the lamentable performance of the Polish economy; but he allowed more freedom of expression than Poland had known since the war. It was said that the Polish dogs crossed into Czechoslovakia to eat, while the Czech dogs crossed into Poland to bark.

In Hungary the freedom of expression was total, though there was little freedom of political organisation. Budapest was crowded with Western tourists, many on day trips by hydrofoil from Vienna. Indeed relations between Hungary and Austria were now so close that one felt the Empress Maria Theresa was once more on her throne. On the other hand the persecution of Hungarians in Transylvania had made Hungary's relations with Romania so bad that they might well have been at war with one another, if they had not both been members of the Warsaw Pact. When I visited the Parliament building, the Speaker showed me Count Karolyi's copy of my book on the destruction of the East European Socialist Parties after the war, *The Curtain Falls*. I expressed surprise, since it included a bitter attack on the Rakosi regime. 'You know Janos Kadar was being tortured in prison at the time you were writing about,' he explained.

East Germany was far less encouraging; it was economically the most successful but politically the most Stalinist of all the East European countries I have visited. For that reason it was the least enthusiastic about Gorbachev; it later banned two of the leading Soviet journals. On the other hand, everyone watched West German television. The regime had to set up a relay station near Dresden, because it could not persuade people to work in Saxony unless they could watch their favourite programmes from West Germany. I had two and a half hours unfruitful discussion with Honecker, who showed no signs of retiring; he was hoping Moscow would at last allow him to pay an official visit to West Germany, so that he could visit his birthplace in the Saar. Once again, as I toured the beautiful eighteenth-century palace in Dresden, painstakingly rebuilt after the allied bombing raids at the end of the war, and looked at the exquisite treasures in the adjoining Grüne Gewolbe, I reflected on the extraordinary unity in diversity of European culture, which has created links between all the peoples living between Dublin and Moscow which are far more enduring than their frontiers or their ideologies.

One proof of this was the popularity of the BBC wherever I travelled. During a visit to the Hermitage in Leningrad I was sitting exhausted in the Matisse room next to a Russian engineer. When he discovered I was Denis Healey his face lit up: 'I listen to the programmes on British politics every night on the BBC World Service'; he asked me to send him books on modern British painting. I was more surprised on a visit to Tiflis to discover that the Politburo of the Georgian Communist Party relied on the BBC for its news. *Yes, Minister* seemed to be popular everywhere. The Hungarians adored it quite as much as the Prime Minister's department in the Netherlands.

My visit to Tiflis was part of a fascinating tour I made of the Soviet Union in the summer of 1986 with a Parliamentary delegation led by Willie Whitelaw, Mrs Thatcher's Deputy Prime Minister. As I was his deputy for purposes of our tour I felt rather like a gentleman's gentleman. We were taken to the beautiful mediaeval city of Zagorsk, the most important centre of the Russian Orthodox Church; services were being held in two of the churches. Our guide was the head of the Soviet Supreme Court, Terebilov; he met his match in the impressive young priest who ran the theological seminary there; they had a tense argument about the obstacles placed before young men who wanted to join the Church.

The same day we were given some insight into the official road to heaven, when we visited Star City, where Soviet astronauts are trained. To our surprise we were allowed to photograph everything except the interior of the latest Mir space station. I treasure a photograph of myself emerging backwards from a tiny space capsule: it looks like the breech delivery of an elephant. On the way back to Moscow we passed a day in the country; it reminded me of England in the twenties.

Gorbachev gave us an interview for three hours in the Kremlin. He was flanked by Dobrynin, who had taken Ponomarev's place as the Party's International Secretary after twenty-four years as Ambassador in Washington, and by other experts; but he hardly ever referred to them. Unlike all earlier Soviet leaders, he did not read out a prepared statement himself, but asked us to raise any issues we liked, making pencil notes as we spoke. Then he dealt in detail with all the points we had raised, never using the old Marxist-Leninist jargon with which I had become so familiar. In the course of his remarks he gave a firm pledge that if Britain gave up its nuclear weapons, the Soviet Union would dismantle the equivalent number of its own. Otherwise he was mainly concerned to answer our questions and to give a clear description of his objectives both at home and abroad.

For me, the most interesting part of that visit was our few days in Georgia; I had never before been outside European Russia. Georgia was indeed another country; it had been an independent state until its conquest by the Tsars in the nineteenth century, and returned to independence for a short time after the Bolshevik revolution. It was immensely proud of its past glories, and of its Christian heritage; indeed its very name was taken from St George of Cappadocia on the other side of the Black Sea. Living standards were higher in its capital, Tiflis, than in Moscow, and life-styles were far more easy-going. In Moscow and Leningrad we had been unable to get even a glass of beer; in Georgia, a great vine-growing region, we had wine at every meal and visited a cellar for a wine tasting. One puzzling item on our programme was down as 'Visit to Sculptor's Studio'; we did indeed visit the studio of Georgia's leading sculptor, but this seemed mainly intended as an excuse for an imperial luncheon at which we drank three or four toasts in brandy during every course. Georgia in fact belonged more to the Mediterranean civilisation than to that of northern Europe; it is significant that Gorbachev himself comes from Stavropol, nearby on the northern foothills of the Caucasus.

By this time Gorbachev had made the main purpose of *perestroika* crystal clear. For years Russia had been a military giant and an economic dwarf – Upper Volta with rockets. Once Krushchev had made his *ex-cathedra* denunciation of the Soviet pope's infallibility, the cement of international Communism was bound to dissolve.

By the eighties there was no Communist Party in the world which still looked to the Soviet Union as an economic or political model. Gorbachev recognised that it was impossible to improve Russia's economic performance without reducing the drain imposed on its scarce resources by its massive arms programmes. Moreover, it would be impossible to persuade the West to give Russia the technological help it needs without drastic changes in Soviet foreign policy.

To buttress these essentially economic arguments, Gorbachev has carried out a searching review of the role of military force in the nuclear age. Neither the United States nor the Soviet Union has gained greater security from its enormous arms expenditure since the Second World War. On the contrary, the arms race threatens to move into new areas, like space and the depths of the ocean, which could destabilise the balance so far maintained. Not one of the fifty thousand nuclear weapons the superpowers now possess could be used in war without the risk of rapid escalation to the thermonuclear holocaust. To the horrors of blast and radiation with which the world has been familiar since Hiroshima, there is now added the possibility of a nuclear winter, as the clouds of smoke created by nuclear fire-storms rise into the upper atmosphere and blot out the sun for months, or even years. In such a war, nuclear-free zones and even neutrality would be a black joke.

Chernobyl reminded us of yet another hazard; the release of radiation caused by the conventional bombing of nuclear power stations could devastate much of the globe even if nuclear weapons were never used. The British Royal Commission on Environmental Pollution estimated in 1983 that if there had been as many atomic power plants in Europe during the Second World War as there are today, large parts of Europe would still be uninhabitable. Sheep are still being slaughtered on the Cumbrian hills for fear of radiation poisoning. Edna and I were passing through the enchanting village of Sirmione on Lake Garda just after the accident at Chernobyl. The mayor had posted a notice in the square warning mothers not to buy green vegetables or to let their children play on the grass. Incidentally, someone had scrawled on the wall next to it 'Viva Madonna': it referred not to the Virgin Mary but to the American pop-star – another example of the technological revolution which is creating a single world.

In his keynote speech to the Communist Party Congress in 1986, Gorbachev used words of which the full importance has yet to be realised. After referring to the fact that nuclear radiation and environmental pollution knew no national boundaries – he was the first world leader to highlight the threat to the ecology – he told his audience of Party functionaries that we have to move, 'groping in the dark as it were, towards an interdependent or even integral world.' The language was as unprecedented as the concept; no previous Soviet leader would ever have admitted that he was groping in the dark about anything. Gorbachev, on the contrary, constantly admits that he is bound to make mistakes in the course of his experiments, and that it will often be necessary to compromise. He has often quoted my favourite saying of Heraclitus: 'Everything is in flux.'

Even as late as 1985 I had a long argument with a leading Soviet spokesman in Stockholm who asserted that, although Russia sought agreement with the West, she still had a political duty to assist revolution anywhere in the Third World. That doctrine has now been formally buried; Moscow is withdrawing from its revolutionary commitments all over the Third World, from Afghanistan through Angola to Kampuchea and Cuba.

Most impressive of all was the opening section of Gorbachev's speech to the United Nations in December 1988, when he put the Russian Revolution in a totally new context, comparing it with the French Revolution as a historical event which 'gave a tremendous impetus to mankind's progress':

'To a large extent, those two revolutions shaped the way of thinking that is still prevalent in social consciousness. It is a most precious spiritual heritage. But today we face a different world, for which we must seek a different road to the future ... We have entered an era when progress will be shaped by universal human interests ... World politics too, should be guided by universal human values.'

Western leaders in the past have rightly given great importance to Marxist–Leninist doctrine as the basis of Soviet foreign policy. They should give equal importance to changes in that doctrine. By abandoning the theory that the Russian Revolution divided the world finally into two camps, which must struggle for supremacy until one or the other wins, perhaps after a world war, Gorbachev has destroyed the doctrinal basis which has helped to determine Soviet foreign policy since 1917. And by reducing the status of the Soviet Revolution to that of a single event which produced simply a spiritual heritage, he has effectively abandoned the whole intellectual apparatus of Marxism–Leninism. This creates opportunities for cooperation between Russia and the West which simply did not exist before Gorbachev.

Perestroika may not succeed in changing Soviet economic performance as Gorbachev hopes. The Soviet state and Party both suffer from enormous bureaucracies which are incompetent and corrupt. The Soviet people is deeply cynical about its political leaders, and is unlikely to see its living standards improve as a result of *perestroika* for some years. Gorbachev may fail, or be replaced. One reason why it is difficult to make radical changes quickly in the Soviet Union is that, unlike Western politicians, its leaders cannot begin public campaigning for their policies until after they are elected.

Gorbachev's new foreign policy, however, is likely to survive, whatever happens to him personally. The bureaucracy which makes and carries out Soviet foreign policy is, as in other countries, comparatively small; the old guard has already been replaced both in the Party machine and in the Foreign Office. The deposed bureaucrats carry no political clout. Meanwhile the economic and technological imperatives which first caused the change in foreign policy are still there, more demanding than ever. Above all, no future Soviet leader could restore the old Marxist–Leninist doctrine to the dominant position it occupied before Gorbachev. Whether the new foreign policy succeeds will depend on whether the Western governments can respond constructively to Gorbachev's challenge, at least in the field of security, where they face the same technological and economic imperatives as he does.

So far, although all the Western leaders now recognise Gorbachev's sincerity, they have failed to adapt their foreign and defence policies to the end of the Cold War. For forty years they have been able to quell criticism and keep the alliance united by brandishing the spectre of the Red menace. Robbed of the Soviet enemy, they are running about like chickens with their heads chopped off. The bureaucrats who control their diplomatic and military machines seem to have lost the capacity for initiative, except in Germany, where the Ostpolitik begun by Willy Brandt is now universally accepted as offering the framework for a relevant response to the new opportunities.

Outside the present governments, however, there are many people in the West with political and military experience who have been exploring new answers to the challenge presented by Gorbachev. I myself have been arguing ever since the fifties that the only way by which NATO can escape from the dilemmas created by its reliance on nuclear deterrence is to build a new security system in Europe based on cooperation with the Soviet Union in arms control. In the sixties the removal of Krushchev and the establishment of the Brezhnev doctrine set back the hopes of such cooperation in Europe, although the seventies saw Nixon and Brezhnev aiming at a global détente between the superpowers and making the first agreements on strategic arms control. However, the agreements between Moscow and Washington on controlling strategic weapons have made the contradictions implicit in NATO's strategy of Flexible Response in Europe even more glaring and more dangerous.

Both Kissinger and McNamara, the most important influences on American strategy since the war, stated soon after leaving office that it was unrealistic for Western Europe to rely on the possibility that any American President would ever risk the survival of the United States for the sake of its allies, by ordering a strategic nuclear attack on the Soviet Union. They also warned Europe that even the limited use of nuclear weapons would probably lead to the thermonuclear holocaust. In 1984 McNamara joined with George Kennan, McGeorge Bundy, and Gerry Smith, all old colleagues of mine in government, in proposing that NATO should abandon its plans to initiate the use of nuclear weapons against a purely conventional Soviet attack. Moscow had already stated that it would not use nuclear weapons first. The slogan of 'No First Use' began to attract growing support in Western Europe too – particularly in Western Germany, which under Flexible Response would be the first nuclear battlefield.

I had been writing and speaking along these lines for many years. In January 1985 I reviewed developments since the war in a Fabian pamphlet entitled *Labour and a World Society*; I argued that Britain should take the lead in moving NATO towards a non-nuclear strategy, and outlined some of the ways in which NATO could build a conventional defence even against an all-out conventional attack by the Warsaw Pact. On the other hand I warned that no possible government in NATO, including a Labour government, would want America to give up all its nuclear weapons while Russia still possessed a nuclear arsenal, and that Russia is bound to maintain a nuclear capability so long as China does the same. A year later I developed these ideas in another Fabian pamphlet entitled *Beyond Nuclear Deterrence*, and then in a long article for the American journal *Foreign Affairs*.

Unfortunately the reception of my argument was often damaged by the belief that I was presenting them only to curry favour with the unilateralists in the Labour Party, because I wanted to be Foreign Secretary; my critics failed to notice that Bob McNamara, Helmut Schmidt and Field Marshal Lord Carver were putting the same points without any such incentive. However, I had great difficulty in persuading Neil Kinnock to accept the need for the American nuclear umbrella, and to make the removal of American nuclear bases from Britain subject to agreement by NATO as a whole. The official Labour Party policy remained an uneasy amalgam between dogmatic unilateralism and a commitment to support the alliance while seeking multilateral disarmament. This Punch and Judy show, in which unilateralism and multilateralism were treated as symbolic absolutes like Virtue and Vice in a mediaeval morality play, confused both the Labour Party and the electorate, and was the despair of our fellow Socialist Parties on the Continent. None of the Russians I met could understand the Party's theoretical commitment to unilateralism; they were certain it would lead us to a crushing defeat in the approaching general election.

When Mrs Thatcher visited Moscow in the spring of 1987, however, Reagan was being propelled willy nilly towards an agreement on getting rid of all intermediate nuclear weapons on both sides, if only because it was the only way he could salvage anything from the ruins of his summit meeting with Gorbachev at Reykjavik. A hair-raising lack of preparation had led Reagan to commit himself there to seek the abolition of all nuclear weapons, starting with all ballistic missiles; he was compelled to retract this commitment when he got back to Washington, in favour of a return to the zero-option for Intermediate Nuclear Forces and a fifty per cent cut in strategic missiles. The strategic mafia throughout the alliance bureaucracy had been hostile to the zero-option from the start, as were Mrs Thatcher and Chancellor Kohl. However, when the politicians realised that their hostility would be electorally disastrous, they reversed it; in the end they actually claimed credit for the final INF agreement, which they had initially opposed. Gorbachev clinched Mrs Thatcher's conversion by rolling out the red carpet when she visited Moscow. I took advantage of the impending agreement to persuade Neil Kinnock that the Cruise missiles should be removed from Britain as part of INF, rather than unilaterally. I was less successful in arguing against his visit to Washington; my point was that, since Reagan was bound to see him only as the opponent of his dear friend Mrs Thatcher, there was no way in which he could gain by visiting the White House, particularly so soon after Mrs Thatcher's triumph in the Kremlin. He nevertheless insisted on going ahead with his journey to Washington; after saying at first that he would not need to take me with him, he finally asked me at a few days' notice to join his party.

When we entered the Oval Office, President Reagan strode immediately towards me, thrust out his hand, and said: 'Nice to meet you, Mr Ambassador!' The real Ambassador murmured plaintively: 'But I've already met him, *eleven* times.' I confess I was nonplussed myself, until I was told by a senator at lunch that, only a week earlier, the President had mistaken General Powell, the immensely able black Deputy to his National Security Adviser, for the janitor. My only compensation for that ill-starred visit to Washington was a long private talk with Paul Nitze, who was still nervous about including the shorter-range missiles in the INF agreement. He thought the Germans would never stand it. I told him that if he meant by 'the Germans' the handful of middle-ranking bureaucrats and staff officers who comprised the strategic mafia in Bonn he was probably right; but the overwhelming majority of the German people would be delighted. And so it proved.

I then paid a short visit to Moscow myself. The Russians had delayed fixing the date, and there was still confusion between their foreign office and the Party Secretariat when I arrived. Gorbachev was visiting the Soviet space centre in Central Asia at the time, but I had useful talks with Shevardnadze and Dobrynin, among others. On my last day in Moscow Mrs Thatcher called the General Election: Macmillan had done the same when I was there with Gaitskell and Bevan in 1959.

During the first few weeks of the election the Labour Party's rating soared. Neil Kinnock proved a brilliant leader: his opening speech at a rally in Llandudno set the tone of the whole campaign – incandescent oratory with an irresistible moral thrust. His most powerful passage, which he improvised on the platform, was his reference to the fact that he was the first Kinnock in a thousand years to have gone to a university. It formed the centrepiece of Hugh Hudson's incomparable first party political broadcast for Labour on television; a year later it was stolen by Senator Joe Biden – the discovery of the plagiarism led to his downfall in the 1988 Democratic Party primaries. An able new team of officials at the Labour Party's headquarters had learned the lessons of its disastrous campaign in 1983. The Tories were badly rattled. In the last week Mrs Thatcher took control of their campaign herself, going straight for the Labour Party's jugular in a brutally effective television broadcast on the Monday before the poll, in which she concentrated on reviving memories of the Winter of Discontent.

I myself caused more than a ripple the next day when I walked out of a television discussion which was supposed to be on the summit conference which had taken place in Venice the previous weekend – the Grand Banal, I called it. Instead I was questioned about the private hip operation Edna had had two years earlier; I was so angry that my loyal research assistant, Len Scott, was able to prevent me from hitting the producer responsible only by interposing his body. The episode brought me hundreds of letters; all but two were strongly supportive.

Neil Kinnock was typically generous about the affair. He brought our final rally in the Leeds Town Hall to its feet by asking Edna to join him on the platform. He also turned the episode to political advantage by using it to demonstrate that the Labour Party had turned its back on the politics of envy.

Nevertheless, Labour lost the election. Mrs Thatcher got a slightly smaller share of the total vote than in 1983, and significantly less than in 1979. Labour did not recover its 1979 share, though improving significantly on 1983. The Alliance vote was significantly down on 1983, with only 23.1 per cent of the total compared with 31.5 per cent for Labour, and 43.3 per cent for the Conservatives.

Subsequent opinion polls suggested that Labour's defence policy lost it a significant number of votes, but not nearly sufficient to account for the scale of its defeat. Moreover, it is possible that some people picked defence policy as their reason for not voting Labour because they were ashamed to admit their real reason – that they thought they would be better off under the Tories. The polls showed that even people with left-of-centre attitudes on trade unions, unemployment and taxation were more likely to vote Conservative if they thought the economy was getting stronger. During the election campaign, 56 per cent of voters believed an economic crisis would be likely under a Labour Government. The miners strike and the Winter of Discontent were still remembered, and a muddle over Labour's tax policy did not help.

The improvement in the economy was in fact the main reason why Mrs Thatcher won the 1987 election. Unemployment had begun to fall. Most of the people in work had seen a significant rise in their living standards. They expected a further rise if Mrs Thatcher won. I cannot recall any general election in which the Government party has lost, when the bulk of the population thought their condition had improved in the previous year and would continue to improve in the next – particularly if they feared that the Opposition would jeopardise their gains.

Had monetarism, then, triumphed after all? Was the British economy set fair to forge ahead of its competitors, at least in Europe? Had the abandonment of Keynesian demand-management, and the withdrawal of government from the economy on both sides of the Atlantic, produced a world invulnerable to the old cycles of boom and slump? Within twelve months it was clear that these questions must be answered in the negative. Bad economic management in both Washington and Whitehall played their part. However, the recent introduction of computer technology into communications and industry had produced changes in the international economic environment as far-reaching as those imposed by nuclear weapons on international diplomacy. It has taken the world forty years to begin coming to terms with the nuclear revolution. We are only just beginning to understand the nature of the electronic revolution – and the way in which it is forcing changes in the structure both of national politics and of international affairs.

CHAPTER TWENTY-FIVE

Economic Disorder in the West

No city in the spacious universe
Boasts of religion more, or minds it less;
Of reformation talks and government,
Backed with a hundred Acts of Parliament,
Those useless scarecrows of neglected laws,
That miss th'effect by missing first the cause . . .

Some in clandestine companies combine,
Erect new stocks to trade beyond the line:
With air and empty names beguile the town,
And raise new credits first, then cry 'em down:
Divide the empty nothing into shares,
To set the town together by the ears.
The sham projectors and the brokers join,
And both the cully merchant undermine . . .

Some fit out ships, and double freights ensure,
And burn the ships to make the voyage secure:
Promiscuous plunders through the world commit,
And with the money buy their safe retreat.

– 'Reformation of Manners (London)' Daniel Defoe, 1702

MRS THATCHER OWED her third term to Nigel Lawson, who managed to produce a classic pre-election boom at exactly the right time. Public opinion was already impressed by Mrs Thatcher's success in curbing the power of the trade unions. Most of British management relished its new freedom from industrial trouble, and had enjoyed exceptionally high increases in salary and reductions in taxation. Although the average family was paying more tax than under the previous Labour Government, its living standards had risen in the previous two years, partly because its earnings had risen faster than its output, partly because it was borrowing more than ever before in history. Inflation appeared to be under control and unemployment had just begun to fall. Rightly seen as the magician who had produced this miracle, Lawson's reputation remained exceptionally high for another twelve months; he was seriously talked about as Mrs Thatcher's successor. Yet by the end of 1988 everything seemed to have gone wrong, and he became the main scapegoat for her failures.

'He trims with such panache.' That was Kit McMahon's not unfriendly judgment on Nigel Lawson's record at the Treasury. Lawson had been a financial journalist before he entered Parliament, and was never happier than when discussing economic theory. I much enjoyed his intellectual exuberance in his early years as a backbencher. He had a raffish insolence which reminded me sometimes of Steerforth in *David Copperfield*, sometimes of a rather tubby Alcibiades.

When Lawson became Chancellor in 1983 he was still besotted with the theories of Milton Friedman; Howe's dismal experience of trying to apply monetarism during Mrs Thatcher's first term had done nothing to dampen his ardour. Indeed Lawson published a careful account of his economic doctrine in his Mais Lecture after his first year as Chancellor. It was sado-monetarism in its purest form. He argued that his only responsibility was to conquer inflation, and that inflation was caused exclusively by excessive growth in the supply of money; changes in costs, like wages or the price of oil, had no direct or long-lasting effect on inflation.

Within two years he had abandoned this theory as completely as he had abandoned neo-Keynesianism a decade earlier. Lawson dropped monetarism partly because he found it impossible to operate; the revolution in the financial markets had produced too many new forms of money, of which plastic credit cards were one example. Thus the money supply rose no less than 50 per cent from 1981 to 1984, twice as fast as he intended. From 1984, instead of slowing down, as he had promised, it accelerated to about 20 per cent a year. Yet contrary to his theories, inflation fell for three years, because of a fall in the price of oil and other commodities. This experience gave Lawson no alternative but to renounce all the ideas he had expounded so confidently in his Mais lecture; needless to say, he has never admitted his U-turn. Unfortunately, his new policies led him into difficulties quite as serious as his old.

His new theory, in so far as there was any intellectual basis for his opportunism, was a sort of 'closet Keynesianism'. During the rest of his time at the Treasury he presided over an enormous explosion of demand, which brought an increase in growth and a fall in unemployment, followed by a rise in inflation and a yawning deficit in the balance of payments. The rise in demand was partly the result of the increases Lawson sanctioned in government spending; he claimed to offset these increases by the receipts from selling off government assets, often at a loss to the taxpayer. Lawson presented such privatisation as 'negative public spending'; Harold Macmillan joined the Labour Party in describing it as 'selling off the family silver to pay the butler's wages'.

Demand was further increased by excessive increases in earnings, and – until Mrs Thatcher overruled him in 1988 – by low interest rates, which led to a fall in the value of sterling, and thus increased foreign demand for our products. However, the main source of the increase in demand under Lawson was an enormous increase in private borrowing. This was the by-product of a revolution in the markets caused by deregulation and information technology, which drove all the financial institutions into cut-throat competition for lending to the consumer. By 1986, households in Britain, taken as a whole, were spending more than they were earning, for the first time since records began. So, in spite of Mrs Thatcher's homilies about 'paying our way', Britain was living on tick, as never before in its history.

By the end of 1988 Britain's balance of payments deficit looked like being four times higher than the £4 billion Lawson had predicted in April. Inflation was rising towards eight per cent, double his budget forecast. And the statistics of past performance were as unreliable as the forecasts – even worse than in my day. No one had the slightest idea how much the economy had grown. Growth is measured in three different ways – by income, by output, and by expenditure, all of which in theory should give the same result. In 1987, if growth was measured by income, it was 4.8 per cent; measured by expenditure it was 2.9 per cent. The discrepancy was greater still in 1988; growth was 2.8 per cent when measured by expenditure, measured by output it was 6 per cent – more than twice as high. There were similar inconsistencies in the balance of payments figures; the official statistics for 1988 showed an unexplained gap of £15.2 billion – even greater than the appalling deficit of £14.7 billion.

In his earlier years at the Treasury, I used to compare Nigel Lawson with the driver who was stopped by the police on a motorway – the M1 or M4 or perhaps the sterling M3. He wound down his window, to be told he was drunk. 'Thank God,' he replied, 'I thought the steering had gone.' Now I think perhaps the steering had gone, after all.

It would have been impossible for Britain to have survived all these disasters without North Sea oil. When I was Chancellor, it had given me little benefit, either in revenue or in foreign exchange, until 1978. During Mrs Thatcher's first nine years it brought the Treasury £62 billion in revenue, while its contribution to the balance of payments was nearly £100 billion. Without it, she would never have won even her second term; Britain would have been bankrupt well before 1983.

In my five years at the Treasury, Britain's growth averaged 2.2 per cent a year. Although North Sea oil alone added five per cent to our GDP, under Mrs Thatcher's first nine years it averaged only two per cent. In 1978, my last full year, Britain achieved 3.4 per cent growth. In Howe's first two years, output actually fell heavily. Since 1981, and particularly after Lawson introduced his 'closet Keynesianism', it has been higher, though the contradictions in the statistics make it impossible to measure with any accuracy. It is, however, fair to say that the recent improvement in Britain's growth rate actually began in 1978; moreover, the economy was then in adequate balance both at home and abroad. Growth suffered a disastrous setback during the monetarist experiment, and did not move back towards the path on which I had set it until monetarism had been abandoned. However, by 1988 Britain was producing less than Italy, our economy was as badly out of balance as at the end of the Barber boom, which the Lawson boom in many ways resembled. There was little chance of restoring balance so long as Mrs Thatcher refused to sanction any instrument of policy except interest rates.

The cost of Howe's monetarism and of Lawson's opportunism was catastrophic; it is still being felt. Howe's holocaust tripled unemployment to over three million; it destroyed a fifth of the jobs in manufacturing industry and a tenth of its capacity. Though this automatically improved manufacturing productivity per head, there has been little industrial training or investment in additional capacity in the last nine years. So Britain is badly prepared for the next twelve years, during which its North Sea oil will be running out.

Relative to growth in France, Germany and the Low Countries the record looks better; but that is because for most of the last decade they have been suffering from what has been called 'Eurosclerosis'. Even so, in 1988 Lord Young had to admit, in promoting his department as 'The Department for Enterprise', that 'Despite rapid productivity growth in recent years, the level of productivity remains, on average, about one third to one half lower than our competitors. Private sector research and development is a smaller proportion of GDP and is growing more slowly than in most major competitors. The training and skills of managers and other employees are low compared with principal competitors.' *The Economist* put it more neatly: 'If every country's GDP per person were to keep growing as fast as it has done since 1982, it would take Britons 16 years to catch up with the French, 59 years with the West Germans.' That is a fitting epitaph on Mrs Thatcher's economic achievements.

As an ex-Chancellor, I found it particularly galling. Since I was Shadow Foreign Secretary during Mrs Thatcher's second term, convention compelled me to speak only on foreign affairs in the House. I had little opportunity to attack the Government's economic performance except in discussions on radio or television. However, the economic changes which were taking place in the Western world as a whole were my direct concern, not least because they were beginning to transform international relations as well as affecting financial behaviour in Britain itself.

The financial disorder of the last ten years is still little understood by the average man and woman, although they are deeply affected by its consequences. It started, I believe, because the oil crisis led to a massive accumulation of bad debt by the private banks, which they tried to offset by increasing their lending to other clients. It then got completely out of control with the introduction of computer technology into the financial markets. This produced a triple revolution in which globalisation was accompanied by deregulation and innovation, making the international financial system exceptionally vulnerable to shock. The United States made less attempt to control this triple revolution than any other country, and managed its economy badly throughout the period. So Japan now has a far stronger economy than the United States, which has come to depend primarily on Japan to finance its deficits. This is bound to have major implications for the balance of world power in every field. Yet it is still difficult to foresee these implications in any detail. The whole subject is complicated and controversial. I am deeply conscious, to adapt Virginia Woolf's words, that I may be wasting my energy in trying to believe in something spectral. But the subject is too important to be ignored even in a personal memoir, particularly since I have spent much of the last ten years trying to understand it.

I had seen the beginnings of the revolution in world finance while in the Treasury, when the 'atomic cloud of footloose funds' in the Euro-markets was a major problem for sterling. The freedom of Opposition gave me the chance to broaden my understanding of the interactions between finance and industry. I became Chairman of the Yorkshire and Humberside Development Association and of the West Yorkshire Enterprise Board; in both roles I was concerned to encourage investment in Yorkshire by foreigners. I attended economic conferences and gave lectures to business and banking audiences on both sides of the Atlantic. This also helped me to keep in touch with old friends in Washington, and to learn something of the dramatic political and social changes which had swept over the United States since I had first come to know it in the fifties.

Soon after leaving the Treasury, in the autumn of 1979, I went to New York as guest of the Council on Foreign Relations to give the Leffingwell Lectures on 'Managing the Economy'. It was a delight to have ten days on my own in the world's most exciting city, after eleven years in which I was rarely able to spend more than a few hours there, always on official business. One Sunday I walked from the Algonquin Hotel, favoured by generations of British actors and American writers, the whole way up Fifth Avenue from 44th Street to the Metropolitan Museum of Art in Central Park. It was Hispanic Day, so the pavements were crowded with Latin American immigrants, cheering an endless procession of bands playing the rumba, dancers in exotic costumes, and floats celebrating the cultures and traditions of every country from Chile to Cuba. When I finally reached the Museum, I found the steps packed with people watching the clowns, acrobats, and mimics who perform there on a Sunday. Carnival was king that day.

Another day I went to Greenwich Village to see a rare production of Yeats' plays about Cuchulain. Bums, drunks and junkies were sleeping in the doorways of the Bowery – a scene of utter dereliction worse than anything to be found in Britain. Just across the road the New York intelligentsia were living the sweet life, in leafy squares and modish houses indistinguishable from those in Hampstead or Chelsea. I found a similar contrast when I went for the first time through the menacing squalor of Harlem's slums to the calm Gothic beauty of the Cloisters. This is a museum of mediaeval art in a church I had visited in the Pyrenees before the war; it had been physically transplanted to America, and set on a cliff overlooking the Hudson river, in a park then glowing with the gold and scarlet of the American fall. Such contrasts are common in New York. Yet that city of infinite diversity contains only a small part of the variety of cultures, climates, and living standards which make it so dangerous to generalise about the United States as a whole.

Arthur Schlesinger gave me a call one morning and invited me to his sixtieth birthday party; he was holding it with Ken Galbraith, who had been born on the same date ten years earlier. I accepted with pleasure, expecting to have a quiet evening of political conversation with a small group of liberal academics. In one respect I was disappointed: the only academics were my hosts. The first guest to arrive was Jackie Onassis, followed swiftly by Lauren Bacall and Leonard Bernstein, and before long the whole of the Democratic Party's social set. It was Radical Chic with a vengeance. As fully paid up members of Camelot, they were all supporters of Teddy Kennedy; but one after another came up to tell me sadly, as the only foreigner present, that Chappaquidick had ruled out Teddy's chances of the Party's nomination the following year. The evening ended with Arthur and Ken singing a round composed for them by Bernstein with the refrain 'History, Economy'; it was not the most impressive performance, since Ken Galbraith is completely tone deaf.

My first two Leffingwell lectures were on the lessons of my own experience in trying to run the British economy over the previous five years. My third, later expanded as an article in *Foreign Affairs*, was on the oil crisis, and the coming crisis over the debts of the developing countries which I foresaw as its inevitable consequence.

At that time aggregate borrowing by the Third World from the multinational banks already amounted to some $190 billion, seventy per cent of which had to be refinanced or repaid by 1982. In addition, about $125 billion was owed to governments and multinational organisations like the World Bank. Meanwhile, most of the Western governments had responded to the second wave of OPEC increases in the oil price by adopting restrictive policies; they were also trying to raise their exchange rates through higher interest rates, in the hope of curbing inflation. The savings ratio in the United States had fallen to about 4.5 per cent, partly because the American banks were aggressively marketing consumer credit, though in most of Europe the savings ratio was between twelve and sixteen per cent. So it was clear that the United States would have to join the developing countries in borrowing abroad to finance its investment and its growing trade deficit.

Recession and rising interest rates in the West meant that the developing countries were unlikely to earn a surplus of foreign currency to finance their debts. On the contrary, those without oil were running enormous deficits. 'The way in which the oil producers have handled the supply and price of oil,' I warned my New York audience, 'and the way in which the consumers have reacted to this, have already reduced world growth and increased inflation. They threaten worse consequences still ... Is it inevitable that we should sit and watch the situation drift, meeting occasionally at massive jamborees of producers and consumers for the ritual exchange of abrasive misunderstandings, or at ill-prepared weekend summits which produce ambiguous communiqués as a substitute for policies?'

Inevitably or not, the situation did continue to drift until September 1982. Then Mexico announced that it could not service its debts. I happened to be speaking at the Anglo-Italian Chamber of Commerce in London that week; I warned my audience, which included Guido Carli and Carlo de Benedetti, the brilliant young head of Olivetti, that a general debt crisis was now inevitable, and that the whole of the Western banking system would be at risk, unless action was taken by the IMF the following week in Washington; de Benedetti agreed with every word I said.

This time my words caused a sensation, and did at least embarrass the Western Governments; but they took no decisions about the debt crisis at the IMF. Catastrophe was averted only by the action of three individuals, each of whom occupied a key position in the Western banking system – Paul Volcker, the Chairman of the American Federal Reserve in Washington, Gordon Richardson, the Governor of the Bank of England, and Jacques de la Rosière, who had succeeded Witteveen as Managing Director of the IMF. Together these three worked tirelessly to persuade the private banks to reschedule their loans so that the system could keep going; meanwhile the IMF imposed conditions for the rescheduling, hoping to enable the debtor governments ultimately at least to service their debts without further loans. No one seriously thought they would be able to repay the principal.

This attempt to deal with the debts of the developing countries case by case was at first seen simply as first-aid in an emergency; but so far the West has not moved significantly beyond it. Later it came to be known as the 'sticking-plaster', or 'band-aid' approach; yet it was obvious that the problem would require drastic surgery. De la Rosière warned the Western governments again and again that the 'band-aid' approach would succeed only on three conditions – if they maintained steady growth at three per cent or more a year, if they reduced interest rates, and if they allowed free entry to imports from the debtor countries. None of these conditions was fulfilled. Growth overall remained below the required level, interest rates shot up, and trade restrictions multiplied to the point at which by 1988 the developing countries were losing twice as much money through Western protectionism as they were getting from all the aid programmes.

Nevertheless, the Western Governments refused to consider anything but the 'band-aid' approach. Their faith in the magic of the market-place produced a system in which the private banks were bullied into lending ever more money to bad debtors by their central banks, which were supposed to guarantee their prudence, not to promote their profligacy. So the volume of debt steadily increased; by the end of 1988 Third World debt was $1,320 billion compared with $800 billion six years earlier, and little over $300 billion when I had raised the problem in 1979. The poorest countries in the world were compelled to export capital to the richest, at the cost of a steady fall in their living standards, which were already pitifully low.

For the Latin American debtors the result was particularly tragic. They had just enjoyed a generation of exceptionally rapid growth which appeared to offer some of them the prospect of catching up with the West by the end of the century. The adjustment programmes imposed by the IMF as the price of rescheduling their debts brought an average drop of seven per cent in their national income between 1982 and 1987; this meant starvation for many of their poor, and the elimination of much of their middle class. The wealthy simply salted away their money abroad; in some cases the volume of this 'flight capital' was as great as the money coming into the Latin American countries in foreign loans. It was the historical recipe for revolution. The Western debt-squads did even more damage to Latin America than its military death squads.

The most worrying case was 'poor Mexico, so far from God, so close to the United States'. Although it should have survived the oil crisis better than most, since it had large oil resources of its own, its living standards fell heavily. In 1988 Washington was so alarmed at the prospect of political disorder sending a tidal wave of Mexicans across the border into California and Texas that it gave Mexico a 'bridging loan' of $3.5 billion. Nevertheless the PRI, which had governed Mexico since the First World War, was defeated in a general election by Cardenas, the son of the man who had nationalised the American oil companies in 1938; Cardenas had fought the election on a pledge to renounce Mexico's debts. The PRI managed to return to power, but only by organising massive fraud at the election counts.

The whole subcontinent is now in turmoil, with democracy in Argentina and Brazil once again at risk. Yet the Western governments have so far taken only one tiny step to produce a real solution to the debt problem; they have begun to write off some of the debts of sub-Saharan Africa, which has never been able to service them anyway – but only on the strict condition that other debtors should not take this as a precedent.

Over the last ten years I have spent much of my time discussing the debt crisis and the oil crisis from which it sprang. I learned much from attending the annual Oil Seminar run by the Alexandrian, Robert Mabro at St Catherine's College, Oxford. The Oil Seminar brought together representatives of the oil-producing and oil-consuming governments, with their oil companies, for a fortnight's intensive discussion of their common problems. It taught me at least one important lesson – that those best qualified to know were invariably wrong in their estimate of the oil price in twelve months' time. It also gave me a chance of meeting my old Private Secretary again; now Sir Patrick Nairne, Master of St Catherine's College.

My exploration of these new worlds renewed many other old friendships, for example with de la Rosière and Paul Volcker. Volcker had been brought to Washington from the New York Fed to run the Federal Reserve Board just after I left the Treasury. He was a gentle giant, six feet seven inches tall, with a small balding grey head, a large cigar usually stuck in his mouth and a sardonic sense of humour. His move to Washington at the age of fifty-one meant a great personal sacrifice; he earned less than at the New York Fed and far less than he could have earned as a commercial banker. Since his wife was ailing he had to commute to Washington from New York. Inevitably the measures he had to adopt to keep the American economy under some sort of control were highly unpopular, and he was the first to admit that they would not have been necessary if the Administration and the Congress had done their duty and shown some fiscal responsibility; they did not, either under Carter or Reagan, so Volcker had to shoulder the whole burden himself, with no instrument available except interest rates.

I also made new friends, particularly among the private bankers, from whom I had been somewhat insulated in the Treasury. Minos Zombanakis had become a leading financial figure on both sides of the Atlantic without losing his passionate devotion to his native Crete. Tall and erect, with the eagle profile and black moustaches of his fellow-islanders, he was as much at home dancing the sirtaki to the thrumming of bouzoukis in a vine-covered taverna, as trading Eurobonds in Wall Street; he counted his real wealth in olive trees rather than paper money. Minos shared my views about the debt crisis and many other problems of international finance; we have spent a few days every summer in Greece with politicians, bankers, businessmen and officials not only from Europe and the United States, but also from Japan and the Middle East; so I have been able to renew many friendships from Saudi Arabia and Tokyo.

After two days' intensive discussions of world politics and economics by the sea near Athens, we would go off with our wives for a weekend somewhere else in Greece. I have been able to show Edna my student haunts in Mykonos, Santorini, Delphi, and Olympia, as well as visiting new wonders like the mediaeval monasteries on the rock pinnacles of Meteora. It was not an unmixed blessing to be able to travel in aircraft, limousines, and luxury yachts; I had enjoyed it more in the espadrilles, buses, and cargo boats of my youth.

The *Small World* so accurately described in David Lodge's novel is inhabited by businessmen and bankers as well as academics. I was lucky to find so many of my meetings in places of exceptional beauty, and to be able to take Edna with me so often – a rare privilege when I was at the Treasury. My speeches to the World Economic Forum at Davos gave us our first chance of seeing the Alps in winter; it was a delight to leave arcane discussions of monetary policy in the conference centre, for a sleigh ride up a dazzling snowy valley, with draughts of steaming glühwein for central heating. A meeting at the enchanting Villa Cipriani at Asolo gave us the opportunity to meet Freya Stark again. The intrepid explorer of the Hadramaut was now a very old lady with a powder-white complexion, in a white dress with an enormous floppy white hat; she took her luncheon regularly at the hotel, where the waiters adored her as much as we did.

At the Aspen Foundation in the American Rockies there was an abundance of distractions – walks in the flowery valleys of Maroon Bells, white-water rafting on the Colorado river with Lee Hamilton, an able and earnest young Congressman of exceptional integrity, who was to make his name as Chairman of the House enquiry into the Iran-Contra affair, dinner with Bob McNamara at his summer home in Vail, where I met Wally Brooks again; he had been a hurdling Blue at Oxford with me, and was now a leading surgeon at Salt Lake City, looking more than ever like Lew Ayres as Doctor Kildare. Meanwhile another old friend, Adam Yarmolinksy, was teaching senior company executives from all over the world to act in Sophocles' *Alceste*. Best of all, we were there during the annual Aspen Music Festival, so we were able to join the crowds of youngsters in the great marquee and hear the tiny Japanese prodigy, Mi Dori, then thirteen years old, playing Ernst's Violin Concerto.

It was at Aspen that I came to know the extraordinary George Soros, said to be the best money manager in the world. He was young, trim, handsome, and a slave to physical fitness. Born in Hungary, educated in England, and settled in New York, his interests and his friendships were protean. Determined to do what he could as a private citizen to encourage greater freedom in the Communist world, he had established a foundation to organise cultural and academic exchanges with Hungary, and has since done the same for the Soviet Union. In *The Alchemy of Finance*, he tried to articulate his exceptional instinct for the behaviour of the markets into a general 'theory of reflexivity', so as to explain the psychology which so often led to irrational behaviour.

Some such guide was badly needed. By the early eighties it was becoming clear that the oil crisis and the debt crisis were only part of a revolution which was shaking the whole of the world economy. The revolution was set in motion by the introduction of computers into every area of finance and industry. It was accompanied by institutional changes throughout the Western world and by innovations in the financial markets, which have completely transformed the psychological climate and structural framework in which economic policy must be made.

Information technology has produced a single global financial market. It is now possible to move billions of dollars in microseconds twenty-four hours a day from almost any part of the world to any other. Way back in 1979 Guido Carli had told me, as Italy's central banker, that only two years earlier he could have named at least nine out of the ten richest men in Italy; now he could not name one. The richest Italians by then all owed their wealth to speculating in commodity futures with money borrowed from the Euromarkets. As I have mentioned, by 1988 the volume of money crossing the exchanges in this way was fifty times what was needed to finance world trade in both goods and services.

These colossal flows of capital from one country to another were managed by young men in the dealing rooms of big companies as well as financial institutions, who had square eyeballs from watching their computer screens. Their minds were square as well; they treated money as a commodity, like coffee beans or grains of rice, and made a market in money without any reference to the underlying economic realities it was supposed to represent. Yet the flows of capital managed by this mafia of gilded young lemmings had become the main influence on exchange rates, and through exchange rates on trade, prices, and interest rates, which in turn influenced the rates of growth in every country.

Not surprisingly, exchange rates became exceptionally volatile. In March 1985 I found it difficult to get more than one dollar for every pound I changed in New York. Twelve months later I got nearly two dollars. These wild swings in exchange rates, combined with the consequences of a decade of stagflation, changed economic behaviour at every level, so that forecasting became impossible. My own misfortunes at the Treasury were as nothing to those suffered by all finance ministers in the eighties. From 1982 to 1984 America's growth was twice as high as predicted, for at least twice as long, while inflation increased only two-thirds as fast as forecast. The dollar rose steadily through most of this period, although America was running the biggest balance of payments deficit in its history. President Reagan won re-election in November 1984 because in the previous two years the American economy had produced seven million more full-time jobs, while inflation had fallen to four per cent from the fourteen per cent he inherited from Carter. Meanwhile Europe had seen its own unemployment rising steadily; when a feeble economic recovery did come, it was very dependent on the unique combination of high American economic growth and a high dollar.

International economic statistics, like national statistics, had become wildly unreliable. The GATT figures for world trade showed a gap of $100 billion between the aggregate trade surpluses and deficits, though these should have been equal. None of the economic rules of thumb seemed to apply any longer. Most European economists argued that the high American internal deficit was responsible for America's high interest rates. Yet in 1984 the Dutch deficit was 10.5 per cent of GDP – twice the size of the American deficit; but inflation in Holland was lower than anywhere else in Europe, and interest rates were among the lowest too. On the other hand Holland had higher unemployment than any other European country. So Keynesian theory was no more reliable than monetarism.

I suspect that many of these changes had their root cause in the uncertainties to which the globalisation of the capital markets had made a major contribution. There were, however, two other changes taking place in the financial markets, which were to increase the dangers presented by globalisation. Most Western governments followed the lead set by President Reagan and Mrs Thatcher in removing the restrictions which had hitherto prevented the various financial institutions, such as banks, insurance companies, building societies, and pension funds, from competing with one another for the same type of business.

This deregulation led to cut-throat competition between all these institutions; they lent money on paper-thin margins, often in areas they did not understand. The great Continental Illinois bank went bust in Chicago partly because it was lending money in the oil market on the assumption that oil would reach $75 a barrel in 1984. Johnson Matthey went bust in Britain for similar reasons. In both cases they were nationalised by highly conservative governments, not because President Reagan and Mrs Thatcher knew what would happen if they did not nationalise them, but precisely because they had no idea what would happen once their collapse hit the international inter-bank market. The competition to lend was most acute in the United States and Britain, because they had carried deregulation furthest, and because their banks had been most deeply involved in the debt crisis; so they wanted to rebuild their balance sheets, which were loaded with bad Latin American debt. This was probably the immediate cause of the collapse of the savings ratio and of the excessive consumer borrowing which were later to confront President Bush and Mrs Thatcher with such serious problems.

As if this was not enough, a third revolution swept the financial markets, on the heels of those caused by globalisation and deregulation. The desire to hedge against unpredictable changes in exchange rates and interest rates led to a feverish rash of new financial instruments, starting with swaps, futures, options, and options on futures, and leading to securitisation; anything which could be defined with numbers – even the toll-charges on motorways in California – was turned into a tradeable security. The securities markets enabled people to borrow without going to the banks at all, and were immune to monitoring or control by governments and central banks. In the USA, there is a market of hundreds of billions of dollars for such commercial paper.

So far, the most sinister of the new instruments produced by the revolution of innovation has been the 'junk bond', which enables a predator to borrow money for a takeover, against no security except what he hopes to earn from his target company, after he has taken it over. This had led in America to the so-called 'leveraged buy-out', organised by a financier for a share of the expected profits, perhaps on behalf of a manager in the target company itself.

The most notorious case so far of a leveraged buy-out was the attempt in October 1988 by Ross Johnson, the chief executive of an enormous American conglomerate, RJR Nabisco, to buy 8.5 per cent of the company which employed him, by putting up only $20 million. The company had revenues in 1987 of $15,800 million; Johnson and the seven colleagues who joined him in the bid stood to gain $200 million when the sale was completed, and $2,600 million within five years. When Johnson's bid became known, rival bidders rushed in; within two months the offering price for the company had climbed above $26,000 million.

Whether or not the company would prove to be worth such a sum was of little concern to the lawyers and investment bankers who organised the buy-out. They stood to earn £1 billion in fees if it succeeded. One of the most disturbing features of the financial revolution is the extent to which, with so much bad debt on their books, the bankers rely increasingly on such fees for their income; this may mean that they personally can be millionaires even if their banks are insolvent. Similarly, the fees they earn for rescheduling bad debts in Latin America give the individuals in the financial institutions little interest in seeking a long-term solution to the debt problem.

The American taxpayers pay billions of dollars to subsidise leveraged buy-outs, because interest payments on the colossal borrowings they involve are deductible as a business expense. Like the merger-mania and takeover-frenzy which gave them birth, they are based on asset-stripping; so they can have disastrous consequences for the workers in the target companies, and the communities in which they live. They also inflict a more general damage on business performance. Because they are fuelled by the greed of shareholders, they make it dangerous for managers to look further ahead than next quarter's stock price; once launched, they demoralise the whole of the workforce in a target company. Whatever good they may have done in improving efficiency in some badly managed companies, they have imposed short-termism on business in the United States and Britain. By contrast, in Japan and Germany managers can afford to look further ahead, because their shareholders have less influence, and both their governments and their banks feel identified with the industrial success of their national companies.

Above all, most of the new activities spawned by the financial revolution, such as leveraged buy-outs, assume that all trees grow up to the sky – that there will never be another recession. If the United States does have a recession, even one as modest as in the Carter years, its whole financial system could collapse like a pack of cards.

This seemed quite possible in October 1987. The whole world held its breath on Black Monday, which brought the greatest stock market crash since 1929. It was totally unexpected by ninety-nine per cent of the business community. The only person I know who foresaw it was George Soros. He thought it would start in Tokyo, not New York; this mistake cost him over $100 million of his personal fortune, though he finished 13.5 per cent up on the year. Everyone was wrong also about the consequences of the crash. All the forecasters thought it would bring a heavy fall in world growth in 1988; on the contrary, 1988 was one of the best years for growth since the war, partly because governments stuffed money into their economies for fear of a recession.

Even now there is no agreement on precisely what caused the crash – and therefore on whether it may be repeated. There is now a general feeling that the stock market had risen so high that the bubble was bound to burst, though few people thought so at the time. The SEC, as official watchdog over the stock markets in the United States, thinks that a major factor was the herd instinct of institutions, such as pension funds, which are now the dominant investors in Western stock markets; they all got out of the market together at the first sign of trouble. Few now believe, as they did at first, that programme trading – the automatic buying and selling of shares by programmed computers – was an important factor. But computers in general certainly had a major responsibility for the crash in New York, and for its lightning repercussions across the globe.

Most financial activity world-wide now depends on the information technology which computers have made available. My own explorations into the financial revolution led me to accept invitations to talk to computer companies in many parts of the world. I have only the most primitive understanding of the scientific principles involved, or of how computers work. Indeed I scarcely survived my first few weeks of writing this book. Trying to operate my word-processor, with no help except from the library of manuals which came with it, almost snapped my reason. The vocabulary alone seemed impenetrable. I could just about learn the meaning of newly invented words like byte and megabyte; what defeated me was the use of familiar words like default or boot to mean something entirely different. As for phrases like 'Allow widows and orphans', my imagination boggled.

However, I can drive a car without understanding the internal combustion engine. And I am told that Greats is the best possible training for some areas of computer research such as artificial intelligence, and even for the invention of new software. I was surprised to find some old friends now engaged in the computer business. After leaving the United States Treasury, Mike Blumenthal had become head of Unisys, which he organised out of a merger between Burroughs and Sperry. Dave Packard returned from his stint in the Pentagon to the great computer company, Hewlett-Packard, which he and a friend had started in a garage in California. There were also some uncovenanted benefits from my explorations of this new world. The occasion of my first visit to the land of my fathers was a talk to a computer company in Dublin; so I was able to pay homage at the Georgian house in Merrion Square where my idol, William Butler Yeats, had lived, and to see James Joyce's lonely tower at

Dun Laoghaire, above the beach where the appearance of a lame school-girl tormented Leopold Bloom with strange desires.

I soon discovered that the computer revolution was developing with such speed that my technical ignorance was shared even by many of the people directly concerned in the field. A thirty-year-old computer expert often finds it difficult to understand what his twenty-year-old colleague is doing; a forty-year-old may find it impossible. Surveys have shown that many British managers do not understand the functions of the computer systems they have spent thousands of pounds to install; they may be as likely to turn to their chauffeur for information. Britain is lagging behind Europe in using computers, Europe behind the United States, and the United States behind Japan. Britain is expected to have a shortage of 50,000 computer technicians in the nineties, and is hopelessly behind in electronic research and development.

Compared with the Industrial Revolution, the computer revolution has advanced with breathtaking speed, and its speed is still accelerating. The first computer, ENIAC, was built in 1946; within thirty years there were half a million computers, costing on average a thousand times less than ENIAC, operating at twenty times the speed, on 3,600 times less power, with ten times more reliability. In the last ten years information technology has exploded, transforming not only the financial world, but also manufacturing and defence. Most experts believe we are now on the brink of a second computer revolution due to the development of superconductor, semiconductor and quantum technologies, and to research into artificial intelligence.

Yet society's growing dependence on computers may carry great dangers as well as opportunities. Computers are liable to failure, fraud, penetration and sabotage. A computer failure in America has recently caused the halting of transatlantic flights; in Britain a government computer has produced the wrong figures for consumer spending. Computer fraud has been costing at least £3 billion a year – probably very much more, since those defrauded are often financial institutions which cannot afford to admit their vulnerability. Computer penetration has opened the secrets of the US Pentagon and the British Royal family to eighteen-year-old schoolboys. Computer 'viruses' and 'logic bombs' have been implanted into the systems of large companies and used for blackmail. There is an obvious risk to the defence, power, communications and financial systems on which all developed countries now rely. Governments now have a common interest in cooperating to protect the international society against such risks, just as they have in cooperation against the risks of nuclear war or ecological disaster.

The financial revolution, and the computer revolution which has made it possible, have produced a world all too reminiscent of Britain two or three centuries ago when greed infected honest citizens with a speculative fever which produced strange collective madnesses like tulipomania and the South Sea Bubble. At that time the consequences of such financial insanity were limited largely to the speculators themselves. Today the consequences of a similar speculative fever have produced a global financial system so fragile and yet so interdependent that it is vulnerable to many possible sources of breakdown, and its breakdown could plunge the Western world into a recession quite as damaging as the Great Slump of the thirties, with political consequences even more dangerous.

At present the most dangerous problem threatening its breakdown is the gross imbalance in world trade caused by excessive borrowing in the United States. The problem is largely the product of President Reagan's eight years in office.

Though Mrs Thatcher often boasted that President Reagan was following her example in his economic policies, I found it fascinating to examine the differences as well as the similarities between them. Reagan won the election in 1980 on a firm undertaking to balance the American budget, while cutting both taxation and government spending. He left office eight years later with a fiscal deficit larger than all previous federal deficits put together. Meanwhile the savings ratio had fallen to under two per cent of GNP. As a result the United States had become the biggest single debtor in the world, and, without drastic changes in policy, was set to owe other countries $1,000 billion in 1991, more than all the other debtor governments put together. It had been able to keep going only because it received massive inflows of capital from its ex-enemies, Japan and Germany.

George Bush was a thousand times right in accusing Reagan of 'voodoo economics' when he fought him for the Republican nomination in 1980. Reagan had been persuaded by the so-called 'supply-side' economists that if he cut the rates of tax on higher earnings he would actually collect more taxes, because people would work much harder and earn much more. It was, of course, nonsense, like the theory that the wealth thus created would 'trickle down' to the rest of the population; Ken Galbraith described the 'trickle down' theory as meaning that, if you stuffed enough oats into the front end of a donkey, enough would come out of the back end to feed the sparrows. So Washington's revenues fell.

At the same time, Reagan doubled defence spending in his first term, and did not offset this increase by cuts in other areas of public spending;

lower revenues and higher expenditure inevitably made his fiscal deficit rise instead of falling. I used to describe his policy as 'Keynes with a crew cut': Reagan thought it was all right to increase demand by cutting taxes for the rich, but quite wrong to do so by raising spending on the poor. Nevertheless, although the federal deficit became horrifically large, it was offset by surpluses in the state and local government accounts. America's PSBR, as we would define it in Britain, was only three per cent of GNP when Reagan left office, substantially less than in most Western countries. The main financial problem in Reagan's United States, as in Thatcher's Britain, has been the collapse of the private saving, out of which governments normally finance their fiscal deficits. In my opinion the prime cause of this collapse in private saving, in Britain no less than the United States, has been frantic competition for business among the deregulated financial institutions, particularly among the banks which had accumulated bad debts in the Third World and were losing much of their traditional business to the securities markets.

At this point, however, Reagan's policy diverged sharply from Mrs Thatcher's. She has tried to offset some of the excess in Britain's private borrowing by increased public saving. To achieve this, in spite of all her election promises, she was taking thirty-seven per cent more tax in real terms from the average family in 1988 than I did as Chancellor. Even so, her enormous budget surplus was essentially the product of her revenue from selling public industries, and of the consequent fall in public investment once these industries were in private hands.

Reagan, however, simply borrowed more abroad. But in both cases private borrowing for consumption remained grossly excessive; so spending increased, and was reflected in enormous deficits on the balance of payments. As a result, the United States has come to depend on financial support by its defeated enemies, while Britain has been able to attract foreign funds only by offering usurious interest rates.

So far, America's current account deficits have been financed by Japan and Germany. When fear of a declining dollar discouraged them from buying American government bonds, they began to buy hard assets in the United States. Japan is now said to own much of Hawaii, and is making vast inroads into the property market on the mainland, particularly in California and New York. Germany seems to favour property in Florida. Japan has also been setting up factories in the United States, above all in the automobile industry. I was told by the head of a big Japanese securities house that any Japanese manufacturing company would be able to make a profit by exporting its own products into Japan from a subsidiary in the United States, once the dollar was down to 110 yen; Honda has been doing so with the dollar at 130 yen.

Meanwhile, for all his free-market rhetoric, Reagan imposed more restrictions on imports than the previous six presidents combined, almost doubling the share of total American imports which are subject to quota or official restraint. Ironically enough, so long as foreigners continue buying dollars to finance America's external deficit, the dollar is likely to remain too high to make American goods competitive abroad; the dollar is also buoyed up by the high interest rates required to cool the American economy, which is already working to full capacity. Such improvement in the American balance of payments as has taken place has been mainly at the expense, not of the surplus countries like Japan and Germany, whose surpluses are still rising, but of the deficit countries like Britain.

Though the details of his country's economic performance are no more familiar to the average American than ours are to the average Briton, there is already a widespread popular feeling that America is losing out to its allies, particularly Japan. The self-confidence which Reagan undoubtedly restored to the American people, after Vietnam and the hostage crisis, now shows signs of flagging. Paul Kennedy's academic study of *The Rise and Fall of Empires* became a popular best seller. I was asked solemnly when I was lecturing at Princeton in 1988 at what precise stage in the decline and fall of the Roman empire did America now stand. There is a general feeling that America is now badly overstretched by its military commitments overseas; in fact, even after Reagan the United States is spending on defence only two thirds as much of its national output as in Kennedy's time, while its national output is twice as high.

However, popular interest, not only in foreign affairs, but in politics generally, is at a low ebb. In the 1988 presidential election about a third of those qualified did not bother to register, and of those who registered, only half bothered to vote. So George Bush was elected President by the votes of fewer than one out of every five American citizens. Voting in the mid-term elections tends to be even lower.

Yet, to use Eric Hoffer's words, 'the American people are lumpy with unrealised potentialities'. The United States is still a unique beacon of hope and opportunity for countless millions all over the world. The hope, the opportunity, and the danger now faced by the United States can be seen best of all in its richest state, California; I have taken every opportunity of visiting California, usually with Edna, since our younger daughter settled in San Francisco some ten years ago.

If California were a sovereign state – and in many respects it behaves as one – it would be the seventh richest in the world. Orange County alone, a small area south of Los Angeles, would be the seventeenth richest. Native-born Californians are a small minority in the state. Until recently, most Californians were immigrants from less sunny and prosperous states in the East or the Middle West of the Union. Today immigration is mainly from Latin America, particularly Mexico, and from almost every country in Eastern Asia. By the end of the century there will be as many Hispanics as people of European origin in California, and a fifth of the population will be Asian.

We first got some sense of the mixture of peoples in 1984, when we spent a few days in the Yosemite valley, surely the most beautiful place on God's earth. I loved swimming under the blazing sun in the icy river at Elbow Bend, beneath the towering mass of El Capitan, three thousand feet of vertical granite. There were usually a few Asian families picnicking with us under the pines, neatly deployed in trim shorts and spotless shirts round portable tables with a glowing barbecue beside them. In full sun, on the sandy bank below, we would see the Hispanic families squatting in the grass, unkempt in their peasant rags, with little to eat except fruit and bread.

The Hispanics compete with the blacks for the lowest paid jobs, and suffer similar discrimination. The Asians mostly go to college, where they tend to win the best degrees. Indeed Berkeley introduced a quota system to limit its number of Asian students, so as to protect its native-born Americans. We made friends later with Dr Sam Yen, one of the world's leading experts on the chemistry of sex at the University of San Diego. As a boy of fifteen in China he had exploited his unusual height to get a pilot's certificate. He spent the war years as a 'Flying Tiger', ferrying supplies into China over the notoriously dangerous Burma Hump. Then he went to California, got his degree and started a new career studying pre-menstrual tension with his friend Bob Jaffe, another immigrant to California, who came from Michigan. When I see what the Asian immigrants have done for California, I sometimes think the economist Harry Johnson was right: there is nothing wrong with Britain that a hundred thousand Chinese could not solve.

Few of the Hispanics achieve such eminence as the Asians; with the blacks, they form a large part of that third of the American people who do not bother to register for the right to vote. If only a small proportion of that third took the trouble to register, and then to cast their vote, the Democratic Party would win every Presidential election. In 1988 a shift of just over half a million votes in the eleven states, including California, where Bush's margin was three per cent or less, would have been enough to elect Dukakis.

Because so many Americans do not use their democratic rights, the richest country in the world contains some of the poorest people. And because government in the United States leaves so many crucial decisions to the market, America's economic superiority and social stability are now both under threat. Richard Lamm, a three-term Democratic Governor of Colorado, has compiled a disturbing list of the problems which confront President Bush. Productivity growth from 1974 to 1987 was a quarter of Japan's and only one third that of France. The average American is poorer than he was in 1973. The United States has a divorce rate twenty-five times that of Japan. Half of all black births are illegitimate. Half of all Hispanic children fail to graduate from high school. The United States has five times as many murders, ten times as many rapes, and seventeen times as many robberies as Japan. The United States spends five times as much on health care as Britain, yet life expectancy there is below that of Spain or Greece.

Most interesting of all, Japan has 1,000 engineers for every hundred lawyers; the United States has 1,000 lawyers for every 100 engineers. One reason for the weakness of America's health service is that the average general practitioner now has to spend half his income on insurance against suits for medical error or malpractice, which are encouraged by the legal right of American lawyers not only to tout for practice, but to take a percentage of any damages which may be awarded. There is little chance of Congress changing the law to prevent this, since most of its members are themselves lawyers.

The startling contrast between the social stability and economic efficiency of Japan, compared with the United States and Britain, led me to learn as much as I could about the secret of Japanese success. I accepted an invitation to the centenary celebrations of the leading Japanese newspaper, *Asahi Shimbun*, in 1979, and in 1986 became a member of the European Advisory Board of the biggest company in Japan, Nippon Telegraph and Telephones, a nationalised industry which was being privatised with glacial majesty, by the sale of ten per cent of its shares each year.

In 1979, despite my few days' visit in 1963, modern Japan was still largely a mystery to me. I had always admired Japanese art, particularly the coloured prints of 'the floating world' by Hokusai and Hiroshige, which made such an impact on French painting when they reached Europe in the middle of the nineteenth century. Postwar Japan first made its impact on me through the films of Kurosawa and the novels of Mishima. Despite his repugnant political views, Mishima seemed to me to combine the sensuous rapture of Colette and the cold rationalism of Montherlant in a disturbing cocktail which reached into the lower depths of the modern psyche. My recent visits to Japan with Edna have given us many pleasures outside the economic and political fields which were their excuse. Kyoto is an ancient city of inexhaustible beauty, like Florence or Isfahan, particularly in the spring, when the cherry blossom foams pink and white among the temples. But how do we relate all this to the Japan of the compact disc and the microchip?

I had already learned as Chancellor, that consensus was the governing rule of Japanese society. No decision can be reached by government or private industry except after a long process of establishing a consensus among all who will be concerned with carrying it out. One reason why it can be so difficult to negotiate with Japanese is that once they have reached a consensus among themselves, they find it difficult to change their position by compromising with outsiders. However, faced with an external *fait accompli*, they are uniquely skilful in adapting to it by establishing a new consensus.

As Chairman of the IMF Interim Committee I had a personal experience of this when I negotiated the redistribution of IMF quotas in 1978. An hour or two after the genial luncheon at which I thought we had settled the matter, we were discussing the communiqué for the concluding press conference; I noticed a great commotion among the Japanese delegation. In the end their leader rose and said, greatly embarrassed, that he had misunderstood the decisions over lunch and wanted to reopen them. I suspected that he had just telephoned Tokyo, to be told that he had conceded too much, so I said: 'I'm afraid that the press is already assembled. We cannot keep them waiting any longer.' So that was that. I never heard another word of complaint.

The most important *fait accompli* to which the Japanese have had to adapt, however, was the constitution imposed on Japan by General MacArthur after its defeat. Carlo de Benedetti has said that the constitution of the United States was the last great political innovation of the Europeans. The constitution of modern Japan was the last great political innovation of the Americans.

At a meeting of the management consultants, McKinsey, I once attributed Japan's postwar success to its cultural and religious traditions. Not so, said Kenichi Ohmae, its Japanese board member, a nuclear physicist who has since become an international guru on business management;

before the war Japan was as torn by social and political conflict as any country in the world. 'But after the war,' he said, 'we knew we faced an economic struggle for survival. So we got together and decided how to solve the problem.' In fact, only the Japanese could talk so naturally of getting together to solve a national problem.

However, without MacArthur's constitution the Japanese would not have been allowed to get together in that way; and due to him they were prevented from spending more than one per cent of their national income on defence. This limitation on its defence spending has been an essential factor in making Japan's economic strength acceptable to its neighbours. It has also helped its economic growth in many ways, particularly in steering Japanese research towards civilian objectives. Partly as a result, Japan's technological progress now exceeds that of the United States, and her national income has grown so much that, with only one per cent spent on defence, in terms of spending at current exchange rates Japan is already the third military power in the world, after the United States and the Soviet Union. It is worth recalling that the United States did not become the world's greatest military power until seventy years after it became the richest nation.

Japan's ability to adjust rationally to external shocks has been proved again and again since the Second World War. It took the so-called 'Nixon shock' of 1969 in its stride. The two OPEC oil price increases of 1973 and 1979 hit Japan harder than any other industrial country, but it adjusted to them faster than any other major power. Though its rate of growth is only half what it was in the early postwar years, it is still the highest in the industrial world. Its rate of inflation is the lowest. It has recently spent a great deal more on improving the quality of life for its own people. Central Tokyo is no longer the noisy building site I saw on my first visit; with its flowery patios and leafy pedestrian precincts it now compares favourably with the centre of most other great cities.

The country is still grossly over-populated, and excessive protection for the rice farmers means that far too little land is available for the rest of the population. My Japanese friends still define their three ambitions as 'Japanese wife, Chinese cooking, and Western style house'. Moreover, the political system has failed to advance with the economy. The quality of Japan's politicians is far below that of its civil servants and businessmen. The ruling party is an untidy collection of squabbling factions, rather like the Christian Democratic Party in Italy, and is no less open to corruption as the Recruit scandal has revealed.

Nevertheless, since these weaknesses are now widely recognised, I believe they too will be surmounted, like the potential loss of competitiveness caused by the rise of the yen. When the yen soared far above the value of the dollar and the Deutschmark, Japanese businessmen did not regard it as a cause for despair, as would businessmen in Britain. They regarded it as a spur to innovation, so as to add more value to their products. The rise of sterling during Mrs Thatcher's first term destroyed a fifth of British manufacturing industry; since the yen rose, Japan has actually increased the share of manufacturing in its total output. Unlike Germany, it has accepted international advice by substantially increasing demand at home. It is also giving more aid to the Third World than any other country, and is planning to increase its aid to more than $50 billion in the period to 1992. The shape of the nineties will depend in large part on whether Japan continues to use its economic and financial muscle with the same enlightened self-interest.

My fascination with Japan was aroused not only by its impact on the world economy. I have been equally concerned to discover whether Japan's success has any features which might be transferable to Britain. One factor stood out above all others, and was very congenial to me. In every field of social and economic endeavour Japan insists on working through consensus. It is no accident that since the war the only European countries which have had a remotely comparable economic record are those which rely like Japan on consensus as the key to progress – Sweden, Switzerland, Austria, and Finland. All are very much smaller than Japan, and all are neutral or non-aligned, though Sweden spends as much of her national income on defence as the average European member of NATO.

The key to Japan's postwar success has been what the leading British student of the Japanese economy, Professor Ronald Dore, has described as 'flexible rigidities'. Egoism is not the touchstone of Japan's economic morality; the Japanese do not believe that you can get an efficient society, still less a moral society, simply by the mechanisms of the market powered by self-interest. Their society is a network of relations which impose responsibilities based on duty, trust and a sense of community. In the economic field these relationships apply between employer and worker, and between producer and supplier, no less than between producer and customer. A firm's obligation to provide lifetime employment to its workers is one example; if managers believe they must move out of a declining industry, they will not do so without first finding alternative work for their employees.

The rigidities imposed by this network of mutual obligations might have proved fatal to Japan in an age of international competition and rapid technological change. Japan has avoided paralysis by seeing that the state intervenes in both industry and finance to represent the residual public interest in the bargaining between organised private interests. Japan's behaviour during the stock market crash of Black October was a good example. By Western standards the Japanese stock market was more vulnerable than any other, because its stock prices were so much higher – NTT shares were actually sold that week at a price/earnings ratio of 162. But when the Ministry of Finance saw that the big financial institutions were all selling together, it intervened and asked them to start buying instead. They obeyed, so the Japanese market fell only half as far as that in New York, and had recovered all its losses within a few months.

Ronald Dore concluded his study of Japanese industry by pointing out that Thatcherism had failed by its own tests; despite its repeated attacks on the welfare state and the trade unions, despite its determination to end intervention in the British economy, it had not restored Britain's nineteenth-century dynamism. Would we not be wise, he mused, 'to ponder the Japanese example and ask ourselves whether we too might not do better by accepting that there is no road back to competitive individualistic atomized markets, and that we had better learn to live with organised capitalism'. I had come to similar conclusions, although I preferred the phrase 'market socialism', which is used in Sweden to describe its form of social democracy.

Modern capitalism has little in common with the system described by Karl Marx. It is the managers, not the owners, who wield the real power in private industry today. In any case, few of the owners are individual capitalists. Private shareholders now own only twenty-five per cent of British industry – less than before Mrs Thatcher launched her privatisation programme in the hope of spreading ownership more widely. The overwhelming majority of shares in British firms are now owned by the financial institutions, which invest their depositors' money in them. The depositors in these banks, building societies, insurance companies and pensions funds are ordinary men and women. The notorious Watergate Hotel in Washington is now owned by the pension fund of the British National Union of Mineworkers.

It would be as ridiculous to describe this system as 'people's capitalism', as to describe the Soviet system today as 'revolutionary socialism'. In fact, both systems now require a drastic reconstruction if they are to become democratically accountable and to satisfy their people's needs. And they must work together to improve the structure of world politics and economics, if they are to prevent a nuclear war or ecological disaster in which they would both perish.

Forty-two years of hard and continuous work in the Labour Party had led me to these conclusions by the time we fought the general election in 1987. When we were defeated I felt I needed a change of pace. I longed for time to reflect on what I had learned. Moreover, my interests outside politics had inevitably languished during nearly thirty years as a front-bencher; I wanted a chance to pursue them. So I decided to return, at least for the time being, to the backbenches.

CHAPTER TWENTY-SIX

The Sunrise of Eternity

Civilisation is hooped together, brought
Under a rule, under the semblance of peace
By manifold illusion; but man's life is thought,
And he, despite his terror, cannot cease
Ravening through century after century,
Ravening, raging, and uprooting that he may come
Into the desolation of reality:
Egypt and Greece, good-bye, and good-bye, Rome!
Hermits upon Mount Meru or Everest,
Caverned in night under the drifted snow,
Or where that snow and winter's dreadful blast
Beat down upon their naked bodies, know
That day brings round the night, that before dawn
His glory and his monuments are gone.

– 'Meru' W. B. Yeats

POLITICS HAS NEVER been the whole of my life. Some of my friends complain that I possess the opposite shortcoming from Mrs Thatcher – I have far too much hinterland. My wife and family have always meant more to me than the House of Commons. I once told an interviewer that I did not need the love of the people because I had the love of my wife. He thought it a somewhat chilling remark; I do not find it so. Nothing is more dangerous than the politician who uses politics as a surrogate for an unsatisfactory personal life. In my experience the best politicians are those with a happy marriage – and with children.

It is not easy, however, for a politician to keep his marriage happy. Too many 'Westminster widows' find that their social life is confined to their weekly shopping at the supermarket. The children of a prominent politician carry an even greater burden; besides seeing their father abused in public, they are liable to feel that they will have failed if they do not achieve the same prominence. Moreover, the absence of their father at critical periods when they are growing up may leave a lasting scar. I have been exceptionally fortunate. Edna shared my political interests, and she concentrated on making good my deficiencies as a father while our children were at home. When the children finally left us, she began to write.

By the time I returned to the backbenches in 1987 her new career kept her, too, away from home a good deal. She had now made a name for herself not only as a speaker and a biographer, but also as a television presenter and writer for radio. Her film on Mary Livingstone had taken her to South Africa and Zimbabwe; it won prizes in Scotland and New York. She went back to Africa to make a film on Mary Slessor, the Dundee mill-girl who became a missionary in Calabar. Besides commanding far larger audiences than I could as a speaker, she had written parallel lives of Jenny Marx, Mary Livingstone, and Emma Darwin, and was now researching a history of Coutts Bank, in which her first subject, Angela Burdett-Coutts, had played a leading part. During the summer of 1987 she was working much harder than I, since on top of everything else she was a member of the jury for the Booker Prize for fiction. While I was walking on the downs she was reading or riffling through some hundred and twenty modern novels. She learned more about sex in those two months than in over forty years of married bliss with me.

My mother was beginning to need more attention. Since my father's death she had suffered from giddy spells. One afternoon, when I went to pick her up for a visit to Glyndebourne, she fell downstairs. I burst in through the kitchen door and found her stretched out on her back, eyes wide open and staring at the ceiling. She was then ninety-two years old. I managed to get her up and tried to put her to bed. But she insisted on making the two-hour journey to Glyndebourne for *Le Nozze di Figaro*. In later years further falls required her to have two hip transplants, so I brought her to our home in Alfriston. One night there was a crash. I rushed into her bedroom to find her on her hands and knees, with blood pouring from a gash on her forehead, where she had smashed it against a glass table-top. When the doctor had put the necessary stitches in the wound, she looked up from her pillow and muttered: 'Denis, I'm in-destructible.' The following year she read all the novels of Turgenev four times. Even at the end, when her memory had gone, her face would light up at the sight of flowers or children. She died on our wedding anniversary just before Christmas 1988; she was then aged ninety-nine, game and happy to the last.

By 1987 Jenny and Tim each had two children, and would come with their families to spend the school holidays with us. Cressida joined us occasionally from San Francisco, where she had become a Black Belt in aikido and was building up a practice in holistic health. My children and grandchildren have provided me with continuing pleasure and education; they have kept me in touch with what younger generations were thinking, though I fear that my appreciation of pop-music has never progressed beyond the Beatles.

Even my family would not have been sufficient to reconcile me to a life in politics if I had not also been able to refresh myself with music, poetry, and painting. Without the arts, politics would before long have encrusted me in a horny carapace; my persona would have taken over from my personality, and the mask would have become the man. Though I found less and less time for playing the piano and for watercolour painting, I remained a passionate photographer, confined, however, to colour slides, since I never had time to do my own processing after leaving Defence.

My political prominence did bring me some opportunities of helping the arts. For example, I played a small role in the admirable Photographers' Gallery, the first museum in Britain devoted exclusively to photography. I also chaired the committee which raised money for a series of concerts on the theme of Mahler, Vienna and the Twentieth Century, which were organised by Claudio Abbado; he lured the public into listening to modern composers such as Berio and Fernyhough, by offering more familiar music from Vienna at the turn of the century. I had first met Abbado when he brought La Scala's opera company to Covent Garden; a handsome young man with immense charm, a quicksilver mind and terrifying dynamism, he was regularly conducting concerts and operas in London, Italy and the United States. His schedule was even more punishing than mine, yet he still had the energy to take an interest in politics, as did many of the other musicians I met. My excursions into music were not always so fruitful. On one occasion, when I was trying to raise money for the Gardner Arts Centre in Sussex by playing a Mozart sonata, I had the shaming experience of breaking down after the first two bars; unfortunately the television cameras did not delete my expletives. But I went on to finish the piece.

My television appearances in comedy programmes were more successful. Starting as the Wizard of Oz in a pantomime with Sue Lawley, I moved on to supporting roles in sketches for Morecambe and Wise and Victoria Wood, recited a parody of *Albert and the Lion* about the Westland affair on *Saturday Live*, and sang a duet with my sister Denise, who bore an uncanny resemblance to Mike Yarwood. At a conference in Venice I did a turn after dinner with Tony Robinson; I was sorry he was not playing Baldrick, since I rather fancied myself as Blackadder. When I took part in person on *Spitting Image* in an interview with a plastic Robin Day, I was distressed to find that people thought I was a puppet too. So far the culmination of my theatrical career has been on a Christmas show for the antipodean megastar, Dame Edna Everage; I did a song and dance routine with a straw hat and a cane, partnered by Secret Agent 007, alias Roger Moore, and the Australian Cultural Attaché at the Court of St James's, Sir Leslie Paterson, alias Barry Humphries.

People sometimes felt I was letting down the side by enjoying myself in such ways. I disagree. Politics should not be seen as 'a bitter abstract thing', and a politician should be more than 'an old bellows full of angry wind'. However, I always took care that I followed such comedy appearances with a serious discussion, for example, about Mrs Thatcher and the money supply; that could be guaranteed to wipe the smile off anybody's face.

My contacts with poets, painters, and musicians have made me think hard about the role of politicians and the place of politics in life. Many artists have a self-sufficient universe in their own work; they can satisfy their deepest needs simply by exploring the infinite possibilities of colour, line and form, or in studying the celestial harmony, counterpoint, and tonality of the great composers. There is a handful of unique spirits for whom their private relationship with their art is enough in itself. Emily Dickinson, for example, found Vesuvius in her little room at Amherst, and dedicated her life to a poetry so bold and penetrating that she refused to have it published. However, most artists need an audience for their work; then they become engaged in politics, whether they like it or not.

The moment they have to compete with others for money, fame, or influence, artists have to become politicians. Artistic politics, like academic or clerical or bureaucratic politics, has nothing to learn in virulence from the House of Commons. Yeats, for example, had to exhaust himself in wrangling on the committees which dealt with his literary, dramatic and occult interests; yet he never realised that he was then engaged in politics. To him, politics was a mystery play in which great men fought against the mob for noble causes. He never understood the political issues of his time; when he became engaged directly in Irish politics he found himself encouraging terrorism and later flirting with fascism. Yet he was obsessed by the relationship between politics and the individual at a deeper level; when he used his poetry to investigate that relationship in general terms, he showed extraordinary insight.

In recent years I have turned more and more often, not only for comfort but also for political understanding, to artists like Yeats, Emily Dickinson, and Virginia Woolf. Besides possessing a depth of human intuition which I rarely find in political writers, they can illuminate the predicament of man with myth and metaphor, reaching areas of experience which are inaccessible to the language and logic of politicians. Through them we can hear what Wordsworth called 'the still, sad music of humanity'.

I have been increasingly fascinated by the personality, as well as the poetry, of Yeats. Throughout my life I found myself stumbling across his tracks. His family was of Yorkshire origin; as a child in Sligo he loved listening to a stable-boy called Johnny Healey reading Orange ballads to him – alas no relative of mine, since he was anti-Fenian! My rooms at Balliol looked across the Broad to where Yeats had lived in the twenties. At the Council of Europe in 1951 I had the pleasant surprise of meeting his son Michael as a Senator; he later served for many years as a member of the European Parliament and Secretariat. The product of Yeats' late marriage to Georgina Hyde-Lees, he had not known his father well. 'Go away, Man!' he bellowed when, as a child of three, he was greeted with a couple of lines of Donne, as he was carried past his father on the stairs. In Leeds I often talked with the leading Yeats scholar, 'Derry' Jeffares. At Bellagio in 1972 I met Sean MacBride, the son of Yeats' beloved Maud Gonne, now a leading jurist – a small, brown, passionate, bird-like man. All this helped me to fill out my picture of the poet as a human being.

I have been delighted to find I have personal affinities with Yeats which have nothing to do with our common background as Anglo-Irish Protestants, or even with our love of poetry. Like me, he had an addiction to detective stories, and loved to boast about his knowledge of them. His sense of humour could be Rabelaisian, and he had a pretty though sometimes savage wit. He described his most famous predecessor as an Irish poet, Tom Moore, as 'that cringing firbolg', and criticised the self-indulgence of some young American poets with the words:

> The heart well worn upon the sleeve may be the best of sights,
> But never, never, dangling leave the liver and the lights.

Yeats was deeply involved in the occult until the end of his life, and as a young man tried to disguise his lack of self-confidence by posturing in the fancy dress of a pre-Raphaelite poet; yet his mind was always powerful and pragmatic. Virginia Woolf met him when he was sixty-five years old – 'very broad; very thick; like a solid wedge of oak. Wherever one cut him, with a little question, he poured, spurted fountains of ideas. And I was impressed by his directness, his terseness. No fluff and dreaminess.' Hopelessly impractical on many issues – he never mastered the telephone – Yeats could also show considerable cunning, especially about money. When they told him he had won the Nobel prize for literature, his first question was: 'How much?' A man after my own heart.

My love for Virginia Woolf had started at school, and was strengthened by working with her husband, Leonard, after the war. When we moved to Alfriston, we found ourselves in the middle of Bloomsbury country. Lydia Lopokova, the ballet dancer who married Maynard Keynes, was still living nearby when we first settled in the area. Visitors would find her gardening at the age of eighty-six, stark naked except for a straw hat. Virginia Woolf's home was a few miles away at Rodmell. Her sister Vanessa, a painter, had settled even closer, at Charleston farmhouse. Vanessa formed an odd *ménage à trois* there with her husband, the critic Clive Bell, and the painter Duncan Grant. I had met her son, Quentin Bell, in Leeds as Professor of Painting; he was an erect figure with wispy white hair, a long white beard, and a disturbingly wide rictus, remarkably like the *Spy* cartoon of Charles Darwin. As a boy he had joined his family in decorating the little church at Berwick with frescoes of the Sussex countryside. His life of Virginia Woolf is one of the great modern biographies, and I find his wife's edition of Virginia's diaries an inexhaustible reservoir of delights. Virginia Woolf has been as much an unseen presence during our years at Alfriston as Yeats was while we were living at Withyham.

While I was on Labour's front bench I found it impossible to pursue all these interests as I wished. Opposition was often even more exhausting than Government. Whenever there was a crisis in foreign affairs I would find myself doing up to a dozen interviews a day on radio or television, as well as all my normal work, which was often more than enough by itself.

January 22nd, 1987, was a typical working day. I woke up at six as usual, listened to the *Today* programme on the radio, had breakfast, and read, marked and cut the newspapers. At nine o'clock a crisis: the Government had just applied for an injunction to prevent MPs from seeing a television programme on the Zircon spy satellite, though details of it had already been published in the *New Statesman*. So I joined Neil Kinnock, Roy Hattersley, and John Smith at a long meeting with Geoffrey Howe and the Tory Chief Whip for a confidential briefing about Zircon. I was far from convinced by the Government's case, particularly since Frank Cooper, my old political adviser at the Ministry of Defence, who had just retired as Permanent Secretary, had already made clear his doubts about it. Then I rushed to lunch at the Israeli Embassy, where Prime Minister Simon Peres told me the conditions his Government was setting for peace talks with the Palestinians in the framework of the United Nations; we also discussed possible developments in the Gulf War. Back to the House of Commons for the Government's statement on Zircon, followed by an interview with an American journalist on Labour's defence policy, and a meeting with an impressive leader of the Solidarity movement in Poland. Dinner at the American Embassy with the indefatigable Phil Habib to discuss Nicaragua, where he had just accepted a new mission, after years of fruitless toil over the Lebanon; he told me of the troubles he had had with the calamitous Colonel Oliver North. As so often, I got to bed well after midnight.

After eight years of days like this in opposition, with no prospect whatever of direct influence on the problems I was discussing, I confess that, although I enjoyed my work immensely, I sometimes wondered whether it was all worthwhile. However, I reflected that even in office my influence on the major new issues then emerging would be severely limited. Moreover, I would have been no better off as a successful poet or painter. At the end of his life Yeats summed up his achievements with the line: '"What then?" sang Plato's ghost. "What then?"'. Even Leonardo da Vinci, the idol of my boyhood, who explored the whole universe of knowledge with pen and ink, would mutter as he traced the delicate whorls of running water or the complex architecture of the human skull: 'Dimmi se mai fu fatto qualche cosa?' – 'Tell me if anything was ever done?'

Such men aimed at a perfection which is beyond the reach of politicians, who must deal with refractory human beings not only as individuals, but also in the mass. Human behaviour is infinitely diverse and unpredictable. A politician can hope only to play some part in moving society broadly in the right direction: he must accept the inevitability of error and the need to change his course when things are going wrong. I have often disappointed my audiences by warning them that it is not possible to produce heaven on earth in the first year of a Labour Government. We shall be doing better than our forefathers if we can prevent hell on earth – which my generation has known twice in its lifetime. However, we can hope to prevent at least some types of unnecessary human suffering; if we know this and do not try to do so, we are abdicating a fundamental responsibility.

A warm heart, however, is not enough. A politician must also learn to cast a cold eye on the realities which confront him. Those realities will not yield to what Nye Bevan called 'an emotional spasm', or to any rigid intellectual doctrine. The scale and speed of the changes now sweeping the world can be followed only by a keen and dispassionate vision, informed by experience and some sense of history.

The challenge which faces politicians today is clear and inescapable, particularly in international affairs, where the explosion of scientific knowledge presents both new dangers and new opportunities. Whatever individualists or pacifists may say, only governments acting together can prevent a Third World War, can deal with the growing threat of ecological pollution, can create the conditions for economic and political stability worldwide. For the first time in history, science has given governments the means of fulfilling these responsibilities, if they can find the wit and will to do so. This is ample justification for a life in politics.

I do not believe we can escape responsibility for trying to prevent the catastrophes which now threaten mankind, by becoming hermits on Mount Meru, as Yeats seemed to think, or by joining Blake in abandoning 'the reasoning power, an abstract objecting power that negatives everything'. Someone must be prepared to wrestle with the dreary abstractions of economics' dismal science, and to master the dreadful equations of the nuclear strategists, even if this means he must 'refuse a heavenly mansion, raging in the dark'.

G. K. Chesterton, at first sight the most romantic and paradoxical of all fantasists, once paid an unexpected tribute to the Fabian Society, and to Bernard Shaw as a Fabian:

> Here was a man who could have enjoyed art among the artists, who could have been the wittiest of all the flaneurs: who could have made epigrams like diamonds and drunk music like wine. He has instead laboured in a mill of statistics and crammed his mind with all the most dreary and filthy details, so that he can argue on the spur of the moment about sewing-machines or sewage, about typhus fever or twopenny tubes. The usual mean theory of motives will not cover the

case; it is not ambition, for he could have been twenty times more
prominent as a plausible and popular humorist. It is the real and ancient
emotion of the salus populi, almost extinct in our oligarchical chaos; nor
will I for one neglect to salute a passion so implacable and so pure.

I believe that the *salus populi* – the well-being of the people – is still the
guiding motive of most politicians in Britain, despite all the vanities,
ambitions, hatreds, and dishonesties which the practice of politics tends
to engender.

The *salus populi* has rarely been under such formidable threat as now. In
international affairs, the immediate priorities are clear enough, although
many governments are fearful of their implications for the longer term.
There is every reason why the West should accept the agenda Gorbachev
has already proposed for building a common security on the ruins of the
Cold War. In Europe we must encourage NATO and the Warsaw Pact to
revise their current strategies and restructure their forces so as to
establish a military posture which is clearly defensive. This means changing our approach to the talks on conventional disarmament in Europe,
and cutting the offensive capabilities on both sides, until each has a
defensive strength which the other's offensive forces cannot overcome.
The traditional search for arithmetical balance is unlikely to succeed
when the strategic situations of the two alliances are incommensurate.

Conventional disarmament in Europe is obviously a problem which
must involve all members of the two alliances. Nuclear disarmament,
however, is still seen mainly as a bilateral problem between Washington
and Moscow. We should now recognise that the current negotiations
between the two superpowers to reduce their strategic nuclear forces are
unlikely to have much direct impact on the prospects for world peace,
until they are broadened to include the other powers which already have
nuclear weapons, like Britain, France, China, India, and Israel, as well as
the growing number of other states which could soon produce nuclear
weapons once they so decided. This means accepting that stopping the
nuclear arms race will also require some control of conventional forces
worldwide, since the main incentive for producing nuclear weapons is
usually the fear of a potential enemy's superiority in conventional weapons. We must also take account of those horrific weapons which are
neither nuclear nor conventional. Several governments in the Third
World are beginning to develop chemical, and perhaps biological, weapons,
and to acquire missiles for carrying them. Iraq has already used chemical
weapons on a large scale.

Thus world peace cannot be achieved simply by cooperation between Washington and Moscow, necessary as that certainly is. Neither the Third World nor the allies of the superpowers are prepared to exchange the constraints of the Cold War for a Soviet-American hegemony. So we must now activate the rusting machinery of the United Nations to fulfil its original purpose, of providing the framework for a world society. That purpose has been frustrated for more than forty years by the Kremlin's refusal to contemplate a single world community, in which the Two Camps could work together with a common aim. It would be tragic if, now that Gorbachev has abandoned the doctrine of the Two Camps, and has put the United Nations at the centre of Soviet policy, the world were to be prevented by prejudice or parsimony in the West from giving the United Nations the role and resources its Charter envisaged.

We must recognise too that, as Washington and Moscow replace confrontation with cooperation, new problems will emerge. During the Cold War, unbridled nationalism was a luxury in which only the non-aligned countries of the Third World could afford to indulge. Wars, and armed conflicts of various types, have already cost them over seventeen million lives since 1945. The decline of the Cold War, and the burgeoning of *glasnost* under Gorbachev, have allowed long-suppressed national feelings to come to the surface – and not only in the Soviet Union. The disintegration of Yugoslavia, for example, calls into question the peace settlement after the First World War as well as after the Second; so do the conflicts between Rumania and Hungary over Transylvania, and between Greece and Turkey over Cyprus and the Eastern Aegean. If NATO and the Warsaw Pact did not exist, they could easily have led to war by now. Western Europe has seen powerful nationalist movements challenging the status quo in France, Spain and Britain; Belgium is in many respects already divided into two.

As in the eighteenth and nineteenth centuries, democracy seems inseparable from nationalism. All of us will have to start thinking again about the best way of persuading communities which feel they have a separate identity to live together with others in a single polity. We may have to consider some surprising precedents. Has the Austro-Hungarian Empire, which is now regarded with increasing nostalgia in Eastern Europe, anything to teach the modern world? Can the Hong Kong settlement, which combines two systems in a single state, provide a precedent which could be followed elsewhere?

All these are issues on which the United Nations should begin to play a central role – as it has already over Afghanistan, Namibia, Kampuchea,

Central America and the Gulf War. There will be a long road to travel. If, as I hope, we can strengthen the United Nations sufficiently to rule out war as a means of settling disputes, we shall also have to give it the means of promoting peaceful change. Otherwise we may find we have simply replaced war by terrorism – and the terrorists of the future may have far more deadly weapons at their disposal than they possess today.

Meanwhile, we in Western Europe are already having to consider how the decline of the Cold War affects the future both of the Common Market and of NATO. The Common Market's attempt to remove all its internal barriers to the movement of goods and services by 1992 is already causing concern among some of the Community's neighbours and allies. Sweden and Austria are considering whether to apply for membership themselves; it is not impossible that the Soviet Union might accept the implications this might carry for their non-aligned status. If so, Finland and even Hungary might follow. Cyprus and Malta are considering membership. Some Mediterranean members of the Community are talking of the accession of countries in North Africa, such as Morocco and Tunisia, and even Algeria and Libya, once Qadaffi disappears. Turkey has been knocking at the door for years.

These developments would produce a Community totally different from the dreams of its founding fathers. However, the future of the Common Market and of NATO depends above all on Western Germany, where the impact of Gorbachev has been most powerfully felt. At the end of 1988 opinion polls showed that eighty per cent of its people wanted a non-nuclear Europe, seventy-five per cent thought there was no military threat from the Soviet Union and forty per cent thought Western Germany should be neutral. Most saw America as a greater threat to peace than Russia. Though there was no revival of the postwar pressure for German reunification, there was a universal demand for better relations with East Germany and Eastern Europe as a whole. The Germans, like the Italians, see 1992 as providing a springboard for their trade with Eastern Europe.

Against this background, even if the commercial objectives of 1992 are achieved, it is difficult to see the European Community developing into a political or military union; the deep divisions between Britain, France, and Germany on defence make this unlikely in any case. Personally I do not regret it. A continental sacro-egoismo could be even more dangerous to peace than a national sacro-egoismo. And it would be difficult to imagine Western Europe forming a distinct political and economic entity, without North America under the United States, and East Asia under

Japan, trying to follow a similar course. Apart from its potential military implications, that would probably lead to a trade war which could do more to destabilise the non-Communist world than Stalin ever dared to hope.

It is no longer unrealistic to aim at ending the postwar division of Europe. The critical question is how *glasnost* and the ending of the Cold War will affect Eastern Europe and the Soviet Union itself. Gorbachev has formally repealed the Brezhnev doctrine; so it is not impossible that the Red Army would not intervene to prevent drastic changes in the relationship of Eastern Europe with Western Europe and with Moscow. Gorbachev himself might welcome such changes if they led to changes in relations between Western Europe and the United States. Nationalist revolt in the Soviet Union itself, however, could be a different matter. The current leadership in Moscow probably accepts the need for drastic changes in the Soviet Constitution to permit greater freedom for the constituent republics; indeed the result of the elections in March 1989 probably makes them inevitable. But, although the Soviet Constitution accepts the right of secession, Georgy Arbatov has told an American audience that if any of the republics went so far as to secede from the Soviet Union, Gorbachev would no more accept it than Abraham Lincoln accepted the secession of the Southern States from the American Republic a century ago.

Yet nothing is now inconceivable. Gorbachev talks incessantly about Russia's 'common European home'. The phrase must sound oddly in the ears of a Tadjik or a Kazakh, who knows that Russia's Asian Empire is no more rooted in antiquity than were the British, French or Dutch Empires. It has so far survived the global tide of anti-colonialism only because of the 'salt-water fallacy', which allows imperialism to expand over land, while rejecting expansion across the seas. In the new world climate that may not be sufficient to protect the Soviet Union against the nationalist forces which are inseparable from *glasnost* and democratisation.

The other great continental empire, of the United States, has also benefited from the 'salt-water fallacy'. It came into existence through the ruthless persecution and expropriation of the native Indian tribes, with whom it fought many colonial wars, and through the purchase or conquest of other European colonies. As late as 1784 most of what is now the United States was part of the Viceroyalty of New Spain.

Except for the Philippines, Alaska, Puerto Rico, Hawaii and a few small islands in the Pacific, United States imperialism overseas took the form of a 'neo-colonial' relationship with the Central American countries it still regards as its back yard. In some ways its problems here resemble those of Russia in Eastern Europe. There are, however, at least two outstanding differences. Although some Presidents, like Kennedy over Cuba, and Reagan over Nicaragua, have used armed intervention to resist revolt in their back yard, others have tried genuinely to escape from the neo-colonial role, like Roosevelt over Mexico and Carter over Panama. More important still, the peoples of Eastern Europe have never sought to emigrate to the Soviet Union and become Soviet citizens; there is an increasing stream of Latin Americans who want to emigrate to the United States and become American citizens.

This stream of Latin American immigrants, many of them illegal, could become an irresistible tidal wave if the debt crisis exploded into violent disorder. Mexican immigration is already upsetting the political balance in states like California and Texas. Immigration from Cuba and Nicaragua now presents Florida with worrying problems. It is easy to construct a scenario in which both the United States and the Soviet Union were distracted for a generation from playing an important role in world affairs by troubles inside or just across their own frontiers.

In that case both the superpowers would find the need for constitutional reform inescapable. It is not easy to administer continental superstates in a world in which political democracy is a precondition of economic advance. As G. K. Chesterton once pointed out, the men who made the great revolutions in eighteenth-century France and America were inspired by the ideals of earlier and smaller societies: 'but no modern state is small enough to achieve anything so great'. Since then, industrialisation and massive immigration are straining the American Constitution to breaking point.

The American people and its representatives seem determined not to open the Pandora's box of constitutional reform. Yet it will be difficult for the United States to deal with its growing problems both at home and abroad unless the federal government is both able and willing to play a more decisive role than it does today. At present the separation of powers between Congress and the Executive makes this more difficult than ever. The Congress has power without responsibility, while the Executive has responsibility without power. Members of the Congress normally serve for many years, and are deeply conscious of their rights and traditions. Members of the Executive often have no previous experience of government at the federal level, and nearly four thousand of the top civil servants who advise them are usually changed every time the President changes – even if he is from the same party. Moreover, it is even more difficult than it was a century ago, when Lord Bryce first identified the problem, for a good man to become President, or even to run for the office.

I raise these spectres, which may come to haunt us before long, not to discourage political action now, but to recall the wisdom of Heraclitus, so recently reasserted by Gorbachev: 'Everything is in flux.' Nothing is more certain than that some of the events which will shape our future are unpredictable. In 1907 no one predicted the First World War or the Bolshevik revolution which grew out of it. In 1922 no one foresaw the Great Slump, or its role in bringing Hitler to power. Even as late as 1937 no one foresaw the nature, length and outcome of the Second World War, least of all that it would bring Russia face to face with America in the middle of Europe for at least half a century. No one foresaw the atomic bomb or the end of Europe's empires overseas, which were also among its consequences.

During my own political career since 1945, the unpredictable seems to have been the norm rather than the exception. None of us foresaw Suez, Vietnam, Hungary, de Gaulle, OPEC, the rise of Islamic fundamentalism, the emergence of the West Pacific rim as the most dynamic area in the world economy, the spread of AIDS as a major threat to health, or the damage done to the world's climate by the depletion of the ozone layer and the so-called 'greenhouse effect'. Above all, no one foresaw Gorbachev.

It was Gorbachev who said that we must move 'groping in the dark as it were, towards an interdependent and even integral world'. Remembering that 'the darkness does not destroy what it conceals', we must look for intellectual tools which will enable us, if not to penetrate the darkness, at least to react in time when the shape of what it conceals begins to emerge.

At present advance of science sets much of the agenda both at home and abroad. Of all the scientists who ever existed, nearly ninety per cent are alive and active today. The volume of scientific knowledge has been doubling every fifteen years or so. Science already offers us the choice between eliminating poverty and eliminating the human race. Before long it may offer us the choice between eliminating sickness and poisoning the planet.

Contrary to the totalitarian nightmares of George Orwell, the scientific revolution has created an irresistible demand for political freedom, rather than the reverse; for without freedom science is crippled. In a world which science has made one, no political system can afford to fall behind in scientific development. Where freedom has allowed science to flourish, living standards have risen faster than ever before, destroying the old class barriers and transforming the social framework in which political and economic life are conducted.

Western science since Aristotle has relied on the concept of cause and effect. Nowadays those who work at the frontiers of science are beginning to use more subtle concepts. In 1988 at the World Philosophical Congress in Brighton, Karl Popper questioned the adequacy of causality, at least in its mechanical form. A whole new science of chaos is beginning to develop, stemming from Einstein's theory of relativity and Heisenberg's indeterminacy principle, which have already played an important role in quantum physics. Mrs Thatcher has already proved one conclusion of the chaologists; they maintain that a simple formula, applied over and over again, can create chaos.

At my humbler political level, I have learned much from the biologists. They make a distinction between analysing a problem in terms of cause and effect, and analysing it as a continuing process – between aetiology and pathogenesis. I find this a fruitful distinction; in many political situations it is impossible to disentangle cause and effect from an infinite variety of data. It may be more useful to look for patterns in a process. For example, the swing of the pendulum is often used to describe shifts of political mood for which no clear single cause can be discovered; such cyclical theories are also used by economists.

Unpredictability and uncertainty play such an important role in both politics and economics that no practical politician should allow himself to be imprisoned in a single systematic theory or doctrine. In the nuclear age it is particularly dangerous when systematic theories are used to justify Messianism – whether of Right or Left – and to present politics as a crusade of good against evil. Another Holy War could mean the end of the human race. I am always uneasy when I hear politicians talk of leading a crusade. The crusaders of the Middle Ages were men of ruthless brutality and unbridled greed; the end result of the crusades was not to spread Christianity to the infidel, but to split the Christian church and bring the Turks to the gates of Vienna.

Then what is socialism, if it is not a crusade? I have already quoted Kolakowski's definition: 'an obstinate will to erode by inches the conditions which produce avoidable suffering'. In my opinion the essential differences in politics concern the priority given to one group of social values rather than another. Socialism emphasises the community rather than the individual, consensus rather than confrontation, public welfare rather than private gain; it puts the quality of life before the quantity of goods. But its priorities are not absolute; it does not deny that the values which it normally puts second will sometimes need to come first, or that its opponents may also give some importance to socialist priorities.

Socialism is based on a belief in the brotherhood of man, and seeks to realise that brotherhood through political action. So defined, socialism has much in common with Christianity – and is no less open to a wide variety of interpretations. Like Christianity, socialism has produced a large number of warring sects, whose internecine conflicts rarely demonstrate much spirit of brotherhood. Socialist parties contain much the same proportion of saints and sinners as their opponents; in all cases the saints are in a minuscule minority.

Socialist values should at least give some sense of direction to socialist politicians. They cannot, however, prescribe what policies should be adopted in every situation. Socialism is not a philosopher's stone; it is simply a compass, leaving the politician to decide for himself the best route and most appropriate vehicle for reaching his objective. Moreover, a large number of the decisions which a politician must take have little to do with any single schedule of moral values; they must be determined by applying simple rules, like the laws of mathematics, to stubborn and irresistible facts. That is true not only of managing a national economy, but also of many issues which now dominate international politics. Few governments in the world are socialist at present; as Nye Bevan once said, a socialist foreign policy is a policy for hermits.

The Labour Party came into being eighty years ago as an alliance of Christian Socialists with Fabians who believed in gas-and-water socialism; they were joined by pragmatic trade unionists who had lost confidence in the Liberal Party's ability to meet their needs. There was only a tiny minority of Marxists. Labour had no systematic ideology, and in government its programmes did not draw on any agreed body of socialist doctrines. When for the first time it achieved an absolute majority in 1945, its policies were based on two concepts – economic planning and the welfare state. Economic planning was first introduced by Colbert, who served King Louis XIV as Finance Minister in seventeenth-century France. The welfare state was invented by Bismarck in nineteenth-century Prussia, and adapted to contemporary Britain by a Liberal, Lord Beveridge. The policies of demand management pursued by Dalton, Cripps, and Gaitskell were based on the theories of another Liberal, Lord Keynes, and had been first applied in the thirties by President Roosevelt to the United States.

The only element in the policies of post-war Labour governments which drew on a specifically socialist theory was the nationalisation of the basic industries; Clause Four of the Party Constitution in 1918 called for public ownership of the means of production, distribution, and exchange. But as Shinwell complained when Attlee made him responsible for nationalising the coal industry, no one had worked out how it should be done. The public corporation, which was chosen by the Attlee Government as the form of nationalisation, is now generally recognised to have failed to meet the nation's needs; it failed even to satisfy the aspirations of those who worked in the nationalised industries themselves.

In any case, the ownership of private industry has changed beyond recognition since Marx made it the first target of a socialist revolution. Industry today is mainly owned by financial institutions, which in theory represent the ordinary people who deposit savings in them. The central problems of private industry now concern management, organisation, and accountability rather than ownership; they include the role of the multinational companies, and the impact of the international financial revolution on industrial performance. That is why privatisation is as much a red herring as nationalisation; the question is how an industry can best serve the people's needs, not what is the form of its ownership. Traditional socialist theory has little to say on these problems, though there is now a growing body of literature about them, notably from Ken Galbraith. Ironically enough, though there are now thousands of books about how to transform a market economy into a socialist system, there are so far no books about what has become the central problem in the Communist world, how to transform what is called a socialist system into a market economy.

Although its obsequies have been celebrated a thousand times, socialism obstinately refuses to lie down and die. Iain Macleod and Norman Tebbit were not the first to announce that socialism was dead, and the Labour Party with it. In 1847, Lorenz von Stein wrote: 'As theories Socialism and Communism have already run their course ... One is no longer wrong in regarding the Socialist and Communist theories as a closed chapter'. A year later the whole of Europe was shaken by revolutions inspired by socialism, and Marx and Engels published their Communist Manifesto.

The last decade of the twentieth century seems likely to see another swing of the pendulum, away from a freedom which has too often turned to anarchy, towards a new form of order both in national and international affairs – away from an individualism which has turned to selfish greed, towards a new sense of social responsibility, in which the quality of life assumes much greater importance. There are already some signs of this in the United States and Western Germany, where concern for the environment is already a political force. Such a swing is long overdue in Britain. The deterioration of our social and economic infrastructure has reached danger point. Demoralisation in our schools, universities, and health service is matched by the breakdown of our roads, railways and airports.

The most striking feature of Mrs Thatcher's third term in power is that she seems to have lost that instinct for the popular mood which marked her first two terms. Every major item in her programme is unpopular. All the opinion polls show large majorities in favour, not of her values, but of those which the Labour Party has traditionally represented. Many of those who have benefited from Mrs Thatcher's policies are now uneasy at the divisions they have created in British society – between North and South, between rich and poor, between the healthy and the sick, between those in work and the retired or unemployed. Neil Kinnock spoke for many outside his own party when he condemned Thatcherism with the words: 'No obligation to the community, no sense of solidarity . . . no neighbourhood, no number other than one, no time other than now, no such thing as society – just me! and now!'

More alarming to many of her own supporters is Mrs Thatcher's growing authoritarianism. She seems bent on undermining most of the institutions which provide social tissue for our parliamentary democracy. The trade unions and local government were her first targets. Since then she has turned her attention to the BBC, the press, the universities, the Church of England, the House of Lords and the House of Commons, and even to the monarchy. Her attacks on the medical and legal professions, both hitherto among the most loyal buttresses of Conservatism, suggest the sort of hubris which has brought so many governments down in the past.

Yet though the British people reject the values of Thatcherism and are increasingly disturbed by the divisions in their society, until 1989 they persistently preferred Mrs Thatcher and her government to any alternative on offer. The reasons why the Labour Party failed for so long to benefit from the unpopularity of Thatcherism were those which had crippled it since the split of 1981 – the image of division, the excessive influence of dogmas which had long since lost their relevance, and the role of the trade unions in deciding both its policy and its leadership.

Once he became Party Leader Neil Kinnock set about ridding the Party of these disadvantages. He shifted the prime responsibility for making policy from the National Executive Committee to bodies on which the Parliamentary leadership predominated. He started to purge the Party of the Trotskyite fronde which had infiltrated some constituencies. He improved the Party machine more than any leader since the war. But the electoral college offered opponents like Tony Benn the chance to challenge his leadership in long campaigns every year, which were successful only in reviving the image of Labour as a divided Party. And the behaviour of some trade union leaders at the Party's Annual Conference made it appear that they, and not its elected political leaders, could always call the tune.

The trade unions are probably the Labour Party's greatest problem; yet there can be no solution without at least their acquiescence. Under Mrs Thatcher the unions have lost a quarter of their membership; and of that membership under half have voted for the Labour Party – less than one in ten of the total electorate. Yet the unions cast eighty-nine per cent of the votes at the Labour Party's Conference, and usually do so without attempting to reflect the views of their members. For example, opinion polls find that sixty per cent of trade unionists want Britain to keep nuclear weapons; but the vast majority of union conferences are committed to unilateral nuclear disarmament, and even those of their leaders who reject unilateralism are reluctant to seek a change in this position except through ambiguous formulas which are all too clearly an attempt to fudge the issue. The real issues of defence and disarmament have always defied discussion in terms of a Punch and Judy show between multilateralism and unilateralism. But for the Labour Party's public image, the fact that its defence policy can be decided by unrepresentative trade union leaders who have no political responsibility is quite as damaging as any defect in the policy itself.

Fortunately there is a new generation of trade union leaders who have come to terms with the new political realities. They recognise that the Labour Party will have less chance of winning an election so long as it remains dependent on trade union money, and so long as the trade unions insist on controlling its policies through their votes at its Annual Conferences. Once Labour does win a general election, I hope it will introduce the public funding of political parties; many European countries have already done so to their advantage.

Labour cannot escape from its problems through alliances with the Centre parties, or through proportional representation. The non-Labour majority is probably as large as the non-Conservative majority; there is no guarantee that members of the Centre parties would vote Labour if their own candidates stood down – or vice-versa. Proportional representation could not be introduced in Britain without years of wrangling over its precise form; previous attempts to change the British constitution, over devolution or the House of Lords, are not an encouraging precedent. The experience of PR in other countries shows that it has many defects. It tends to give excessive influence to tiny political parties, such as the religious parties in Israel, and rarely produces a government which can act decisively in a crisis; in the Netherlands it has often taken months to produce any government at all.

In any case, if the Labour Party can not defeat the Conservatives on its own, it is unlikely to do so in alliance with the Centre or Nationalist parties; it is even less likely to form an effective government with them if it did. The Centre parties are deeply divided both on their values, their policies and their leadership; and each Nationalist party has only one aim, which none of the other parties share.

The Labour Party's social values are reflected in practical policies on health, education, and welfare which already command popular support. Its economic policies are now coming to grips with some of the changes in the modern world. Democratic parties of both Right and Left have always accepted an economic role both for the market and for government; they have argued essentially about where the line between the market and government should be drawn. Even Adam Smith, the great theorist of the free market, saw the state as having a vital role in providing the economic infrastructure, such as roads, canals, ports and bridges, which were 'of such a nature that the profit could never repay the expense to any individual or small number of individuals'. He favoured control over interest rates so that 'sober people are universally preferred as borrowers to prodigals and projectors'. He would be as surprised to witness some of the follies now perpetrated in his name by Conservative governments, as would Marx by the follies of those who call themselves 'Marxists'.

Government still has an indispensable role in managing the economy and in guaranteeing the provision of a people's basic needs and services. On the other hand, as prosperity increases, the market becomes far superior to a government bureaucracy in satisfying people's less essential needs; no Communist state has yet succeeded in producing a store which can satisfy consumers remotely as well as a Marks and Spencer's or a Sainsbury's. For most people, the greatest single advantage of rising living standards is the increase in personal freedom which they offer; they open the gates to an immense variety of new pleasures from which every individual should have the right to choose what he likes best. Middle-class intellectuals may sneer at this as rank materialism. In fact nothing has done more to liberate women from dehumanising drudgery than the washing-machine and the vacuum cleaner. The telephone and television have done much to make old age less lonely. The best, as well as the worst, of past and present culture is now available to everyone in his own home; millions of people are able, for the first time, 'to dig for this submerged sunrise of wonder' in Chesterton's words. But of course no one can make them dig if they do not want to.

Socialists should welcome this new consumer society, and the new freedoms it offers. They will be unable to attract the young unless they do so. Some of the Left have done immense harm to the image of socialism in recent years by trying to impose a puritanical uniformity on their supporters; Karl Marx himself far preferred a glass of claret to the mug of tea affected by some of his recent converts.

The market-place need not be the battlefield of the class war. On the contrary, a modern democracy cannot adapt to the speed of technological change through confrontation between employer and worker. The advantage of consensus as the lubricant of change has been proved a thousand times over, not only in Japan, but also in Sweden, which has a culture much closer to that of Britain. The Labour Party could learn much about a constructive symbiosis between government and the market from the experience of Sweden's Social Democrats, who have earned over half a century of almost uninterrupted power by managing their economy with exceptional efficiency. Their output per head is twice that of Britain. They have combined full employment with low inflation throughout the turbulence of the last fifty years; high public spending on the most advanced welfare system in the world has not prevented them from nurturing some of the most innovative private companies, such as Ericsson and Volvo, in one of the smallest national markets.

Sweden can teach us other lessons too. Some thirty years ago Hugh Gaitskell toasted Tage Erlander, the wisest of all Swedish Prime Ministers, and asked him for the secret of his success. 'Don't ask me,' replied Erlander. 'Ask the opposition parties.' The Liberals, Conservatives, and Farmers' Party in Sweden have always been racked by the most bad-tempered political and personal divisions. The Social Democrats have also had fierce arguments among themselves, but have managed to conduct them without arousing the personal animosity and sectarian virulence which have poisoned so many of the Labour Party's internal debates. All the British parties are prone to these weaknesses, not least the Liberals and Social Democrats, who destroyed for ever their reputation for being nice in two appalling months after the 1987 general election; the Tories wisely prefer the stiletto and the bowstring to the public punch-ups of the Labour Party.

The next British Government, of whatever party, will face exceptionally difficult problems in managing the economy. Nineteen eighty-eight saw the children of the postwar baby boom reaching the age of forty. Britain's population is now shrinking, like that of most developed countries. There will be an increasing number of pensioners to support with a declining labour force, and the cost of caring for the elderly will increase rapidly as they live longer. On the other hand, there will be a desperate shortage of young men and women entering the labour market – two million fewer than now, as against two million more middle aged.

Britain has made far less preparation for these demographic changes than Japan and Germany, which will be even more affected. Our education and training has been notably deficient, particularly over the last ten years. We have done far too little training for the new technologies on which we will depend to manage the changing balance in our population. Like the United States, we have fallen far behind in new investment, and are wasting our resources on a consumption boom which is fuelled by excessive personal borrowing.

In such a situation, the need to divert resources from consumption into new investment will be paramount – and require immense political courage. This is one problem which cannot be solved simply by allowing the market mechanisms to operate, particularly when they are distorted by a financial system which rewards short-term speculation rather than long-term investment. Only the Labour Party is likely to accept the need for a return to government leadership in these areas; that is why I believe that anyone who wants a government in Britain which will confront the challenges of the modern world with courage and humanity will find the Labour Party, with all its weaknesses, the best vehicle for change.

When I look back on my political career I am convinced that a life in politics has never been more worthwhile than it is today. In the international field, for the first time the world faces a real opportunity of ending war as an instrument of policy. When I went to Oxford, Yeats had just written 'Meru', the poem I have used to open this chapter. My generation knew in its bones that war with Hitler was inevitable – and we had no confidence of surviving it. For more than forty years after the defeat of Hitler our lives were dominated by the fear that the Cold War might end in a nuclear holocaust. That prospect is fading fast. We can now concentrate on the far more constructive task of organising a world society through the United Nations. In Britain our domestic problems remain severe; through the sort of absolute poverty which afflicted a third of the nation in the thirties has almost disappeared, there is now a small but growing minority suffering real destitution. Yet, science now offers us the tools to eliminate most of the physical evils from which mankind has suffered, providing we can find the political will and administrative skill to use them properly. Politics is the key to our survival.

Nevertheless, politics will remain, as ever, a difficult and sometimes disappointing business. Fighting to change your country and the world as a member of any political party inevitably involves compromises and frustrations. But in a parliamentary democracy change can be achieved only through working inside a party. This means accepting its constraints and disciplines. It means acquiescing in policies you dislike until you can persuade your party to change them. It will often bring defeat – and sometimes personal humiliation.

Fortunately, personal ambition has never been my consuming passion. I have always wanted to do something rather than to be something. When I have fought for leadership my motive has been less the desire for my own victory than an unwillingness to see victory going to someone I judged unsuitable. And however disagreeable the bickering which disfigures so much of politics at every level, I find my faith constantly revived by evidence of the genuine idealism which inspires hundreds of thousands of men and women who give up night after night to sit in bare and draughty rooms, so that they can play their part in a great national and international movement. When they sing Blake's great triumphal anthem, 'Jerusalem', they mean every word of it.

Only historians can say for sure whether what a politician sees as his great achievement really has a lasting value – and too many historians seem to be frustrated politicians, judging what little they know of the past by the partisan prejudices of their own age. Fortunately, in Britain a good constituency MP can usually find satisfaction in some unequivocal successes. Persuading an ignorant or indifferent bureaucracy to provide a family with decent housing, to pay essential benefits, to reunite an immigrant husband with his wife, means far more to those concerned than speeches in Parliament about intermediate nuclear weapons or the crisis of sovereign debt.

During my first election campaign in 1945, I called on a Roman Catholic priest at his home in Otley. A small, youngish man called Father Mawson, with a brown and wrinkled face, he was quite content to spend his whole life serving humbly as a parish priest in the same small Yorkshire town. We fell to talking about our respective callings. I told him that after five years in the army I wanted to help my fellow-men and prevent another war. But though I was standing for the Labour Party, and had once been a Communist, I now realised that I did not really know very much either about the Labour Party as an organisation, or about the intellectual arguments for socialism. Father Mawson said without hesitation: 'But you must do whatever you do for the greater glory of God.'

Though I did not share his faith, I knew exactly what he meant. Politics must be in some sense a vocation. Otherwise it would be intolerable. But if you think you understand something of Britain and the world, and want to change them for the better, you will find no more rewarding vocation – providing you do not seek your reward in power or money, and providing you do not make political success your only touchstone of personal achievement.

The bleakness of Yeats' icy dawn is not inevitable. Throughout my life I have said with William Blake:

> He who bends to himself a joy
> Doth the winged life destroy.
> But he who kisses the joy as it flies
> Lives in eternity's sunrise.

Epilogue

In the preface to his poem, *Milton*, William Blake addressed the painters, sculptors and architects of his time in words which carry an everlasting message for politicians too:

'Rouse up, O young men of the New Age! Set your foreheads against the ignorant hirelings! For we have hirelings in the camp, the court, and the university, who would, if they could, forever depress mental, and prolong corporeal war . . .'

> And did those feet in ancient time
> Walk upon England's mountains green?
> And was the holy Lamb of God
> On England's pleasant pastures seen?
>
> And did the countenance divine
> Shine forth upon our clouded hills?
> And was Jerusalem builded here
> Among these dark satanic mills?
>
> Bring me my bow of burning gold!
> Bring me my arrows of desire!
> Bring me my spear! O clouds, unfold!
> Bring me my chariot of fire!
>
> I will not cease from mental fight,
> Nor shall my sword sleep in my hand,
> Till we have built Jerusalem
> In England's green and pleasant land.

'Would to God that all the Lord's people were prophets.' (Num. xi. 29.)

Index